TREASON
AGAINST
GOD

Also by Leonard W. Levy

Against the Law: The Nixon Court and Criminal Justice
Judgments: Essays on Constitutional History
Origins of the Fifth Amendment: The Right Against
    Self-Incrimination
Jefferson and Civil Liberties: The Darker Side
Legacy of Suppression: Freedom of Speech and Press in Early
    American History
The Law of the Commonwealth and Chief Justice Shaw

Edited by Leonard W. Levy

The Supreme Court Under Earl Warren
The Fourteenth Amendment and the Bill of Rights
Blasphemy in Massachusetts
Essays on the Making of the Constitution
Freedom and Reform
Judicial Review and the Supreme Court
American Constitutional Law: Historical Essays
Freedom of the Press from Zenger to Jefferson
Parties and Pressure Groups
The Judiciary
The Congress
The Presidency
The American Political Process
Jim Crow in Boston: The Origin of the "Separate but
    Equal Doctrine"
Major Crises in American History: Documentary Problems
Essays on the Early Republic

LEONARD W. LEVY

TREASON AGAINST GOD

A History of the Offense of Blasphemy

SCHOCKEN BOOKS · New York

First published by Schocken Books 1981
10 9 8 7 6 5 4 3 2 1   81 82 83 84

Copyright © 1981 by Leonard W. Levy

Library of Congress Cataloging in Publication Data
Levy, Leonard Williams, 1923–
Treason Against God.
Includes bibliographical references and index.
1. Blasphemy — Great Britain — History. 2. Blasphemy —
History. I. Title.
KD8073.L48   345.41'0288   80–15063
Manufactured in the United States of America

ISBN 0–8052–3752–6

Dedicated with love
to the memory of my mother-in-law,
Estelle S. Gitlow,
a woman of exceptional
compassion and courage

CONTENTS

Preface		ix
Acknowledgments		xvii
Part One: Religious Foundations		1
1.	The Offense and Its Origins	3
2.	The Jewish Trial of Jesus	29
3.	The Age of Christian Heterodoxy	63
Part Two: Continental Precedents		101
4.	Compelling Heretics to Come In	103
5.	Protestantism Rediscovers Blasphemy	122
Part Three: England to 1700		159
6.	The Fires of Smithfield	161
7.	Snatching the Socinian Palm	188
8.	Antinomianism Running Amok	224
9.	The Quakers Ungod God	258
10.	Christianity Becomes the Law of the Land	297
Epilogue		331
Notes		340
Index		403

PREFACE _____

The verdicts of time mock judgments and alter sensibilities. Socrates, Aristotle, Jesus, Michael Servetus, Giordano Bruno, George Fox, William Penn, and Tom Paine were condemned for blasphemy. Protestantism in the sixteenth century seemed blasphemous to the Roman Catholic church; in the next century Protestant countries punished Unitarians, Baptists, and Quakers as blasphemers. Beliefs that once staggered society achieve respectability as fighting faiths.

Perhaps these are no longer times that try men's souls. In some respects we have become a numb society. Today almost anything seems endurable. What appears to be a debasing permissiveness may well be worth the freedom it affords in the various forms of human expression. Freedom is often a condition of enlightenment. Adolescents of my generation furtively read Joyce's *Ulysses* or Farrell's *Studs Lonigan* as dirty books. Unashamed and exploitative pornography has replaced movies that were censored as "blue." How many of us remember what that word meant? By 1971 the Supreme Court of the United States, when reversing a conviction for offensive conduct, quipped that "one man's vulgarity is another's lyric." The case concerned a young man who wore in public a jacket stenciled with the words "Fuck the Draft" to proclaim his opposition to the war in Vietnam. The Court understood that the First Amendment protects the emotive as well as the cognitive force of words. One may now openly say, without fear of prosecution, that Jesus was a bastard who entertained no notion that he was divine, or that the doctrine of the Trinity is unscriptural and breaches the unity of God. Celebrated theologians and New Testament scholars commonly profess beliefs that once provoked not only coercion of dissent but execution of dissenters.

We live in a society in which the citizen has the duty of preventing the government from falling into error and in which the business of government is no longer whether citizens lapse into errors of opinion or taste. Most Americans probably do not accept the dictum of Justice Oliver

Wendell Holmes that the principle of the Constitution that most im-
peratively calls for our attachment is "not free thought for those who
agree with us but freedom for the thought that we hate." Most,
however, would agree with Justice Robert Jackson's declaration: "If
there is any fixed star in our constitutional constellation, it is that no official, high or petty, can prescribe what shall be orthodox in politics,
nationalism, religion, or other matters of opinion or force citizens to
confess by word or act their faith therein." Blasphemy is surely the expression of thought that we hate, and government in seeking its suppression enforces orthodoxy and forces citizens to stifle their beliefs
about religion.

Freedom of expression was never freer than now, but it is not
limitless. In matters of religion, atheists have the same rights as theists,
but not everyone may worship as he pleases, let alone put his beliefs into practice. He might conceivably engage in the murderous rites of the
goddess Kali or unroll his prayer rug in the middle of highway traffic.
Cultists who fondle venomous snakes to demonstrate the faith of the
true believer (Mark 16:18, Luke 10:19, Acts 28:3–6) can be arrested,
because public safety in this instance is a greater value than freedom of
faith. One may not exercise one's religion at the expense of the public
health, order, or welfare, nor plead conscientious objection to evade
civic obligations. Caesar's conscription laws, for example, encompass
all with such exceptions as only Congress may make. No one, however
sincere, will prevail in alleging that his duty to God makes him decline
the importunities of the IRS. Some who have claimed the immunity of
their religious beliefs have been convicted for fortune telling, breach of
the peace, polygamy, draft evasion, nudity, practicing medicine
without a license, and blaspemy.

Blasphemy is still a crime in most states of this country, although
prosecutions are no more frequent than the sighting of snarks. In Great
Britain, however, a country that values freedom of expression as highly
as the United States does but where Christianity is still part of the law
of the land – Judaism and other non-Christian beliefs cannot be
blasphemed – a court of appeals sustained a conviction for blasphemy
in 1978. The culprit was the editor of a magazine who published a
poem (James Kirkup's "The Love That Dares to Speak Its Name") that
reads as if it were written by the Roman centurion at the foot of the
cross. In the poem, the centurion and Jesus are homosexuals, and the
intercourse between them is explicit and undoubtedly shocking to
believers. Blasphemy, the British court ruled, is an offensive or vilifying
assault on Christian sensibilities. It is, therefore, and has been, a subjective offense. In the United States, however, in recent years several

movies, including *The Passover Plot, Oh God!,* Zeffirelli's *Jesus of Nazareth,* and Monty Python's *Life of Brian,* have been freely shown, although censured as blasphemy by orthodox vigilante groups. Given the state of the First Amendment today, no blasphemy law could possibly withstand appellate scrutiny. The federal courts would surely find a violation of the free exercise of religion or of free speech in any prosecution for blasphemy (see the Epilogue of this book).

Historically the word "blasphemy" has functioned as an epithet to aggravate or blacken an opinion on sacred matters that is objectionable to one who differs. He may genuinely feel that his religion has been assaulted, yet the "blasphemy" may exist only in his mind and not necessarily in that of the offender. One of the nation's most distinguished historians of Christianity regarded the manuscript of this book as blasphemous — "written," he said, "with a deep animus against orthodox Christianity," and filled with "gratuitous digs about Christian beliefs such as the Trinity and about Christian theologians." My critic then obliged me by giving me a private reading of the first five chapters, the ones he found objectionable, and he enumerated all the "offensive" matter. Having no intention to offend, I modified many statements and deleted the "digs" (e.g., "Innocent III would not only die for his religion but would also kill for it"), but found that I was not able to alter my basic viewpoint. If a blasphemer of a pagan god should be spared, because that god can avenge his own honor (Judg. 6:32), why should not the blasphemers of God also be spared? I do not consider that question to be offensive as my critic did. My sympathy for Arian and Unitarian beliefs and for Christian victims of Christian persecution remains evident. St. Augustine of Hippo doubtless wrote religious classics, but he also formulated a theory justifying religious persecution, and St. Thomas Aquinas endorsed it. Martin Luther, when confronted by religious differences, could be a foul-mouthed, ill-tempered bigot, and John Calvin was responsible for Geneva's execution of Servetus.

Having very considerably revised the manuscript to avoid giving unnecessary offense, and having reached a rapprochement with the expert on Christian theology, I resubmitted the work. An anonymous reader, who is not a New Testament scholar or theologian, angrily condemned the manuscript as unworthy of publication because my writing was filled with gratuitous sniping at Christianity and horrific hyperbole aimed at exposing the sins of the church. The reader, referring to "the Divinity of Christ," found "outrageous" my statement that the historical Jesus did not claim to be divine and that he probably did not speak of himself as the Son of Man. The reader invoked the support of "a billion people"

who have concluded that the texts in question support the divinity of
Christ. Of course, I do not doubt that and state as a fact that the books
of the New Testament take the divinity of Christ for granted; I simply
speculate about the historical Jesus' sense of his own role and try to
make available to a lay public the skeptical interpretations of modern
New Testament scholarship. Demythologizing, even after sixty years of
respectability among experts on the Gospels, is not yet a practice to
which believers, unfamiliar with modern New Testament scholarship,
can extend their toleration. Even a specialist on Stuart England and
English legal history, whose work I admire, devoted most of his critique
of the manuscript of this book to the early chapters, arguing for a more
orthodox position. I learned that biblical literalists cannot be placated.

Jefferson referred to "the incomprehensible jargon of the Trinitarian
arithmetic, that three are one, and one is three." Santayana wrote that
"Christianity persecuted, tortured, and burned. Like a hound it tracked
the very scent of heresy. It kindled wars, and nursed furious hatreds and
ambitions. It sanctified...extermination and tyranny." Whitehead said
that he considered "Christian theology to be one of the great disasters of
the human race.It would be impossible to imagine anything more un-
Christ-like than Christian theology." I had thought that such sentiments
were Voltairean clichés and that the few pale imitations of them that I
have cautiously allowed myself would not have brought down on me a
chorus of epithetical denunciations. Nevertheless, many readers, including New Testament scholars, have not found the book offensive.
And I am not aware that I have blasphemed in writing it. If one man's
vulgarity is another's lyric, one man's blasphemy may be another's
freedom of expression. That does not mean that there is no such thing
as blasphemy. Reviling God is blasphemy and, in Western Christendom, reviling Christianity and the Bible is blasphemy too.

This is a book about the suppression of freedom of expression in the
field of religious belief and experience. It is an unfashionably Whiggish
book. The past depicted here should not be forgotten or emulated.
James Madison stated:

> Whilst we assert for ourselves a freedom to embrace, to profess
> and observe the Religion which we believe to be of divine origin,
> we cannot deny an equal freedom to those whose minds have not
> yet yielded to the evidence which has convinced us. If this freedom
> be abused, it is an offense against God, not against man: To God,
> therefore, not to man, must an account of it be rendered.

Abuse, as distinguished from appropriate use, or licentiousness as opposed to liberty, has always been the rationale for suppression. What society deems to be blasphemy may differ with time and place, but whatever is condemned as blasphemy is always regarded as an abuse of liberty.

Any definition of the freedom of religious (or irreligious) expression necessarily requires the drawing of lines and limits. Perimeters against the impermissible, separating blasphemy from the expression of lawful opinion on religion, reveal what society will not and cannot tolerate. Blasphemy is a litmus test of the standards a society feels it must enforce to preserve its unity, its peace, its morality, and above all its salvation.

The period covered by this book, about three thousand years from Moses to the England of 1700, is one in which very few blasphemers were irreverent. This is not a book in which the victims of blasphemy laws are atheists and irreligious scoffers. On the contary, the book concerns devout Christians, although they were obnoxious to the majority of Christians among whom they lived. Even the homosexual centurion in Kirkup's poem who described his feeling toward Jesus recognized him as the Son of God. The decision of the British court sustaining the conviction of the publisher of that poem was rooted in Old Testament law, in Mark 14:62 and 15:39, in Calvin's prosecution of Servetus in 1553, in Parliament's trial of Nayler in 1656, and in *Rex* v. *Taylor*, where the King's Bench ruled in 1676 that Christianity is part of the law of the land. History, Maitland said, is a seamless web.

The history of the offense of blasphemy originates, at least for us, for Western Christendom, in Exodus 22:28: "You shall not revile God." The understanding of blasphemy in ancient Jewish thought did not progress much beyond that injunction. The Gospels of the New Testament retained the God-centeredness of the Mosaic code but expanded the concept of blasphemy to cover rejection of Jesus and the attribution of his miracles to satanic forces. During the next three centuries, when many variant and conflicting Christianities existed, Christians struggled among themselves to define the true faith. That faith emerged by the close of the fourth century, when it had the backing of the Roman Empire. A standard of orthodoxy finally prevailed by which Christianity, or the church, could measure blasphemy. But Christians characterized other Christians as heretics as well as blasphemers. The offense of heresy and that of blasphemy were nearly synonymous; theologians used the two as if they were interchangeable. Heresy, however, became the more encompassing offense, blasphemy its most execrable and aggravated form.

By the Middle Ages blasphemy had for all practical purposes become indistinguishable from heresy; heresy simply superseded it. Canonists and theologians who sought to be systematic and comprehensive sometimes dealt with blasphemy as if it were a separate offense against religion, but they invariably described it as a subspecies of heresy. I assume that heresy was what the church defined it to be: obstinately held differences of opinion about the true faith as determined by the church. Any error of opinion, recalcitrantly maintained, concerning the church, its creeds, saints, hierarchy, rites, symbols, sacraments, and doctrines, constituted heresy. I know of no case in which a person was convicted and executed for the crime of blasphemy during the Middle Ages. Gratian, Innocent III, Aquinas, and Bernard Gui said nothing about blasphemy significantly different from Tertullian and Augustine. Accordingly I skip lightly over the Middle Ages. This is not a book about heresy. Medievalists may register dismay and amazement because Chapter 4 is so brief and encompassing: it spans the period from Augustine to the Inquisition. Heresy, the Middle Ages, and the Inquisition are not subjects that I can ignore, but I see no reason to digress overmuch from my subject and to recapitulate the work of such excellent scholars as Norman Cohn, Austin Evans, M.D. Lambert, Gordon Leff, Robert E. Lerner, R.I. Moore, Jeffrey B. Russell, and Walter L. Wakefield.

The Reformation brought about a revival of the concept of blasphemy. The first generation of Protestant reformers in the sixteenth century tended to gag on "heresy," of which they stood accused. To describe and condemn the dissidence within their own ranks they preferred the scriptural term "blasphemy," which had yielded to "heresy" under Roman Catholic usage. Consequently the primary sources deliver an increasingly larger payload as I reach England in the seventeenth century.

The first half of this book, covering the history of the offense of blasphemy from ancient Jewish thought to the Reformation, provides essential background to the history of that offense in England, which is the subject of the second half. In the course of defining themselves religiously, the English used the offense of blasphemy as a way of enforcing orthodoxy. The history of the offense in Tudor and Stuart England and during the Interregnum is indispensable to an understanding of the offense in America, indeed, to an understanding of the history of religion and the state of religious liberty in America. America is not even mentioned in the main text of this book. But the English founded America, and the ideas of English Anglicans, Puritans, Baptists, Socinians, Quakers, and Antinomians became American ideas.

This book ends with the closing of the seventeenth century. By then, heresy had become a strictly ecclesiastical offense, punishable at most by excommunication. Blasphemy, as defined by the common-law courts and Parliament, had become a crime against the state. The last execution for blasphemy in Great Britain occurred in 1697 under Scottish law; in 1698 the English Parliament passed a new act against blasphemy, reducing the penalties and aiming them at Christian antitrinitarians. Milton, Newton, and Locke ended their careers as antitrinitarians and helped introduce the Enlightenment to Britain. A new era of freedom of religious expression coincided with the next century, although it began with the prosecution of a Unitarian for blasphemy and closed with the prosecution of Paine's publisher. By that time the victims of the blasphemy laws tended to be freethinkers, rationalists, agnostics, and atheists, and they had begun to rely for their defense on the freedom of the press as well as freedom of religion. The year 1700 closed an old era, making that date a natural point to end this book.

In a sequel I shall continue my study of the history of the offense of blasphemy, covering the span of American history from the colonial period to the present, as well as the British history of blasphemy from the point where I leave off here. The sequel will return to the more familiar ground of Anglo-American legal history, the immediate origins of First Amendment rights, and their development to our time.

The subject of blasphemy, which historians have neglected, forms the basis, at least implicitly, for a study of the struggle for intellectual liberty in general and of religious liberty in particular. The origins, scope, and limitations of freedom of expression have concerned me in several books. The history of the offense of blasphemy has lurked in the background. My first book included a chapter on the blasphemy case of Abner Kneeland in the 1830s. When I wrote a study of the origins of the free-speech and free-press clauses of the First Amendment, I focused mainly on seditious libel but discovered that another major category of libel was blasphemous libel. When I studied Jefferson's record on civil liberties, I learned about his lifelong interest in opposing blasphemy laws and the rule that Christianity was part of the law of the land. When writing *Origins of the Fifth Amendment*, I learned that persons resorted to the claim that they should not be forced to incriminate themselves in cases of political crimes (seditious libel and treason) and in cases of religious crimes (heresy and blasphemy). The subject of blasphemy has pursued me for nearly three decades. This book, in which I pursue my pursuer, treats European religious history, an unlikely subject for a student of the American Constitution. I have been asked why I switched to a new field of interest. I have not. The study of

European and especially English religious history continues my longstanding interest in the origins and present state of First Amendment problems. In our time, as in the past, this is not a subject of merely academic interest.

ACKNOWLEDGMENTS_____

If, as someone said, history is the study of the mistakes of others, I ought not add any of my own. Thomas G. Barnes of Berkeley, Martin Marty of Chicago, Jaroslav Pelikan of Yale, and Krister Stendahl of Harvard reviewed the manuscript of this book. Professors Barnes and Pelikan, whose disagreements with me were strong on many points, generously saved me from mistakes, improving a book whose viewpoint they did not share. Chapter two also benefited from the criticism of Father Thomas Curry and my colleagues of the Department of Religion of Claremont Graduate School and its Institute of Antiquity and Christianity, including James M. Robinson, Hans Dieter Betz (now of Chicago), Burton Mack, and James Brashler. Professor Brashler and Father Curry also assessed chapter three. My foremost gratitude belongs to colleagues in my own department of history, Robert Dawidoff and Henry J. Gibbons, who read the entire manuscript with care and offered invaluable encouragement, when I needed it, as well as incisive criticism. Both know how to hit a platitudinous thought when it is down and help a friend when he is. Ariel Glucklich and Ben Winters also encouraged me. On the whole I found that many of my critics think I use any stigma to beat a dogma, and some people whose names I have mentioned will be relieved to know that I confess this book to be mine — viewpoint, faults, and all; my expression of thanks in no way incriminates them. They revealed "truth" to which I was blind.

Three university administrators earned my appreciation for their encouragement of scholarship: Barnaby Keeney, Joseph B. Platt, and Paul A. Albrecht. Toni Tosch and Karen Clobes typed and retyped the manuscript of this book as it underwent revisions. They too helped. I enjoyed generous institutional support over the years I worked on this book, including a senior fellowship from the National Endowment for the Humanities, a merit fellowship from the American Bar Foundation, and summer fellowships from the American Council of Learned Societies and from the Salvatori Center of Claremont Men's College. In no previous book have I felt the need that I now do to thank my publisher, especially Mr. John J. Simon, editorial director of Schocken Books. In every previous book I have acknowledged my daughters, Wendy Ellen and Leslie Ann, both of whom expressed monumental disinterest in this book. My acknowledgment of special thanks to Professors Dawidoff and Gibbons notwithstanding, I have never depended so much upon my wife, Elyse, for loving support. I did this book for myself; had I done it for anyone else, she would have been the one.

PART ONE

RELIGIOUS FOUNDATIONS

1

THE OFFENSE AND ITS ORIGINS

In *After Strange Gods,* T.S. Eliot lamented that genuine blasphemy, "a symptom that the soul is still alive," is no longer within man's capability. When God is dead to man's religious perception, blasphemy too is dead, Eliot believed. He was not wholly wrong, for blasphemy could not exist in a society of atheists. Ours, however, has been a monotheistic society whose law still punishes blasphemy as a crime. Eliot knew little and cared less about criminal prosecutions; the law of blasphemy simply did not interest him. He used blasphemy like a compass, only to take a fix on the religious direction of our culture. When he claimed that modern society could no longer generate genuine blasphemy, he did not mean that our law protects scurrilous defamations of God, the Bible, or the Christian religion. He meant, rather, that blasphemy is possible only in an age of reverent belief, and he yearned for a more congenial past when speaking evil of the Deity or of things sacred provoked the horror that used to be felt in the presence of spiritual corruption.[1]

In the twentieth century, scorning God, even reviling Him, T.S. Eliot reflected, is merely a breach of good taste, not of deep-seated faith. The logic is that a man who exclaims "Go to hell!" does not really curse if he does not believe in an afterlife. He may be offensive but does not profane the faith. Blasphemy should be "not a matter of good form but of right belief," Eliot thought. If people are still schocked "by any public impertinence towards a Deity for whom they feel privately no respect at all," the bad taste of the impertinence rather than the offense to right belief shocks them. The blasphemer, moreover, "unless he profoundly believes in that which he profanes," no more blasphemes than a parrot mimicking speech curses. "I am reproaching a world in which blasphemy is impossible," Eliot complained, adding maliciously that not even George Bernard Shaw could blaspheme.[2]

If Eliot were right the law would hold only the faithful accountable for the crime of blasphemy. In times past, the rejection of God by a heathen or of the divinity of Jesus by a Jew might unleash the hellhounds of persecution, but not a criminal prosecution for an offense against religion. There never was a time, however, when only a person raised as a Christian could commit the crime of blasphemy by denying the Trinity or some Christian dogma. In law and religion only a believer can be a heretic, but anyone, even an unbeliever, can blaspheme. Historically, blasphemy has been a complex and protean offense whose dragnet has ensnared men of no or little faith as well as the unorthodox faithful. At various times in the past, blasphemy was nearly indistinguishable from the crimes of idolatry, sacrilege, heresy, obscenity, profanity, sedition, treason, and breach of the peace. The meaning of blasphemy has ranged from the ancient Hebrew crime of cursing the ineffable name of God to the modern crime of ridiculing Him or professing atheistical principles in a way that outrages the feelings of others. Blasphemy is not just an irreligious crime; political considerations have often tinged prosecutions, as have considerations of the public welfare and morality.

The core concept of blasphemy, nevertheless, derives from religious belief. The crime is basically a verbal assualt on the most sacred values. Thus, a seventeenth-century English lawyer said, it "is speaking Treason against the Heavenly Majesty, the belching out of execrable words against God, whereby the Deity is reproached." [3] Similarly a Scots jurist in the same year, 1678, referred tersely to the crime of "divine laese majesty or treason," and he joined blasphemy to witchcraft and heresy as "treason against God." [4] Prosecutions for blasphemy, however, have often been "treason" against intellectual liberty and, paradoxically, "treason " against freedom of religion. Over the centuries the sanctions against blasphemy have muzzled not only religious but artistic, political, scientific, and literary expression.

A criminal law, even if only a vestigial relic, never dies until it is repealed or held unconstitutional. The laws against blasphemy in the United States in Eliot's time and now are still on the books and occasionally are enforced. The twentieth century may not be as great an age of faith as the times when men burned witches, blasphemers, and heretics; but the shock of bad form, if not of wrong belief, periodically stirs some avenging prosecutor. The First Amendment as construed by the Supreme Court might now bar the prosecutor, but not in Eliot's time. The Court has never adjudicated a case involving the constitutionality of a blasphemy law. A legal authority who was a contemporary of Eliot declared that any reading of the First Amendment that protected a vile attack on the legitimacy of Christ and the virginity of his mother "would be an enormous perversion of the meaning of the constitution." [5] That bit of wisdom has probably passed out of date.

Prosecutions against blasphemy violate protections of intellectual liberty as much as blasphemers overstep the bounds of civility.

During Eliot's heyday in the 1920s and 1930s, although he for his own reasons deplored the demise of blasphemy, England jailed a blasphemous atheist for his coarse ribaldry about the Gospels and, in particular, for his description of Jesus entering Jerusalem "like a circus clown on the back of two donkeys."[6] In the United States, Maine imprisoned a radical for his contumelious rejection of religion generally and of the doctrines of virgin birth and incarnation especially.[7] Similarly, Massachusetts prosecuted another radical for simply denying the existence of God and the divinity of Jesus.[8] The same state jailed the author of a book on freemasonry for referring to Jesus as immoral and issued a warrant for the arrest, also on a blasphemy charge, of the distinguished philosopher Horace Kallen, who said in a public lecture that if Sacco and Vanzetti were anarchists, "so was Jesus Christ."[9] Arkansas convicted the president of the American Association for the Advancement of Atheism for possessing literature that ridiculed the Bible's depiction of the creation.[10] Canada found blasphemy in a pamphlet virulently attacking the Roman Catholic church and, in another case, imprisoned and deported the editor of an agnostic journal for his facetious references to the "frenzied megalomaniac boastings" of a "touchy Jehovah whom deluded superstitionists claim to be the creator of the whole universe."[11]

In the Canadian "Jehovah" case, the trial judge, when charging the jury, observed that because "nothing is more sacred to us than our religion," any disrespectful language or writing tht God-fearing people resent is blasphemy. Summarizing modern Anglo-American law on the subject, he declared:

A blasphemous libel consists in the publication of any profane words vilifying or ridiculing God, Jesus Christ, the Holy Ghost, the Old or New Testament or Christianity in general, with intent to shock and insult believers, or to pervert or mislead the ignorant and unwary; and if a publication be "full of scurrilous and opprobrious language, — if sacred subjects are treated with levity, if indiscriminate abuse is employed instead of argument, — then a design to wound the religious feelings of others may be readily inferred.But where the work is free from all offensive levity, abuse, and sophistry, and, in fact, the honest and temperate expression of religious opinions conscientiously held and avowed, it is not blasphemous libel." . . . Publications which, in an indecent and malicious spirit, assault and asperse the truth of Christianity or the Scriptures, in language calculated and intended to shock the feelings and outrage the belief of mankind, are properly to be regarded as blasphemous so as to be fit subjects for criminal prosecution.

The views of cultural conservators like T. S. Eliot might reflect theology but not the law; law is indifferent to the question of whether a culprit blasphemes from the wellsprings of belief. Eliot was correct, however, in his patrician understatement that the history of blasphemy would be "an interesting subject of investigation."[12]

Blasphemy is taboo where organized religion exists, and monotheistic systems hold no monopoly on the concept of blasphemy. Any pagan society, whether as civilized as ancient Egypt or as primitive as idol-worshipping savages on Papua, can imagine superior beings or spirits that influence man's destiny; every religious society will punish the rejection or mockery of its gods. Because blasphemy is an intolerable profanation of the sacred, it affronts the priestly class, the deep-seated beliefs of worshippers, and the basic values that a community shares. Punishing the blasphemer may serve any one of several social purposes other than setting an example to warn others. Punishment propitiates the offended deities by avenging their honor, thereby averting divine wrath: earthquakes, infertility, lost battles, floods, plagues, or crop failures. Public retribution for blasphemy also vindicates the witness of the believers and especially of the priests; it reaffirms communal norms; and it avoids the snares of toleration.

Toleration of blasphemy poses problems even for a society that can imagine gods sufficiently powerful to defend their own reputations and discriminating enough to do so by a judgment on the offender only. But if vengeance belongs to the supernatural governor of life, why invoke the criminal law? The reasons are that toleration seems to sanction the offense, inviting others to commit it; reflects adversely on orthodox truths, shedding doubt on them if blasphemers escape punishment; and endangers the unity of society. Even if sanctioning blasphemy did not risk divine wrath on the whole community, failure to punish the blasphemer might lead to public disturbances by provoking violence against him and perhaps even aginst those who tolerate him. Believers whose sensibilities he has injured might seek private retribution when official justice has failed. Fundamentally, however, the blasphemer incurs punishment because society regards his scandalous crime as a form of high treason against the highest powers in the universe. Even societies that cherish liberty have denied it to blasphemers.

Athens in the fifth century B.C. reached cultural peaks that rivaled the finest achievements of mankind for about two thousand years. Freedom of expression was an Athenian boast and a source of accomplishment, but the taboo against reflecting on the gods, whom the Greeks invented in their own image, jeopardized even the highest placed citizens. Impiety was the Greek equivalent of blasphemy. The penalties for impiety circumscribed the prevailing spirit of free inquiry. One could criticize the state but not mock or repudiate its gods, or defile the customary manner of honoring them. The ancient Greeks, having no fixed theology, did not demand obeisance to religious creeds. In general the externals of religion counted most. What a man believed was of little importance if he did not sin against the gods by violating the respect due to them or to the forms of worship. Observing the conventional ceremonials "without omission or innovation," declared Demosthenes, and not giving religious offense in any other way sufficed to keep one on the right side of the law. The law punished those guilty of impiety for two reasons, according to Demosthenes: "first that they may pay the penalty for their crimes; and, secondly, that others may take warning, and may fear to commit any sin against the gods and against the state." When a priest offered a sacrifice on a day not appointed for that rite, or when a priestess should properly have performed it, he died for his crime. Because Athenians regarded an adultress as defiled, she risked death by viewing sacred spectacles or offering public prayers. Drunkenness or violence during a Dionysian service, black magic or sorcery, novelties in religion, the introduction of foreign divinities or ceremonials, and sacrilege or the desecration of holy places and objects were all capital forms of impiety or blasphemy.[13]

The offense that impinged most on intellectual liberty was expression of disbelief in the gods, their religious servants, or the efficacy of conventional worship. Disbelief or impious opinions challenged the cult by impeaching its foundation. The public honoring of the gods could not be fulfilled unless men accepted their existence. Greek scientists and philosophers could speculate about the origins and constitution of the universe as long as they ascribed natural phenomena to the familiar gods. Plato, as Plutarch oberved, merited acclaim in his time partly because he "subjected the compulsions of the physical world to divine and more sovereign principles." By contrast some of his more skeptical or daring predecessors learned that their theories ran them into a sacred area patrolled by the ban against impiety. Any act or expression contemptuous of the gods or depraving holy matters was impiety.[14]

Anaxagoras (ca. 500–428 B.C.), the first philosopher to reside in Athens and one of the earliest Greeks to write a scientific book, was probably the first free-thinker to be condemned for his beliefs. A modern scholar has described him as "one of the truly great philosophers of mankind." Anaxagoras held that a superior intellect had imposed a purposeful order on the physical world. The Athenians, however, saw in his primal organizing force, which he called "Nous" or Mind, no resemblance to their own gods; he regarded their gods as mythic abstractions endowed with anthropomorphic attributes. He speculated about the spatial infinity of the universe, the infinitesimal particles that compose matter, the rotation of the earth, the causes of eclipses, and the nature of the sun, moon, and stars. The fall of a great meteor seemed to confirm his astrophysical theories, inspiring him to publish his book. Long after, when Socrates was being tried for his crimes, his prosecutor sought to associate him with the guilt of Anaxagoras by claiming that Socrates too was an atheist who did not believe that the sun and moon were gods; rather, like Anaxagoras, he believed that the sun was a fiery mass of stone or iron and the moon an earth-like sphere. Socrates replied, "You must think you are accusing Anaxagoras," whose book could then still be bought for a drachma. That book had led Anaxagoras to a dungeon, charged with impiety, probably about the year 450 B.C.[15]

Plutarch claimed, "Men could not abide the natural philosophers and 'visionaries,' as they were called, because they reduced the divine agency down to irrational causes, blind forces, and necessary incidents." The observation accurately described superstitious men and their attitude toward Anaxagoras. His "Nous" set in motion not irrational causes but natural laws which he sought to define. Therefore he attributed godly powers to something other than the conventional gods, making his work seem blasphemous.[16]

Diopeithes, a superstitious priest and fanatical opponent of new ideas, secured from the Athenian assembly a law that called for the indictment "of such as did not believe in gods, or who taught doctrines regarding higher matters," thus, said Plutarch, "directing suspicion against Pericles by means of Anaxagoras." Pericles, who became the preeminent statesman of Athenian democracy at the time of its foremost glory, seemed vulnerable because he was a pupil of Anaxagoras and closest to him. According to tradition, Anaxagoras had taught Pericles his loftiness of thought, his majestic demeanor, and his habit of spicing his oratory with scientific allusions. From Anaxagoras Pericles "seems to have learned to despise those superstitious fears which the common phenomena of the heavens produce in those, who ignorant of their cause, and knowing nothing about them, refer them all to the immediate action of the gods." The indictment of Anaxagoras was, therefore, an effort to cut down an impious radical and, simultaneously, to discredit the rising Pericles. He himself represented the frail, old philosopher at the trial, and the celebrated Periclean oratory saved Anaxagoras from a sentence of death. He had to pay a fine and, by some accounts, was banished. In any case, Pericles, fearing for the philosopher's safety, sent him away; Anaxagoras spent his remaining years in exile, teaching in peace.[17]

About the same time as the trial of Anaxagoras, Pericles also had to defend his mistress, Aspasia, against a charge of impiety. A former courtesan, she was a brilliant woman who made Pericles' home a center of Athenian intellectual life. She held court for Anaxagoras, Phidias the sculptor, Euripides the dramatist, Hippocrates the physician, and others who exchanged uninhibited opinions. Socrates later became a habitué of her salon and sometimes brought his pupils to listen to Aspasia. So unusual a woman may well have been a freethinker who attracted a spurious charge of impiety. Fortunately for her, Pericles' eloquence, embellished with his tears, swayed Aspasia's jury and won her an acquittal.[18]

Pericles was unable, however, to rescue his intimate friend Phidias from the misfortunes that befell him on being charged with sacrilege. Phidias, reputedly the greatest artist of the classical era, designed the interior of the Parthenon and was the sculptor of the colossal statue of the goddess Athena that dominated it. On her shield he carved recognizable figures of himself and Pericles, as a way of signing his work and acknowledging his patron. Since Athena was the guardian deity of Athens and the Parthenon her temple, Phidias's egotistical depiction of himself and his friend, the first citizen of the city-state, was more than the sin of pride; it was a form of impiety and a dangerous one, for any profanation of the protecting gods of the state was implicitly an attack on the state itself, akin to treason. Phidias probably died in prison, while awaiting trial, in about the year 433 B.C.[19]

A few years later Euripides, the tragic poet of the theatre, faced the same charge as Phidias. Cleon, the demagogue who had risen to power on a path paved with oracles, sought to discredit intellectuals like Euripides. The dramatist's record of associations made him suspect, and his plays made him vulnerable. He had studied with Anaxagoras, supported the Periclean party, frequented Aspasia's salon, and fraternized with foreigners who espoused strange, rationalist ideas. Diagoras of Melos and Protagoras of Thrace, whose unorthodoxy eventually approached the scandalous, were friends of Euripides. His own plays revealed a streak of skepticism, if not of latent agnosticism. "We are slaves of gods, whatever gods may be," he said in *Orestes*. His characters did not, of course, necessarily voice his personal beliefs, and he was conventional enough to depict a thunderbolt from Zeus dispatching Bellerophon for his bold atheistic blasphemies. Still, several of Euripides' plays seemed irreligious and shocked his Athenian audiences. He questioned some of the divine legends and daringly exposed the baneful influences that the deities exercised over the lives of mortals. When he seemed to doubt the sanctity of oaths, he passed the threshold of tolerance. In *Hippolytus* he had a character say, "My tongue is sworn, but my mind is unsworn," thus giving the impression of condoning perjury, a form of impiety. Even in pagan Greece oaths were sacred, because they called upon the gods to witness an obligation. Cleon instigated a charge of impiety against Euripides, but he managed to escape the penalty by affirming his belief in oaths and explaining that the oath in question lacked divine sanction. Aeschylus, the illustrious precursor of Euripides, also had to defend himself against a charge of impiety. Regrettably, the facts of his case have not survived.[20]

During the Peloponnesian War, when Athens and Sparta fought for Greek supremacy, the charge of impiety destroyed many lives and careers. Among the victims were Protagoras, the sophist philosopher, and Alcibiades, the statesman and general. Like Anaxagoras, Aspasia, Phidias, and Euripides, both Protagoras and Alcibiades had connections with Pericles. Protagoras had been his friend; Alcibiades, who had been brought up in his household, was a kinsman and protégé. With dozens of others they stood accused of impiety for complicity in the mutilation of the Hermae and the profanation of the Eleusinian Mysteries, the holiest of the Athenian sacraments. The affair of the Hermae, followed immediately by that of the Mysteries, caused a furor. In its frenetic hunt to find and punish the guilty, and thus restore Athens to the good graces of the gods, the city took vengeance on many who were innocent.

The terror occurred in 415 B.C. As the Athenians were preparing a huge expeditionary force to sail against Sparta, the city awoke one morning to an appalling discovery: nearly every statue celebrating Hermes, son of Zeus, the king of gods and men, had been desecrated during the night. There were statues of Hermes everywhere in Athens—before temples, by the doors of private homes, in the city squares, and in front of public buildings; hardly one escaped mutilation by sacrilegious vandals. Impiety on so vast a scale was obviously the work of a conspiracy. Thucydides, the chronicler of the Peloponnesian War, lived through the event which, he recorded, "was taken very seriously; for it seemed to be ominous for the expedition and to have been done withal in furtherance of a conspiracy with a view to a revolution and the overthrow of the democracy." After the Council of the Assembly offered rewards for information leading to the discovery of the culprits, informers implicated Alcibiades and dozens of others, including an aristocratic orator named Andocides. Many were imprisoned, some were executed, and others under suspicion fled.[21]

Further investigations uncovered a second crime of impiety. If the first was comparable to smashing statues of the Madonna in all the religious shrines in a Catholic town during the Middle Ages, the second was comparable to a Black Mass. According to informers, one night when spirits had been high and flagons low, Alcibiades had led a blasphemous parody of the sacred Eleusinian Mysteries, which honored Demeter, the earth goddess. Impersonating the high priest, Alcibiades had revealed and mocked the secret rites. The accusations against him seemed plausible because he was notorious for his escapades, and as an initiate he knew the rites. But the demand for accusations made them cheap. One man, the Titus Oates of his time, named forty-two people and implicated about three hundred in the conspiracy. Andocides, who bargained for a pardon in return for turning state's evidence, confessed his guilt and testified against numerous people, some of whom were executed for impiety.[22]

Alcibiades, one of the commanders of the army, was too important to be condemned summarily. He denied complicity in either of the sensational impieties but never got the chance to clear his name. Although he demanded the right to be tried at once, his political opponents, who had stirred public opinion against him and perhaps instigated the accusations, cleverly contrived to postpone his trial indefinitely. They knew that they had only circumstantial evidence supporting his guilt and that the army remained loyal to him. Accordingly they argued that to delay the departure of the expedition risked too much and that it could not sail without its most vigorous commander. Having no choice, Alcibiades obeyed the council and went off to war.

During his absence his political enemies convinced the public of his guilt; the objective of his blasphemies, they claimed, had been to weaken and overthrow the government, establishing an oligarchy with himself at its head as chief tyrant. The charge gathered credibility from the fact that Alcibiades was a blunt critic of democracy. At length the Assembly dispatched a ship to fetch him home to be tried for his crimes of impiety, but he eluded arrest. He would trust his city, he said, with everything but his life. For his failure to stand trial, Athens convicted Alcibiades by default; the sentence was death and the forfeiture of his properties. On hearing the verdict he renounced his Athenian citizenship and went over to the enemy. At home the priests and priestesses cursed his name publicly and to ensure his everlasting damnation engraved their curses on stone pillars. Although those curses called on the gods to punish him, Alcibiades successfully led the Spartans against Athens.

Protagoras had no connections with Alcibiades or with the impieties of 415 B.C., but the terror led to his destruction. In that year he was over seventy, an illustrious philosopher and teacher of rhetoric. Protagoras was the first and "the greatest sophist," as Cicero said nearly four centuries later. His principle that "Man is the measure of all things" revealed his relativistic outlook and challenged the orthodox belief in universal truths; to Protagoras truth had no fixed meaning, not even for each individual, who was, in his theory, the final determiner of what is true for himself at a particular moment. He taught how to attack any proposition and was the earliest to maintain that every question has two sides. Yet his analytical skills failed him when he turned to the most fundamental question of religion. At a public reading of the introduction of his book, "On the Gods," while in the home of Euripides, Protagoras confessed that he could not argue both sides of the question; his speculations had led him to agnosticism: "As to the gods, I have no means of knowing either that they exist or that they do not exist." At a time when Athens was in a frenzy because of the outrageous impieties against the Hermae and the Eleusinian Mysteries, and was at war as well, Protagoras' philosophy seemed to subvert the public morale. Tolerating him tempted the gods to visit disaster on the city. Athens saved itself by confiscating and publicly burning his books. To avoid a trial for his life, he fled the city. Divine judgment, the Athenians believed, brought him to his fate: he perished at sea when his ship sank in a storm.[23]

More dangerous still was Diagoras of Melos. Once an inoffensive poet, he suffered some tragedy in his personal life, causing him to turn to sophistical philosophy and atheism. So sensational were his alleged impieties of belief that his very name connoted a repudiation of divine justice, and men spoke of him as "Diagoras the atheist." Twenty-four centuries later a historian influenced by the views of the ancients surmised that the title of a nonextant work by Diagoras, "Crushing Speeches," afforded "a glimpse into the blasphemous disposition of the orthodox poet now turned revolutionary." His disposition, rather, seems rational. Once a friend called his attention to the existence of many votive pictures as proof that the gods protected persons from stormy seas. Diagoras retorted that there were "nowhere any pictures of those who have been shipwrecked and drowned at sea." As evidence of his mockery of the gods, he threw into a dying fire a wooden image of

Heracles, facetiously remarking that the heroic deity would perform his thirteenth miracle. Such a man naturally drew accusations that he was in the conspiracy to profane the Mysteries and mutilate the Hermae. Diagoras sensibly fled for his life. Athens published in bronze the notice of his outlawry and of a huge reward for his capture dead or alive. In the safety of Spartan territories, he eluded his Athenian hunters and lived out his life in obscurity.[24]

The last of the Pericleans to be tried for blasphemy was Socrates, who, in Plutarch's poignant but misleading phrase, "lost his life because of philosophy." When he drank the compulsory cup of hemlock in 399 B.C., he closed a lifetime of intellectual subversion and a long history of associations that contributed to his unpopularity, making him more vulnerable to attack after his enemies regained political power in his old age. In the prime of his life, when his rapier-like intellect earned him a place at Aspasia's soirées, Socrates fell in love with Alcibiades, then the most pampered and beautiful adolescent boy in Athens. Socrates became his teacher, and the two remained close friends long after the affair between them ended. No one did greater injury to Athens than Alcibiades, whom the city drove to treason, and it never forgot that he had been a pupil of Socrates. If anyone rivaled Alcibiades as Athen's nemesis, it was Critias, who sat at the head of the Thirty Tyrants, the rulers of the city during the brief Spartan hegemony. Critias was a close friend of Socrates, as was his next in command Charicles, a former pupil of the notorious teacher. The Thirty Tyrants probably executed more Athenians, mostly members of the democratic party, than the Spartans had killed in battle in a decade. Socrates had no share in the tyranny, but his lack of sympathy for democracy was well known. The public identified him with its enemies and believed that the lives of Alcibiades, Critias, and Charicles personified his teachings. After the democrats regained power, their tolerance for his corrosive criticism soon wore out. His enemies would have been satisfied with his exile; he chose death instead. He died "because of his philosophy" in the sense that it made him uncompromising, religiously different, and politically obnoxious.[25]

Except for that of Jesus, the trial of Socrates for blasphemy is the best known in history. Plato, the young aristocrat who was Socrates' greatest pupil, wrote the dialogues that are the chief source of our knowledge of him. Socrates himself wrote no books. Like Jesus he upset his universe by his tongue alone, but his method of teaching as much as his teachings did the damage. To be sure, Socrates was the earliest proponent of a morality founded on the compulsions of individual conscience rather than in obedience to law, even if democratically made. But he was a moralist who professed not to know the path of morality, and he was not religious in the conventional sense. Worse still, perhaps, he was unbearable, because he sought truth by a pitiless inquisition into accepted beliefs. His method made him seem insufferably superior and abrasive. Although he pretended to be a humble seeker of truth who meant to lead men to find it by first understanding the error of their beliefs, Socrates gave the impression of tearing down beliefs without salvaging much. He respected no man and no convictions, no matter how deep-seated. His questions exposed unsupported or false assumptions, leaving people hurt, angry, and not knowing what to think or why. To Socrates, every premise was questionable, every question had two sides or more, and nothing could be confidently believed because truth was unknown. His skepticism shook faith in conventional values, religious and political. What emerged from Socrates' teachings seemed negative, agnostic, and dangerously innovative. The public saw him as a destructive critic and a subversive elitist.[26]

After the treason of Alcibiades, disastrous military reverses, and the bloody rule of the Thirty Tyrants, Socrates seemed to be undermining the already shaken self-confidence of Athens. Little wonder then that he had to stand trial for impiety. The indictment was that he corrupted the youth, did not believe in "the gods of the state," and advocated new deities of his own. The charge meant that he taught oligarchy and sedition, as well as unconventional religious beliefs; he was the intellectual leader of a conspiracy that drew its main support from young aristocrats whom he had indoctrinated with his contempt for democracy as well as for the old religious ways. Socrates was a dangerous man who from a legal standpoint was guilty as charged. The surprising fact is that the Athenian citizenry who were his jury divided so closely in their verdict. He was certainly no crowd pleaser. When arguing that he should not be sentenced to death, he arrogantly claimed that he was so important to Athens as an intellectual gadfly that he should pay no more than a small fine for his guilt. He claimed too that by ridding itself of him, Athens would not expunge what he stood for—an implied threat that oligarchy might prevail over democracy. As every schoolboy knows, his death was the result of his refusal to accept exile or be smuggled out of prison.[27]

That the Athens of the fifth century B.C. could drive Socrates, Phidias, and Protagoras to their deaths and drive away Anaxagoras, Alcibiades, and Diagoras proved rather early in the history of the West that religion when supported by the state can be hostile to enlightenment and personal liberty. Not even in the case of Diagoras "the atheist" do we have a record of any victim of Athenian persecution having reviled the deities. That any even engaged in deviant religious practices is doubtful.

The cases tended to be as much political as religious in character. Treason against the gods was close to treason against the state. The threshold of tolerance for the former was lower than that for the latter. Athens could accept a charge for impiety more easily than it could a political charge. Its targets of attack were mainly intellectual dissidents, and without exception their cases raised fundamental issues of freedom of expression — literary, artistic, scientific, philosophical, religious, and political. And without exception, proof of treason or sedition against the state was harder to come by than proof of deviant religious opinion. Nor did that situation change in later Athenian history. Aristotle, for example, fled Athens in 323 B.C., when he was indicted for impiety; his crime was writing an inscription for the statue of a political patron whom he compared to the immortals, thus insulting religion.[28]

Impiety served as an easy way to reach a religious offense that was little more than an exercise of free speech by a strong-minded intellectual whose politics, like his religious views, were objectionable. Athens honored its cultural leaders who celebrated its values. Those who challenged its values risked the charge of impiety, especially if their expression had an unpopular political coloration.

The Athenian character of impiety, mixing religion with politics at the expense of intellectual liberty, was not radically different from that of blasphemy under Christendom. But the West's law on the crime of blasphemy derived from a quite different source. It was a divine ordinance supposedly revealed to Moses for the governance of the Israelites soon after the Ten Commandments.

Exodus 22:28 declares, "You shall not revile God, nor curse a ruler of your people." The second half of that injunction, which lays the foundation for lese-majesty or treason against the crown, may be a composition of the tenth century B.C., describing events of Moses' time half a millennium earlier. By the tenth century the Davidic monarchy rested on firm foundations; that the people should be warned not to curse a ruler seems less anachronistic at that later date. If the warning was in fact an ordinance of Moses' time, he was probably its originator and surely its beneficiary. Jewish history, like Athenian, suggests that a charge of blasphemy reflected politics as well as religion.[29]

The people who followed Moses out of Egypt were a loose confederation of tribes united by their religion, their adversity during the long sojourn in the Sinai, and their acceptance of Moses as their leader. He was their chief priest, judge, and ruler. But the people so bitterly blamed him for their hardships in the desert that Moses could not cope with their "faultfinding." He cried out to the Lord, "They are almost ready to stone me," an ancient method of capital punishment. They even "put the Lord to the proof" by demanding additional miracles to save them (Exod. 17:2–7). Moses' exclusive access to God, who made him the sole instrument for performing the miracles, vested him with a majesty, divinely derived, that made cursing him equivalent to rejecting the Lord. Moses alone knew His law and sat, a desert ruler, to judge his people. As he explained to his father-in-law, "the people come to me to inquire of God; when they have a dispute, they come to me and I decide between a man and his neighbor, and I make known the statutes of God and his decisions" (Exod. 18:13–16). An appeal to Moses was in effect an appeal to God, who disclosed His law only through Moses. Even when the task of judging became so burdensome that Moses had to devise a system of assistant judges, his people still came to him on all "great matters" and with "hard questions." His decisions carried divine authority. "You shall not revile God, nor curse a ruler of your people" shows the intimate relationship between God and ruler, although the Israelite ruler in Moses' time and ever after possessed no claim to popular respect independent of that relationship.[30]

One case, which is reported in Leviticus 24:10–26, required a decision by Moses himself. During a quarrel, a man "blasphemed the Name, and cursed." We do not know exactly what he said, but he apparently pronounced the personal name of God, for which the conventional rendering is "Yahweh," and spoke contemptuously about Him, thereby shocking and frightening the people within earshot. The Israelites held the name of God in great awe and probably believed that it possessed some magical properties because they associated it with the giving of life and the making of miracles. To curse God by name was a horrendous crime that might bring divine wrath down on the people of Israel. The Bible says that they put the offender in ward or custody until God's will could be made known to them, meaning that Moses had to sit in judgment.

That a crime had been committed was beyond doubt, but this un-precedented case of blasphemy seems to have raised novel questions. The mother of the offender was an Israelite, but his father was an Egyptian; the account of the case refers to the culprit as a "sojourner" rather than a "native." Was he subject to the same laws as natives? Could he be punished for blaspheming a deity in whom he may not have believed? What was the punishment for blasphemy? The ordinance "You shall not revile God" fixed no sentence. The Bible presents Moses' opinion as the words that God spoke to him:

And the Lord said to Moses, Bring out of the camp him who cursed; and let all who heard him lay their hands upon his head, and let all the congregation stone him. And say to the people of Israel, Whoever curses his God shall bear his sin. He who blasphemes the name of the Lord shall be put to death; all the congregation shall stone him; the sojourner as well as the native, when he blasphemes the Name, shall be put to death.

Leviticus 24:16 fixed the precedent in Judeo-Christian history for punishing blasphemy as a crime. Subsequently Moses promulgated a general ordinance that there should be one law for all persons, whether natives or not.

The method of inflicting the death sentence on a person found guilty of blasphemy had a ritual significance similar to sacrifice. When the people shared a collective guilt for a sin violating a divine commandment, they had to make a "sin offering" by sacrificing a bull. The elders of the congregation, representing the people, laid their hands on the head of the sacrifical animal before slaughtering it; thus they acknowledged their responsibility for the sacrifice and sought atonement for the community's sins. So too the witnesses to the crime of blasphemy placed their hands on the head of the blasphemer whom they offered as a sacrifice to God in the hope that He would be forgiving; and the whole congregation, meaning all those who had been present at the trial, had to stone the condemned man to death as a way of sharing responsibility for the sacrifice and atoning for his sin. The sentence and the means of carrying it out signified the way a God-fearing people sought to avert divine wrath.[31]

After the Israelites abandoned their nomadic life and settled in Canaan (Palestine) around the twelfth century B.C., they strayed from monotheism and "went after other gods, from among the gods of the peoples who were round about them, and bowed down to them... They forsook the Lord, and served the Baals and the Ashtaroth" (Judg. 2:12–13). The Canaanites, whose agricultural economy and culture the Israelites assimilated, worshipped local deities or Baals, represented by idols or graven images. The struggle of Yahweh's adherents against idolatrous foreign cults and the prophetic thunderings against them constitute a major theme of biblical history, showing how powerfully the Baal cults gripped the Israelite imagination. There were many Baals — of springs, of mountains, of the soil, of towns, and of various places — but generally they were symbols of the reproductive powers of nature and in particular represented the life-giving rains. The Baals, a superstitious people believed, had the supernatural power of fertilizing the land and providing bounteous rains on which the crops and livestock depended. Ashtaroth or Astarte was the female deity associated with the rain gods. Yahweh was forever punishing the Israelites for their idolatry by turning them over to their enemies, and then, when He heard their contrite prayers, would mercifully raise up a leader to save them.[32]

In the twelfth century B.C., Gideon was one of those leaders, chosen to drive out the Midianites, who had oppressed the Israelites. The Lord instructed him to pull down the altar of Baal belonging to his father and to cut down the grove nearby that represented Astarte, the mother goddess, and then to build an altar to the only true God. Gideon carried out the divine orders, but at night, for fear of the people in the community. In the morning, when they saw what he had done, his blasphemy outraged them, and they demanded his death. Gideon's father saved him from the angry crowd by demanding to know why the people should defend Baal's cause. "If he is a god, let him contend for himself, because his altar has been pulled down" (Judg. 6:25–32). The argument was effective. Yahweh was more than a tribal god and had promised that if the Israelites kept His covenant He would make them "a kingdom of priests and a holy nation" (Exod. 19:6). Insulting Him offended the national honor and invited divine judgment on the people. But a Baal who was merely a local god was apparently expected to avenge his own honor by sending a bolt of lightning against the defiler, by drying his well, by parching his crops, or by some other way within his power — if he possessed it. Gideon's case shows that biblical law regarded as the high crime of blasphemy only the reviling of the one living Deity. Other gods were fair game for blasphemers. A man could curse or destroy the sanctuary of his idol or of a local god without Jewish law taking cognizance of his act. Baal, Astarte, and the others had to look out for themselves. Death by stoning awaited him who blasphemed the true God. The Bible does not explain why Yahweh did not contend for Himself or why men must murder each other to avenge an avenging God's honor. His ways were unfathomable to mortals, and they did not dare question His judgment.

Gideon blew his trumpet, vanquished the Midianites, and for forty years ruled over Israel, restoring the people to Yahweh. After his death, however, "the people of Israel turned again and played the harlot after Baals. . ." (Judg. 8:3). By the time of King Ahab, who died about 851 B.C., the Baal cult threatened to obliterate Yahwism. Ahab's reign receives more space in the Bible than that of any other since Solomon's, yet the chronicler of the first book of Kings did not mention Ahab's role at the battle of Karkar, which checked the advance of the Assyrians. The dominating focus in the book of Kings is religious. We learn that Ahab supported his wife's effort to supplant Yahweh with a foreign deity, Malkart, the Baal of Phoenicia whom Jezebel, a Phoenician princess, worshipped. At his new capital in Samaria, Ahab built a great temple to the Baal and kept, at royal expense, a huge entourage of Baal's priests — eight hundred fifty no less. Jezebel desecrated the sanctuaries of Yahweh and killed almost all His prophets. Closely related to the main thread of the narrative is the tragedy of Naboth. Jezebel plotted his death on false charges of blasphemy and treason, proving the immorality of the royal apostasy from Yahweh and the intimacy between law, politics, and religion.

Naboth, a prosperous elder of Jezreel, had a vineyard adjacent to the royal summer palace. Ahab coveted Naboth's land and made him a reasonable offer for it, but Naboth, claiming that the Lord had forbidden him to part with any of his inheritance, adamantly refused to sell. Ahab, recognizing the ancient right of a subject to hold onto his patrimony, could do nothing but sulk. On discovering the cause of her husband's depression, Jezebel promised to secure Naboth's land for him. She represented a foreign tradition of despotism that recognized no rights in the subjects; she did recognize, however, that the Yahweh cult and the personal liberties of an Israelite landowner could not in this instance be overcome unless the appearance of law supported the crown. She therefore corrupted the courts of justice by influencing the elders of Jezreel to accept the perjured testimony of two "base fellows" who accused Naboth of having cursed God and the king. According to a Talmudic tradition, the charge of treason reinforced the unlikely one of blasphemy in the minds of the elders who sat as judges, while the charge of blasphemy was calculated to ward off popular resentment against royal tyranny. Each charge supposedly made the other more heinous and believable. The court summarily found Naboth guilty and he died by stoning, the customary punishment for blasphemy. Ahab then took possession of his land, either because Naboth's property escheated to the crown or because as a distant relative the king was the surviving heir — a situation ensured by the slaying of Naboth's sons. What follows is one of the Bible's most terrible stories of divine retribution (1 Kings 21:20–4; 2 Kings 9:21–37, 10:6–28).[33]

The story shows not only the vindication of Yahweh but the enormous indignation of the people against the crimes of the royal house. They would not accept the unjust murder of a servant of the Lord nor see their old liberties trampled upon. Naboth's case also revealed the need for a careful investigation of criminal charges and eventually led to

elaborate procedures that hedged the accused with protections intended
to prevent miscarriage of justice.

An episode of 701 B.C., during the Assyrian siege of Jerusalem,
became the basis of a peculiar Jewish ritual, the tearing of one's clothes
on hearing blasphemy. More than seven centuries later that ritual
figured in the trial of Jesus before the Sanhedrin, according to the accounts in the Gospels. In 701 King Sennacherib of Assyria captured and
sacked all the fortified towns of Judah, except Jerusalem, the capital.
King Hezekiah of Judah paid Sennacherib an enormous tribute in an effort to save the city from assault, but the Assyrian demanded un-
conditional surrender. With his army encamped on the outskirts of
Jerusalem, Sennacherib's emissaries, led by one known only by his title
of Rab-Shakeh, engaged in psychological warfare. Shouting in fluent
Hebrew so that he could be understood by the soldiers and people of
Jerusalem, Rab-Shakeh ridiculed Hezekiah's ability to save the city; he
threatened its destruction and the enslavement of its inhabitants if they
did not capitulate. "Do not," he warned, "let Hezekiah make you rely
on the Lord by saying the Lord will surely deliver us." The gods of
many other lands, Rab-Shakeh reminded his frightened listeners, did
not save them from utter destruction. "Do not let your God on whom
you rely deceive you by promising that Jerusalem will not be given into
the hands of the king of Assyria." Rab-Shakeh's speech grew blasphemous. He spoke "against the Lord God" and "cast contempt" on Him.
The accounts refer to mocking and reviling, although we know only
that he compared Yahweh to the gods of various conquered peoples
whose deities, by Jewish standards, were "no gods but the work of
men's hands, wood and stone," like idols.[34]

Hezekiah's representatives rent their garments as a sign of the grief
and horror they felt on being exposed to blasphemy. They reported the
Assyrian ultimatum and utterances to the king, who also tore his
clothes, covered himself in sackcloth, and went to the temple to pray
for divine aid. He also sent for the prophet Isaiah, who assured
Hezekiah that the only true and living God had heard his prayers and
would save the city by turning away the enemy. According to biblical
accounts, Yahweh sent an angel (more than likely it was a plague) who
destroyed no less than a hundred eighty-five thousand Assyrians;
history has known many a conquering army conquered by disease. Sennacherib retreated to his capital at Nineveh where, in fulfillment of
Isaiah's prophecy, he met assassination.

The blasphemy of Rab-Shakeh did not conform to the Levitical requirement that blasphemy consist of cursing God or His name, unless
cursing be taken loosely to include abusing, rejecting, and deriding. In

the biblical sense, to curse ordinarily means to utter an imprecation or invoke evil, usually by calling on God's power. "God damn," the most familiar curse, is now mere profanity. Notwithstanding the characterizations of Rab-Shakeh's speech as contemptuous, reviling, and mocking, the only specific evidence in three biblical accounts is that he regarded Yahweh as no different from the deities worshipped by idolators. Apparently blasphemy had come to mean showing disrespect for God, doubting His powers, and even disobeying His commandments. Indeed, we read that as long ago as Moses' time anyone who knowingly sins "reviles the Lord." The blasphemous nature of the sin was a considerably less serious offense that that of damning or cursing God, for the punishment was merely that "that person shall be cut off from among his people," or exiled (Num. 15:31). Similarly, in the time of Ezekiel (about 580 B.C.), the chronicler reports God as saying, "Your fathers blasphemed me, by dealing treacherously with me," and the context makes clear that the offense was worshipping idols (Ezek. 20:27). By contrast the verbal crime of blasphemy, which was a capital crime, consisted essentially in speaking evil of God. The Hebrew word for "curse" can mean "show disrespect," which conceivably can be manifested in any irreligious or immoral way, but blasphemy was a crime of utterance.[35]

The Rab-Shakeh episode shows that blasphemy encompassed a considerably broader range of offensive utterances than did cursing in the literal sense; therefore, the incident illustrates a shift in the understanding of the crime. Long after, when the Talmud was being compiled, the rabbis agreed that rending one's garments and leaving them unsewn was the proper reaction of a God-fearing person exposed to blasphemy, although only when coming from the mouth of a Jew. Rab-Shakeh was a Gentile, a fact that the Talmud explained away by alleging, without evidence, that he was an apostate Jew. Apparently the rabbis reasoned that only a person raised as a Jew could have spoken Hebrew as fluently as he.[36]

None of the numerous scriptural references to "blasphemy" actually quotes a blasphemous utterance. Those who composed the Old Testament would not dare offend God by repeating the thought, let alone the very words, of such an utterance. Generally the Hebrew Bible declares that blasphemy, like idolatry, is not to be endured. In Daniel 3:29, for example, Nebuchadnezzar, awed by the rescue of Yahweh's servants from the fiery furnace, decrees that no one shall blaspheme their God on pain of being torn limb from limb. In the original Hebrew version the decree enjoins "speaking anything against God," although in the Septuagint, the Greek translation of the Scriptures, the verb is "blaspheme." Greek usage favored "blasphemy" where the Hebrew tended to prefer a circumlocution or a more exact word. Thus, Isaiah 66:3 in the Septuagint connects blasphemy with idolatry in a passage where the Hebrew simply compares an abominable offering to blessing an idol. Or, in an Apocryphal text, 1 Maccabees 2:6, the Greek relies on "blasphemy" where the Hebrew more appropriately uses "sacrilegious."[37]

The scriptural term for "blaspheme" in Hebrew is *nakob*, which literally means to specify, enunciate, or pronounce distinctly; but Leviticus 24:10–23 uses *nakob* in conjunction with *killel* or *qillel*, which means curse. The word's connotations include "pierce" (the name of God), "rail," "repudiate," "derogate," "speak disrespectfully," "denounce," "insult," and "abuse." Although the Septuagint tended to use "blasphemy" as a broad term for offenses against religion, it did not basically differ from the Hebrew Scriptures. Begun as a Greek translation of the Pentateuch for the benefit of Greek-speaking Jews of the Diaspora, the Septuagint extended over time to include all the Old Testament and the Hebrew Apocrypha (a dozen additional books which, although composed before the Christian era, were omitted from the rabbinical canon as too recent in composition). The Greek-Jewish tradition also encompassed the Pseudepigrapha, an indeterminable number of still more recent extracanonical writings, yet that tradition did not significantly depart from the fundamental Hebrew definition of blasphemy.[38]

In Jewish thought the word invariably denoted verbal abuse of God. 2 Maccabees, which was originally composed in Greek, uses "blasphemy," "blasphemer," or "blaspheme" much more frequently than 1 Maccabees, which derived from a Hebrew version. The two books depict roughly the same events of the Maccabean struggle for Jewish independence during the years 175–161 B.C. 2 Maccabees, dating from about 124 B.C., contains the most references to "blasphemy" in all the Apocryphal literature. In this chronicle describing how the Hellenizers sought to eradicate Judaism and replace it with idolatrous worship, the text contains various references to offenses against religion — forced apostasy, sacrilege, and "acts of impiety" such as killing mothers who had their sons circumcised, compelling Jews to eat forbidden foods, and building a pagan temple on a sacred Jewish site. Within such a context, described in 1 Maccabees also, the references to blasphemy suggest that the Hellenizers also reviled the living God in words not fit for quotation. In 2 Maccabees 15:3, Nicanor questions whether there is a "ruler in the sky who has ordered the sabbath day to be observed," giving us the closest approximation to blasphemous words that a Jewish chronicler would permit.[39]

With the exception of Sirach 3:16 no Greek-Jewish text uses "blasphemy" or any form of it, that is not God-centered. The thought in Sirach is that to reject or despise one's father "is like blasphemy." The aberrant analogy recalls the disobedient son of Deuteronomy 21:18–21 who must be stoned. Every other usage of "blasphemy" whose meaning can be inferred occurs in the context of idolatry or a rejection of God. Nowhere in the entire corpus of Greek-Jewish sacred books (Septuagint, Apocrypha, and Pseudepigrapha) is blasphemy a synonym for heresy. Indeed, heresy is not a Hebrew term at all, and no equivalent for it appears in the pre-Christian era. Christianity, although greatly influenced by the Septuagint, would use the two terms as equivalents and as more than a God-centered offense. Not until Christianity began did the meaning of blasphemy change.[40]

When the rabbis composed the Talmud in the Christian era, they narrowed the meaning of blasphemy at the very time, and probably because, Christianity expanded it. The Talmud, a sprawling temple of learning that is a commentary on the Old Testament, contains the ultimate expression of Jewish law on the subject of blasphemy. To understand scriptural provisions and apply them to daily life, the "People of the Book" developed an ever-growing body of law that was passed on by oral tradition for approximately fifteen centuries. From about the time of the generation before Jesus to the third century, rabbinic scholars compiled and codified that body of law as a sort of interpretative Corpus Juris and encyclopedia of Jewish culture and religion, which was itself subject to further exegesis and commentaries. The entire authoritative compilation became the Talmud, the English edition of which extends to over thirty volumes. Because it came into existence after Christianity became systematically anti-Semitic (the Talmud itself would later be burned as a mountain of damnable blasphemies), the Talmud's discussion of blasphemy represents a road not taken by Christendom. Scriptural rather than rabbinic law is the source of Anglo-American law on blasphemy; but the rabbinic law represents the culmination of a formative Jewish tradition.[41]

Jewish law avenges God's honor but not that of the Jewish religion. The Old Testament and the Talmud restrict the crime of blasphemy to defamation of the deity, which had the resonance of high treason against the king of kings, the creator and lord of the universe. But reviling sacred customs, beliefs and institutions — whether Judaism itself, the Temple, the sacerdotal hierarchy, particular rituals, or holy dogmas — did not constitute blasphemy. The Rab-Shakeh incident and 2 Maccabees reflected an enlarged view of the crime, yet only in relation to God. The Talmud, however, focused on the original injunction from Exodus 22:28, "You shall not revile God," and defined the crime as tightly as possible. It was essentially a capital sin, an offense against religion, as was idolatry; both signified a rejection of God, the one by worshipping a created thing and the other by cursing Yahweh. In the Talmud, as in the Rab-Shakeh incident, blasphemy and idolatry were inextricably related: "Wherein lies the enormity of these offenses? Because they constitute an attack on the fundamental belief of Judaism," the existence and unity of God. Significantly, they attacked "the" fundamental belief— belief in God — not "a" fundamental belief, for there was only one and it alone could be described as a dogma of Judaism, a religion notably devoid of dogmas. We can interpret the criminal nature of blasphemy and the capital punishment for it as an effort to placate Yahweh in the hope of saving the people from His judgment; He could be vengeful as well as merciful. But the Talmud itself condemned the offense for purely religious reasons: blasphemy offended God contrary to His express will as revealed to Moses. Neither scriptural nor rabbinic law refers to the need for appeasing the deity.[42]

In his codification of the Mishnah Torah, the basic Talmudic exegesis of the Pentateuch, Maimonides, the foremost Jewish scholar and philosopher, wrote that whoever accepted idolatry repudiated "the whole of the Torah," the Mosaic law of God, and "whoever acknowledges that idolatry is true, even if he does not worship an idol, reviles and blasphemes the honoured and revered name of God. The idolator and the blasphemer are in the same class . . . I have accordingly included the law of the blasphemer among the laws of idolatry, since both the blasphemer and the idolator deny the fundamental principle of our religion." Although blasphemy was a form of idolatry, the Talmud explicitly confined blasphemy to cursing God, as in "May Yahweh smite Himself," and additionally restricted it to a particular utterance: "the blasphemer is punished only if he utters (the divine) Name." Thus, to say "God damn" was to curse profanely but was not a curse against God, while to say "May God smite Himself" or "Damn God" implied a rejection and reviling of the deity but did not meet the requirement that God be cursed by His name. Indeed the Talmud, which often defined a crime in a way that would make its commission nearly impossible or at least extremely unlikely, specified that the blasphemer must curse "the name by the name," or else he would not be guilty of the capital crime. Neither cursing God nor saying His name fulfilled the Talmudic requirement.[43]

The belief nevertheless persisted among some scholars and theologians that the mere utterance of the name of God was, in Jewish law, blasphemous. According to the Talmud one who pronounced the name as it is spelled would have no share in the world to come, but a better reason for the misleading belief is that a literal translation of Leviticus 24:16 commands death for whoever "pronounces" the name of the Lord. The Hebrew for "blaspheme" has a variety of meanings including "pronounce distinctly," but the name of God is not known for certain, and its actual pronunciation must forever remain a mystery. A four-letter Hebrew name know as the "Tetragrammaton," for which the English equivalent of the letters is YHVH, represents the name of God. The original Hebrew lacked vowels, leaving doubt as to the sound of the name, although it is commonly spelled "Yahweh" or "Yahveh." Its meaning is, roughly, "I am who I am," leaving doubt whether God disclosed his personal name to Moses in Exodus 3:14.[44]

Although the Talmud requires that in order to commit blasphemy one must curse God's name, indeed, curse the name by the name, the belief that merely uttering the name constituted blasphemy drew strength from the fact that use of the name atrophied over the centuries. In the last three books of the Old Testament, which were compiled after 300 B.C., the Tetragrammaton appears only seven times, although almost six thousand times previously. The reverence of the Jews for that ineffable, sublime, and awesome name caused them to recoil at hearing it except, perhaps, when praying or reading the Scriptures; they thought it too sacred to be uttered and adopted substitutes for it, chief among them being "Adonai" (the Lord) and "Elohim" (God). By the time of Jesus, only the priests in the Temple in Jerusalem used the name and only during religious observances.[45]

The decreasing frequency of the use of the name can also be attributed to other circumstances, unrelated to a belief that pronouncing the name was blasphemous. When Yahwism had rivals among the Baal cults and other forms of idolatry, a need existed to emphasize the name as that of the only true God. Later a simple reference to God or the Lord sufficed as proof that Yahweh had prevailed over all false deities. His name, however, remained sacred. Confining its use to Temple rites diminished the possibility that the name might be profaned, taken in vain (false swearing), or desecrated by falling into the hands of sorcerers who believed that uttering it in incantations enhanced their magical powers. Whatever the reasons, superstition and reverence enveloped the name, making its use exceptionally rare and possibly dangerous, giving rise to the assumption that its utterance was blasphemous.[46]

The simple fact, however, is that the Talmud required at the very least that the utterance of the name be accompanied by disrespect or contempt, and some of the rabbinic scholars demanded proof that the accused had cursed the Tetragrammaton by invoking the name to revile it. So sacred had the name become that the Talmud employed far-fetched euphemisms when describing blasphemy. For example, the witnesses to the crime could not testify in open court by stating exactly what they had heard. That would repeat the holy name and the abhorrent crime itself. Accordingly, although the trial was open to the public, the court instructed the witnesses to employ a four-letter substitute for YHVH, as in the Talmudic illustration, "May Jose (Joseph) smite Jose." Because the court could not convict on the basis of such evidence, the judges cleared the room of spectators at the end of the trial and commanded the eldest witness, "State literally what you have heard." When he repeated the actual utterance, the judges arose and ripped their robes to show their profound grief on hearing blasphemy. The witnesses, having torn their clothing when they first heard it, were exempted from the courtroom ritual. Only one witness repeated the blasphemy; others had only to state, "I too have heard thus," thereby avoiding unnecessary use of the name and the crime itself.[47]

So horrifying was the thought that anyone might curse Yahweh by name that the rabbis, when arguing that the name must be cursed by the name, resorted to an antonym for "curse" by saying, "The Name must be 'blessed' by the Name" if the utterance was to deserve death. Some early rabbis taught that reviling God, even without using the Tetragrammaton, was a capital crime, although later sages decreed that a blasphemous utterance employing any of the substitutes for YHVH was punishable only by flogging. If the offender was a heathen, however, the prescribed penalty was decapitation whether he used the name or a substitute; the Talmud offered no satisfactory reason for the discrimination against heathens. On the other hand rabbinic law was moderate in construing the rule "He is not guilty unless he cursed the Tetragrammaton." From that the rabbis deduced that a two-letter substitue such as El for Elohim or YH for YHVH was not punishable at all.[48]

The Talmud's narrow definition of blasphemy was in keeping with its criminal procedure, which seemed calculated to exonerate the accused unless a guilty verdict could not be avoided. Probably no system of jurisprudence reflected a more humane concern for human life and liberty by interposing so many roadblocks against the conviction of an innocent man — and even the guilty. There was no public prosecutor to manage the indictment, marshal the evidence, and present the case for society. Witnesses to a crime brought an accusation before the Sanhedrin, a court of at least twenty-three rabbinic judges whose jurisdiction included criminal cases; the Sanhedrin conducted a blasphemy trial, like any capital case, as if the witnesses against the defendant might be guilty of lodging false accusations against him. The court's inquisitorial cross-examination of the prosecuting witnesses constituted the bulk of the trial. The accused could testify on his own behalf but never against himself; the Sanhedrin would not accept even a voluntary confession of guilt, nor any self-incriminatory statement. The witnesses against him — Scripture required two or more (Deut. 19:15) — testified with the knowledge that they faced harsh penalties for false or refuted testimony and that in the event of a verdict of guilty, they would be the executioners.[49]

The Sanhedrin applied stringent rules of evidence and refused to accept conjecture, hearsay, or circumstantial evidence. As an example of the latter, the Talmud gave this judicial admonition to a witness: "Perhaps ye saw him running after his fellow into a ruin, ye pursued him, and found him sword in hand with blood dripping from it, whilst the murdered man was writhing [in agony]: If this is what ye saw, ye saw nothing." The court would even reject the evidence of unimpeachable eyewitnesses if their testimony differed on an essential point. A discrepancy in their testimony resulted in an acquittal. The accused benefited from a presumption of innocence until the proof of his guilt was certain, yet even then he was not liable to execution unless the case against him showed that he had committed the offense willfully. If the character and circumstances of the crime permitted, proof of willfulness or criminal intent could be satisfied by demonstrating to the Sanhedrin that two people, "admonitors," had forewarned the accused that he was about to commit a capital crime, that he had acknowledged the warning, and that he had defiantly ignored it. The rabbis had so intense an aversion to the death penalty that they made its infliction nearly impossible.[50]

The Talmud described a Sanhedrin which gave a verdict for death once in seven years as a "destructive tribunal." Some rabbis said, rather, "once in seventy years," and others that they would never vote to inflict capital punishment. For practical purposes the penalty for blasphemy was flogging, especially after A.D. 70, when the Romans destroyed the Temple. Thereafter the Sanhedrin lost the power to inflict death. Accordingly the Talmudic commentaries on trial procedures in capital cases and on the four modes of execution, including stoning for blasphemy, had historical and ethical values; but as far as practice was concerned, those sections of the Talmud had become a fossilized collection of exquisite distinctions derived from an exegetical scholasticism that bore no relation to a functioning world. Capital punishment by Jewish courts had become obsolete more than a century before the Talmud provided manuals for the four modes of execution. In time the penalty for blasphemy became excommunication. A ninth-century rabbinic scholar summed up Jewish law already old when he declared:

> It is not necessary that the blasphemy be in Hebrew, and it makes no difference whether the Ineffable Name or the attributes of God be mentioned, whether the offender be a Jew or a non-Jew, whether the language be Hebrew or any other. The former distinctions were made to distinguish the capital offense from the lesser transgression. But for the purposes of excommunication it makes no difference whether the blasphemer be a heathen or a Jew, whether he use the Sacred Name or the attributes, nor what language he uses; he must be excommunicated.[51]

In sum the Jewish law on blasphemy remained severely God-centered, but its Talmudic interpretation was a law made for a world that had all but disappeared in the late first century A.D. Christian nations would seize upon the scriptural definition of blasphemy as a point of departure for drastically enlarging the definition of the crime.

2

THE JEWISH TRIAL OF JESUS

The most famous and influential blasphemy trial in history was a religiously inspired fiction. The Jewish Sanhedrin, the great council of seventy presided over by the high priest, neither tried Jesus for blasphemy nor convicted him of any crime. The depictions of the formal trial of Jesus by the Sanhedrin in the Gospels of Mark and Matthew really mean to convey with dramatic force the Jewish rejection of Jesus. Theologically, the trial scenes in Mark* and Matthew are crucial, because they reveal the identity of Jesus as the Christ. Readers understand that he had not blasphemed God and that the blasphemers were those who found him guilty, for they refused to accept him as Son of God and Messiah.[1]

Although only Mark and Matthew depict a formal trial and condemnation by the Sanhedrin, all four evangelists (the writers of the Gospels) employ the motif that the Jewish rejection of Jesus was blasphemy. The Synoptics — the first three Gospels, whose similarity of viewpoint is especially evident when they are compared in parallel columns — describe a scene in which Jesus forgives a man for his sins and cures him of paralysis, provoking some "scribes" to say, "It is blasphemy! Who can forgive sins but God alone?" (Mark 2:5–8, Matt. 9:2–3, Luke 5:21). In that scene Jesus relies on his authority as Son of Man to heal and forgive. Thus, he acts from a divinely inspired commission, making the charge of blasphemy warrantless. When Jesus restores the power of speech to a dumb man, Jewish onlookers (Pharisees in Matthew, scribes in Mark, and unidentified members of the crowd in Luke) allege that his miraculous power comes from the prince of demons. Such scenes set the stage for the infamous Jewish trial. They are, like the trial, devices for demonstrating Jewish rejection of Jesus and a new meaning of

---

*When I refer to Mark, Matthew, or any of the other Gospel accounts by name, I mean the account and not its author; we do not know the identities of the Gospels' authors.

blasphemy. Jesus declares that to ascribe to the devil a work of the Holy Spirit is an unforgivable blasphemy (Mark 3:22–29; Matt. 12:24–31; Luke 11:15, 12:10).[2]

In reality, Jews in ancient Palestine assumed the omnipotence of God and the commonplaceness of a religious man's having the power to heal and forgive in the name of God. Jesus himself never claimed to act on his own authority. His healing on the sabbath and forgiving sins did not violate Jewish law. An assertion by a holy person, relying on scriptural precedents, that he was doing God's will would not likely have been subject to criticism, let alone be called blasphemous. The frequent Gospel assertions that the people and even Jesus' apostles were "astonished" show what was probably the Jewish reaction to Jesus. The Gospels are ambivalent on this point. When, for example, he cured multitudes by the sea and then fed five thousand with five loaves and two fishes, there was no talk of blasphemy. In the fourth Gospel, John says of the feeding miracle that the people took it as a sign that a prophet had come, and they wanted to make him a king (John 6:14–15).[3]

John, however, also uses the theme that Jewish rejection of Jesus was blasphemy. When Jesus performs a healing on the sabbath, "the Jews" want to kill him "because he not only broke the sabbath but also called God his Father, making himself equal with God." Jesus appropriately silences them by saying, "The Son can do nothing of his own accord . . ." (John 5:18–19). On another occasion Jesus says, in accord with John's high christology, "Before Abraham was, I am," so the Jews began to stone him — a symbolic execution for blasphemy. On another occasion Jesus declares, "I and the Father are one," and again they stone him. In this scene, Jesus stops them with Old Testament sayings, which give a Jewish coloration to the story, to prove that, far from blaspheming, he acts with divine authority (John 10:30–38). These episodes in John echo the blasphemy charge in Mark's account of the Jewish trial. Their point, of course, is that Jesus is God or Son of God, as Christian readers of the Gospels, reflecting a christology that did not exist at the time of the historical Jesus, readily understood. The Gospels broke with the Jewish understanding of blasphemy — reviling God by name — but from a Christian standpoint, they did not break with its God-centeredness.[4]

The chasm between history and theology separates the historical Jesus, who lived the life of a human being, and the historical Christ, who is the object of Christian worship as God's self-revelation. Each of the evangelists is a "witness" only in a religious sense, expressing Christian faith, in James M. Robinson's words, as "an inward participant in the history he narrates." But the history he narrates was not intended to be a factual record of what actually happened to the historical Jesus, whose life cannot be recovered. Religious propaganda is the object of all four Gospels. A New Testament scholar recently claimed that because the evangelists did not even think in historical terms, "the historian has to treat these sources as he would treat propaganda material." The Gospels christianized the truth of what happened, and the problem of the Gospels' truth derives also from the fact that they are supernatural or superhuman miracle stories, depicting the human life of a divine being. The narrative about Jesus serves the purpose of making the religion of Jesus a religion deifying him. Every purported fact has a spiritual or theological motive and, in canny ways, sometimes a political one.[5]

As the controversial Catholic theologian Hans Küng recently wrote, the whole Passion narrative is an "absurd story" that "becomes comprehensible as the expression of God's mysterious imperative. " Because the Gospels are testaments that convey a message deriving from Christian faith, history, a reconstruction of what happened founded upon verifiable facts, cannot get much enlightenment from the evangelists. The chapters dealing with the trials of Jesus before the Sanhedrin and then before Pilate have purposes unrelated to accurate reporting founded upon original and credible sources. The Gospels, incidentally, are so difficult to comprehend that even Jesus' own apostles did not always understand his message and identity. If Jesus had to rebuke Peter's misunderstanding by saying "Get thee behind me, Satan" (Mark 8:33; Matt. 16:23), the misunderstanding of the Pharisees, or of the Sanhedrin, or even of Pilate, should not be surprising, and none can be blamed, not even Judas, for fulfilling roles assigned by an inscrutable God.[6]

The chief priests of Judea doubtlessly collaborated with the Roman occupation authorities and believed Jesus to be guilty of political crimes. They governed the Temple and influenced the Great Sanhedrin, which constituted the supreme religious court of the Jews and as a senate governed Judea subject to Roman policies. It was a political council even more than a religious or judicial one. The chief priests of the Sanhedrin were implicated in Jesus' fate, but from his arrest and trial to his execution Jesus was probably a victim of the Romans. As Oscar Cullmann, an eminent New Testament scholar, declared, "From the beginning the entire action proceeds from the Romans." The inscription attached to Jesus' cross explained the crime for which he died; he supposedly had proclaimed himself to be "King of the Jews." Under Roman law one claiming to be king in place of the emperor was guilty of treason, a capital crime. Jesus died by crucifixion, a Roman punishment and most certainly not a Jewish one.[7]

According to the four Gospels, however, Jesus never called himself

king of the Jews, a title that only non-Jews would use. Jesus was a Jew.
He was born a Jew, lived as a Jew, and died as a Jew. The fact that the
historical Jesus was Jewish, and a devout Jew at that, means a good
deal, most of all that he was not a Christian. Christianity did not exist
during the lifetime of Jesus. In the words of Rudolf Bultmann, the most
influential Protestant New Testament scholar, "Jesus was not a Christian but a Jew, and his preaching is couched in the thought forms and
imagery of Judaism, even when it is critical of traditional Jewish piety."
The Jews awaited a messiah who would be king of Israel, not king of
the Jews. But Jesus did not call himself king of Israel either, nor did he
ever use any regal title for himself in a political or temporal sense. In
fact, with one exception (Mark 14:62), he did not even call himself the
Messiah, although he did not reject that title. When he asked his
disciples whether they realized who he was, Peter replied, "You are the
Christ." "Christ" is a Greek translation of the Hebrew word for
"messiah." Jesus responded by warning his disciples to keep his identity
a secret, and he predicted that he would be killed but would rise again
in three days (Mark 8:29–31, Matt. 16:6–21, Luke 9:20–22). At the
trial before the Sanhedrin, the high priest asked Jesus point-blank, "Are
you the Christ, the Son of the Blessed?" On this occasion only and nowhere else in the New Testament, Jesus replied directly and affirmative-
ly: "I am; and you will see the Son of man sitting at the right hand of
Power, and coming with the clouds of heaven" (Mark 14:61–62).[8]

That was the putative blasphemy for which the Sanhedrin supposedly
condemned Jesus. In Matthew, Jesus' response to the high priest is indirect. Jesus replied, "You have said so," and then he continued with
the saying about the Son of Man (Matt. 26:63–64). In New Testament
scholarship, construing his evasive answer as an affirmation, as in "You
are right," is common but disputed.[9]

According to the Gospels, Jesus never claimed any title for himself
except that of "Son of Man." This is a difficult expression derived from
the Old Testament. Of all the titles by which Jesus is known in the New
Testament — Lord, Son of God, Prophet, Rabbi, Savior, Son of David,
King of the Jews, and King of Israel, among others — the only one that
he used to describe himself and the only one not attributed to him by
others is "Son of Man." "It expressed," said Vincent Taylor, a conservative New Testament scholar, "the very idea of lordship, of rule over
the messianic community, and its associations are supernatural." As
"Son of Man," Jesus supposedly felt himself to have divine authorization as a worker of miracles and a forgiver of sins. Although the title invoked God's authority, it described a human being.[10]

"Son of Man," in the sense that Jesus used it of himself, if he did, came from the book of Daniel where it is eschatological in character, yet carries distinct messianic overtones as numerous theologians have suggested. Daniel predicts that the "Son of Man" will come on the Day of Judgment: "And to him was given dominion and glory and kingdom, that all peoples, nations, and languages should serve him; his dominion is an everlasting dominion, which shall not pass away, and his kingdom one that shall not be destroyed" (Dan. 7:13–14). Like Daniel, the New Testament presents the eschatological concept of the Son of Man, but Daniel places the prophecy in a political context, the Babylonian captivity. He was predicting the liberation of the Jews as well as depicting an apocalypse when the Son of Man would pass judgment on human sins. Old Testament imagery should not be taken in an exclusively religious sense, especially of a time when the Jews were in bondage to conquerors. Politics and religion were inextricably entwined throughout Jewish history from Moses to Jesus — and after. For Mark himself, and in the tradition he received, "Son of Man was a messianic title."[11]

Jesus probably did not speak of himself as Son of Man, although the Gospels may preserve a tradition that he believed that he would become the Danielic Son of Man after his death. The earliest traditions probably used honorific titles that stressed Jesus' extraordinary powers as a teacher and healer, implying nothing about his status after death or his relation to God. Mark, however, found in the obscure term "Son of Man" a useful vehicle for depicting Jesus as Messiah in a way that his readers might understand, while allowing Mark to confound the characters in the story who were closest to Jesus. "Messiah," like "Son of God," "Lord," or "King," could have raised false expectations among Jesus' fellow Jews, who would not be able to accept the crucifixion or failure of their beloved leader. When Peter recognized Jesus as the Christ, Jesus taught his disciples that the Son of Man must suffer, be rejected by the Jewish authorities, and be killed. Then, according to Mark and Synoptic parallels, Jesus preached about the hardships of discipleship: one who followed Jesus must deny himself, take up the cross, and prepare to die, although he would win life everlasting as a reward (Mark 8:31–38, Matt. 16:21–28, Luke 9:22–27). Thus the Son of Man title, which figures prominently in the blasphemy scene in the trial before the Sanhedrin, was a theological device for presenting Jesus as a messianic figure without implying the normative Jewish meaning of Messiah; indeed, Son of Man became in the Gospels an eschatological heavenly figure divorced from all this-worldly political implications.[12]

The Gospels depoliticize all the titles ascribed to Jesus and present each in an exclusively spiritual sense. The evangelists used the titles of "Christ," "Messiah," "Savior," and "Son of God" to describe a deity.

Yet as Vincent Taylor conceded, Son of God "does not describe a divine being" in Jewish thought, which was the only thought that Jesus knew. Son of God referred rather to a person who had an especially close relationship to God, as in the Danielic usage (Dan. 3:25). Attributing divinity to any human being would be a cardinal violation of the Jewish concept of monotheism. Ascriptions of divinity to "Son of God" and to other titles describing Jesus probably originated in the Hellenistic or gentile world of the postcrucifixion period. [13]

Except in the Gospel of John, Jesus did not claim to be divine in any sense, nor did Peter or any of the other disciples understand the historical Jesus to be divine. When they called him Messiah (Christ) they were using an Old Testament word associated with kings, patriarchs, prophets, priests, and the scion of the House of David. Although Jesus did not use Christ or Messiah to describe himself, he did recognize and accept the title when used by others to describe him (Mark 14:61–62, 15:61–62; Matt. 16:16; John 4:26). The Gospels were composed in Greek primarily for a gentile world that would not easily have understood the term "Christ," which is the reason that even the evangelists employed it infrequently. Whether rendered in Hebrew or Greek, "messiah" was a Jewish concept that referred primarily to the Davidic king, a national deliverer who, with divine assistance, would save Israel from gentile oppressions. The word "messiah" in Hebrew meant "anointed." God anointed every Jewish king, figuratively. Most Jews at the time of Jesus thought of the Messiah as a king, favored with the miraculous intervention of God, who would usher in a great kingdom through which God would rule the world. Others thought the Messiah would usher in the Day of Judgment, inaugurating the time when God, assisted by the Son of Man, would judge everyone since Adam's time and raise the innocent dead to heavenly glory. The Sadducees, incidentally, did not believe in this Pharisaic concept of resurrection. A messiah, no matter how conceived, would preach that the kingdom of God was at hand. That could have here-and-now or otherworldy dimensions, or both in succession. In any case Roman domination of Israel would be threatened, and so would Sadducean control over the Temple and Jewish affairs. Anyone claiming to be the Messiah or acclaimed as such could expect opposition from the chief priests and crucifixion by the Romans as a Zealot or political rebel. [14]

Not only was the Messiah a mortal man of flesh and blood, notwithstanding his special relationship to God, so too was the son of God. Our versions of the Gospels capitalize the word "son," but the earliest manuscripts capitalized no words, and where the translation is given as "the Son of God," it could equally be rendered as "a son of

God." In the Jewish world of the historical Jesus every man was a son of God, who is the Creator of Life. The Jews, as God's chosen people, spoke figuratively of Israel as the son of God (Exod. 4:22, Hos. 1:10). But the Old Testament usage of son of God referred in particular to the ancient kings — Saul, Solomon, and above all, David. Yahweh said of Solomon, "I have chosen him to be my son" (1 Chron. 28:6), and of King David, "You are my son, today I have begotten you" (Ps. 2:7). The Gospels made a point of tracing Jesus' ancestry to David to prove his royal lineage (Matt. 1:1, 9:27; John 7:42). Luke says of the infant Jesus that God "will give him the throne of his father David" (Luke 1:32). The "son of David" was a Jewish equivalent of the Messiah, conceived of as the royal deliverer who combined military prowess, justice, righteousness, and holiness. As Geza Vermes wrote, "the only kind of Messianism Jesus' audience would have understood, and the only kind that might have possessed applicability in the world and context of the Gospels, is that of the Davidic King Messiah." Yet the Gospels surely do not depict Jesus as the warrior-king, nor do we have any reason to believe that he thought of himself that way. Indeed, John's Gospel has Jesus say to Pilate, as the governor privately interrogated him, "My kingship is not of this world" (John 18:36). The remark is in keeping with the ordinary understanding of Jesus and with his Galilean ministry.[15]

To the Romans, any claim to kingship conveyed distinct political overtones, as it would to the Jewish authorities of Judea. The Romans, of course, did not understand the metaphysical aspects of Jewish messianism or Jesus' "Son of Man" claim based on the book of Daniel. But the Romans knew politics. Even if Jesus' message was purely eschatological, concerning only the imminent coming of the kingdom of God and the judgment thereafter, he was preaching that Roman dominion, like all else, would soon pass away. His message, as Luke said in the Acts of the Apostles, "turned the world upside down" (Acts 17:6). Clearly the chief priests understood that, just as they understood, but did not believe, the messianic claim. The Romans, like the Sadducean chief priests, understood the political implications of turning the world upside down.

The Sadducees, an aristocratic sect that derived its wealth from land and from control of the Temple's commercial activities, monopolized the high priesthood. They were collaborationists, charged by the Romans with the responsibility of maintaining law and order. They collaborated out of choice as well as necessity. Their relationship with the Romans was based on a desire to remain in power and save the Jewish populace from still greater oppression by the world's conquerors.[16]

The Roman governor of Judea appointed the high priest of the Temple, who also presided over the Sanhedrin. One Sadducean family, that of Annas, dominated the high priesthood from A.D. 6 to the outbreak of the great war in A.D. 66 when the Jews overthrew the Sadducees and rebelled against the Romans. Annas, five of his sons, and his son-in-law each served as high priest. They bought the position from the Roman governor and kept it by making further payments as well as by appeasing him. The powers and privileges of the high priests depended upon Roman sufferance. Former high priests retained their titles as a courtesy and sat on the Great Sanhedrin. Annas's son-in-law, Joseph Caiaphas, had been high priest when Pilate became governor and continued in that office throughout Pilate's rule, which ended in A.D. 36. Annas, Caiaphas, their clan and coterie, collectively the Sadducean chief priests, maintained an effective working relationship with Pilate. When the Jews protested Pilate's oppressions or profanations of their religion, the chief priests did not speak for the Jews or side with them.[17]

A point requires emphasis. Caiaphas, the high priest at the time of the trial of Jesus, was the religious leader of the Jews, but not because they or their priests and elders had selected him. He was Pilate's choice. Judea was an occupied land, governed by the military might of the Romans, who acted through Quisling agents, the Sadducean chief priests. They controlled a police force of their own and maintained a vigilant watch for would-be messiahs and troublemakers.

As Bultmann said, although Jesus did not claim to be the Messiah, the movement he headed among the Jews "may, and really must, be described as a Messianic movement," even if subject to misinterpretation. "To those who stood outside it, the movement must have appeared like any other of the Messianic movements which in those decades convulsed the Jewish people and finally led to war with Rome and the destruction of Jerusalem. The Roman procurators suppressed such movements with blood, and Jesus fell victim to the intervention of the procurator Pilate." The Gospels all agree, however, that Jesus first fell victim to the Jewish authorities.[18]

In John's Gospel the Sanhedrin never convened to try Jesus. After the Romans arrested him, the high priest, Caiaphas, privately interrogated him and then turned him over to Pilate. But long before the account of Jesus' triumphal entry into Jerusalem, John depicts a meeting of the Sanhedrin to consider the problem of Jesus. One member of the council asked, "What are we to do? . . . If we let him go on thus, everyone will believe him, and the Romans will come and destroy both our holy place and our nation." Caiaphas replied that expediency required Jesus' death "that the whole nation should not perish" (John 11:47–53). The scene conveys the impression that Jesus somehow threatened the Temple establishment and might even trigger Roman retaliation against the Jews for condoning a treasonous enterprise. The scene shows no Jewish alarm at any blasphemy on Jesus' part; indeed, Caiaphas evinced no concern for the *religious* character of Jesus' teachings. Jesus may have advocated radical reforms of the Temple cult and its sacrificial system. He believed in the old prophetic principle that love of God was far more important than burnt offerings and sacrifices (Mark 12:28). His hostility to the Temple as a place not fit for worship and as "a den of robbers" may be surmised from his cursing of the fig tree, which is a symbol of the Temple (Mark 11:12–17; Matt. 21:18–19).[19]

According to the Gospels, Jesus went to Jerusalem for the Passover festival, which memorialized the liberation of the Israelites from an earlier bondage. As pilgrims heard about the new Messiah and joined him, Jesus warned them that anyone who followed him might be crucified. When they approached the capital almost on the eve of the holiday that symbolized national independence, Jesus consciously acted out the prophecy of Zechariah 9:9. He rode into Jerusalem confident that God would cut off the chariots and war horses of the enemy by upholding Zion's sons. The triumphal entry was like a royal procession. The crowds, who acclaimed Jesus as "Son of David" and "King of Israel," strewed leafy branches (a symbol of royalty) in his path and shouted "Hosanna," the Hebrew invocation to God to save His people (Mark 11:7–10; Matt. 21:8–9; Luke 19:35–38; John 12:13).[20]

While Jesus was in Jerusalem during the Passion Week, an uprising of some sort occurred. It may have had something to do with the "cleansing of the Temple." It may have involved a Jew named Barabbas who lay in prison for his part in "the insurrection" (Mark 15:7; Luke 23:19). Mark's cryptic reference to "the" insurrection sounds as if he had described it in an earlier passage that was lost or deleted in the transmissions of the text. Several of Jesus' disciples (five, according to Oscar Cullman) had Zealot associations. In Luke 13:1 there is a mysterious allusion, placed on Jesus' lips, to "the Galileans whose blood Pilate had mingled with their sacrifices." The Gospels retain only muted echoes of the cleansing of the Temple, an episode that most New Testament scholars construe as merely symbolic or eschatological. Still, Jesus himself behaved with uncharacteristic violence during that episode. In John's Gospel he wielded "a whip of cords" against the sacrilegious, driving out the animals intended for sacrifice and overturning the tables of the money changers (John 2:14–15). Mark omits the whip but shows Jesus as able to prevent anyone from carrying anything through the Temple — a feat that could not be accomplished without controlling a large area, supported by the usual "multitudes" (Mark 11:15–16). That Jesus controlled the sanctuary as well as the road and courtyards is possible, because he taught in the Temple "day after day" (Mark 14:4). Consonant with this picture of militancy are some of Jesus' sayings, such as his instructing his disciples to buy swords (Luke 22:36) and his declaring that he had come to bring not peace but the sword (Matt. 10:33).[21]

This conflation from the Gospels suggests that violence lurks in the background of Jesus' Jerusalem ministry. However, each item in the conflated pastiche can be explained away by New Testament experts who see in the essentially religious no political implications. But there is no explaining away the fact that Jesus was crucified for a political crime and that he himself understood the charge against him as a political one, for the Gospels have him protest indignantly to his captors, "Have you come out as against a robber, with swords and clubs?" (Mark 14:48; Matt. 26:55; Luke 22:52). "Robber" or "brigand" in the Gospels is the customary translation of a Greek word that anti-Zealots used to describe Zealots or insurrectionaries. Jesus himself described the reason for his arrest: his opponents regarded him a political rebel.[22]

After his arrest, he was brought to the home of the high priest, according to all the Gospels, although only Mark and Matthew depict an emergency meeting of the Sanhedrin at night and on the eve of a religious holiday in that impossible locale (Mark 14:65; Matt. 26:66; Luke 22:54; John 18:15–16). The Sanhedrin had scriptural authority to convene for a capital charge only in the dwelling place of God, and the tribunal never met except in its special council hall within the Temple precincts. Mark and Matthew fixed the familiar story of a formal trial leading to a judicial condemnation for blasphemy deserving death. Their reference to "the whole council" means that the entire membership of seventy was present in this capital case, yet the first two Gospels do not specify the charge against Jesus. That it concerned his cleansing of the Temple, which many people had witnessed, is a justifiable inference. But the first two Gospels tell a strange story. Mark 14:55 says, "Now the chief priests and the whole council sought testimony against Jesus to put him to death; but they found none." Matthew 26:59 intensifies the Sanhedrin's prejudice by writing that they "sought false testimony against Jesus, that they might put him to death, but they found none, though many false witnesses came forward." The statement is self-contradictory. A tribunal that seeks false testimony and gets many false witnesses has what it wants. Mark 14:56 more carefully notes that although many false witnesses testified, "their witness did not agree."[23]

The testimony supposedly concerned a remark by Jesus about the destruction of the Temple. Both Mark and Matthew reported earlier that Jesus prophesied that at some future time the Temple would be destroyed (Mark 13:1–2; Matt. 24:1–2; also, Luke 21:5–6). At the trial before the Sanhedrin, however, the witnesses swore to having heard Jesus say that he personally would destroy the Temple and in three days build another. Mark 14:58 has witnesses report Jesus' words as "I will destroy this temple," while Matthew 26:61 completely eliminates the threat: "I am able" to destroy it. Matthew, content with the attribution to Jesus of miraculous powers, does not include Mark's version of the false testimony about rebuilding a temple "not made with hands." Matthew drops the point, having left the impression that Jesus was innocent of the charge concerning the Temple. Mark insists on explaining that the testimony of the witnesses did not agree. Amazingly the Sanhedrin rejected the testimony, although anyone not knowing the outcome of the story would assume that a tribunal bent on a judicial murder would not scruple to discard perjured testimony, or that it could have found witnesses whose evidence was acceptable. Nevertheless, the Sanhedrin did not pursue the charge concerning the Temple, although intent on convicting Jesus. Thus, a "trumped-up" trial resulted in utter failure on the only charge. Caiaphas, the Sadducean high priest, had convened the entire Sanhedrin on a holy night in his home to listen to witnesses whom he failed to coach carefully, although he staged the trial to procure the death of Jesus.[24]

Equally amazing is the fact that the evidence had to be thrown out because the witnesses "did not agree," proving that a procedural rule of the Pharisaic Talmud, the earliest part of which was not codified until about A.D. 200, was in effect in A.D. 30, or at least was known to Mark, who wrote about A.D. 70. Agreement among the witnesses was not a scriptural requirement. Yet the Sadducees differed from the Pharisees mainly on the interpretation of the Mosaic law. The Sadducees were scriptural literalists, the Pharisees interpreters and transmitters of the Oral Law, which the Sanhedrin followed in Mark's account.[25]

One of the Ten Commandments enjoins against false witnesses (Exod. 20:16), while another rule of the Mosaic code requires the testimony of two or three witnesses to a crime before a court can convict for "any crime" (Deut. 19:15) and especially a capital one (Deut. 17:6). Nothing in the Mosaic code requires the testimony of the witnesses to correspond substantially in all details. That is a Pharisaic interpretation not codified until the Talmud, yet said in the New Testament to be known and followed at the time of the trial of Jesus. That the Talmudic rule of the Pharisees operated in the time of Jesus is surprising in view of the assumption by many scholars about the inapplicability of Talmudic rules on trial procedure at so early a date.[26]

The charge against Jesus was a threat to destroy the Temple, because the witnesses testified only to that crime. If such a threat was a crime, it was neither capital nor blasphemous. But was it a crime? The Old Testament, which the Sadducees followed literally when possible, teaches that perhaps it was not. Mark and Matthew echo the story in Jeremiah 26:1–19, where the prophet stood in the Temple and predicted its destruction. Those who heard him demanded his death, but Jeremiah defended himself by claiming to speak in the name of the Lord; he was acquitted. Micah made the same prophecy, and he too was acquitted. In the next verses, however, Uriah was slain for prophesying against Jerusalem, not the Temple (Jer. 26:20–23). Prophets of doom crowd the pages of the Old Testament with dire threats and predictions, but Uriah alone suffered death. The parallel of Jesus and Jeremiah concerning the Temple was too close for even a Sadducean high priest to permit a death sentence, unless he distinguished between a threat and a prediction. But the court that tried Jesus, although determined in advance to convict him on a capital charge, was too stupid to make distinctions or rig the prosecution, or too honest to accept false testimony, or too punctilious to break a rule requiring the testimony to be consistent in every respect. Perhaps the principle charge failed because the threat to destroy the Temple not only was far-fetched; it was erased by the accompanying promise of a miracle: Jesus would rebuild the Temple in three days.[27]

According to Mark and Matthew, the high priest, although defeated on the Temple charge, the very reason for the prosecution, next asked Jesus to answer the witnesses. Jesus remained silent to a request that defied the Sanhedrin's rejection of their testimony. Then Caiaphas asked, "Are you the Christ, the Son of the Blessed?" (Mark 14:61). The question was un-Jewish. Although the Jews scrupulously avoided any reference to the actual name of God, YHVH, except by the high priest once a year during religious services, none of the Jewish circumlocutions in the Old Testament or in the Greek-Jewish texts refers to God as "the Blessed One." In Matthew, Caiaphas asks the question correctly, although redundantly: "tell us if you are the Christ, the Son of God" (26:63). The Jews in A.D. 30 would have regarded "the Christ" (the Messiah or Anointed) as God's son, like David.[28]

In Mark 14:62, and only there, Jesus replied, "I am," and continued with his saying about the Son of Man from Daniel 7:13. In Matthew 26:64, the saying is prefaced by "You have said so." At that point Caiaphas tore his robes and said, "Why do we still need witnesses? You have heard his blasphemy. What is your decision?" Mark added, "And they all condemned him as deserving death" (14:63–65). Matthew's account relies on Mark's (Matt. 26:65–66). Both Gospels then portray a mockery of Jesus: "some" or "they" spit at and strike him. Such outrageous conduct by the supreme judiciary is unthinkable, but does not render the scene invalid; the culprits were probably servants or police, and the scene might have occurred out of the Sanhedrin's sight, if it occurred at all. The crucial passage in the accounts is Jesus' statement, which is understood by the Sanhedrin to be blasphemous. Thus, Caiaphas tore his garment in horror or grief.[29]

That Jews at the time of Jesus, and long before, tore their garments on hearing blasphemy is undeniable. Equally undeniable is the fact that in as early as the first book of the Bible Jews tore their garments in moments of grief, whatever the cause. Joseph's brothers did so on learning that Benjamin, the youngest, would be sent into slavery (Gen. 44:13); Moses' scouts did so on learning that the people wanted to return to Egypt. (Num. 14:6); Joshua did so on learning about the defeat of his men in battle (Josh. 7:6). There are at least a score of Old Testament scenes of Jews tearing their clothes in grief over matters that had nothing to do with blasphemy. Nor had the ritual become "a formal judicial act in the case of the high priest." Josephus related that "the leading men and the chief priests rent their clothes" in A.D. 66 because they believed that the people would provoke the Roman governor to commit another atrocity.[30]

Jesus had not blasphemed, and if Caiaphas nevertheless tore his robe, his grief or horror had a different cause. Jesus had just admitted that he was the Messiah. To Caiaphas, a Sadducee, that would have no eschatological significance, and he would not think that he was gazing at the human embodiment of a deity or that the person before him claimed to be the incarnation. Caiaphas, rather, would have seen standing before him a Davidic pretender. To the high priest that would mean that the Romans would kill Jesus and perhaps other Jews. The Jews had not forgotten the mass crucifixions of A.D. 6, which occurred after the Romans suppressed the Zealot uprising led by Judas of Galilee. According to the Acts of the Apostles, soon after the death of Jesus a member of the Sanhedrin, the great Gamaliel who was the leader of the Pharisees, spoke of the deaths of the followers of Judas of Galilee and of the four hundred who followed another messiah, Theudas. Significantly, Gamaliel's advice to the Sanhedrin on that occasion, which involved the apostle Peter, was to tolerate such people: "keep away from these men and let them alone." He reasoned that if their plan "was of men" it would fail; that is, the Romans would kill them. But "if it is of God, you will not be able to overthrow them. You might even be found opposing God." The Sanhedrin took his advice (Acts 5:33–40), which is probably closer to the truth of what happened in the case of Jesus than the Gospel according to Mark or Matthew.[31]

If Caiaphas tore his robe, assuming that the scene ever happened, he did so not because he had heard blasphemy, but because he had heard a messianic pronouncement which he construed as an omen of catastrophe — more Roman pogroms or crucifixions, perhaps the crucifixion of a Jew honored by the people as a miracle worker, a prophet, or a Davidic king. Despite his own animosity against Jesus, Caiaphas would not likely welcome his crucifixion, a form of execution execrated by the Jews. Yet Mark shows a unanimous judicial verdict: "And they all condemned him." All the Pharisees, including Gamaliel, Joseph of Arimathea, and Nicodemus, supposedly joined with the Sadducees in plotting Jesus' death and then voting for it, against their religious conviction that crucifixion violated the Torah.

The trial of Jesus by the Sanhedrin, as portrayed in Mark and Matthew, leaves a puzzling question. If they condemned him for blasphemy, why did they not execute him by stoning, the prescribed punishment? The Gospels do not answer the question, but they present the story as if the Sanhedrin had no power to execute or as if the conspiracy against the innocent Jesus was diabolical enough to procure his conviction and murder by Pilate. Yet neither alternative can be true. The New Testament also abundantly shows the Sanhedrin acting as if it could try and punish capitally, and it shows that Pilate was so reluctant to crucify Jesus that the chief priests could not have confidently believed they could shift the responsibility for his death to the Romans. Indeed, all four Gospels teach that the Jews alone were responsible for the death of Jesus, despite the Roman crucifixion.[32]

Mark and Matthew "solve" the problem by continuing with the theme of Jewish conspiracy. The Sanhedrin, having tried and convicted Jesus during the night, met again in the early morning for a "consultation." They had tried, convicted, and sentenced, but did not carry out the sentence. Why the consultation? We must assume that they had no power to conduct the trial in the first place without Roman consent, or that they could not inflict the death penalty without Roman consent, or that they decided to ignore their own condemnation for blasphemy and press different charges against Jesus before Pilate. They followed the last course of action. The Roman governor would have dismissed a silly Jewish dispute about a prophetic threat to the Temple accompanied by a promise to rebuild it miraculously. The governor would have been still more contemptuous if confronted by a purely religious issue concerning a supreme insult to some invisible god. So the "consultation" resulted in devising related but different charges of a political character that would engage Pilate's interest. Yet, going to Pilate risked the crucifixion of a fellow Jew and was altogether unneccessary if the Sanhedrin could act independently.

Did the Sanhedrin have capital jurisdiction at that time? The Gospels provide three different answers. Mark and Matthew describe the Sanhedrin as exercising capital jurisdiction but failing to inflict the death penalty. Why not? The inference forced upon us is that the Romans must authorize it or that the Sanhedrin decided to press wholly different charges before Pilate. Luke's story of the Jewish trial differs significantly. The Sanhedrin met only once, in the morning on the Passover holiday and in Caiaphas's home, but Luke does not mention a charge concerning the Temple, false witnessing, blasphemy, or the tearing of judicial robes. The crucial question was simple and Jewish: "If you are the Christ, tell us." It provoked Jesus' Son of Man answer. The Sanhedrin took that as a confession of an unnamed crime and immediately brought Jesus before Pilate on explicit political charges (Luke 22:66–71, 23:1–2). Thus, in Luke the Sanhedrin neither tried nor convicted Jesus. It merely conducted an inquiry; on hearing Jesus' messianic claim it turned him over to Pilate for prosecution on political accusations. Luke allows no conclusions about the capital competence of the Sanhedrin, except that it possessed no jurisdiction over a political crime against Rome. In Acts 7:58 the same author does, however, depict the Sanhedrin as exercising capital jurisdiction in Stephen's case.

John's narrative omitted both a trial and a hearing by the Sanhedrin. John has only a private inquiry by one or two high priests. Like Luke, John says nothing about blasphemy. He reports Pilate's telling the Jews to judge Jesus by their own law. One might then conclude that the governor recognized the Sanhedrin's capital jurisdiction. But the famous Jewish reply is "It is not lawful for us to put any man to death" (John 18:13, 19, 24, 28–31). Pilate then examined Jesus, found no guilt in him, yet expressly authorized the Jews to execute him (John 19:6). When the chief priest and their supporters chanted "Crucify him, Crucify him," Pilate commanded, "Take him yourselves and crucify him, for I find no crime in him" (John 19:6). From the context of the story, Pilate had not authorized a particular form of execution that the Jews found unacceptable on account of its being contrary to their law. Clearly, the Gospels present Pilate as yielding to Jewish pressure yet seeing a way to exculpate himself from any participation in the deed. "Crucify him yourselves" means "execute him yourselves." Luke 23:25 confirms this, for the evangelist there declares that Pilate delivered Jesus "to their will." Yet the Jews neither stoned him nor protested that their law did not permit them to crucify anyone. From John, then, we may conclude that the Sanhedrin either had Roman authorization to try capital cases or required and received Roman approval to inflict the death sentence. Yet there is no Jewish trial at all in John.[33]

The overwhelming preponderance of scholarly opinion is that the Sanhedrin did not possess capital jurisdiction. That opinion rests on two facts. The Talmud records a tradition that the Sanhedrin lost its capital jurisdiction forty years before the destruction of the Temple in A.D. 70. But that tradition is suspect because it originated much too late, lacks substantiation, and is an apologetic. Forty years before the destruction of the Temple puts the date back to the year A.D. 30, when Jesus was crucified. If the Sanhedrin had no capital jurisdiction then, it could not have tried Jesus. That alone would make the Mark–Matthew account of the Jewish trial a Christian fiction. It is, but not because of the Talmudic tradition.[34]

The Talmud, both the Palestinian and Babylonian versions, was composed over hundreds of years, recording oral traditions of the law, but no part of the Talmud was written down before about A.D. 200. The tractate *Sanhedrin*, which deals with criminal law and procedure, is excessively idealized, yet its many rules include some that were once vital and operative. That the witnesses against the accused must testify alike on every significant point or be repudiated is a rule that Mark (ca. A.D. 70) knew. But the Talmud includes much that is not believable. It was composed long after all four Gospels were written, at a time when the Jews were being blamed for the death of Jesus. Having no knowledge of a Sanhedrin trial of Jesus, the Talmudists defensively invented a "tradition" to exculpate the Jews by ending the Sanhedrin's capital jurisdiction at just the right moment in history.

That tradition cannot be traced back earlier than a rabbinic saying about a century *after* the destruction of the Temple. Similar sayings are much later still. But the Talmud also includes another set of rabbinic sayings that established a different tradition, which conflicts with the apologetic one by fixing the date for the end of the Sanhedrin's capital jurisdiction in the year A.D. 70, when the Temple was destroyed. Modern experts on the Sanhedrin fix the actual date in A.D. 66, when the war broke out and the rebels overthrew the Sadducean priesthood. The date accords with Old Testament law (Deut. 17:8–10) directing that criminal cases be decided in the dwelling place of the Lord. In the post-Temple period, the rabbinic successors of the Sanhedrin sometimes exacted the death penalty in violation of the scriptural injunction, because although the Temple no longer existed, the need did.

Thus, the guiltlessness of the Sanhedrin cannot be deduced from a worthless and alternative Talmudic tradition.[35]

The second reason for believing that the Sanhedrin had lost its capital jurisdiction at the time of the trial of Jesus is that the Roman conquerors controlled the judicial power over life and death. Judea was subject to Roman law; therefore, its native courts required the approval of the Roman governor before executing a death sentence. The theory that no capital verdict of the Sanhedrin was valid without Roman confirmation necessarily implies that Jesus would have died by stoning if the Sanhedrin had convicted him of an offense against the Jewish religion. The Romans rarely, if ever, interfered with Judaism's purely internal matters. Blasphemy violated the Torah, not Roman law. A threat to the Temple did not contravene the Torah. If construed as a public disturbance or breach of the peace, such a threat could have violated both Jewish and Roman law, but in Jewish law it was punished only by a fine.[36]

The most common scholarly contention is that although the Sanhedrin had lost its capital jurisdiction under the Roman occupation, it still functioned as an inferior tribunal that could arrest and hold hearings somewhat like a grand jury. That is, it could bring accusations. This grand jury or preliminary investigation theory is especially popular with Anglo-Americans. They ignore the fact that neither Jewish nor Roman law knew anything like a preliminary hearing or a grand jury. They have a penchant for construing the Gospels to make them come out "right," despite contradictions, inconsistencies, and improbabilities. The Gospels portrayed a Roman crucifixion of Jesus that originated in a Jewish trial. Consequently the Sanhedrin at the very least must have preferred the charges. Mark and Matthew, according to this view, erred in depicting a formal trial and judicial verdict. The unlikely time and place of the Sanhedrin's meeting, as well as the supremacy of Roman law, supposedly fall into place if the Jewish trial was only an informal hearing for the limited purpose of bringing charges before the Roman governor. Such a view overstretches the evidence.[37]

The New Testament shows that the Sanhedrin possessed capital jurisdiction before A.D. 66 and exercised it without Roman confirmation, if the crime merited death under Jewish law and was no concern to Roman law. Offenses against religion by Jews came within the Sanhedrin's jurisdiction. Offenses against the Roman state did not. Many crimes, such as murder, robbery, or rape, were punishable under both systems. In any case of a conflict of jurisdiction, Roman authority prevailed, although if the criminal and his victim were both Jewish, the

Sanhedrin might try the case. Its law would also prevail if the charge was blasphemy, apostasy, idolatry, or some other religious matter of no concern to the Romans. In the case of a political crime such as sedition or treason, Roman law claimed exclusive competence. In such a case the high priest had an obligation to report any information to the state, and he might do so to preserve his own position. Pilate would have dismissed and punished Caiaphas had he concealed vital information affecting the security of the state or the majesty of the emperor.[38]

Mark, followed by Matthew, presented the original Gospel account of a formal Sanhedrin proceeding that ended in a judicial verdict. Mark's account is the only one that is contemporary with the Jewish war against Rome. If the Sanhedrin possessed capital jurisdiction at or right before the time he wrote, his account would seem plausible to his readers. Luke's morning inquiry by the Sanhedrin and John's omission of the Sanhedrin in favor of an inquiry by just the high priest suit compositions written well after the Sanhedrin disappeared. Mark, however, fixed the Sanhedrin in the Christian mind as the Jewish supreme court with capital jurisdiction.

The Acts of the Apostles, for example, sustains the tradition that the Sanhedrin possessed capital powers. Acts 5:33 shows the Sanhedrin wanting to execute the apostles Peter and John but stopped by the advice of Gamaliel. Acts 6–7 tells the story of the Sanhedrin's trial and execution of Stephen about A.D. 36. Those who contend that the Sanhedrin had no lawful authority to put him to death interpret his execution as the result of lynch law by an angry mob, but no mob is part of the story.[39]

The verses preceding the trial scene depict people maliciously spreading the rumor that Stephen spoke "blasphemous words against Moses and God" (Acts 6:11). As a result the Sanhedrin summoned him for trial. The analogy to the trial of Jesus, from which the account was concocted, is apparent. False witnesses testified that Stephen had said that Jesus "will destroy this place, and will change the customs which Moses delivered to us." The account is all the more remarkable because it depicts a period when the Nazarenes worshipped at the Temple, in peace with other Jews; but it was written much later, at a time when the schism between Jews and Christians had become irreparable. Stephen's long speech before the Sanhedrin is irrelevant to the charge against him. It reads like a jeremiad of the Old Testament and is not even Christian in character until the sudden disjointed climax when Stephen said he saw Jesus and repeated the Son of Man saying. The "whole speech," wrote Foakes-Jackson, "is a free composition" by the author of Acts or of the lost source which he used.[40]

All that can be said for certain about the case of Stephen, if it happened, is that a tradition existed which depicted him as being called before the Sanhedrin and then being executed. What happened *at* the trial and what he said there are unknown. What Acts depicts as having happened after the trial is believable: "Then they cast him out of the city and stoned him; and the witnesses laid down their garments at the feet of a young man named Saul" (Acts 7:58). That shows a formal execution according to Jewish law, which required the witnesses to be the executioners. The young man, incidentally, was Saul of Tarsus, who became St. Paul. "It has long been recognized, although often not frankly admitted," Morton S. Enslin wrote, "that the Stephen incident — especially Paul's tenuous connection with it — is unlikely history. It would seem definitely a Lukan invention."[41]

Elsewhere Luke has Paul himself testify that as a young Pharisee in Jerusalem he participated in the persecution of Nazarenes, and that "when they were put to death I cast my vote against them" (Acts 26:10). Luke's exaggeration of Paul's role in Stephen's death and Luke's unhistorical depiction of Jews persecuting Nazarenes are not the point. It is that Paul and the author of the account of Stephen's trial did not doubt that the Sanhedrin exercised its capital powers and inflicted the death penalty. Had the Sanhedrin acted illegally or by lynch law, the Acts of the Apostles would have additionally denounced the Jews for their crimes. Indeed, the victims of the Sanhedrin or their friends would have protested to the Romans, leaving us some historical trace of Roman punishment of the Sanhedrin for having usurped the *jus gladii* or sovereignty of the emperor.

Several chapters of Acts (22–26) present a clear jurisdictional conflict between the Romans and the Sanhedrin in the case of Paul himself, which occurred in the 50s. The Jewish charge against him, defilement of the Temple, originated when he took a gentile into the sanctuary. The gentile's fate is not reported, but the Sanhedrin unquestionably had power of life and death over him. Barriers around the sanctuary bore stone inscriptions warning gentiles not to pass further lest they die. The warning applied even to the Romans themselves. In A.D. 70 Titus, the Roman general, when berating the Jews for their rebellion, exclaimed: "And did we not permit you to put to death any who passed it [the warning barrier], even were he a Roman?" This special Roman concession to the capital jurisdiction of the Sanhedrin in the cases of non-Jews implies that that tribunal had exclusive jurisdiction in the cases of Jews who defiled the Temple or committed other capital crimes of a religious nature.[42]

The case of Paul, a Jew but not a citizen of Judea, indeed a Roman citizen by birth (according to Acts), merits consideration. Its relevance is that the Jewish tribunal sought jurisdiction over him and failed, but not because it lacked capital powers. Paul successfully claimed the right of a Roman to be tried before Caesar; the Roman charge against him was probably political, not religious: inciting Jews throughout the world to commit treason against Caesar. Tertullus, the spokesman for the Sanhedrin, declared, "and we would have judged him according to our own law for defiling the Temple" (Acts 24:6 note z, R.S.V.). Nowhere in his speeches defending himself did Paul deny the Sanhedrin's capital powers.[43]

In a case not recorded in the New Testament, the Sanhedrin in A.D. 62 executed the leader of the Nazarene synagogue, James (Jacob) the Just, who was Jesus' brother (Gal. 1:19). We know only what happened, not why. The supposition that James was allied with the Zealots seems warrantless. Eusebius (260–340), the first great church historian, contradictorily acknowledged that James was acclaimed by the Jews for his holiness and devotion to the Temple yet was hated because of his inevitable saying about the Son of Man, which was a motif in early Christian martyrology. In Eusebius, James was the victim of a Jewish lynching. A modern scholar who analyzed alleged Jewish persecution of Christians rejected the lynching as well as religious motivation in this and other cases. Josephus, who lived in Jerusalem at the time of James, reported that Annas, the son of the elder Annas of the Gospel of John, became high priest at a moment when his power was unchecked. One Roman governor had died and another had not yet replaced him. Annas, the head of the Sadducees, who were "more heartless than any of the other Jews . . . when they sit in judgement," accused James and certain others "of having transgressed the law and delivered them up to be stoned." The Pharisees, deeply offended by this unjust act against innocent men, protested to the incoming governor. Annas lost his position. Josephus' explanation for his deposition is that Annas had no authority to convene the Sanhedrin before the arrival of the new governor. The account shows a miscarriage of justice, not an execution that was illegal because the Sanhedrin lacked capital powers.[44]

A miscarriage of justice could have occurred in Jesus' case. As C.G. Montefiore observed, "There have been illegal trials at all times, and even the flimsiest legal forms have sufficed to get rid of an enemy." Yet the historicity of the trial of Jesus by the Sanhedrin is impossible, and no fact about Jesus is better attested than that Pilate convicted him and ordered his crucifixion by Roman soldiers for claiming kingship. If the Sanhedrin had convicted Jesus, he would have been stoned. If the Sanhedrin had tried and condemned him yet required Roman authorization to inflict the death penalty, again the execution would have been by stoning. Pilate did not confirm a Jewish sentence. He tried the case as if it had never been tried by any other court. The Sanhedrin did not try Jesus or conduct a preliminary hearing. Mark and Matthew wrote or transmitted an imaginary account of a Jewish trial. Luke assumes that "the council" of the Jews met in Jesus' case to hold an inquiry. Significantly, Luke refers only to "the chief priests and scribes," without referring to the Pharisees. John described a simple inquiry in Caiaphas's home, attended, no doubt, by a scribe and perhaps a few of the Sadducean chief priests, including Annas the elder. The remark attributed by John to "the Jews" about the Sanhedrin's not having the lawful authority to execute is unique and either wrong or abridged. The high priest could have said, "It is not lawful for us to put any man to death for a political crime against Rome." On the one hand John depicts a Roman arrest and on the other has the Jews charge Jesus, with unbelievable vagueness, as an "evildoer." John should be understood theologically. He explains the saying "It is not lawful for us to put any man to death" as follows: "This was to fulfill the word which Jesus had spoken to show by what death he was to die" (John 18:32). Crucifixion was not a punishment that the Jews could inflict, and they had no authority in a case of treason. Even the Roman arrest, which could have happened, has theological significance in John. The evangelist was depicting not what happened, but what it meant. To him the Roman arrest, which English versions of the Bible keep veiled, was a theological necessity: the arrest of Jesus would require a Roman cohort, but not even such a military force could overwhelm him unless he voluntarily acquiesced (John 18:7).[45]

Luke alone reports the charges brought by the high priest against Jesus. Immediately on delivering Jesus to Pilate, Caiaphas "began to accuse him, saying, 'We found this man perverting our nation, and forbidding us to give tribute to Caesar, and saying that he himself is Christ a king' " (Luke 23:2). In effect, the three parts of the charge describe Jesus as an insurrectionist or Zealot. Caiaphas and his coterie, it must be remembered, were Pilate's deputies and collaborators, not spokesmen for the Jewish populace. The charge was exclusively political in character. To the Romans, it described treason.[46]

The third part of the charge, that Jesus said he was "Christ a king," has the ring of truth because it is a rare New Testament usage of "Christ" in the Jewish sense: the messiah as the Davidic king. The second part of the charge, that Jesus forbade the payment of tribute, also sounds authentic; Jews in A.D. 30 would have understood the saying about the tribute money — "Render to Caesar the things that are Caesar's, and to God the things that are God's" (Mark 12:17) — as meaning "don't pay Roman taxes." The first part of the charge, that Jesus was "perverting our nation" might mean anything if taken by itself; but in the context of the rest of the charge, it meant that Jesus was seditiously turning the people against Rome. So the high priest would have reasoned. To Luke, of course, the charge was false in all parts. He could therefore reveal it, having no need to distort or spiritualize it. The fact that this was the charge Caiaphas made against Jesus is the only thing that renders intelligible Pilate's first question to Jesus in the Synoptic Gospels: "Are you the King of the Jews?" In all probability Pilate already suspected Jesus of treason, thus the Roman arrest. The treason had something to do with both the trivialized "cleansing of the Temple" and "the insurrection" to which Mark alluded. [47]

If the Sanhedrin had tried and convicted Jesus, it would not have done so at the expense of its legal and religious practices. Caiaphas and his party were law abiding. On bringing Jesus to Pilate, they refused to enter the praetorium "so that they might not be defiled, but might eat the passover" (John 18:28). A trial utterly perverting justice and contradicting the Sanhedrin's rules on procedure and evidence, as Montefiore acknowledged, is hypothetically conceivable. A bench consisting of a few members might be so corrupt that it could subvert all its usual regularities, but not likely one as large as the Great Sanhedrin, which consisted of seventy men representing diverse factions and sects. The Talmud later codified the exacting procedures of the Pharisees, who opposed the Sadducees in interpreting the Torah. By no means did all or even many of the Talmudic rules operate as early as A.D. 30, but at least one did, even in a court that included the Saducean chief priests. Mark shows that the Sanhedrin carefully honored the Talmudic rule, which is not in the Old Testament, requiring accord in the testimony of witnesses. The rule against false witnessing came from the Old Testament. So did the rules that the witnesses against the accused must perform the execution (Deut. 17:6–7) and that the execution for blasphemy must be by stoning (Lev. 24:16).

The Talmudic rule that the Sanhedrin could not accept a confession of guilt probably originated after the destruction of the Temple, but can plausibly be traced to the Old Testament injunction that guilt could not be pronounced except on the testimony of witnesses. The inference is logical but not historical. That is no reason to assume, as Vincent Taylor did, that the high priest tried to incriminate Jesus, or to assume, as Richard W. Husband and Haim Cohn did, that the question about Jesus' identity gave him an opportunity to deny the accusations of messiahship. A claim to messiahship constituted no crime. The question was not incriminatory in Jewish law, although Caiaphas, Jesus' "cunning inquisitor," supposedly used the answer to lay the basis of a charge before Pilate. That charge, however, did not derive from the words ascribed to Jesus. If he had done no more than preach religion to the people and perform his wonders, Jesus would never have come into conflict with the chief priests or Pilate.[48]

No court that included Pharisees could have unanimously convicted Jesus on the evidence in the Gospels. The Pharisees relished sharp disputation, and the Gospels are right in supposing that they frequently disagreed with Jesus. Nevertheless, their argumentativeness should not be taken as enmity or as the basis for a conjecture that they hated Jesus enough to participate in a mockery of justice. Was the Jewish trial so corrupt that the seventy judges had to meet in the high priest's home to avoid sacrilege in the Temple? The Sadducees honored the Old Testament, as did the Pharisees, who had a passion for justice, tolerance, and ethical behavior. The Gospels picture the Pharisees as formalists who doted on legal and religious niceties. They were hardly a sect that would break the law to serve the ends of a kangaroo court. Significantly, the Synoptic Gospels mention the Pharisees frequently and not always unfavorably before the arrest of Jesus, but not at or after it; John mentions their presence at the scene of the arrest but not after. The Sadducees appear in John just once, long before the arrest. John was probably unfamiliar with the importance of the Sadducees in A.D. 30. They had disappeared when John composed his Gospel, leaving the Pharisees dominant after A.D. 70.[49]

Josephus described the Pharisees as "naturally lenient in the matter of punishments." They saved Jesus from death at the hands of John the Baptist's murderer (Luke 13:31). Not long after the death of Jesus, they convinced the Sanhedrin to free Peter and John (Acts 5:40). Paul, himself a Pharisee, appealed to the Pharisaic members of the Sanhedrin when he appeared before it, knowing that they too believed in resurrection after death. His appeal provoked the Pharisees to quarrel with the Sadducees, deadlocking the Sanhedrin in his case. "We find nothing wrong in this man" was the Pharisaic judgment (Acts 23:6–9). The Pharisees also protested the judicial murder of Jesus' brother, James. D.E. Nineham, the Regius Professor of Divinity at Cambridge, commenting on Mark's statement that they "all" condemned him, drew the conclusion that Joseph of Arimathea was probably not present at the proceedings. He was indeed a Pharisee, as were Gamaliel, Nicodemus, and many other members of the Sanhedrin. The conclusion that should be drawn is that the Sanhedrin did not meet, not that its vote was unanimous. Whatever part the Jewish authorities took, said Bultmann, "cannot now be made out, since the Passion narrative is so thickly overgrown with legend." Later, the evangelists regarded the Jews as the enemy. Bultmann continued, "It is, of course, possible that the Jewish Court . . . had some part in the tragedy, but we are not entitled to assume that Jesus' ethical teaching so roused the Pharisees and scribes against him that he finally fell victim to their enmity. That the steady opposition of the Pharisees and scribes rests upon the artificial and schematic conception of later Christians has already been shown."[50]

Herbert Danby, who translated the *Mishnah*, the first codification of the Talmud, declared that the Mark–Matthew account of the Jewish trial showed a violation of at least sixteen Talmudic rules — "the grossest examples of irregularities." From that fact Danby, followed by a host of other scholars, concluded that the rules could not have been in force in A.D. 30 or did not apply to a preliminary investigation as in Jesus' case. The Sanhedrin, however, did not hold preliminary investigations. Such a procedure has no precedent in the Old Testament or in the Talmud. Haim Cohn, an Israeli judge who rejected the pretrial or grand jury interpretation of the Sanhedrin meeting, concluded that because the Talmud codified existing law, it incorporated those rules "which must be presumed to have been practiced at the period when criminal (that is, capital) jurisdiction was still actually exercised, and it was exercised until the year 70 only." But it cannot be so presumed. Unfortunately we do not know when each of the sixteen rules originated. Only the evidence in both Testaments can be accepted. Because the Sadducees were scriptural literalists, Old Testament evidence is conclusive. As a matter of religious scruple they would have accepted the practices prescribed by the Torah. At least five are relevant to the Jewish trial of Jesus: meeting only in God's designated place (Deut. 17:8–10); no false witnessing; severe punishment for false witnessing (Deut. 19:18–19); the requirement of two or three trustworthy witnesses; and, above all, the definition of blasphemy. Additionally, the Gospels show that the witnesses must agree, the only Talmudic practice followed in the account of the Jewish trial.[51]

The unreliability of the Gospels as history seems evident at other points respecting the trial. They make the Sanhedrin meet hurriedly at night on a religious holiday or its eve. That would have been politically inexpedient as well as religiously unlikely. As soon as Jesus cleansed the Temple, the chief priests plotted his death, but "Not during the feast, lest there be a tumult of the people (Mark 11:18, 14:1–2; Matt. 26:5). The conspirators felt helpless, "for all the people hung upon his words," and the chief priests "feared the people" (Luke 19:47, 22:1–2). The Passover season was a particularly inexpedient time to procure Jesus' death, because Jerusalem was swollen with his Galilean supporters as well as the crowds of pilgrims who had welcomed him joyously as their king when he entered the city. And yet the Sanhedrin is supposed to have met on a holy day and carried out its scheme, despite the fear of a tumult. A Sanhedrin maliciously disposed toward Jesus would have held him in jail until Passover ended and the pilgrims left the city. After the holiday they could have met by day in the Chamber of Hewn Stone adjacent to the Temple.[52]

As William R. Wilson wrote,

> In order to accept Mark's account, we must believe that the supreme Sanhedrin of Jerusalem — the nation's leading religious and political body — gathered furtively at night and conducted hasty and prejudicial proceedings against Jesus; and that they did so in the very season when its members would have been especially preoccupied with the most careful observance of religious and civil regulations, namely, the Passover season. The Synoptic Gospels agree that Jesus was arrested and tried on the day of the Passover feast. From the standpoint of probabilities, there was no day in the year when the Sanhedrin would have been less likely to engage in such clandestine and illegal activity. The Passover was observed according to the strictest rules; it called for the most careful exercises of piety. Yet the Sanhedrin's members are found violating every rule of moral and judicial ethics under cover of darkness.

The trial, Wilson accurately said, was either illegal or unhistorical, and the evidence "overwhelmingly substantiates the latter view."[53]

The most important evidence concerns the Jewish substantive law on blasphemy, not procedural law or the time and place. The conviction for blasphemy was groundless. It was not only impossible as a matter of law; it was ludicrous. Even D.E. Nineham declared that neither the prophecy against the Temple nor Jesus' reply to Caiaphas constituted blasphemy. Ferdinand Hahn, having studied the origins and development of "Christos," said of the Old Testament's depiction of messianic expectations that variant themes cropped out: "Throughout, however, and this is the constant characteristic feature, the Messiah is a human figure, is a successor to David, takes over a political kingdom and completes his task in the sphere of earthly realities." The Sadducean high priest could not have construed an affirmative reply in accordance with a later Christian understanding of Messiah. Significantly the trial of Jesus before the Sanhedrin was unprecedented. The council had never before tried or convicted anyone for blasphemy. Jesus' trial would be unique except for Stephen's, which is an apparent imitation and is thoroughly misleading if not fictive.[54]

The fact is that no Jewish court of authority at the time of Jesus would have deemed blasphemous a messianic claim or a claim to be Son of God or Son of Man. In John, the Jewish officials, immediately on being empowered by Pilate to execute Jesus, say illogically, "We have a law, and by that law he ought to die, because he made himself Son of God" (John 19:7). That statement cannot be taken in the christological sense of the later church. No Jew in the year 30 could comprehend a human deity. If the claim to be "Son of God" was the Jewish charge against Jesus, as John states, then Pilate would have had no jurisdiction or interest in a purely religious case, and the Jews could not have convinced him to order the crucifixion. John's depiction of the Jewish charge, that Jesus made himself Son of God in the Christian sense, or equal to God, is proleptic.

Had Jesus claimed divinity, his crime in Jewish law could have been false prophecy — leading the people from the one and only God to worship a competing god. Claiming to be the son of God, however, was not blasphemy or any crime, for the Jews regarded all men as God's sons (Deut. 14:1). For a Jew at the time of Jesus to claim before other Jews that he personally was the deity, or that God or the Holy Spirit was his biological father in a literal rather than a figurative sense, would have met with derision. The Talmud preserves a saying: "If a man say to thee 'I Am God,' he is a liar; if (he says 'I am) the Son of Man,' in the end people will laugh at him; if (he says) 'I will go up to heaven,' he saith, but shall not perform." Blasphemy, however, was a very special crime to Jews: it was cursing God by name or, in the laxest Old Testament view of the crime, denying Him or His attributes, honors or powers. Assuming that Jesus made a wholly unprecedented claim that he was equal to God or was God's exclusive son, and assuming that the Jewish authorities took him seriously, they could have believed that he derogated from God's majesty by breaking the unity or uniqueness of God. But the assumption that Jesus made such a claim is founded on a serious anachronism. It endows the historical Jesus with an understanding of himself attributed to him by Christians of the later first century and requires the authorities in the year 30 to receive Jesus' affirmative answer to Caiaphas (in Mark only!) in terms of subsequent Christian theology. We might as well assume that Matthew understood the

Nicene Creed or that John could distinguish *homoousion* (same substance) from *homoesousion* (similar substance) concerning the nature of Christ.[55]

Father Gerard S. Sloyan interpreted Jesus' appearance before the Sanhedrin as a literary composition by Mark enabling him to state a religious belief, not a historical happening. Mark inserted the entire sequence "as an epiphany or manifestation of him who has come as the Messiah and will come again as the Son of man." Mark made the Sanhedrin reject Jesus as the Messiah to symbolize Jewish rejection. By Mark's time the Jews had rejected a christianized Jesus. Jesus' answer to Caiaphas should be understood not as something he said but as post-Easter theology. Father John R. Donahue more bluntly and elaborately argued that Mark created the entire trial narrative, including the blasphemy charge and condemnation, for the purpose of explaining the Roman destruction of the Temple as evidence of divine judgment on the Jews who had rejected Jesus as the Messiah; the nonhistorical Jewish trial, with its anti-Temple theme, "thus becomes a way for Jewish Christians to come to terms with the destruction of the cult center and to view the (Christian) community as its replacement." Sloyan and Donahue have few rivals in their understanding of the trial of Jesus by the Sanhedrin as described in Mark.[56]

Even Josef Blinzler found little to support the Gospels on the point that Jesus' answer to Caiaphas was blasphemous. Blinzler was the weightiest of the pre–Vatican II Catholic scholars, who wrote on the trials of Jesus as faithfully as possible. He completely accepted the historicity of both the high priest's lone inquiry and of the Sanhedrin trial as depicted in conflicting Gospels. Blinzler thought that Jesus' "absolute authority" must have been "incomprehensible and could only be regarded as blasphemous in the light of Jewish religious thought." He didn't explain why. He also observed that Jesus meant to bring about the destruction of the Temple. That would seem to the Sanhedrin "a crime deserving of the death penalty; a vindictive court could easily make it out to be a blasphemy." The innuendo is clear enough, but because the Gospels located the blasphemy in Jesus' affirmative reply to the question of whether he was the Messiah, Blinzler had to backpedal:

In what did Jesus' blasphemy consist in the view of the Sanhedrin? Definitely not in the utterance about the Temple, which, moreover, was not pursued further because of a lack of agreement among the witnesses; nor in speaking the name of God straight out, since Jesus avoided the name of God and used the term

'Power' instead. No, He incurred the charge of blasphemy wholly
and solely by his solemn affirmative to the high priest's question,
i.e., by His confession of His messianic dignity.[57]

Aware of the scholarly objections against his literal reading, Blinzler
found an ironic way to bolster his interpretation. He turned the equally
literal Sadduceans into broad constructionists and the strict crime of
blasphemy into "a very elastic conception." Nevertheless, Blinzler
acknowledged, "The Messiah awaited by the Jews was not a supernatural or superhuman, but a human being; therefore it seems doubtful
whether a claim to be he could be regarded as an infringement of the
majesty of God." But the person who claimed to be the Messiah was imprisoned, abandoned by his friends, and "helpless" before his enemies
(*pace* John). To the Sanhedrin, such a person making that claim "could
not fail to be a blasphemer who dared to deliberately make a mockery
of the great promises given by God to His Chosen People."
   Blinzler admitted that although his interpretation of the charge was
"not quite identical with a charge of blasphemy, it is only a small step
from it." Without bridging the step, he then concluded that "there can
be no doubt whatsoever that the only ground for the death sentence by
the Sanhedrin was the messianic self-testimony of Jesus, which was
regarded as blasphemy." Blinzler rejected all argument that the
blasphemy was a claim to divine attributes, utterance of the sacred
name, or anything else. Thus, because Jesus was the Sanhedrin's
prisoner, it took his claim to be a mockery: he had failed to deliver as
the Davidic king and so blasphemed — or, perhaps, had come "a small
step from it." In the end, Old Testament law had nothing to do with the
issue; only politics, military weakness, and the lack of divine intervention on Jesus' behalf explain the blasphemy, according to Blinzler. Yet
never before or after was a failed messiah condemned by the Jews as a
blasphemer.[58]
   David R. Catchpole, a Protestant scholar who specialized in Jewish
accounts of the trial of Jesus, offered an elaborate "evaluation" of the
charge of blasphemy. Catchpole reasoned that nothing in the Gospels
"suggests that the trial of Jesus hinged on his alleged claim to destroy
the temple," but added without proof that Blinzler was "probably correct" in saying that such a claim would have been regarded as
blasphemous. Blinzler said no such thing. Catchpole decided that a
messianic claim (not a failed one) would bring about the condemnation,
but added: "Here it must be agreed that Jewish scholars are correct in
declaring that a messianic claim is not blasphemous," even under a
"looser definition" than the Talmudic one. Contrary to Catchpole, the

Talmudic definition is irrelevant. The real point is that under Old Testament law, no Jewish court could possibly have condemned Jesus for blasphemy. According to Catchpole, though, Jewish scholars have tended to ignore the possibility that by answering "I am" Jesus pronounced the actual name of God, thus committing the crime of blasphemy as defined in the Talmud (Sanh. 7:5).[59]

Catchpole assumed that the Talmudic definition operated in A.D. 30, that "I am" was *the* name, and that Mark — and only Mark — quotes Jesus verbatim (Mark 14:62). According to the Talmud, which nearly defined away the crime of blasphemy, one must invoke the name represented by the Tetragrammaton for the purpose of denouncing, piercing, or cursing it; thus: May YHVH damn YHVH. Catchpole, having elaborately considered his "I am" theory, finally shelved it for seven reasons. None dealt with Talmudic definition, or the fact that "I am" in Greek, the language of Mark, was not the Hebrew or Aramaic name, or the fact the "I am" is a simple subject and predicate used in daily speech. The "I am" theory dies hard, because New Testament scholars desperately try to find the blasphemy that the Gospels say existed in the minds of the Sanhedrin's members.[60]

Catchpole relied on a Talmudic saying of about A.D. 300 to show that some rabbis objected to the idea of a man sitting in heaven. Supposedly they thought the idea "sacrilegious," which led Catchpole to conclude weakly "that there is the possibility that such a claim as that in Mark 14:62 (the Son of Man saying) might have been regarded as blasphemous." Presumably neither the Sanhedrin nor the later Talmudic rabbis could distinguish sacrilege from blasphemy. Jesus' Son of Man saying at the trial was part of his answer to the question from the high priest as to whether he was the Son of God. On that crucial issue, Catchpole followed Vincent Taylor, Ferdinand Hahn, and many others when he could detect no blasphemy in Jesus' affirmative answer "I am." Catchpole concluded his analysis by vaguely declaring, "The one place where Jesus can be shown to have caused offense is in matters religious." Luke, for Catchpole, somehow contains the answer, but Luke makes no reference to blasphemy.[61]

J. Duncan Derrett, who took "law in the New Testament" as his subject, rejected the Sanhedrin trial as unhistorical, yet construed Jesus' Son of Man saying as "unequivocally blasphemous" to "the dominant school of Jewish law" (Pharisaic or Sadducee?). Derrett's explanation is that blasphemy in the Old Testament means "piercing" the name of god or diminishing His honor. Even if so, that has nothing to do with the meaning of Son of Man in Jewish thought. Derrett reasoned that Jesus, by predicting that he would sit at God's right hand, had usurped the

place of Moses, and, still more blasphemously, put himself into a position from which he could gaze upon the face of God, which not even
Moses was permitted to do. This explanation botched the facts.
Blasphemy was a verbal crime; the Danielic Son of Man acted for God
and did not dishonor him; and in Isaiah 52:8 the people rejoice, "for
eye to eye they see the return of the Lord to Zion."[62]

Another theory is that blasphemy had many meanings. Blinzler said it
was an "elastic" conception. Haim Cohn did not think so, but he construed Leviticus 24:15–16 to mean that one who curses God "bears his
sin" in the sense that God will punish him, while the blasphemer who
must be put to death is the one who pronounces the sacred name *and*
curses it. This distinction, based on a disjunction of Leviticus 24:15
from Leviticus 24:16, assumes that he who bears his sin is not subject to
execution. In any case the distinction is not relevant to Jesus, since no
one alleged that he cursed God, whether by name or not. The distinction also depicts blasphemy as a sin as well as a crime. However broad
the construction, Jesus did not knowingly sin or despise the word of
God in violation of Numbers 15:27–31.[63]

Still, distinguished theologians and biblical scholars must find the
blasphemy somewhere, no matter how, even if they do not differentiate
different crimes. Hans Küng, for example, abandoned the effort to
define blasphemy. He concluded that the Sanhedrin heard it, but he did
not say what it was. In the midst of an ecumenical interpretation which
distinguishes the Jewish populace from their collaborationist leaders in
the time of Jesus, Küng repeatedly refers to Jesus as a "heretic" whom
the Jewish hierarchy tried to "unmask." They "had to act against the
heretical teacher, false prophet, blasphemer and religious seducer of the
people. . . . " Their political charge was a "cover" for their "religious
hatred." Küng simply misunderstood Jewish law and ethics, and he
assumed that the crime of heresy, which Christians later invented, was
known to Jews in the year A.D. 30. It was not, although they did
distinguish the other crimes referred to by Küng.[64]

Douglas R.A. Hare showed a better understanding of law and Jewish
toleration when he examined whether the Jews hated and persecuted
the early churches. Hare believed that at the time of Jesus blasphemy
had a less technical meaning than the one in Leviticus 24:15–16. He
held that "any attack on the Torah or Temple was regarded as
blasphemous, but this is not to say that such attacks could be treated as
blasphemy in the technical sense and punished as capital crimes." Hare
insisted that despite a popular conception of blasphemy, "some relatively narrow" one of a legal character controlled the disposition of prosecutions. Otherwise "all the Pharisees were liable to capital prosecu-

tions by the Sadducees," because the Pharisees changed the customs of Moses (Acts 6:14). Among the Jews of Jesus' time, only the Essenes believed that Moses could be blasphemed. Nazarene claims on behalf of Jesus, Hare asserted, were blasphemous only in the popular sense, for no legal prosecutions could be founded on those claims. If Jesus had been condemned for capital blasphemy, Hare reasoned, "*the profession of Christianity was from the beginning a capital crime* from the point of view of the Jewish judiciary." But the Acts of the Apostles shows the contrary, and little evidence supports the view that verbal attacks on the Temple and Torah "constituted blasphemy in the legal sense." Hare concluded that the Jewish charge against Jesus was not capital, but only a "serious" breach of the peace. In sum, Hare distinguished the popular or elastic concept of blasphemy from the legal crime, and he discovered no blasphemy in the charge or condemnation of Jesus or of Stephen.[65]

J. C. O'Neill vividly illustrated the difficulty, widespread among scholars, of capturing the blasphemy of Jesus as the Sanhedrin understood it. O'Neill rejected the Temple charge as constituting any part of the blasphemy because Jesus coupled his threat with a miraculous promise to rebuild the Temple. O'Neill also rejected the Son of Man saying as a basis for the charge. Even if the Son of Man was considered "the exalted heavenly figure," O'Neill said, such sonship would not have been viewed by the Sanhedrin as a capital offense. Everybody expected him to appear, and the title was not a divine one. O'Neill also rejected as invalid the Gospel suppositions that Jesus had on earlier occasions faced accusations of blasphemy. The claim to forgive sins, he observed, was a claim "to pronounce validly that *God* had forgiven the sinner." He rejected the "I am" theory too. Similarly, he pointed out that however the healing on the sabbath is construed, it had no part in the trial; John's depiction might be inauthentic. O'Neill also observed that no blasphemy could have been implied or inferred "in calling the Messiah whom God has sanctified and sent God's Son." He showed Old Testament evidence for the Jewish belief that Son of God was an acceptable designation for the Messiah.[66]

The blasphemy, according to O'Neill, consisted in Jesus' "temerity of using any title at all before God the Father had himself announced the enthronement of his annointed one." That invented a new Jewish law on blasphemy. In any event, O'Neill declared, Jesus did not claim to be the Messiah. His claim to be the Son of Man "could have been interpreted as blasphemous," although Jesus made the claim in a form that assured that God alone could announce his enthronement. O'Neill showed that Jesus avoided encroaching on God's prerogatives, as when he denied the sons of Zebedee seats of honor in the kingdom: "To sit at my right hand or at my left hand is not mine to give" (Mark 10:40; Matt. 20:23). The saying attributed to Jesus, that no one knew the Father except the Son, signified that the Father revealed the Son; the Son did not reveal himself. "Jesus observed this law strictly and took care not to blaspheme" by infringing divine majesty. Having said all this, O'Neill contradictorily concluded:

> The technical charge upon which Jesus was condemned to death by the Sanhedrin may well have been that he blasphemed in making himself God (John 10:33) by presuming to say he was the Son when the Father alone knew who the Son was (Matt. 11:27, Luke 10:22). He was condemned for making himself the Son of God (John 19:7). The charge was probably false, but the Sanhedrin would regard Jesus' defense as a mere technicality, he behaved with such regal dignity and spoke with such assurance. [67]

C.H. Dodd, a major New Testament scholar, advocated much the same view in his mature reflections on "The Historical Problem of the Death of Jesus." What, he asked, was the blasphemy for which Jesus was condemned? All four Gospels take the view, he concluded, "that Jesus was charged with blasphemy because he spoke and acted in ways which implied that he stood in a special relation with God, so that his words carried divine authority and his actions were instinct with divine power." That, said Dodd, is what the charge of blasphemy "really stands for, rather than any definable statutory offence." In the "stylized account" of the trial before the Sanhedrin, the crucial phrases are "Son of the Blessed" and "at the right hand of God," which for Dodd constituted a messianic claim "plus." [68]

All the conjectures and straining derive from the pursuit of a red herring. Jesus' blasphemy did not exist: it was a symbol of the Jewish rejection of Jesus and was the only capital charge that the evangelists could put in the mouths of Jesus' Jewish opponents. The Sanhedrin trial itself has no historicity at all. It was a creation of Mark, imitated by Matthew and rejected by Luke and especially by John. Even in Mark, the question is not what happened but what did it all mean? As Hans Conzelmann said, any attempt to reconstruct the actual course of events is doomed to failure. "Methodologically it is misleading to interpret the present report (the Passion accounts) as such a record. It is a witness of faith." None of the Gospels is reliable as history and none purports to be. They propagate faith in Jesus. Most of what actually happened is unknowable, except that the Romans crucified Jesus for treason after the chief priests pressed the charge. [69]

New Testament scholars and liberal theologians have long claimed that the Passion story should be read as theology rather than as a record of actual events. Yet the same men freely pass judgments based on the record as if it were a transcription of minutes of the trials and eyewitness accounts. Cullmann, for example, held that on "the principal question," whether the Jews or Romans condemned Jesus, the Romans were legally responsible, the Jews morally. Like Küng, Cullmann differentiated the Jewish populace from its hierarchy yet said that the Pharisees "made common cause with the Sadducees" — as if the Pharisees would favor a Roman crucifixion of a Jewish religious leader on the flimsy reason that he "embarrassed" them and was "popular with the people"! Neither Cullmann nor Küng had any understanding of the Pharisees nor could they escape the Gospels' interpretation of history. History and theology in the Passion story seem to be fused together forever. Not even men of great intellect and the best of intentions can separate what happened from its religious meaning, because what happened is, in James M. Robinson's phrase, "theologically understood history."[70]

What happened has been lost forever, but some things did *not* happen. Gospel history is sacred mythology that depicts what did not happen as having happened, and does so on the bases of prejudice and politics as well as theology. The climactic culpability of the Jews, for example, depends on the inventing of a nonexistent custom, the pardoning of a prisoner at festival time. The Jewish crowd chose Barabbas, a notorious insurrectionist and murderer, over Jesus — thereby symbolizing their ultimate rejection of him. But any New Testament scholar knows that an important mystery surrounds the identity of Barabbas. His first name was "Jesus," a fact suppressed in the authorized Gospels, and Barabbas was a nickname that meant either "Son of the Father" or "the Teacher." The possibility, not at all fantastic, exists that only one Jesus is in the story. He might somehow have been mixed up in "the insurrection," and a crowd of his supporters might have shouted for his release.[71]

Pilate did not pardon him, nor did the chief priests stir up the crowd to seek the pardon of a rebel leader. The Pilate of the Gospels is not the Pilate of history. The real Pilate was a cruel despot who slaughtered unarmed civilians, Jewish and Samaritan. The real Pilate had the legal authority, backed up by troops, to acquit a man whom he thought innocent. He could have freed Jesus even *after* he pardoned Barabbas — if he did pardon anyone. The Pilate of the Gospels is wise but spineless; he knows that Jesus is innocent, but the bloodthirsty Jewish crowd intimidate him with their threats, forcing him to surrender to their wishes.[72]

The trial before Pilate is not the subject here, but it is not irrelevant.

The point is that the real Roman trial was portrayed falsely, an extension of the false Jewish trial and the false blasphemy charge. The two trials are in some respects striking parallels. In both Mark shows Jewish testimony against Jesus, an interrogation of the accused, and abuse of him. The pattern of similarity supports the hypothesis that the first trial was a recast version of the second. Mark probably invented the scene of the formal Jewish trial out of a primitive tradition that the Jewish authorities delivered Jesus to Pilate. Some scholars have speculated that the pre-Markan tradition included no Jewish trial, no Gethsemane story, no references to the Temple, and no apology for the fact that Jesus was condemned by the Romans as a political revolutionary.[73]

The Jewish trial reflects the early Christian belief that the Jews, not the Romans, were responsible for the death of Jesus. More than half a century ago, A.E.J. Rawlinson, an Anglican priest, wrote, "It was important, from the point of view of Christian propaganda in the Roman Empire, to establish the fact that Jesus, in spite of the fact that He had been condemned by the Roman Governor, was nevertheless innocent of any political offence, and that the primary responsibility for the judicial murder of which He was the victim rested with the Jews." S.G.F. Brandon, also an Anglican priest, made this point one of the themes of three books. In brief, the anti-Semitism of the Gospels and their exoneration of Pilate — the whole Roman problem (the Romans appear in the Gospels but in friendly terms) — resulted from self-serving apologetics.[74]

Although the Gospels are theology, they had practical or political functions too. Their pro-Roman stance was intended to sever the early churches from the Jews and their Jewish origins. The Jews and Romans were military enemies. They were at war from 66 to 73, from 115 to 117, and from 132 to 135. The Romans persecuted the Christians, whom they confused with the Jews, as early as Nero's time (A.D. 64) and long after. The safety of the early churches depended on their identification with a pacifistic Savior who never opposed Rome and who had been crucified at Jewish instigation. Gentile readers were given to understand that Jesus opposed the Pharisees, the Temple, and the Jewish cult, and above all that his real crime was not treason but blasphemy in the minds of the Jewish Sanhedrin. The Gospels also taught that the rejection of Jesus as the Messiah or Son of God is blasphemous. At first the story sought to protect the Christians by appeasing the Hellenistic and Roman world. It also proved enormously helpful in softening the gentiles for conversion. Along the way, Jesus became Christ, the Jews the villains, and blasphemy a new sort of crime under Christianity. And so, as Paul Winter said, "The trial of Jesus goes on. His is a trial that is never finished. . . ."[75]

3

THE AGE OF CHRISTIAN HETERODOXY

For the first four centuries after the crucifixion and before Christianity became the state religion of the Roman Empire, blasphemy prevailed as a concept of primary concern to Christians. Paradoxically, under Christianity "blasphemy" became so bloated with meanings that it burst all bounds, becoming almost meaningless; by 400 "blasphemy" was hardly more than a vile epithet and in a confused way similar to the concept of "heresy." During early Christianity, blasphemy was the initial and broader concept: blasphemy generated heresy. The word "heresy" originally meant factionalism, which was a form of blasphemy because it exposed the true faith to contention, even scorn. In time, however, heresy became the more encompassing, formal term, eclipsing blasphemy. Not until the time of Thomas Aquinas in the thirteenth century did the church coherently define blasphemy, although even then as a peculiar species of heresy. Long before — before there was a Roman Catholic church, or a formally canonized New Testament, or an authorized creed on the Holy Trinity, or a body of doctrine that could be described as orthodox, or a secular power that could enforce the church's wishes — blasphemy was the cardinal sin. *The Shepherd of Hermas*, an early second-century patristic work, referred to "blasphemy or treason," treason against God.[1]

Christianity in the pre-Nicene period, before the fourth century, was heavily Greek in thought as well as in language. Accordingly, "impiety," which was the Greek equivalent of blasphemy, rivaled blasphemy as the name of the sin. To the Greeks, blasphemy meant any sort of speaking evil, verbal abuse, or defamation, especially profane speech. In English the word "impiety" has a soft sound, calling to mind a lack of piety or something faintly irreverent, but in Greek impiety signified shocking and abhorrent ideas about religion. Impiety, after all, was the crime for which Athens killed Socrates and prosecuted, Anaxagoras, Phidias, and Alcibiades. In early Christian thought, impiety was as vague and broad in meaning as in Athenian thought. The Jewish meaning of blasphemy was certainly narrow and fairly clear: reviling God by name. Impiety or blasphemy, which were synonymous in early Christian thought, gathered numerous and complex meanings. Blasphemy became more than just cursing or reproaching God. It rapidly came to signify breaking the unity of Christianity. What was blasphemous or impious was any viewpoint or utterance that deviated from the true faith.

The true faith, however, differed in meaning to early Christians. They embraced Jewish monotheism and accepted the Old Testament as divinely inspired Scriptures, which they reinterpreted in the light of Jesus. He was the risen Christ through whom salvation became possible for all humanity. Beyond that, Christianity was protean, heterodox and fluid. In the absence of orthodoxy, distinctions between blasphemy and heresy became difficult if not impossible, while both blurred in meaning and blended with faction, sedition, schism, apostasy, and sacrilege.

The principal problem of early Christianity was to define itself even as it had to establish itself. To do either it required an authority or standard for its faith, deviation from which was a form of blasphemy. The difficulty of determining the standard for the true faith derived from the fact that Christianity's earliest traditions were oral, Jewish, and varied. The writing of gospels preserved some of the traditions, but the four Gospels presented different theologies as well as different histories of Jesus, and so did the other writings that ultimately became canonized as the New Testament. The Gospels themselves, which originally belonged to the local churches for which they were written, underwent alterations as time passed and needs changed. Although there were a great many apocryphal gospels and books of acts and of epistles, the first structuring of the New Testament canon, which occurred toward the end of the second century, included most of the twenty-seven books.[2]

Fixing their authority was less a problem than the fact that the twenty-seven books spoke differently among themselves and differently to different people. What one man took as a cardinal reproach to the Christian religion or to a particular doctrine or to Christ himself, and called blasphemy, was another man's sacred belief. Heresy to one was orthodoxy to another. All Christians agreed on the need for unity of belief, but they could not find what did not exist. Jesus' own apostles did not always agree with him, understand him, or concur among themselves. Christianity had to establish itself against rivals from without and against dissident proclamations of orthodoxy from within. It had to establish and define itself even as it continually evolved, during the centuries when it existed as an illicit religion and then during the reformative period after it became the established religion of the world state.[3]

Until at least 325 when the Council of Nicaea formulated the first creed at an ecumenical meeting of bishops mainly from the eastern division of the Roman Empire, there were Christian churches but not *a* Christian church, that is, not a catholic or universal church. Nor did Nicaea settle anything. The dissident parties, who were condemned as blasphemers and heretics by the emperor and the council, soon became dominant, winning the support of the state and controlling most of the churches. That reversed the definition of orthodoxy, until another emperor made possible a reaffirmation of the Nicene Creed at the Council of Constantinople in 381. The trinitarian victory was not secure until confirmed by the Council of Chalcedon in 451. Not until the fifth century was there a Roman Catholic church with the power to enforce its interpretation of orthodoxy.[4]

As long as Christianity remained decentralized, many Christianities existed within the Roman Empire. Religious beliefs based on Jesus as the Christ had fanned out across the Mediterranean into Asia Minor, Europe, and North Africa. Judaism, paganism or Hellenism, and Gnosticism successively affected Christian thought in dissimilar ways in different places at various times. Credal lines of evolution veered and clashed. Orthodoxy in one place was heterodoxy in the same place at a later date, while the orthodoxy of one place was the heterodoxy of another at the same period of time. In A.D. 359 councils of bishops in the East and the West reached contradictory declarations on the Christian creed. In Rome, Constantinople, and Alexandria in the 350s, the Nicene orthodoxy of thirty years later was regarded as heretical, schismatic, and blasphemous. The orthodoxy that finally prevailed at the close of the fourth century was syncretistic in character but Nicene. It controlled most people's minds, the writing of history, the making of theology, and the definitions of offenses against religion.[5]

The cliché that the heresies of the past become the orthodoxies of the future is only half the truth. The other half, much less appreciated, is the converse fact: today's heresy was yesterday's orthodoxy. Nazarene Christianity, a form of Judaism, was once the sole and orthodox form of Christianity, and Nicene Christianity was once merely a heresy. Judaism, Christianity, and Gnosticism impregnated each other with incredible fecundity in the first century or so after the crucifixion, resulting in a swarm of beliefs and exotic blends of beliefs. The centralization of Christianity in the late fourth century terminated most of the surviving permutations; the Roman Catholic church gradually managed to impose uniformity, which was inevitably syncretistic, despite the multiplicity of Christianities that the canon enshrined. Indeed Catholicism could not have become catholic without combining different, even irreconcilable, elements.

The New Testament reflects dissidence and dissonance in its various

theologies. They allow ample room for the luxuriant growth of subsequent "heresies," yet at the same time numerous dicta provide the foundation for their condemnation and for identifying them with
blasphemies. That "the church" originated in unity and possessed a
timeless uniformity of doctrine is a post–New Testament myth concocted to justify unity and the persecution of dissenters. The earliest
Christianity was Jewish and probably had its own gospel. It was resis-
tant to Hellenistic ideas such as virgin birth, the preexistence of Christ,
his divinity, and the repudiation of the Torah as a means of saving
grace. The first Christians, who participated in the Temple cult and
were received as Jews by other Jewish sects, believed in Jesus not as God
incarnate but as the risen Messiah imminently to return. Traces of the
mother church of Jerusalem survived in the Ebionite and Nazarene
"heresies" of a later era; ecclesiastical histories preserve them like
aborted fossils from a primitive time and place that sought to
monopolize a human Jesus for the circumcised.[6]

Paul had the world-shattering inspiration of preaching the gospel to
the uncircumcised, the gentiles, and exempting them from the Torah.
Given his special mission and the fact that the mother church in
Jerusalem spoke in the authoritative name of the original apostles, Paul
felt compelled to distinguish his message from Judaism. Although he
was a self-proclaimed Pharisee who observed the Law or Torah in the
company of Jews, Paul preached that God freely offers his universal
grace to anyone, Jew or gentile, who accepts Jesus and believes in God
through him as mediator. Only believers would be resurrected on Judgment Day, which Paul long expected to witness in his own lifetime. The
death, resurrection, and imminent return of Jesus were for him the
transforming facts of history, abrogating the Torah as the source of
salvation for gentile converts. Paul modified his near antinomianism or
emancipation from the Mosaic law by recognizing it as the basis of
righteousness and the avoidance of transgressions; he advocated faith
alone as the way of redemption. The Paul of Luke–Acts fused the
Messiah with the Son of Man who suffered and died, much like the
Christianized Jews of Jerusalem. The real Paul, however, presented
Christ as the exalted Son of God in the divine sense. Paul raised the Son
of God concept to divinity, making divine mercy the source of salvation. For gentiles, he jettisoned the Jewish idea of salvation which
allegedly was dependent on merit attained by good works and obedience to God's commandments in the Law. Paul's revolutionary gospel
provoked opposition from Judaizers in the Christian churches during
his lifetime and even centuries after.[7]

No greater contrast exists in the New Testament than between a
Pauline epistle and the one attributed to James, the brother of Jesus and

head of the mother church in Jerusalem. James is an echo of primitive Christianity, so very primitive that it seems Jewish. Christological theology is absent in James. His two references to Jesus Christ must, in their context, be intended in the Hebrew sense of Messiah as the anointed one. James even addresses himself to the Jews of the Diaspora, not to the gentiles. His focus is on righteous living, and he rings out ethical exhortations. He advocates good works, against Paul's exclusive reliance on justification by faith. For James, faith without works "is dead . . . my works will show you my faith. . . . You see that a man is justified by works and not by faith alone" (James 2:17–18, 24). James is rabbinic in his opposition to men who pass judgment on the "evil thoughts" of others or who speak against the law of Moses.[8]

Mark presents a more familiar Christian message, although scarcely like Paul's. In many respects Mark is as different from Paul as James. Paul focused on the risen Christ and showed no interest in the historical Jesus. Like the other Synoptic evangelists, Mark gives Jesus' earthly ministry saving significance. Although Jesus will become Son of Man after his death, his life as the suffering servant of god and his apocalyptic message about the in-breaking Kingdom of God bring salvation. Mark's Gospel has Paul's eschatological force and a polemic against Jewish Christianity. In Mark, Jewish Christianity is represented by the disciples, especially Peter. The twelve are persistently uncomprehending and, still worse, faithless. That they slept at Gethsemane shows their religious blindness; that they fled shows apostasy, confirmed by Peter's triple denial of Jesus. Mark's parables also show how the historical Jesus, a Jew, was rejected by his own people, even those closest to him. Thus Mark set the pattern for the other Synoptics, in explaining why the Kingdom became populated with gentile believers. But Mark's catholicity is comparatively stunted and veiled, and his christology less developed than his successors'. In Mark, Jesus' death is inevitable and he fears it, yet Mark makes nothing of the resurrection and little of redemption. He has only a passing although significant reference to a saying of Jesus that the Son of Man will give his life "as a ransom for many" (Mark 10:45). The narrative ends with an empty tomb and a mysterious young man saying that Jesus has risen and would be seen later.[9]

Matthew's Gospel is an expansion of Mark's, intercalated with proverbs, parables, and ethical precepts drawn from the Old Testament, all calculated to prove that Jesus is the culmination of God's work on earth as foretold. Contrary to Paul, Matthew continues and intensifies the demands of the Torah. The Sermon on the Mount, unique in Matthew, makes ethics subordinate to God's will and to salvation. Although the Jesus of Matthew's Gospel conducts his ministry among the Jews, the risen Christ directs a mission to the gentiles. The Jesus of Matthew is a divine person, a prophet and lawgiver unparalleled in Jewish history, whose mission reconstructed the way to the Kingdom, which is imminent. In its time Matthew's Gospel was a polemic against rabbinical Judaism, arguing that the church had become the true Israel. Matthew's christology is more developed than Mark's and even Luke's. The young man at the empty tomb in Mark becomes an angel in Matthew who then depicts Jesus as being seen and worshipped by his disciples after the crucifixion. He declared to them that he had received "all authority in heaven and on earth." The end of the world is still close in Matthew, who ends his Gospel with the bare ingredients of the Trinity in the remark of the resurrected Christ that his disciples should go to "all nations, baptizing them in the name of the Father and of the Son and of the Holy Spirit . . ." (Matt. 28:18–19).[10]

Luke's Gospel is the first of a two-volume work of which the Acts of the Apostles is the second half; it is the first history of the new church. Luke's is a gospel of salvation but has lost much of the eschatological fervor of the earlier Synoptics, because Luke did not live in the expectation of seeing an apocalypse and the return of Christ in his glory. His Gospel, although finding salvation in the historical Jesus' earthly ministry, is one in which the church is entrusted with the continuing redemptive task that Jesus began. Luke, much more than Mark and Matthew, saw Christianity as a universal religion. The ascension at which he hints at the close of his Gospel becomes a vivid scene at the beginning of Acts, as the rising Christ leaves his church in the care of his disciples. In the face of increasing Jewish rejection, converts were sought among gentiles. The anti-Jewish polemics in Luke are muted, compared to those of his predecessors. He is more interested in exonerating the Romans toward whom he is apologetic. For Luke accommodation with Rome is important but the battle with the Jews is over; Christianity has clearly superseded Judaism. Thus the great Jewish Christians, Paul and Peter, are for Luke figures of the past who are scarcely distinguishable. Luke's Paul, like his Peter, sounds as if he believes that the cross and baptism are not crucially different from the Torah because Jesus fulfilled the Torah. Compared to the Paul of the Epistles, Luke has no theology of the cross or of justification by faith alone. His Jesus is the Savior of the world and the pivotal figure in its history as planned by God.[11]

The Son of God as the Christ is John's focus. Thus he omitted the nativity and baptismal scenes, because he was the least interested among the evangelists in the historical Jesus. His Gospel of the incarnation is the most supernatural, verging at times on docetic christology, the view that Jesus was so nearly indistinguishable from God that one might be led to question his humanity. Denying his manhood became one of the great heresies which John avoided in his eucharistic and crucifixion scenes. Otherwise John tended to make Jesus human in appearance only, knowing that appearance can be deceiving. To John, Jesus was Logos, the Word, existing before the creation and taking flesh for the benefit of worshippers who could not otherwise see him. The emphasis in John is on the divine and glorified Christ through whom humanity has direct revelation. The Son of Man, whose identity was something of a mystery to the earlier evangelists, is no problem for John, because he knows Jesus is the Son of Man; John also slights eschatological expectations, because the resurrection has fulfilled all promises. John universalizes Jesus. Having descended to earth to establish the Kingdom — it is already an accomplished fact in John — Jesus reascended triumphantly, his work done. Thus the Kingdom is always present, confronting everyone with the need to understand the meaning of his existence in Christ or remain a "Jew." Metaphorically John makes "Jews" out of all nonbelievers. He amplified the postresurrection scenes of Christ dining with his disciples, but the meals have sacramental significance at most. Doubting Thomas believes only after touching the stigmata and finally proclaims Jesus as God, but Jesus replies with the Johannine message: "Blessed are those who have not seen and yet believe" (John 20:29). To the earlier evangelists, Jesus teaches about God; to John, his teaching reveals God wholly apart from time and place. John's Jesus is Savior in perpetuity. [12]

Through all the New Testament variations a common theme reverberates in the form of a question that Günther Bornkamm defined as "not so much who he *was*, but of who he *is*." Still the "discords" remain, Bornkamm said, "producing interpretations of faith which tend to error, even to downright misinterpretation." Thus Paul lamented that his flock in Corinth was split by factionalism and heresies (1 Cor. 11:18–19). He feared that one had come who "preaches another Jesus than the one we preached . . . a different gospel" to which the church in Corinth might submit (2 Cor. 11:4). Paul warned another church, "If anyone is preaching to you a gospel contrary to that which you received, let him be accursed" (Gal. 1:6). Paul was full of anti-Judaizing denunciations. Having been "entrusted with the gospel to the uncircumcised," he would not allow them to believe that anyone could be justified by the Torah instead of faith in Christ. "For all who rely on the works of the law are under a curse . . . Christ redeemed us from the curse of the law" (Gal. 2:7, 16; 3:10). Avoid "strife, seditions and heresies," Paul counseled, by fulfilling only the "law of Christ" (Gal.

5:20 K.J.V.). Of those who deceived the faithful the worst were the circumcision party; "they must be silenced. . . . " The reference is not to
the Jews but the Jewish Christians, the Nazarenes (Tit. 1:10–11).
Deutero-Paul demanded that only "sound doctrine" be taught, glorify-
ing "our great God and Savior Jesus Christ" (Tit. 2:1, 13). After due admonition a factious person or "heretic" must be rejected (Tit. 3:10
K.J.V.). "Paul" also advised against "diverse and strange teachings"
(Heb. 13:9). "Philosophy" produced them, he believed, meaning pagan
theories of *gnosis*, the secret knowledge of the mysteries of the universe
(Col. 2:8).[13]

The first epistle attributed to John seems to have Gnostics in mind as
the "antichrists" who denied the Father and Son. John exhorted against
unsound doctrines but not always consistently. One who sinned, he
taught, was "of the devil," yet no one born of God sins "for God's
nature abides in him, and he cannot sin because he is born of God" (1
John 2:18–24; 3:8–9). That proved to be the basis of the later doctrine
of the indwelling Christ, a heresy thought to justify antinomianism or
libertine lawlessness. Although John also proclaimed that men should
love one another ("God is love"), he meant Christians only, and he condemned false prophets, adding that everyone who "does not confess
Jesus is not of God. This is the spirit of antichrist . . . " (1 John
4:1–3). So it proved to be. To John anyone who hated his brother yet
said he loved God was a "liar" (1 John 4:7, 20); John himself lacked
love for brothers who became false prophets and antichrists by deceiving the faithful with the doctrine that Jesus had not "come in the flesh"
(2 John 4:7–8). John's targets here were the Gnostic or Docetic Christians, blasphemers and heretics all, who taught that Christ was purely
divine and therefore undefiled by flesh.[14]

Interspersed with the warnings against heretics are those against
blasphemers. But the crime of blasphemy for which the Sanhedrin supposedly condemned Jesus — his claim to be the Son of God — is not the
crime of the New Testament. To be sure, if anyone but Jesus made that
claim, he would be blaspheming, for the title belongs to Jesus alone. In
Jewish thought only God can be blasphemed. After the crucifixion,
Jesus joined Him as a divine majesty, in Christian thought. Cursing,
reproaching, challenging, mocking, rejecting, or denying Jesus Christ
became blasphemy. Doubting his miraculous powers, his teaching, or
the true Christian faith became blasphemy. Posing as Jesus, claiming to
be equal to him, and asserting the powers or attributes that belonged
only to him became blasphemy. On the other hand Jesus himself taught
that a blasphemy against himself could be forgiven, but not a deliberate
and unrepentant rejection of God's redemptive or miraculous work.

Jesus eternally damned statements that his own miracles were the work of Satan. To attribute evil or immoral inspiration to any work of God or of the Holy Spirit which moved Jesus is blasphemy. That is the meaning of Matthew 12:22–32. Jesus had exorcized the evil spirit from a blind and dumb man, healing him. Pharisees who heard of his miracle supposedly said, "It is only by Beelzebul, the prince of demons, that this man casts out demons." Jesus, replying that he performed his miracles by the "Spirit of God," declared: "Therefore I tell you, every sin and blasphemy will be forgiven men, but the blasphemy against the Spirit will not be forgiven. And whoever says a word against the Son of man will be forgiven; but whoever speaks against the Holy Spirit will not be forgiven, either in this age or in the age to come." In Luke, speaking evil of the Holy Spirit also became blasphemy (Luke 12:10).

As components of the Holy Trinity, Jesus and the Holy Spirit can be seen as divine in their natures, making the step from God to them logical. Still another step, however, had to be taken to elevate the Christian religion to such sacrosanctity that criticism of it could be thought of as blasphemy. Yet another step made particular doctrines beyond dissent by any but blasphemers. Paul and the author of Acts of the Apostles took those extra steps. Before his dramatic conversion on the road to Damascus, Paul claimed to have been a persecutor of Christians. Later he supposedly denounced himself as a blasphemer. That is, he confessed his guilt for blasphemy because he had once persecuted Christians by trying to force them to renounce their faith in Jesus. The tradition, historically valid or not, taught that for a Christian to deny Jesus or his teaching became blasphemy (Acts 26:11, 1 Tim. 1:13).

Stephen's case is a very special one, illuminating both Christianity and Judaism. As a young man named Saul, Paul held the garments of the witnesses against Stephen when they executed him by stoning, "Paul consenting to his death" (Acts 7:58–59). The charge against Stephen was "blasphemous words against Moses and God" (Acts 6:11), although the only evidence we have is Stephen's statement that he had seen Jesus as the Son of Man at the right hand of God. Stephen, who was either a Greek-speaking Jew or more likely a Greek gentile, had converted to the Nazarene sect in Jerusalem. That they accepted converted pagans is known from Galatians 2:3 where Paul wrote that "Titus, who was with me (in Jerusalem) was not compelled to be circumcised, though he was a Greek." Stephen probably "blasphemed" Moses — an impossibility for any Jews except for the isolated Essenes — in the sense that he preached an inflammatory speech in a synagogue, repudiating the entire Mosaic Law, the Torah. His offense was an extravagant antinomianism, not preaching Jesus as Savior although possibly preaching Jesus as a divinity who superseded the Law. To supersede the Law would be to reject God, from a Jewish standpoint. The mother church at that time, still part of Judaism, kept the Torah, participated in sacrificial rites, observed the sabbath, and practiced circumcision – all condemned as heresies by Christians a century later. For a Greek gentile to use a synagogue to condemn Judaism wholesale by demanding repudiation of its fundamental religious code was comparable to Luther's using the pulpit of St. Peter's to censure Roman Catholicism with all his prodigious invective.[15]

Whatever really happened in Stephen's case, it was unique. The Nazarenes, the members of the mother church, probably never suffered persecution from their fellow Jews. The Acts of the Apostles relates that from the day of Stephen's execution, "a great persecution arose against the church in Jerusalem; and they were all scattered. . . except the apostles. . . . But Saul [Paul] laid waste the church, and entering house after house, he dragged off men and women and committed them to prison" (Acts 8:1–3). If the Sanhedrin had persecuted the Nazarenes, its first victims would have been their leaders, the least likely to have been left unmolested. Apart from the fact that Saul was then a young man of no standing or power whatever, the account in Acts cannot be true if Paul's own accounts are the least credible. Paul's conversion occurred no later than A.D. 37, probably earlier, making Stephen's case fall between 33 and 36. Paul testified that he did not return to Jerusalem until three years after his conversion, "And I was still not known by sight to the churches of Christ in Judea" (Gal. 1:18–22). The Jerusalem church, led by James "the Lord's brother," was flourishing. Consequently the "great persecution" against the Jerusalem church was not great at all; it had probably been limited to a few gentile converts who followed Stephen's antinomianism. Paul himself shared it, but he boasted of being an observant Jew when among Jews or writing to them (Acts 21:15–26, 23:6; Rom. 7:1, 11:11; 1 Cor. 9:20).[16]

In Matthew, Jesus himself had announced that he had come "to fulfill the law, not to destroy it" (Matt. 5:17). Despite Paul's professed persecutions of Christians and his claims that the Jews persecuted him, neither the authorities in the Jerusalem church nor in the Temple excommunicated him or prosecuted him for his deviant beliefs. The word *minim*, loosely construed in the post-Temple era as a Hebrew usage to describe "heretics," was not leveled at Paul. The statement in Acts 24:5 that Paul was called "a ringleader of the sect of the Nazarenes" is an inaccurate description of a later date. Acts was written when Paul was dead. He was not a Nazarene in the sense of being a member of the mother church. The Sanhedrin sought to prosecute him only after he defiled the Sanctuary by bringing a gentile into it (Acts 21–28). At no time in his career, despite all his anti-Judaic and anti-Torah pronouncements, was Paul charged with an offense against religious opinion. The report of Stephen's prosecution for blasphemy, Paul's role in it, and the subsequent persecutions is inexplicable and unbelievable. Whatever Stephen's crime was, it was not blasphemy. But after Luke's description of Stephen's case, blasphemy became in Christian thought any attempt to persecute Christians and any denial or renunciation of the faith by Christians.[17]

The deutero-Pauline epistle to the Ephesians drums on the theme that there must be "unity of the faith." As there is one God, he wrote, so there is "one body and one Spirit . . . one Lord, one faith, one baptism . . ." (Eph. 4:4–6, 13). Yet, discord and false doctrines kept cropping out in the churches he had planted. "Paul" instructed Timothy, one of his disciples, to remain in Ephesus for the purpose of supervising the purity of the faith there. Uproot everything "contrary to sound doctrine," he counseled. He himself had had to excommunicate Hymenaeus and Alexander "that they might learn not to blaspheme." Although baptized in the true faith, they had made a shipwreck of it by spreading divergent beliefs (1 Tim. 1:3, 10, 19–20). "Paul" also commanded that the name of God "and his doctrine be not blasphemed" (1 Tim. 6:1 K.J.V.).[18]

The belief that dissent from or defamation of Jesus' teachings was blasphemy laid the basis for a nearly limitless expansion of the concept, particularly because Paul or his disciples had a habit of distinguishing "truth" or "true" faith from counterfeit versions. The author of the second letter to Timothy also lamented that people were falling away from "sound teaching" and "the truth." Hymenaeus and Philetus, he declared, had "profaned" and "swerved from the truth by holding that the resurrection is past already. They are upsetting the faith of some." Others also "oppose the truth, men of corrupt mind and counterfeit faith . . . " (2 Tim. 2:16–18, 3:8, 4:3–4).

To Titus, whom he counseled to reject heretics, "Paul" wrote that sound doctrine inspired a moral life and thus avoided blasphemy or the discrediting of "the word of God" (Tit. 2:2–5, 3:10). That, like the blasphemy against doctrine, allowed any difference in the interpretation of "the word" to be considered blasphemy. Elsewhere, letters ascribed to Paul equated apostasy with denial of the faith and with crucifying Christ by holding him up to contempt (Heb. 6:5). Recalling that the penalty for violating the Mosaic code was death, "Paul" added that a man who profaned the covenant of the faith deserved still worse (Heb. 10:28). Paul also thought that any behavior that made enemies of

Christianity calumniate it by blaspheming the name of God was tantamount to blasphemy (Rom. 2:17–24). Similarly, "Peter" warned of "false teachers among you" who spread "destructive heresies" and "reviled" the "way of truth," meaning that heretics blasphemed Christianity. Unlike Paul, "Peter" was not referring to Judaizers, Gnostics or apostates. "Peter" meant Christians who had gone "astray" (2 Pet. 2:1–3, 15). The connection between heresy and blasphemy continued in Christian thought for at least fifteen centuries.

Clement, reputedly an associate of Paul and head of the church in Rome, shows the continuity between the New Testament writers and the church fathers. Writing during the 90s to the church in Corinth, Clement tried to persuade a rebellious group, which had taken over the leadership of the church, to submit to the authority of the elders who had been deposed. Although politics and personal ambitions seemed to be the problem in Corinth rather than religious differences, Clement condemned the malefactors for sedition and schism. By overthrowing the presbyters, he declared, "you bring blasphemy on the name of the Lord." About fifty years later "Clement II" made the same point. He regarded as blasphemous anything that contravened the wishes of ecclesiastical authority. Blasphemy, he announced, consists in that "you do not do what I desire." This view that blasphemy consisted of any religious belief contrary to the policy of the church or its leaders, became a fixed position in Christian thought.[19]

In *The Shepherd of Hermas,* a tract written in Rome on Christian ethics, the references to blasphemy are numerous but inexplicable, like those in Revelation (Rev. 2:9; 13:1, 5, 6; 16:9, 11, 21; 17:3). The writer obviously regarded blasphemy as something quite terrible, even beyond repentance, but except at the point where he joined blasphemy to apostasy and treason to describe the crime of those who, when persecuted, betrayed "the servants of God," there is no divining his understanding of the term.[20]

In an early Christian apology by "Mathetes," whose purpose was to differentiate Christians from Jews at a time when the Jews had again rebelled against Rome, the author, a Greek Christian, equated "impiety" with "speaking falsely of God." He meant that Jewish beliefs like the necessity of circumcision and observing the sabbath showed impiety, especially the supposed prohibition against doing good on the sabbath (which was not a Jewish belief at all). Christians had more than religious reasons for their anti-Semitism. The Jews of the Diaspora had engaged in a major rebellion against Rome during 115–17, and Judea was in rebellion again from 132 to 135. Over half a million Jews were slaughtered in each rebellion, and each was followed by severe Roman persecutions. The Romans razed Jerusalem, rebuilt a new town filled with pagan temples and statuary, and banned Jews from the place. The Christians, who had suffered persecutions under Nero in the 60s, under Domitian in the 90s, and under Hadrian during the Jewish revolt of 115–17, felt compelled to differentiate themselves from the Jews. Christians stressed their pacifism and their enmity to the Jews partly in the hope that the Romans would be able to distinguish submissive friends from the incessant insurrectionists whose God and ancient Scriptures the Christians professed.[21]

The Christians were scarcely better off when the Romans finally learned to distinguish them from Jews, although because of religious differences Christian anti-Semitism did not abate. Sporadically, and usually on a local basis, the Romans continued their persecution of Christians. The Romans disliked Judaism but tolerated it as an ancient religion of a nation. Separated from Judaism, Christianity became a stateless and atheistic novelty to the Romans. Polycarp, the bishop of Smyrna, was burned alive after spurning a Roman offer of freedom conditioned on his reproaching Christ. Polycarp declared that he would never "blaspheme my King and Saviour." Denial of Christ or of Christianity was, for Christians, blasphemy. To the Romans, Polycarp's crime was blasphemy in a wholly different sense. His being a Christian meant that he taught against and overthrew their gods. Although Christians rejected war, they were as militant about their religion as the Jews. Exhorting his fellow Christians never to return "railing for railing," Polycarp contended that whoever did not confess Jesus was "antichrist; and whosoever does not confess the testimony of the cross is of the devil. . . ." Romans took that sort of talk as blasphemy against their gods, although Polycarp in this instance was not speaking against pagans. He referred to the Docetics, who called themselves Christians but thought of Jesus as so purely divine that he could never have come in the flesh, suffered and died.[22]

Justin Martyr, whom the Romans executed in 165, about a decade after executing Polycarp, explained that the Christians looked like atheists to their persecutors. "And we confess that we are atheists, so far as gods of this sort are concerned, but not with respect to the most true God. . . ." For refusing to sacrifice to the gods, Justin Martyr and his friends were decapitated; their crime was atheism or blasphemous insult to the gods. Christian apologists had to defend themselves against other heinous charges such as cannibalism and incest. In about 177, Athenagoras disposed of such charges by refuting the one about atheism. Tertullian, a Christian apologist of the early third century, summed up the Roman charges: "I am a practiser of incest (so they

say). . . . I am an infant killer. . . . I am guilty of crimes against the
gods, against the Caesars." "So," he concluded, "we are accused of
sacrilege and treason. This is the chief ground of charge against
us. . . ." The Romans, apparently, were no more precise in specifying
the crime or in making distinctions than their Christian victims. Justin
also accused Bar Kochba, the Jewish rebel leader, of persecuting Christians because they would not "deny Jesus Christ and utter blasphemy."
Bar Kochba was doubtlessly ruthless, but he executed Jews as well as
Christians for refusing to support his revolt against Rome. Political
considerations rather than religion probably dominated Roman
persecutors too. From the time of Ignatius, who was martyred about
110, to the time of Eusebius, the fourth-century church historian,
Christians regarded persecution and anti-Christian charges as
blasphemy.[23]

Ignatius of Antioch condemned heresies which he identified as
Docetism and Judaism; by the latter he may have meant Ebionism,
which was a form of Jewish Christianity. The Docetists, he wrote,
"blaspheme my Lord by not admitting He carried living flesh about
Him." Ignatius regarded heretics as atheists and probably as
blasphemers, if they were ashamed of the cross, mocked the Passion,
jested about the resurrection, disputed the virgin birth, or alleged that
Jesus was not divine. Such abominable opinions caused schism, sun-
dering the unity of the church, because there was only one Christ and
one true faith. Anyone who said that the Lord was a mere man, according to Ignatius, was "a Jew" and no better than a murderer of Christ.
Letters misattributed to Ignatius, probably later forgeries, described as
heresies and blasphemies the doctrines of Simonianism, Menanderism,
Basilidism, and Nicolaitanism, early forms of Gnosticism named for
their founders. Christian Gnosticism, like Jewish Christianity, became
a formidable rival to the line of Christian development that ultimately
triumphed as orthodox. Incredibly, Judaism itself was still regarded as
a heresy against Christianity as late as the time of Hippolytus of Rome,
who wrote *The Refutation of All Heresies* about 220. He included
many forms of paganism as well as Judaism, showing that heresy was
not yet understood as a Christian deviation from some orthodox
standard.[24]

The varieties of Christianity before the fifth century were probably as
numerous as those of today. They included, among others, Paulinists,
Johannines, Gnostics, Marcionites, Docetists, Montanists, Samosatans, Sabellians, Meletians, Arians, Semi-Arians, Nicenes or Athanasians (Catholics), and Donatists. They also included Jewish Christians.
Even varieties of Jewish Christianity existed. Jesus and his disciples, of

course, were a Jewish sect, as were the members of the mother church in Jerusalem before the destruction of the Temple. Later there were Ebionites and Jewish Gnostic Christians, "Jewish" on matters like circumcision, the sabbath, diet, and the humanity of Jesus, but bewilderingly different on many theological points. Most Gnostic Christians were not only not Jewish; they were "radically anti-Semitic." So too, most "Jewish Christians" were not Jewish at all.[25]

The orthodoxy of the Nazarenes, which any Christian theologian would probably concede to the church of Jesus' apostles (as long as we have no records to document its theology), became regarded as heretical and blasphemous as early as the second century. Justin is proof of that. He called the Jews blasphemous for not accepting Christ and even argued that they rejected God because they rejected Christ. Justin was as severe or more so with "some who are called Christians, but are godless, impious heretics, [who] teach doctrines that are in every way blasphemous, atheistical, and foolish." Unfortunately the rift between early Christians and Jews was so great that Justin did not understand Judaism. He even tried to prove by analogy that many "Christians" were no more Christians than Sadducees, Galilaeans, Pharisees, and Baptists were Jews.[26]

Not the Jews or Jewish Christians but the Gnostic Christians constituted most of the "false" and blasphemous Christians of whom early fathers like Ignatius, Justin, Irenaeus, Tertullian, and Hippolytus wrote so vitriolically. Gnosticism, which might have originated in Zoroastrianism a millennium before Christianity, expressed itself in many cultural forms, but in any form it was bafflingly complex and fantastic in its mythology, yet formidable: it confronted the problems of existence, evil, and salvation. Usually, Gnosticism depicted an unknown, ingenerate, transcendent Supreme Being and a polytheistic pantheon of numerous lesser deities in a dualistic universe of opposites—spirit against matter, good against evil, heaven against hell, light against dark, divine against demonic.[27]

The Supreme Being, who was Spirit only, had nothing whatever to do with this world of matter. It and life on it was the creation of a demonic lesser deity who rules over it. To the Gnostic, life on earth is hell, but not hopeless if an individual can reawaken the spirit deep within him which is the part of his nature that links him to the pure cosmic Spirit. The usual response to man's condition was ascetic withdrawal or libertine self-indulgence, but both speak only to the body: corrupt matter. The solution to the human dilemma was to seek redemption from this world, but redemption can be only in the form of revelation or self-knowledge, *gnosis,* which can be assisted by a divine messenger. The Gnostic *knows* he will be saved because he has discovered his true inner self or spirit; one who knows has no need of faith. On his death he will be released from demonic bondage and his soul will ultimately yield up his spirit, allowing it to unite with the primal Spirit.

In the second century, Gnostics who were exposed to Christianity and Christians who were exposed to Gnosticism spawned an extraordinary variety of theosophies. Their common nexus was Jesus as the Savior who brings revelation and salvation, thus rescuing people from this hellish world. But Gnosticism was blasphemous: God did not create Earth and its life; Jesus was a lesser deity, about thirty times removed from the Supreme One; his parents were also minor deities; no deity could suffer and die; Jesus had not been resurrected; he and the Holy Spirit were the last and least in rank among the deities; only the spirit could be resurrected, not body or soul; a pure spirit or deity could not be seen by people; the primal Spirit was incomprehensible to lesser deities; only those who had *gnosis,* not those who had faith or lived by the Law, would be saved; the Old Testament was, on the whole, irrelevant. The possibilities within Gnosticism for blasphemous opinions were limitless. Still worse, the number of people who blended Gnostic and Christian elements into a new religion possibly exceeded by the mid first century the number who reinterpreted the Old Testament in the light of the Gospels and the Pauline epistles. The Gnostic Christians or Christian Gnostics "style themselves Christians," Justin bitterly objected, but because they taught such "impious and blasphemous things," Christians called them by the name of their "particular doctrine" — Simonians, Basilidians, Saturnilians, Marcionites, Valentinians, and the like. Justin also called them atheists, heretics, sinners, and "spirits of error." Although the church fathers, who represented the line of development that triumphed as orthodox, rejected the Gnostics, Gnosticism, according to Adolph Harnack, was "analogous to the Catholic embodiment of Christianity, in doctrine, morals, and worship." The Gnostics "hellenized" Christianity and rejected the Old Testament, while the Catholics retained it but more gradually reached a similar hellenization. Harnack admired the Gnostics because they "undertook to present Christianity as the absolute religion, and therefore placed it in definite opposition to the other religions, even to Judaism." Gnostic Christians made Christianity the *gnosis,* but that did not immunize them from the polemics of the anti-Gnostic Christians. On the contrary, the closer Gnosticism came to Christianity, the greater it loomed as a rival and as a heterodoxy.[28]

The most formidable antagonist of the Gnostics was Irenaeus, the bishop of Lyons in the last quarter of the second century. His huge polemic, *The Detection and Refutation of False Knowledge* [Gnosis], is usually called *Against Heresies*. To call it *Against Blasphemies* would be as accurate, for Irenaeus used "heresy" and "blasphemy" interchangeably and with about the same frequency. He despaired of the possibility of condemning them all, because "they differ so widely among themselves both as respects doctrine and tradition, and since those of them who are recognized as being most modern make it their effort daily to invent some new opinion, and to bring out what no one ever before thought of, it is a difficult matter to describe all their opinions." Irenaeus cannot be faulted for failing to make the effort to help believers "avoid such an abyss of madness and blasphemy against Christ."[29]

Valentinus and Marcion, who were both active in Rome in the 140s and 150s, received Irenaeus's fullest attention. All roads may have led to Rome but not to orthodoxy. Valentinianism was probably the most popular of all the Gnostic religions. Valentinus himself had many disciples who modified and perpetuated his beliefs. Irenaeus began his book not with the first Gnostic but with Valentinus, the most important. He had no gospel, said Irenaeus, that was "not full of blasphemy." His "system is blasphemous above all" because he represented Jesus as the product of a "defect or apostasy" from the "Pleroma," the fullness of all divine spirits. Valentinians "utter blasphemy, also, against our Lord, but cutting off and dividing Jesus from Christ, and Christ from the Saviour, and again the Saviour from the Word, and the Word from the Only-begotten." In one passage, when summarizing Valentinianism, Irenaeus denounced them for blasphemy eight times within two paragraphs, only twice for heresy. The very concept of *gnosis* he thought to be an "impudent" blasphemy of the Creator.[30]

Marcion, whom Irenaeus treated as a Gnostic, was the most Christian of all the Gnostics; indeed, he was in a sense more Christian than Irenaeus. Harnack even refused to classify Marcion as a Gnostic because he carried to their logical extremes positions explicit in the Christian tradition, and he was an effective organizer of churches in the empire. He rejected the usual Gnostic mythology but adopted its Docetism, for he accepted the Gnostic principle of dualism: divine spirit versus corrupt matter. Thus he regarded the Passion as an illusion and rejected the humanity of Jesus. Virulently anti-Semitic, Marcion sought to purge Christianity of its Judaic origins and traces. To him, the God of the Old Testament personified the evil Creator, while the God of the New represented salvation and all that is good — another example of Gnostic dualism. Marcion seems to have been the first person to develop a Christian canon; his New Testament included only a bowdlerized Luke and Paul, none of the Old Testament. He regarded the other Gospels as Judaistic.[31]

Irenaeus thought Marcion was the author of "the most daring blasphemy" against God by declaring Him to be the author of evils and being contrary to Himself. By "mutilating" the Gospels he had also blasphemed, according to Irenaeus. But the bishop found consolation in the thought that "the very heretics themselves bear witness" to the Gospels, even though dismembering and misinterpreting them. In Marcion's Docetism, of course, Irenaeus found hideous blasphemy. As for the Old Testament, it foretold Jesus and proved his divinity. Therefore, to reject Scripture was blasphemous too. Throughout Irenaeus, no illumination can be had on the distinctions, if any, between blasphemy and heresy. He used the words as epithets to signify any heterodoxy of which he disapproved. When he wrote that Satan raised up blasphemers against God by means of all the heretics, or that every heretical, godless, impious doctrine should be shunned, he was intelligible by being specific as to doctrine he opposed, but never as to the differences among schism, atheism, apostasy, impiety, blasphemy, sacrilege, and heresy.[32]

Tertullian, a presbyter of the church in Carthage in the early third century, had the stylistic flair of a great propagandist, but although he had legal training, he mixed concepts with the same ease as Justin and Irenaeus. At one point, in his *Prescription Against Heretics,* he seized a fundamental idea that the church later developed, and he thereby advanced the cause of clarity by light-years. Speaking of "false doctrines," he said that they were "called in Greek *heresies,* a word used in the sense of that *choice* which a man makes when he either teaches them (to others) or takes up with them (for himself)." The heretic, therefore, condemned himself, because: "We, however, are not permitted to cherish any object after our own will, nor yet to make choice of that which another has introduced of his private fancy. In the Lord's apostles we possess our authority; for even they did not of themselves choose to introduce anything, but faithfully delivered . . . the doctrine which they had received from Christ."[33]

Unfortunately Tertullian lost the thought when he denied that there was a difference between idolatry and heresy and when he said that every lie against God was "a sort of idolatry." When he wrote that the teachers of false doctrine were blasphemers without demonstrating the blasphemy and explaining how it differed from the heresy, he had lapsed into the epithetical diatribes of Irenaeus. To Tertullian, every heretic was a blasphemer and vice versa. In *Against Marcion,* Tertullian forgot his own definition of heresy and had none for blasphemy or any other offenses against religion. Thus, he could refer to the same Gnostic dualism as a heresy in one place, a blasphemy in another. Having clearly labeled Marcion a heretic, he wrote that "every" opinion of Marcion was "impious and sacrilegious." After tracing Marcion's Docetism to the Jews, whom Tertullian despised as much as Marcion, Tertullian then resorted to the Old Testament, whose authority he relied upon, to prove that the Jews blasphemed Christ. At no point did Tertullian refer to Leviticus for an understanding of what blasphemy might mean.[34]

By the middle of the third century, no change was discernible, although the early stages of the Trinitarian Controversy had begun. The task of Christianity was to define itself positively by explaining the Holy Trinity as well as negatively by differentiating itself from blasphemers, heretics, and schismatics. Although the fathers mixed up blasphemy and heresy on the one hand and heresy and schism on the other, their incapacity to see the difference between blasphemy and schism showed that the identity of the true church had not yet been established. Heresy might mean the willful choice of a false doctrine by a factious party of dissenters who might claim to be the true church and break away to form their own. Such a schism rent the unity of the church, but without necessarily advancing a theology that significantly differed. The most important schismatic movements of early Christianity, the Montanists of the late second century, the Novatians and Meletians of the third, and the Donatists of the late fourth, claimed to be orthodox. But every heresy, like every schism, has represented itself as the true Christian faith, and every schism, especially if durable, develops blasphemous and heretical deviations in doctrine, in the eyes of its opposition.[35]

Before the Council of Nicaea in 325, every heresy and every schism affected only local churches. No "church" existed until an international council, representing mainly the churches throughout eastern Christendom, defined a "creed," a body of religious dogma bearing the stamp and sanction of ecclesiastical authority. In the absence of a church and its creed, no orthodoxy exists. Thus, after the Roman persecutions under Decius (249–51), the Novatians, who had remained most steadfast in the Christian cause and suffered for refusing to turn over sacred writings for Roman bonfires, regarded themselves as the pure communion. To the Novatians, everyone who had surrendered the faith to the Roman persecutors had defiled himself. Therefore the Novatians, who would not recognize sacraments performed by lapsed churchmen, demanded the rebaptism of recovered "heretics" by Novatian authority.

Yet Dionysius, the bishop of Alexandria, representing the traditional but less pure position against the Novatians, claimed that they "rent the Church," drew away brethren "to impiety and blasphemies," and "calumniated" Jesus Christ as if he were "unmerciful." [36]

At about the same time, A.D. 250, another Dionysius, the bishop of Rome, condemned Sabellius for numerous blasphemies in advancing a theory of the Holy Trinity that persisted for centuries. From the six-teenth through the nineteenth centuries, people were still prosecuted for "Sabellianism." Sabellius tried to preserve the unity of God by subor-dinating the Son and the Holy Spirit to the Father. Dionysius of Rome wrote: "For he blasphemes in saying that the Son Himself is the Father, and *vice versa*; but these in a certain manner announce three gods, in that they divide the holy unity into three different substances, absolute-ly separated from one another." The Sabellian view that the Son was born a man rather than a begotten of God, in the opinion of Dionysius, was also a blasphemy, "not ordinary, but even the highest." Sabellius believed that Jesus gradually became the Son, but to Dionysius that meant that there was a time when he was not and when he did not even exist; yet, "He was always. . . ." That is, he preexisted his birth as Jesus and was present before the Creation as the Logos. Thus, disagree-ment among devout Christians with different interpretations of the mystery of the Trinity was "the highest" blasphemy. This characteriza-tion of Sabellius differed not at all from that imposed on Mani, the founder in the third century of a lasting form of Gnostic Christianity that bore his name, Manichaeism. In about 277, Archelaus, a bishop of Mesopotamia, wrote that one could not look at Mani's system "without stumbling on blasphemy." About a thousand years later, the Albigen-sian Crusade murdered much of the population of southern France, and an Inquisition lasting into the next century finished off the survivors, the spiritual descendants of the "Manichean heresy."[37]

In the third century the weapons in the contest were the mildest — preaching, writing, censure by local synods, and excommunication. Christianity, itself a sporadically but cruelly persecuted religion, had no means of employing stronger measures. In self-defense against the Romans, Christians had to argue for toleration, and except during brief periods of persecution, they were in fact free to worship as they pleased and to publish their opinions. As the religion evolved, the controversy among Christians became more intense, while the doctrine of the Trini-ty increasingly moved to the forefront of their differences as the focal point of blasphemies.[38]

Everyone who professed to be a Christian of whatever kind regarded Jesus as the means by which God made himself known to man. Jesus

Christ was the Savior who by God's grace offered resurrection of the flesh to all believers. The books of the New Testament took the divinity of Jesus for granted. Even doubting Thomas accepted him as divine when addressing him as "My Lord and my God" (John 20:28). Justin, Irenaeus, Tertullian, Origen, and other fathers into the third century were more preoccupied with developing a christological theology than with cursing heretics, although their compulsion to defend the faith from heretics and pagans influenced their definition of it. The Logos of the fourth Gospel came to dominate the thought of the early fathers: "In the Beginning was the Word [Logos], and the Word was with God, and the Word was God. He [Logos] was in the beginning with God; all things were made through him . . ." (John 1:1–2). Irenaeus and Tertullian construed the passage to mean that Christ as a separate person preexisted from the beginning of time; explaining the Jesus who really lived as a man proved more complicated. Still more complicated was explaining the Holy Trinity without derogating from either God or Jesus Christ as a deity and yet allowing room for the Holy Spirit.

Through the time of Origen (184–254), the fathers advanced interpretations and used terminology that in the fourth century the Nicene church deplored as heretical. Not that the earlier fathers from Ignatius to Origen were heretical; rather, they represented an earlier point in the evolution of Christian theology. No historian would condemn Jefferson's theory of the Union according to a standard fixed by Lincoln. But the fathers of the fourth century were not historians, nor were their predecessors. [39]

Historically, the Holy Trinity was not the basis of a creed. The simple reference in Matthew to the Father, the Son, and the Holy Ghost and to other "slogans and tags" became consecrated by usage in Christian liturgy. Jesus was a man in whom the Logos, or the Spirit, or the Christ, or the Father dwelt. There was no consensus on the right way to make the point, although all agreed that Jesus was finally exalted and possessed godlike honor. Some thought he was a heavenly spirit who had assumed a human body. [40]

Whoever he was or is, the problem posed by his existence is that Christians worshipped one God *and* Jesus Christ. Some theologians called "adoptionists," trying to preserve the monotheism of Christianity, understood Jesus to be divine in some way but not as God Himself. Jesus was subordinate to Him; God the Father, they said, adopted him. They were desperately trying to avoid three gods like Dionysius or "the blasphemy of two Gods," which they thought was the result of acknowledging Jesus Christ as God or as a divine Son who was a separate person. Novatian, a disappointed aspirant for the seat of Rome, in his book *On the Trinity* (256), ascribed to the Adoptionists the argument, "If the Father is one and the Son another, and if the Father is God and Christ God, then there is not one God, but two Gods are simultaneously brought forward, the Father and the Son." The crisis in Christian theology in the third and fourth centuries turned on the need to retain the unity of God without sacrificing the divinity of Christ.[41]

In the end, the authority of the church, backed by the coercion of the state, settled the controversy in the sense of fixing on a creed which became the test of orthodoxy as a matter of faith — and, therefore, the tests of blasphemy and heresy. The creed "settled" the faith but did not end the controversy. Nor did the creed, supported by the intricate christological metaphysics which churchmen developed, explain an incomprehensible mystery. If the human mind cannot fathom the God of the Old Testament, notwithstanding the simple *Shema* — "Hear, O Israel, the Lord our God, the Lord is One" — still less possible is it to understand one Godhead and three persons.[42]

If Jesus lived and died, he was a creature of the Creator, and no creature should be worshipped; but Jesus was the Christ — in his time the anointed one but divine after his ascension. Was he divine during his life? Was he God? At what point did the incarnation begin? The fourth Gospel has Jesus say, "Before Abraham was, I am," "I and the Father are one," and "I am in the Father and the Father in me. . . . the Father . . . dwells in me. . ." (John 8:58; 10:30; 14:10). Did the Father beget Himself, suffer and die on the cross, and sit at His own right side? If "I and the Father are one," what is the meaning of "My Father is greater than I. . ." (John 10:28)? Who is meant by the pronoun "He" in John's reference to the Logos? Is the Holy Spirit also a person? If Father and Son are one, *is* there more than one person in the Trinity? Speculative answers to such questions caused acrimonious debate among Christians who viciously denounced each other for blasphemy, heresy, and other offenses against religion whenever confronted by an answer with which they disagreed.

Although no secular issue is comparable or can be to the christological one, in effect all Christians through the time of Augustine in the fifth century (and even long after) were debating a religious problem roughly analogous to the problem that plagued political philosophy for a thousand years: What is sovereignty? The comparison is not far-fetched because the theologians were seeking to define the sovereignty of the Supreme Being. Indeed some of the "heresies" of the third century are called "monarchianism," meaning the rule of one God, because their supporters like Noetus and Praxeas sought to protect the divine unity or sovereignty. "Modal monarchianism," so called because it depicted God as revealing Himself in different modes at different times, was popular enough to be a rival to the position represented by Dionysius, the bishop of Rome. Modal monarchists believed that Christ was God, but there was only one God; therefore, the Father and Son were the same. That led to "patripassianism," the absurd idea that God the Father died on the cross, but it preserved the unity of God by denying the existence of any persons in the Godhead except God Himself. An indivisible single God divided into three persons is as paradoxical as an immortal God dying. Sabellius developed a modal monarchianism that avoided patripassianism and also took the Holy Spirit into account; he described the Father, Son, and Holy Spirit as the same person or essence who by different modes revealed himself successively as Creator and Lawgiver, then as Redeemer, and finally as the Spirit to inspire and bestow grace. This was the view that Hippolytus of Rome called a pagan heresy and a blasphemous folly, that Bishop Dionysius denounced as the highest blasphemy, that Peter, who held the same chair in 306, called an impiety, and that Athanasius still later coupled with Arianism as the worst of blasphemies. Yet some bishops of Rome from 198 to 222, during the lifetime of Sabellius, gave him their support. Later a bishop withdrew support and had him excommunicated, but the fundamental of his doctrine, that God is the only person in the Trinity, lived on. [43]

Paul of Samosata, who was formally condemned by a synod in Antioch in 269, also presented an interpretation of the Trinity that reverberated across the centuries. He was an even more uncompromising Unitarian than Sabellius. One church historian called him "the most famous of these rationalistic Unitarians." Unfortunately, his writings, like those of Sabellius, did not survive; we know him only through the writings of his enemies. Somehow most of the work condemned by the church disappeared, despite the survival of a huge body of ante-Nicene work by "church fathers." "Roman" fires in more than one sense were at work. In the 260s Paul of Samosata was the bishop of Antioch, the highest see in the East. He sought to restore the earlier view of Christianity that Jesus was a mere man, although exercising the divine office of the Redeemer. The synod that deposed and excommunicated him pronounced the only true faith as that which recognized three persons of the Trinity, all equally united in the Godhead. [44]

Paul, who could not accept the preexistent Logos, acknowledged the Trinity in form only. For him it was a Trinity of revelation not of persons or essences. He thought of Christ as Son of God in the sense of being an impersonal and invisible power like the Holy Spirit. Jesus, the man, was inspired by the Logos of God which dwelled within him. But

God being one was the only person of the Godhead. "Paul's thought," said J.N.D. Kelly, "is notoriously difficult to evaluate, but the view that he was a strict unitarian, denying any subsistence of personality to the Word and teaching that the Son and the Spirit were merely the Church's names for the inspired man Jesus Christ and the grace which God poured upon the apostles, is probably accurate." The incarnation having become a fundamental of Christain belief denied by the bishop of Antioch, three synods between 264 and 269 addressed themselves to anathematizing his antitrinitarianism. They never did sort out his "heresies" from his "blasphemies." Athanasius, who led the anti-Arian forces in the fourth century, compared the Arian heretics to Paul, connected him with both Sabellius and the Jews, and found the roots of Arianism in Paul's thought. Naturally, Athanasius perpetuated the condemnation of the "blasphemies of Paul" and his "heresy" too. Denying the incarnation and calling the Son of God a creature remained blasphemies in the Protestant world until this century, and in the Catholic world are blasphemies still.[45]

In the early fourth century Christians were still trying to understand the idea of God, which they made phenomenally complex by the worship of a being who was once a man; more mystical still, Christians added a third dimension to the divinity, the Holy Spirit. They had to protect their faith in the Father, Son, and Spirit yet maintain the integrity of one God, and at the same time defend themselves from persecution. The persecutions ended in the West with the abdication of Diocletian in 305, but continued under Galerius in the East until 311. Then Constantine united the entire empire after winning the victory that allowed Christianity to become a catholic or universal religion. A superstitious man who worshipped the sun god Sol Invictus, Constantine before the decisive battle saw the sign of the cross blazing in the sky under the words "By this sign, conquer." He did, and out of gratitude to Christianity the emperor lavished wealth and power on it, having extended to it complete freedom. In Rome and in Constantinople (Byzantium), the eastern capital of the empire, he built churches and endowed them with magnificent estates and tax revenues. Eusebius, the bishop of Caesaria in Palestine and the most famous ecclesiastic of his time, ended his great history of the church with a rhapsody, because "the whole human race was freed from the oppression of tyrants" and Christians worshipped together "in complete harmony." The harmony did not last long, for Christians were soon accusing each other of blasphemy. Eusebius's later biography of the emperor is a panegyric, but none who accepted Constantine's favors accused him of idolatry or blasphemy for having built both in Rome and in Byzantium colossal statues of the sun god.[46]

Theology was not one of the emperor's strong points. He could comprehend the only Supreme God *or* Jesus Christ as the source of his victory, and he was familiar with polytheism, but the Holy Trinity held mysteries for him. Theological distinctions about the persons within a triune Godhead and disputes about their relations and natures were matters that Constantine preferred to leave to the more subtle bishops around him, especially Ossius the principal court bishop. Peace and unity were Constantine's values, and he did not want them shattered by churchmen any more than by politicians or military rivals. In Alexandria, however, where the see ranked in importance with Rome and Antioch and the bishop was called "pope," the church knew neither peace nor unity.

In 318 Arius of Alexandria accused his bishop, Alexander, of Sabellianism for having used a Greek term referring to "the same essence" of the persons of the Trinity. Arius used "Sabellianism" as an epithet; soon "Arianism" became one. Although Arius lived almost twenty years more at the center of a theological controversy, none of his writings survived. His name became the most execrated in Christendom for about fourteen centuries, yet his words survive only as quoted by his antagonists, Alexander and the next bishop of Alexandria, Athanasius. Athanasius's writings against Arius and the Arians fill a volume of almost 600 pages of double-column small type.[47]

From him and Alexander we learn that Arius began with the proposition that God was the Father and He was one, infinite and indivisible. He was uncreated, existed forever, and ruled as sole sovereign and judge. No other God existed but He. Given His nature, He could not impart it to any other being. He had no equals. Accordingly the other elements of the Trinity, whom Arius recognized, had to be subordinate.

Subordinationism was an old view and probably the original one of the earliest Judean Christians. Even Origen, the third-century father, was a subordinationist who concluded, paradoxically, that the Son, although God, is not "true God," only his image. Athanasius recoiled in horror at the Arian rejection of a preexistent Logos or Son of God. Arius believed that the Son did not exist until his creation by the Father: ". . . there was a time when He was not. For the Son is a thing created, and a thing made; nor is He like to the Father in substance; nor is He the true and natural Word of the Father. . . ." To Arius, "the Word is a creature and a work, and foreign and unlike the Father in essence. . . . Wherefore the Son is not true God." Bishop Eusebius, the historian, held the same view. It is an extrapolation of the words ascribed to Jesus: "the Father is greater than I" (John 14:28).[48]

In a sense Arianism, then as orthodox as any other interpretation of the Trinity, proved the dictum of Ecclesiastes 1:9 that "there is nothing new under the sun." Arius devoutly believed that his was a truly Christian view advanced to save the church of Alexandria from his bishop's error. But by the fourth century, many christologists who took Christ's divinity as axiomatic found Arianism un-Christian. They were shocked by Arius's thesis that the Son, whom he conceded to be "first begotten of all creation," was a "creature," although a "perfect" one, who once did not exist, who had a beginning, and who was "alien" from God. "God," said Arius, "is ineffable to His Son." Although the Son was "God-only begotten," he could not know or understand the Father. To call the Son God, Arius held, was to confuse the Son with the Father in ignorance of the fact that the Son was God only by God's grace and in name only: Acts 2:36, "God has made him both Lord and Christ." The Son was not eternal; he was inferior to God. Arius rested his case exclusively on the Scriptures and refused to accept any view or word that was unscriptural. For him the Trinity was figurative, there being only one God, the Father whose substance or essence could not be shared. In effect Arius divided Father and Son; he reduced Christ to the historical Jesus and the Holy Spirit to the divine inspiration in man. This, Arius thought, was "our faith from our forefathers."[49]

Bishop Alexander could also rely on Scriptures. They yield what the mind wants or can understand, for Satan, it has been said, can also quote Scripture. Alexander was convinced that Satan had taken root in Arius's soul, arraying him against "the Godhead of Christ." Arius had been talking about the Godhead of the Father, and Alexander saw opprobrium and infamy cast upon the Christian religion. Arius, he reported to his namesake, Alexander of Constantinople, had drained the dregs of impiety. By imitating the Jews, the Ebionites, and Paul of Samosata, Arius had engaged in "impious and unscriptural blasphemy against Christ," "publicly derided the Christian religion," and created "a most disgraceful and Antichristian heresy." Accordingly, in 321 Alexander called a synod of the bishops of Egypt and Lybia, nearly a hundred, who found that Arius and his numerous followers, including two bishops, taught "an apostasy, which one may justly suspect and designate as a forerunner of Antichrist." They also called it heresy, blasphemy, and impiety, and they anathematized it. Alexander had the synod"s support in deposing Arius, then in excommunicating and exiling him. Nevertheless Arius spread his doctrine with the sympathetic support of powerful bishops, including Eusebius of Caesaria, the historian, and Eusebius of Nicomedia. The latter was related by marriage to the imperial family who maintained an imperial residence in Nicomedia. The dispute between Arius and his bishop became notorious as it spread through Egypt and echoed across Libya, Palestine, and Asia Minor.[50]

Arianism was an atavistic reversion of Christianity to its primitive apostolic age, but the clock could not be set back. Although Catholic Christianity had not yet fully emerged, the time had long since run out when it could recognize and accept its past. Alexander and Athanasius, his successor as bishop of Alexandria, projected the Catholic future. The Arian or Trinitarian Controversy was a turning point in the history of Christianity, the most decisive since Paul undertook to preach the Gospel to the gentiles. Although the fourth century can be termed the Age of the Trinitarian Controversy, it can with equal validity be called the Age of Blasphemy, judged by the incessant use of "blasphemy" or "impiety" to describe the position of an opponent who disagreed.

If all the contestants in the theological battles of the fouth century had represented polar extremes, Arianism versus Athanasianism, one might easily understand the ferocity with which they anathematized each other. In a single generation, however, the extremes produced a variety of fellow travelers and middle-of-the-road compromisers, so that the controversy quickly reduced to quibbles. Yet each variant and compromise became the object of the same sort of vile abuse that the extremes showered upon each other.

The reason for the peculiar intensity of the controversy seems clear. Not only was the future development of Christianity at stake; the right road to salvation was the issue. It was a matter on which the slightest mistake or deviation from the "true" faith, as the contestants variously understood it, could mean the damnation of all the souls of Christendom. Thus, antichrist, blasphemer, atheist, un-Christian, heretic, apostate, idolator, and epithets of such force seemed appropriate characterizations for a misstep.

The controversy was inherently complex because of its focal question: What is the true Christian understanding of God? The complexity derived from confronting a matter that surpasses human understanding. But a difference in language complicated the problem. Slightly over half the bishops in Christendom spoke Greek, the rest Latin. A word in one language carried different nuances in another. Still worse, many crucial terms were ambiguous enough in meaning to be understood in different ways. Two bishops agreeing that Christ shared the same "essence" of God could mean contradictory things. Fundamental clashes also existed. The Arians said the essence was different, not the same. The Semi-Arians thought it was similar, at least in some respects. The degree of similarity and the points of dissimilarity divided bishops who agreed in principle. Men who believed that the Father and the Son shared a similar essence fought each other on the differences that remained between them. Two substances alike in some ways may be unlike in others, allowing theological ideologues to zero in on the fine distinctions, as if every tone in a chiarascuro had to be identical. Conformity on everything, not on most points, was the test — the test of salvation — and of blasphemy and heresy. Thus the Greek and Latin words for same, similar, and different became battle cries in a dispute about substances, consubstantiality, natures, hypostases, existences, properties, persons, coessentiality, essences, and subsistences within the Trinity.

Emperor Constantine, valuing a unified church as a bulwark of his domains, sent his court bishop, Ossius of Cordoba, with a letter to Alexander and Arius, chastening both for their quarrel. Taking no sides at this point, Constantine saw only a dispute "about matters of small or scarcely the least importance," involving no "heresy." Yet, he commanded, "let there be one faith." Both parties must "hold one and the same judgment" on the faith lest the people be confronted by a choice of "blasphemy or schism." On returning from his mission, Ossius advised Constantine that the rift was serious and that Alexander's position should be preferred. Constantine then called the first ecumenical council in Christian history, inviting Arius and all eighteen hundred bishops of the empire to meet the next summer, in 325, at Nicaea, then a thriving town twenty miles south of the imperial residence at Nicomedia near the Bosphorus. Only about one-sixth of all the bishops attended the council, and only seven from the 800 bishops of the Latin churches of the West; Rome sent no bishops, only two priests. Presbyters and deacons, including the young Athanasius who backed his bishop, swelled the membership of the council to almost two thousand. The emperor himself, assisted by Ossius, presided over the sessions that lasted over six weeks.[51]

Initially both the Arians and Alexandrians were insignificant minorities. The overwhelming majority of bishops preferred a comprehensive definition of the faith that would exclude no one, the more ambiguous the better. Few wanted to depart from scriptural authority or take sides, but Constantine would agree to ambiguity only on Alexandrian terms. Bishop Eusebius, the historian, disliked the Alexandrian position as did Eusebius of Nicomedia, an uncompromising Arian. The historian, seeking a middle way, introduced a creed used in his church, to which the Arians could have subscribed by construing its meaning in their way. The emperor assented to the historian's creed on condition that a Greek term meaning "of the same essence" or "consubstantial" be added to show the relationship of the Father and Son. And the emperor demanded a unanimous vote.[52]

The Nicene Creed as modified to please the Alexandrians, later known as Nicenes or Athanasians, defined the faith as belief in God the

Father and in Jesus Christ, "the Son of God, begotten of the Father, Only-begotten, that is *from the essence of the Father*; God from God . . . begotten and not made, One *in essence with the Father*," who came to earth for the salvation of men, "was made flesh," suffered, and ascended to heaven to judge the quick and the dead. Almost as an afterthought, on the heels of the elaborate definition of Jesus Christ came the terse affirmation of belief "in the Holy Ghost." The Logos disappeared, the Holy Spirit shriveled, and the Son of God became consubstantial, that is, ranked "in essence with the Father."[53]

Eusebius the historian had difficulty in accepting the drastic revision of his creed, and he surely represented the great majority. He never was convinced by the Nicene faith which he took more seriously than Constantine. The emperor cared little for metaphysical meanings; to him, unanimity, a triumph of form over substance, meant good politics and proof of divine approbation. Therefore, Bishop Eusebius was able to secure the emperor's approval for an interpretation by the council to the effect that the Son was not "a part" of the Father although of His essence. Eusebius took that to mean that "the Son was from the Father, not however a part of His essence." Thus, he construed away the objectionable although ambiguous word.[54]

Arianism recognized Jesus Christ and the Holy Spirit as divine by the Father's grace, although not in actuality of essence. Semi-Arianism saw a crucial distinction between the Son having an essence from the Father but not being an essence of the Father, not, that is, of the same essence. Later, Semi-Arians spoke of a similar essence. With the council's approval, Eusebius construed "begotten, not made" to mean that the Son far excelled all ordinary creatures, thus allowing the conclusion that the Son was a creature begotten "of" the Father but not by him. That staked out a position midway between the competing claims that Christ was really divine or really Jesus the man inspired by the Spirit. Having adopted Alexander's language and a Semi-Arian interpretation, Eusebius and all the bishops — fifteen unwillingly — subscribed to the Nicene Creed. Five recalcitrant Arians refused to subscribe to a condemnation of Arius, and their opposition rankled. The council, intimidated by the emperor, took drastic measures. They anathematized "every impious heresy," meaning Arianism generally but in particular its unscriptural doctrines about the Son, for example, that "once he was not." They had to swallow the unscriptural term "essence," which they interpreted to mean what Alexander and Athanasius did not mean.[55]

Constantine's temper required Arius's excommunication. The emperor himself ordered Arius's books to be burned in front of the council. Curiously, in its letter to the church in Alexandria, the council did not again refer to "heresy," although it did speak of "pestilential error." By contrast it used "blasphemy" three times and "impiety" three times, each time in reference to a specific unscriptural Arian opinion or phrase, including a reference to the Son as a "creature" or "work" who could sin. Constantine too wrote to the church of Alexandria where Arianism had first been vented; condemning Arian "blasphemies," he stressed the "unanimous" opinion of over three hundred bishops in affirming the only true faith. Their opinion was unanimous, because Constantine coerced fifteen and by imperial decree deposed and exiled the leading Arian bishops, including Eusebius of Nicodemia and Theognis of Nicaea. He also commanded the burning of all books by Arius throughout the empire "in order that not only his depraved doctrine may be suppressed, but also that no memorial of him may be by any means left." The decree concluded that anyone caught with Arian books would be treated as a "criminal" and suffer "capital punishment."[56]

Thus, for the first time Christians, who had long been victims of persecution, began to persecute each other. Constantine's edicts against the Arians fixed the precedent for temporal punishment of offenses against the Christian faith. In this instance Constantine named the crime as "licentious treatises against religion" by "impious persons." On the other hand, a church document of this period called *The Genuine Acts of Peter* referred to Arius as "the heresiarch, the divider of the consubstantial and indivisible Trinity" who dared "to blaspheme the Lord and Saviour, beyond all other heretics. . . . " Associating heresy and blasphemy had become habitual among ecclesiastics. Not surprisingly, Constantine revealed the same confusion. In 312 he had guaranteed religious liberty. After Nicaea, he issued an edict against heretics but specified only Novatian schismatics and Gnostic Christians (Valentinians and Marcionites). For their "criminality" and "pernicious errors," he deprived them of their right to hold religious assemblies, but he imposed no sanctions. The edict invited all heretics to enter the "Catholic Church." Lest anyone misunderstand the targets of his decree, Constantine declared, confusingly, "I mean the impious and wretched double-mindedness of heretics and schismatics."[57]

The writings of Athanasius, fifth-century church historians, and many modern ones misleadingly depict the Nicene Creed as having established Catholic orthodoxy. Yet orthodoxy was impossible without unity between the Eastern and Western churches. The Latin churches of the West had not committed themselves in 325. Hilary of Poitiers, later a Nicene, declared that he had been a bishop for many years without having heard of the Nicene Creed. It was the product of imperial and ecclesiastical politics, not of free consent. In any case the creed, judged by results, enshrined heterodoxy, because Arians and Semi-Arians alike could read their own meanings into it and Athanasian meanings out of it. Moreover, the wily bishops of Nicomedia and Theognis of Nicaea pretended to recant and reingratiated themselves with the emperor. On being restored to their bishoprics, they allied with Eusebius of Caesaria to control a majority at a succession of councils at Caesaria, Tyre, Jerusalem, and Constantinople during Constantine's last years. They arranged the condemnation and exile of Athanasius and several other bishops who had championed the Nicene Creed. The Nicomedian even obtained for Arius a new hearing before Constantine who agreed that the former archenemy of Christianity should be restored to the communion of the church. Indeed, one of the counts against Athanasius was his adamant refusal to accept Arius on the ground that "Christ-opposing heresy had no fellowship with the Catholic Church." In 337, when Constantine was on his deathbed, he received baptismal rites from the leading Arian bishop in Christendom, Eusebius of Nicomedia. Thus by 337 the Nicene party had lost the confidence of the emperor, its major sees, and for over forty years the battle on whose outcome depended the definition of orthodoxy. As Jaroslav Pelikan said, the Nicene consensus was an "illusion" from the beginning.[58]

About 440, Socrates Scholasticus of Constantinople, a defender of the Nicene Creed who wrote an ecclesiastical history from the point where Eusebius of Caesaria had left off, coolly described the bewildering hostilities among Christian bishops a century earlier. After Nicaea, Socrates wrote,

> the term *homoousios* [of the same essence] troubled some of them. So that while they occupied themselves in too minute investigation of its import, they roused the strife against each other; it seemed not unlike a contest in the dark; for neither party appeared to understand distinctly the grounds on which they calumniated one another. Those who objected to the word *homoousios*, conceived that those who approved it favored the opinion of Sabellius and Montanus; they therefore called them blasphemers, as subverting the existence of the Son of God. And again the advocates of this term, charging their opponents with polytheism, inveighed against them as introducers of heathen superstitions. . . . In consequence of these misunderstandings, each of them wrote as if contending against adversaries: and although it was admitted on both sides that the Son of God has a distinct person and existence, and all acknowledged that there is

one God in three Persons, yet from what cause I am unable to divine, they could not agree among themselves, and therefore could in no way endure to be at peace.

In Socrates' account, the two bishops whose Christian names were Eusebius called the Athanasians blasphemers.[59]

The fortunes of the party triumphant at Nicaea worsened after Constantine's death. When his sons divided the empire, the principle that prevailed was that the emperor's religion determined the standard of orthodoxy within his realm. In the West under Emperor Constans, the Nicene Creed was orthodox, at least until 350. The East repudiated that creed at several councils. From 350 to 361, Emperor Constantius reunited East and West under the Arian banner. Athanasius and his Nicene Creed were condemned at councils in Arles (353), Milan (355), Sirmium (357), and Constantinople (360). The Council of Sirmium was noteworthy because exclusively Western bishops brought Arianism as far as it could go. Church historians, following Hilary of Poitiers and Athanasius, have made a cliché out of the phrase "the blasphemy of Sirmium," because the bishops rejected "of one essence" and "of like essence." The Sirmium Creed expressed belief in Jesus Christ as Lord and Redeemer, the only Son of God, "but two Gods may not and shall not be taught." Such was the blasphemy.[60]

In the 350s a dozen Western bishops including the bishop of Rome were deposed and replaced by Arians. Athanasius, having regained his see in Alexandria under Constans, lost it again under Constantius. Rome, Antioch, Alexandria, Constantinople, and the remaining great sees of Christendom fell to victorious bishops who denied the sameness and even the similarity of the Son's essence with that of the Father. "Orthodoxy," for the time being, severed Christ from God. Jerome (340–420) the great scholar in Rome, lamented: "The whole world groaned and marvelled to find itself Arian."[61]

Although the Arian church jettisoned even the Semi-Arian position that the essences were "similar," Constantius finally favored that position for reasons of state: Arianism jeopardized peace and unity. Worshippers believed in the divinity of Christ, and the Semi-Arians, recoiling from the extremism of the Arians, began moving toward an alliance with the old Nicene party. At Ariminium (359) and Constantinople (360), councils condemned the Arian heresy for having reached "beyond every pitch of blasphemy," but the latest creeds omitted the term "essence" as unscriptural and provocative of misunderstandings. The Council of Ariminium declared simply, "The Son is like the Father in all things. . . . " From 358 to 380, before the coronation of

Theodosius, varieties of Semi-Arianism prevailed, making deviations on the left and right heresies and blasphemies. But the Semi-Arians could not agree among themselves whether the Father and Son were alike in essence or just alike, although they still rejected the Athanasian interpretation of the Nicene Creed. The terminological muddle had become hopelessly confusing, not that it had ever been clear. After Athanasius, the last survivor of the Council of Nicaea who died in 373, his epigones debated whether the essence was a single hypostasis (self-subsistent being) or whether there were three hypostases in a single essence. Chaos seemed to exist on every side, as Christian bishops cursed each other for being antichrists and atheists.[62]

Athanasius, the foremost defender of Catholicism before Augustine, is a good case study. His polemical flights were commonplace. A victim of verbal scourging as well as the inflictor of it, he was deposed and exiled three times as an enemy of the church, once on false charges of mutilation and murder. In 339, while in exile, he retailed from hearsay livid accounts of outrages committed in Alexandria by Bishop Gregory. Because his successor in Alexandria was an Arian, Athanasius conceived of no crime that Gregory's blasphemy was incapable of provoking. Athanasius alleged that in concert with city officials, Jews, heathens, and above all the notorious Arian bishop of Nicomedia, Bishop Gregory plundered churches and set them on fire, raped nuns, killed monks, and committed other atrocities, all to show "blasphemy even in the churches of our Lord" and to mingle Arian impiety with the true faith. Athanasius especially liked to refer to "the impious heresy of the Arian madmen." He coined the word "Ario-maniacs" to describe them. He was convinced that a "blasphemous conspiracy" masterminded by Eusebius had prejudiced Constantine against him and inspired a church council to remove him. His removal too was an act of impiety, he thought.[63]

As a Greek scholar, Athanasius usually preferred "impiety" to "blasphemy," although he used the terms synonymously. Indeed, he used synonymously all words that described an offense against religion, although they might be as different as idolatry and schism. In a passage on Arianism under Constantine, Athanasius spoke of "impiety" twelve times and heresy less than half that often. In this context he meant by impiety the deposing of bishops faithful to his view of the creed. When, however, he spoke of Constantine's persecution of Arius and his followers, Athanasius exulted in upholding the true faith. Although a favorite gambit of the various anti-Nicenes was to call the Athanasian view Sabellian because Sabellius had employed the term "of the same essence," Athanasius retorted in kind by attributing "Sabellian blasphemy" to those who rejected the crucial term. Sabellianism and Arianism, he said, were "both heresies equal in impiety." The worst "crime" of the "godless heresy of the Arians" was their alleged "blasphemous" rejection of Christ, for which the guilty deserved the "hatred" of all Christians.[64]

Athanasius preserved two credal statements by Arius himself and headed them "Blasphemies of Arius." Some of Arius's points seem unexceptionable. The first, obviously missing a preface, is: "God Himself, then, in His own nature, is ineffable by all men." Athanasius construed that to mean that Jesus the man did not know God. Athanasius could nit-pick any credal statement not of his own devising and find blasphemy, if he wanted to. Yet he did not assault all who differed from him if they supported him. Bishop Marcellus of Ancyra (in Turkey), one of Athanasius's firmest supporters at the Council of Nicaea, held eccentric ideas which in an opponent of Athanasius would have been proof of heresy or blasphemy. Athanasius loyally defended Marcellus against their common enemies. The Athanasians even defended the "heresiarch" Photinus, the bishop of Sirmium, whom the Arians also deposed for opinions that seemed Unitarian to the scholar who translated Athanasius's writings into English. Athanasius himself tried to ignore Photinus by name while refuting his opinions, only once and reluctantly referring to him as a heretic.[65]

By contrast Athanasius described his enemies, by no means all Arians, as "Arian heretics" or, synonymously, as "Jewish blasphemers." He repeatedly claimed that those who opposed him and his interpretation of the Nicene Creed were "modern Jews and disciples of Caiaphas." To Athanasius the contention even of Semi-Arians that Jesus was "unoriginate," meaning "created" or "not preexistent with the Father himself," was "diabolical irreligion" whose perpetrators deserved to be stoned. Anyone who rejected the Athanasian understanding of the Nicene reference to "the essence of the Father" engaged in a "crime," not just a sin. Even Eusebius of Caesaria, the historian, was guilty of that crime according to Athanasius. He freely called even conservative Christian bishops "Jews," "heathens," "Arians," "antichrists," and "blasphemers" as if the names had no differences in meaning. As a matter of fact, however, many of the Christian bishops whom Athanasius condemned also condemned Arianism and were as reverent in their beliefs and practices as Athanasius himself. The Arians, for that matter, were as zealous and devout in their Christian beliefs as the Athanasians.[66]

To Athanasius, Arius had first "vomited forth the poison of this impiety," rejecting the "same essence" and thus rejecting Christ. Then

Eusebius "defended his blasphemy," and finally it spread until entire councils of bishops endorsed it. Athanasius managed very successfully to make Arian and Semi-Arian councils look absurd as they inconsistently turned out creed after creed at different councils from Antioch in 341 to Antioch in 361. His gift for ridicule matched his penchant for invective, but he debased the language by censuring any non-Athanasian creed as blasphemy and Arian heresy. The deluge of Athanasian vituperation, which opponents reciprocated, registered the tremendous importance that creed-makers attached to their task. The true faith was at issue, and on it depended the road to salvation.[67]

In the end, the bishops of the fourth century deserve no credit for fixing a creed. An emperor and ordinary priests and Christian worshippers settled the most important issue before the Reformation. No creed that diminished or derogated from the sovereign divinity of Christ had a chance of remaining dominant. Athanasius won not because his invective was stronger or his theology was more persuasive; he won because Christians worshipped Jesus Christ as God from very early times. "The law of prayer here," as R.P.C. Hanson wrote, "decided the law of belief." Liturgy was decisive because in churches throughout the empire, baptismal rites, confessions, and prayers invoked Christ as God. People wanted a divine Savior. Neither grace nor salvation could emanate from one who was only the most perfect creature among others or had a nature different from the Father.[68]

Theodosius, who became emperor in the East in 379 and subsequently reunited East and West for a time, was a devout Athanasian and a merciless ruler. His own religion coincided with his political understanding of which religion most likely would maintain unity in the empire. The Council of Constantinople in 381 reaffirmed the Nicene Creed but expanded on the section describing the Holy Spirit. When a new heresy, monophysitism, arose in the next century (there was never an end to new heresies) advancing the doctrine that Christ had a single nature, the Council of Chalcedon in 451, supported by Pope Leo of Rome, fixed the Nicene-Constantinople creed as the authoritative one. By that time the pope was a temporal as well as a spiritual leader. Some things do not change. The creed remains authoritative even today and of heresies there have been no end — old ones with new names and new ones based on old principles.[69]

Although Theodosius and Christian liturgy settled the creed of the church, establishing Catholic orthodoxy, the fourth-century bishops prepared state and church for persecuting heterodoxy. The bishops, following earlier church fathers, popularized the heinous character of blasphemy and heresy. As a result transgressions against the faith became crimes against the state. Hebrews 10:28 had first pointed the way when its anonymous author declared that profaning the faith deserved worse than death. Clement, Ignatius, Irenaeus, Dionysius, Origen, Alexander, and Athanasius used heresy and blasphemy interchangeably. On the other hand, none advocated the use of force in matters of conscience. Tertullian flatly opposed coercion. A persecuted minority naturally argues for its freedom. In power, however, its perspective may change. Constantine, backed by the Nicene bishops, fixed the precedent for burning licentious books, commanding death for concealment of blasphemy, and banning heretical worship. Athanasius's litany of hate and his references to the "crime" of heresy or blasphemy also helped fix a course for the future. Theodosius followed it with repeated legislation. Christian truth did not yet come from the blade of an executioner's axe, for the ordinary penalty consisted of the imposition of civil disabilities. First the church anathematized, then turned the offender over to the state. Heretics lost their property and their civil rights, and so the purity of the faith was nourished.

The union of church and state made secular punishment possible. The Theodosian legislation of 380 enthroned Catholic Christianity as the exclusive religion of the empire. The state then committed itself "to the religion which was taught by St. Peter to the Romans, which has been faithfully preserved by tradition, and which is now professed by the pontiff Damasus of Rome. . . . We order that the adherents of this faith be called *Catholic Christians*; we brand all the senseless followers of other religions with the infamous name of *heretics*, and forbid their conventicles. . . . Besides the condemnation of divine justice, they must expect the heavy penalties which our authority, guided by heavenly wisdom, shall think proper to inflict." Thus religious intolerance rapidly became a Christian principle. The "heavenly wisdom" offered by the church was to terrify everyone into communion with Catholicism. Within fifteen years of 380, imperial edicts deprived all heretics and pagans of the right to worship, banned them from civil offices, and exposed them to heavy fines, confiscation of property, banishment, and in certain cases death. By 435 there were sixty-six laws against Christian heretics plus many others against pagans.[70]

Only Manichaeans, some dissident monastic sects that opposed marriage, and, peculiarly, certain Eastern Christians who celebrated Easter on the Passover faced the possibility of death. Death was a measure of last resort that was exacted with great rarity, for it did not suit the church's spiritual profession nor achieve the objective of converting the heretic. The whole purpose of persecution was to force conversion. Imposing the death penalty on any and all pertinacious heretics was a thirteenth-century invention.[71]

The first instance of capital punishment for heresy occurred in 385 when the pious Bishop Pricillius of Spain and six of his followers were tortured and decapitated with the approval of a synod in Trier. Never before had ecclesiastical authorities resorted to the ultimate secular power against a heretic. The Pricillian heresy was a form of Manichaeism. Rome had rejected Pricillius but did not approve of his execution. Rome did approve of the persecutory legislation; otherwise it would not have been enacted. When Theodosius herded seven thousand pagans into an amphitheater and slaughtered them, Bishop Ambrose of Milan refused the emperor communion in the church until he submitted to ecclesiastical discipline. He submitted. Theodosius did not pile up edicts against heretics without the encouragement of the church. The mass of persecutory legislation inspired lynch law. In Alexandria alone, Christians under the patriarch Cyrillus engaged in murderous pogroms, killed off Novatian schismatics, and, in 415, kidnapped the foremost Platonic philosopher of her time, Hypatia, stripped her in a church, and tore her limb from limb. Rome did not approve of lynch law. It lacked the obligatory formalities. The Theodosian code, by contrast, had official sanction.[72]

From the time of that legislation, "heresy" became the formal name of the great crime against Christianity, although Tertullian's definition of the early third century was not improved upon. The idea of false doctrine or willful error of opinion covered much more ground than "blasphemy," because "blasphemy," however loosely used, retained a core connotation of cursing or scorning. "Heresy" as the newer generic term, being unfreighted with Old Testament origins, was intrinsically more flexible and spacious. True enough, blasphemy had been used as the equivalent of heresy and virtually every other offense against religion, but it was best reserved as a descriptive epithet that conveyed the ultimate abhorrence. The one "unforgiveable sin" according to Jesus himself was a particular blasphemy: "blasphemy against the Holy Spirit," or attributing to demonic forces a saving work of God or the Spirit (Matt. 12:31). Augustine in the early fourth century freely mixed blasphemy, impiety, heresy, apostasy, schism, and sacrilege, but even he declared that the church could forgive an Arian or any other heretic, a schismatic, or even a Jew if entering the holy communion; never, however, could the church forgive a blasphemy against the Holy Spirit.[73]

On the other hand, "blasphemy" retained its generally epithetical character. It was also a useful term for denigrating a fellow Christian whose fundamental orthodoxy was indisputable but who had somehow misspoken about the Holy Trinity, any of its members, the Virgin,the symbols of the church, its sacraments, its doctrines, or its officers. "Heresy" served as well for that purpose but seemed ludicrous applied to one whose reputation was impeccable. The famous dispute between Rufinus and Jerome about the year 400 is an example. Rufinus, a presbyter, scholar, and founder of monasteries, had been an intimate friend of Jerome, the incomparable Christian scholar and translator of the Scriptures. Taking offense at something Jerome supposedly said about his work, Rufinus countered savagely to prove that he was more orthodox than Jerome. In a text on the "bride of Christ," Jerome had referred to the "mother-in-law of God." Rufinus called that heathenism, sacrilege, impiety, and a "blasphemy" so "great and foul" that it was "worthy of death." That sentiment, foreshadowing a dark stain in Christian thought, showed that the concept of blasphemy, once a description of an exact crime, had all but lost its meaning. Rufinus's use of "blasphemy" closed an era that had begun with the Gospel story of the trial before the Sanhedrin.[74]

PART TWO

CONTINENTAL PRECEDENTS

4

COMPELLING HERETICS TO COME IN

For twelve centuries after the Trinitarian Controversy, blasphemy had almost no history because Christianity confronted a "crime" with a different name, heresy. From the standpoint of the church it was substantially the same crime; only the name was different. The authors of the New Testament sometimes differentiated heresy from blasphemy. Heresy to them meant a seditious spirit within the church, that is, factionalism or the formation of a sect. It also meant the holding of a false doctrine on a matter of Christian truth. But early Christians also regarded a seditious spirit and false doctrine as forms of blasphemy, so that the two terms, from New Testament beginnings, became indistinguishable. By the end of the fourth century the engulfing term had become heresy, while blasphemy signified its most reprehensible expression. Heresy finally superseded blasphemy as the description of the offense against religion because the church faced a proliferation of competing doctrines about the faith, challenging its mastery. The preoccupying problem of the church was not abusive speech about God or the Holy Trinity but different interpretations of the faith.

Internal disagreements about the faith had always existed, but the triumph of the Catholic church and its Nicene Creed altered the situation. With the state supporting the church's standards of orthodoxy, the church was in a position to enforce its will wherever the writ of the state was enforceable. Heresy was more than the name of a sin against the church and a crime against the state. It became a reason for the persecution that was intended to make the church "universal" and monolithic. Separate sections of the Theodosian Code applied to Jews and pagans, making heresy a crime that only Christian deviants could commit. The church's hatred of heresy would in time drench Christendom with the blood of Christians. No matter how devoutly they believed in Christ, heretics suffered because their beliefs differed from the church's. By remorselessly persecuting them, the church attained and long kept its catholicity. Its monopoly as the only recognized or established religion was built on murder as well as the exclusivity of its control of salvation. Ironically, the first Catholic theologian who advocated systematic persecution had been a libertine and a Manichaean heretic, and he genuinely opposed the death penalty for offenses against religion.

Augustine, the bishop of Hippo Regius (now in Algeria), converted to Roman Catholicism in 387 when he was thirty-three. Between then and his death in 430, his contributions to the church made him the most revered figure in its postapostolic history prior to the time of Thomas Aquinas in the thirteenth century. No person except Paul had such a shaping influence on Christianity. Augustine also became the most authoritative name in the history of the theory of persecution. Although he did not originate that theory, he gave it substance and the force of his extraordinary imprimatur. He led the way to the medieval mentality and to the Inquisition.[1]

For the church to have had a direct hand in murder would have been un-Christian. Augustine understood that. Although he opposed the death penalty, he justified it. The church had to maintain the appearance of charity, but the state had to inflict death when necessary. The church merely turned offenders against religion over to the secular arm. That required the cooperation of the state. Indeed, that required an elaborate rationalization for church–state cooperation against dissenters. Its premise was that the offender against religion, by being a rebel against God, rebelled against the state. The state protected itself and society by using force against the heretic.

Augustine's theory of persecution developed in connection with the Donatists, a schismatic group in North Africa that passed itself off as the orthodox Catholic church. The Donatists were orthodox in the sense that they subscribed to the same creed and dogmas as the Church of Rome, reproduced its organization, and administered the same sacraments. But the Donatists, who constituted a large majority of the Christians of North Africa, Augustine's home, were stricter than the Church of Rome, whose authority they rejected. The schism had developed early in the fourth century, when Donatist purists took the position that any Christian who had cooperated with Roman persecutors defiled the faith; Christians who were Donatists rejected sacraments performed by defilers. To be in communion with the church, the Donatists believed, required rebaptism or rebirth as a Christian under Donatist auspices. As the schism developed throughout the fourth century, Donatists came to regard all communicants of the Church of Rome as defiled Christians, and the Church of Rome came ultimately to regard the Donatists as the worst sort of heretics—

blasphemers, because they knew the absolute truth yet rejected it from the one true church.[2]

Before the empire condemned Donatists as heretics in 405, Augustine described their schism as heresy and blasphemy. He was not fastidious in his choice of words. The Donatists were heretics, he wrote, because they rejected "the primacy of the Apostolic chair of Rome" and had set up a "rival altar." "Thus, then, when God wills to stir up powers [the state] against heretics, against schismatics, against those that scatter the Church, that blow on Christ as if they abhorred Him, that blaspheme baptism, let them [the Donatists] not wonder." The state had no alternative but to use force against the Donatists. "How otherwise should they [Christian kings] give an account of their rule to God? . . . it concerns Christian kings of this world to wish their mother the Church, of which they have been spiritually born, to have peace in their times." Nebuchadnezzar had provided a model for Christian kings when he decreed that any who blasphemed God should be "cut off." The Donatist blasphemers, Augustine declared, "slay souls," and for that must suffer physically. They "cause everlasting deaths, and yet they complain that they themselves suffer temporal deaths." Coercing them by the temporal powers of Catholic princes inflicted mere "bodily suffering, not the suffering of spiritual deception." By severing themselves from Rome and Christian unity, Donatists engaged in "heinous impiety" or "sacrilege."[3]

In Augustine's thinking schism, heresy, blasphemy, and treason were strands in a twisted cable. He and his teacher, Bishop Ambrose of Milan (340?–97), recognized two spheres of jurisdiction, the spiritual and temporal, and although they differed on the demarcation between the two, they agreed that the temporal was subordinate to the spiritual in any matter concerning the unity of the church. "The maintenance of civil law," Ambrose told Theodosius, "is secondary to religious interest." By humbling Emperor Theodosius, Ambrose prepared the way for Henry IV's barefoot penance in the snows of Canossa in 1077 before Pope Gregory VII. Salvation and imperial politics were an old mix. The Church of Rome taught that life on earth is a fleeting moment compared to the future life, which is in Christ's charge acting through the church. To the Donatists Augustine wrote, ". . . we are calling on your soul to grasp everlasting life and avoid everlasting death." Salvation came from the Church of Rome alone. As long as the church could sustain its claim to exclusive power over salvation, it controlled the policy of the state on any issue concerning an offense against religion.[4]

The theory of the church was that a society forfeits the protection of heaven by offending the divine powers that protect against disasters. A wrathful God could inflict droughts, famines, plagues, poverty, and military defeat. Christianity, perpetuating such ideas from the Jewish and Hellenistic worlds, held the state to be under an obligation to prevent its subjects from holding religious beliefs or recognizing a spiritual jurisdiction other than the church's. Rulers, said Augustine, do not use the sword in vain, for "they are the ministers of God, avengers unto wrath against those who do evil." Rulers had established the church by law, recognizing it as the only true faith and the sole jurisdiction over the state, thus ensuring the possibility of future rewards. Because the heretic stood athwart the path of salvation, he constituted an immortal danger to himself and a mortal one to state and church. As a public enemy the heretic had to be corrected by force for his own benefit and society's or be removed. His contagion was worse than that of a plague, because carnal death counted for nothing compared to the everlasting life of those saved by their adherence to the church. It alone administered divine grace; thus the power of kings and the health of the body politic depended on spiritual unity.[5]

The purity of the faith was incomparably more important than the "coercion of exile and loss of goods," Augustine declared. No one owned earthly goods except by divine law, according to which the just possessed all things; sinners, heretics, and the impious owned nothing. Indeed, the purity of the faith required the prayers of the church so that its adherents not be "pierced to the heart by the sword of spiritual wickedness. . . ." Let Christians die whatever death they must and "let us have greater fear that the purity of faith be destroyed . . . than that women be violently raped in the flesh, for chastity is not destroyed by this violence if it is preserved in the heart. . . ." Rape, torture, and temporal death were nothing compared to rejection of the faith. The death to be feared is "not a temporal death, which is bound to happen sometime; we fear their eternal death, which can happen if we do not guard against it and can be averted if we do guard against it."[6]

Salvation was the strongest trump of the church and the fount of persecution. If salvation did not exist outside the church, the state had to cooperate with it in compelling everyone to worship in the one true faith. The state had the authority of the apostle Paul (Romans 13:2–4) to use its power against offenders of the faith. When "the saving doctrine is added to useful fear," truth drove out error and caused rejoicing, because those who blessed God with the church had been saved. Some, like the Donatists, argued that no one should be *forced* to do right. To them Augustine preached his favorite text: "compel them to come in" (Luke 14:16–23). Force could free a man from destructive error. The shepherd called his wandering sheep back to the fold "by using the lash." The mother was "harsh and stern" with her children, using punishment "to heal by love, not to injure by hatred." So too with the mother church. Her intentions made all the difference. As if illustrating his point, Augustine added that Jezebel killed the prophets, Elijah the false prophets. "I think," taught Augustine, "there was a difference between the doers as between the victims." Paul had damned men eternally "that they may learn not to blaspheme." From this Augustine reasoned that it was "a good work to correct evil men by evil."[7]

History showed that the bad had persecuted the good and the good the bad, but the good did it "to bring about amendment by punishment . . . out of love." When the impious killed the prophets and the prophets killed the impious, "what else is to be noted except to ask which of them served the cause of truth, which that of sin; which . . . to injure, which . . . to convert?" Under the faithful kings of his time, Augustine happily observed, "now the impious suffered instead of the Christians." He taught that Christians, when persecuted, had to plead conscience and the obligation of wicked magistrates to tolerate Christian truths, but that when Christian magistrates were in power their duty was to sustain the church by persecuting errors of faith. The Donatists, who complained about persecution, claimed that theirs was the true church because it suffered, while the Catholic church, which persecuted, was false. To that Augustine replied that the Donatist did in fact belong to the true church, but: "The reason why we say he belonged to the true Church was not that he suffered persecution, but that he suffered it for justice' sake, while, on the other hand, they have been estranged from the Church not because they persecuted, but because they persecuted unjustly." In the same vein, Augustine argued, "there is an unjust persecution which the wicked inflict on the Church of Christ, and there is a just persecution which the Church of Christ inflicts on the wicked." The church persecuted "out of love," he reminded, "to reclaim from error to save souls."[8]

In the case of the Donatists, their "impiety" surpassed even "idolatry." Augustine made that extraordinary observation about all heretics who were "as well versed" in Christianity as the Donatists. And so he justified secular decrees against heretics and schismatics. He saw no immorality in coercion. The question for him was whether force was being used for good or evil, and being a practical man he asked whether force worked. To a Donatist he wrote, "We see that . . . many cities which were formerly Donatist are now Catholic, now detest the diabolical separation, and now ardently love unity. These became Catholic by the effect of that fear which displeases you, through the laws of the emperors. . . ." Conceding that he had first opposed forcing "the unity of Christ" and had preferred "that we should act by speaking, fight by debating, and prevail by reasoning," Augustine observed that he had changed his mind: "First of all, the case of my own city [Hippo] was set before me, which had been wholly Donatist, but was converted to Catholic unity by the fear of imperial laws. . . ." Seeing many other cities "converted" too, he had finally come to realize the meaning of Paul's truth that all power was from God; "therefore he that resisteth the power, resisteth the ordinance of God. For princes are not a terror to the good work, but to the evil." Scripture also taught that the father should beat his headstrong son "with a rod and deliver his soul from hell" (Prov. 23:14), proving that coercion was necessary against the heretic "lest he perish eternally."[9]

Toleration was no mercy to the heretic for it merely intensified his damnation. Still worse it passed his guilt to church and state for allowing him to contaminate others. Thus, more than the vindication of God's honor was at stake, because toleration of the heretic multiplied his eternal fate among the faithful. Augustine's reasoning was simple. Those who absolutely knew the revealed truth and accepted it, yet permitted disloyalty to it, committed a greater crime than those who did not know it or rejected it. Thus, toleration could bring a curse to state and church; indulging willful error in a matter of salvation betrayed the revealed faith and risked the worst calamities that could befall mankind in this life and the afterlife. From the standpoint of the state, no one who betrayed the faith could be a dutiful subject. The heretic stirred up wars and treasons. How much worse, then, for society was a blasphemy against God, or Christ, or his church, for blasphemy was the most "diabolical heresy." The traitor betrayed only his king, the heretic and blasphemer the King of Kings.[10]

Nebuchadnezzar, Paul, the shepherd with his lash, and the father with his rod were repetitive motifs in Augustine. But his most powerful argument showing that "it has been a blessing to many to be driven first by fear of bodily pain, in order afterwards to be instructed," came not from what he called "experience"—the success of persecution—but from the preeminent model of Christ himself, as Augustine understood him. Donatists claimed that Jesus had not used force on anyone. Augustine repudiated them first by recalling the case of Paul. Christ not only compelled him by words "but used His power to strike him prostrate. . . ." Christ also blinded him because Paul, as Saul of Tarsus, seeing nothing through his open eyes, was filled with dark unbelief. "Paul was forced by Christ; therefore, the Church imitates her Lord in forcing them [heretics], although in her early days she did not expect to have to compel anyone in order to fulfill the prophetic utterance."[11]

In the same way, Augustine reasoned, "the Lord Himself commands the guests first to be brought in to His great supper, but afterwards to be compelled. . . ." When there were empty seats at the banquet, the Lord commanded: "Go out into the highways and hedges and whomsoever you find, compel them to come in" (Luke 14:16–23). Augustine concluded that the church "in the era of kings" exercised a power received by divine gift, "and if those who are found in the highways and hedges, that is, in heresies and schisms, are compelled to come in, she is not to be blamed for compelling them, but they for waiting to be compelled." He opposed the death penalty, favoring lashings, exile, and confiscation of worldly goods. Thus he recommended that the devout Christian emperor should prefer a reformation of "impious aberrations" by stringent laws short of death, but should use force "to force those who carried the standard of Christ against Christ to return to Catholic unity, under stress of fear and compulsion, rather than merely . . . leave them free to go astray and be lost."[12]

Augustinian thought represented the final stage of Roman Catholicism under the old Roman Empire. Even as Augustine completed the writings that made him the most popular of the church fathers for over a thousand years, the empire was crumbling under the onslaughts of Germanic invaders on all borders. In 410, when the weakened imperial forces attempted to enforce the Theodosian Code in Numidia (Algeria) against the Donatists, who fanatically resisted, Rome itself was sacked by the "barbarian" Visigoths. They were, in fact, Arian Christians who persecuted Catholics with the same ferocity as Catholics and Donatists had persecuted each other. In North Africa neither of the old contestants won. Orthodox successes faded away beginning in 429 when the Vandals, who were also Arians, began to sweep across the Numidian plains. Eventually Islam replaced Christianity in the Berber homeland.[13]

Roman Catholicism triumphed in Europe, despite the capture of the Eternal City in 476 by the Arian Goths and the end of the old empire in the West. Unlike the Greek Arians and the Donatists, the Germanic Arians had little capacity for theology or ecclesiastical organization. The church in Rome had a genius for both plus the prestige of being the residual legatee of ancient Roman culture. In time the church "civilized" the Arians, while its allies conquered them. The Franks, who accepted Roman Catholicism, defeated the Arians in Burgundy, while the Byzantine Empire defeated them in North Africa and Italy. Before the close of the sixth century the Visigoths in Spain accepted conversion. Thus by war, conversion, and propaganda the church prevailed against Arianism and a succession of other heresies.

In Byzantium, the eastern half of the old empire, where the Greek Orthodox church dominated, Emperor Justinian I sponsored a massive codification of the laws, called the *Corpus Juris Civilis*. It greatly influenced subsequent legal developments in Europe. Its provision on blasphemy, dating from 529, alleged that "famine, earthquake, and pestilence" occurred because a failure to punish blasphemy "provoked God's wrath." Although blasphemers would ultimately lose their souls, the code fixed the punishment in this world as death in order to bring offenders into "anguish." Imperial officers who were slack in enforcement would be damned by God and subject to the emperor's displeasure. Charlemagne, who in 800 founded what became the Holy Roman Empire in central Europe, endorsed this provision in Justinian's code, as did successors. What blasphemy meant and the frequency of its punishment during the Middle Ages cannot be easily determined. Penalties short of death also existed, including imprisonment on bread and water (then a lingering substitute for death), cutting off the lips or slitting them, burning through the tongue, and tearing it out or cutting it off. From the early Middle Ages to the outset of the Reformation, Christian thought on heresy and blasphemy remained static. Theologians who discussed blasphemy in the times of Bede, Gratian, Aquinas, Bernard Gui, and Bellarmine said nothing significantly different from Augustine. Blasphemy engaged their attention hardly at all. Heresy was the offense against religion that progressively preoccupied them and the energies of the church in crushing dissidence.[14]

Punishments for heresy became increasingly common, for blasphemy, rare. The first burnings for heresy in the West probably did not occur until the eleventh century; some were burned by the "secular arm" with episcopal approval in that and the next century. Sometimes the fires consumed heretics singly, sometimes in wholesale batches, but not all heretics were burned. Lesser punishments included branding, scourging, and imprisonment for life. No pattern of punishment for obdurate heresy existed before the thirteenth century, nor is there any way to differentiate heretics from blasphemers, especially if the facts showed no cursing or reviling. Even in the thirteenth century (for which the facts are abundant) and when the death penalty for obstinate heresy became routine, the Christian habit of identifying blasphemy as heresy, or as equating the two as one, persisted. Heresy, long the generic crime, supplanted blasphemy as the offense for which the state was obligated to punish those condemned by the church. Blasphemy, in fact, nearly disappeared as a legal concept or a separate crime; heresy engulfed and superseded it. The history of heresy in the Middle Ages, having been the subject of numerous scholarly books of distinction, need not be recounted here. All that needs be shown is that an offense that contemporaries could have classified as blasphemy was deemed heresy and that theologians scarcely distinguished the two offenses.[15]

The Albigensian Crusade of the early thirteenth century, followed by the Inquisition, had a genocidal effect upon the Cathars of southern France. If blasphemy had any meaning beyond cursing or reviling God, the Cathars should have been condemned as blasphemers by Catholic standards. Yet the Cathars — a name deriving from the Greek for "purified" — were called heretics. They were neo-Gnostic dualists who believed that God was the primal Spirit and first cause but that Satan created the world and that the spirit, which was pure, was imprisoned within a corrupt body. Christ, to them, was a deity, one of many, whose pure spirit could not have been born of Mary or crucified. He had a human appearance only to fool Satan while he rescued human spirits. As Docetists, the Cathars also rejected incarnation. They were a neo-Manichaean version of Gnostic Christianity that regarded Roman Catholicism as the church of Satan. The church waged war on them as heretics, although by Catholic standards the Cathars were not even Christian. The paradox was that only a Christian could be considered a heretic. Because the church operated in a closed society, one who professed Christ was a member of it and had to conform or pay the penalty; one who rejected Christ, as did the Jews and Moslems, was regarded as an unbeliever who was outside the society and had no rights except by sufferance.[16]

Thomas Aquinas (1225–74), the greatest of the medieval theologians and philosophers, laboriously expounded on the various offenses against religion, yet he left the penumbra connecting heresy and blasphemy scarcely diminished. To his credit he sought distinctions and did not merely use the terms "heresy" and "blasphemy" as interchangeable epithets, as had Augustine. Nevertheless, he brought those terms only a step beyond Tertullian, who had preceded the sainted scholastic by a thousand years. Thoman Aquinas started with Tertullian's definition of heresy as a deliberate choice of "false or new opinions" on matters of faith. On such matters the truth had been revealed, abrogating the right of anyone to make a choice. Accordingly a man might "deviate from the rectitude of the Christian faith" in one of two ways. If he had an evil will and rejected Christ, he was an unbeliever like the Jews. Or, "he intends to assent to Christ yet he fails in his choice of those things wherein he assents to Christ, because he chooses, not what Christ really taught, but the suggestions of his own mind." Accordingly, those who professed the Christian faith "but corrupt its dogmas" were heretics: "Wherefore heresy and sect are the same thing. . . . " Relying on Augustine against the Manichees, Thomas

Aquinas added that the proof of heresy is the heretic's stubborn refusal to conform when rebuked; he maintained his pernicious doctrines "contrary to the dogmas of faith" even after instruction in the "truth." The authority to define "what Christ really taught" rested in the "Sovereign Pontiff." One who defied that authority adopted "a species of unbelief."[17]

To Thomas Aquinas several "species of unbelief" existed, among them heresy, paganism, Judaism, apostasy, and blasphemy. Some thought, wrote Aquinas, that because blasphemy referred to the utterance of an "insult against the Creator," it pertained to "ill-will against God rather than to unbelief." On the contrary, he maintained, blasphemy opposed "the confession of faith" and therefore was a species of unbelief. He accepted, initially, the principle that blasphemy denoted "disparagement" not just of God but of "some surpassing goodness. . . . Consequently whoever either *denies* anything befitting God, or *affirms* anything unbefitting Him, disparages the Divine goodness." Because the blasphemer "strives to hinder the honour due to God" and because the saints praised God, blasphemy against them redounds against Him. To Aquinas, a distinction between the faith and God as "the object of faith" confused one and the same thing. The faith affirmed God. Therefore "to affirm unfitting things, or to deny fitting things of God," or "to ascribe to creatures things that are proper to God" amounted to the same blasphemous, mortal sin, severing the blasphemer from God's charity. Leviticus 24:16 taught that the blasphemer should suffer death, the penalty inflicted only for mortal sins. Surprisingly Aquinas maintained that a person who asserted "something false about God" took His name in vain even more than one who knowingly perjured himself under oath. Given the extraordinary sanctity with which oaths were regarded in the thirteenth century, Thomas Aquinas's finding that "blasphemy is worse than perjury" is startling until his reason becomes clear: the perjurer "does not say or think something false about God, as the blasphemer does. . . ."[18]

But to "say or think something false about God" was heresy as much as blasphemy. Indeed, both were species of unbelief or deviance from the faith; both sprang from a willful or evil intent (Aquinas distinguished blasphemy from the venial sin of impulsively or passionately uttering profane words); both asserted a falsity about God; both were mortal sins, and neither could be tolerated. Heresy could not be tolerated even though executing the heretic deprived him of the opportunity of repentance. The obstinate heretic deserved not only the excommunication which separated him from the church; he had to be "severed from the world by death." Aquinas employed similar reasoning against blasphemers. Other evildoers, such as forgers of money and murderers, were executed. Heresy and blasphemy were worse than counterfeiting coins and murder; therefore, heretics and blasphemers too must be executed. Thomas Aquinas not only defined blasphemy in terms of heresy, he condemned all heresies as blasphemy. Heretics, he declared, "by right . . . can be put to death and despoiled of their possessions by the secular [authorities], even if they do not corrupt others, for they are blasphemers against God, because they observe a false faith. Thus they can be justly punished [even] more than those accused of high treason. . . ."[19]

In the thirteenth century such logic was irrefutable because temporal crimes were insignificant compared to spiritual crimes. Thomas Aquinas, like Augustine, was concerned with life or death not just as a penalty for wrong opinion but as a matter of salvation everlasting. The heretic who remained pertinacious was beyond salvation; he was lost to the church. It had to look "to the salvation of others" by delivering him to "the secular tribunal to be exterminated. . . . Arius was but one spark in Alexandria, but as that spark was not at once put out, the whole earth was laid waste by its flame." The heretic really intended "the corruption of the faith," endangering all souls: "eternal salvation takes precedence of temporal good, and . . . the good of the many is to be preferred to the good of one." The heretic twice admonished could not be given another chance, because he might relapse and infect others, tempting them to join his heresy.[20]

The reasoning about the blasphemer was similar. Blasphemy was "the most grievous" and "the greatest sin." By conflicting with the "confession of faith" blasphemy reflected unbelief, like heresy. Comparing murder with blasphemy, Thomas Aquinas held that "blasphemy, which is a sin committed directly against God, is more grave than murder, which is a sin against one's neighbor." The gravity of the sin depended on the intention of the doer. As the blasphemer "intends to do harm to God's honor," he was the worst sinner. "In comparison with blasphemy, every sin is slight." But Aquinas admitted that blasphemy "can do no harm to God." He was really concerned about the harm it would do by infecting others and tempting them to the blasphemer's damnation. Yet he advocated the death penalty even if heretics did not in fact infect others and blasphemers could not hurt God, and his reason for severity was that "heretics . . . blaspheme against God by following a false faith."[21]

Thus, having begun with the element of disparagement as the basis of a distinction between blasphemy and heresy, Thomas Aquinas ignored it thereafter and left heresy and blasphemy as interchangeable as ever.

Disparagement itself turned out to be nothing more than heresy or false doctrine — attributing to a creature that which belonged to God, denying God that which belonged to Him, or attributing to Him that which was "unfitting." Because blasphemy and heresy were different aspects of the same thing — a deviation from the faith as defined by the church — calling the Cathars heretics rather than blasphemers apparently did not matter, although they regarded Satan as the Creator, scorned the Old Testament, denied Jesus' humanity, and vehemently reviled the church. What did matter was that the Cathars had to be exterminated. [22]

Because only Christians could be heretics, the Jews were the only group officially regarded as blasphemers rather than heretics in the late Middle Ages. Beginning in the thirteenth century, when the papacy was at its zenith and popes regarded themselves as rulers of the world — "The world is an *ecclesia*," declared Innocent III — popes habitually described Jews as blasphemers. The church identified Jesus Christ as God. No greater blasphemy existed than rejecting him, except the greatest blasphemy of all, deicide. The Jews were considered guilty of both. The first accusation was true in the church's sense of what constituted rejection; although the second was spurious, it was and surely is the teaching of the Gospels. [23]

The blasphemy of the Jews posed a special problem for the church. Alexander of Hales (d. 1245), the theologian of the University of Paris whom contemporaries called "the Unanswerable Doctor," confronted the Jewish problem. "On the face of it," he argued, "it appears that they should not be tolerated." Their blasphemies against Christ and the Virgin Mary were notorious; their very religion persecuted Christianity and its sacraments. By their own law, blasphemy was a capital crime; it was immeasurably worse when committed against the true faith. Logic seemed to require the extinction of the Jews. But, Alexander counterargued, they were unique. Jesus himself had prayed for them, and both Testaments spoke of them as the saving remnant. Therefore their survival was necessary as a testimony to the Christian faith. The existence of Jews proved the truth of the story of the Gospels. What stronger testimony for the faith than from its enemies! Although they did not understand their Scripture, they were its guardians and it predicted Christ's advent. Their conversion must be awaited; its occurrence would be Christianity's triumph. Their blasphemies had to be understood as deriving from their belief that the Messiah had not yet come, but such blasphemies could not be publicly tolerated; the church was obligated to urge princes to suppress them without mercy and burn the books that nourished them. On the other hand, their religion must be tolerated, for "we have accepted the Old Law from them, Christ issued from their seed, and the promise was given of their ultimate salvation." Thomas Aquinas agreed. Judaism foreshadowed the true faith and bore witness to it. "For this reason," Aquinas concluded, "they are tolerated in the observance of their rites."[24]

Judaism was tolerated, but not the Jews. Theological reasoning, not humanitarianism, saved them from official extermination. But because of their perpetual blasphemies they had to be systematically degraded. Pope Innocent III presided over the Fourth Lateran Council of 1215 which stripped Jews of civil rights and forced them to wear special marks of identification so that no Christian would unknowingly deal with them. They were technically the serfs of the Christian princes in whose lands they resided by sufferance. They were subject to boycotts, confiscation of properties, and expulsion. But Innocent III would not allow Jews to be killed. The popes protected them, officially, yet not even popes and princes together could protect them from periodic massacres or pogroms. A crusader considered himself unworthy of redeeming the Holy Land from the Moslems until he first killed a Jew, for the crusader believed that avenging Christ by killing Jews earned a crusader remission of his sins. For centuries the church taught that all Jews bore a hideous hereditary guilt. The Gospel was witness to the fact that they themselves had crucified Christ and cried, "His blood be on us and on our children!" (Matt. 27:23). The pogroms began with the First Crusade in 1096 and continued without end. During the Shepherd's Crusade in 1251, almost every Jew in southern France was slaughtered. In 1348–9 when the bubonic plague wiped out one-third of Europe's population including its Jewish population, religious fanatics blamed the Jews; in German cities entire communities were murdered on a scale not exceeded until modern times. Bishops and popes who had poisoned the minds of the people with hatred of Jews could not stop the mobs bent on revenging the Jewish blasphemies against Christ.[25]

The age was incredibly savage. There was nothing uniquely cruel in the persecution of the Jews or even the pogroms against them. The Inquisition, which Innocent III inaugurated and his successor systematized, left a trail of tortured bodies, shattered minds, and smoking flesh for centuries. In Spain thirty-one thousand "heretics" were burned at the stake, and in the Netherlands the Inquisition condemned the entire Protestant population, including children; at least a hundred thousand people were killed for being Christians of the wrong persuasion. The Albigensian Crusade, which Innocent III also launched, turned into a final solution of the Cathar problem. The crusaders indiscriminately massacred Moslems and Jews in the Holy Land, not sparing women and children. Roman Catholic Europeans even slaughtered Coptic Christians, and during the sack of Constantinople in 1204 killed Greek Orthodox priests and raped nuns. In 1282 at least eight thousand Normans in Sicily were slaughtered during the Easter week called Sicilian Vespers. In 1365 during the pillage of Alexandria, native Christians suffered with Jews and Moslems. The Vatican's war against the House of Hohenstaufen caused the deaths by papal violence or in papal dungeons of ten children and grandchildren of Emperor Frederick II, whom Innocent IV had publicly denounced as a blasphemer.[26]

Annihilation on a scale so vast as to exceed any precedents of Nero, Attila, or Genghis Khan makes individual cases of formal prosecution by the Inquisition look trivial and the burning of books nothing compared to the value of human life. But book burning was part of the church's campaign against Jewish blasphemies. The church took the matter with the utmost seriousness, and the Jews lamented the loss or desecration of their holy books. Gregory IX ordered the Talmud to be burned throughout Christendom for its alleged blasphemies against Christ and Mary. The first public *auto-da-fé* occurred in Paris in 1242 when twelve thousand manuscript copies of the Talmud and other rabbinic writings were burned. Louis IX delighted in burning the Talmud. In 1248 another huge batch went up in flames in Paris. The sainted king knew how to treat blasphemous Jews. He told the story of a knight who was present at the Abbey of Cluny when a great disputation was held between monks and Jews. The knight intervened, asking the leader of the Jews whether he believed that the Virgin Mary was the mother of God. The Jew replied negatively, whereupon the knight "laid him low." Explaining the moral of the story, the king declared that no one ought to argue with the Jews except very good scholars, "but the layman, when he heareth the Christian law reviled, should not defend it but by his sword, wherewith he should pierce the vitals of the reviler as far as it will go." Louis, on return from a crusade, confiscated all Jewish properties including synagogues. Five Jews were burned by the close of the fourteenth century in France.[27]

In Aragon, where the Talmud was not burned, it was confiscated and censored. Jews were required to turn in all their writings under sentence of death for blasphemy if they failed to comply, and for speaking evil of Christ they faced the threat of capital punishment and forefeiture of all properties. Expurgation and mutilation of the Talmud were more common than putting it to the bonfire. Only in France, before the Catholic Counterreformation, did the fires consume Jewish writings. That happened with systematic regularity at the urging of the popes from the thirteenth century and on command of the Inquisition. In 1415 a papal bull forbade Jews to have, study, or read the Talmud. In 1442 Eugenius IV ordered magistrates to fine Jews and impose "more severe penalties as they may see fit," because Jews "blasphemed God, the most glorious Virgin his mother, or some saints, or else in some other way commit transgressions of this kind." The charge of blasphemy was also used by authorities to extort Jews into paying a fortune into the royal treasuries to escape the penalties. The worst burnings occurred during the Roman Inquisitions in Italy in the sixteenth century, by which time the invention of printing presses had simplified the manufacture of books. In the 1550s Jewish books as well as rare rabbinic manuscripts were burned by the hundred thousand in Italian cities. Incredibly, a bull of Clement VIII in 1593 forbade Jews to have not only "impious talmudic books or manuscripts" but even writings that "tacitly or expressly contain heretical or erroneous statements against the Holy Scriptures of the *Old Law* and Testament." As late as 1629 an Italian cardinal boasted of having collected ten thousand outlawed Jewish books for destruction.[28]

Real blasphemies existed in the late Middle Ages, although not in the crude sense of reviling God. The church did not have to look to the Jews had it wanted to find blasphemy. Periodically, religious psychopaths cropped up who claimed to be divine. For over two hundred years, beginning in the thirteenth century, the Free Spirit movement existed throughout Europe. Next to Arianism, it was the longest lasting, widest spread blasphemy in Christian history. In the seventeenth century a muted form of it called Ranterism appeared briefly in England. Adherents of the Free Spirit movement sometimes congregated together, but they were rarely organized as a sect and they differed from place to place; not all members even of the same group in the same place agreed on all the various doctrines associated with the Free Spirit. But its adepts, sharing a core of common beliefs, circulated freely among brethren from place to place, even across national borders. Zealous vagabonds, who tended to live a life of poverty, dependent on alms, were the most common carriers of the Free Spirit. They were called Beghards, from which we derive the words "beg" and "beggar." Their female counterparts were Beguines, laywomen who devoted themselves to good works among the poor. Probably only a small fraction of Beghards and Beguines were committed to the doctrines of the Free Spirit, although many were infected with some of those doctrines.[29]

The movement seems to have begun in France among a group of clerics led by Amaury of Béne, a theologian of the University of Paris. Although they were basically pantheists, they were particularly interested in the nature and powers of the soul. Soul liberty or spiritual liberty (liberty of the *spirit* in a Gnostic sense) became the fundamental characteristic of the movement. About a dozen members of this initial group were burned for heresy. Innocent III in 1215 denounced the "most perverse dogma of the impious Amaury" but added that his "doctrine is to be considered not so much heretical as insane." The pope probably referred to the doctrine that "all things are One, because whatever is, is God," from which later adepts of the Free Spirit concluded that they were God. Some claimed to be each member of the Trinity. They perverted the doctrine of incarnation by claiming that incarnation occurred within each of them.[30]

During the next two centuries, as Free Spirits traversed Europe and spread their beliefs, the church ordered the Inquisition to capture, interrogate, and condemn them. Occasionally the word "blasphemy" or "impiety" was used to characterize Free Spirit beliefs, but believers were burned for the crime of heresy. Two historians have investigated this phenomenon of religious lunacy; both use the same chapter heading, "The Heresy of the Free Spirit." The heresy was, rather, a compound of blasphemies. Pantheism was not its central tenet. All Free Spirits, despite the many differences between them, agreed that because a person's spirit or soul was "one with God," God or Christ dwelt within him. Their pantheism and perhaps even their wholesale antinomianism and libertinism may have been derived from pagan philosophy, but the "religion" of the Free Spirit was suffused with Christian concepts, more often than not turned inside out or utterly perverted in meaning. Gnostic Christianity and Manichaeism or Catharism had blended paganism with Christianity, but they were genuinely spiritual or holy in character.[31]

Christianity itself is founded on the idea that a man who was once flesh and blood should be worshipped as God. And the New Testament has enough statements in it, especially when ripped out of context or out of an ambiguous context, to nourish any heresy and, apparently, even the blasphemy of the Free Spirit. The existing accounts do not show that its adepts relied on Scripture, but a movement passing itself off as the true Christianity and Roman Catholicism as its perverted antichrist had to fall back on some texts to justify itself. Paul said, "I have been crucified with Christ; it is no longer I who live, but Christ who lives in me; . . . if justification were through the law, then Christ died to no purpose" (Gal. 2:20–21). "For freedom Christ has set us free; stand fast therefore, and do not submit again to the yoke of slavery. . . . You are severed from Christ, you who would be justified by the law. . . " (Gal. 5:1, 4). John 10:38 depicts Jesus as saying, "the Father is in me and I am in the Father." An Epistle of John adds,

"No one born of God commits sin; for God's nature abides in him, and he cannot sin because he is born of God" (1 John 3:9). A disordered mind with religious delusions of grandeur, sick of the church's sexual suppressions, hostile to its wealth, power, worldliness, and visible corruptions, can lose itself in such texts and conclude that one must cast off the Roman yoke by allowing the divinity living in him to express itself freely without recognizing any law, religious or civil.

Meditation and self-exaltation, according to the Free Spirit, led to what the Gnostics called *gnosis*, a self-revealing understanding of the cosmic mysteries. The Free Spirit regarded himself as "perfect." The Gnostics had preached that eventually every spirit would find its way back to God and become reabsorbed in His essence or substance. The Free Spirits taught that they had made that great leap in this life, indeed that there was no afterlife, no heaven and no hell except in man's imagination. Having received direct revelation and self-understanding, they believed that heaven was here and now for the liberated soul. Life itself was the incarnation and the resurrection. "The divine essence is my essence and my essence is the divine essence," said a Free Spirit. Another said he was "wholly transformed into God" so that not even the Virgin Mary could tell the difference. "Rejoice with me, I have become God," announced a third.[32]

A French abbot decried the "profane novelties" of his time, calling their adherents "disciples of Epicurus rather than of Christ," but no Free Spirit invoked Epicurus. "With most dangerous deceit," said the abbot, "they strive secretly to persuade people that sinners shall not be punished, saying that sin is nothing, so that nobody shall be punished by God for sin." He called it "supreme madness," not blasphemy, "that such men should not fear nor blush to say that they are God." Some Free Spirits disavowed Christ and the Holy Spirit as being less perfect than they, and some diminished and even debased Christ for not being perfect. A perfect man could lie, cheat, steal, and even kill without the least remorse, because he was emancipated from conscience. All that he did was perfect and godly. Adultery before the altar, or still better, incest with mother or sister, reaffirmed the Free Spirit; they called the act the divine sacrament of "Christerie." They also believed that intercourse with a Free Spirit increased a woman's chastity, even her virginity.[33]

Albertus Magnus, the great theologian who was Thomas Aquinas's teacher and later bishop of Regensburg, compiled ninety-seven propositions of the Free Spirit. The liberated soul claimed to be co-eternal with God and equally omnipotent. Another proposition was that every act, however immoral to others, is sanctified. Another was that the Free

Spirit not only became equal to God but surpassed Him and was entitled to the same or greater reverence. He was beyond a state of grace; he
was God in his own body; God was created in the image of man; only
the Free Spirit, not Christ, need be obeyed. Naturally the Free Spirit
had no need of the church, its heirarchy for which he had contempt, or
its sacraments, which were less holy than his. The Free Spirit, by definition, was emancipated from the church's slavery; he recognized no
authority but his own free will and could do as he pleased, knowing he
was divine beyond divinity.[34]

Popes issued bulls against the Free Spirit and sometimes called it
blasphemous, but rarely. The first heretical error listed in the bull of
1311 was: "That a man in this life can attain to such perfection that he
is incapable of sinning or surpassing his present degree of grace, since to
do so would make him more perfect than Christ." Some archbishops
and inquisitors spoke passingly of blasphemy, and a chancellor of the
University of Paris said that the doctrines of the Free Spirit were "the
most impious and foolish since the world began." Clearly, they had to
be punished. Some adepts of the Free Spirit were allowed to die in jail
because they were regarded as insane, but most, when caught, were
burned as heretics. A report of 1317 by the bishop of Strasburg
classified Free Spirit doctrines under seven branches of heresy. The
first, "Against God," was blasphemous in the extreme, but heresy was
the standard description. The other branches were against Christ, the
church, the sacraments, heaven and hell, the Gospel, and the saints. In
a case of 1458 that ended in a burning, Johannes Becker of Mainz confessed that since he was united with God (he meant that literally) he was
more perfect than Christ; he was God by nature, in contrast to Christ
who was God only by grace. At the same time, said Becker, he was not
obligated to observe God's decrees, for as Paul said, "The letter kills,
but the spirit gives life" (2 Cor. 3:6). The inquisitors convicted him on
all counts for heresy. Becker may have blasphemed God and Christ, but
blasphemy was not a threat to the church.[35]

Heresy was. A blasphemer had to be killed, of course, for his crimes
against God, but the heretic, although called a traitor against God, was
executed by the state for his crimes against the church. God could not
be harmed, although He might avenge Himself on those who tolerated
blasphemers. The heretic, however, could harm the church by dividing
it and winning away its adherents. Free Spirits, even if psychopathic
zealots, created envy because of their emancipated and immoral life
outside the church. In all probability the church concentrated on them
as heretics rather than blasphemers for that reason; similarly, it had
condemned the Cathars as heretics, although they too held

blasphemous doctrines, because they had captured the affections of most of southern France. Since the church was capable of recognizing blasphemy when confronted by it, only this quasi-political interpretation explains why the Cathars and Free Spirits were condemned for heresy. What surprises is that their condemnation was not reinforced by the church's calling attention to the blasphemous character of their doctrines.

Throughout the history of the Inquisition, the church turned blasphemers over to the secular arm to be burned at the stake for "heretical pravity." The sentence invariably was for the crime of heresy, a practice in keeping with Thomas Aquinas's teaching that while all heretics blasphemed God, blasphemy or disparagement was not in principle different from heresy. Actually, most heretics were not blasphemers at all, because they were as reverent in their beliefs and worship as the pope. From the late twelfth century to the Reformation, the Waldensian heresy, so named after its originator, Peter Waldo, flourished despite persecution. The Waldensians were proto-Protestants, precursors of the Reformation. So too were the followers of John Wycliffe in England and John Huss in central Europe. The church unquestionably considered them to be blasphemers. A papal bull of 1418 against the sects founded by such "archheretics" denounced them because they "blaspheme the Lord God," although in fact they disparaged only the church. Jerome of Prague, a Hussite, was burned for heresy even though he allegedly taught "very blasphemous" doctrines such as denial of the Real Presence in the Mass. His doctrines, like those of most proto-Protestants, come from a different reading of the New Testament instead of from Rome. That was the real nature of his heresy — and of his blasphemy. In the sixteenth century the church began to speak of "blasphemous heresies" and "heretical blasphemies." When doing so the church followed the practice of the heretics themselves, the Protestants, who would, in a sense, reinvent the crime of blasphemy. Condemned as heretics, they sought a different term and found it in "blasphemy," but they really followed Paul, Augustine, and Thomas Aquinas in the sense that they applied the name to what they conceived to be false religious doctrines.[36]

5

PROTESTANTISM REDISCOVERS BLASPHEMY

The major Protestant denominations of the Reformation — Lutheranism, Calvinism, and Anglicanism — repudiated the Roman Catholic church but quickly established their own standards of orthodoxy and ecclesiastical polity. In effect several establishments of religion superseded the single historic one in the areas they respectively controlled. However, the Reformation once unleashed could not be contained. To a minority of sixteenth-century Protestants the Reformation was a deformation. They believed that the rebirth of the simple church of the Gospels had died aborning under Luther and Calvin. With the assistance of the printing press, the Reformation made the Bible available to every person who could read or listen to his own language; it taught the supremacy of the Bible over hierarchies and theologies, and it offered the saving grace of God directly to every individual without the intervention of any church or religious officials. In effect the Reformation gave to every Christian the hope, however illusory where establishments of religion existed, that he could serve as his own priest by finding Christ his one way. Schisms, sects, and heresies were inevitable as individuals rediscovered the Bible in the vernacular and reinterpreted it for themselves, whether mystically, literally, allegorically, or rationally. To use the vivid phrase of an intolerant Puritan of the next century, private readings of the Bible swiftly produced "a multimonstrous maufrey of heteroclytes and quicquidlibets."[1]

Although the varieties of religious experience within Protestantism's dissidence ranged from divinely inspired ecstasies to withdrawn pietism, two main streams of belief diverged from the officially sanctioned Protestant churches. One was Arianism, the other Anabaptism, both names imposed by derisive enemies. Arianism, which ultimately called itself Socinianism and Unitarianism, referred loosely to any species of antitrinitarianism, including Sabellianism, and was named after the hated fourth-century heretic, Arius. Lutheranism, Calvinism, and Anglicanism followed the Nicene or the Athanasian Creed: "God the Father, God the Son, and God the Holy Spirit." Accordingly,

Arianism was as execrable to Protestant establishments of religion as to Rome. Arians tended to be rationalistic scripturalists who pointed out that the standard creeds were extrascriptural and that the injunction of Jesus to baptize in the name of the Father, the Son, and the Holy Spirit (Matt. 28:19) said nothing about the three persons of the Trinity sharing the same essence. Arians accepted Jesus as serving a divine office on behalf of God, but they denied his divinity or identity with God, believing that God was one and indivisible. Other Christians, even most Anabaptists, found this denial and the Arian rejection of the doctrine of the Trinity to be atheistic and blasphemous.[2]

Only the Anabaptists were as loathed as the Arians by the rest of Christendom. "Anabaptism" meant "rebaptism," a term rejected by those to whom it was applied. Referring to themselves simply as "the Brethren" or by some other nondescript term, the Anabaptists disagreed on many points and eventually split into several sects, although the name stuck to the bulk of them in the form of "Baptists." They believed that children, being in a state of innocence, would be received into the kingdom of heaven without baptism. Baptism was therefore reserved for persons of maturity who understood and accepted the Gospel. Such persons were regenerated by their faith *before* baptism. The Dutch Anabaptist Menno Simons (1493–1559), after whom the Mennonites were named, explained that baptism was not a sacrament, but only an external ceremony that signified internal Christian birth and acceptance of membership in the church. To believe that baptism in itself could obtain regeneration, he declared, was "blasphemy." "We are not reborn," said Simons, "because we have been baptized . . . but we are baptized because we are reborn by faith and the Word of God. Regeneration, indeed, is not the result of baptism, but baptism is the consequence of regeneration." Infant baptism rather than baptism of believers was to the Anabaptist an abomination invented by Rome to keep everyone within fealty to the pope. Anabaptist aspersions against infant baptism, which most other Protestants held as dear as Rome did, provoked enmity; baptizing an adult who had already been baptized as a child seemed insulting as well as ridiculous. But the Anabaptists were scriptural fundamentalists. The Bible taught them that Jesus received baptism as an adult and that he had commanded, "He that believeth and is baptized shall be saved. . . " (Mark 16:16).[3]

Anabaptism, which spread faster than Arianism and attracted far more adherents, emerged in the 1520s in Lutheran Germany and in Zwinglian Switzerland. In Germany a few atypical Anabaptists incited a class war in 1525 and others in 1533 briefly captured the city of Münster to make it their New Jerusalem. Those freak incidents associated Anabaptism with revolution. The "Peasants' Revolt" and the tragedy of Münster gave Anabaptism a terrible reputation throughout Europe as a seditious conspiracy against governments as well as against established churches. The overwhelming number of Anabaptists were extraordinarily peaceable, righteous, hardworking, pious, and humble folk. They shared with other Protestants an abhorrence of Rome, its sacerdotal hierarchy, its administration of sacraments, its worship of relics, its veneration of Mary and the saints, and its staggering worldliness and corruptions. To Catholics, therefore, Anabaptists were revolutionary Protestant heretics. Michael Sattler, an evangelical Anabaptist, whom Ulrich Zwingli, the leader of Swiss Protestant reform, expelled from Zurich, was caught by Catholic authorities of Rottenburg, Austria. They called him an "archheretic," convicted him on eight counts of heresy, and executed him in a peculiarly grisly way. His tongue was cut out; red-hot tongs were used to tear pieces from his body; he was then burned to ashes.[4]

Protestant establishments regarded Anabaptists with fear and loathing too, although ironically the Anabaptists sought to emulate the primitive church of the original apostles as they imagined it to have been. They were despised for their virtues. They believed that no true Christian should serve the state, which they considered a necessary evil administered by sinful men. They would not take any oaths, not even oaths of allegiance. As pacifists they would not kill, countenance the death penalty, or serve in armies. They passively resisted any form of coercion as contrary to the love which man owed his fellows. Believing that the state had no religious duties, they refused to pay tithes or ecclesiastical taxes for the support of established churches. For them religion was a wholly private and voluntary affair. They wanted only to be left alone to worship as they pleased and live apart from an unChristian world. They asked of government only that it keep peace for the pious. Their apparent rejection of civil officers, courts, the military, taxes, and established churches made them seem as dangerous to Lutherans and Calvinists as to Catholics. The judgment in 1527 against Felix Manz by the town council of Zurich was as follows:

> He has administered baptism in a way contrary to Christian rule; in spite of all the admonitions he could not be made to repent; . . . he and his followers have severed themselves from the Church, and with seditious intention forming groups in order to bring about a schism, they have constituted an independent sect under cover of a Christian gathering; he has rejected the death-penalty and boasted of having certain revelations concerning the

epistles of St. Paul, and all that to acquire more support. Such teachings are contrary to the general custom of Christianity, and lead to scandal, turmoil and rebellion against government; they disturb the general peace, brotherly love, civic concord and provoke every kind of evil.

For those crimes Zurich, the stronghold of Zwingli, executed Manz by drowning him. He was the first Protestant martyred by Protestants. Interestingly the Zwinglians did not call him a heretic or a blasphemer. His religion, clearly, was taken as civilly seditious.[5]

In 1530 Sebastian Franck, one of the great Protestant mystics for whom the church of Christ was invisible and internal, estimated that two thousand Anabaptists had been executed. A recent scholar who examined the history of Anabaptism in central Europe concluded that Catholics were responsible for 84 percent of all the death sentences inflicted on Anabaptists, although only 16 percent of the Anabaptists lived in Catholic areas. Usually Catholics punished unrepentant Anabaptists as heretics and burned them alive. Protestant localities tried to avoid condemning them as heretics, because heresy was a papist description for Calvinism and Lutheranism. Drowning or decapitation was the usual form of Protestant execution, but it was a last resort. Protestants preferred imprisonment, mutilation, and exile as punishments. They executed, in general, only when Anabaptism was compounded by sedition or blasphemy — public criticism of infant baptism or of the established church. An Anabaptist who "rebaptized" contrary to a civil decree was a seditionist or rebel, as was one who defiantly returned to a locality after having been exiled from it. Significantly, 80 percent of all Anabaptist executions in central Europe before 1618 occurred before the Münster episode of 1533, that is, before the tiny lunatic fringe of Anabaptists had captured that city and earned a reputation for freak excesses that included communism, polygamy, and egalitarianism. Münster merely confirmed the worst fears of Christendom about the Anabaptists.[6]

For Martin Luther (1483–1546) the turning point came earlier with the Peasants' War of 1525, an uprising of the poor against the nobility. Before then the great religious reformer was one of the first Christian advocates of religious toleration. Others, notably the early Anabaptists, had claimed that conscience should be free but they had not developed a theory of religious toleration, for they advocated it mainly for themselves. Luther was a vehement, impulsive, and contradictory man. He hated the papists more, if possible, than they hated him, and argued that they blasphemed the name of God, a crime which Paul, he said, deemed worthy of death. "Not that we should slay the papists," he added. "One can do more than enough with words and letters. Neither hewing nor stabbing is necessary." He believed, at least before 1525, that Augustine and Aquinas were wrong: "Christ did not wish to compel men into the faith by force and fire." Argument based on the Bible, he naively believed, would triumph over heresy. If, he quipped, getting rid of heretics by fire was right and effective, the executioner would be the best theologian. Luther clearly passed through a stage in which he advocated liberty of conscience even for those whom he detested.[7]

In his treatise "On the Scope of the Magistrate's Authority" (1523), Luther wrote eloquently on the autonomy of private judgment in matters of conscience, arguing that the government has sovereignty only over men's bodies and property, none over spiritual affairs. His clear division of the spiritual and temporal realms led him to the precocious position that religious liberty could exist only when church and state were separated. "Every man should be allowed to believe as he will and can, and no one should be constrained." To the claim that heresy would flourish if the civil government had no authority to compel faith or punish false doctrine, Luther answered: "Heresy is a spiritual thing which can be cut with no iron, burned with no fire, and drowned with no water. Only with the Word of God can it be cut, burned, and drowned. . . . " In 1524, when some fanatical Anabaptists began preaching revolution, Luther urged a strong stand against sedition but appealed to princes on behalf of the peaceable Anabaptists: "Do not prevent the ministry of the Word. Let them preach boldly as they like and against whom they like, because it is necessary that there are sects. . . ." Even in 1525 he insisted that heretics and false teachers should neither be rooted out nor killed; "Christ makes this perfectly plain, when he says, 'Let both [tares and wheat] grow together.' " When the chancellor of Nürnberg asked his advice on how to deal with the Anabaptists, Luther replied, "I do not yet consider them to be blasphemers, but to be like the Turks, or apostate Christians, who are not to be punished by secular authority, especially not by means of corporal punishment." If, however, they did not acknowledge and obey the government, they forfeited all rights to life and property because "rebellion and murder" would be in their hearts.[8]

A Jesuit historian has wisely observed that Luther's words were meant for Catholic princes. That is, the position of Luther's own church was insecure until a prince sympathetic to it succeeded as Elector of Saxony, which occurred in 1525. But that does not wholly explain his early tolerance of the Anabaptists or even of Catholics. In 1522 Luther wrote, "Don't tear the priests from the altar. Tell the people to withdraw financial support, and with such preaching the Masses will in time fall of themselves. Show consideration to the weak." From one who considered Mass to be a blasphemy that could not be tolerated, indeed that toleration of Mass was blasphemy, the advice was not that of a persecutor. However, after 1525, Luther, supported by the government for the first time, advocated the exclusive establishment of Lutheranism and the suppression of Mass by the government. In 1525, too, the Peasants' War reached its pitch, and Luther took the side of the princes. When news of the atrocities of the peasants reached him he called them blasphemers as well as murderers, although he never condemned the atrocities of the princes who killed over one hundred thousand peasants. Princes had "the sword" by divine decree. "In my opinion," he wrote, "it is better that all of the peasants should be killed rather than that the sovereigns and magistrates should be destroyed, because the peasants take up the sword without God's authorization." To justify the peasants, he declared, "would be the same as to deny and blaspheme God, and to throw God out of heaven." He knew that he was called "a toady to sovereigns," and he was one, although he considered that title one of Satan's blasphemies.[9]

The shock of the Peasants' Revolt and the corruptions of power, which came from having a prince ready to impose Lutheranism by force, explain Luther's abandonment of his earlier opposition to the role of the government in religious affairs. He did not change overnight nor did he end up wholly on the side of persecution, but he surely ceased his advocacy of religious liberty. "Freedom of conscience," a term which he virtually invented, became by casuistic reasoning different from freedom of worship. In 1526, he insisted that people might believe as they pleased but that all must be compelled to attend his church, because conscience "must be instructed from Scripture. If they object that they are forced to faith, that's not the idea. Public offence alone is forbidden them. They may stay in the land, and in the privacy of their rooms pray to as many gods as they like."[10].

At a time when the Inquisition was employing torture to expose men's secret thoughts, Luther's position was still progressive. Although he declared that one could not be a Catholic without being a murderer and a persecutor — "one judges the tree by the fruits" — he proudly added, "We do not kill, banish, and persecute anybody who teaches other than we do. We fight with the Word of God alone. If they don't want it, we let them go and separate ourselves from them and let them stick to any belief they like...and let them live among us...." Two years later, he advised against killing false teachers. "I am slow in a judgment of blood even when it is deserved." The example of the persecutory papists "terrified" him; the saintly and innocent were killed. "I cannot admit that false teachers are to be put to death. It is enough to banish." That signified a major change in his position. Having come to believe that Protestant dissidents and Catholics must be compelled to worship in his church or be banished, he no longer allowed them to "live among us." When the death penalty was proposed for Anabaptists in 1528, the tolerant Luther reemerged: "It is not right and I am deeply troubled that the poor people are so pitifully put to death, burned, and cruelly slain. Let every one believe what he likes. If he is wrong, he will have punishment enough in hell fire. Unless there is sedition one should oppose them with Scripture. . . . With fire you won't get anywhere."[11]

In 1529 an imperial decree capitally condemned Anabaptists without requiring ecclesiastical examination, and a year later Luther endorsed the death penalty; but he convinced himself that his opinion had not changed, for he argued that the Anabaptists were blasphemers and seditionists. They taught that "no rulers are to be tolerated; that no Christian may occupy a position of rulership. . . ." That was seditious. They also taught "doctrines contradicting an article of faith clearly grounded in Scripture and believed throughout the world by all Christendom, such as the articles we teach children in the Creed — for example, if anyone were to teach that Christ is not God, but a mere man and like other prophets, as the Turks and Anabaptists hold — such teachers should not be tolerated, but punished as blasphemers. For they are not mere heretics but open blasphemers." He believed too that anyone who taught that Christ did not die for the sins of mankind, or that there was no resurrection of the dead, or that there was no heaven and hell was a blasphemer. All such people, Luther urged, should be condemned "out of hand" without a defense, because they were blasphemers. Leviticus 24:16 prescribed death for blasphemers; Luther extended that passage to "false teachers," whom he thought no different from blasphemers. His discourse clearly showed that he had neither Jews nor Catholics in mind when he spoke of preachers "who are not willing to cast the poison of their blasphemy upon any except those who are baptized and are called Christians." Whom he meant besides Anabaptists and Arians is not clear. What he meant is clear: although the ancient Jews had killed "true" prophets, "we must not abolish or hide the commandment to stone false prophets. . . ." To those who believed that his persecutory teaching strengthened Catholic tyrants who "pretend" that duty compelled them to punish "us" as blasphemers, he answered first that the Gospel should not be abandoned because of fear and, second, that "pious rulers will punish no man without first seeing, hearing, learning, and becoming certain that he is a blasphemer." That cannot be reconciled with his injunction that "open blasphemers should be condemned without a hearing and without defense. . . ." Luther regretted the cruelty of death, but he had come to believe that dissent from his church was equivalent to persecuting it (a form of blasphemy), making the dissenters "crueler" than the executioners. By 1536 he advocated capital punishment even for Anabaptists who were not seditious, because their beliefs were blasphemous.[12]

Luther fixed upon the term "blasphemy" and invested it with his enormous prestige. The Protestant reformers were being killed by the Catholic church as heretics, and he himself was called a heretic; so he tended to choke on the word "heretic." He had written and preached for years about the futility and evil of punishing heresy. Accordingly he preferred not to use "heretic" as a description of his Protestant enemies, although in fact he did call them heretics. But the word that came easily to him was "blasphemy," as if it differed from "heresy." It did not, especially not as Luther used it. He used it indiscriminately to describe anything that he disliked or disagreed with, just as the church had used "heresy."

Luther always believed that the Jews were blasphemers, but in 1523 he was tolerant toward them. "What good can we do the Jews when we constrain them, malign them, and treat them as dogs? When we deny them work and force them to usury, how can that help? We should use toward them, not the pope's, but Christ's law of love." As Luther aged he became a vicious persecutor of the Jews. For their infinite blasphemies against Christ, he insisted that they could not be tolerated. He urged that their synagogues, Talmuds, and prayerbooks be burned, their houses destroyed, their monies confiscated, their rabbis forbidden to teach, and that no Jews be allowed to use the name of God under penalty of death. All must be put to forced labor, or better still, exiled. Had he the power, he said, he would cut out their tongues because of their blasphemies and force them to accept Christianity. A Jewish historian observed that thanks to Luther's anti-Semitism "Protestants became even more bitter against Jews than Catholics had been."[13]

Luther also raged against Catholicism as a blasphemy against God, although he hesitated advocating the use of the Mosaic law on blasphemy against Catholics; he did not hesitate in the case of Anabaptists and Jews. On the other hand he so vehemently despised Catholics that in his ranting against them he even called them heretics, but, more characteristically, blasphemers. Their Mass was blasphemous. Their popes were blasphemers and antichrists. Their church was a synagogue of Satan, "full of blasphemous lies" and "terrible idolatry." They must be compelled to worship in Lutheran churches and if they failed to attend, their very absence was blasphemy and should be met with excommunication and exile. By 1536 he finally endorsed imprisonment and death for Catholic blasphemies to prevent the spread of their contagion. Mercy existed in heaven, said Luther; on earth, the sword.[14]

He ranted endlessly against the Catholics. In Roman churches "you hear the doctrine of Satan. Nothing is proclaimed there except lies, and the prayer is downright blasphemy." His description of the pope fit himself: "Oh, how he bellows, rages, raves, and foams, just like one possessed by many thousand of devils. . . ." The papal "asses," he said, "are such stupid asses that they cannot and will not distinguish between God's word and human doctrine, but hold them both as one. . . . Here one sees so well how they have set themselves above God like blaspheming Antichrists, and how they regard doctrine as true only as long as they want it to be. . . . They expect such filthy blasphemy of us. . . ." He was speaking of "the pope and cardinals" in 1545 when he said, "they believe that there is no God, no hell, no life after this life, and die like a cow, sow, or other animal. . . That is why it would be best for the emperor and estates of the empire to let the blasphemous, abominable rascals and damned scum of Satan in Rome just go to the devil." "Oh, my dear brother in Christ," he added, "when I here or elsewhere speak so coarsely about the loathsome, accursed, atrocious monster in Rome, be sure to credit it to me. . . . I can with neither words nor thoughts do justice to the abominable, desperate blasphemy he commits with the word and the name of Christ. . . ." In the same treatise against Catholicism, he used the words "blasphemer" and "blasphemy" with such frequency that they either lose all meaning or make one lose count.[15]

Impartially, if promiscuously, Luther condemned Anabaptism, Arianism, and Catholicism as blasphemies, Judaism and Islam too. Any denial of an article of Christian faith as he understood it was blasphemy, as was speaking against the faith; so too, sin was blasphemy, opposing Luther was blasphemy, questioning God's judgments was blasphemy, persecution of Protestants by Catholics was blasphemy, Zwinglian dissent from Lutheranism was blasphemy, missing church was blasphemy, and the peasantry's political opinions were blasphemy. Luther abused the word but revived and popularized it. It became part of the Protestant currency.[16]

Philipp Melanchthon, the interpreter of Lutheranism to the intellectuals, joined Luther in condemning "blasphemous doctrine" as a capital crime to be punished by the magistrate. Justus Menius, the reformer in Thuringia, declared that "preachers of false doctrine must be severely punished by the secular authority as public blasphemers and murderers of souls." In Wurttemberg, John Brenz announced that the magistrate was bound not only by his office but "by his soul's salvation to placate the wrath of God by the suppression of the blasphemous abuse of the Mass." In Strassburg, Caspar Hedio held that "those who denied the right of the magistrate to punish a false and blasphemous worship of God are merely seeking an opportunity to indulge their own dissension and sedition." Otto Brunsfels of Strassburg was more tolerant when he said that he did "not object if anyone feels that the magistrates, who have the sword as ministers of justice, should punish manifest blasphemers."[17]

In Geneva, Protestantism's greatest theologian, John Calvin (1509–64), also revitalized the concept of blasphemy, although, like Luther and the other reformers, he still clung to the concept of heresy and did not clearly differentiate the two. The early Calvin, like the earlier Luther, was relatively tolerant, perhaps because the French authorities had hounded him and prosecuted his brother and several friends for heresy. In the first edition of his *Institutes of the Christian Religion* (1536), he advocated leniency toward persons subjected to ecclesiastical discipline and even toward "Turks and Saracens, and the rest of the enemies of true religion." He explicitly condemned punishing them with "fire and water . . . and . . . pursuing them with the sword." Later editions dropped these and similar passages. As he aged and achieved power in Geneva, becoming that little republic's civil as well as ecclesiastical dictator, his bigotry and inhumanity intensified. Calvin, the most Hebraic of the reformers, possessed an absolute belief in the Mosaic code and the Old Testament's vision of a vengeful Jehovah. He was, in a sense, the Protestant Moses, and he surely thought of himself as God's truest representative, identifying his teaching with God's. His Mosaic fierceness and his doctrine of predestination (only the saints, whom God unfathomably chose, were destined for the life everlasting) allowed him to say of the children killed in the destruction of an impious city, "We may rest assured that God would never have suffered any infants to be slain except those who were already damned and predestined for eternal death." Roland Bainton, the Reformation scholar, remarked, "Calvin scarcely yields the palm to Arnold Amalric, the papal legate, who when there was doubt as to how to distinguish the Catholics and the Cathari, exclaimed, 'Kill them all. God will know which are his.' "[18]

Not suprisingly Calvin abhorred all offenses against religion. Impartially he called both heretics and blasphemers "traitors to God." He applied a similar term to persons convicted of witchcraft, saying they had committed the "*crime de lèze majesté divine au plus haut chef.*" He also called the pope "the high priest of all impiety." Yet Calvin distinguished various degrees of blasphemy. Swearing by the name, blood, or body of Christ, taking frivolous oaths, engaging in impious imprecations and incantations, or calling on a divine power to assist in magic or sorcery were not nearly as serious as denying, defying, or renouncing God. Although Calvin did not expressly recommend the death penalty for serious blasphemy, he justified its use among the Israelites. "Judges and magistrates," he taught, "ought not to slacken the rein when God is mocked, his name put in shame, his religion fouled under foot. We have seen heretofore that blasphemies were more grievously punished than murder." In his commentary on Leviticus 24:16 he observed that stoning the blasphemer to death was the will of God. Dishonoring God, Calvin thought, was the worst crime anyone could commit, and teaching false doctrine (any doctrine but his own) dishonored God.[19]

Traditionally, of course, false doctrine was heresy, not blasphemy, although Calvin did not make such fine distinctions. Of heresy he declared, "If we rightly consider what it is to speak falsehood in the name of Jehovah, it will certainly appear to us more detestable than to kill an innocent man, or to poison a guest, or to lay violent hands on one's own father, or to plunder a stranger [all capital crimes]. . . . Now to corrupt pure doctrine, is it not the same as if to put the devil in God's place?" Putting the devil in God's place was another way of expressing what Jesus had called the one unforgivable sin of blasphemy. In the ordinances adopted by Geneva in 1541, the punishments for blasphemy did not include death, not even for repeated offenses. Heavy fines, jail, bread and water, the stocks, and exile were the specified penalties. "If anyone contradicts the Word of God, he shall . . . receive punishment, according to the exigencies of the case."[20]

In the case of Pierre Ameaux who drunkenly criticized Calvin's teaching, the punishment was public humiliation. In the case of his wife, who advocated sexual license and committed adultery, the punishment was life imprisonment. In the case of Jacquet Gruet, who was accused of blasphemy *and* treason, the punishment was death. These three cases of 1546–7 were probably as enmeshed in politics as in offenses against religion. At that time Calvin still confronted formidable opposition from a party in Geneva that he described as the Libertines. They included well-to-do burghers like Ameaux and Gruet, some of whom, including Ameaux himself, were council members. They disliked Calvin because he was a stern moralist who sought to impose the letter of the Decalogue on everyone and because they preferred the spirit rather than the letter of the law on many points of religion. Geneva's Libertines were basically a political faction but their religious opinions made them seem kin to the Spiritual Libertines, notoriously dissolute antinomians of western Europe; they espoused doctrines reminiscent of those of the Brethren of the Free Spirit, whom the Inquisition had not quite extinguished after more than two centuries of persecution and executions.[21]

In 1544 Calvin wrote a tract against the Spiritual Libertines, whom he identified with his Genevan enemies. Condemning their licentious behavior as subversive of Christian liberty, he characterized their "heresy" as the embodiment of "wretched and horrible blasphemies." They held that the soul was not eternal, attributed creation to the devil, and stressed the divinity of the spirit within each person. Calvin thought they were devoid of morality because they did not believe in sin. "The consequences are," he wrote, "first the blasphemous position, that God is the devil himself, not providence; secondly, that men have no conscience or ability to distinguish right from wrong; thirdly, that all kinds of sin are to be praised, and that none are punishable, all being the work of God." The Libertines were also Docetists, who believed that Christ's death on the cross occurred in appearance only, and, still worse, each claimed to be Christ — or so Calvin alleged. That the Ameauxes and Gruet were Spiritual Libertines is uncertain. The charge of treason against Gruet was very probably trumped up, but a document in his handwriting, found under the roof of his house after he was executed, seemed to validate the Calvinist charge of blasphemy against him. He is supposed to have written that the founders of Judaism and of Christianity were deceivers and that Jesus was justly crucified.[22]

The evidence produced at Gruet's trial in 1547, after his house was searched and he was tortured daily for a month, showed that he had favored the abolition of ecclesiastical discipline, described Calvin as a man who wanted to be adored like the pope, written "all nonsense" in the margin of a copy of Calvin's tract against the Libertines, and corresponded with Calvin's enemies in France; and in a Latin manuscript found in his study, said Calvin, "he made a mock of Scripture altogether, and abused the Saviour. Immortality he called a dream and a fable, and struck at the very root of all religion." Gruet was beheaded. Three years later Calvin wrote of Gruet, "Not only did he oppose himself to our holy religion, but he poured forth such blasphemies that they make the hair stand on end."[23]

The Protestant preference for describing opponents as blasphemers, compared to the Catholic preference for condemning religious deviants as heretics, represented a distinct tendency, but only a tendency. Neither side was consistent. Desiderus Erasmus, the great Catholic humanist, wrote, "What does it matter if there be no blasphemy of the tongue, if the whole life breathes blasphemy against God?" The thought remained ambiguous. Erasmus deplored the excesses of the Inquisition, but whether he believed that a sinful life was worse than a mere utterance or that the one deserved punishment as well as the other cannot be determined. Erasmus was orthodox when he added that no more "detestable blasphemy" existed than calling the Beatitudes a lie. He believed that it was "heretical" of Luther to question any point that the church had authoritatively decided. When Erasmus seemed too tolerant and was criticized for it, he demanded, "How could anyone infer . . . that I do not approve of killing heretics. . . ?" He maintained that he had never taught that heretics should not be executed, but only that princes should "not be severe." There was heresy that was "manifest blasphemy" and heresy that was "sedition," Erasmus declared. "Shall we sheath the sword of the magistrate against this? To kill blasphemous and seditious heretics is necessary for the maintenance of the state." Thus, Luther and the Protestants were not alone in urging death for blasphemers, but interestingly Erasmus the Catholic spoke of "blasphemous . . . heretics." In the Catholic world the genus was still heresy, blasphemy a species of it. [24]

Catholic practice was to convict for the crime of heresy even though the criminal charges might include articles on blasphemous utterances. In the case of Ludwig Hatzer, for example, the magistrates in a small town in southern Germany charged him with blasphemy on a number of counts. As an antitrinitarian he believed that Christ was not equal to God and was of a different essence — the conventional Arian belief — and he excoriated the worship of images as idolatry. In 1529 Constance executed him for heresy. In both respects he could have been called a Judaizer. That happened in the case of Katherine Weigel, one of the first antitrinitarians of Poland. At the age of seventy she had been accused of apostasy for endorsing allegedly Jewish beliefs, although she recanted and was readmitted to the communion of the church. Ten years later, however, the bishop of Cracow tried her for apostasy and blasphemy, because she again maintained Jewish beliefs, a charge she denied. She also denied that Christ was begotten from the substance of God and that he was the Son of God in the Catholic sense, and she protested against the Mass. Such ideas were commonly described as Jewish or Arian or both. In 1539 Cracow burned her as a heretic. In 1546 Paris burned Étienne Dolet who, by adding levity to antitrinitarianism, seemed so dangerous that he was widely reputed to be an atheist. [25]

These rare cases of blasphemous heresy in the Catholic world scarcely have significance compared to the frequency of the death penalty for ordinary heresy. Countless thousands died for religious beliefs that the church deemed ordinary heresy. Dolet's execution, for example, should be compared to the deaths inflicted on twenty-four Lutherans in Paris in 1535. The educated ones had their tongues slit and they were all slowly roasted alive, suspended over the fires. In 1545 the French Catholic authorities, at the instigation of Cardinal de Tournon, attacked some peaceable villages and slaughtered about three thousand Waldensian, including women and children. The pope rapturously congratulated the military commander for his pious work and made him Count Palatine. On the Protestant side, the execution of Gruet in Geneva must be seen in the context of Swiss executions of Anabaptists and the craze against witchcraft; Geneva alone burned about fifty-eight people as witches between 1542 and 1546. The fears, hatreds, and savageries of the Middle Ages toward offenses against religion did not wane until the eighteenth century.[26]

Étienne Dolet, the antitrinitarian, had been a friend of Michael Servetus (1511–53), probably the most celebrated martyr of the sixteenth century. Servetus was a Protestant victim of Calvin's Geneva, which burned him at the stake in 1553 for both blasphemy and heresy. He was also the precursor of Unitarianism. The tradition of antitrinitarianism preceded Arius, but Servetus was the first systematic antitrinitarian theorist. A quixotic Spaniard, he challenged the established churches, Catholic and Protestant, to return Christendom to its pre-Nicene purity. In his time he was notorious throughout Europe as an Arian heresiarch. The systematic suppression of his masterwork, *Christianismi Restitutio (Christianity Restored)*, minimized even his posthumous influence on religious thought. Faustus Socinus (1539–1604), an Italian of the next generation who lived most of his adult life in Poland, became the principal influence on antitrinitarian thought. The suppression of Servetus's book incidentally suppressed his discovery of the pulmonary circulation of the blood. He was a genius of multiple talents. Although Servetus was not forgotten, men remembered his death, not his accomplishments. His martyrdom triggered the first great controversy over toleration.[27]

Servetus was only a teenager when his biblical studies convinced him that Luther, Calvin, and Zwingli were not revolutionary enough, because they accepted the doctrine of the Trinity. He discovered that "not one word is found in the whole Bible about the Trinity, nor about its Persons, nor about an Essence, nor about a unity of the Substance, nor about one Nature of the several beings. . . ." In language often offensive, he assaulted the traditional belief and presumptuously tried to reeducate the leading scholars and theologians of the reformation. Having failed to engage Erasmus in debate, Servetus sought out Johannes

Oecolampadius in Basel, only to be driven away with the warning, "By denying that the Son is eternal you deny of necessity also that the Father is eternal. . . .I will be patient in other matters but when Christ is blasphemed, No!" Oecolampadius alerted other Protestant leaders, and Zwingli urged that they convert or silence the young Spaniard or risk the danger that his "false and evil doctrine, would, if it could, sweep away our whole Christian religion." Do everything possible, Zwingli urged, to end "such dreadful blasphemy." Rebuffed in his efforts to persuade the reformers, Servetus determined to write a book that would reveal the truth of his discoveries to all Christians. In 1531, only fourteen years after Luther had posted his theses on the church door in Wittenberg, Servetus published *De Trinitatis Erroribus (On the Errors of the Trinity)*. It made him a despised and hunted man, although he was not yet twenty-one. The Inquisition sought him in Spain and France. The Protestants banned his book and closed their cities to him. Martin Bucer, from his pulpit in Strassburg, thundered that Servetus should "have the guts torn out of his living body."[28]

Servetus "disappeared" and assumed a new identity. In a few years Catholic France was talking about a brilliant young humanist named "Michel de Villeneuve." Villeneuve was the French rendering of the name of the village in Aragon where Servetus had spent his childhood. Monsieur Villeneuve, a master of Hebrew and Greek, as well as Latin, was a gifted student of astronomy, geography, law, mathematics, medicine, philosophy, and religion, and he lectured on most. At the University of Paris he ranked with his colleague Vesalius as an anatomist. Servetus was still a medical student when he observed from his dissections that Galen, the Greek physician of the second century and still the text for the sixteenth century, had incorrectly described the circulation of the blood. Physicians, relying on Galen, thought that the liver generated blood through the body. Servetus was the first to report that the heart pumped the blood and the lungs aerated it. As Dr. Villeneuve, externally a Catholic, Servetus the heretic became personal physician to the archbishop of Lyons, who had been fascinated by his lectures on comparative ethnology and geography. The doctor settled in Vienne, a town near Lyons, and developed a profitable practice. On the side he continued his studies by working as an editor for a publisher in Lyons. He did two editions of Ptolemy's *Geography* and, most notably, a definitive edition of Pagnini's Latin Bible in seven volumes with extensive revisions and a preface that had traces of heresy. The Council of Trent in 1546 passed over it in favor of the Vulgate as the authentic church text of the Bible, although the Vulgate was inferior in style and scholarship. Servetus's edition of Pagnini ended up on the Index of prohibited books, but he had resumed his biblical scholarship. He was at work on a new book.[29]

His ambitions for the book were boundless. It would, he hoped, rejuvenate Christianity by restoring it to the innocence and simplicity it had in the time of the Gospels. Restoration, not mere reformation, was Servetus's objective. The very title of the book, *Christianismi Restitutio,* would be a reproach to the Reformation. It had failed because it had not sought a return to Christianity as it was before becoming corrupted in the early fourth century by pagan doctrines, by the church's possession of temporal power, by the state's encroachments on the spiritual realm, by the Council of Nicaea's dictation of an erroneous trinitarianism, and by the un-Christian practice of infant baptism. Servetus would purge all the corruptions. The Reformation had repudiated the papacy but not its teachings and sacraments that had no biblical foundation. The Reformation had failed to confront Trinity, incarnation, and redemption, essential matters of Christian theology. Servetus's theology became increasingly radical; he was inclining toward a mystical pantheism and toward the fundamental tenet of the Anabaptists or rebaptizers, whom Christians on both sides of the Reformation abhorred and murdered. God the creator, Servetus believed, fills all things and is knowable only through devotion to Christ, in whom He revealed Himself. One became a Christian by being baptized after experiencing Christ and repenting one's sins. Becoming a Christian meant sharing a spiritual communion that no infant could understand. Christ himself was not baptized until he was an adult.[30]

Servetus's soul burst with his rediscovery of Christianity. He could no longer withstand the spiritual torment of suppressing his secret religion. Villeneuve the Catholic could not betray himself to those who sought the death of Servetus. But after fourteen years as Villeneuve, he must, at least, find someone, if only a correspondent, to whom he could reveal himself and discuss his religion. In his desperation, he convinced himself that John Calvin would understand and encourage him. Calvin and Servetus were about the same age, considerably younger than the Protestant leaders whom Servetus had encountered before being forced to flee from them. Geneva, during Servetus's fourteen years in France, had become the new center of Protestantism and Calvin, its foremost theoretician, had dominated Geneva since 1541. In 1546 Servetus opened a correspondence with him.

Signing his real name, Servetus wrote letter after letter. At first Calvin tolerated him, answering at length, correcting his errors. Servetus, never deferential, became increasingly condescending and critical. He parsed Calvin's replies, revealing their inconsistencies and their conflicts with the Scriptures. Calvin was wrong on the Trinity, wrong on regeneration, wrong on baptism. Servetus dared to instruct Calvin on theology and, for Calvin's better guidance, sent him a manuscript copy of part of his book-in-progress, *Christianismi Restitutio*. Calvin had recommended his own book, the monumental *Institutes of the Christian Religion*, only to be sent an annotated copy of it by Servetus with the errors exposed in marginal comments. "Servetus seizes my books," Calvin wrote a friend, "and defiles them with abusive remarks. . . ." Not a page was free from his "vomit." Belatedly Servetus realized that he had gone too far, although he did not understand that he had roused in Calvin a murderous hatred. "Since you fear I am your Satan, I stop," declared Servetus. "So then return my writings, and farewell." Yet he could not stop: "If you really believe that the Pope is Antichrist," he added, "you will also believe that the Trinity and infant baptism according to the teaching of the Papacy are the doctrine of demons." Calvin did not reply or return the manuscript, but did not betray him to the Inquisition either. Servetus, he wrote to William Farel, had sent him "a great volume full of his ravings" and offered to come to Geneva, "but I shall not pledge my faith to him; for if he did come here, I would see to it, in so far as I have authority in this city, that he should not leave it alive." Like a man possessed, Servetus turned to one of Calvin's Genevan colleagues. Receiving no reply, he exclaimed in a final letter, "Your gospel is without God, without true faith, and without good works. Instead of a God you have a three-headed Cerberus. . . ." Prophetically he added that he knew he would die for his beliefs.[31]

The rejection by Geneva meant that Servetus's last hope to shuck off his Catholic masquerade vanished. He could fulfill himself only by writing his book, which he finished in 1552. Luckily he found a local publisher in Vienne, a man of secret Protestant sympathies, who agreed to undertake the risk of printing; the doctor could afford to pay the heavy costs and handsome bonuses. They burned the manuscript page by page as it was set in type, and they ran off a thousand copies of the huge anonymous book. Servetus shipped most of the edition to a warehouse in Lyons and some copies to bookdealers in Frankfurt and Geneva. Calvin got hold of a copy and recognized it as the work of Servetus, whose manuscript he still retained. Instead of denouncing the book from the pulpit as a danger to Christendom, Calvin betrayed Servetus to their common enemy, the Inquisition, which was responsible for the deaths of so many Protestants.

Calvin worked through an intermediary, an intimate friend and neighbor, who wrote the following letter to his Catholic cousin in Lyons:

You suffer a heretic, who well deserves to be burned wherever he may be. I have in mind a man who will be condemned by the Papists as much as by us or ought to be. For though we differ in many things, yet we have this in common that in the one essence of God there are three persons and that the Father begat his Son, who is eternal Wisdom before all time, and that he has his eternal power, which is the Holy Spirit. So then, when a man says that the Trinity, which we hold, is a Cerberus and a monster of hell and when he disgorges all possible villainies against the teaching of Scripture concerning the eternal generation of the Son of God . . . when this man blatantly mocks all that the ancient doctors have said, I ask in what place and esteem will you hold him? This I say to obviate any reply which you may make that we are not agreed as to what is error. You will admit that what I have told you is not merely error, but such detestable heresy as to abolish the whole Christian religion. I must speak frankly. . . . One is not content simply to put these men to death, but they must be most cruelly burned. And now here is one who will call Jesus Christ an idol, who will destroy all the fundamentals of the faith, who will amass all the phantasies of the ancient heretics, who will even condemn infant baptism, calling it an invention of the devil. And this man is in good repute among you, and is suffered as if he were not wrong. Where I'd like to know is the zeal which you pretend? Where is the police of this fine hierarchy of which you so boast? The man of whom I speak has been condemned by all the churches which you reprove, yet you suffer him and even let him print his books which are so full of blasphemies that I need say no more. He is a Portuguese Spaniard, named Michael Servetus. That is his real name, but he goes at present under the name of Villeneuve and practices medicine. He has resided for some time at Lyons. Now he is at Vienne where his book has been printed by a certain Balthazar Arnoullet, and lest you think that I am talking without warrant I send you the first folio.

The letter had its intended effect. Soon, Matthieu Ory, inquisitor general of heretical pravity for the realm of France, was in Vienne, but his investigation turned up no evidence incriminating Dr. Villeneuve, who indignantly denied his connection with *Christianismi Restitutio* and Michael Servetus. Archbishop Palmier vouched for his friend and physician. Inquisitor Ory then dictated a letter to the informer in Geneva, asking for proofs. Calvin supplied them: seventeen letters from

Servetus which were published in the blasphemous book and the manuscript copy of it. "If you show him the printed book he can deny it, which he cannot do in respect of his handwriting."[32]

Servetus was imprisoned and held for trial, but he tricked his jailor and escaped. The Inquisition condemned him *in absentia*, sentenced him to be burned, and carried out the sentence using a picture of him as an effigy. The five bales of his book which he had consigned to Lyons were burned with the effigy. His printer, in an effort to obliterate traces of his complicity, asked his agent in Frankfurt to destroy the copies there. Calvin had the same objective: when he learned of the existence of a bale of the books in Frankfurt, he urged the ministers there to find and burn them. Scattered through the pages of the book, he warned, were "prodigious blasphemies against God. . . . Imagine to yourselves a rhapsody made up of the impious ravings of every age; for there is no impiety which this wild beast from hell has not appropriated." Only three copies of the *Restitutio* survived.[33]

After hiding in France for four months, Servetus decided to start a new life in Italy, where Protestant unorthodoxy was, at the time, reputedly rampant. Inexplicably he made the fatal mistake of choosing the route through Geneva. On the day after his arrival, he attended church there, heard Calvin preach, was recognized, and at Calvin's instigation was imprisoned.

The trial of Servetus dragged on about two and a half months, interrupted by numerous delays. During that time he was kept in solitary confinement in degrading conditions. The lice, he complained, ate him alive; he had no change of clothing, a bowel disorder sickened him, and the essentials for personal hygiene were denied him. In the early stages of his trial, he was calm, reasoned, and respectful, but as the weeks wore on and his physical condition worsened, he became angry, frenzied, and abusive. He "vomits many insults" upon Calvin, complained the ministers of Geneva — murderer, monster, criminal, and every epithet his crazed, frightened mind could summon. The judges were aghast at his tirades against their Christian leader, who sat there in his starched black robes, frostily watching his victim discredit himself. Twenty-five judges, the city council of Geneva sitting as a criminal tribunal, tried him.[34]

First in the complicated process against Servetus came the preliminary indictment or "articles," framed by Calvin, consisting of thirty-eight charges drawn from the prisoner's writings. Then followed a series of oral interrogations based on his written replies to the charges. His crimes consisted exclusively in his wrong and horrible opinions, technically, "heresy, blasphemy, and disturbance of the peace of

Christendom." His *Restitutio*, Calvin charged, contained "an infinity of blasphemies." Calvin was specific. Servetus had blasphemed against God, against the eternal divinity of Christ, against the Trinity, against the Church of Geneva, against infant baptism, and even against Calvin himself. For one who sought to avenge God's honor, the great theologian seemed unable to distinguish blasphemy from personal defamation, let alone from heresy. Servetus's views of the Trinity offended him most. Professing to believe in the Father, the Son, and the Holy Spirit, Servetus claimed to understand them differently. He knew only one God, the Creator; Jesus, the son of God, was not eternal; the Holy Spirit was only the spirit of God in man's heart, and not a distinct being. Anyone, like Calvin, who destroyed the unity of God by some tripartite division was, Servetus charged, a trinitarian and an atheist. "Trinitarian," a word of reproach that Servetus coined, referred to one who worshipped some metaphysical abstraction rather than God.[35]

The give and take between Servetus and Calvin convinced the judges that there was a basis for a formal trial. The prosecutor, at that point, supplanted Calvin, the accuser. "I hope," Calvin now wrote of Servetus, "that he will at least be sentenced to death, though it is my wish that he be spared needless cruelty." Before the trial proceeded Calvinist Geneva formally requested Catholic Vienne, the site of the Inquisition against Servetus, to supply records of the evidence that had been used to condemn him there. Vienne asked for the prisoner's extradition so that he might suffer the penalty already adjudged. Geneva declined, giving assurance that justice would be done. Servetus petitioned his judges for a dismissal of the charges against him on the ground that doctrine should not be subject to criminal prosecution. He denied that he was seditious or a disturber of the peace. If he must be tried, he declared, he should have legal counsel because he was a foreigner ignorant of Geneva's customs. The prosecutor twisted the points of his petition, alleging that his plea for toleration of doctrine was a confession of guilt. As a most dangerous heretic, not in the least innocent, he did not deserve counsel. In the next series of examinations the prosecutor sought to prove him guilty of heresy, sedition, a life of crime and wantonness, and sympathy for Jews, Turks, and Anabaptists.[36]

The next stage of the case, the compiling of a Latin record of a written debate between Servetus and Calvin on points of religion, was intended for the benefit of other cities of the Swiss confederation. Calvin's "Refutation of Servetus's Errors" purported to show that the prisoner at Geneva meant to "overthrow all religion," surely a grotesque perversion of his unorthodox beliefs. Yet to Calvin, Servetus was a real threat to religion. By deifying humanity, he degraded God; by rejecting infant baptism, he undermined the continuity of the church as an institution; by denying the eternal deity of Christ, he rejected God. Yet Servetus was no Anabaptist. He did not advocate separation of church and state, reject the authority of the magistrates, or oppose oaths. He did not exalt the inner light above the Scriptures. He did not contend against ceremonies. For Protestants to put such a man to death was unprecedented. Geneva needed support. So a copy of the theological records of the trial, a copy of the prisoner's *Restitutio*, and a request for advice went to Bern, Basel, Schaffhausen, and Zurich, and Calvin paved the way with his own letters. Not one of the cities openly advocated death, although some of their ministers did. All agreed, however, that Servetus was guilty, and they expressed their confidence that Geneva would defend the faith. Basel, for example, declared that he had exceeded all the old heretics by spewing their combined errors in one blasphemous mouth. Schaffhausen said, "We do not doubt that you, in your wisdom, will repress his attempts lest his blasphemies like a cancer despoil the members of Christ."[37]

The verdict of Geneva was that Servetus had spread "heresies and horrible, execrable blasphemies against the Holy Trinity, against the Son of God, against the baptism of infants and the foundations of the Christian religion." He had confessed to calling the Trinity a three-headed monster of the devil and believers in the Trinity trinitarians and atheists. He had blasphemed by saying that Christ was not the Son of God. "His execrable blasphemies are scandalous against the majesty of God, the Son of God and the Holy Spirit. This entails the murder and ruin of many souls." He had maliciously persisted in his errors, calumniated true Christians, and obstinately sought to infect the world with his "stinking heretical poison." For these reasons, read the verdict, "we . . . give final sentence and condemn you, Michael Servetus, to be bound and taken to Champel and there attached to a stake and burned with your book to ashes." The court sentenced him on October 27, 1553. He asked to be beheaded, lest the flames persuade him to recant. Calvin endorsed his request, but the court refused. Sentence was executed at noon of the following day. They gave him nothing to deaden the pain. He was chained to a post in a seated position, his neck tied to the post with ropes, and his head crowned with a wreath filled with sulfur. A copy of his book and the manuscript he had sent to Calvin were tied to his body. The executioner used green wood which burned slowly. Servetus screamed continuously, imploring God for mercy, as the lower half of his body broiled while he remained conscious. He passed out and died in about a half hour. His last recognizable words were, "O Jesus, Son of the Eternal God, have pity on me." They took that as final proof of his guilt, for he had not referred to the "Eternal Son of God."[38]

Theodore Beza, Calvin's confederate, grumbled that Servetus's ashes were not yet cold when a dispute arose on the question of whether heretics should be executed. The dispute occurred because one man, and he alone, had the courage to protest in print against the bloodletting in Christendom over points of doctrine, and even he, Sebastian Castellio of Basel, did not dare put his real name to his book. Dissent raised a suspicion of heresy. Those who agreed with Castellio discreetly kept their thoughts to themselves. Sixteenth-century Europe was inhospitable to religious toleration. On both sides of the Reformation, political and religious leaders believed that the safety of the state and the preservation of the faith required the execution of obstinate and blasphemous heretics. They saw nothing un-Christian in punishing capitally for a crime against the majesty of God. Had an epidemic among livestock annihilated as many pigs and sheep as the number of people slaughtered for their religious opinions, governments would have bemoaned the loss. But they would have thought themselves traitors to their faiths if they had not rid the world of its Servetuses. France burned Calvinists and Lutherans indiscriminately; England, under Mary, newly come to power, followed suit. Melanchthon, now the leader of Lutheranism in Germany, exuberantly congratulated Calvin for putting a blasphemer to death.[39]

Nicholas Zurkinden, the chancellor of Berne, regretted the heinous form of Servetus's death yet conceded the necessity of the execution. Still, he protested the widespread use of excessive cruelty. With his own eyes, he told Calvin, he had seen an eighty-year-old Anabaptist woman and her daughter, the mother of six, dragged to their execution "for the single crime of having refused to have the children baptized. . . ." Beza disagreed with Zurkinden's protest. He made allowances for impulsive blasphemies and for blasphemies that derived from ignorance, as in the case of Jews. But deliberate blasphemies were unendurable; they were worse than the worst crimes against the state. The supreme offense was blasphemy combined with heresy, said Beza. "If together with blasphemy and impiety there is also heresy, that is, if a man is possessed of obstinate contempt of the Word of God, of ecclesiastical discipline and by a mad frenzy to infect others," no torture, said Beza, would be great enough to suit the crime. Calvin agreed. He thought that "whole towns and populations" and "the memory of the inhabitants" had to be "destroyed" in such a case to prevent the spread of their contagion. Sounding Catholic, Calvin rigidly opposed allowing "heretics" to murder souls and poison others with false doctrine, yet he denied that he thereby justified the Inquisition; the papists, he reasoned, had no right to persecute, because they taught false doctrine and murdered souls.[40]

One man's heresy was another's blasphemy. In denouncing the doctrine of the Trinity as atheistic, Servetus had passionately cared for the well-being of Christianity, and in that he had been no different from and no less fanatical than his executioners. Although men differed on heresy, no one would champion a blasphemer or the right to blaspheme. Still, Calvin felt the need to defend the execution. He demanded implacable severity to show "devotion to God's honor." When he threatened, "Those who would spare heretics and blasphemers are themselves blasphemers," he meant to silence dissent. The teachings of Servetus, he complained, were spreading; he knew too that the execution had stirred up an undercurrent of criticism. Even among the faithful there were formal requests for information about the crime that merited burning. Accordingly Calvin justified his views on the case and on crimes of religious opinion generally by publishing, in 1554, a book, *Defense of the Orthodox Faith Against the Prodigious Errors of Michael Servetus*. In the Lutheran world Alexander Alesius of Leipzig published *Against the Horrible Blasphemies of Servetus*.[41]

Castellio's book, *Concerning Heretics*, which he published in Latin, French, and German under different pseudonyms, appeared immediately afer Calvin's *Defense*. A professor of Greek at Basel, Castellio wrote epic poems in classical languages and did translations of the Bible. His preface to one edition, in 1551, contained an unprecedented argument against persecution. Calvin pestered the authorities at Basel to punish him as an enemy of religion. In the manuscript of another volume by Castellio, which Calvin managed to suppress, Castellio said there were three professors at Basel "whom the Calvinists openly regard as followers of Servetus," and he named himself as one. His *Concerning Heretics* was the sixteenth century's first book on religious liberty, and although not as analytical or systematic as Jacobus Acontius's *Satan's Stratagems* of 1565, Castellio's book deserves W.K. Jordan's praise as "the most important work favouring religious toleration to be published on the Continent during the century." The modernity of much of his argument is striking, and for that reason much of it seems pedestrian. We take for granted what was then incisive, original, and even shocking. To the Calvinists the argument was both heretical blasphemy and blasphemous heresy.[42]

Castellio wrote to "stanch the blood" so wrongfully shed by those called heretics. After carefully investigating the meaning of "heresy," he concluded "that we regard those as heretics with whom we disagree." Each sect looked upon others as heretics, "so that if you are orthodox in one city or region, you must be held for a heretic in the next." Persecution derived from the diversity of religious opinions, the certainty of each sect that it was right, and the arrogant desire of each to rule the rest. In fact, however, the points of religion over which Christians disagreed and persecuted each other were intrinsically uncertain. The persecutor might be as mistaken as his victim, if the issue that divided them was the Lord's Supper, free will, justification, baptism, the Trinity, predestination, or other mysterious matters on which the Scriptures are unclear. Were these matters obvious, as that there is one God, all would agree. The course of wisdom, then, was to condemn no one — Jew, Turk, or Christian — who believed in God.[43]

Conduct alone, Castellio concluded, was punishable, but never religious belief or worship. (Jefferson reached the same conclusion over two centuries later.) Men could agree, Castellio reasoned, that robbery, murder and treason are crimes; they would never agree on religious matters. That a Christian believed in God, in salvation through Jesus, and in the Bible was "enough." Religion, to Castellio, did not consist of "dubious or ambiguous doctrine," of ceremonies, of "indifferent matters," or of points that transcended human understanding and for which there was no indisputable scriptural authority. On all such matters, like the doctrine of the Trinity, "each may be left to his own opinion and the revelation of the Savior." Thus, no one should be molested for religion, "which above all else should be free, since it resides not in the body but in the heart, which cannot be reached by the sword of kings and princes." Faith could not be compelled, and so coercion was futile. To claim that loyalty to a true faith demanded coercion of those who differed confessed a lack of confidence in that faith. A ruler ought to content himself with the punishment of injury to persons and their property. If anyone disturbed the public peace by an assault under the color of religion, "the magistrate may punish such an act not on the score of religion, but because he has done damage to bodies and goods, like any other criminal." But the punishment of a religiously motivated offense ought to be limited to fines, imprisonment, and banishment — never death. The church should restrict itself to admonition and, in the last resort, excommunication.[44]

One danger in prosecuting heresy was that the victim might not be a heretic. Christ and his disciples, Castellio claimed, died as heretics and seditious blasphemers. "This ought to fill us with fear and trembling when it comes to persecuting a man for his faith and his religion." Another danger in prosecuting heresy was that the punishment exceeded the crime. There was, moreover, a real danger of letting loose a war of extermination among Christians. Some people argued, said Castellio, that to suffer heresy caused sedition and disseminated false doctrine. Persecution, he answered, caused those evils. "Seditions arise from the attempt to force and kill heretics rather than from leaving them alone, because tyranny engenders sedition." He admitted the danger of dissemination of false doctrine, but maintained that the remedy should not be worse than the disease. Here too, persecution spread the evil to be averted. People saw the constancy of heretics in martyrdom and joined their faith. Servetus, for example, had fought with "reasons and writings" and should have been answered the same way. His books could have been sold without disturbance, "but now that the man has been burned, everybody is burning with a desire to read them."[45]

Castellio emphasized that the sword and the stake did not and could not protect sound doctrine. For him sound doctrine was that which made men good, endowed them with love, and gave them a conscience. He judged religion by its fruits, not by the names of sects or by their appeal to authority. "Take a good Papist, one who fears God and does not swear, commit adultery, bear false witness, or do to another what he would not have done to him. I say that such a man should by no means be called impious and killed. He worships idols. Well? He does so in error and not with malice, just as we all worship." Not even Milton or Locke over a century later tolerated "Papists."[46]

Distinguishing heresy and blasphemy, Castellio found that the first was mere error of opinion and should be exempt from the law. "To err is not to blaspheme." Blasphemy, as far as the law is concerned, should be governed by its definition in the Mosaic code. It was consciously reviling God or His Scriptures. Had Servetus said that God is the devil, that would have been "real blasphemy," meriting punishment. But he had merely expressed an opinion about religion. His having said that the Calvinists did not know God and worshipped a false god was a comment against men, not God. He had simply interpreted the Bible differently, as was his Christian right. The greatest blasphemers, Castellio declared, "are those who confess God with their lips and deny him with their lives." But not even Castellio would tolerate "real blasphemy." Nor was he consistent in his Mosaic definition, for he regarded the denial of God or Christ as blasphemous. "I do not classify under the name of heretic the impious, the despisers of sacred Scriptures and blasphemers," Castellio wrote. "These in my judgment are to be treated as impious. If they deny God, if they blaspheme, if they openly revile the sacred teaching of Christianity, if they detest the holy lives of godly men, I leave such offenders to be punished by the magistrate, not on account of religion — they have none — but on account of irreligion."[47]

To Calvin and Beza, Castellio was a real blasphemer and deserved Servetus's fate. They quickly uncovered his authorship of *Concerning Heretics* and tarred him with the vilest eptithets. He replied in a stinging, satirical polemic, *Against Calvin's Book* (1555), in which he answered Calvin's *Defense* point by point. His enemies suppressed his book by seeing that no publisher would print it; it circulated only in manuscript until about 1612, when it was published for the first time in Holland. For a decade the Calvinists hounded Castellio and in 1563 managed, at last, to institute a proceeding against him. His death deprived them of a triumph.[48]

Concerning Heretics initially influenced liberal Protestants, who stood to gain most from a policy of toleration. Among them was a band of refugees from the Italian Inquisition who sought a haven in the Swiss cities. As early as 1542 they had founded an Italian church in Geneva, which Calvin welcomed until he became aware that some of its members were sympathizers of Servetus and friends of Castellio. They included men who helped found the Unitarian movement, which on the continent was called Arianism or Socinianism after Faustus Socinus. Three of these Italian refugees published books on toleration that directly reflected the work of Castellio. Most members of the Italian church in Geneva were, however, orthodox Calvinists. In 1558 they enlisted Calvin's assistance in stamping out the spread of heresy among the Servetians and Socinians. All persons under suspicion had to sign a confession of faith repudiating opposition to the Trinity, predestination, the divinity of Jesus, and the sacraments. Six who resisted finally subscribed, under coercion. Among them was Giovanni Valentio Gentile, a teacher of Latin who was a bold advocate of antitrinitarianism. Calvin himself "converted" him, but he proved to be obdurate in his offenses against religion, and eventually ended up on the executioner's block.[49]

Gentile was first arrested for heresy in Geneva in 1558. The town council, which had condemned Servetus five years earlier, tried Gentile. Brazenly, he defended his religious opinions and criticized Calvin's. Although threatened with death, Gentile persisted for a while in claiming that he had not feigned his subscription to the Calvinist confession of faith. He had simply changed his mind and would not change it again, he claimed, unless Scripture taught him otherwise. At length, however, Gentile recanted on realizing that Servetus's fate awaited him. Once again he confessed to a belief in the orthodox doctrine of the

Trinity. He repudiated all his heresies "and especially those blasphemies, which I have written with my own hand, in which among other errors, I asserted a quaternity, and made Christ the Son of the One God of Israel, so as to rob him of his Eternal Divinity." He promised that he would sooner die than repeat his blasphemies against the Trinity.[50]

Gentile's judges, believing that he had recanted out of fear rather than belief, despite his professions to the contrary, were intransigent. They voted for his execution. The sentence stirred considerable opposition among Italian refugees in Geneva and other Swiss cities. Without endorsing Gentile's views, they begged that the council grant him clemency. The council finally commuted the death penalty and in its place substituted a degrading penance. Gentile had to confess his crimes publicly on bended knees, beg for mercy, subscribe once again to the true faith, throw his writings into a fire, and walk barefooted through the streets in a penitential garment while a trumpet announced his humiliation. He also had to promise that he would never leave Geneva without permission. Two weeks later Gentile escaped from the city.[51]

He became a wanderer, finding no rest for very long wherever he went, for he could not refrain from advocating the beliefs that he had renounced in Geneva. In Lyons, Grenoble, and Bern, among other cities, Gentile was apprehended and briefly jailed, but he talked his way out of trouble. Calvin, on learning that he was proselytizing in Poland, denounced him in a letter of 1561 to the Protestant churches of that country. Its temporary policy of toleration allowed Gentile freedom until a royal edict of 1563 expelled foreign heretics. After more wanderings Gentile returned in 1566 to Switzerland. Because Calvin had recently died, Gentile mistakenly believed he would be safe. He had become either foolish, fanatical, or demented. In a town near Bern he publicly challenged all the Protestant ministers to debate him on religion, the loser to suffer death "for false religion." The authorities held him in prison while awaiting instructions from Bern. In Geneva the news of Gentile's arrest caused Beza, Calvin's successor, to thank God for the delivery of an enemy. But Bern, the most liberal of the Swiss cities, lacked Geneva's fiery zeal. At Gentile's trial in Bern the clergy made a strenuous effort to make him recant. Although he pleaded insanity, "the craziness of his Heart," this time he remained obstinate, defending his religious opinions to the end.[52]

The evidence against him was conclusive. Benedictus Aretius of Bern, a supporter of Beza, published a book against Gentile to justify Bern's course of action to the world. The prisoner had condemned himself in a scurrilous libel against the doctrine of the Trinity, calling it a "mere human invention," for which Bern charged him, tautologically, with having "impiously blasphemed God." Another count in the indictment was that Gentile had "dissented from us and all the Orthodox" by advancing his Arian doctrines. His calling "our church heretical" constituted still another count, and his books containing numerous "impious Blasphemies" were the main proofs. Gentile had denied for example that the father of Christ was an individual named in the Trinity; he had maintained, rather, that "the Father of our Lord Jesus Christ is that one God, is God alone." He flatly rejected the doctrine of the Trinity, saying "The Father is God of himself, not begotten, Maker of all things." To Gentile the Nicene and Athanasian Creeds were "cant" and "sophistry." He regarded Christ as a "different sort of God" who was a "secondary" or "subordinate inferiour God." Thus, he adopted "the Blasphemies of Arius." Aretius's account reads as if Bern thought it was trying that fourth-century enemy of Athanasius.[53]

The trial of 1566 ended in a sentence of death by beheading for attacks on the Trinity: ". . . he acknowledges the Father only to be that infinite God, which we ought to Worship, which is plain Blasphemy against the Son . . . and by relapsing into the Erroneous Opinions he had once Abjur'd . . . hath been guilty of the vilest Scurrility, and most horrid Blasphemies against the Son of God, and the Glorious Mystery of the Trinity." Gentile is supposed to have said, when putting his head on the executioner's block, that many had died for Christ but that he died a martyr for the one God.[54]

In the Low Countries, which Spain controlled and which instituted an Inquisition rivaling Spain's itself for severity, the duke of Alva's armies and the Inquisition murdered about eighteen thousand Protestants between 1567 and 1573. Individual cases seem inconsequential against the numbing total. One case that both Mennonite and Unitarian martyrologists remembered, probably because an account of the inquisitional proceedings against him survived, was that of Hermann Van Flekwyk. He stood accused of having "blasphemed against the true body and blood of God, by speaking against the Mass" and by professing antitrinitarian beliefs. He acknowledged the Trinity in a Servetian sense — "One God, the Son of God, and the Holy Spirit" — but refused a demand that he subscribe to the Athanasian Creed of "God the Father, God the Son, and God the Holy Spirit." His refusal was taken as a denial of the divinity of both Christ and the Holy Spirit, although he protested, "God forbid I should deny the Divinity of Christ! We believe that he is a divine and heavenly person. . . ." Still, he maintained a scriptural literalism in speaking of Christ as the Son of God rather than God and of Mary as mother of Jesus rather than Mother of God. He also seems to have had a Docetic view of the body of Christ, denying his humanity, an extraordinary position for an antitrinitarian. The inquisitor pelted him with epithets—"blasphemer against the Holy Ghost" as well as against God and Christ, "diabolical Antitrinitarian," and "enemy of the Mother of God." Van Flekwyk died at the stake for heresy in 1569, in Bruges.[55]

Of all the blasphemy cases of the sixteenth century that of Francis David was the strangest and least likely: his persecutors were Socinians, the most rational and tolerant of sects, and he was the head of their church. The locale, moreover, was the most liberal in Europe, the eastern region of Hungary known as Transylvania. A decree of 1557, intended to promote religious peace between Catholics and Lutherans, provided that "every one might hold the faith of his choice, together with the new rites or former ones, without offense to any." Reenactments benefited Calvinists and even antitrinitarians or Unitarians, as they came to be known. Transylvania was the only place on the continent where the Socinians would call themselves Unitarians. It was also the only place where Unitarianism became an established religion and the only place ever to have a Unitarian monarch. The man mainly responsible for the Unitarian triumphs in Transylvania was a charismatic minister named Francis David (David Ferencz).[56]

David ran through religions as if apostasy were fashionable. After renouncing the Roman Catholicism of his origins, he became a Lutheran pastor in the city of his birth, Kolozsvar (now Cluj, Rumania), then a seat of the government. David achieved fame as the leader of the orthodox position in a theological debate on the Trinity. His rhetorical powers, commanding personality, and unusual learning quickly brought him to the position of superintendent or head of the Hungarian Lutheran churches. Within a few years Calvinism split the Lutheran churches, and David converted to the new reform movement. By 1560, when he was superintendent of the Calvinist churches in Transylvania, he was questioning the Trinity and the divinity of Jesus. His only consistency was a constant evolution toward radicalism in religion. Dr. Giorgo Biandrata, the lay head of Unitarianism in Hungary, found in David a man receptive to innovation and capable of leadership.

Biandrata was one of the Italians who had refused to sign the Calvinist confession of faith in Geneva in 1558. He was a canny politician and controversialist whose medical skills made him sought after by royalty. From Poland, where he helped spread the doctrines of Faustus Socinus, he went to Hungary as physician to the dowager queen and quickly won the confidence of her son, John Sigismund II, prince of Transylvania. Biandrata used his influence at court to push David's career, at the same time nudging David from Calvinism to Unitarianism. By

1567 David became court preacher and a year later led the reformers in a marathon disputation against the Calvinists; it was, said the historian of Unitarianism, "the greatest debate in the entire history of Unitarianism." Victory was David's. In quick succession, Unitarianism became legal, the prince converted, and the new religion, with its rallying cry, "God is One," spread throughout the land. Unitarianism received formal recognition as one of Transylvania's four "received" religions, and the new superintendent of the numerous Unitarian churches was the former superintendent first of Lutheranism and then of Calvinism, Francis David. Even after Stephen Blathory, a Catholic, became the next prince, Unitarianism remained an established church in Transylvania. Significantly, however, Blathory outlawed further innovations in religion. Although David lost his position as court preacher, he remained influential as the head of Unitarianism and as the preacher of the great church at Kolozsvar.[57]

David, who never reached a theological stasis, embraced innovations. The most controversial was his rejection of the invocation of Christ. David believed that there was no scriptural authority for invoking Christ's name in prayer. Royal admonitions against repudiating the invocation did not silence David. At a general synod of the Unitarian churches of Transylvania in 1578, before an audience of over three hundred ministers, David opposed prayers to Jesus because he was not divine. On this issue, Biandrata and David, who had cooperated so fruitfully for a dozen years, opposed each other. Conscious of the royal decree against innovations and especially against repudiation of the invocation, the doctor worried whether Unitarianism might be discredited by David's heresy. Biandrata prevailed upon his old friend, Faustus Socinus, the foremost divine of the faith in Europe, to visit Kolozsvar. Socinus stayed as a guest in David's home for almost five months, but neither could sway the other. In early 1579 David called another synod. Socinus and Biandrata vainly sought to confute David's new belief that Christians should not worship Christ. When the synod supported David, Biandrata grew alarmed. Still the court physician, he denounced David to Prince Bathory for innovations and blasphemy. The prince commanded the town council of Kolozsvar to suspend David as preacher and hold him under guard. Before the royal order could be executed David defiantly took to his pulpit. He informed the congregation that his arrest was imminent and preached his new views. For a month he was under house arrest, while the government, with Biandrata as accuser and prosecutor, prepared the case against him. Socinus framed a document which became the basis of an indictment, invidiously contrasting David's views with those of orthodoxy.

David had become what his enemies described as a "semi-Judaizer."

The epithet was a curious one since he conceded that Jesus was the Messiah promised by God in the Old Testament, whom the Jews would not receive and killed. But his new views were even more curious. He not only denied the Virgin Birth and the belief that Jesus' teachings came from the mouth of God, views then accepted by Unitarians; he also claimed that the Christ promised by God was to have no kingdom but an earthly one. That led him to the conclusion that until Jesus returned again to this world as the Christ, he could no longer be rendered divine homage, be adored, or be prayed to. Invoking him was as useless as invoking Mary or any of the saints. Christians should keep his precepts but to worship him offended the one God. Jesus would return as the Messiah, David believed, but until his return he was in a "quiescent state." During that state his words and those of his apostles were to be rejected if found contrary to the Old Testament. In Biandrata's opinion, to imply that a Christian could not find salvation through Jesus Christ was blasphemous.[58]

Prince Bathory summoned David under armed guard to be tried before the Hungarian Diet at the capital. Its members included nobles of the four received religions — Catholicism, Lutheranism, Calvinism, and Unitarianism. The trial lasted two days. The prince himself presided. His chancellor opened for the prosecution, but Biandrata conducted the case for the state thereafter. David denied not only the charge of blasphemy, but even the charge that he had violated the decree against innovation. His defense was that to worship anyone but God was unscriptural, but Biandrata derided him for his Jewish interpretations in which he had openly tested the New Testament by the Old. The members of the Diet, with some Unitarian nobles dissenting, voted for a verdict of guilty. Although a Calvinist urged the prince to condemn David to death under the Mosaic law for the crime of false prophecy, Blathory sentenced him to life imprisonment in a dungeon for execrable blasphemies and innovations. He died of illness in prison, probably within a year, an eccentric quester denied the religious liberty he had won for so many. The Biandratas who were responsible for his persecution doubtless acted to save the reputation of their church and defend its faith. In that regard they were little different from their counterparts in Rome or Geneva.

Rome burned the foremost philosopher of the Italian Renaissance, Giordano Bruno, in 1600. Neither a scientist nor a theologian, he sought to reconcile science and religion, but his philosophy subverted basic theological premises. He said of himself that he had "given freedom to the human spirit and made its knowledge free. It was suffocating in the close air of a narrow prison-house, whence, but only through chinks, it gazed at the far-off stars. Its wings were clipped, so that it was unable to cleave the veiling cloud and reach the reality beyond." Bruno could pierce the reality of the stars from the depths of a dungeon. He had a genius for intuition.[59]

Theology repelled him because he hated dogmas. Yet the Dominicans, the "hounds of Christ" who specialized in scenting out heresy, educated him and admitted him to the priesthood in 1572. Bruno was unreliable. As he later confessed to the Inquisition, he began to doubt the Trinity at the age of eighteen. Even as a young monk he multiplied his impieties. He despised religious symbols, especially the images of saints. Worse, he could not conceive of God as three persons, accept the doctrine of incarnation, or believe in transubstantiation. When the Dominicans began a process against him for heresy, he fled his native Naples. He shed his monastic name and religious habit but not his intellectual habit of skeptical inquiry. He claimed a right to "philosophic freedom" and exercised it boldly.

From 1576, when he was about twenty-seven, until 1592, Bruno roamed from city to city in western Europe, studying, teaching, and writing. After earning his doctorate at Toulouse, he wrote book after book. Honors began coming his way. He turned down a chair at the University of Paris because attendance at Mass was obligatory, but "I got me such a name," he reported, that the king of France personally awarded him a special lectureship in philosophy. Subsequently he lectured at London, Oxford, Wittenberg, Prague, Zurich, and Frankfort. In England, where he published seven books in two years, he frequented Elizabeth's court. Rome had denounced the Protestant queen as a heretic and would remember his admiration for her. Bruno never became a Protestant, nor was he a practicing Catholic. He found all denominations mean and narrow, preoccupied with rituals, dogmas, and petty disputes. His business was to get at the truth of the cosmos.[60]

Science had destroyed Ptolemaic conceptions but had not addressed itself to man, his world, and the worlds beyond. Bruno derived from the Copernican revolution a wholesale assault on the prevailing Aristotelianism and the basis for constructing a "New Philosophy," as he called it. Although Copernicus had displaced the earth from the center of the solar system, he never speculated about what extended beyond that system. Kepler did not doubt that the universe was fixed and finite. Galileo, another of Bruno's younger contemporaries, declared that he could not conceive of infinity and that no one had proved the universe to be finite or infinite. Galileo was right. No one had proved infinity, but Bruno did not concern himself with empirical proofs. He did not map the stars or calculate orbits. He was a metaphysicist, not a physicist. He knew Copernicus's work; intuition and imagination led him the rest of the way.[61]

Bruno's massive assault on Aristotelianism brought him into direct conflict with the church, which had made man the center of the world. The church was concerned with how to go to heaven, not with how the heavens go. One heaven and one hell was all that it could conceive. To think otherwise violated Scripture. Bruno, however, swept man and salvation from center stage. "Man is no more than an ant in the presence of the infinite," he said. "And a star is no more than a man." Each star was a sun with its own worlds, and there was an endless number of stars stretching forever in infinite space. Although Bruno undermined some conventional premises of religion, he was a God-intoxicated man. The infinite universe was the result of an infinite divine power, whose work was manifest in a grain of sand, in all life, in human reason, and in the limitless number of worlds. God caused all and was in all, and He alone was Absolute, Infinite, the One, the soul of the world, the spirit of the Universe. On and on Bruno went, rhapsodizing the supreme being who brought unity to the seeming chaos of human existence and Nature. To the church, of course, a form of pantheism would seem like a new dress for an old heresy.[62]

Bruno fell into the hands of the Inquisition when he dared to return to Italy in 1592. A Venetian patrician, whom he served as tutor, denounced him for uttering numerous blasphemies against the Trinity and the majesty of God. One of the alleged blasphemies was that Bruno had accused the Catholic church of many blasphemies. Bruno at first defended himself vigorously. He denied all charges of blasphemy and heretical errors. He claimed philosophic freedom to argue "according to the principles of Nature and by its light, not chiefly considering what must be held according to Faith." He conceded that his philosophy might be indirectly opposed to truth according to the faith, but he had never meant to impugn that faith. On being asked whether he believed in the Trinity, he construed it in terms of metaphysical abstractions — creative power, intellect, and love. When asked whether he believed that the Father, Son, and Holy Spirit were one in essence but distinct persons, he admitted, "I have never been able to grasp the three being really Persons and have doubted it." His inquisitors at Venice managed to make him fall to his knees and beg for mercy. "I hate and detest all the errors I have at any time committed as regards the Catholic Faith and decrees of Holy Church," he declared, "and I repent having doubted anything Catholic." The entreaty failed, and he stayed in prison.[63]

The chief inquisitor at the Holy Office in Rome demanded that

Bruno be delivered there for trial. He was no ordinary heretic; he was an apostate monk who praised Protestant princes, and he was a "heresiarch" — an originator and leader of heresy. Venice reluctantly extradited him to Rome. Eight months after his capture in Venice, Bruno was in the dungeon of the Roman Inquisition, where he stayed for seven years. We know nothing about his treatment or his interrogations for most of that time. Early in 1599 several cardinals examined him on eight heresies they had extracted from his books. No records remain that describe those heresies. The presence of Cardinal Robert Bellarmine, S.J., who had denounced the Copernican theory as heresy and persecuted Galileo, suggests that Bruno's philosophy was at issue. Near the end of the year, at a final interrogation, Bruno declared that he would recant nothing. In January of 1600 a meeting presided over by the pope decreed that Bruno be turned over to the secular arm to be burned at the stake. The sentence referred generally to his "many various heretical and unsound opinions." On February 17, 1600, the sentence was executed. Bruno's last utterance is supposed to have been "I go to carry the Divine in us to the Divine in the Universe." A Catholic witness who described the burning concluded, "he is gone, I suppose, to recount to those other worlds imagined by himself the way in which the Romans treated blasphemous and impious men."[64]

During the seventeenth century blasphemy increasingly became a secular crime on the continent. It remained, as always, a religious offense, but the state began to supplant the church as the agency mainly responsible for instigating and conducting prosecutions. The association of religious crimes with political ones such as sedition and treason had its roots in Exodus 22:28, which declares, "You shall not revile God, nor curse a ruler of your people." The intimacy between *laesa religio* and *laesa maiestas*, crimes against religion and crimes against the state, was a feature of Athenian law and then of Roman law both before and after Christianity became the state religion of Rome. The Reformation, especially in Protestant countries, reinforced the belief of sovereigns that they were "the images of God, representing in the governance of their several States that authority which is exercised by God in the governance of the Universe." In the seventeenth century the belief that a nation's religious unity augmented its peace and strength accounted, at least in part, for the rising dominance of the state in policing serious crimes against religion. The connection of religious dissent with political subversion was old, but governments intervened more frequently to suppress nonconforming intellectuals and sectarians. Political considerations began to supersede religious ones in justifying persecution, first in Protestant countries and then in Catholic countries, where the sovereign was not the head of the church and the Inquisition still prevailed. Even when bigotry motivated a prosecution for blasphemy, rather than concern for security, unity, or peace, the state led the church. In earlier times the state had usually followed the church or cooperated with it. The cases of Tyszkiewicz and Vanini are examples of fanatic zeal by secular authorities.[65]

In Poland, the scene of Socinus's major mission, Iwan Tyszkiewicz became an ardent Socinian. His abandonment of Catholicism, his prosperity, and his spirited advocacy of his new faith in an area dominated by Catholics made him a marked man. His refusal to swear an oath by the Trinity or on a crucifix led to his conviction by a local court. On an appeal that went all the way to the royal court in Warsaw, in 1611, the public prosecutor pressed the charge of blasphemy. The Catholic sovereign influenced the judges to return a verdict of death. The executioner cut out Tyszkiewicz's tongue, because of his blasphemy, before burning him for blasphemous heresy.[66]

The case of Julius Caesar Vanini in 1619 carried echoes of the Bruno affair. Vanini, who earned his doctorate at the University of Naples, was a wandering monk like Bruno. For several years he too visited the capitals and university towns of Europe, supporting himself as a teacher. He too wrote books on philosophy, touching religion, science, literature, and all the subjects of interest to a learned, skeptically minded humanist. But Vanini, for all his independence of spirit, was a minor figure in his time and would be forgotten but for his martyrdom. He settled in Toulouse, an arch-Catholic citadel, yet the Inquisition showed no interest in him, not even after the Sorbonne revoked the imprimatur for one of his books. A royal official who was secretary of the city parliament instituted before that body a blasphemy proceeding against Vanini. He is supposed to have written mockingly about religion and made the mistake of calling Nature "Queen of the Universe," thereby derogating from God's sovereignty. The charges against him made no mention of heresy, although the entire trial consisted of an examination of his religious beliefs. He insisted that he believed in the Trinity, as defined by the church, as well as in God, whom he described as the creator of Nature. He was convicted on the testimony of a witness who swore that Vanini had privately confided his disbelief in God and really credited natural laws for the governance of the physical world. The Toulouse Parliament found him guilty of "atheism, blasphemies, impieties and other crimes," unstated, and ordered that he be taken to his place of execution wearing a placard with the words "Atheist and Blasphemer of the Name of God." After his tongue was pulled out with pincers and severed, he was garrotted and his body burned at the stake.[67]

Although Bruno had been charged with blasphemy and sentenced for heresy, Protestant precedents were not without some influence. When the Catholic states of Poland and France prosecuted Tyszkiewicz and Vanini, the sentences were for the crime of blasphemy, contrary to conventional Catholic precedents. The church condemned for heresy, the state increasingly for blasphemy. Blasphemy prosecutions continued in continental Europe into the present century, although the death penalty for the crime died out during the eighteenth century.[68]

PART THREE

ENGLAND TO 1700

6

THE FIRES OF SMITHFIELD

Until the later fourteenth century England was so isolated from the heresies of the continent that punishments for religious offenses were unusual. Catholic orthodoxy peacefully reigned over the English church, which escaped the Waldensians and the Cathars, the Albigensian Crusade, and the Holy Inquisition. The instances of heresy that cropped out in England were isolated and rare; always excepting the Jews, religious persecution did not exist because there was no need for it. When that need arose, the response of the ecclesiastical courts was decisive. In 1166, for example, about thirty people from Flanders, probably Cathar heretics fleeing from persecution, sought refuge in England. Their proselytizing brought them to the attention of the authorities at a time when Henry II, having broken with Thomas à Becket, was eager to prove his orthodoxy. With the king himself presiding, a council of bishops convened at Oxford and condemned the heretics whose religion seemed un-Christian enough to be blasphemous. The heretics rejected baptism, matrimony, and the Eucharist, disparaging the church. Innocent III and Frederick II had not yet made pertinacious heresy a capital crime even on the continent, although cases of burning alive were known in 1166. In England, however, no legal basis for the death penalty existed for any offense against religion — not till 1401. The Oxford ecclesiastical court of 1166 met the heretical challenge by ordering that the heretics be branded, flogged, stripped to the waist, and sent out into the winter fields to die, "and they perished miserably." By royal command, "if any one shall have received them, he will be at the mercy of the lord king, and the house in which they have been shall be . . . burned."[1] This, said the historian of the Inquisition, was "the first secular law on the subject . . . since the fall of Rome."[2]

Ecclesiastical courts with their canon law had taken root in England in the aftermath of the Norman Conquest, and they eventually achieved control over offenses against religion. They reached into the daily lives of the English people, regulating their beliefs as well as their conduct.

161

Ecclesiastical jurisdiction glutted itself with all sorts of cases. One category covered the various sins of the flesh; "immoralities" of a wholly different kind, as disparate as breach of contract, disorderly conduct, usury, and defamation, constituted another category. Still another was "spiritual" affairs, reaching cases on matrimony, wills, clerics, and church properties. Offenses against religion encompassed a variety of sins, from desecration of the sabbath and failure to attend church to profanity, sacrilege, and witchcraft. The gravest offenses against religion, touching the security of the church and the salvation of souls, were errors of religious opinion. As on the continent, heresy was the generic name for such errors. It included within its spaciousness everything from a trival difference on some point of faith to speaking evil of God. Defamation of God's church, its sacraments, its sacerdotal hierarchy, its discipline, or any of its doctrines or saints was a form of heresy — blasphemous heresy, but heresy nevertheless. Distinguishing one kind of heresy from another did not matter. Any heresy, blasphemous or not, was high treason against God. Its punishment was intended to keep believers in uniformity and the church in power, rich and influential.[3]

The orthodoxy of England during the thirteenth century was unsullied except for tantalizing glimpses of heresy. In 1210 there is a reference to a solitary Albigensian's being burned in London; nothing more is known about the case, which would be unprecedented in English history if true. A dozen years later occurred the strange case of the deacon who, having converted to Judaism for the love of a Jewess, was condemned for apostasy by an ecclesiastical court presided over by Stephen Langton, the archbishop of Canterbury. In consonance with a canon-law pretense of the church that it never stained itself with blood, the prelates turned its victim over to the sheriff for execution by burning. The same court in the same year, 1222, also decided a peculiar blasphemy case. A couple who represented themselves as Jesus and Mary, thereby assuming divine attributes, were condemned to solitary imprisonment for life, on a diet of only bread and water. Before the middle of the century, a Jew who converted to Christianity relapsed; although the outcome of his trial is not known, anyone baptized as a Catholic was liable to the church for his religious errors. Another Cathar heretic refused to attend church, declared that the devil was loose, and said blasphemous things about the pope. There is a reference, finally, to the Dominican fathers of Yorkshire hunting for heretics but thwarted by a sheriff who thought the power of arrest belonged to him. At the close of the century, the author of *The Mirror of Justices,* a lawbook of questionable repute, described heresy as the crime of high treason against God and its punishment as excommunication and cremation; but the author was theorizing about what should be done in the event that heretics turned up in England.[4]

Ireland's first experience with heretics occurred in 1325, when Richard Lederede, the bishop of Ossory, armed with a decretal of Boniface VIII as his authority, introduced the Inquisition. The bishop discovered an arcane form of heresy, the blasphemous belief that demons have power attributable only to God. The criminals, who were reputed to be sorcerers or practitioners of witchcraft, confessed under torture, and the bishop had the satisfaction of burning some as heretics. The confusion in styling their crimes — heresy, blasphemy, sorcery — was enormous. So great was the secular opposition to the bishop, because of his methods and the fact that some of his victims were kinsmen of powerful chiefs, that he himself had to flee into exile to escape a countercharge of heresy. A more conventional case was that of Adam Duff O'Toole, who in 1327 was burned alive in Dublin as a heretic and blasphemer. He is supposed to have denied that the person of Jesus embodied the divine spirit, and he rejected the doctrine of the Trinity. He also made improper remarks about the mother of Jesus and called the stories in the Bible fables. O'Toole was possibly the first antitrinitarian in what is now Great Britain to die for blasphemous heresy.[5]

Heresy as an organized movement did not exist in England until the late fourteenth century, the time of John Wycliffe and his followers, the Lollards, a name of contempt signifying mumblers at prayers. Wycliffe was the preeminent English heretic before the Reformation. Although he meant to purify, not divide, the church, his teachings led to a sect that plagued it ever after. Wycliffe attacked the authority of the pope and the priesthood, repudiated auricular confession, and denied the doctrine of transubstantiation, according to which, by the teachings of the church, the bread and wine used in the holy communion literally became the body and blood of Christ. Wycliffe also advocated the translation of the Bible into English on the theory that men, without the intervention of the clergy, should read and understand the holy book for themselves. Although he did not advocate freedom of conscience, he believed that the church should not have prisons to punish transgressors. In many respects he anticipated fundamental Protestant convictions. His heresy was clear; the pope himself, Gregory XI, condemned him for "heretical pravity, tending to weaken and overthrow the status of the whole church, and even the secular government." Acting on the papal bull, William Courtney, archbishop of Canterbury, presided over an ecclesiastical convocation that enumerated all the damnable opinions of Wycliffe and his adherents. One of the beliefs ascribed to him without supporting proof and of which he was doubtlessly innocent was plainly blasphemous: "That God ought to obey the devil." That he blasphemed Christ's vicar on earth was clear to the church, for he implied that the pope could be "a reprobate and evil man, and consequently a member of the devil," without power over the faithful of Christ. The prelates, faced with such heresies, called upon the secular authorities to assist in their extirpation; those heresies were infecting many Christians, causing them to depart from the faith "without which there is no salvation." An earthquake, which occurred at that very time, proved to the heretics that divine judgment sided with them. Wycliffe, although hounded, had the support of a powerful duke, and so died peacefully in 1384. Forty years later his remains were dug up on orders of the church, his memory reviled, and his bones given to the flames.[6]

Wycliffe's followers paid the penalty of his heresies. England was a devout Catholic nation in an age that was convinced of the duty of the state to support the church's infallible judgments on spiritual matters. As a partner of the church, the state too was responsible for protecting the souls of its subjects against heresy. Its existence threatened eternal damnation for all who were victims of its contagion; as Archbishop Courtney declared, heresy could "destroy the tranquility of the realm," as well as subvert the church.[7] There was one fixed body of revealed and absolute truth. To permit deviations reflected doubt on the purity of the faith and the sincerity of the convictions of true believers. The sovereign must, therefore, obey the command of the church on matters of faith or be excommunicated as a heretic and have his people absolved from their allegiance to him. The trouble, however, was that the hazy precedents on heresy in England showed no lawful authority for the prelates or the prince, acting separately or together, to order anyone burned for a religious crime.

Courtney and his bishops audaciously rose to the occasion; they forged a statute of Parliament providing that on certification by the prelates, sheriffs should arrest and imprison heretics, holding them for "the law of the holy church." Later in 1383, the House of Commons asked the king to annul the law "never assented to nor granted by the Commons." By 1386, however, the spread of Lollardy at last provoked Parliament to outlaw heretical writings and make their teaching a crime, punishable by forfeiture of properties and imprisonment. The prelates, not satisfied, sought fuller cooperation from the state and, on the advice of Pope Urban VI, vainly asked for the death penalty. Meanwhile, Lollard leaders, especially at Oxford, the seat of Wycliffe's influence, suffered from the archbishop's inquisitions. Much later John Foxe, the indefatigable Elizabethan martyrologist, complained that although the church quickly condemned for heresy, "In times past [before the Lollards] it was not accounted as a heresy, except it did contain blasphemy, and did bring in some great peril to the faith, or where the majesty of Christ was hurt: such as were the Donatists, Manichees, Appollinarists, and Arians." But those heresies of the early church were no more blasphemous than the Lollards'.[8]

William Swinderby, the foremost Lollard priest in Lincoln, faced an accusation in 1391 of having preached "many heretical, erroneous, blasphemous, and other slanderous things contrary and repugnant to the . . . holy catholic church." Unfortunately the charges against him did not distinguish which "things" were heretical and which blasphemous. Swinderby denied transubstantiation, claiming that Christ was only figuratively, not really, present in the sacrament of the altar. He described as the "very Antichrist" any doctrine, even if taught by a pope or a cardinal, that was against Christ's scriptural laws. He denied too that the pope had power to remit any man's sins, for only God could do that, and he claimed that the pope's assumption of such power "makes himself Christ, and blasphemeth in God as Lucifer did. . . ." When sentenced for heresy — the sentence always referred to the generic crime, "heretical pravity" — Swinderby appealed to king and council. The king's courts, he claimed, were above those of the bishop; an ecclesiastical court could put no man in jail but with a writ from the secular authority. Heresy, Swinderby conceded, was punishable by death, but not without justice from the king's courts. Christ's law, he reminded, bid us to love our enemies, while "the pope's law gives us leave to hate them and to slay them." Denying that he was a heretic, Swinderby complained, in a remarkable confusion of concepts, that the sentence of excommunication against him, by damning him to hell, was "a foul heresy of blasphemy." So too, John Purvey, a close associate of Wycliffe and the probable author of the Lollard Bible, accused Innocent III, "the head of Antichrist," of having "invented a new article of our faith," transubstantiation, which Purvey ridiculed and damned as "blasphemy" as well as heresy. Purvey recanted and was imprisoned. Swinderby, edified by the spectacle of dry wood being gathered for his burning, also recanted for "dred of death." Soon afterward he relapsed into heresy, but when cited to appear for an inquisition he escaped to Wales.[9] The authority for his death sentence was so baseless as a matter of law that both church and state determined to resolve once and for all that the power to punish capitally for heresy was beyond dispute.

The case of William Sawtre, a parish priest, provided the occasion for legislation. Sawtre, having recanted his Lollard heresies and sworn to be faithful to the church, began preaching the very criminal doctrines he had renounced. Thomas Arundel, the archbishop of Canterbury, meant to make an example of Sawtre, who not only had flaunted his religious convictions, but also had mocked his inquisitors at his trial in 1401. Arundel condemned Sawtre as a relapsed heretic and committed him to the secular power for burning. The archbishop was aided in his policy by the accession to the throne of Henry IV, whose orthodoxy was beyond question. Henry made a tacit agreement with the prelates to persecute the Lollards in return for the church's support of his dubious claim to the throne. During Sawtre's trial, Parliament had been considering a bill, long urged by Arundel and his predecessor, that would make heresy a capital offense. Papal decrees and precedents notwithstanding, there was still no law in England that authorized the execution of heretics. Before Parliament could enact its bill, Henry IV hurriedly issued a writ that ingratiated him with the church. Proclaiming himself "a cherisher of the Catholic faith, willing to maintain and defend Holy Church . . . and to extirpate radically such heresies and errors from our kingdom of England," the king commanded that Sawtre "be burnt in the flames, according to law divine and human, and the canonical institutes customary in that behalf. . . ." The writ was dated February 26, 1401; Sawtre was roasted alive on March 2, before Parliament passed its act. The king and the archbishop hurried to burn their victim to show that they could send a heretic to the stake whenever they wished, without relying on statute; Parliament could neither give nor take the authority to burn a heretic. If the scepter supported the miter, canon law prevailed.[10]

Parliament, far from objecting, assisted the church by belatedly passing the statute, *De Haeretico Comburendo* (on the burning of heretics) which neglected to define heresy because it was a canonical offense. Consequently the ecclesiastical courts had a blank check to condemn as heresy anything they pleased. In addition Parliament did not require the ecclesiastical courts to seek a royal writ for the execution of their judgment as was the practice for other capital crimes; church authorities could arrest, imprison, try, and condemn as they pleased for the crime of heresy and oblige the sheriff to execute the victim without further delay or formality. Burning was the mandatory sentence for an obstinate or relapsed heretic, "to the intent that this kind of punishment may strike a terror on the minds of others. . . ." An act of 1414 reinforced that of 1401 and extended the punishment to "lollardies."[11]

The church's victory in 1401 extended the Inquisition into England, although neither on the scale nor of the severity as the continent. From

1401 to 1534, when Henry VIII ended Rome's spiritual supremacy in England, about fifty persons were burned as obstinate heretics. For every one who was burned, many recanted and suffered lesser penalties which ranged from long sentences of imprisonment to a peculiar form of penance — carrying fagots, or firewood, to symbolize their deaths by burning. For every one who was punished there were undoubtedly thousands who were put to an inquisition for their religious beliefs. The ecclesiastical courts functioned as accuser, prosecutor, judge, and jury; they met in secrecy and compelled self-incrimination. Between 1518 and 1521 in just the diocese of Lincoln, those courts convicted 342 people; for the crime of "not thinking catholickly," five relapsed heretics were burned, forty-six were sentenced to life imprisonment, and the remainder were burdened with lesser forms of penance.

The extant records show that the crime of blasphemy almost disappeared without trace, swallowed by the crime of heresy which it had spawned in the days of the apostolic church. That many of the heretics must have been accused of blasphemy is highly probable. In 1418, for example, a papal bull against the "sectaries and followers" of those "arch-heretics," John Wycliffe of England, John Huss of Bohemia, and Jerome of Prague, declared that they "cease not to blaspheme the Lord God," yet the bull focused on the need to extirpate their "heretical pravity." Huss's case shows no charge of blasphemy, although in Jerome's there is an accusation that he taught heretical doctrines, "some being very blasphemous." Yet Jerome was burned for heresy, the generic crime that encompassed the more specific one of blasphemy. The two crimes were confusingly treated as the same offense and, indeed, overlapped. Transcripts of the trials hardly mention blasphemy; heresy simply superseded and engulfed it. Early in the reign of Henry VI, a woman named Joan was accused of being "a diabolical blasphemeresse of God," but here blasphemy took the form of sorcery.[12]

Soon after, about 1432, Bishop William Lyndewood, the foremost expert on the canon law of England, finished his great compilation. He warned of the penalties for anyone who observed any sacrament "otherwise than it is found discussed by the Holy Mother the Church," or doubted anything decided by the church, or spoke "blasphemous words about the same," or engaged in any heresy. Lyndewood defined none of the crimes, nor did he distinguish them. Yet their seriousness is evident from his saying that "though there be a certain likeness and equalness in divers laws between the crime of heresy and treason, nevertheless the offense is unlike, and it requireth greater punishment to offend the majesty of God than of man."[13]

The English reformation of religion began with the heresies of

Wycliffe and the Lollards. The Henrician Reformation was chiefly political; the king substituted himself for the pope as the head of the church in England but was otherwise as orthodox as the pope. On matters of heresy Henry VIII differed from other Catholic rulers of his time, if at all, only in his greater severity and intolerance. He meant to make himself undisputed sovereign of the English church as well as the state, and to that end encouraged measures that turned the people against the pope's supporters. He also welcomed to England antipapists from the continent if they were industrious subjects and supported the crown. They began to stream in, especially from Holland. Dutch Protestants saw England as a refuge from Spain, which ruled the Low Countries, and from the Spanish Inquisition. In England under Henry anyone who kept his mouth shut and attended the English church was tolerated, but not Protestants who wished to worship in their own way and certainly not the proselytizing, anti-Catholic foreigners whose bizarre notions about religion set them apart from most Christians. The unwanted were promiscuously denounced as Arians or Anabaptists whose beliefs were said to blaspheme Christianity, but they were not an organized sect, nor deemed as dangerous as the Lollards seemed to have been in the early fifteenth century. On the other hand, Lollardy, although persecuted, still seethed among the lower classes and would become the seedbed of Puritanism; but fragmented and undisciplined, it was hospitable to novelties like the alleged power of personal revelation over scriptural literalism, or the aspersions cast on the doctrine of the Trinity, or the claims that the bread and wine of the holy sacrament were no more than a remembrance of Christ's sacrifice, and that infant baptism was a practice of the antichrist. These blasphemies and others were received with abhorrence by Henry's church, their carriers designated as heretics.[14]

As early as 1528, under Henry, the "Defender of the Faith," the church imprisoned seven Dutch "Anabaptists," a term of reproach which at that date could signify any antipapal Christian who differed from Luther. Two of the seven were burned. There is no knowing whether they were antitrinitarians who denied the divinity of Christ or his coessentiality with the Father, or were "Donatists new-dipped" who rejected certain sacraments like infant baptism. The government issued edicts against "Anabaptists and Sacramentaries, being lately come into this realm," and warned against their heresies. But they kept coming, Rhinelanders and Dutchmen, who were said to dispute in taverns yet lurked in secret places, stirring the king's subjects to their opinions about baptism and the holy sacrament of the altar.[15] According to a sixteenth-century chronicler:

The five and twentieth day of May, was in S. Paules church at London examined nineteen men and sixe women borne in Holland, whose opinions were: first, that in Christ is not two natures, God and man: secondly, that Christ tooke neither flesh nor blood of the Virgine Marie: thirdly, that children borne of infidels shall be saved: fourthly, that baptisme of children is to none effect: fiftly, that the sacrament of Christs bodie is but bread onely; sixtly, that he who after his baptisme sinneth wittingly, sinneth deadly, and cannot be saved. Fourteene of them were condemned, a man and a woman of them were burned in Smithfield, the other twelve were sent to other townes there to be brent.[16]

Two more were burned in 1538, while others who repented in time bore fagots for their penance. At least half of the people burned as obstinate heretics under Henry VIII were "Anabaptists," reputed throughout Christendom to be the most despicable blasphemers. Their doctrines and reputations aside, the crime for which they died was heresy, or perhaps blasphemous heresy. The name of the crime scarcely mattered. They died for their religion.[17]

The government made distinctions of a different sort. The king, having become supreme head of the English church, took any deviation from his new religious order as a threat to royal supremacy. Whether loyalty to the former "bishop of Rome" or conscientious belief in any of the deviant new Protestant doctrines, the expression of dissent blended heresy and treason into almost indistinguishable crimes. The government branded Protestant heterodoxy as seditious and traitorous, but only those who continued to support the authority of the pope went to the executioner's block or the hangman to be punished for a secular offense. Those who preached blasphemous or heretical novelties went to a fiery death to avenge God's honor. The form of execution differed with the belief. The crime was essentially the same — disagreeing religiously with the king — but one offense was called treason, the other heresy.

Thomas Bilney, a London priest who prematurely became a Protestant — before Henry VIII did — was arrested on suspicion that he was a Lutheran. He "blasphemed most perniciously the immaculate flock of Christ, with certain blasphemies," "blasphemed the efficacy of the whole church," and affirmed "blasphemously, that the bishop of Rome is the very Antichrist. . . ." Bilney repeated good Lutheran belief when he declared that papal "miracles" came from Satan rather than God, but his remark was taken as another blasphemy. He abjured and did penance, but two years later, in 1531, he openly preached all that he had renounced and so died as a relapsed heretic.[18] In that year, James Bainham, a lay scholar and lawyer, was prosecuted by the lord chancellor, Sir Thomas More, for the same offense as Bilney. Bainham too identified the pope as the "Antichrist." He also rejected transubstantiation as "idolatry to the bread," mocking the possibility that Christ "should dwell in a piece of bread," when he was sitting in heaven on the right side of God. Bainham too was burned as a heretic, yet not a word in the accusation against him or in the record of his inquisition mentions blasphemy. According to Foxe, More had Bainham whipped, then racked in the Tower of London, and kept in the stocks in irons for a fortnight, yet More does not seem to have multiplied the heinousness of Bainham's offense by calling it blasphemous. Although More verbally scourged Protestants in his writings, he thought "heresy" was sufficient as the word with which to condemn them. "Treason" was the word that Thomas Cromwell, More's prosecutor, later used to condemn him, although Cromwell conceded that the difference in the crime was the difference between beheading and burning.[19]

Elizabeth Barton, known as the nun of Kent, together with twenty-four coconspirators, also died for treason, in 1534, although the government also denounced her for blasphemy. Under the pretense of a direct communion with God, she had trances during which she revealed prophecies, carefully schooled by a papal faction, inimical to the crown. If Henry VIII divorced Catherine of Aragon, the nun predicted, he would die the death of a villain. When the conspirators confessed their fraud, the nun's feigning a divine commission struck some of her judges as a blasphemous imposture, but the offense against the king's majesty took precedence over that against God's.[20] There was, however, no shortage of obstinate heretics. Fifty-one were burned between 1534, when Henry VIII began his reformation, and his death in 1547 — as many as were burned in the whole period from 1401, the date of the statute *De Haeretico Comburendo,* to 1534. In that latter year Parliament abrogated the act of 1401 and other laws connected with the bishop of Rome, but the king as a matter of royal prerogative authorized his sheriffs to issue the old writ for burning.[21]

The death of Henry VIII in 1547 passed the crown to his young son, Edward VI, and to the Protestant cause, although Thomas Cranmer, who had been an obedient archbishop of Canterbury since 1533, continued in office. In an age of unspeakable cruelty, the short period of Edward's sovereignty, 1547 to 1553, was notable for its comparative mildness. Religious persecution, which was taken for granted and even counted a duty on the part of believers of whatever persuasion, hardly existed by any comparison with the immediately preceding and succeeding reigns. Foxe, the anti-Catholic martyrologist, lightly skipped over the Edwardian burnings. "Briefly," he wrote, "during all this time, neither in Smithfield nor any other quarter of this realm, were any heard to suffer for any matter of religion, either papist or protestant, either for one opinion or another, except only two, one an English-woman, called Joan of Kent, and the other a Dutchman, named George, who died for certain articles not much necessary here to be rehearsed."[22] During the Marian burnings of the next reign, the Catholics delighted in citing those two cases as precedents that justified their roaring fires. A modern Catholic historian searching for evidence of real persecution under Edward discovered only the heresy provisions of a proposed canon-law revision that was never enacted, two burnings that he admitted would have occurred under Henry or Mary, and the plunder of Catholic properties.[23] He might have added that ecclesiastical inquisitions into religious belief slowed but did not abate.

One inquisition under Edward VI uncovered the remarkable heresy of John Assheton, a cleric. His views were even more repugnant than those of the execrated Arians, who accepted the eternal divinity of Christ, although assigning him an inferior station beneath God. The later Socinians, whose blasphemies were notorious, agreed that Christ was less than God but saw him as a human being whom God made divine. Assheton's antitrinitarianism was still more radical; he anticipated Unitarianism. Recognizing only one God and no divine persons, neither Christ nor the Holy Spirit, Assheton thought of Christ as a holy prophet, beloved of God, but only a man. Assheton was probably the first Englishman to be charged with such opinions. They were surely blasphemous, more so than Servetus's, but Assheton's timely recantation, saving him from the fire, referred only to "detestable errors, heresies, and abominable opinions." That clearly showed the demise of "blasphemy" as the legal designation of the crime, or, rather, that heresy had become its name.[24]

Joan Bocher, whom Foxe called Joan of Kent in his history of martyrs, was a "lady of quality" who was received at Edward's court. Archbishop Cranmer protected her for a while, but her opinion on the incarnation became too fantastic for him to tolerate. She denied the humanity of Christ by claiming that because his mother's own flesh "was sinfully begotten" he did not get his body from her but passed through her as light through a glass. Cranmer and his ecclesiastical commission condemned her as an obstinate heretic, but kept her in Newgate prison for a year, mercifully hoping she would recant. She could not be pursuaded to abandon her "Anabaptisicall opinion." Before her execution at Smithfield in 1550 she told the bishops that not long ago they had burned Anne Askew, her friend, "for a piece of bread," that is, for denying transubstantiation, "and yet you came yourselves soon after to believe and profess the same doctrine for which you burned her. And now forsooth you will needs burn me for a piece of flesh. . . ." When Cranmer finally sought a writ for her execution, he argued from the Mosaic law that blasphemers must be stoned to death and that this woman was guilty of capital impiety.[25]

Denying that a divine Christ could have been human was unusual; denying his divinity was not. That had been Assheton's heresy in 1548, and others shared it. Immigrants were thought to be responsible for its introduction into England. London in Edward's reign had about three thousand Protestant refugees, mostly from the Low Countries. The majority were Lutherans and Calvinists, but an alarming number were reputedly Arians — the word then common for any sort of antitrinitarians. In 1549 the discovery of an Arian manuscript led to the publication of the first book in English defending the faith from attacks on Christ's divinity; it was the beginning of a literary genre of works against antitrinitarianism. The author believed that Arianism was "rife," so many were the people who impiously held that Christ "is not true god, but a mere creature, a passable man only."[26] George van Parris, a Dutch physician who belonged to London's Church of Strangers (foreigners), held that view; his reverent beliefs notwithstanding, he scandalized his own congregation. The government ordered an inquisition; Archbishop Cranmer himself was in charge. Van Parris, who knew little English, defended himself through an interpreter, one of the bishops who accused him. Relying on his reading of the New Testament, Van Parris held that Christ was not divine and that calling the Father the only God could not be heresy. When informed that it was heresy, he stubbornly refused to retract. The king's journal includes the laconic entry, "In 1551, April 7. A certain Arian of the strangers, a Dutch Man, being excommunicated by the congregation of his country men, was, after long disputation, condemned to the fire." Van Parris's inquisitors, calling him "a child of the Devil," felt obliged to burn a foreign Arian as an example to others. Their victim's constancy to his faith and his devoutness to God awed those who had come to Smithfield to jeer.[27] No reference to blasphemy appears in the superficial accounts of the case. When Calvin burned Servetus for blasphemy two years later, he showed Protestants how to describe heresy in the most horrific way.

Mary's accession to the throne in 1553 ushered in a Catholic restoration and a persecution unique for its ferocity and extent, at least in England. A distinguished Catholic historian, Philip Hughes, declared:

The facts are, that in the last four years of Mary's reign, between February 4, 1555 and November 10, 1558, something like 273 of her subjects were executed by burning, under laws which her government had revived, for the capital crime of obstinately adhering to beliefs that contradicted the teaching of the Catholic Church, of which Church they were all presumed to be members. In this respect alone, namely of so many executions for this particular offense in so short a time, the event is a thing apart, in English history: never before, nor ever since, was there anything at all quite like it.[28]

According to Hughes, the revulsion that one feels must be tempered by the understanding that the Marian period differed, in the main, only quantitatively. Heresy everywhere in Christendom was accounted the greatest crime. The foremost leaders of the Reformation — Luther, Zwingli, Calvin, Melanchthon, Beza, and Bullinger on the continent, and Cranmer, Knox, Latimer, Ridley, and Coverdale in England — believed that the failure to persecute betrayed God's true faith, the version they professed. In England, however, the Protestants under Edward burned only two people, both of whom were regarded as fanatical extremists. Even the Edwardian inquisitions were not directed against Catholics. Under Mary, in less time, the 273 included not only Arians and Anabaptists, who by Hughes's count may have accounted for a maximum of 111 of the victims; the rest were Anglican Protestants and among them were the leading bishops of the Edwardian reformation. As for the 111 supposed extremists, Hughes does not prove a single case, although undoubtedly there were some, including blasphemy cases.[29]

The case of the first victim, John Rogers, who had been the prebendary of St. Paul's Cathedral under Edward, is typical of the Marian persecutions. Rogers denounced the Church of Rome as "false and antichristian," and he denied the doctrine of transubstantiation. He was burned alive at Smithfield for "heretical pravity and execrable doctrine."[30] The "sentence definitive" from the pope for the condemnation of Thomas Cranmer, primate of England, was also restricted to heresy in accordance with conventional practice. But his trial began with the pope's representative announcing: "Thomas archbishop of Canterbury! appear here and make answer to that shall be laid to thy charge; that is to say, for blasphemy, incontinency, and heresy. . . ." Cranmer, although denying the charges, threw them back at the Church of Rome. He even accused the pope of having "brought in gods of his own framing, and invented a new religion. . . . O Lord,

whoever heard such blasphemy?" Cranmer's ow blasphemy, as defined
by his prosecutor, was his denial that in the sacrament of the altar,
"Christ's body is there really. . . ."[31] John Philpot, who had been archdeacon of Winchester under Edward, also denied the "real presence" of
the body and blood of Christ during the sacrament, but in his case, as in
many others, his crime was designated as heresy. The other charge
against Philpot was that he had "blasphemously spoken against the
sacrifice of the mass, calling it idolatry and abomination." In this case,
at least, the distinction between blasphemy and heresy was that the
former involved reviling, the latter only a denial. But it was a distinction that held only for the statement of charges, because Philpot
repeatedly, during the trial, reviled the Catholic view of the sacrament
as blasphemous. Indeed, he defamed the Church of Rome more openly
than Cranmer.[32] Several Protestant prisoners denounced their
persecutors for blasphemy. They reviled Roman Catholicism and died
for heresy.[33] Philpot was freer than most with his abuse. When he
claimed to speak in the spirit of God, one of his inquisitors replied, "All
heretics do boast of the Spirit of God, and every one would have a
church by himself; as Joan of Kent and the Anabaptists." Philpot
retorted, "As for Joan of Kent, she was a vain woman (I knew her well),
and a heretic indeed, well worthy to be burnt. . . ."[34]

In prison, while awaiting his execution, Philpot had an argument
with a fellow prisoner who declared that God was not in Christ. Philpot
reacted by spitting in the man's face. On being criticized by one of his
own church for conduct unbecoming a Christian, he wrote a tract explaining that he had spit for the honor of Christ, whom the other
prisoner blasphemed. Philpot made his tract "an Invective against the
Arians." They were the antichrists "whom the Devil hath sh - - out in
these days to defile the gospel." By robbing Christ of his "infinite majesty," the Arians were blasphemers who cut themselves off from Christian
fellowship. Philpot reminded his readers of biblical examples of pious
people tearing their garments to express grief on hearing blasphemy. So
too, he had spit to show his sorrow and to demonstrate to other
prisoners who were present that a blasphemer is to be abhorred by all
Christians. Philpot, who was more learned than most on the subject of
blasphemy, was, not surprisingly, an admirer of Calvin, whose books
he recommended to his inquisitors. When one of them replied with a
criticism of Calvin, Philpot declared, "I am sure you blaspheme that
godly man, and that godly church where he is minister; as it is your
church's condition, when you cannot answer men by learning, to op-
press them with blasphemies. . . ."[35] They sentenced him as an
obstinate heretic, as he might have sentenced them, given the chance;

doubtlessly he would have aggravated the offense by adding blasphemy to it.

Elizabeth's succession to the throne in 1558 began an era of relative tolerance. Men like Philpot honeycombed the church, but reasons of state, not of church, prevailed. England had not embraced an official policy of toleration. That was still impossible in an age that could not conceive of a state without an established church to which all, without exception, must conform, if not for the greater glory of God, then for the greater security of the monarch, national independence, and public order. By subordinating religion to politics Elizabeth's government quenched the fires of Smithfield. Treason against the state, not against God, was the crime for which nonconformists died under the Anglican establishment. The distinction, however nice, theoretically advanced the cause of toleration; and the government, in fact, repealed all the laws against heresy. It professed to abhor even the appearance of persecution for the cause of conscience. Yet the inquisitions continued against Catholics and Puritans as well as some Arians and Anabaptists, whom Catholics, Puritans, and Anglicans alike loathed murderously. But only Arians and Anabaptists suffered for their religion alone. All others suffered because their religion, in the eyes of the state, led them into political offenses. The church under Elizabeth was remarkably latitudinarian; it included men whose beliefs ranged from Catholicism to Calvinism. For over a decade an astonishing variety of practices prevailed within the church, despite official disapproval, and when Parliament finally, in 1571, adopted a binding body of doctrine, the Thirty-nine Articles, the laws were not rigorously enforced. Some clergymen conducted authorized public services and then privately celebrated Mass. Catholic laymen, for the most part, attended the established church on Sundays and holy days, or paid the small fine for recusancy, and went to Mass in private. The government scarcely knew the names of recusants — and did not want to know them. All that was required, however much it injured Catholic or Puritan consciences, was an outward conformity. Although the openly contumacious put themselves in jeopardy, the law demanded only a pro forma obedience — not for spiritual reasons, but to sustain the political supremacy of the crown.[36]

In that state of affairs, heresy began to die as a capital crime in England. In fact, heresy as any erroneous doctrine of faith or any departure from a prescribed religion died with Mary. Under Elizabeth heresy became what the vast majority of people regarded as so monstrous a contradiction of the cardinal principles of religion that the guilty party must be deemed anti-christian and irreligious. He might profess a belief in God and appear pious and law abiding, but if he denied the fundamentals of Christianity, he was a heretic. In effect, there was no such thing as a heretic under Elizabeth or ever after in English history unless blasphemy suffused his heresy, so aggravating it that most outraged Christians felt that the state had no choice but to rekindle the fires with fresh fagots. When that happened in Elizabethan England, the victim always was an accursed Arian or Anabaptist of the sort that provoked Philpot to spit on the blasphemer. The state saw such a person as a blasphemous heretic who had to be "cut off" from the flock of Christ lest he infect it with a contagion and sicken the realm.

John Knox, who introduced the Genevan system into Scotland, revealed the new-dawning Protestant understanding of heresy. He had read the work of an Anabaptist who relied on Castellio to reproach all religious persecution as un-Christian, and in particular to castigate the burnings of Joan of Kent and Servetus. The Anabaptist condemned the cruelty of all who affirmed "it to be lawfull to persecute and put to death such as dissent from them in controversies of Religion, whome they cal blasphemers of God." He would say no more about such persecutors, he wrote, because God had already revenged the blood of the true martyrs by serving some of the persecutors "with the same measure where with they measured to others." To Knox this aspersion on the memory of Cranmer, Ridley, and Latimer was "horrible blasphemie in the eares of the godlie." In 1560 he published *An answer to a great number of blasphemous cavillations written by an Anabaptist*. With Proverbs 17 as his text — "he that justifieth the wicked, and he that condemneth the innocent, are alike abominable before God" — Knox justified the persecution of blasphemers. One who had the lawful authority to kill, he reasoned, yet allowed a murderer to live, was a murderer. As with the murderer, so with the blasphemer. The Anabaptists justified Servetus, a blasphemer; "therefore ye are blasphemers before God, like abominable as he was."[37]

That blasphemers must be executed was clear from the Mosaic law. Blasphemy, Knox wrote, providing a complex definition that did not even refer to heresy, "is not onely to denie that there is a god, but that also it is lightly to esteme the power of the eternal God. . . ." Although distinguishing blasphemy from heresy, he defined blasphemy in a way that corresponded to the conventional definition of heresy. Blasphemy also consisted in spreading such opinions "as may make his Godhead to be doubted of" and departing from the religion of God "to the imagination of man's invention's," which was Knox's characterization of the Anabaptist doctrine of grace from inner light. Blasphemy, additionally, was the obstinate defense of "diabolicall opinions plainely repugning to God's truth; to judge those things which God judgeth necessary of our salvation, not to be necessarie; and finally, to persecute the trueth of God, and the members of Christes bodie."[38] On the final point alone Knox and his Anabaptist adversary agreed, although they were as night and day on "the trueth of God." From both Old and New Testaments, Knox garnered examples to illustrate each category of blasphemy and then explained Servetus's guilt under each. Significantly, Knox found blasphemous only those opinions of Servetus, and of Joan, concerning "the Godhead."

> For what is more blasphemous, then to affirm that such as beleve in the Godhead three distinct Persons, have no true God, but the illusion of the Devilles: that Christ Jesus is not the Eternal Son of the Eternal Father: That there is no distinction betwixt the Father and the Sonne, but in imagination onely: that Christ hath no participation of man's nature, but that his flesh is from heaven; yes, that it is the flesh of the Godhead: That in stockes, stones, and all creatures, is the substantial Godhead?[39]

Drawing on bloody stories of the prophets' endorsing the murder of the priests of Baal and the children of Moloch, Knox defiantly justified persecution; "convict us if ye can by Scriptures," he demanded.

> We say [he concluded] the man is not persecuted for conscience, that, declining from God, blaspheming his Majestie, and contemning his religion, obstinately defendeth erroneous and fals doctrine. This man, I say, lawfully convicted, if he suffer the death pronounced by a lawful Magistrate, is not persecuted, (as in the name of Servetus ye furiously complein,) but he suffereth punishment according to God's commandement, pronounced in Deuteronomie, the xiii. chapter.[40]

As blasphemy, the reviling of God, had ballooned into heresy and nearly disappeared under the influence of the Roman Catholic definition of heretical pravity, so, in Knox's thinking, heresy almost vanished as it was absorbed into the definition of blasphemy that had emerged in the days of the apostolic church. To differ on a doctrine of a much later date, such as transubstantiation, was no crime; to deny any aspect of the Trinity, or any matter involving the Godhead, was blasphemous.

Elizabeth's church rejected the fierce Calvinism of Knox as well as his zealous hatreds, but was influenced by his definition of blasphemy. Characteristically, compromise, the middle road between Catholicism and Calvinism, was the Elizabethan response. Heresy became blasphemous heresy, which was directed against the Godhead. Five times under Elizabeth, possibly a sixth time, and twice again under her successor, blasphemers were executed. The first two victims were foreigners, Dutch by birth. They were among the thousands who fled from Spanish atrocities in the Low Countries. Probably fifty thousand Dutch refugees sought asylum in England during Elizabeth's reign. Most were Calvinists, but some belonged to lesser Protestant sects and others to no recognized communion at all. Among these were the Anabaptists and the Arians, religious eccentrics who met in secret conventicles and lacked the organization of a sect, and also the Familists or members of the Family of Love founded by Henrick Nicklaes or Nicholas. In 1568 the queen ordered an inquisition in London, which at that time had over five thousand Dutch refugees, to find any who held "heretical opinions, as the Anabaptists do hold." Those detected were banished, but more refugees took their places. In 1574 the government captured and banished another batch of Anabaptists. A conventicle of Familists was discovered in the same year; some publicly recanted and others were imprisoned.[41]

On Easter Sunday, 1575, the government uncovered an Anabaptist meeting in a private home. Of the twenty-seven people arrested, eleven were at first condemned to the flames. Terror tactics succeeded in bringing some to abjure. The form of recantation by which they renounced their "Anabaptistical" errors specified their "most damnable and detestable heresies," giving us a glimpse of their beliefs. The first was Joan of Kent's blasphemous heresy: Christ did not take flesh of the Virgin Mary. The second was that infants should not be baptized. The others were more in the nature of affronts to the state than to religion: Christians should not serve as magistrates, bear arms, or swear oaths. Those who would not recant were kept in prison, where one died. Ministers of the Flemish church in London and the queen's ecclesiastical commissioners tried unsuccessfully to convert the prisoners. The queen regarded the Anabaptists as atheists, opposed to all religion and government, but she and her council eventually consented to the banishment of the women, children, and those who had recanted, leaving five intransigents in the dungeons. Two of them, Jan Peeters, a wheelmaker, and Henry Turwert, a goldsmith, the leaders of the conventicle, proved to be so contumacious that the queen and her council would not spare them. Turwert wrote a petition for clemency, which was denied. It was a plea for toleration, based on the commandment "Thou shalt love the stranger as thyself," and on Jesus' teachings. Persecute none, Tuwert wrote, "who have the one true gospel doctrine," but the government thought his doctrine worse than wrong.

The writ *de haeretico comburendo,* which had not been used for seventeen years, directed the sheriff of London to burn the two men at Smithfield for their wicked, corrupting Anabaptist heresies, as an example to others.[42]

John Foxe, the martyrologist, whom Elizabeth favored, interceded on behalf of the condemned men. Pleading for their lives, he argued that to "roast the living bodies" of those who erred in judgment "is a hard-hearted thing, and more agreeable to the practice of the Romanists, than the custom of the gospellers." Reminding the queen that she had punishments short of death, Foxe suggested imprisonment, banishment, burning just the hand, whipping, "or even slavery." "This one thing I most earnestly beg; that the piles and flames of Smithfield, so long ago extinguished by your happy government, may not be revived." Elizabeth, relentless, allowed only a month's reprieve to see if the two would recant. They did not. The queen said that her severity was necessary, because she had already executed men for treason, so for "now sparing these blasphemers, the world would condemn her, as being more in earnest in asserting her own safety than God's honour."[43] At the scene of the execution, an Anglican preacher told the crowd, "These people believe not in God," yet Peeters's reply was an orthodox confession of the Trinity. Turwert, in his petition, also embraced Christ and the Holy Ghost as divine. The wonder is that such reverent believers could have been so execrated. Bishop Edward Sandys believed that the Anabaptists were "of no religion, of no church, godless and faithless people," yet their real offense, one is tempted to say, was, in Sandys's words, that they were people who "condemn all superiority, authority, and government in the church." Similarly, John Whitgift, the master of Trinity College, Cambridge, and later the archbishop of Canterbury, declared that while the Anabaptists pretended the glory of God, "they assert, that the civil magistrate has no authority in causes of religion and faith, and that no man ought to be compelled to faith and religion. . . ." Although their religion led them to treasonous opinions, church and state saw them as blasphemers and burned them as heretics.[44]

Turwert proved to be right in arguing that the execution of a man for his religion would convince no one. The number of Anabaptists continued to swell. Their offshoot, the Familists, grew so numerous that by 1579 the Privy Council redoubled efforts to suppress them. Nicholas, the founder of the sect, was a disciple of David Georg, reputed to be one of the great Anabaptist heresiarchs. In his youth, Georg's tongue was bored with an awl, because he had blasphemed by publicly criticizing the church for idolatry. Georg fled from Münster to Amsterdam and then, under an alias, to Basel. He spent his last years there quietly, risking discovery only once when he wrote a letter eloquently pleading for Servetus's life. The authorities discovered Georg's real identity soon after his death in 1556, dug up his corrupted body, and burned it with his writings as punishment for his blasphemous heresies. Nicholas, his follower, fled from Amsterdam to England, where he somehow escaped detection. His disciple, a Dutch carpenter named Christopher Vittel, had spent several years in prison for professing Arian doctrines, but on recanting was released. Vittel, who had a good knowledge of English, translated several of Nicholas's books, which had been written in German. The appearance of the translations from 1574 to 1578 alarmed both state and church. In 1578 and the following year, several tracts appeared by orthodox writers who exposed the Familist connection with Georg and denounced Arian and Anabaptist principles, in livid language, as both heresy and blasphemy. The Familists supposedly denied both the doctrine of the Trinity and the divinity of Christ. Vittel's natural death in 1579 and Nicholas's in 1580 denied the government the chance of burning the leaders. But their books were burned, and they had many followers, especially in the Norfolk area of East Anglia.[45]

Matthew Hammond or Hammante, a plowmaker of Dutch origins who lived in a village near Norfolk, may have been a member of the Familists. The authorities, who did not know what to make of his religious convictions, also called him an Anabaptist or an Arian or an atheist, as if the names did not differ. Hammond was certainly no atheist, nor did he fit the other categories; unlike the Anabaptists he dismissed the need for baptism and unlike the Arians he repudiated not only the doctrine of the Trinity but Christ and the Holy Spirit as well. The little that we know of Hammond — all of it from hostile sources — makes him seem something like a precursor of the Deists. Whatever his sect he was a religious man. William Burton, an Anglican minister who witnessed his execution, remarked:

> I have known some Arian heretiques, whose life hath beene most strict amongst men, whose tongues have beene tyred with scripture upon scripture, their knees even hardened in prayer, and their faces wedded to saddnesse and their mouthes full of praires to God, while in the meanetime, they have stowtly denied the divinitie of the Sonne of God . . . such were Hamond, Lewes and Cole heretikes of wretched memorie lately executed and cut off in Norwich.[46]

John Lewes and Peter Cole, artisans of the same locality, may have been
members of the same Familist conventicle as Hammond. We know
scarcely more than that they shared his religious views and, later, his
fate.

Hammond first got into trouble for seditious and slanderous words
against the queen. He probably came under suspicion as a foreigner,
was questioned about his religious beliefs, and boldy claimed that they
were not the queen's business. That led to an inquisition by Edmund
Freake, the bishop of Norwich, acting for the Court of High Commission for Ecclesiastical Causes. Hammond openly professed the following convictions, each of which the bishop condemned as blasphemy and
heresy:

> That the new Testament and Gospell of Christ are but mere
> foolishness, a story of men, or rather a mere fable.
> That man is restored to grace by the meere mercy of God,
> without the meane of Christ's blood, death and passion.
> That Christ is not God, not the Saviour of the world, but a
> meere man, a sinfull man, and an abhominable Idoll.
> That all they that worship him are abhominable idolaters; and
> that Christ did not rise againe from death to life by the power of
> his Godhead, neither, that he did ascend into heaven.
> That the holy ghost is not God, neither, that there is any such
> holy ghost,
> That baptisme is not necessary in the Church of Christ, neither
> the use of the Sacrament of the body & blood of Christ.[47]

The bishop, having found Hammond guilty, turned him over to the
secular authority of Norwich. For his utterances against the queen and
her council, Hammond was sentenced to stand in the pillory and have
his ears cut off. For his denials of Christian beliefs, he was taken to a
ditch and burned at the stake. That was in 1579. Lewes and Cole, who
are also supposed to have denied Christ, were burned in the same ditch,
the first in 1583, the latter in 1587.[48]

The case of Francis Kett, who suffered the same fate in 1589, was different. He was a native Englishman of good family and well educated.
He had a Master of Arts degree from Corpus Christi College in Cambridge and was elected a fellow in 1575. For at least ten years his
religious convictions were orthodox; he may even have served as an
Anglican minister. About 1586 he returned home to Norwich, where he
underwent a conversion, perhaps under the influence of the Familists or

from reading the works of Henry Nicholas. The Reverend William Burton, who regarded Kett as another Arian heretic like Hammond, described him as a "holy" man, "the sacred Bible almost never out of his hands, himselfe alwayes in prayer," yet Burton found his opinions "more monstrous" than those of Hammond. That charge seems strange, since Kett embraced rather than rejected Christ, but not a Christ who is God. Kett mixed a mystical chiliasm with Unitarianism. Utterly rejecting the Church of England and its authority, he believed that Jesus had suffered only as a man for his own sins, but had returned to Jerusalem as the high priest, with his apostles, and was gathering the true church. He would suffer again as Christ and then be without sin. No man could find salvation unless he was first baptized as a believing adult and visited Jerusalem before he died. Such preaching made Kett notorious in Norwich.[49]

In 1588 Edmund Scambler, Freake's successor as bishop of Norwich, summoned Kett for an examination of his beliefs. Scambler condemned Kett as a heretic whose "blasphemous opinions" merited an order from the Privy Council that he be executed at once as a "dangerous" person. The "Blasphemous Heresyes of One Kett" include the following charges, of the fifteen of which he was found guilty:

> That the Holie Goste is not god, but an Holyspirite.
> That there is no such persone and that God is no person.
> That Christ is only man and synfull as other men are.
> That no Children ought to be baptized before their full age and to knowe what they should beleave.
> That no man ought to be put to death for heresies, but that the wheate and tares should both growe together.
> That no man as yeat doth preach the trewe Gospel of Christ.
> That he is even gatheringe his people togeyther at Jerusalem in his owne personne.[50]

Burton, who witnessed the execution in 1589, thought that Kett acted like "a devil incarnate." He went to his death in the flames leaping and dancing, clapping his hands, and blessing God, "and so continued until the fire had consumed all his neather partes, and untill he was stifled with the smoke."[51]

Kett was the last Protestant executed for his religious opinions during the reign of Elizabeth. Like Hammond, Lewes, and Cole, he died for heresies of a blasphemous nature. Many other Protestants, like those implicated in the Marprelate controversy, as well as scores of Catholics, died for their religion in the late sixteenth century, but they were convicted because their religious beliefs made their political opinions treasonable. Essentially secular considerations, rather than spiritual ones, dictated Elizabethan policy. When nonconformity or recusancy was unobtrusive and respectful, the government preferred, as the queen herself reputedly said, to look the other way, rather than make windows into men's souls and their secret thoughts. Those whom she burned for their blasphemies were guilty of such heinous crimes, by sixteenth-century standards, that they might have been burned almost anywhere in Christendom. To believers, the denial of the divinity of Jesus seemed so execrable an outrage that exceptions to a comparatively mild policy seemed necessary to avenge God's honor. In general, the gallows of Tyburn and the executioner's axe replaced the fires of Smithfield. They would flare again for the last time in 1612, when James I executed two more people for reasons of religion alone. The two last martyrs were, like those of Elizabeth's time, radical Protestants whose crimes included the blasphemous Unitarian heresy, refusal to regard Jesus as on a plane with God.

The first of the two was Bartholomew Legate, a cloth merchant from Essex whose business took him to Holland, where exposure to advanced Unitarian thought turned him to religion. Convinced that there was no true church to be found anywhere, Legate began preaching in London. His views were similar to those of Francis David in his last years. Legate believed that Jesus was "a meere man," not literally the son of God, yet born free of sin because he was God's anointed one, that is, the Messiah. Specifically rejecting the Nicene Creed, Legate argued that Jesus was not divine in essence or substance; his office, rather, was divine, for through it he represented God's righteousness and gave salvation. But there were no persons in the Godhead. Thus prayers must be directed only to the one God. Legate explicitly repudiated the invocation of Christ. The Church of England might tolerate a man of such "Arian" beliefs, as they were inaccurately described, if he conducted himself quietly. But Legate had a mission. His preaching denied the authority of the established church and its doctrines. In effect he forced himself on the attention of the church.[52]

King James, a man of enormous conceits and considerable learning, fancied himself to be a skilled dialectician and theologian. He told Parliament that kings were not only God's "lieutenants upon earth, and sit upon God's throne, but even by God himselfe they are called Gods. For if you will consider the attributes to God, you shall see how they agree in the person of a King."[53] Nothing Legate believed was as blasphemous. Since James's bishops obsequiously backed his assertions of divine right, James, who had been a Presbyterian in Scotland, embraced Anglicanism and took its enemies to be his. His favorite aphorism, "No Bishops, no King," reflected his conviction that the fortunes of church and crown were the same. On hearing about Legate, James decided that he would personally convince him that his religion was founded on errors. He summoned Legate several times in 1611 and engaged him in debate, hoping to convert him. Although Legate apparently had never gone to college, he was "of bold spirit, confident carriage, fluent tongue, excellently skilled in the Scriptures. . . ." The king got nowhere with him. On one occasion James, not realizing that his heretic opposed the invocation, tried to trick him into a tacit confession of the divinity of Jesus by asking whether Legate did not pray to him daily. When Legate replied that he used to pray out of "ignorance, but not for these last seven years," the king kicked at him in a fury and turned him over to the bishop of London for trial.[54]

The bishop too tried persuasion to exact from Legate a confession of his errors, but failed. The prisoner came to trial in 1612 before "many reverend bishops, able divines, and learned lawyers" at St. Paul's. Legate steadfastly held to his opinions, while denying that the church had any authority over him. The formal charge of heresy was based on thirteen "blasphemous opinions" advanced by Legate. They included his contentions that the Trinity was not a true Christian profession, that Christ was not God, and that he was not to be prayed to. Both the indictment and sentence treated heresy and blasphemy as if they were synonymous. The sentence closed by describing him as a "blasphemous heretick."[55]

The king wanted Legate burned and ordered that a writ be issued authorizing the sheriff to execute the fiery sentence. Some of the common-law judges, however, doubted whether the old statute *De Haeretico Comburendo* was still in force and, even it if was, whether the consistory, the ecclesiastical body that tried Legate, properly had jurisdiction over him. Punctilious on the legal points in this case, James commanded the archbishop of Canterbury to tell the lord chancellor to appoint a commission of a few judges to settle the issues; the chancellor was to make certain that he appointed judges "who make no doubt that the law is cleere to burne them ['blasphemous heretikes']."[56] Legate was reduced to ashes at Smithfield before a huge crowd, "for the manifest example of other Christians, lest they slide into the same fault."[57]

Within a month Edward Wightman of Burton-on-Trent was burned at Lichfield "for far worse opinions (if worse might be) than Legate maintained," as an Anglican minister said.[58] How Wightman came to his opinions, some of which were bizarre, is unknown. He had been a member of the established church, and as recently as two years before his trial his opinions were orthodox. Then, after questioning the doctrine of the Trinity and the sacrament of the Lord's Supper, he underwent a strange conversion from which he emerged with a religion that was, in part, a rational Unitarianism mixed with the equally rational tenet that only adult believers should be baptized; but he also thought that he was the prophet spoken of at different points in the Old Testament and that he was the Holy Ghost. He even claimed to be the Holy Ghost of whom Jesus spoke when saying that the one unpardonable and eternal sin was blasphemy against the Holy Ghost – attributing to the devil a miracle by Christ or charging Christ with being the devil incarnate. To believers, Wightman blasphemed by claiming that he was himself of a divine nature. Wightman, however, did not believe that the Holy Ghost was divine, but that surely was a distinction that James I and his episcopacy could not understand.[59]

Given his message, that he alone professed the only true Christianity, only a maniacal zeal explains Wightman's presentation to the king of a manuscript revealing his beliefs. The result was inevitable. James ordered Wightman to be imprisoned and instructed Richard Neile, the bishop of his diocese, to examine him. Neile, assisted by numerous divines – including his chaplain, William Laud, the future archbishop – held many conferences with the prisoner "to make him see his blasphemous heresies, and to reclaime him." But, Neile later reported, Wightman "became every day more obstinate in his blasphemous heresies." On learning of his obstinacy, the king ordered the bishop to take his prisoner to Lichfield, where a consistory, the same kind of tribunal of divines that tried Legate, should condemn him formally.[60]

The articles against Wightman charged him with holding that there is no Trinity, that Jesus was not the natural son of God and "of the same substance, eternity and majesty with the Father in respect of his Godhead," that Jesus was only a man, that the Holy Ghost was neither divine nor equal to the Father, that the Nicene Creed is un-Christian, that the Lord's Supper should not be a sacrament, and that infants should not be baptized. In addition there were a series of charges relating to Wightman's belief that he was the Holy Ghost and the Comforter spoken of in John 16:7–8. Bishop Neile, who conducted the trial in the Lichfield Cathedral, decided not to pass sentence before giving the prisoner a final chance to recant. The bishop himself delivered a sermon confuting Wightman's blasphemy against the Trinity, with a different divine assigned to each of the other blasphemous points, so that collectively they covered the sixteen counts of blasphemy in the articles. "To all which," Neile reported, "He no way relenting, but p'sisting in his blasphemies, I read ye sentence against him to be a blasphemous heretique, and to be accordingly certified to ye secular power, whereupon his matie's [majesty's] writ was directed to ye sheriffe of ye county. . . to burn him as a heretique." The king's writ, commanding that Wightman be burned, at one place described him "as a blasphemous and condemned heretic," as if blasphemy were a form of heresy, and at another place condemned him for "heresies and other detestable blasphemies," as if heresy were a form of blasphemy.[61]

Neile's report of the case almost concludes with a respite from the gruesome end. As the flames began to burn Wightman, he cried out in pain that he would recant. "The people thereupon ran into the fire, and suffered themselves to be scorcht to save him." The authorities kept him chained to the stake until he signed a hastily framed recantation. They then escorted him back to prison. A couple of weeks later, the consistory court reconvened and required Wightman to make a proper recantation. He surprised them with his bold refusal. James, on being informed, commanded that the execution be carried out at once. On April 11, 1612, Wightman "died blaspheming," the last person in England to be executed for his religious beliefs. Not that England embarked on a new policy of toleration. Hardly. The seventeenth century witnessed Laud's persecutions of nonconformists, a civil war of religious character, and Presbyterian persecution of dissenter sects; in 1698 Parliament passed an act against blasphemy, and prosecutions under statute or common law continued for over two more centuries. The burnings ceased after 1612 in deference to the public reaction against them. A "Spanish Arian" condemned about the same time as Legate and Wightman was allowed to live out his remaining years in prison, because James did not wish to risk stirring up public sympathy for him by a burning. Besides facing the growing revulsion against the hideousness of the punishment, the government learned that it had little to gain from making martyrs. The people, being unable to distinguish between obstinacy and constancy of faith, "were ready," said Bishop Thomas Fuller, "to entertain good thoughts even of the opinions of those heretics, who sealed them so manfully with their blood." Consequently, James shrewdly preferred that "heretics hereafter, though condemned, should silently, and privately waste themselves away in the prison. . . ."[62]

The burning of Legate and Wightman ended an era during which English law showed a distinct movement from heresy to blasphemy. In 1553, when Geneva burned Servetus, Archbishop Cranmer proposed the first Protestant codification of the ecclesiastical law in England. It was the first, ever, to have a separate title on blasphemy.[63] The Calvinists, those zealous students of the Old Testament, were responsible for reviving blasphemy as a crime distinct from heresy. In Elizabethan England, where a middle way between Catholicism and Calvinism prevailed, blasphemy did not displace heresy; rather, it supplemented and modified it, giving rise to confusion in usage. Thus we read of convictions for the simultaneous crimes of blasphemy and heresy, or for blasphemous heresy, or for heresy resulting from blasphemous opinions. The nomenclature of the crime was of slight importance compared to the character of the crime. The infliction of death was restricted to denials of "the Godhead," geneally speaking to some form of antitrinitarianism, as in the cases involving those called Arians, Anabaptists, or Familists; all were regarded as atheists. They did not deny the existence of God, but "atheism" at that time meant also denial of any person of the Trinity. About 1607 Sir Francis Bacon, who was more sophisticated than most of his contemporaries, wrote, "All that impugn a received religion, or superstition, are, by the adverse part, branded with the name of atheists."[64] As late as 1632, Thomas Richardson, the lord chief justice of England, remarked, "I say they are Atheists that scoffe at religion in others."[65]

From the time of Elizabeth, however, the law did not inflict death merely for holding different religious opinions, no matter how obstinately. One had to reject the divinity of Christ or some other principle equally fundamental. Sacramental differences, which led to the deaths of most of the Marian martyrs, were no longer capital offenses under Elizabeth and her successors. In a peculiar way the renaissance of Old Testament studies in Protestant England assisted the cause of toleration; the Old Testament renewed interest in the crime of blasphemy yet restricted its application. If Elizabeth had emulated her father and sister by burning people for heresy, which was defined as any deviation from her church, multitudes of English Catholics and Protestants would have died for reasons other than political crimes against the crown. Elizabeth and James inflicted the ultimate penalty for crimes against religion only upon those regarded as loathsome by Catholics, Anglicans, and Puritans alike.

7

SNATCHING THE SOCINIAN PALM

Prosecutions for blasphemous heresy or for any sort of erroneous religious opinions all but expired in England after 1612 and did not revive until the 1640s, when the Presbyterians rose to power. The burning of Legate and Wightman occurred when James I was passing through a phase of Calvinist righteousness. It soon subsided and he became the most tolerant monarch England had known. James never abandoned his belief "that it is one of the principall parts of that deutie which appertaines unto a Christian King, to protect the trew church within his owne dominions, and to extirpate heresies," but he resorted to extirpation of antitrinitarians only when his very belated discovery of Arminianism in Holland provoked in him a rage for orthodoxy.[1]

England and Holland were allies, bound together by Protestantism, trade, and common enemies. Holland was England's doorway to an extraordinary diversity of reformationist currents from Calvinism to Socinianism. Dutch Protestants of every sect fled from Spanish tyrants to England. After the Dutch gained independence with England's aid, English nonconformists, persecuted at home, found refuge in the Netherlands. There were English churches in Holland and Dutch churches in England. The cultural connections between the two countries were so close that when the Arminians solidified their control of the endowed chair of divinity at the University of Leyden, the Dutch Calvinists turned to the Church of England for support and James I presumed to interfere in the affairs of the Dutch church. The king had never heard of Jacobus Arminius, the preeminent leader of religious liberalism in Holland, until the excitement surrounding the appointment of his successor, Konrad van den Vorst. Vorst espoused the Arminian heresy of free will in opposition to the basic Calvinist doctrine of predestination. James read his books and those of Arminius — and erupted. He denounced Arminius as "an arch Anabaptist," "a blasphemer," and "the enemy of God," reserving equally choice epithets for his successor at Leyden. The king burned Vorst's books as "monstrous blasphemie" and called his followers "Atheisticall

Sectaries." Through his ambassador at the Hague, James presented a list of the Arminian blasphemies suckled by "the Disciples of Socinus." Graciously conceding that the professor need not be sent to the stake if he recanted his blasphemies, although none "ever deserved it better," James demanded Vorst's expulsion. The tolerant Dutch allowed him to retain his emoluments but moved him to a different university. The controversy occurred in 1611–12. By the end of James's reign in 1625, the Arminian heresy infected the Church of England, setting it on a collision course with Puritanism.[2]

James acted as God's avenger again on discovering the existence of the Racovian Catechism. The Latin edition of 1609, which Faustus Socinus and his Polish brethren wrote as an explanation of their faith, was dedicated to England's Protestant monarch. When the book came to his attention in 1614, he assailed it as "satanic," and Parliament ordered the public hangman to burn it. Socinianism, or Unitarianism which it later became, was the seventeenth century's scapegoat for almost everything that trinitarians deemed detestable in radical Protestantism.[3]

In the sixteenth century, Christians execrated Anabaptism; in the next century, Socinianism. The two were alike in some respects, yet very different in others. Both believed in the primacy of the Scriptures, but the Socinians professed to construe the Bible in the light of reason while the Baptists, as one offshoot of the Anabaptists came to be known, preferred the guidance of an inner light derived from the promptings of God and private conscience. Notwithstanding their stress on reason, the early Socinians accepted a great deal of biblical supernaturalism, such as the virgin birth and miracles. The Baptists remained literalists in such matters, while the Socinians evolved in the direction of rationalism and eventually toward the abandonment of a formal creed. In the seventeenth century, however, the Socinians had as little in common with modern Unitarianism as the English Baptists with the Anabaptists of revolutionary Münster. The distinguishing tenet of Socinianism was antitrinitarianism or rejection of the doctrine of the Trinity and the deity of Christ, on which the Baptists were orthodox Christians. Socinianism inconsistently emphasized both the humanity of Jesus and the divinity of his office, but distinguished divinity from deity. One God and no incarnation was the tenet, yet Socinians invoked Christ's name in prayer, as did the Baptists. Socinianism disavowed the Christian theory of atonement and the doctrine of original sin, which Baptism embraced.[4]

The distinguishing tenet of Baptism was that the church is a voluntary congregation of believers who signify their acceptance of Christ as savior by undergoing the rite of immersion. Socinianism agreed with Baptism on the sovereignty of private judgment and the voluntary character of church membership, but regarded baptism, whether of infants or of believing adults, as unnecessary for salvation. Both Socinianism and Baptism looked upon most sacraments as superfluous, the Lord's Supper as a mere commemorative service. Excluding the Particular Baptists, a later faction that reconciled Calvinist theology with adult baptism, Baptists and Socinians rejected predestination in favor of free will. The most important tenet common to both was that religion is a private matter between the individual and God. Thus, no external authority, political or ecclesiastical, could impose a church or any beliefs upon a Christian; Christian liberty meant freedom to worship as one pleased. The Baptists were the only sect to advocate the free exercise of religion not only for themselves but for everybody, without exception. The Socinians shared the same principle, but in seventeenth-century England lacked organization as a sect. The Baptists were intensely evangelical, believing in the efficacy of individual efforts to achieve a state of grace and the promise of salvation. By the end of the seventeenth century English Socinianism, which tended to avoid proselytizing, was still a movement, both within and outside the established church, rather than a separatistic group or church. The Socinianism of which James I read in the Racovian Catechism was, like early Baptism, pacifistic, against capital punishment, democratic in church organization, and utterly opposed to the interference of the state in matters of spiritual concern; unlike Baptism, Socinianism repudiated Christ as God.

The king hated Socinianism and Baptism alike, but he grew to distinguish one from the other. Always excepting those like Legate and Wightman whom he did not regard as Christians, James understood that persecution could not create Christians or a body of unified church doctrine. Like Thomas Aquinas and Calvin he declared that heresy was much more dangerous than a plague by the same degree that the soul was more important than the body. Yet, his imprisonment of separatists notwithstanding, he gradually turned a blind eye and deaf ear toward all but the most aggressive and vociferous who insisted on worshipping outside his church. He preferred to believe that the Church of England would become national in fact as well as name by ignoring most differences within it. He hated the Puritans, not because of their theology which for the most part he accepted, but because they insisted on exaggerating differences and demanded that their way be imposed on everybody else. James wanted as many Christians as possible to embrace his church. Believing that compulsion could control behavior but not conscience, he realized that he could force a subject to attend the established church or imprison him for attending another, but could not make him have faith in anything against his will. The sovereignty of church and state could not prevail over private judgment in matters of faith.[5]

James did not realize, however, that England already had such a diversity of religions that uniformity was a hopeless objective. The Catholics, whose suppression James wished to ameliorate for reasons of foreign as well as domestic policy, were an unpopular but strong minority. Religion in England also included Arminians and Calvinists within the Protestant establishment, plus a bewildering variety of sects, some of which, like the Baptists, wanted to withdraw peaceably from the national church and form their own congregations, with permission if it was forthcoming, without it if necessary; others, like the Puritans, sought to control the national church and persecute any who differed. Sectarianism had become a permanent force in England, irreconcilable with the principle of one nation, one church. The government would not tolerate the separatists, because they seemed subversive: they rejected the king as head of their churches. They suffered harassment and imprisonment not because they endangered the souls of true believers, but because as nonconformists they challenged the royal prerogative. But James's persecution, however harsh to its individual victims, was sporadic; it was certainly not systematic and suppressive.

As early as 1615 James and his archbishop of Canterbury, William Abbot, demonstrated their understanding that even a separatist, if he acknowledged Christ as his savior, was not a heretic. Bishop John Jegon of Norfolk, having captured a separatist named William Sayer, asked permission to burn him for denying Christ and the Holy Ghost. Abbot refused. He replied, in effect, that Sayer espoused Barrowist, Baptist, Brownist, and other separatist opinions, but he was not an Arian or an atheist deserving the stake. The moderates who controlled the government distinguished between those who agreed on fundamentals and those who did not. The godly, all of whom the Church of England claimed, included anyone who accepted Christ as the divine Son of God offering salvation. That included, by orthodox reckoning, all Christians except Arians and Socinians, deniers of the Trinity. This view of the matter allowed the separatists to exist, certainly not free to worship as they pleased with official toleration, but free to survive and grow.[6]

Thus, as early as 1611, Thomas Helwys, perhaps more with a spirit of martyrdom than with good sense, returned to England from his exile in Holland to bear witness to his Baptist convictions. Helwys established the first permanent Baptist church in England — and in London, no less. He sent King James a copy of his book, personally inscribed: "The King is a mortall man and not God, therefore hath no power over the immortall soules of his subjects to make lawes and ordinances for them and to set spirituall Lords over them." That got Helwys a term in Newgate prison, and John Murton, who took his place as the head of the congregation, followed him there. But Baptism won converts; by the close of James's reign the first Baptist church in London had about one hundred fifty members, and there were several other Baptist churches in southeastern England.[7]

Helwys's book, *A Short Declaration of the Mistery of Iniquity* (1612), was the first work in England to claim religious liberty for all subjects. Castellio's *Concerning Heretics* (1554) and Acontius's *Satan's Strategems* (1565) were Latin works that were later republished in various languages, including Dutch which the early Baptists knew, but neither of those pathbreaking books on toleration existed in English during their time. Helwys presented their thesis in English. No state, he argued, had a lawful authority to force conscience or even to foster religion; church and state should be separated. Christ's domain must be protected from temporal authority, no matter how beneficent, because every individual is responsible to God for his own salvation. Erroneous opinions on religion were no concern of anyone, least of all the state and its established church, except the individual who held them. "For men's religion to God, is betwixt God and themselves; the king shall not answer for it, neither may the king be judge betweene God and man. Let them be heretikes, Turcks, Jewes, or whatsoever it apperteynes not to the earthly power to punish them in the least measure." Much as Helwys abhorred the church of Rome, he made no exception to his principle: Catholics must be as free as any to worship as they pleased. Leonard Busher, a Baptist layman who wrote *Religion's Peace; or, A Plea for Liberty of Conscience* (1614), presented the same argument. Busher systematically summarized every reason that religious liberty was beneficial to believers and unbelievers, and to government and society as well as individuals.[8]

John Murton's *Objections Answered* (1615) also sought to prove that government had no jurisdiction in matters of religion. Murton stands out because he fully developed a point not adequately treated by Helwys and Busher. In opposing secular punishment of erroneous opinion, they advocated the "spiritual sword" of excommunication as the punishment of last resort for heretics. They did not address themselves to the problem of blasphemy. Nor had Acontius. Castellio's tolerance had withered when he faced the problem of blasphemy that took the form of atheism. Murton not only opposed secular punishment for heresy and blasphemy; he even questioned ecclesiastical punishments. He treated blasphemy as a special problem. It was the worst of all offenses against religion, because the atheist merely denied God, while the blasphemer reviled Him, and the Old Testament explicitly prescribed death for the blasphemer. Murton believed, however, that Christ's law had abrogated the Mosaic law. Excommunication, like death, sent a condemned soul to hell. Accordingly, it was a punishment not rightfully available to ecclesiastical authority, any more than the temporal authority could rightfully imprison or harm a person for his religious beliefs. Christ taught gentleness and charity, reserving to himself the punishment even of those who blasphemed him or his Gospel. God's way, Murton believed, surpasses human understanding. We must, therefore, leave blasphemers to the mystery of His divine purpose. Moreover, every person, no matter how unregenerate, possessed within him the potential for grace. To expel anyone from the church shut him off from possible salvation. St. Paul himself had blasphemed before he discovered the light. Had he been cut off, God's purpose would have been thwarted. The Jews were "fearfull blasphemers of Christ and his Gospel," but by Christ's commandment were to be persuaded by the power of spiritual truths. So too all blasphemers. Later libertarians of the seventeenth century, such as Roger Williams and William Penn, sound derivative when compared with Helwys, Busher and Murton.[9]

The early Baptist theorists were pathetically out of joint with their time. Persecution increased after the death of James I. His successor, Charles I, gave a free hand to the one formidable man in his government, William Laud, who, after the death of Abbot in 1633, became archbishop of Canterbury. Abbot had grown tolerant and neglectful with age. While Abbot lived, Laud, then bishop of London, was kept on a leash; after he died, Laud's repressive temper knew no restraints, and the Puritans felt its full severity. Under Laud the Church of England was never more influential in molding government policy. He dominated the Privy Council, the Court of High Commission, and possibly the Court of Star Chamber; he even managed to get one of his bishops appointed lord treasurer and lord high admiral. Although he tended toward Arminianism and rationalism in matters of theology, his interests in theology were perfunctory. He had no drive for certainty in religious truths and therefore lacked the theological bigotry and fanaticism of his Puritan antagonists. They could not conceive of more than one true religion, which they must force on everyone else, while Laud could not conceive of anyone's being sure about the mysteries of divine truth.[10]

Although Laud knew he could not coerce uniformity of belief, he held that if all men worshipped in the same way, using the same words and ceremonies, a spirit of communion might unite them. Laud, like the Puritans, believed in uniformity but thought that it derived from external conformity. He was, above all, an obedient servant of the law, and it required uniformity of worship. Laud ruthlessly enforced its letter and spirit. He had resolution of purpose, incredible energy, and a sense of mission in exactng the last jot and tittle of obedience to the Book of Common Prayer and the Thirty-nine Articles of Faith. He could allow no exceptions and so drove thousands of his countrymen out of the national church, many more to America, and others toward revolution. His enforcement of high-church Anglicanism had the unintended effect of causing the people to think that Puritan nonconformity represented English Protestantism and national independence from Rome. To Laud's victims, most of whom were far more narrow and mean spirited than he, he was dissolving the Reformation in England. His religious policies were unrepresentative of his church as well as his country. Yet he knew, rightly, that the Puritans matched his zeal; they meant, if given the chance, to remodel the national church in the image of Calvin's Geneva, destroying the episcopacy and derogating from the royal supremacy, whose obedient servant he was.

One difference between Laud and his Puritan victims was that he controlled the ecclesiastical powers of the government and mightily influenced the civil. Another difference was that the Puritans professed obedience to the letter of the Mosaic law. Laud was too enlightened and shrewd to prosecute for erroneous opinions, heretical or blasphemous. To have done so would have staggered public opinion, which knew that men who accepted the divinity of Christ could not be enemies of God or religion. Laud did not persecute for the high purpose of saving souls from contagion or preserving the purity of doctrine. He persecuted because the peace, order, and uniformity which he cherished derived from obedience to the law. The crimes of the dissenters, he believed, sprang from their willful opposition to the laws of church and state. Nonconformity was the crime, and nonconformity he meant to extirpate — because it was factious, not erroneous. Thus, in the 1639 case of John Trendall, a Dover separatist who held conventicles in his home and rejected the national churtch, Neile, the archbishop of York, and members of the Privy Council considered whether he should be sent to the stake as a "blasphemous Heritique." Laud, however, would not burn him. Trendall's crime was nonconformity, not blasphemy, and his punishment was fine and imprisonment. The government severely treated nonconformists of every kind — Baptists, Brownists, Congregationalists, Familists, and Presbyterians — for reasons of state. They were, Laud knew, seditious people who, given the opportunity, would overthrow the established church and undermine the royal prerogative.[11]

Laud's engines of repression were the Court of Star Chamber and the Court of High Commission for Ecclesiastical Causes. The Star Chamber, although it was the judicial arm of the Privy Council, which could do as it pleased, deferred to the High Commission in cases of offenses against religion. In 1596 when the Star Chamber heard a case of "blasphemous heresy" arising from a man's statement "that Christ was no savioure and the gospell a fable," the court declined jurisdiction and turned the prisoner over to the prelates for punishment. In 1606 when considering the case of a person accused of a variety of misdemeanors, the Star Chamber heard evidence of his "great blasphemye"; he had declared that if God came down from heaven and threatened him, he would not obey. The court took notice of the fact that its own jurisdiction did not extend to matters of religion, but sentenced the defendant to three years for his misdemeanors in order to punish his blasphemy. Vicar's case of 1631 was also unusual. The High Commission, in this instance, described a separatist's Calvinist doctrines as "hereticall blasphemous and scandalous," and then punished him for his "seditions." Generally the Star Chamber had discretionary jurisdiction over any acts that it chose to regard as offenses, excepting treason and felonies. It could imprison, fine, and punish by mutilation short of dismembering a limb, but it could not inflict death, which was the sentence for treason and felonies; jurisdiction over those crimes belonged to the regular common-law courts.[12]

The common-law courts deferred to the High Commission in cases involving religious offenses. The law, as summarized by Sir Edward Coke, was that "in causes ecclesiastical and spiritual, as namely blasphemy, apostacy from Christianity, heresies, schism and others (the conusance of whereof belongs not to the common laws of England,) the same are to be determined and decided by ecclesiastical Judges. . . . " In Attwood's case of 1617, however, the King's Bench, which was the highest common-law court on felonies and treason, took jurisdiction for the first time in a matter belonging to the ecclesiastical judges. Attwood had declared that the established religion was a recent innovation and that preaching was but prattling. The King's Bench sustained his conviction by the lower trial court, because his words were "seditious against the state of our Church and against the peace of the realm." Since the king was the head of the church, an attack on it was an attack on him as well as the law establishing the church. Nonconformity and erroneous opinion could, therefore, be converted into sedition either in the common-law courts or in the Star Chamber, whenever the judges of either were so minded. Normally, however, offenses against religion belonged to the High Commission.[13]

That court, which emerged by royal authority in Elizabeth's time, had jurisdiction over violations of any statute enacted on the subject of religion, of all cases within the cognizance of ecclesiastical law, and of cases dealing with religious errors, recusancies, schism, and any preaching contrary to the Book of Common Prayer and the Thirty-nine Articles defining the Anglican establishment. In addition the High Commission shared jurisdiction of cases on seditious utterances, conspiracies, and contempts. The High Commission was a formidable prerogative court not only because its authority was so broad and it operated throughout the realm, but also because it employed inquisitorial procedures and had an array of effective punishments. Although it could not torture, it could force a party to incriminate himself or find him guilty as charged if he refused; it acted as his accuser, prosecutor, judge, and jury. Its powers of search and seizure, like those of the Star Chamber, were unfettered, and it could fine and imprison for indefinite terms. The High Commission also exercised powers of censorship, granted by the Star Chamber, against "all heretical, schismatical and seditious" works, offensive to state or church, and against any works published without prior license. When the Star Chamber prosecuted a clergyman, it first turned him over to the High Commission to depose him from the ministry; the Star Chamber, in turn, inflicted gory physical punishments for the High Commission. In theory an ecclesiastical court should not shed blood. The Star Chamber and High Commission operated in such close collaboration, especially under Laud, that the two became indistinguishable to the public.[14]

When Laud was archbishop of Canterbury the High Commission decided no cases of blasphemy. He preferred for reasons of expediency to prosecute on other charges. Under his lax predecessor, the High Commission had only one blasphemy case, in 1631. Richard Lane, a tailor, stood accused of blasphemy, wholly apart from heresy, because he supposedly claimed divine attributes. Laud, then bishop of London, menacingly said to Lane, "I hear you are a high Familist, and you hould it very lawful to equivocate. Did you not say you were as Christ was God and man?" The prisoner explained that he thought Christ dwelled in every believer; God, through Christ, accepted him as perfect. Archbishop Abbot replied that if Lane did not fall to his knees and ask forgiveness for his blasphemy, he would receive a sentence that would make him an "example to all the world." Laud thought Abbot was too lenient in allowing Lane to escape by offering him a chance at repentance. "This will not serve his turne," said Laud, because Lane deserved "*ultimam poenam*," the ultimate punishment, but if he tasted the severest discipline of Bridewell prison until the last day of the court's term, he could then make his submission. The High Commission agreed. As Abbot's successor, Laud arranged that the charges against dissenters should be brought for nonconformity and seditiousness.[15]

The cases of Bastwick, Burton, and Prynne demonstrate how Laud treated his enemies and gained the odium of the populace. Dr. John Bastwick, a Puritan physician, the Reverend Henry Burton, a Puritan preacher, and William Prynne, a Puritan lawyer, were tried together in 1637 for seditious libel. Each of the defendants had committed the crime by publishing vitriolic attacks against Laud, his prelates, and the established church. Bastwick and Prynne were violent extremists who would have inflicted death for heresy and blasphemy not only on Anglicans and Catholics but even on Baptists and the independent Puritan sects that opposed a Presbyterian establishment. Burton would have exempted the Calvinist sects from the ultimate penalty. Both Bastwick and Burton had composed their seditious tracts while in prison under sentence from the High Commission. Prynne also had a conviction record. The Star Chamber had punished him in 1633 by disbarring him, exorbitantly fining him, and ordering the hangman to hack off his ears. In 1637 the Star Chamber pronounced the three Puritans guilty of the offense charged and imposed a punishment meant to terrify others who might repeat their offenses. They were fined five thousand pounds each and sentenced to life imprisonment in distant fortresses, and the hangman cut off their ears. Prynne had already suffered that grisly punishment, but the court discovered that he had stumps which could be severed — and they were. The hangman also branded Prynne's cheeks with the letters "S.L." for seditious libeler — "*stigmata Laudis*," the scars of Laud, Prynne said. When he had been mutilated in 1633, few people cared. By 1637 Laud's policies had created popular sympathy for his victims. Hundreds watched their bloody torment and with tears and cries shared the religious ecstasy of their martyrdom.[16]

Three years later the country was on the edge of rebellion. The Short Parliament, the first in eleven years, dissolved after three weeks, having achieved nothing; the king refused to redress grievances, without which the House of Commons refused their approval of new revenue measures. Laud's attempt to force Anglicanism on Presbyterian Scotland had led to war with the Scots, and riotous crowds in London cheered Presbyterian victories as their own. Laud convened a synod that adopted new canons for the church, reinforcing his policy of uniformity. One canon, taking aim at "the spreading of the damnable and cursed Heresie of Socinianism," sought to curb its "blasphemous errours" by strengthening censorship decrees. Another canon, directed against "Sectaries," named Baptists, Brownists, and Familists among the destroyers of the church. Late in 1640 a mob of "2000 Brownists," as Laud called the separatistic Calvinists, tore apart the High Commission's courtroom as one of their number was about to be sentenced. The Privy Council was afraid to prosecute the ringleaders, and a grand jury refused to indict them. The government was breaking down. When the Long Parliament met in November 1640, the Puritans dominated it. They repudiated Laud's recent canons, emptied the jails of dissenters, imprisoned the archbishop himself and executed him in 1645, and abolished the Star Chamber and the High Commission. By the summer of 1642 the civil war between royalist and parliamentary forces had begun. [17]

A majority of the House of Commons favored Presbyterianism. They had the strength to destroy the episcopacy and suppress Catholicism within the area controlled by their armies, but they could not muster a majority to establish their own religion. They disagreed among themselves on the question of whether Parliament or the presbyters should control the new church. The politicians, who championed their own prerogatives against the ministry, realized too that a narrow establishment could lead to their own overthrow: the hodgepodge of dissenting sects that had mushroomed within the Puritan movement made up the rank and file of the army. The sects feared any uniformity of religion; their dedication to the principle of congregational independency made them gravitate toward the Baptist position of separation of church and state.

Thwarted in their foremost aim to make Presbyterianism a lawfully established system of exclusive, infallible truths, the emulators of Geneva vented their suppressionist tendencies in books and tracts. Francis Cheynell's *The Origin, Rise, and Growth of Socinianisme* (1643) regarded the case for persecution as unanswerable. The author was able to discover Socinianism in any opinion the least different from Presbyterianism. Adam Steuart conceded that persecution could not alter religious beliefs but pressed the obligation of the state to ensure that God's name and honor were not outraged by heretics and blasphemers. The magistrate could "cut away an ill tongue," even if an ill-will could not be prevented. Error must perish or the godly would be exposed to its infection. "God in the Old Testament granted no toleration of divers religions, or disciplines." Because the New Testament established a much holier covenant, it required a firmer union among

Christians than the Old Testament did among the Jews. Ephraim Pagitt's *Heresiography* (1645), demanding death for blasphemous opinions, reasoned that if a man should be executed for poisoning drinking water, death was all the more necessary for those who "poyson mens soules." He was speaking not just of Socinians but of the congregationalist sects as well. John Bastwick, one of Laud's martyrs who had returned to London from his distant prison amid the roars of an approving crowd, also recommended persecution for any who disagreed with Presbyterianism. The Bible, Bastwick argued, expressly prohibited toleration; God himself demanded death for "atheism, blasphemy, profanation of the Sabbath, and all manner of impiety and toleration of all religions . . . " That many of the sects who opposed God's true church professed Calvinist doctrine only veiled the dangers of their heresies. Thus, the Presbyterians, knowing that there could be no prosecutions for nonconformity when there was no established religion with which to conform, sought to revive prosecutions for erroneous opinions.[18]

Presbyterian threats alarmed the sects, but they had the army's protection — indeed they were the army, in a large sense. Socinianism, however, was vulnerable. Socinian books were being imported into England; their importers and disseminators had been the target of Laud's abortive canon of 1640. Parliament's rejection of it did not reflect sympathy for Socinians. The House of Commons had rejected the anti-Socinian canon only because, by its failure to define Socinianism, it allowed the prelates to decide who was guilty of it. Parliament reserved that decision to itself. Having removed the prelates, it was free to punish advocates of that "most vile and damnable heresy." In 1645 both houses of Parliament condemned John Archer's *Comfort for Believers*, a treatise whose thesis was that true believers, although weak in faith, "should not be opprest, or perplext in heart." Both houses agreed that the book was "blasphemous Heresy." There being no way to reach its author, a London preacher who had recently died, Parliament had to content itself with a search for its printers and an order to the common hangman to burn copies of the book at various places in London, with ministers present "to declare to the People the Abominableness of it."[19]

The imprisonment of Paul Best in 1645 was the first blasphemy case in many years and the first of many during the Puritan hegemony. Best, a man of mettlesome intellect and spirit, was the first Englishman to write a Socinian work, although he had to smuggle the manuscript out of prison to get it published — and Parliament summarily ordered that the hangman burn it in public. A country gentleman with an excellent education in theology at Cambridge, he had money enough to indulge his intellectual interests. For over a decade he had traveled on the continent, searching out people and books that exposed him to new religious ideas. No Englishman before him had studied Socinianism firsthand in Poland and Transylvania, its places of origin. On his return to England, Best, who had had experience as a soldier abroad, joined the Parliamentary army. He also began writing on the subject of religion. Renewing an old friendship with his former roommate at Jesus College, Cambridge, Best showed him a manuscript on the doctrine of the Trinity and some Socinian books imported from abroad. The former roommate, who had become a Puritan minister, was horrified by what he read and reported Best to the military authorities. In early 1645, Best was in prison, probably in York. He soon became notorious.[20]

The ministers of York complained about Best's "blasphemous opinions" to the Westminster Assembly of Divines. That body, a ministerial group established by Parliament in 1643 to recommend and supervise a new religious settlement for England, determined to make a test case of Paul Best. The Presbyterians, who dominated the Westminster Assembly, admired the Scottish church as a model of ecclesiastical organization and discipline. They abhorred sects, of course, and saw in religious diversity a threat to the success of their objective, the imposition of Presbyterianism on all England. People like Best stood in their way. If they could make an example of him, they might snuff out the rising demand by the autonomous congregationalists for a policy of toleration. Best was proof, to the Presbyterians, that toleration led to defilement of the true church, opened the door to soul murder, and resulted in schism, satanism, and sedition. Lord Fairfax, in whose army Best had served, sent him to London for interrogation by the Westminster Assembly. Its committee examined his books and writings, and they recorded his replies to their interrogatories.[21]

On June 10, 1645, the Westminster Assembly, "vindicating the honour of God and of Jesus Christ," condemned Best's "horrid blasphemies" and demanded the speedy suppression of the "liberty of all opinions and religions, under the pretence of liberty of conscience, maintained in books and otherwise . . . which hath been the occasion of those and the like blasphemous opinions." On the same day the entire assembly appeared before the House of Commons to press their case. They accused Best of blasphemies "against the Deity of our Saviour, Jesus Christ, and of the Holy Ghost," produced their evidence, and requested Parliament to execute "condign punishment" on so terrible an offender. The Commons, promising condign punishment, turned the matter over to a committee to investigate Best's blasphemies. The committee was enjoined not to "meddle with any other Business, until they have dispatched this," and to bring its recommendation to the house "with all Speed." The matter was much too complex to be settled speedily, though, and Best remained a close prisoner, not permitted to speak to anyone except members of the committee. Despite the naggings and promptings of the Westminster Assembly, which complained that Best still vented his "blasphemous heresies," the committee did not report till seven months had passed.[22]

An unprecedented legal predicament explained the delay and also the reason that the House of Commons in September added lawyers to the committee of Best's case. When the committee reported at the end of January 1647, its chairman told the house that Best was guilty, yet the law did not provide for his punishment. The man continued pertinacious in his opinions. He denied the Trinity, rejected the deity of Christ and of the Holy Ghost, and engaged in "several other monstrous and unheard-of Blasphemies." In "former Ages," the punishment was clear; the chairman reminded the house of the fate of Bartholomew Legate. But in those times the jurisdiction over offenses against religion belonged to the ecclesiastical courts. Parliament, however, had abolished them all in 1641, when it demolished the Laudian system. Thus, "the former Course of Proceeding against Hereticks is, by the Taking away of the Power of Ecclesiastical Courts, defective," leaving no way of punishing the crimes of a man like Best. No statute reached him, and the common-law courts had always denied that their jurisdiction extended to such matters. The committee lamely asked Parliament for guidance. The House of Commons ordered that Best be kept under close restraint and resolved that an ordinance be framed "for punishing with Death Paul Best, for his abominable, prodigious, horrid Blasphemies." The course of procedure, at least at that stage, was to be a bill of attainder: Parliament would outlaw the crime, apply its statute retroactively to Best, and then conduct the trial against him in order to provide a semblance of due process of law. To work out the details, the Commons augmented its committee by adding "all the Lawyers of the House." They were to report in one week.[23]

They did not report, however, for two months, and still the proceedings foundered. A bill was introduced demanding Best's death by hanging for his denials of the Trinity, the deity of Christ, the Holy Ghost, and for other "execrable Blasphemies, not fit to be named," but the bill was merely read twice — not thrice and enacted — "and nothing more done at this Time." Uncertainty is evident from the fact that the House of Commons also voted to examine Best and at the same time deputized a committee of ministers to visit him in jail "to make him sensible of his Errors." He remained obdurate.[24]

On April 4, 1646, Best's jailor brought him to the House of Commons. It was the day appointed for his trial, but they condemned him first and tried him next. The chairman of the committee which had been deliberating his case for nearly a year read the charges "proved against him," and then Best got his chance to speak. Adroitly defending himself, he claimed to acknowledge the Holy Trinity by which he hoped to be saved. He had simply denied "the Tripersonality of Athanasius" (who in the fourth century contended against Arianism), which he denounced as "Popish," and he would hold to his opinion unless otherwise convinced. Most members of the Puritan house, who opposed anything "Popish," knew little about ancient heresies. Best baffled them, even after he conceded that he did deny that Jesus Christ "is co-equal, co-eternal, and co-existent, with the Godhead of the Father." After the house sent him back to jail, the members indecisively resolved to deliberate "what shall be done with him." Not knowing, they appointed a new committee to bring in a recommendation. At least two of its five members opposed Presbyterianism, and one of them, Sir Henry Vane, had argued "for a full libertie of conscience to all religions. . . . " Five members of the Westminster Assembly were commissioned to assist, if need be. Although they included two Presbyterians who believed that blasphemy merited death, another member was the foremost Independent leader in the assembly, Thomas Goodwin, who could not tolerate intolerance.[25]

The reason for the inconclusive deliberations on Best is that he had become a pawn on a chessboard in a match between those who sought a uniformity of religion and those who saw in uniformity a threat to themselves. The religious situation in England had swiftly changed during the 1640s. Once the Puritans pulled down the Church of England under Laud, the persecutions, which had kept them fraternal, ended and they split apart. As a minister who supported the Presbyterians complained, "Every one that listeth turneth preacher, as shoo-makers, coblers, button-makers, hostlers and such like, take upon them to expound the holy scriptures, intrude into our pulpits, and vent strange doctrine, tending to faction, sedition and blasphemie." Sectarianism had rampantly spread throughout the country and in the army and Parliament as well. Although the Presbyterians had gained the upper hand by the middle of the decade, they were not strong enough to impose their will on all the other Protestant sects. By one Presbyterian count, the sects had multiplied from three to forty within a couple of years. Collectively they were known as the Independents, because they insisted on their own tenets, congregations, and governance. All shared some Calvinist beliefs, but they differed among themselves. Only a common dread of Genevan rigidity held them together, and of necessity they rallied around the principle of toleration of religion for all but Catholics, Socinians, and atheists. Cromwell supported the Independents. After his victory at Naseby, he wrote a famous letter to the speaker of the House of Commons, demanding liberty of conscience to anyone who served in Parliament's army against the king. When choosing men to serve, said the general, the state took no notice of their opinions.[26]

To the Presbyterians, if Best, a "blasphemer," could not be convicted, no one could. The Presbyterian author of *Hell Broke Loose* complained that Best was a source for the opinion that the doctrine of the Trinity was "a mystery of Iniquity," and Thomas Edwards, that fierce Calvinist, singled Best out as the man responsible for numerous other blasphemies. Edward's huge and abusive book, *Gangraena*, purported to be a "catalogue and discovery of many of the errors, heresies, blasphemies, and pernicious practices of the sectaries of this time." The prevailing toleration, he complained, was Satan's work, resulting in innumerable sects and no less than 176 heresies and blasphemies, about twenty-five of which were of the worst kind, Arian or Socinian. As the recorder of the Westminster Assembly lamented, while blasphemous heresies spread in England with unprecedented velocity and variety, the army and the Independents had become "pleaders for libertie almost to them all." Even the House of Commons, the greatest pulpit in England, invited Independents to preach before it. For the time being the best the Presbyterians could do was to keep Best imprisoned; the chessboard was in a position of stalemate.[27]

Intermittently through 1646 the House of Commons fretted about its prisoner, examined him, returned him to jail, and reached no decision. That he had influential supporters is evident from the fact that he was able to publish a brief tract addressed to the Westminster Assembly. Someone who had access to the closely guarded prisoner supplied the pen, ink, and paper, and arranged for the printing. In his tract Best cleverly argued against the death penalty: only a live heretic could repent, and "Paul Best (what-ever his errours be at present), as well as Paul the Apostle, once a blasphemer, may one day become a convert. . . . " He also wrote a petition to Parliament, which he managed to get published, requesting that he be given a speedy judgment or be set free. Parliament resolved at the end of 1646 to fix the death penalty for anyone tried and convicted "by the judges of the land" for the crime of saying anything against "the attributes of God." The ambiguity of this purported condemnation of atheism showed the continuance of the stalemate, while the reference to a regular judicial trial showed that the House of Commons had abandoned its attainder procedure. The committee in charge of Best's case complained that he had access to pen and ink, and his jailor had to answer for that.[28]

Notwithstanding security procedures, Best somehow published a little book, *Mysteries Discovered*, which did not reveal the mystery of how he did it. That was in mid-1647. He did, however, take note of the fact that over one hundred petitions on his behalf had been sent to Parliament. Although Parliament was debating passage of a bill to punish blasphemy, the army submitted proposals that would have guaranteed religious liberty to all but Catholics. Important people openly supported Best. John Selden, the foremost legal scholar and parliamentarian of the age, reportedly said, on hearing Best, "that he was a better man than he understood himself to be." Another eminent member thought that Best showed himself to be a moderate man willing to reason. Outside of Parliament the Levellers, who were the first group in modern history to battle for libertarianism and democracy, opposed all coercion of conscience. William Walwyn, one of the Leveller leaders, answered the Presbyterians by saying that if they could not convince Best's conscience, they should not punish his person. Edwards, the Presbyterian leader who collected such remarks in his *Gangraena* as evidence of blasphemy, also reported that John Goodwin spoke on behalf of Best. Goodwin, one of the leading Independent ministers, reputedly demanded "a full liberty of conscience to all sects, even Turks, Jews, Papists. . . . " He claimed that Best's imprisonment did "no good at all" and that no force should be used against him, " even should he gather a church and vent Arian opinions. . . . "[29]

Despite the gathering support for Best and for toleration, Best's illicit book was a challenge Parliament could not ignore. The Presbyterians, still the majority party, were enraged by his open Socinianism. He subordinated Christ to God, condemned the Nicene multiplication of the Deity, and even claimed that to detract from its Unity was "blasphemy." Acknowledging the Father to be God "essentially," the Son "vicentially," and the Holy Spirit "potentially," Best argued that "to make Christ coequall to his Father, is to make another or false Christ, or . . . an Idoll Christ, or two Gods. . . . " To regard Christ as both God and man, Best believed, conflicted with both "reason and Scripture." His reliance on "reason" was characteristically Socinian. Refusing to make the "creature" equal to the Creator, he rejected the Nicene Creed as a "semi-Pagan" innovation of ancient times "made Catholike by Imperiall decree. . . . " Real blasphemy, which he compared to treason, consisted in multiplying the Deity or detracting from His Unity. Arius, Best contended, had a much better understanding of Christianity than Athanasius. Best also argued that the experience of

Holland and Poland showed that toleration was beneficial, and he showed esoteric learning when he described the 1560s in Transylvania, Lithuania, and Poland as a "reformation of the Reformation" and a time of liberty.[30]

The House of Commons condemned Best's work as blasphemous and ordered that copies be "burnt by the Hands of the common Hangman" on three separate days at different points in London. An inquiry to determine "by what Means this blasphemous Pamphlet came forth" got nowhere. Best himself suffered no additional punishment. The last reference to him in the House of Commons was in September when his case was joined with that of a man named "Biddle." John Biddle would become "the father of the English Unitarians" and his "blasphemies" troubled England for many years. Best, however, simply faded out of the picture. Sometime before the close of 1647 he was quietly released. Cromwell is supposed to have been influential in securing his liberty. In all likelihood Best had to promise never again to publish his religious opinions. He retired to his estate in Yorkshire, where, unmolested, he wrote voluminously about religion until he died ten years later, leaving many manuscripts. He had no disciples, although he probably influenced Biddle.[31]

Biddle too was a lone intellectual. Although he had a congregation for a short time during the few years he was left at liberty, he did not found a church or lead a sectarian movement. He was very much the creation of his persecutors. His enduring reputation as "a very conspicuous Heresiarch," a characterization that follows the judgment of his contemporaries, seems unmerited. His martyrdom more than his own contributions to Unitarianism accounts for that reputation. Although his publications attracted attention even on the continent, he owed far more to the continental Socinians, whose writings he introduced to English readers, than he gave in return. His own writings were remarkably independent-minded and restrained in doctrine and tone. That so mild, moderate, and scholarly a person could have aroused such hatred as a reputed blasphemer is evidence of the bigotry of his time. Many hundreds of his contemporaries, especially among the frenzied Ranters, who did blaspheme by cursing, reproaching, or repudiating God, Christ, or religion — crimes with which Biddle had no remote connection — suffered comparatively mild harassment. They seemed to be more crazy than dangerous. The extraordinary response to Biddle suggests that England's leaders in government and religion saw in him a man of awesome intellect and character that made him capable of subverting received religion, if not of leading a new reformation. We cannot know whether their estimate of him was exaggerated, as it appears, because the seventeen years of his persecution succeeded in quashing him. On the one hand persecution drove him further into opposition and gave him a name; on the other it denied him the opportunity of commanding a reform movement, if ever that was his desire.[32]

In 1644 when Biddle first got in trouble he was twenty-eight. Nothing in his previous life indicates any departure from orthodoxy. He was still a teenager when his English translations of Latin poets stimulated predictions that he would be a gifted scholar. At Oxford, where he earned an A.B. in 1638 and an M.A. in 1641, he specialized in classics and philosophy, and he knew the New Testament so thoroughly that he could repeat it verbatim, through Chapter 4 of Revelation, in both Greek and English. He continued his scriptural studies after he became master of a grammer school in Gloucester. In 1644 he reached the conviction, based entirely on his own reading of the New Testament, that the Holy Ghost of the Trinity was the principal angel but not divine. His views, expressed in conversation, were reported to Presbyterian authorities who accused him of "dangerous opinions," but he subscribed to a confession of faith that satisfied them. That was the only occasion that Biddle, who was a quiet but extremely obstinate man, backed down.[33]

In the following year, to clarify his own thinking on the subject of the Holy Ghost, he composed a short treatise and indiscreetly showed the manuscript to some friends. Again, one betrayed him, and parliamentary commissioners in Gloucester arrested him. Another friend bailed him out of jail, pending his being summoned before the House of Commons for an examination. In the spring of 1646, James Usher, the lord archbishop of Ireland, stayed in Gloucester on his way to London and decided to convince the bright young scholar that he was in "damnable Error" or else all Christendom "had been guilty of Idolatry." Usher relied only on the church fathers, while the sole authority Biddle relied on was the New Testament. In London, Usher reported his opinion that the presumptuous schoolmaster believed that everyone else was guilty of idolatry. Soon after, Parliament summoned Biddle to London. When examined by a committee, he admitted that he had denied the divinity of the Holy Ghost but refused to express an opinion on the divinity of Christ. In June 1646 they sent him to the Gatehouse prison in Westminster, where Paul Best was locked up. The two probably met in prison, and Best, the most learned Socinian in England and twenty-five years Biddle's senior, may have awakened him to a literature that he had not known to exist. Biddle's unorthodoxy up to that time had been limited to his own idiosyncratic interpretation of the third person of the Trinity. While Best's case agitated and perplexed the House of Commons, Biddle's was ignored. His "crime," like Best's, was not punishable under the law as it then stood. So, the Commons neglected him. He tried to get a hearing by petitioning Sir Henry Vane, a parliamentary tolerationist. Biddle related the facts of his case, explained his beliefs about the Holy Spirit, and concluded that he had relied solely upon "the principles of reason and scripture." His placing reason before Scripture showed a Socinian characteristic. Vane was unable to get Biddle discharged or even bring his case before the attention of the house.[34]

Over a year after his arrest, in May of 1647, the Commons at last resolved that a committee which had been drafting an ordinance against blasphemy should look into the case of "one Biddle, a Schoolmaster of Gloucester, that has written a Treatise against the Divinity of the Holy Ghost." Nothing further happened, though, and Biddle continued in jail, with neither bail nor trial. Desperate to capture attention, he resorted to a daring strategy. He published the manuscript that was responsible for his plight. The little tract appeared in September 1647 under the title *Twelve Arguments drawn out of the Scripture; Wherein the commonly-received Opinion, touching the Deity of the Holy Spirit is clearly and fully refuted.* It got him the attention that he wanted but gravely worsened his situation. The house condemned the tract as blasphemous, ordered that it be publicly burned, authorized a search for its printers, and instructed the committee on Best's case to examine Biddle. When he would not renounce his opinion, a committee of the Westminster Assembly was deputized "to remove him from his blasphemies and dangerous opinions," but no one could satisfy him that he was wrong. So they kept him where he was, without trial; he was too dangerous to let loose and impossible to prosecute.[35]

The order to burn Biddle's tract had the effect of advertising it. Its secret printers ran off a second printing for sale later that year. The orthodox rushed into print to refute Biddle. In 1647 *God's Glory Vindicated and Blasphemy confuted* was on the streets. Biddle, of course, had not questioned God's glory. *A Testimony to the Truth of Jesus Christ,* which attacked the blasphemies of both Best and Biddle, received the signatures of fifty-two London ministers. Almost as many from York in the next year signed *Vindiciae Veritas* (Truth Vindicated). Two Presbyterian tracts of 1648 bore the same main title, *Blasphemoktomia.* One was subtitled, *The Blasphemer Slain; or, a Plea for the Godhead of the Holy Ghost vindicated from the cavils of J. Bidle;* the other, too, purported to be a vindication of the Holy Ghost. While the pamphlet warfare was in progress, a Presbyterian board of visitors at Oxford discovered and seized Socinian literature in the possession of John Webberley, the subrector of Lincoln College, leading to his ouster and imprisonment.[36]

The seeming spread of Socinianism, the most detested heresy in

Christendom, spurred Parliament to legislate. First Best's case, then Biddle's and Webberley's, showed the absence of any lawful course against alleged blasphemers. For about two years the Independents, fearing that the Presbyterians might use legal sanctions against them, had blocked passage of an act. But by 1648 the situation had changed. The Congregationalists were undergoing the transformation whereby a heretical sect becomes a respectable church alarmed by religious anarchy. And the threat of a monolithic, bigoted Presbyterian establishment was vanishing. Even moderates of that denomination had come to realize that a uniformity of religion was simply no longer possible in England. The country was too divided religiously. Independents who stood closer to Calvinism than to the heterodox fringe sects had reached high places and had the support of the army; they were no longer afraid of a bill that would outlaw the most reprehensible of religious offenses. Secure in the knowledge that they had achieved toleration for themselves, they believed that they could vote against blasphemy without installing presbyter in place of priest or prelate as inquisitor of heretical pravity. If an occasional Socinian as well as outright atheists had to be sacrificed, the price seemed well worth paying to secure toleration of most religious differences. There was no chance that the punitive character of the bill would intrude upon the consciences of any recognized Protestant communion. A sop to placate Presbyterian moderates, moreover, would prove the fitness of the bill's Independent supporters to share the reins of government; they favored neither toleration for blasphemers nor the extreme sectarianism of the lower classes. On May 2, 1648, Parliament, without serious Independent opposition, passed "An Ordinance for the punishing of Blasphemies and heresies."[37]

The act of 1648 had two sections. The one on blasphemy fixed the death penalty, to be determined by regular judicial procedure, for anyone advocating "that there is no God," or that "the Son is not God, or that the Holy Ghost is not God, or that they Three are not one Eternal God, or that . . . Christ is not God equal with the Father," or that Christ did not rise from the dead and ascend to Heaven or was not the Son of God, or that Holy Scripture is not the word of God, "or that the Bodies of men shall not rise again after they are dead, or that there is no day of Judgment after death. . . ." But for the clause against atheism, the capital provisions of the act focused primarily on Socinian doctrines. The heresy section of the act was far milder in its punishment but more comprehensive in its coverage. It reached Arminians, Baptists, and most critics of Calvinism by declaring unlawful the advocacy of any of the following beliefs: that all men shall be saved, that man has free will, "that man is bound to believe no more than by his reason he can comprehend (another Socinian belief), that the moral law of the Ten Commandments is not a rule of Christian life, that believers should not pray for pardon of sins, that the sacraments of baptism and the Lord's Supper are not "commanded by the Word of God," that infant baptism is wrong and that only believers should be baptized, that the Churches of England are not "true churches," or that "the Church government by Presbytery is Antichristian or unlawfull." These provisions against heretical "errors" were, in the main, concessions to Calvinist church discipline. Anyone convicted of any of these errors by the testimony of two or more witnesses had to recant or be sent to jail until he found two "suffient Sureties" who would be liable in the event that he maintained the same errors.

The chief sect that denounced the act of 1648 was the Baptists. The argument that complete religious liberty would inundate England with pernicious heresies and corrupt the faith did not convince them. To them it showed little faith in true religion, which in time would prevail over error. Erroneous opinions, they thought, were inevitable. God permitted them and He alone reserved judgment over them. The Baptists did not condone blasphemy but believed that the persecution of anyone professing God was evil. To the claim that blasphemy was irreligious, thus not deserving the protection afforded religion, they answered that persecutors always saw truth as blasphemous, thus justifying their coercion of conscience. Christianity flourished when men were left alone to advocate whatever religious views they wished. Christ had not planted his church by force. To exact an unwilling and hollow conformity was the real blasphemy. Persecution convinced no one; it only hardened souls. Any limitations on religious belief or any punishment for it destroyed the foundations of liberty, opening the way to further persecution. The Baptists acutely sensed the possibility that they stood next in line if Socinians or papists or anyone suffered for conscience' sake. They remembered history and knew that "blasphemer" was, like "Papist," a term of reproach which men with bitter hearts indiscriminately used to assail their opponents. They recalled that Christ himself suffered the reproach of blasphemer and that his followers were accused of sedition and heresy. The most awful sin of the Christian churches was persecution. Baptists genuinely believed that the church should use only spiritual weapons, ranging from persuasion to excommunication, and that the civil magistrate had no business with anything touching religion. They would spare even blasphemy from molestation if only because no one, civil or ecclesiastical, was sufficiently infallible in his judgment to justify punishment. If the government could punish even a Socinian for religious reasons, rather than because he had created a civil disturbance, anyone dissenting from a prescribed religion could suffer the same fate.[38]

The same tolerationist arguments came from a motley group of thirty autonomous congregations in London who published their petition to Cromwell, urging that he declare the Blasphemy Act of 1648 "Null and Void" and liberate John Biddle. The petitioners maintained that "the most mistaken Christians," if peaceable, should be protected in the "exercise of their Religion." Biddle, "though differing from most of us in great matters of faith," deserved "liberty of Religion." If he could be punished under the "Bloody Ordinance" of 1648, so might anyone who had "begun already to reject the Traditions of men, the unscriptural words and notions of Trinity in Unity, & Unity in Trinity, of three persons in one essence, of the hypothetical union of two natures in one person. . . ." All should be free to profess their faith, or dissenters would be "left out" of the liberty Cromwell had promised to "godly men of different judgment." If Biddle did in fact differ on vital points of faith from the petitioners, they had taken a principled stand on the right of every peaceable Protestant to freedom of religion, while anxiously warning that Biddle's fate foreshadowed that of any heterodox believer.[39]

The act of 1648, despite the provocations that led to its passage, remained dormant on the books, but not because tolerationist arguments prevailed. At the close of 1648 Pride's Purge cleaned the Presbyterians out of Parliament, quelling the demand for enforcement. The Independents now controlled the government.

Shortly before the purge, however, Biddle defied the penalties of the "Draconic Ordinance" against blasphemy by smuggling out of prison for publication his *Confession of Faith touching the Holy Trinity* and, soon after, his *Testimonies* [of the Church Fathers]*concerning the One God and the Persons of the Holy Trinity.* How he got the necessary materials for his research is unfathomable. The new books revealed that he had become a convinced Socinian, familiar with the literature of which he had been ignorant when first imprisoned. He believed "the Father only to be One God" and contended that the leaders of the Reformation had failed to go far enough by having failed to reject the "Idolatrous Pollutions of the Romane Antichrist" on the subject of the Trinity. Repudiating the Nicene Creed, he declared that it introduced "three Gods, and so subverteth the Unity of God. . . ." To Biddle, Christ was the Son of God and of divine nature, but was not God. Prison was radicalizing him. His views tempted death; he could not know that he was safe, because enforcement of the act of 1648 would have brought within its penalties officers of Cromwell's army.[40]

The expulsion of the Presbyterians from Parliament eased Biddle's treatment. At one point he briefly got out when a Staffordshire justice of the peace, who admired his work, posted bail. Biddle returned with him to Staffordshire in his first position as preacher to a congregation. But John Bagshaw, the head of the Rump Parliament's Council of State, secured from the house an order for Biddle's reimprisonment. He stayed in jail, more closely confined than before and on the verge of starvation, until February 1652 when an act of "oblivion," dictated by Cromwell, freed him. He had spent five and a half years in jail, without ever having seen a judge, for the crime of denying the divinity of the Holy Spirit. Three years later he would again be charged with blasphemy.[41]

During Biddle's long incarceration the House of Commons discovered an antitrinitarian in its midst. The house had difficulty enough coping with an eccentric Yorkshireman, Best, who had been to Transylvania, and with a young Gloucester teacher, Biddle. John Fry was a tougher antagonist. A seventeenth-century antiquary described him as "a man of more than ordinary parts." He was an army captain, a prosperous gentleman with friends in high places, and, since Pride's Purge, a member of Parliament, sufficiently important to be appointed one of the commissioners to try King Charles. He could be blunt on his feet and satirical with a pen.[42]

In 1649 a fellow member of Parliament asked him to help free Biddle. Another member, overhearing Fry consent, objected that Biddle deserved to be hanged. In the argument that ensued over the Trinity, Fry admitted that he was "dissatisfied with those expressions of three distinct Persons or Subsistences in the God-head." He denied that there could be any persons in the Godhead, meaning that God is not a "person"; the word, he said, referred only to people. If God is a person, he added, "I might be said to be God too, as well as Jesus Christ, and the like might be affirmed of all other creatures whatsoever." The remark sounded like double-barrelled blasphemy; Fry's adversary took him to mean that Jesus was not divine and that he, Fry, and everyone else had divine attributes. The charge of blasphemy led to Fry's suspension from the house until an investigating committee reported. His denial that he claimed to be as much God as Christ was, satisfied the committee, leading to his reinstatement. He would not, however, let the matter rest.[43]

To clear his name from the charge of blasphemy, Fry published a detailed account in which he repeated his rejection of the "Persons or Subsistences" of the Trinity, and he denounced that doctrine as a "chaffy [worthless] and absurd Opinion." Finding no scriptural basis for the doctrine of the Trinity or for "the forcing of a man's conscience by civil

Power," he favored toleration for antitrinitarians. In the course of his argument he ridiculed and condemned the Westminster Assembly, adding that he would as soon put a sword in the hands of a madman "than a high-flying Presbyter."[44]

Before its final session the assembly asked Francis Cheynell, one of its highest flyers, to answer Fry. Cheynell was one of those Presbyterians who specialized in seeing Socinians under the bed. In 1643 he had published *The Rise, Growth, and Danger of Socinianism*, and in 1648 he had found Socinian books under John Webberley's bed. As a reward for his labors Cheynell was appointed to the most richly endowed professorship of divinity and became president of St. John's College, Oxford. His response to Fry became a huge book, *The Divine Trinity* (1650), but before it could reach print, others rushed out tracts against Fry. One had the title *Mr. Fry his blasphemy and error blown up and down the kingdome* (1649). Cheynell's theme was that for the past century "there have been many blasphemous bookes to the great dishonour of the blessed Trinity printed in England." He classified Fry with "Atheistical Libertines" with whom communion should not be held. Socinians, like Fry, he claimed, maintained that Jesus was a mere man, "and therefore they are blasphemers," as were all who claimed to be as much God as Christ was. Fry "had too much acquaintance" with such "high swelling blasphemies." If he thought that Christ was a mere man to be worshipped as divine, he was an idolator; if he thought Christ should not be divinely worshipped, he was a blasphemer.[45]

Fry promptly replied in a second tract, *The Clergy in their Colours* (1650). He confessed that he had been adequately answered if "foul-mouthed language be a sufficient confutation." He made his defense of his views on the Trinity an assault on the clergy. They taught many things as truth that were not. People who took their religion on faith or authority were no wiser than parrots. He commended men who did their own thinking and rejected clerical teachings "if after a careful and conscionable search, they find no footing for such things in the Scripture." A rational man, especially a Christian, should profess nothing without first determining its truth for himself. The clergy were full of tricks, and if you put a hard question to them, they answered, "'tis a thing above reason, and yet you must believe what the received opinion is of it." Fry would have none of that. "Every man that knows anything, knows this," he answered, "That it is reason that distinguisheth a man from a beast: if you take away his reason you deny him his very essence. . . ." That Socinian passage would be quoted against him in Parliament. Fry concluded by writing: "I drive at this, that men may reflect upon those things which are taught, not believing anything, because their teachers say so; but because what is taught, is rational and grounded upon the Scriptures."[46]

Fry's attack on the clergy was so provocative that not even his friends in the House of Commons could down the clamor against him. Early in 1651 both his little books were cited against him and went to a committee for examination. The committee reported that the first one, by denying the Trinity, contained blasphemous matter. The second was scandalous and tended to the "Overthrow of the Preachers and Preaching of the Gospel." Both books "throughout" were against the doctrine of "the true Religion." Substantial quotations from both were introduced in evidence to support the charges. Fry got no chance to defend his position; the only questions asked of him concerned his authorship. Two days later the house debated Fry's case from morning to night. On the "Matter of Blasphemy" the house resolved that Fry's first book was "erroneous, profane and highly scandalous." The book against the clergy was similarly condemned. Both were ordered to be burned. Fry himself, however, was not molested. His punishment was limited to expulsion from Parliament. He was too important a person to be imprisoned for a crime that Cheynell advertised as infecting high places in the realm. The last word in print came from Cheynell. His tract, *A Discussion of Mr. Frye's Tenets lately condemned in Parliament,* purportedly proved Socinianism "to be unChristian Doctrine." Proof does not exist for the tradition that Fry joined John Biddle's congregation. A few years after being expelled from Parliament, Fry died.[47]

Biddle, the former schoolteacher, had begun preaching the Gospel in London after being pardoned in early 1652. His congregation was small but his notoriety occasionally attracted Sunday crowds, causing the orthodox to complain that he vented his blasphemies in public. The government, which was committed to a policy of toleration for anyone who publicly worshipped God through the Christian religion, preferred to take no notice. No loyal subject of peaceable deportment was molested. Biddle's literary productions attracted attention, but, not bearing his name, drew only suspicion. In 1652 he published the first English translation of the Racovian Catechism, with a preface containing a plea for religious toleration.[48]

Biddle's edition of the Racovian Catechism was an especially bold project. The name came from the city in Poland, Racow, which was once the "capital" of Socinianism with a flourishing religious press that distributed antitrinitarian books throughout Europe. The Racovian Catechism, although in question-and-answer form, was scarcely for children. It was a systematic manual of Socinian doctrines. When James I saw the first Latin edition, he ordered it burned as a heretical work.

All orthodox Europe knew Rakow as a source of spiritual contagion until Poland cauterized it. In 1638 the Polish government, under the influence of the Jesuits, abolished Racow's press, college, schools, and churches; dispersed its congregations; and exiled its ministers under penalty of death. So died a remarkable center of intellectual liberty and religious liberalism. For a short time John Biddle made London the new Racow — or so his hysterical enemies said. In 1652 the secret presses in London turned out a new Latin edition of the Racovian Catechism. What an Anglican king saw as heresy in 1614, a Parliament of Independent Puritans condemned to the flames as blasphemy in 1652. Unfazed, Biddle freely translated the Latin into English a few months later, interspersing the text with his own unmistakable emendations. He followed with unsigned translations of several Socinian tracts and a biography of that really great heresiarch, Faustus Socinus.[49]

Biddle's works reached readers as far away as Danzig. A Calvinist scholar in Holland, after studying Biddle, concluded that London "seems to be snatching the palm from . . . Rakow." In London a Presbyterian wrote "that Socinianisme hath fixed its metapolitical seat here in England, and displayed openly the Banners of its Impiety." The "prime man" behind it all was John Biddle. John Owen, a preeminent Independent minister, and vice-chancellor of Oxford University, devoted hundreds of pages to a refutation of Biddle's works, and even Owen, a sensible man, panicked before Biddle's supposed influence: "the evill is at the doore; there is not a Citty, a Towne, scarce a village in England, wherein some of this poyson is not poured forth." The Reverend Matthew Poole, who kept bringing out revisions of his book, *The Blasphemer Slain,* in order to keep up with Biddle's productions, found it all "most lamentable to rehearse":

> . . . the whole body of Socinianism, that hydra of Blasphemies, that Racovian Catechism (which walked only in the dark, and in the Latine tongue in the Bishops times) is now translated into English, for the more speedy corruption of the people; many bold Factors for these Blasphemies, which in those times durst not appear, do now both publickly, and from house to house, disseminate their Heresies without fear: amongst these is Mr. John Biddle. . . .[50]

In 1653 Biddle brazenly published an anthology of his own works, including those burned earlier as blasphemous. His final work and masterpiece was *The Twofold Catechism,* which appeared in 1654, exasperating even a Parliament of Independents. The newest book was probably the most radical assault on conventional Christianity ever seen in England. Biddle, following Fry's suggestion, simply threw out sixteen hundred years of theology, council edicts, and church confessions; he went back to the source of Christianity. Not even the Racovian Catechism satisfied him. It was too marred, like all its sectarian counterparts, by running commentaries on early church fathers and disputes with authorities. Biddle determined to rediscover "the chiefest things" concerning Christian belief and practice, "whilst I myself assert nothing (as others have done before me) but onely introduce the Scripture faithfully uttering its own assertions." He restricted his own commentary to an introduction, saying he wrote for "meer Christians" rather than for one sect or another; the paradoxical result was that in his effort to avoid sectarianism, he wrote the ultimate sectarian catechism. It covered the whole field of Christian doctrine.[51]

In effect, by distilling Christianity from the New Testament, Biddle produced an epitome of what later would be called Unitarianism. Although he urged that the Scripture should be taken "in its plain straightforward sense" with no twisting or construction, where doubt arose in meaning he relied on "Reason." On the whole, he stayed with a literal interpretation, even to the point of describing God as a person with anthropomorphic features and dwelling in a particular place. In an attempt "to reduce our Religion to its first principles," Biddle discarded all glosses on the Bible as well as the "Babylonish confusion of language" and "intricate expressions" that had accumulated with the "traditions of men." By speaking of original sin, the Trinity, hypostatical union, and transubstantiation, theologians abandoned the Bible and common sense, making religion unintelligible to the ordinary man for whom Biddle wrote. The Bible, Biddle held, was "plain enough to be understood, even by the simple." It taught the unity and love of God, salvation through God, the sonship of Jesus Christ who was a mortal, and the free will of man. It taught nothing about original sin, predestination, the co-essential divinity of Christ, justification by faith alone, the resurrection of the body, or much else that passed for Christianity.[52]

Parliament, on receiving complaints about Biddle's last two books, which bore his name, resolved "to suppress his School" and arrest him. The first book, anthologizing his earlier works, was familiar. Again the house condemned it for "blasphemous Opinions against the Deity of the Holy Ghost" and ordered it burned. On December 13, 1654, the house examined Biddle, who admitted writing both books, but said that he had no congregation and refused to identify his printers. "The Law of Christ," he explained, enjoined him "not to betray his Brethren." He denied the divinity of the Holy Ghost, as earlier, and when asked whether Jesus Christ was God "from Everlasting to Everlasting," he denied that the Bible said so. The house committed him to the Gatehouse prison, as before, ordering close confinement "without Pen, Ink, or Paper, in order to a further Proceeding against him." *The Twofold Catechism* was, of course, burned.[53]

A month later the house adopted the report of its committee which had been studying Biddle's last two books. In the same language each was found to be "full of horrid, blasphemous, and execrable Opinions; denying the Deity of Christ, and of the Holy Ghost." The thirteen "Particulars" cited from *The Twofold Catechism* and the half dozen more from the other book contained many flat denials but no reviling; John Biddle was a temperate, reverent, and rationalistic Christian. The list of his blasphemies concerning Jesus Christ were, in Parliament's language, as follows: He claimed Christ had a "divine Lordship, without a Divine Nature," that he was not "a Priest, whilst he was on Earth," and that he did not die "to reconcile God to us." He claimed that "Christ is the Second Cause of All Things pertaining to our Salvation, And that the Son is not equal with the Father." He claimed that Christ had "no other than a human Nature," was "not the Most High God, the same with the Father, but subordinate to him," and finally that "Christ is not the supreme and independent Monarch Jehovah."[54]

Parliament's prosecution of Biddle was lawless. The proceedings against him awaited a report from "the Committee on Printing," which the house ordered to "bring in a Bill for the Punishment of the said John Biddle." He had published his books without prior license, in violation of the censorship law, but the proper course for prosecuting such an offense was trial before a magistrate and the maximum sentence was a fine. In exceptional cases the Council of State had jurisdiction. Even if Biddle had committed a capital crime, indeed, especially if he had committed such a crime by violating the act against blasphemy passed in 1648, jurisdiction over the offense belonged, by the terms of that act, to the ordinary courts of justice. Conviction by a legislative attainder was the only purpose of ordering a bill against him. Revolutionary oppression often takes the form of an improvisation that has the color of law.[55]

In the late 1640s when Parliament had first jailed Biddle, he was an unkown. At that time only the Baptists and a few Independents like John Goodwin would have exempted antitrinitarian beliefs from sanctions against blasphemy. By 1655 Biddle was a celebrity with a congregation, some influential friends, and the support of many who believed that if so reverent though misguided a man could be punished for his religion, so might they. On the other side were those like the majority of Parliament who believed that toleration should go far, but not far enough to protect "blasphemy." Those favoring Biddle's prosecution by Parliament also demanded severer penalties for breaking the act of 1653 against unlicensed "scandalous" publications "to the great dishounour of God . . . and insufferable contempt of all good Order and Government." One faction that demanded stronger press regulation to prevent blasphemies like the Racovian Catechism complained that prosecutors had "no standing penal Law" on which to rely. As the public awaited Parliament's disposition of Biddle's case in January 1655, the question of censorship and that of toleration linked together.[56]

John Goodwin, who had spoken up for Best's liberty, saw the connection between censorship and toleration. Although he deplored Biddle's antitrinitarianism, Goodwin believed that "liberty of the Press" permitted no censoring of any religious opinions. In a *Fresh Discovery of the High Presbyterian Spirit,* he opposed censorship laws as unscriptural, dangerous, and ineffective; they hampered learned men like Goodwin himself from rebutting Biddle. Although none of Biddle's publications had been licensed, Goodwin perversely blamed the censors for them. The printing of Biddle's "most enormous and hideous notions, and conceits about the nature of God," wrote Goodwin, was the fault of those who sought to suppress the liberty of the press. Blasphemous writings had to be publicly exposed "to become the loathing and abhorring of all men." Error, he reasoned, flourished in "spiritual darknesse" but died in the light of open controversy. "The Gospel and the truth never flourished, prospered, and triumphed at a higher rate in the world, than when errors and heresies were no otherwise restrained, punished, or opposed, than by those spiritual means, which God himself hath sanctified . . . as *viz.,* by effectual preaching of the Gospel." Opposition to the liberty of the press was "Anti-Christian," an inheritance from priests and prelates, preventing the learned and godly from having free access to printed opinions like Biddle's so that he could be rebuked and confuted. Licensing laws, Goodwin claimed, worked either to the benefit of the "Orthodox," who authorized only their own version of religious truth, or to the benefit of men like Biddle who had to resort to secret presses. The Bible clinched Goodwin's argument. He found "neither footing nor foundation in the Scriptures" for licensing laws, and he demanded to know where Christ or the Holy Ghost had authorized anyone to decide what "shall publickly go forth into the world. . . . What ground is there in the Word of God . . . to stifle or slay what books they please"? No one, civil or ecclesiastical, could be trusted with a sovereignty over the press. Censorship was inconsistent with the interests of a free government and true religion. Licensing laws inevitably tended toward the establishment of "a State Religion." Goodwin saw no reason for "a power of gagging the Press." It did no good, did a lot of damage, and did not even work. It was like coercion of conscience. Punishments and restraints were no answer. "If you saw the Books [by Biddle] that you speak of burnt by the hand of the hangman, do you think that the Errors, Heresies and Blasphemies, contained in them, would burn with them?" Goodwin concluded that the ashes of Biddle's books would propagate his opinions more than the books themselves.[57]

Biddle, although not fortunate enough to have Goodwin as his judge, had a momentary stroke of luck. Cromwell, for reasons of his own, dissolved Parliament before its attainder process got far. A few weeks later, on February 10, 1655, he allowed a court to fix bail for Biddle, pending his appearance at its session next May. At that time, on finding that Biddle was not under indictment, the court dismissed the case against him. He returned to his congregation, which began to grow. Some of the converts came from a Baptist congregation whose jealous minister challenged Biddle to an old-fashioned theological dispute. On June 28, 1655, the rival sectarians before an audience of about five hundred people disputed the question "whether Jesus Christ be the most High or Almighty God." Biddle denied the divinity of Christ throughout several hours of debate, scandalizing a faction of Presbyterians who were present. They reported the affair to the Council of State, complaining about Biddle's argument and the fact that the debate was scheduled for continuation a week later. The Council of State, with Cromwell himself in attendance, ordered the lord mayor of London to prevent the intended meeting, if necessary by arresting Biddle. The Presbyterians took their testimony to the mayor, who promptly jailed Biddle.[58]

The mayor, in concert with his aldermen and recorder, who was a magistrate, reluctantly consented to a hearing. The prisoner had the support of a small group of his friends, who included a lawyer. Because Biddle was held without a warrant, his friends demanded a specification of the charges against him. The mayor, equivocating, replied that the Council of State had ordered his commitment, to which Biddle's counsel replied that not even the council could imprison someone without a transgression of the law. The mayor asked Biddle whether he had denied Christ to be "the most High God." This time Biddle equivocated, and when the recorder handed him a copy of his *Twofold Catechism* and asked whether he wrote it, Biddle refused to answer the incriminating question. He would answer no questions against himself, he declared, "because we finde, that even Jesus Christ himself, when he was questioned before the High Priest, refused to answer in this sort." When an alderman retorted, "What Christ?" Biddle replied, "My Lord and Saviour Jesus Christ, that sitteth at the right Hand of God in the Heavens." A report of the case, written by one of Biddle's partisans, asserted that Biddle acknowledged Christ "to be his Lord and God," which sounds unlike the Biddle of 1655. Notwithstanding Biddle's conformity, the recorder produced a copy of the 1648 act against blasphemy with certain passages marked that were pertinent to the case.[59]

Biddle was the first victim of the act of 1648, because it had never been enforced. Not even Parliament's proceedings against Biddle had referred to that act. Biddle "desired the Recorder, if that were a Law, to shew him how he was liable to it." The recorder replied that many passages reached him but refused to specify which. Biddle replied with a quibble that the act did not cover his denial that "Jesus Christ was the Almighty, or the most High God." In fact his *Twofold Catechism* at many points violated the prohibitions against advocating that "the Son is not God, or that the Holy Ghost is not God, or that they Three are not one Eternal God, or that . . . Christ is not God equal with the Father." Nor could Biddle have taken the negative position in the public disputation of June without having violated the same provisions of the act. If it was still law, his guilt seemed clear to the authorities, although the recorder conceded that Biddle had not used the "very words" proscribed by the act; yet his words were "tantamount," and that was enough to bring them within the intentions of Parliament. The mayor then recommitted Biddle by a warrant dated July 10, 1655, "for publickly denying, That Jesus Christ was the Almighty or most High God." Biddle's friends tried to post bail for him, but the city authorities ruled that the accusation, being a capital felony, was not bailable. They sent him to Newgate prison where he awaited trial in the dreaded Old Bailey criminal court.[60]

Biddle's reimprisonment, this time under the act of 1648, caused consternation among the sectarians and tolerationists. Within two weeks, hawkers were selling unlicensed tracts denouncing the government and spreading alarm. Two tracts in particular, vividly describing the proceedings against Biddle, sent a shiver through sectarian readers. Their very titles attracted attention. One was *A True State of the Cause of Liberty of Conscience in the Commonwealth of England, Together with a true Narrative of the Cause, and Manner, of Mr. John Bidle's Sufferings;* the other was *The Spirit of Persecution Again broken loose, by An Attempt to put in Execution against Mr. John Bidle Master of Arts, an abrogated Ordinance . . . for punishing Blasphemies and*

Heresies. . . . The anonymous author of *The Spirit of Persecution* observed that Biddle's exact words did not match those prohibited by "the Draconic Ordinance" of 1648. If he could be brought within its terms of death by inferences, as the recorder claimed, then by the same reasoning "all Christians" breached it, "for thus we argue, he that saith Christ dyed, said that Christ was not God, for God could not dy. But every Christian saith that Christ dyed, therefore every Christian saith that Christ was not God, and so becomes guilty of death by this ordinance."[61]

Less contrived was the argument that the Instrument of Government, which was the constitution that established Cromwell's First Protectorate in December 1653, guaranteed religious liberty and rendered the act of 1648 obsolete. The Instrument of Government provided by Article 37 that Christians (anyone believing in God through Jesus Christ) "though differing in judgement from the Doctrine, Discipline, and Worship, publickly held forth, shall not be restrained from, but protected in the profession of their faith and exercise of their religion. . . ." Article 38 provided that "all acts and ordinances to the contrary are to be esteemed null and void." The catch was that Article 37 did not conflict with the orthodox contention that blasphemy was antireligious; the liberty granted was not to be abused to the injury of others or disturbance of the peace, and it did not extend "to Popery or Prelacy, nor to such as, under the profession of Christ, hold forth and practise Licentiousness."[62]

The popular understanding, however, was that Cromwell had promised liberty of conscience to all Christians. "Oh! what miserable desolations would be made in this Land, were not Liberty of Conscience allowed! It had been better for us, never to have seen a day of Liberty, than now again to return to Bondage." If Biddle suffered for his conscience, "the old Presbyterian designe of persecution" would again prevail, forcing all people to be of their opinion. That would destroy the Commonwealth and Cromwell by sapping "the foundation of our Government . . . libertie of conscience in Religion a fundamentall."[63]

A True State of the Case of Liberty of Conscience considerably amplified the argument of *Spirit of Persecution.* The anonymous author of *A True State,* who claimed to know Biddle well, described him as a peaceable and righteous Christian, although quite mistaken on some "high points" of the doctrine of the Trinity. Biddle's differences notwithstanding, he was no heretic or blasphemer. *A True State* vividly reminded readers that under the episcopacy, the grossest errors had passed for religious truths, and opinions once persecuted were now taken as orthodox. If Biddle suffered for conscience' sake, "let no man, differing from the multitude, think to go free; nor let those that now, by reason of their consent with those in power, enjoy present Liberty, dream of keeping it, except they resolve to change with the changeable Spirits of men, or the vicissitude of times." The only proper course was to emulate the example of Jesus, who fought error with argument even among those mistaken in the "highest points of Religion."[64]

From prison Biddle wrote letters on his own behalf, first to Cromwell himself, then to the president of the Council of State. He described his religious opinions and relied on the Instrument of Government for his freedom. His letters were read to the council and, for the time being, ignored. One night in the middle of August, a few weeks after, copies of an incendiary pamphlet were scattered about the streets of London: *A Short Discovery of His Highness the Lord Protector's Intentions Touching the Anabaptists in the Army*. Amid its main argument, that Cromwell was weeding the Baptists out of the army, was the claim that the Instrument of Government had become a worthless piece of paper. If it could not save Biddle from prison, might not Cromwell, a "dissembler" and a "persecutor," lock up all sectarians? The lord protector replied to the libel with a stringent new order against "Dangerous, Unwarrantable, Seditious, Blasphemous, and Scandalous" publications. Clearly Cromwell did not regard his Instrument of Government as having abrogated the act of 1648 or as having extended protection to blasphemy.[65]

On September 5, after Biddle was indicted, his case came to trial in Old Bailey. He refused to plead to the indictment unless granted counsel, but the court threatened to take him as standing mute. That meant that he could be spread-eagled on the ground, pressed with more weights than he could bear, and starved — until he pleaded. The purpose of that punishment was to extort a plea, not a confession; the law did not care whether the prisoner pleaded guilty or not guilty. Biddle pleaded not guilty and, without counsel, attacked the indictment, using the arguments his friends had employed against the lord mayor and in their tracts on Biddle's behalf. The exact words charged against him, he argued, did not coincide with the language reached by the act of 1648; anyway, the Instrument of Government had abrogated that act. At that point the court belatedly granted the prisoner counsel and took the case under advisement. Until the court met the next month, Biddle was remanded to Newgate.[66]

In the middle of September, Parliament reconvened, which raised the possibility that if the court freed Biddle, the House of Commons, not having finished with him, would again arrest him. A week later a group of his supporters, including some of his congregation, Baptists, and a few other sectarians, got an audience with Cromwell and the Council of State in order to present a petition on the prisoner's behalf. The petition described Biddle as "a man, though differing from most of us in many great matters of faith, yet by reason of his diligent study in the Holy Scripture, sober and peaceable conversation, which some of us have intimate good knowledge of, we cannot but judge every way capable of the liberty promised in the Instrument of Government." Cromwell's reply was that because the Instrument "was never intended to maintaine and protect blasphemers from the punishment of the lawes in force against them, neither would hee." He rebuked them for defending a man who held that Christ was "but a creature." Thomas Firmin, who had given Biddle room and board and paid for his lawyer, was one of the petitioners. Later he would become a great merchant-philanthropist and the leading Unitarian layman in England. In 1655 he was only twenty-three. When he pleaded for Biddle's release, Cromwell is alleged to have retorted, "You curl-pate boy you, do you think I'll show any favor to a man who denies his Saviour, and disturbs the government?" The petitioners got the last word; they published their statement for all London to read.[67]

About a week later a tract entitled *The Protector, so called, in Part Unvailed* appeared on the streets. It was the work of an anonymous ex-soldier who claimed to be a witness to the events he reported. He accused Cromwell of having "cheated and robbed his People of their Rights and Priviledges." He told how the protector had treated the petition for Biddle who lay in prison, his books burned, with none allowed to see him and death around the corner. The author blamed Cromwell for having chosen a persecuting Parliament and for having allowed "the doing of such things." Then Biddle's friends added to the public's excitement by publishing his letters of the preceding July to Cromwell and the president of the Council of State. The campaign of agitation against the government was becoming unbearable as the day for Biddle's trial in Old Bailey approached.[68]

On October 5, immediately before the court was scheduled to give its opinion on the question of whether the indictment against Biddle was defective, Cromwell took the case out of the hands of the court and decided it for himself. He banished Biddle for life, sending him under armed guard to a castle-fortress on one of the Scilly Islands about forty miles off the southwesternmost point of England. There Biddle received mild treatment, had an allowance of one hundred crowns a year for his subsistence, and had the privilege of books and writing materials.[69]

Biddle's exile was the best solution for the government's dilemma. If the court freed him, Parliament would get him. If the court convicted him, he would face the death penalty. Cromwell could not afford to have him acquitted or convicted, nor did he welcome a formal ruling on whether the Instrument of Government abrogated the act against blasphemy. If the case continued, its outcome, no matter what, would antagonize loyal subjects. Cromwell could neither jeopardize his support in Parliament nor alienate the sectarian tolerationists. He himself hated persecution and drew his strength from the sects, yet could not tolerate what he believed to be Biddle's excesses. Making him a greater martyr for the great cause of conscience risked demoralization of the radical Protestants and tempted sedition. Freeing him would outrage the conservatives and many moderates who drew distinctions between liberty and licentiousness. Biddle at liberty on a far-away prison-island satisfied no one but infuriated none.

His friends continued to work for his freedom, he periodically petitioned the protector, and for a time tracts on his behalf continued to be published. After almost three years, when Biddle was all but forgotten, Cromwell relented. Liberated but chastened, Biddle returned to London. Although he continued preaching, he published no more, and when Parliament was in session he prudently sought the safety of the countryside. A parliamentary committee, soon after Cromwell's death, sought to revive his persecution, but no report was ever made on the inquiry "how Biddle came to be released, being imprisoned for blasphemy." After the Stuart Restoration in 1660 Biddle did not dare preach in public. The prelates were once again in power as if Laud had returned from his grave to Canterbury. The Act of Uniformity in 1662 prescribed the Anglican Book of Common Prayer for every pulpit. No one might lawfully preach contrary to it, nor preach except following ordination by the episcopacy. Two months after the passage of the act, agents of the crown burst into Biddle's home while he was conducting religious service for some friends. All were arrested, tried, and fined. Nonconformity, not blasphemy, was the issue. There was nothing special about the episode. During the Stuart Restoration thousands of nonconformists, ranging from Quaker to Presbyterian, died in jail. Biddle was merely one of them. Unable to pay his £100 fine, he was kept in prison under sickening conditions. He caught a fatal malady and died in 1662 at the age of forty-seven. His congregation did not survive him, and Socinianism, once supposedly raging in every nook and corner of the realm, almost disappeared from it.[70]

8

ANTINOMIANISM RUNNING AMOK

Reminiscing about the years 1649 to 1651 when he was called "Captain of the Rant," Laurence Clarkson wrote:

> I brake the Law in all points (murther excepted:) and the ground of this my judgement was, God had made all things good, so nothing [was] evil but as man judged it; for I apprehended there was no such thing as theft, cheat, or a lie, but as man made it so; for if the creature had brought this world into no propriety [property], as *Mine* and *Thine,* there had been no such title as theft, cheat, or a lie; for the prevention hereof *Everard* and *Gerrard Winstanley* did dig up the Commons, that so all might have to live of themselves, then there had been no need of defrauding, but unity one with another.

The reference by the Ranter Clarkson to Everard and Winstanley, the Digger leaders, showed a kinship. They did not believe in private property or in sin as organized religion taught it, although they differed radically about the meaning of sin. In the spring of 1649, the Diggers, those religious mystics who sought to establish a Christian communist community, had occupied St. George's Hill in Surrey. They dug the ground and planted vegetables, because, as Winstanley explained in *The True Levellers Standard,* "the great Creator Reason made the Earth to be a Common Treasury" for all mankind. The government fined them for trespass and prosecuted them for both unlawful assembly and disorderly conduct; soldiers destroyed their little utopian community.[1]

"Digger," like "Ranter" and "Leveller," was a term of contempt. In a political tract of 1647 advocating the sovereignty of the common people, Clarkson spoke of the "True Levellers," a name which the Diggers adopted. Cromwell despised them all — Levellers, True Levellers, and Ranters. "Did not the levelling principle," he asked, "tend to reducing all to an equality . . . to make the tenant as liberal a fortune as the landlord?" Winstanley, knowing that poor people worked for only four pence a day and that the price of flour was high, remembered the prediction "The poor shall inherit the earth," and he added, "I tell you, the scripture is to be really and materially fulfilled . . . you jeer at the name Leveller. I tell you Jesus Christ, who is that powerfull Spirit of Love, is the Head Leveller."[2]

Men of the "true" levelling principle, Diggers and Ranters, were a tiny minority who posed no military or political threat, but their theory resonated subversion of Christian society. Even the Socinians, as well as the Baptists and other autonomous congregational sects, could agree on that. If Paul Best, John Fry, and John Biddle had converted much of the nation to their antitrinitarianism, England's momentum toward intellectual freedom and an open society would have accelerated, but the future would not have significantly differed. If the Levellers, the constitutional radicals led by John Lilburne, Richard Overton, and John Wildman, had triumphed, political democracy would have come swiftly, followed by some amelioration of the injustices of the class system and the economic order. If Winstanley, Clarkson, and Abiezer Coppe had prevailed, law and order, the Protestant ethic, private property, the class system, and even Christianity itself might have disintegrated in a revolutionary and blasphemous upheaval. Although the threat of such an upheaval remained rhetorical, the government summarily squashed it. The Ranters could not be ignored; they were too blatantly offensive, deliberately going to extremes to shock, to show contempt for society, and to scorn its right to judge them. As political radicals, the Ranters had the clout of pipsqueaks, but as antinomian libertines, they stirred envy, disgust, and hostility, as did their late-medieval precursors, the Brethren of the Free Spirit.

Antinomianism defies definition even more than Puritanism or Independency. The word in its narrowest sense means being against the law — generally, the moral law, specifically, the Ten Commandments. But antinomianism need not be taken in its narrowest sense except, perhaps, in the case of those who, like the Ranters, wholly repudiated the concept of sin. Too narrow a definition of antinomianism misses its religious argument, namely that God's grace being unbounded, eternal salvation is open to all, that salvation begins here on earth and not beyond the grave, and that the righteous or moral man does not, or cannot, sin. A world of difference exists, of course, between "does not" and "cannot." The antinomians lived in that contradictory world and could not consistently resolve its contradiction.

Antinomianism begins with the proposition that human nature is perfectible and is perfected even in this world through the gift of divine grace. God makes the moral law subordinate to His grace or love, just as He makes the spirit of the Bible transcend its letter. Antinomians such as Behmenists, Familists, Grindletonians, Seekers, and Quakers, believed that divine inspiration and spiritual regeneration perfected the soul, making the acts of a righteous or perfected man correspond with and even supersede the moral law. In Christ none can sin; sin is a temporary aberration pardonable through spiritual regeneration. Antinomians magnified the compelling nature of grace. They emphasized man as redeemed, not man as the fallen and depraved Adam. They focused on Paul's doctrine that salvation is attained not by observance of the Law but by faith inspired by the divine spark within the soul. Christ, Paul proclaimed, lived within him (Gal. 2:20). The "Father is in me" is also a doctrine of the Gospel of John 10:38. An Epistle of John reinforced antinomianism's mystical principles: "No one born of God commits sin; for God's nature abides in him" (1 John 3:9), and "God abides in us and his love is perfected in us" (1 John 4:12).[3]

Antinomian readings of such texts were intensely exalting, personal, and liberating. Antinomianism was not easily communicable or understandable to someone not on the same spiritual wavelength. Antinomians scarcely agreed among themselves. Perhaps there were as many brands of antinomianism as there were inner selves. The Ranters reflected an extreme: antinomianism run amok into religious anarchism. Not that there was a different sort of rant for every Ranter, but Ranters differed sharply. Joseph Salmon, George Foster, Laurence Clarkson, William Franklin, and John Robins were dissimilar Ranters but definably Ranters. A former Ranter fancifully classified seven types of schools of Ranters and to each gave an exotic name — Familists, Shelomethes, Clements, Athians, Nicholartanes, Marcions, and Seleutian Donatists. The Ranters themselves made no such distinctions, did not worship in churches of any sort, and never organized into sects.[4]

The conduct and opinions of Abiezer Coppe suggest why he became the most notorious of the Ranters, although he was no more "typical" than any other Ranter. The repressions of Coppe's early life suggest reasons for his later libertinism. So puritanical was his upbringing that thoughts of hell consumed him; he kept a daily register of his sins and "did constantly confess." His tears, he wrote, were his drink; ashes, his meat; and his life, "zeal, devotion, and exceeding strictness." At seventeen, he entered Oxford as a "poor scholar" to study for the ministry, but the Civil War ended his formal education. An enthusiast for the parliamentary cause, he became a preacher to an army garrison. Drifting from Presbyterianism to Baptism, he continued his search for religious satisfaction. The histrionic powers that Coppe later displayed as a Ranter must have been at his command as an itinerant Baptist preacher, for he claimed to have "dipped" about seven thousand people.

In 1649, a year that began with the execution of Charles I and ended in the sudden emergence of Ranterism, Coppe underwent a spiritual conversion that was not at all uncommon at the time. He heard terrifying thunderclaps, saw a light as dazzling as the sun and as red as fire, and "with joy unspeakable in the spirit, I clapt my hands and cryed out, *Amen, Halelujah, Halelujah, Amen.*" Trembling and sweating, he felt divine grace sweeping over him. "Lord," he shouted, "what wilt thou do with me," and the "eternal glory" in him answered that he would be taken into the everlasting kingdom after first being thrown into "the belly of hell." He was among all the devils, he reported, but "under all this terrour, and amazement, there was a little spark of transcendent, transplendent, unspeakable glory . . . triumphing, exulting, and exalting itself," till at last he saw the "Eternal Majesty" and heard a voice saying, "The spirits of just men made perfect." It was the antinomian message: a pure or sanctified man can do no evil. After four days and nights of revelations, Coppe received his divine commission; he must go to the great city of London to spread his new gospel. Thus, he explained his conversion to Ranterism as a spiritual experience, although by conventional standards of morality and religion Ranterism was obscene, blasphemous, and seditious.[5]

In London Coppe preached his antinomian version of the doctrine of the Free Spirit — Christ's death liberated mankind from sin, God dwells within everyone, and all shall be saved, all except perhaps the prosperous and powerful. Coppe's theology was saturated with a hatred of the rich. He assaulted "men and women of the greater rank" in the city streets, ranting and gnashing his teeth at them, while proclaiming that the day of the Lord, the "great Leveller," had come. He embraced the poor and the diseased, and he became a libertine. "Twas usual with him," recorded an Oxonian biographer who knew him, "to preach stark naked many blasphemies and unheard-of Villanies in the Day-time, and in the Night to drink and lye with a Wenche, that had been also his hearer, stark naked." He was imprisoned for fourteen weeks, possibly for similar conduct. In London he fell in with Laurence Clarkson and an orgiastic group of Ranters who called themselves "My One Flesh," probably to symbolize their unity with all God's creatures. A 1650 vignette of "Ranters ranting" depicts Coppe, "their Ring-leader," as having drunkenly "bestowed an hours time in belching forth imprecations, curses, and other such like stuffe, as is not fit to be once named among Christians." He was supposed to have retired that night with two of his "she-Disciples." The rumor was that "he commonly lay in bed with two women at a time." The cursing, nudity, adultery, drunkenness, and generally immoral behavior (none of it sinful to Coppe), reflected the Ranter repudiation of Puritan middle-class conventions.[6]

Coppe's eloquent and cadenced biblical rhetoric was a mix of mystical ravings and social radicalism. Antinomianism (a repudiation of the moral law), millenarianism (the imminence of the second coming), pantheism (the doctrine that God dwells within all creatures), and a repudiation of private property suffused Coppe's utterances. In late 1649 he wrote his sensational tracts, A Fiery Flying Roll [of Thunder] and its successor of the same title. The two tracts purported to be Coppe's witness to a divine warning issued against "all the Great Ones of the Earth." Their dreadful day of judgment was at hand. God would save England with a vengeance. The gospel, according to Coppe, was "I overturn, overturn, overturn." The bishops, lords, and king had had their turn, and the surviving great ones would be next. Although Coppe identified God as "Universal Love," served by "perfect freedome, and pure Libertinisme," the love did not extend to those who could not endure "levelling." "Behold, behold, behold, I the eternall God, the Lord of Hosts, who am that mighty Leveller, am comming (yea even at the doores) to Levell in good earnest . . . putting down the mighty from their seats; and exalting them of low degree. . . ." God would level riches and bring "parity, equality, community" to avenge the deaths of the army Levellers who had been shot for mutiny. Coppe himself was a pacifist who repudiated "sword levelling, or digging levelling"; rather than fight he preferred to be drunk "every day of the weeke, and lye with whores." The real sins, he declared to the great ones, were wealth, pomp, and property — and taking the "enslaved ploughmans money from him." Coppe would rather starve than do that, although stealing from the rich was no sin.

Mine eares are filled brim full with cryes of poor prisoners, Newgate, Ludgate cryes (of late) are seldome out of mine eares. Those dolefull cryes, Bread, bread, bread, for the Lords sake, pierce mine eares, and heart, I can no longer forbeare.

Werefore high you apace to all prisons in the Kingdome,

Bow before those poore, nasty louisie, ragged wretches, say to them . . . we let you go free, and serve you,

Do this or (as I live saith the Lord), thine eyes (at least) shall be boared out, and thou carried captive in a strange Land.

. . . undo the heavy burdens, let the oppressed go free, and breake every yoake. Deale thy bread to the hungry, and bring the poore that are cast out (both of houses and Synagogues) to thy house. Cover the naked: Hide not they self from thine own flesh, from a creeple, a rogue, a begger, he's thine own flesh. From a Whoremonger, a thief, &c. he's flesh of thy flesh, and his theft, and whoredome is flesh of thy flesh also, thine own flesh.[7]

In an anticlerical passage, Coppe represented God as demanding that branding with the letter "B" for blasphemy be ended. The clergy could not judge "what is sinne, what not, what evill, and what not, what blasphemy, and what not." They served God and Jesus for money, and for all their learning could not understand the real meaning of sin: oppressing the people. Coppe reversed orthodox values when he declared his belief that what was called good was evil, "and Evill Good; Light Darknesse, and Darknesse Light; Truth Blasphemy, and Blasphemy Truth." To the pure, all things are pure. Cursing by some was more glorious than praying by others. What God cleansed should not be called unclean.[8]

The second *Fiery Flying Roll* warned those who had "many baggs of money" that the Great Leveller would come "as a thief in the night" with sword drawn, and say "deliver your purse, deliver sirrah! deliver or I'll cut thy throat." The rich should turn over their wealth to the cripples, lepers, rogues, thieves, whores, and to all the poor, "who are flesh of thy flesh, and every whit as good as thy self in mine eye. . . ." The "fat swine of the earth" would soon "go to the knife," if they did not obey the command to "give, give, give, give up, give up your houses, horses, goods, gold, Lands, give up, account nothing your own, have ALL THINGS common, or els the plague of God will rot and consume all that you have." In other chapters Coppe explained how he had found "unspeakable glory" in the basest things, how he had found God in gypsies and jailbirds ("mine own brethren and sisters, flesh of my flesh, and as good as the greatest Lord in England"), and how the path to salvation lay in abandoning "stinking family duties," biblical laws, and personal possessions. The presence of God within him filled his life with joy and beauty, not to mention "concubines without number." In his final chapters Coppe returned to the theme that kings, princes, and lords, "the great ones," who pleaded "priviledge and Prerogative from Scripture," must yield to "the poorest Peasants" to fulfill the grand design: "equality, community, and universall love." His closing jeremiad (from James 5:1)—"Howl, howl, ye nobles, howl honourable, howl ye rich men for the miseries that are coming upon you"—revealed Coppe's utopian vision: "For our parts, we that hear the APOSTLE preach, will also have all things in common; neither will we call any thing that we have our own . . . wee'l eat our bread together in singleness of heart, wee'l break bread from house to house." The same thought is in Winstanley.[9]

Abiezer Coppe was a religious eccentric and a spiritual anarchist, but he was not demented and, judged by his time, was not a capricious sport. Millenarian and mystical traditions reached back into the Middle Ages. The foremost doctrine of Ranterism, that God lives within every creature, was an old heresy bolstered by scriptural evidence. That heresy thrived in the thirteenth and fourteenth centuries in most of Europe as the Free Spirit movement, and it cropped out in an entirely different form in Elizabethan England when Dutch and German immigrants imported Henry Nicholas's Familist beliefs. Christopher Vitells, a disciple of Nicholas, translated his works into English. The Familists survived royal persecution and the libels of even radical sectarians. Henry Ainsworth, a Separatist, in 1608 said that no one wrote "more blasphemously" than Nicholas; and Edmond Jessop, who despised English Anabaptists, described the Familists as "the most blasphemous and erroneous sect this day in the world." Yet Nicholas explicitly repudiated libertinism and preached that personal righteousness bears witness to a new life, which showed that one has experienced the inward revelation that God or Christ is within his spirit. Such mystical knowledge led to the Familist belief that regenerated people, in whom Christ dwells, have reached perfection and cannot sin; that belief opened Familists to the antinomian charge. They also invited denunciation by exalting the spirit above Scripture. Anabaptists advocated similar principles, and so did the Behmenists. Others, called Seekers, believing that there was no true church yet, wandered in search of a revelation of God's glory. Even John Murton, the tolerant Baptist leader, condemned Familists and Seekers (although he would not silence them) for advocating the "libertine doctrine" that people need not hear preaching nor read the Bible. Gilbert Roulston, who was once a Ranter, designated a particular school of them as Familists or members of the Family of Love which he traced to a German of Elizabeth's time. Another anti-Ranter writer entitled his tract *The Bottomles Pit Smoaking in Familisme*.[10]

Familism influenced Coppe and the Ranters. In 1649, the turning point in the history of Ranterism, four of Nicholas's English books were reprinted. But Ranterism was more directly a product of the Civil War of the 1640s and of the revolutionary upheavals that accompanied it. The period was both disruptive and creative. The overthrow of the episcopacy and of their ecclesiastical courts, which had maintained law, order, and status, and helped keep people in subjugation to state and church, snapped religious restraints. People formed "gathered churches" or voluntary congregations and separated from society. They advocated universal grace and took up all sorts of old heresies as if they were new revelations. The inner light in the soul of the individual believer, whatever he believed, became the highest standard of authority in spiritual matters. Judging what was sinful was left to personal conscience, and men were saying that the clergy, with the support of the rulers, had invented sin as a means of suppression. People felt emancipated. They were free from sin and from prosecutions for sin; they were free to form their own congregations, to preach as they pleased, or to choose lay preachers. They felt free to argue against and reject the orthodoxies of the past. In the absence of effective censorship, those who dreamed of new worlds freely expressed themselves. Infinite liberty and utopia seemed within the realm of possibility, especially in religious matters. Next to instinctual needs, religion was still the most important aspect of life — and of death. John Biddle, the Socinian, rationally rejected original sin and eternal damnation, while uneducated people — herdsmen, tinkers, soap makers, and weavers — instinctively came to the same conclusions.

In 1644 a conservative identified "Antinomians and Familists" as "enemies of civil government, who seek to overthrow the eternall Law of God, on which the civil law is built. . . ." He was saying, in effect, that religious questions contain or mask political and social issues. That is also an inference that can be drawn from a sermon preached before the House of Commons by Thomas Case in 1647. Case warned that if liberty be granted to sectaries, people would claim their birthright to be free from Parliaments and kings and even rebel against them. "Liberty of conscience, falsely so called," Case added, "may in good time improve itself into liberty of estates and liberty of houses and liberty of wives." Within a year Levellers mutinied in the army, and in the next year a king was beheaded, while Diggers, Ranters, and others proclaimed that property should be shared in common and that there should be free love. The free exercise of religion, coming almost all at once in the 1640s, after the sudden breakdown of the usual controls, burst forth in a torrent of exotic and eccentric religious opinions, many of which were precursors of Ranterism. And many openly or impliedly expressed political positions.[11]

In that, nothing was new. When there was a dispute, provoked by Laud, within the Church of England on the placement of the altar, the issue was as much over who should control the church as it was theological. If the altar was at the far end of the church, above the congregation and railed off from them, the people received the sacrament from the priest on their knees before the railing; if the altar was a table within the nave, on a level with the congregation, they could take the sacrament closer to God, seated, and on equal terms with the priest. Presbyterians wanted the elders to select the minister, while the Independents said that the whole congregation should choose him: the theological issue pitted ecclesiastical oligarchy against congregational democracy. So did the sectarian demand for lay preachers, especially because the pulpit was a public rostrum for the expression of political and social ideas. Thomas Edwards, the Presbyterian cataloguer of the heresies and blasphemies that infected England in 1646, believed, rightly, that many disorders attributable to wrong opinions and practices derived from "mechanics taking upon them[selves] to preach and baptize, as [did] Smiths, Taylors, Shoo-makers, Peddlars, Weavers," and even women.[12]

The Calvinist doctrine of predestination was obviously theological but was as surely political in its implications. Sin having corrupted human nature, eternal damnation was the just reward for all mankind. God in His mercy, however, had for His own reasons predestined some people for salvation; they were the elect. Although they could not know they were the saints, their spiritual rigor and material prosperity were a sign, that made them best qualified to govern church and state. But if Christ had died for all mankind and all were saved, then all were equally qualified to govern. Amid the "gangrene" in Protestantism, Edwards reported, was the common doctrine "That by Christs death, all the sins of all the men in the world, Turks, Pagans, as well as Christians committed against the morall Law and first Covenant, are actually pardoned and forgiven, and this is the everlasting Gospel," meaning universal salvation. Edwards listed corollary doctrines that the Ranters would popularize. The Creator was responsible for people's sins and for the "Pravity, Ataxy, Anomy" which is in them. God loves them whether they pray or sin, do good or evil. It could not stand with the goodness of God to damn his own creatures eternally, "nor would he pick and choose among people in showing mercy, for if he manifested his love to only a few, "it is far from being infinite."[13]

Two other "errours" in Edwards's catalogue concern Ranterism. One was the argument for religious liberty made by Roger Williams in a book of 1644 which Parliament ordered burned. Some "eminent sectaries" endorsed the argument, Edwards said, and they added that where conscience was concerned, "the Magistrate may not punish for blasphemies, nor for denying the Scriptures, nor for denying there is a God." The second, in Aesopian language, was "That God the Father did reign under the Law, God the Son under the Gospel, and now God the Father and God the Son are making over the Kingdon to God the holy Ghost, and he shall reign and be poured out upon all flesh." That was remarkably like the message of *A Rout, A Rout,* the first Ranter tract of early 1649, by Joseph Salmon. He believed that God had progressively manifested himself: first, when he gave the Law to Moses, then when he revealed himself through Jesus, and finally in the present age, when he destroyed the monarchy and was spreading his spirit upon all the people of England. But Parliament and the army, Salmon wrote, had made themselves "as absolute and tyrannicall as ever the King"; the "Grandees," he warned, should watch out, "for the Lord is now comming forth to Rip up your bowels." If the Grandees laid down their swords and sought deliverance, they would replace oppression with "a blessed Freedom."[14]

Salmon wrote shortly after Charles had been beheaded, when the Rump Parliament — the approximately fifty Independents who survived Pride's Purge of the Presbyterians — and the Council of State governed England. For people like Salmon, Clarkson, and Coppe, "the fall of the monarchy," as A.L. Morton recently observed, "was only the first stage in vast changes by which the whole social order would be turned upside down." Radicals versed in the Bible expected that "the world would be turned upside down" (Acts 17:6). England had become a republic; even the House of Lords had been abolished. Yet the country was governed as autocratically as ever. The government represented substantial property owners and the generals of the New Model Army. "We were before ruled by King, Lords, and Commons," said a Leveller leader, "now by a General, a Court Martial, and House of Commons: and we pray you what is the difference?"[15]

Ranterism probably developed because the difference was so very little, blasting the expectations of many people and leading them back to religious expression as their only consolation — and their only way of venting defiance against everything their rulers stood for. The "tyranny" of the generals and of Commons was a Ranter theme. For a time there had been a reasonable expectation that a New Jerusalem would arise in England. The constitutional radicals, the Levellers under John Lilburne, demanded popular sovereignty, a genuinely democratic government, and civil and religious liberty. The common soldiers of the New Model Army constituted the rank and file of the Leveller movement and of the gathered churches of the sectaries. The Civil War seemed to them a revolution signalizing the reconstruction of society. William Dell, one of the leading preachers of the army, told his congregation of soldiers, "the power is in you, the people; keep it, part not with it." He said of them, after a victory over royalist forces, "Poor illiterate, mechanic men turned the world upside down." Leveller leaders encouraged the vision that the ordinary people were on the threshold of inheriting the earth. Richard Overton, in his *Appeale . . . to the . . . free people in general*, wrote, "I am confident that it must be the poor, the simple and mean things of this earth that must confound the mighty and strong." But the Levellers miscalculated their strength when negotiating with the generals, "the Grandees," for a united front in securing their program from Parliament. The people, a Leveller despairingly wrote, grieved: "they are deceived, their expectations . . . frustrated, and their liberty betrayed." A royalist commentator pointed to the reason: "The Grandees and the Levellers can as soon combine as fire and water; the one aim at pure democracy, the others at an oligarchy."[16]

When the generals rejected the Leveller program, the radicals had no choice but to submit or rebel. Their leaders repudiated the government and the generals in a manifesto calling for the abolition of the Council of State because it was a front for military despotism. The House of Commons condemned that seditious tract as tending to cause mutiny in the army and branded its authors as traitors. On the next day, Cromwell arrested Lilburne, Overton, and two others, sending them to the Tower of London on a charge of treason. From the Tower they published further incitements, including the third Agreement of the Free People, the climax of Leveller thought. A week later mutiny broke out in the army, but Cromwell responded with overwhelming force. His defeat of the Levellers at Burford destroyed their military power. By no coincidence, Ranterism soon became prominent. "You have killed the Levellers," Coppe accused the "Great Ones," and "Ye have killed the just." That refrain, like his assault on the rich, was an echo from James 5:6.[17]

Ranterism was a religious phenomenon among the defeated and disillusioned political left. Politics had failed, pamphleteering had failed, mutiny had failed. Only religion remained. When the Stuart tyrant was beheaded in January 1649, there had been talk about King Jesus succeeding King Charles. Regicide, the defeat at Burford, and the dispersion of the Diggers later the same year were shattering events that provoked a crisis of faith. If the time of deliverance was at hand, millenarian expectations and social radicalism required further revelations. George Fox began his travels throughout England in 1649, proclaiming his "Quaker" message of love and the divinity within all persons. Those who became Fifth Monarchists first insisted in 1649 that the kingdom be turned over to them, to be governed by officers appointed by the power of Christ. Others survived their despair by becoming Ranters.[18]

The Ranter message was a peculiar one to be cast in religious terms; but religion was then the universal language, and Ranterism was an expression of religious conviction, not a loss of religion. The Ranters shared the universal craving for a communion with God, although they understood Him differently. They saw the inhumanity of man to man, and they could not stand their pain. They lost their revolution and could not stand their grief. And they reacted extravagantly in a form of religiously inspired surrealism, which was anchored in the familiar Familist heresy of the immanence or indwelling of God as the activating force of the universe.

What set the Ranters apart, though, was the surrealist way that they translated their visions. They acknowledged no authority but their own intuition and emotional satisfactions. They allowed their subconscious to reveal itself in their theology and in the uncensored conduct of their daily lives. Their imagery was nonrational, their style frenzied, their subjectivity intense. They exaggerated everything for emotive purposes. Their fantasy, that they were truly liberated people, led them from spiritual ecstasies to crude and energetic sensationalism. They made a principle out of unsocial conduct, sexual promiscuity, and even madness. And, of course, they raved vehemently and interminably, giving rise to the name by which they were called. They smoked tobacco even as they preached, drank and cursed heavily, fornicated lustily, ate gluttonously, tended to shiftlessness, and in every way imaginable tried to be shocking. If a Ranter had known French, he would have shouted, "Épater le bourgeois!"

Their extravagent flouting of normative conduct also reflected the Ranters' belief that the normative principles were no longer right and authoritative. Depression, war, revolution, and betrayal led to an erosion of confidence in the guides that conventionally defined conscience. The Fifth Monarchist, the Familist, the Behmenist, the Leveller, the Digger, the Seeker, the Quaker, and other radicals were not libertines, although each in his own way, like the Ranter, was a symptom of and a response to widespread social breakdown. Only the Ranter greedily practiced a rejection of the moral law. The values and institutions of England no longer commanded the respect of tens of thousands of people, but all radicals except the Ranters belonged to the overwhelming majority who still professed the conventional standards of morality. The majority determined what was eccentric, crazy, and dangerous; the same majority defined blasphemy. By every standard but their own the Ranters were blasphemous. A basically Puritan society had to prosecute them. Yet Ranter blasphemy, although calculated, perverse, and threatening, was usually harmless defiance. Its harmlessness did not mitigate its offensiveness. But its offensiveness was chiefly a matter of sensibility. Cursing, whoring, and theft appalled moralists, but war, profit making, and poverty were at least as shocking to Ranter sensibilities as Ranter blasphemy was to Puritan sensibilities. Ranter blasphemy, which is to say, Ranter theology, was a symptom of anomie, unlike Socinian blasphemy, which was a reflection of rationalism. Ranters believed that people were not responsible for the "pravity, ataxy, anomy" within them. In that belief they were not wholly wrong. But they did not blame society for their abnormal convictions and behavior. They blamed no one. They gave credit where credit was due: all that is in man, all that he feels, all that he does, is God-given, for God is the creator, omnipotent and all-wise.

God was that and much more to the Ranters, because they carried every principle to its logical extreme — and beyond. John Holland, "an eye and ear witness" who wrote a reliable description of their theology, not surprisingly condemned their "Atheistical blasphemies." They maintained, he wrote, that God is as much in a leaf as in an angel. He heard one Ranter say that God did not exist except in creatures and that men should pray to no god "but what was in them." They called God "the Being, the Fulnesse, the Great motion, Reason, the Immensity," and one Ranter said that if there was any god, he was it. When Holland called that blasphemy, because man could not create as God could, the Ranter replied, "he was not The God, but he was God, because God was in him and in every creature in the world. . . ." Jacob Bauthumley, who spoke reverentially for a Ranter, had their usual pantheistic view; he saw God in every flower, indeed in "Man and Beast, Fish and Fowle, and every green thing from the highest Cedar to the Ivey on the wall." God was the life and being of all, "doth really dwell in all," framed men's thoughts and was in all their acts — all of them. Like other Ranters, Bauthumley abandoned an anthropomorphic concept of God as well as a God who favored an elect of any sort. His god was little more than a divine spirit suffusing everything alive. To some Ranters God was even in inanimate things, incarnate in the furniture in the room. One reasoned logically that if God was in all things, "then he is sin and wickedness; and if he be all things, then he is this Dog, this Tobacco-pipe, he is me, and I am him. . . ." Bauthumley said that man could not know, believe in, or pray to God. Richard Coppin concluded that if God was perfect and was in every man, each person was perfect; so, none could sin. To Abiezer Coppe, God was not only the great Leveller; he was base things, unspotted beauty, and the divine Being. "My spirit dwells with God," said Coppe, "sups with him, in him, feeds on him, with him, in him."[19]

Whatever God was to the Ranters, he was never evil to them or connected with it. They attributed God to everything useful or enjoyable—a table, sex, children, a daisy, comradeship. They did not find godliness in the things they opposed—war, disease, wealth, inequality, churches. Yet they insisted illogically that God created everything and dwelt in everything. Christ had no significance for them, except as a rarely used synonym for God; the Christ of the Bible meant as little to them as the Bible. Laurence Clarkson "really believed no Moses, Prophets, Christ or Apostles, no resurrection at all."[20]

The Bible laid down the moral law, the Ten Commandments. To Ranters it was merely the work of men, a human invention, a figment of the imagination. Some Ranters construed the Bible as a collection of allegories. The Resurrection, for example, was spiritual, not of the body. Christ's coming meant the saving of all men or free grace. For others, who rejected the Bible altogether, scriptural truths had no meaning. The sense of God within man should be his guide, not the Bible. It was, they said, a "dead letter," a "piece of Witchcraft," and "but a meer Romance." One said that it consisted of tales "to keep People in subjection," and had as much truth in it as the history of Tom Thumb. The Commandments of both Old and New Testaments were "fruits of the curse" from which the grace of God freed mankind. Heaven, hell, the afterlife, and sin were fictions, said the Ranters, to enslave people and make them content with their lot. Clarkson thought there was nothing after death. He would "know nothing after this my being was dissolved." Even as a stream was distinct from the ocean till it entered the ocean, he said, so he was distinct from God until death returned his spirit to God and "became one with God, yea God it self." He spoke too of death as no more than rot and corruption. Heaven was pleasure in this world; hell was poverty, sickness, or in Bauthumely's phrase, "an accusing conscience." The Ranters had fun with the concept of the Devil. He was, they said, just an old woman stuffed with parsley or the rearend of God and not really a bad fellow, because he too was a creation of God.[21]

Sin, another fiction, was the invention of churches to make a living for priests. Ranters were fond of the royal motto "Evil to him who evil thinks," and insisted, like Coppe and Clarkson, "To the pure all things are pure." "Whatever I do," said Clarkson, "is acted by that Majesty in me." From that he concluded that "Scripture, Churches, Saints, and Devils are no more to me than the cutting off of a Dog's head." God was good; He was in every act; therefore every act was good. Clarkson applied his simple logic to swearing, drunkenness, adultery, and theft. He drew the line at murder and, perhaps, at praying in church. All else was the product of God and perfected by His wisdom. The very name "sin,"

Clarkson said, was but "a name without substance, hath no being in God, nor in the Creature, but only of the imagination." Men reached perfection and grew closer to divinity if they could commit "sins" with no remorse or shame. None could be free from sin "till in purity it be acted as no sin." Clarkson clinched his point by claiming that a man would continue to feel sin until he "can lie with all women as one woman, and judge it not a sin." In an anti-Ranter tract by "a late fellow-Ranter," an eyewitness described a Ranter meeting in a tavern as affirming

> that that man who tipples deepest, swears the frequentest, commits adultery, incest, or buggers the oftenest, blasphemes the imprudentest, and perpetrates the most notorious crimes with the highest hand, and rigedest resolution, is the dearest darling to be gloriously placed in the tribunal Throne of Heaven, holding this detestable Opinion, (equalizing themselves with our blessed Redeemer) that it is lawful for them to drink healths to their Brother *Christ*, and that in [drinking] their liquor, each Brother ought to take his Fellow-Female upon his knee, saying Let us lie down and multiply. . . . *O most horrible blasphemy*!

People believed that Ranters regarded sexual intercourse as the highest sacrament and, therefore, that they supposed it was no sin for "hundreds of Men and Women (savage like) to lie with each other, publickly all together, either in Houses, Fields, or Streets, which is their constant course. . . ." Pornographic woodcuts depicting lascivious conduct by Ranters illustrated *Strange Newes from Newgate and the Old Baily,* a tract that retailed the sensational evidence given at the trial of two Ranters charged with blasphemy. Ranters were amusing as well as repellent. One of them took a candle and in broad daylight began hunting about the rooms of a tavern, saying "that he sought for his sins, but there were none, and that which they [the police] thought so great unto him, was so small, that he could not see it."[22]

Ranters liked to meet in taverns — houses of God, Clarkson called them. Ephraim Pagitt, in a clever phrase, called Ranters "the merriest of devils." They sang bawdy songs, often to the tune of church hymns; they whistled, danced, clapped hands, and reputedly enjoyed orgies. One critic spoke of their "prodigious pranks, and unparalleled deportments," and another entitled his comic, anti-Ranter play *The Jovial Crew, or the Devill turn'd Ranter* (1651). Dining was a ritual that some Ranters turned into a travesty on the Christian Mass. One police informant testified that he saw a group in a tavern eating a piece of beef and "one of them took it in his hand, tearing it asunder said to the other, *This is the flesh of Christ, take and eat.* The other took a cup of Ale and threw it into the chimney corner, saying, *There is the bloud of Christ.*" They discussed God over their meal, and one said he could go to the outhouse *"and make a God every morning,* by easing his body."[23]

Some Ranters were undoubtedly scatalogical and coarse, and much in Ranterism was outrageous and deliberately disrespectful. But by pushing the doctrines of free grace and human perfection to the outermost limits of antinomian practice, the Ranters seized upon what was for them an enormous truth — organized religion stifled human expression. They blamed religion for muzzling people's emotional lives. Using theological terms disabled the Ranters from saying that religion had failed man; they intended what Freud meant when he said religion was the universal neurosis. Their intense subjectivity, which was based on hopelessness, was no program, but it was no more unrealistic than the Diggers' economics or the Levellers' politics, both of which had failed. By vomiting away moral repressions, Ranters sought to emancipate the inner lives of people. Their lifestyle was an invitation for all to live out relatively harmless but socially disruptive fantasies; Ranterism was a purge for sickening anxieties and for an oppressive sense of guilt, especially about sex. Coppe and Clarkson, wild as they were, spoke to the alienated person, alienated from his own inner life as well as from his "fellow Creatures."

The Ranter fantasy was that man could return to Eden, the godly inheritance which religion denied. Before the Fall, God was a benefactor, the world was good, and man did not know evil. After the Fall, the Ranters were saying, the God of theology appeared, vengeful and arbitrary; it was he whom they rejected. Orthodox theology represented Adam as the sinner and Eve as temptation, not as love or fulfillment. The Ranters offered an alternative theology as well as an alternative lifestyle. Unfortunately we have no Ranter statements by women, but the sexual content of the writings of the Ranter men and even of the anti-Ranter writings implies that Ranter women were willing believers and partners. The first Ranter sermon that Clarkson heard was preached by a Mary Lake. In a titillating pamphlet, *The Ranter's Last Sermon,* "Mistress E.B.," in mixed company, went to one of the men and offered "to unbutton his Cod-piece." When her partner asked why, she is supposed to have replied, "For sin: whereupon . . . in the sight of all the rest, they commit Fornication." If she did reply "For sin," she was jesting, because as the author of the pamphlet acknowledged, Ranters believed that "whatsoever they did was Good and not Evill, there being no such thing as sin in the world."[24]

The England of the Ranters was a Puritan society in which the foremost connotation of sin was sexual. John Holland, an accurate though hostile reporter, depicted the women as equal beneficiaries of free love. "They say," he wrote, "that for one man to be tied to one woman, or one woman to one man, is a fruit of the curse; but, they say, we are freed from the curse, therefore it is our liberty to make use of whom we please." Another critic, in *The Routing of the Ranters*, claimed that "the woman doth commonly make choice of the man she will dwell with." The lack of contraceptives doubtless robbed women of that equality. Gerrard Winstanley, the Digger, warned women to "beware this ranting practise." It burdened them with excessive childbearing. The mother and the children were likely, he said, "to have the worst of it, for the man will be gone and leave them . . . after he hath his pleasure." Winstanley was probably right, but he missed the point that the Ranters hungered for an emotional expression, of which sex was a part, that religion inhibited. He did not understand, either, that the Ranter advocacy of extreme individual freedom represented a desperate search for psychological health. It was present even in Jacob Bauthumley's attempt to understand God: "If I say I love thee, it is nothing so, for there is in me nothing can love thee but thy self; and therefore thou dost but love thy self: My seeking of thee is no other but thy seeking of thy self: My delighting enjoying thee, is no other but thy delighting in thy selfe, and enjoying of thy selfe after a most un-conceivable manner." Bauthumley's narcissistic illusion that he loved the God within him expressed a drive to fulfill himself through someone else.[25]

The Ranters fed a hunger in people. John Taylor wrote in 1651 that heretics used to emerge one by one, "but now they sprout by huddles and clusters (like locusts out of the bottomless pit). They now come thronging upon us in swarms, as the Caterpillers of Aegypt." He was speaking of the Ranters. Samuel Sheppard, who thought the devil had turned Ranter, claimed that same year, "All the world now is in the Ranting humour." In 1652 Durand Hotham, a justice of the peace, told George Fox, the founding Quaker, that "all the justices of the nation" could not have prevented England from being "overspread with Ranterism." These were doubtlessly exaggerated statements; although Ranters existed throughout England, in both town and country, their strength lay in London among the teeming poor. They attracted un-skilled workers, petty artisans, the unemployed, vagabonds, former soldiers, and underworld elements. Ranterism had a lower-class character. Coppe romantically identified with thieves, whores and beg-gars. Salmon addressed *A Rout, A Rout* to fellow soldiers "of inferior rank and quality." The caterpillars of Egypt notwithstanding, Ranters usually congregated in small groups. Even before the government launched its campaign to suppress them, they tended to be a secretive underground movement. When Clarkson first tried to meet the Ranters who called themselves "My One Flesh," he had to be given introductions to one intermediary after another. In London the Ranters probably numbered thousands, but their constituency never competed with the organized denominations or with the gathered churches. Ranterism was more boisterous and articulate than truly dangerous. Focusing on what their leaders said can make them sound dangerous. A. L. Morton observed that leveling as the Ranters understood it "involved a far greater social upheaval than the political changes advanced by Lilburne and his associates, or Winstanley's quite limited proposals for a joint cultivation of the commons and waste land." But for all their militancy, Ranters were pacifists and appealed "only to the defeated and de-classed, the lower strata of the urban poor, and upon these no substantial movement could possibly be built." They were also badly organized, if organized at all, and schismatic. They did not even have a program. Men who left the movement revealed that a "Ranters' Parliament" in London lost half its attendance of three hundred when the speakers could not satisfactorily answer questions about the problems of poverty. People should borrow money without paying it back, the leaders said, and steal and, "not only make use of a Man's wife, but of his Estate, Goods, and Chattels also, for all things were common." Even the poor understood that this "stratagem" was "no wayes feasible."[26]

Most people perceived the Ranters as spiritual fanatics and libertines. Their critics usually lambasted them as "Atheistical blasphemers," but a few who condemned them for having abandoned all religion spoke contradictorily. One referred to their "irreligious Religions." The titles of some anti-Ranter tracts show the same ambivalence: *The Ranters Religion, The Ranters Creed,* and *The Ranters Bible.* One writer, noting the dualism in Ranter thought, perceptively defined a particular gang of Ranters as "Marcions," an allusion to second-century Christian Gnostics; the "Marcions," like the old Gnostics, believed in two deities, one of which was the creator of all evil. Another writer, appalled by the "horrid" blasphemy that sin was imaginary, said, "These Ranters are but the Gnosticks of former Ages brought backwards amongst us. . . ." Yet the Presbyterian divine, Richard Baxter, although esteemed for his learning and his attempts to be tolerant, discerned in Ranterism no more than its run-of-the-mill opponents did. The Ranters, Baxter claimed, made it their business, "under the Name of Christ in Men," to dishonor all churches, the Bible, the clergy, and worship. They demanded that men and women should "hearken to Christ within them," Baxter wrote, but

> they conjoyned a Cursed Doctrine of *Libertinism,* which brought them to all abominable filthiness of Life: They taught, as the familists, that God regarded not the Actions of the Outward Man, but of the Heart; and that to the Pure all things are Pure, (even the most forbidden): And so as [if] allowed by God, they spoke most hideous Words of Blasphemy, and many of them committed Whoredoms commonly . . . and this all uttered as the Effect of Knowledge, and a part of their Religion, in a Fanatick Strain, and fathered on the Spirit of God.

Quakers and Presbyterians agreed on Ranters, although the early Quakers often suffered the indignity of being confused with Ranters. George Fox first encountered Ranters in a Coventry prison in late 1649. When he met them, "a great power of darkness struck me," he recorded. They began to "rant, and vapour, and blaspheme," and they said they were God. Fox asked them whether it would rain tomorrow; they did not know. God knew, he rejoined, and after reproving them for their blasphemies, he left because "I perceived they were Ranters, and I had met with none before."[27]

Although Gerrard Winstanley and the Ranters shared some fundamental tenets, he publicly repudiated them to still the slanders that Diggers and Ranters were indistinguishable. Winstanley believed that man should earn his bread by the sweat of his brow; labor, hard and productive, was a virtue with him. He scorned the Ranters as slothful and condemned them for cheating others of their earnings. Winstanley, who was very Quaker-like, condemned libertinism. Righteous and quietistic, he spurned the Ranters' materialism. Theirs, he wrote, was the "Kingdome that lies in objects; As in the outward enjoyment of meat, drinke, pleasures, and women; so that the man within can have no quiet rest, unless he enjoy those outward objects in excess." They believed, he complained, only in the life of the senses, "which is the life of the Beast." Overindulgence, he warned, impaired the "Temple" of the body and brought eventual "sorrow of mind." He thought too that "excessive copolation with Women" broke up families, caused quarrels, and burdened women with childbearing. Winstanley was the only critic of the Ranters who did not castigate their theology; nor would he suppress them. Let him who was without sin, he wrote, "cast the first Stone at the Ranter." He counseled patience and righteous living, "and thou shalt see a returne of the Ranters."[28]

The government pursued a different policy. Coventry was probably the first town to jail its Ranters. Among the group that George Fox visited in prison there in late 1649 was Joseph Salmon, the former soldier and itinerant preacher who had written *A Rout, A Rout.* Abiezer Coppe, who had just written the two installments of his lurid *Fiery Flying Roll,* was probably in the same Coventry prison with Salmon and his group. The charge against them may have been based on a provision in the Blasphemy Act of 1648 for punishing the heretical belief that the moral law of the Ten Commandments is not a rule of Christian life. Too little is known about the Coventry case to be certain. In January 1650 the two *Fiery Flying Rolls* were republished as one, adding to their notoriety. The authorities in Coventry did not know they had its author in custody, nor did the House of Commons know that Coventry had him when, on February 1, the house directed that a search be made for him. The house censured the book for its "horrid Blasphemies" and ordered that all copies be seized throughout the realm and be burned by the public hangmen. According to George Fox the Coventry Ranters won their release by recanting their beliefs "not long after" he encountered them. Salmon had to promise to put his recantation into public print. Coppe, who was probably using an assumed name to escape detection, recanted orally; he and Salmon were at liberty in mid-1650.[29]

Ranters had not the stuff of which martyrs were made. They renounced their beliefs with comparative ease. Believing in neither heaven nor hell, that even the soul died with the body, and that there was no afterlife, they had nothing to win by standing fast by their beliefs and nothing to lose by repudiating them. Life was to be enjoyed, here and now, rather than be wasted in prison. Anyway, the Ranters were amoral enough to say what had to be said to gain their freedom. As Justice Hotham told Fox in 1652, they would have said and done as the magistrates commanded "and yet kept their principle still." Salmon in his book of recantation professed a "sincere abdication of certain Tenets, either formerly vented by him, or now charged upon him." The very title of his *Heights in Depths and Depths in Heights* was a clue that he had not fundamentally changed. Ranters were fond of oxymorons, rhetorical figures that joined contradictory and incongruous meanings, as when Coppe spoke of his "filthy, nasty holiness" or said that one could not know unspotted beauty without knowing base things. The oxymorons reflected Gnostic dualism.[30]

Salmon recanted after he suffered "above halfe a years imprisonment under the notion of a blaspheamer; which through want of air, and many other conveniences, became very irksome and tedious to my outward man. . . ." Those are Ranter sentiments. Similarly, Salmon, supposedly repentant, defined God as "one simple, single, uncompounded glory: nothing lives in him or flows from him, but what is his pure individual self." A minister, commenting on the Ranter practice of using Aesopian language, declared that they say "one thinge and mean another. . . . They will say and unsay in one breath." Their expressions had "wayes and windings, to keep themselves from being known, but to their owne."[31]

While Coppe was being hunted, Clarkson published his libertine manifesto, *A Single Eye All Light, no Darkness; or Light and Darkness One.* The "Devil is God, Hell is Heaven, Sin Holiness, Damnation Salvation, this and only this is the first Resurrection," Clarkson announced. The House of Commons, in June 1650, after listening to a reading of *A Single Eye,* empowered a committee that was investigating "a Sect called Ranters" to find and imprison them. The house also ordered the committee to prepare a bill to suppress such blasphemies "and to make the same Offences capital."[32]

New legislation was needed because the Blasphemy Act of 1648, having been passed before the emergence of the Ranters, did not speak to their principles or conduct. The heresy clause on the denial of the Ten Commandments, the only one applicable to the Ranters, allowed recantation as an alternative to a prison term. The act of 1648, a Presbyterian product, required death for a conviction of any of the blasphemies that it proscribed, and in the main they were Socinian in character. The heresy clauses of the same act were so broad that if enforced they would have ensnared Cromwell, members of the Rump Parliament, and a large part of the army. The Independents, who controlled the government, were reluctant to enforce a Presbyterian measure, especially at a time when Presbyterian Scotland was engaged in a war against England for the purpose of placing Charles II on the throne. As the House of Commons debated a new measure on offenses against religion, Scottish divines charged that the English Independents were guilty of blasphemies and heresies. Repudiating that charge, Cromwell declared that he abhorred the detestable blasphemies "lately broken out amongst us," and he called attention to the fact that "We have already punished some among us for blasphemy, and are further ready to do it. . . ." On the same day in July that the House of Commons received a copy of Cromwell's declaration, it voted against death as the punishment for Ranter blasphemy by accepting a six-month prison term for a first offense. The house also voted against a proposal that punishment for the second offense should be boring through the blasphemer's tongue with a hot iron. Banishment was to be the recidivist's sentence; death was reserved only for those who, having been banished, returned to England without permission from the house.[33]

On August 9, 1650, the house passed its "Act against several Atheistical, Blasphemous and Execrable Opinions, derogatory to the honor of God." By comparison with any previous standard in English history, this was not an enactment into law of bigotry; it was carefully framed to cover only Ranter professions and practices. No persons whose religious beliefs were recognizably Christian, not even the Familists, who upheld the teachings of Henry Nicholas, or any of the novel and recent sects such as the Quakers and Fifth Monarchists, came within its terms. From the standpoint of its framers, the target of the statute was not the unorthodox but the irreligious or those who made a religion of immorality. John Milton supported the act of 1650 because, he said, blasphemy "or evil speaking against God" was not a reflection of religious conscience. He offered the act of 1650 as a definition of blasphemy that was plainer and more judicious than the clergy had produced "in many a prolix volume." Actually all the act did was to catalogue Ranter precepts and call them blasphemous.[34]

The act applied to anyone who maintained any of the following opinions: that he or another living person was God, was equal to God, or possessed His attributes; that God dwells within man "and no where else"; that unrighteousness or sinfulness was not immoral; or that heaven and hell, or salvation and damnation, did not exist or could not be distinguished. The act also applied to anyone who denied or blasphemed God, cursed Him, or swore falsely or profanely in His name; and to anyone who claimed that it was not sinful to speak obscenely, or steal, cheat, and defraud, or commit adultery, fornication, incest, or sodomy, or that any of the enumerated sins were as holy as praying or preaching. In addition, the act covered anyone who professed that whatever he did, "whether Whoredom, Adultery, Drunkenness or the like open Wickedness," could be done without sin or expressed the God within him; and anyone who professed that heaven consisted in acting out the things that were sinful, or that one committing them was closer to God or reached perfection by feeling no remorse, or that sin had God's approval, or that there was no such thing as sin.

A month later the same House of Commons passed an act that repealed all enactments requiring uniformity in religious belief and practice, or establishing any form of religion in England. That statute of September 1650 also advanced the cause of religious liberty by implying that no establishment of religion should exist and by allowing every variety of Christian worship. As an alternative to Sunday worship, one might privately preach, pray, read the Bible, or discuss it. In effect, toleration existed for anyone not subject to the provisions of the blasphemy acts of 1648 (Socinianism) and 1650 (Ranterism). The toleration act was fittingly denoted an act for the relief of "religious and peaceable people."[35]

On the very day of the passage of the toleration act, the house tried two Ranters who had been arrested, Laurence Clarkson and Major William Rainborough, a former Leveller. Clarkson was a great prize, for his *Single Eye* was the immediate provocation of the Blasphemy Act of 1650, although Coppe claimed credit for it. He too had been captured and awaited his turn to be examined. The house's committee on Ranters had already examined Clarkson. He was a difficult witness, for he admitted nothing, demanded that his accusers prove that he wrote the book whose title page bore only the initials, "L.C.," and refused to answer incriminatory questions. The committee, however, reported that he had confessed, and the house summarily condemned him as guilty and ordered the burning of his book. They sentenced him to a month in jail, following which he was to be banished "and not to return, upon Pain of Death." The sentence of banishment was not carried out, probably because it was illegal. Indeed, the trial of Clarkson by the House of Commons was illegal. By the terms of the Blasphemy Act of 1650, the accused was to be held for trial before a judge, a justice of the peace, or a mayor, and the sentence of banishment could be imposed only after a second lawful conviction. Clarkson was released from prison after about fourteen weeks. Rainborough, for his Ranter conduct, was simply stripped of his rank and discharged from the army.[36]

When the same committee of the house examined the author of the *Fiery Flying Rolls,* "the wild deportment of Mr. *Copp* the great Ranter" made news. He disrupted the proceedings by acting like a lunatic— talking to himself and flinging fruit and nuts about the room. His having "disguised himself into a madnesse" was rational, because the act of 1650 exempted persons "distracted in brain," and Coppe apparently believed that appearing mad was the appropriate response of a sane man in an insane world. The tactic failed; they returned him to Newgate prison and left him there. Although the statute of limitations had run out on Coppe's offense, the House of Commons did not stickle at a legal nicety. Like Biddle, he received no trial, not even a formal condemnation by the house, and they had already done him the honor of burning his book.[37]

In Newgate, Coppe was as feisty as ever, at first. He received visitors with éclat and converted some fellow prisoners. But he had little of Biddle's courage and consistency. Ranters were not cut out to suffer for a cause. After a few months, Coppe published a hemidemisemiquaver of a recantation; it was a protest, denying that he held blasphemous opinions and complaining that he had been defamed. The government paid no attention to him. After fourteen months of incarceration, Coppe published his *Return to the wayes of Truth,* begging Parliament's pardon. He renounced his blasphemous opinions, although he retained his social radicalism. While damning the conventional sins, he emphasized hypocrisy, a lecherous heart, and tyranny over the poor as the worst sins. If a "fellow creature" hungered, Coppe would feed him: "If I have bread it shall, or should be his, else all my religion is in vain. I am for dealing bread to the hungry, for cloathing the naked, for breaking of every yoak, for the letting of the oppressed go free." Doing otherwise was sinful. But he was on the side of the angels on the issue of righteous living, so the government set him free. As part of the bargain, he had to preach a recantation sermon at Burford, where Cromwell had suppressed the Leveller mutiny. A minister who heard Coppe's sermon remained unconvinced. Coppe, he wrote, used "melting words, Honeysweet, smoooth as oyle, but full of poison."[38]

The act of 1650 punished the Ranter conviction that if God was in man, man was God. Some Ranters took that literally, among them William Franklin, a ropemaker of London. His spiritual adventure and apprehension occurred before the passage of the statute. Its "Franklin clause" was intended to remedy a gap in the law. Franklin had been a pious Congregationalist, but on recovering from an illness that affected his mind, he announced that he was God and Christ. In 1649 he fell in with Ranters, abandoned his wife, and began practicing free love. One of his women, Mary Gadbury, was a religious eccentric given to visions. That Christ had been reborn in Franklin came to her in a revelation, and she spread the glad tidings. When a minister questioned the morality of her living with Franklin, she replied that Adam and Even had lived naked in their innocence and had been unashamed till sin brought shame into the world; but Christ had taken sin away. She called herself the spouse of Christ and claimed to be equal to God. In late 1649 Franklin and Gadbury left London to bring their gospel to the Southampton countryside. They made converts and even found disciples. "Now," wrote an eyewitness, "doth this poysonous infection begin to amaine [at full speed] to spread itself, having gotten many, and these also very active persons, to be the Preachers, Spreaders, and publishers of it abroad to the people. . . . They perswade others to imbrace and entertain also, that . . . this Franklin is the Son of God, the Christ, the Messiah." Millenarians expected King Jesus but not his spouting Ranter doctrines. Franklin, Gadbury, and their disciples were arrested in 1650. At first they all claimed, and Franklin agreed, that he was literally Christ. The disciples, having been reborn when they met him, dated their ages from that event. They were steadfast in their new beliefs until their leader betrayed them. Confronted with prison, he recanted, angering his disciples and causing them to abandon him. Mary Gadbury, unrepentant, was sent to Bridewell prison, where she was whipped on and off for several weeks. The men received prison sentences but were released on giving sureties for good behavior. Franklin, who was penniless, joined Gadbury in Bridewell. When the next imposters came along, the law was readier to deal with them.[39]

The act of 1650 and the imprisonment of Salmon, Clarkson, Coppe, and Franklin did not intimidate some Ranters. George Foster published his *Sounding of the Last Trumpet,* apocalyptically restating the social doctrines of the early Coppe. Foster presented God as the Great Leveller who would usher in King Jesus' communist utopia after over-throwing the rich, the clergy, and Parliament — all oppressors of the poor. Jacob Bauthumley's *Light and Dark Sides of God* was quietistic but antitrinitarian and pantheistic. Bauthumley, once a cobbler from Leicester, wrote his little book when he was a soldier. The army, fol-lowing its own law, made an example of him: he was punished by being bored through the tongue with a hot iron. The army suppressed its Ranters remorselessly. Cromwell himself cashiered one Ranter officer for denying that man could sin. Ranter officers lost their commissions and like rank-and-file Ranters were publicly whipped. Some soldiers were suspended by their thumbs, and one, a "W. Smith," was hanged by the neck at York, at the close of 1650, "for denying the Diety, Arian-like," and for other unnamed Ranter practices. Following the act of 1650, the police cracked down on civilian Ranters. Systematic raids re-sulted in scores of arrests. In one case eight Ranters, taken in a London tavern, were sent to Bridewell to beat hemp, and the two who were the most offensive were put on trial at Old Bailey, the seat of the central criminal court in London, and sentenced to six months in prison. Another gang of Ranters were sentenced to be whipped at Bridewell. The police raids continued into 1651. We may disbelieve one report that a Ranter, supposedly in league with the devil, escaped after he "called for . . . a pissepot, and in an instant, upon a great flash of fire, vanished, and was never seen more."[40]

Undoubtedly some Ranters were mentally deranged. One writer classified "these Atheistical Creatures" as either Free Will Ranters or "your mad Ranters, for they are lunatics very often." They were pun-ished anyway, because of the enormity of their blasphemous conceits.

Two women, both named Elizabeth Sorrell and related to each other, were arrested for blaspheming the "Holy Trinitie" and claiming the power to raise the dead. Four of their followers were also arrested, and at least one of the Sorrells was sent to jail. Messianic delusions were not uncommon among Ranters. In the same year, 1651, Richard King was imprisoned for the blasphemous claim that his pregnant wife was about to give birth to the Holy Ghost. Mary Adams also went to jail for claiming that her unborn child was Jesus Christ, although Joan Robins contested that claim by saying the same about her own child; she too earned a sentence for blasphemy, also in 1651. It was a vintage year for messiahs. The two most notorious were Joan's husband, John Robins, and Thomas Tany.[41]

John Robins was a blasphemer who inspired blasphemy in. others. Thomas Tidford, first arrested as a follower of the Sorrells, transferred his allegiance to Robins and, like Robins, whom he called "God the Father, and the Father of our Lord Jesus Christ," landed in jail for blasphemy. Robins, as well as the Sorrells, claimed the power to raise the dead, but he went further. By his own statement he had already raised Cain, Benjamin the son of Jacob, the prophet Jeremiah, and Judas; he had not only raised but redeemed them. Lodowick Muggleton, then an associate of Robins and later a great heresiarch, recorded that he had had "nine or ten of them at my house at a time, of those that were said to be raised from the dead. For I do not speak this from a Hear-say from Others, but from a perfect Knowledge, which I have seen and heard from themselves." Robins, whom an enemy called "the Shakers god" and "the Ranters' god," allowed his followers to worship him. He was fluent in the Scriptures, claimed to have been Adam and then Melchizedek in previous incarnations, and came by his Hebrew, Greek, and Latin, he said, "by inspiration." He had a plan to lead 144,000 people out of England to the Mount of Olives in the Promised Land. Joshua Garment, his Moses, would part the waters of the Red Sea for the pilgrims, and Robins would feed them with manna from heaven. In May 1651, Robins with his wife and eleven disciples, including the Kings and the Sorrells,.were imprisoned. After a year in jail, Robins addressed a letter of recantation to Cromwell, which won him a discharge.[42]

Thomas Tany, an associate of Robins, spent six months in Newgate for his blasphemies. He had abandoned his business as a goldsmith to proclaim that God had personally spoken to him, giving him to understand that he was a Jew of the tribe of Reuben whose mission was to lead the Jews back to the Promised Land and rebuild the Temple. By divine command, Tany changed his name to Theaurau John and, according to Muggleton, circumcised himself. Tany had many silly ideas, some of them sublime. He claimed to be the earl of Essex, heir to the throne of England, and in a pamphlet of 1651 debated Magna Carta "with the Thing called Parliament." He ranted madly in the streets about his mission as high priest of the Jews and about the indwelling of God. Following his prison term he was quiet for several years, but in 1654 he was claiming that as a descendant of Charlemagne, he was entitled to the crown of France.As that year closed, he publicly burned the Bible and then assaulted the House of Commons while it debated the fate of John Biddle. With a long, rusty sword Tany hacked away at the doors of Parliament, slashing at people nearby. After he was subdued and brought before the bar of the house, he explained, irrationally, that the people were ready to stone him (the Old Testament punishment for blasphemy) because he had burned the Bible. Asked why he burned it, he said it deceived him; it was only letters and idolatry, not "Life" and "the word of God." But he "did it not of himself: And being asked, Who bid him do it; saith, God." The house, taking him for a Quaker, resolved that for drawing his sword, burning the Bible, and declaring that it was not the word of God, he be committed to the Gatehouse prison. After his liberation some months later, he revived his project for restoring the Jews in Jerusalem. There being no Jews in England, Tany sailed to Amsterdam but perished at sea.[43]

Robert Norwood, a friend of Tany, was a more conventional Ranter, if Ranters of any stripe can be said to have been conventional. A former army captain, he came to the Ranter way of thinking by abandoning belief in the immortality of the soul, the physical existence of heaven and hell, and the literalness of the resurrection. Convicted in Old Bailey in 1652 for the crime of blasphemy, he was sentenced to six months' imprisonment under the act of 1650. Richard Faulkner of Petersfield was lucky that Parliament did not get him before the criminal courts did. He not only drank a toast to the devil; he said "our saviour Christ was a bastard," and, with the class consciousness of a Ranter, added that Joseph was only a poor carpenter. He too got six months.[44]

When Parliament got hold of William Erbury in 1652, it was scraping the barrel. Although Erbury's record made him a likely suspect, he was no Ranter. After attending Oxford he had been an Anglican priest frequently in trouble with the Court of High Commission. In 1640 he became a Puritan, later an Independent. During the Civil War, he was a chaplain in the army. Thomas Edwards charged that he vented antinomian doctrines, which could mean merely that he advocated universal salvation. Cheynel, another Presbyterian, debated Erbury publicly and accused him of Socinian blasphemies. Like Biddle, Erbury denied the divinity of Christ while preaching the "inner Christ," a doctrine of universal incarnation in believers. He defied all labels, except that of Seeker. His politics were as radical as his religion. Although he flirted with Ranterism and shared some of its views, much in Ranterism offended him. When examined by the parliamentary investigating committee he denounced the Ranters, but that occurred in 1652, after the law had turned against them and the craze had subsided. The fact that the committee examined Erbury is proof that by that date the Ranter heresiarchs had been silenced or driven underground. There were still Ranters around, but if they did not keep to themselves they risked being caught, like Henry Walker, a tavern keeper who pronounced "a poxe on Jesus Christ" and said he would rather be in bed with his girlfriend than in paradise with Jesus.[45]

The prosecution of John Reeve and Lodowick Muggleton under the act of 1650 was as misdirected as the investigation of Erbury. Worse, their prosecution, like that of Biddle, reflected religious prejudice against mere doctrinal novelty. Reeve and Muggleton were upright men with exceedingly strange ideas, too strange to countenance. The two, who were cousins, were not Ranters, although Reeve had briefly consorted with John Robins and Thomas Tany, and Muggleton had been fascinated by them. Muggleton had also avidly read the works of Jacob Boehme, one of the mystics who believed in the indwelling of God and in universal salvation. By 1653, however, when Reeve and Muggleton were arrested, they had completely repudiated Ranterism; indeed, they felt so repelled by it that they cursed its advocates — and when they cursed anyone, he was damned everlastingly.[46]

Thomas Babington Macaulay amusingly referred to a "mad tailor, named Lodowick Muggleton, [who] wandered from pothouse to pothouse, tippling ale, and denouncing eternal torments against all those who refused to believe, on his testimony, that the Supreme Being was only six feet high, and that the sun was just four miles from the earth." Muggleton, who knew nothing of astronomy, was more sober than Macaulay and no madder. His logic told him that if God made man in his own image, God was human in form and size, exactly like Jesus Christ. Muggleton, and Reeve too, was only a tailor. If the Old Testament prophets could have been herdsmen and Christ's Apostles fishermen, he asked, then why couldn't tailors be the Two Witnesses mentioned in Revelation 11:3? Reeve and Muggleton, like the new faith they had the boldness to imagine, were Interregnum period pieces fashioned by the religious turbulence of their time, but "Muggletonianism" survived it. Of all the sects spawned in that period, only two have endured, Quakerism and Muggletonianism, the two which in the

seventeenth century hated each other. The Muggletonians are doubtlessly the most obscure and tiny sect in all Christendom.[47]

Reeve and Muggleton no more advocated sin than a believing
Presbyterian did. No Ranter shared their fantastic opinion that Eve, the
Ranter's sex symbol, was the devil come to flesh. The Two Witnesses,
Reeve and Muggleton, thought that prosecuting them for their beliefs
was blasphemous. The act of 1650 aimed at those who made a religion
out of immorality or who justified sin by blasphemous opinions. Reeve
and Muggleton, by contrast, were puritanical; as men of rectitude, they
were industrious, believers in Christ, faithful to their wives, and opposed to drunkenness and gambling. Muggleton, who died at the
patriarchal age of 89, proudly recorded that he had never lived off the
gospel as the apostles had; he always earned his livelihood from his
craft as a tailor, accumulated property, paid his taxes, and had no
debts. Although he was not given to religious enthusiasm, spiritual fires
smoldered within him. He had lost his zeal as a Calvinist after the Civil
War fractured Puritanism into squabbling factions, and he stopped the
habit of praying. If anything followed death, he wrote in his autobiography, he would leave it to God to do "what He would with me."
God did not wait for Muggleton's death. In 1651 he began getting
revelations that opened to him "the Paradise of heaven, within man
upon earth," and he began reading the Bible again. Reeve, long envious
of his serenity, finally experienced similar revelations. Reaching a state
of peace, the two thought they would never again dispute with anyone
about religion. Then, in 1652, Muggleton recalled, "we were made the
greatest meddlers in Religion of all Men in the World. Because our
Faces were against all Mens Religion in the World, of what Sect or Opinion soever. . . . "[48]

Reeve first got the message. As he recorded in a tract of 1652, the one
that got them into trouble for blasphemy,

> . . . the Lord Jesus, the only wise God, whose glorious person
> is resident above or beyond the stars, . . . spake unto me
> Reeve, saying, I have given thee understanding of my mind in the
> Scriptures, above all men in the world. . . . I have chosen thee
> my last messenger for a great work unto this bloody unbelieving
> world; and I have given thee Lodowicke Muggleton to be thy
> mouth. . . . I have put the two-edged sword of my Spirit into
> thy mouth, that whoever I pronounce blessed through thy mouth
> is blessed to eternity, and whoever I pronounce cursed through
> thy mouth is cursed to eternity.

Reeve and Muggleton had a divine commission to teach the Word as they understood it, and they were armed with a unique power. In compliance with other messages from the Lord Jesus, they pronounced curses of damnation upon Theaurau John Tany and John Robins. The curse on Robins, a marvel of hellfire and brimstone, damned him eternally as the antichrist. Robins, who was in Bridewell prison at the time, put his hands on the grates of his cell and uttered, "It is finished; the Lord's will be done," and soon after he recanted. The new prophets began attracting the crowds that had thronged around Tany and Robins.[49]

In their revised version of Christianity, Reeve and Muggleton renounced the trinitarian principle. No point was clearer at the time of their arrest in 1653. Reeve until his death in 1658 and Muggleton thereafter continued to develop their theology without ever resolving some contradictions. From the beginning, though, they believed that the Father, the Son, and the Holy Ghost were synonymous expressions for one real person, the God Jesus Christ. In the beginning, when He was the Creator He was Spirit, but He came to earth as Jesus the man, to die so that He would understand the human predicament. On the cross He cried out to Elijah whom He had left on the throne of glory as his representative while He was mortal. When Jesus died, God died, but rose again body and soul, and thereafter paid no further attention to man. Having set everything in motion, God would not concern Himself with the human race again until Judgment Day. So wars, plagues, famine, and human cruelty were the work of the devil, a fallen angel who had planted his seed in Eve and lived in all her descendants through Cain. God, having fixed a conscience in man's heart, allowed him to work out his own destiny. Thus every person had within him both the spirit of God and that of the devil; as the voice heard by Reeve had said, the kingdoms of heaven and hell were in man's body. On Judgment Day God would resurrect the righteous, body and soul. Till then He would do nothing. After that time this earth would become hell, inhabited by the damned. One need only believe and live righteously. All else was pointless: worship, churches, sacraments, ceremonies, clergymen and their ordinances. Anyone who heard the message of God's last prophets, Reeve and Muggleton, and willfully disbelieved was damned.

Some angry readers delivered copies of Reeve's book to the lord mayor of London, and demanded an arrest. Reeve and his "mouth," Muggleton, said that God had died, repudiated the doctrine of the Trinity, and claimed that the soul was mortal. It was too much. The mayor ordered their arrest. When the Two Witnesses appeared before him, he had a copy of their book and copies of their letters to the Presbyterian ministers of London ordering them to quit preaching or be damned eternally for the unpardonable sin of blasphemy against the Holy Spirit. Reeve admitted writing the book, Muggleton the curses. "You are accused," the mayor said, "for denying the three Persons in the Trinity: You say there is but one Person Christ Jesus, you deny the Father." Reeve replied that they accepted the Trinity as "all but one Person." When the mayor answered that the devil had spoken to Reeve, the prisoner damned his lordship and demanded an explanation of God. He was an "infinite, incomprehensible Spirit," the mayor said, with "no Body or Person at all." Reeve insisted that Jesus had a body "in form like Man, Sin excepted." Then the mayor read from the act of Parliament "newly made against Blasphemy," which condemned any man who said that he was God and that God was nowhere else. Reeve and Muggleton had not, of course, made that claim. Muggleton informed the mayor that as a mere temporal magistrate, he was "not to judge of Blasphemy against God; nor those that made this Act neither." And, with stupefying arrogance, Muggleton added that God had chose only his Two Witnesses to be judges of blasphemy. The mayor sent them to Newgate.

After a month in jail, they were tried before a jury, with the mayor presiding, at Old Bailey. The charge of blasphemy was based on the denial of the Trinity in Reeve's book. After a few questions and direct answers, the trial was done, "and the Jury laid their Heads a little together" and found them guilty. They were sentenced to six months in Bridewell. When they got out, they wrote *A Remonstrance from the Eternal God*, which they addressed to the government. They restated their mission as the Lord's messengers and lamented their unjust sentence, but in the main they pleaded for liberty of conscience. They did not understand that the power they claimed, to damn willful disbelievers, conflicted with conscience, "which belongs not to man to judge, but to God only that knows the heart." But they made a ringing plea on behalf of "the free people of England, that they should not only enjoy their civil liberties, but the liberty of consciences towards God. . . . " For "all the prisoners . . . that suffer purely for their conscience towards God," Reeve and Muggleton demanded immediate liberty.[50]

The government, which paid no attention to their demand, did not understand that in Reeve and Muggleton it had had behind bars a pair of heresiarchs whose opinions violated the act of 1648, not the one of 1650. When Reeve died four years after coming out of prison, Muggleton took command of the new sect. He survived until 1698. He would be troubled three times more with the charge of blasphemy, but he was a witness with a divine commission. He could not be stopped by a government that did not impose crippling sentences and could not distinguish a Muggletonian from a Ranter.

The government never did stamp out all the Ranters. In time they faded away; they were never more than a passing craze. Coppe changed his name, became a physician, and was buried in the town church. As late as 1655, he reciprocated a visit that George Fox once paid to him in a Coventry jail; when Fox was in jail, Coppe and Bauthumley and a company of Ranters visited him. Fox called Bauthumley a "great Ranter" in 1655, but he too lapsed into respectability; he became keeper of the library in Leicester. Salmon emigrated to Barbados. Coppin became a Seeker and Clarkson a Muggletonian. That Ranterism survived throughout the 1650s is evident from occasional glimpses of it. In 1655 R. Forneworth, a Quaker, published a denunciation of blasphemous Ranterism in this sketch of Robert Wilkinson of Leicester:

. . . he said he was both God and Devill, and he said there was no God but him, and no Devill but him, and he said whom he blest was blest, and whom he curst was curst, and he said he was a serpent, and so he is, and he said the Apostles were lyars and deceivers, and I gave him a Bible to prove that, and he said the Bible was a pack of lyes, and there was neither heaven nor hell but here, and yet he was both in heaven and hell, and he had as lieve be in hell, as in heaven, and he said he was a serpent, and a whoremaster, and before he said he was born of God, and could not commit sin.

That is Ranterism, straight and pure. As late as 1659, Richard Hickcock, another Quaker, also published a tract "against the People call'd Ranters," in which he complained about those who cursed, lied, fornicated, believed that one sinned only if he thought so, and who contended that God is the author of sin.[51]

When Ranters surfaced publicly, the government prosecuted. Richard Coppin, a founding Ranter, would never have served time for blasphemy if he had shunned publicity. His first tract, *Divine Teachings* (1649), for which Abiezer Coppe wrote the preface, became a source that other Ranters looted for ideas and imagery. After the act of 1650 Coppin was quiet for a while. He claimed later that he had never abandoned his beliefs of 1649, although he explicitly repudiated Ranterism as well as Quakerism and every other religion but his own. Coppin the Seeker was an antinomian but no libertine. For him Scripture had become "dead letter" unless understood through the revelation that God had given to the Christ in Coppin. Yet his God was as much in everyone as in Christ and made every person perfect. Coppin also denied the physical existence of heaven and hell. A Worcester jury convicted him of blasphemy in 1652, but the judge, noting that the beliefs proscribed by the act of 1650 did not precisely correspond with those charged against Coppin, bound him over for retrial. A jury in Oxford found him guilty too, but again a judge, disagreeing, persuaded the jury to reconsider its verdict; it divided indecisively. That was in 1653. In the next year Coppin was again arrested for blasphemy because he preached in violation of the act of 1650, but once more a judge strictly construed the statute in his favor. Coppin had clearly repudiated Ranterism, but few conventional Christians could tell the difference.[52]

In 1655 Coppin foolishly agreed to a public debate in Rochester on theological matters, against a Presbyterian no less. Major General Thomas Kelsey heard Coppin. Assisted by justices of the peace, Kelsey accused him of blasphemy for having declared that Christ as a human being had been defiled by sin, that all men would be saved, and that heaven and hell existed only in man. Kelsey recommended to Cromwell that Coppin should be banished like Biddle, but Cromwell let the law take its course. Belatedly Coppin received the statutory six months' sentence.[53]

The same fate awaited two weavers in the village of Lacock in Wiltshire. William Bond and Thomas Hibbord rantingly maintained in public that there was no God, no Christ, only the sun overhead. Bond said that his friend, Tom Lampire of Melksham, could write better Scriptures than the Bible. Heaven was good fortune in this world, and hell was poverty. Hibbord, who believed that God was in anything thought sinful, said he "would sell all religions for a jug of beer." That was in 1656. The grand jury that indicted them deplored the fact that there were "many" people wandering about spreading such blasphemies.[54]

Ranterism could persevere in a free and disordered society like that of the England of the Interregnum, but not in Presbyterian Scotland. The Scots did not have the problem that Kelsey described to Cromwell after Coppin's arrest: " . . . people are ready to cry out for liberty of conscience, and not backwark [sic] to say it's persecution worse than in the bishops time, and the like." Uniformity in religion and severe persecution flourished in Scotland like heath and thistle. To a Scot of the established church, a sentence of merely six months for treason against God was coddling blasphemers. Alexander Agnew of Dumfries, a vagrant known as Jock of Broad Scotland, found that out. He was an atheist with the Ranter habit of talking too much and too offensively, but without sense enough to know when to shut up. His blasphemies, as his indictment stated, were frequent, uttered wherever he went. When asked whether he desired to attend church, he replied, "Hang God." God had given him nothing, and he was just as indebted to the devil, whom he thought the more powerful. When asked how many persons were in the Godhead, he replied that only one person, God, made all; Christ, a mere man, was not God. He denied that he was a sinner, scorned God's mercy, and mocked all worship. Declaring that he never had any religion and never would, he flatly said "there was no God, nor Christ." Only Nature reigned. Heaven and hell did not exist, the Bible was false, and man had no soul. On that evidence the jury found him guilty. On May 21, 1651, Jock of Broad Scotland was hanged from a gibbet.[55]

9

THE QUAKERS UNGOD GOD

In the 1650s the Ranter and the Quaker were allied in antinomianism and opposed in all else. One was the libertine antichrist, self-indulgently reveling in sin, the other the primitive Christian self-righteously overcoming sin — and demanding, in the shrillest possible tone, that everyone else must find Christ exactly his way and no other. To the Quaker, no other way was possible. Linking Quakers with Ranters and even with blasphemy sounds preposterous to modern ears, but the Quakers of the mid-seventeenth century were not like their descendants. The first Quakers had the fiery temperament of Old Testament prophets, and they trumpeted the message of the New Testament as if no one had done so since Christ's apostles. They made extravagant claims that offended and infuriated people. In conduct and belief the first Quakers had about the same effect upon their contemporaries as Holy Rollers would have in a quiet Friends' meeting today.

The Quaker founder George Fox, and his captains, James Nayler, Francis Howgill, and William Dewsbury — all condemned for blasphemy — were pentecostal, puritanical, proselytizing zealots. Quakers obeyed no sacrament, no law, no ministry, and no custom that conflicted with the indwelling Light of Christ that guided their lives. They were militant, intolerant, and vituperative; they invited persecution, and they gloried in it as a sign of their witness to Christ. They saw themselves as the only true, infallible church and saw all Christians of the preceding sixteen centuries as apostates. The Protestants of England, whether Anglican, Presbyterian, Congregationalist, or Baptist, belonged, Fox said, to the "Synagogues of Satan."

> And therefore in the name & power of the Lord Jesus was I sent to preach the everlastinge gospell which Abraham saw & was preached in the Apostles days. . . . And since has the Apostacy gonne over all nations. . . . Nowe wee haveinge the false prophetts antichrists deceivers whore false Church beast & his worshippe in the dragons power betwixt us and the Apostles . . . I

say the everlastinge gospell must bee preacht againe to all nations
& to every creature: which bringes life & immortality to light in
them that they may see over the Devill & his false prophetts & antichrists & seducers & deceivers & the whore & beast & before
they was. And in this message of this glorious & everlastinge
gospell was I sent foorth to declare & thousands by it are turned
to God & have received it & are come Into the order of it.[1]

Fox and his Quaker preachers engaged in "the Lamb's War." The
Lamb, of Revelation 5:1–14, is the victorious Christ, exalted by God to
govern the world after conquering the antichrist. Edward Burrough,
one of Fox's soldiers for Christ, proclaimed that the Lamb "hath called
us to make War in righteousness for His name's sake, against Hell and
death, and all the powers of darkness. . . . And they that follow the
Lamb shall overcome. . . . " Dewsbury spoke of the Lord's gathering
a mighty host exalting Christ as King of Kings. The Quaker army raised
in the north of England would march southward, reinforced by the
mighty power of the word of God, as sharp as the two-edged sword, to
cut down anyone, rich or poor, who disobeyed the righteous law.
England would be conquered, but the victory would come "neither by
sword nor spear, but by the Spirit of the Lord." Although the message
was purely spiritual, its military coloration made the Quaker preacher,
as Burrough acknowledged, look like a "sower of sedition, or a subverter
of the laws, a turner of the world upside down, a pestilent fellow." No
wonder that the members of Parliament thought that Theaurau John,
the demented Ranter, was a Quaker when he flailed his sword against
the great doors of the House of Commons.

Quakers were not yet thoroughgoing pacifists, although they were incapable of harming anyone. While Fox was in Darby prison for his first
blasphemy conviction, he demonstrated such charismatic qualities of
leadership that he won the devotion of the common soldiers who heard
him preach from his cell; the army offered him a captaincy if he would
take up arms for the Commonwealth, but he declined, saying his was
"the covenant of peace." His celebrated "flaming sword" was the sword
of the Spirit, forged he said in the "pure fires" that lit up his soul. Still,
he later censured the army for discharging Quakers as unreliable, and
he lamented the army's failure to attack Spain, end the Inquisition,
march on Rome itself, and continue into the lands of Islam, everywhere
planting the true religion. Nayler, who had extensive military experience, presented the militant Quaker message most disarmingly
when he wrote in his tract, *The Lambs War,* that everyone should
discover Christ the Quaker way and so find a life of gentleness,

faithfulness, and truth. The war was not directed against the government or the social order, and was only indirectly aimed against all the churches and sects of England. The war was, rather, directed at everyman; it was an inward war, exhorting the individual to crucify his spirit by confronting the Spirit of God within him and to find salvation.[3]

The Lamb's War was a full-time occupation for Quaker preachers. They were not Sunday Christians. Indeed, the sabbath day had no special significance for them. They abominated even the pagan names of the days of the week and months; when they redesignated the months and days as numbers (e.g., fourth day, second month), they were acting religiously. Matters of indifference to most people were for Quakers suffused with religious meaning. They rejected all oaths on the theory that a religious man would not perjure himself or affirm falsely; an oath implied that he spoke the truth only when he was sworn. But their first reason was that Jesus had said, "Do not swear at all" (Matt. 5:34). Quakers would not even swear an oath abjuring papal authority and the doctrine of transubstantiation, which they hated as they would the antichrist.[4]

"Moreover," Fox wrote, "when the Lord sent me forth into the world, he forbade me to 'put off my hat' to any, high or low; and I was required to Thee and Thou all men and women, without any respect to rich or poor, great or small." Quakers, who in the first generation almost invariably came from humble origins, enraged the gentry and magistrates by refusing "hat honor." Uncovering was the usual mark of deference or respect, but to the Quaker it was the sin of vanity. Similarly, they used "thee" and "thou" in addressing any individual, no matter how high his station, at a time when "thee" and "thou" were customarily used by superiors toward inferiors as marks of command and between equals as a mark of familiarity. "Plain speech," as the Quakers called it, was not a symbol of class warfare, nor a thing indifferent. Their refusal to kneel, remove their hats, use titles, or say "you" to a gentleman were deliberate acts of insubordination that conscience prompted. The Quakers were not really "levellers" in a political or social sense. Rather, they acted in the belief that God, before whom all were equal, was no respecter of rank. "Thee" and "thou" did not exalt the humble; the usage, like other Quaker customs, was an assault on the sin of false pride before God. Quakers owed loyalty only to the Spirit and to other "convinced" Quakers as signs of the Spirit. Every Quaker affront to a judge, a member of the gentry, a "priest," a government official, or an army officer was a self-testing by the regenerate against the unregenerate and a purposeful provocation of the unregenerate to see his own sins and thus become receptive to the Light of God within. Plain speech, plain clothing, and plain manners rebuked the world's vanities, set righteous standards, and, if necessary, led to the Cross.[5]

Quakers eagerly exposed themselves to martyrdom and suffered cruelly, needlessly in the minds of others, as proof that the Spirit within conquered one's own spirit or willful bent. "Being faithful to the Light," instructed John Audland, ". . . will lead you to the Death upon the Cross, and Crucifie you unto the World and worldly things, and raise you up into the pure Life, to follow the Lamb whethersoever he goeth." Self-crucifixion, figuratively, was a Quaker specialty — "follow the Lamb whethersoever he goeth . . . and therefore all come to the Cross and love it, and rejoyce in it." Prison became an almost normal form of Quaker self-crucifixion. Addressing a magistrate as "thee" instead of "your honor" or refusing to uncover before him could be taken as contempt of court. Quakers conscientiously opposed tithes for the support of an ungodly ministry, refused to pay fines, and failed to put up sureties for good behavior, and so they were jailed. They were stoned — the biblical punishment for blasphemy — and beaten by mobs so frequently and put into the pillory or flogged by court order so often that self-crucifixion became a way of life. In 1656 Fox estimated that "there were seldom fewer than one thousand in prison in this nation for Truth's testimony, — some for tithes, some for going to the steeplehouses, some for contempts, as they called them, some for not swearing, and others for not putting off their hats, etc." Included in Fox's "etc." was the woman who went to the "steeple-house," that is, challenged the parish minister for un-Christian teachings; she was tried for blasphemy and acquitted, but preferred to spend the winter in jail rather than promise that she would not disturb the worship of others.[6]

"Going to the steeple-houses" was probably the most provocative Quaker witness to the Spirit. Fox introduced the practice in 1649 when a steepled church in Nottingham appeared to him as an "idolatrous temple." The Lord instructed him, he reported, to "cry against yonder idol, and against the worshippers therein." Entering, he heard the minister say that the Scriptures decided all matters of religion, and Fox "could not hold, but was made to cry out and say, 'Oh, no, it is not the Scriptures,' and was commanded to tell them God did not dwell in temples made with hands." The Holy Spirit, he declared, had inspired the Scriptures and was the source of all religion. For disrupting divine service Fox was jailed, the first of many such occasions. Thereafter Fox and his converts to the indwelling Light invaded churches to denounce the preachers and their sinful congregations. God, the Quakers said, dwelt in the Spirit and the Spirit dwelt within every individual. The true church was a congregation of believers, not a building. Houses of worship, with or without steeples, became abominations to the early Quakers, as did ministers who taught falsely, or were ordained, or preached for money. Even the gathered churches of the separatist sects and their lay preachers, if paid, became targets of Quaker disruptions. "The disturbance of ministers in their sermons and alleged blasphemies," wrote William C. Braithwaite, the foremost historian of the early Quakers, "were the most usual grounds of complaint — the Quaker was frequently guilty of the first, and his innocence of the second, though clear to himself, was not easy of proof to a prejudiced and unsympathetic judge, who put the worst construction possible on unguarded statements about the indwelling life of Christ."[7]

William Penn entitled one of his books *Primitive Christianity Revived* (1696). That was Quakerism, or, rather, primitive Quakerism. Fox sought a return to the primitive church, as he understood it, purified of its accretions of sixteen centuries. Christianity in England was false, vain, and did not lead to the Cross, Fox preached. His mission was to bring the "pure religion" of Jesus to the people. One way of doing it was crying down and disrupting false worship, which the Quakers could not tolerate. There being so many souls that must be saved, errors in worship or in points of faith, "contrary to or different from the perfect Truth of the Gospel of Christ," required direct exposure and censure. Since the Lord accepted only His own worship, "here all Indifferency hath an end." Although the first Quakers were among the foremost advocates of liberty of conscience, it was not for them an end in itself but a means of propagating their faith. Their claim to infallibility matched that of the Roman Catholic church or of Calvinism, except that Quakerism made its advocates incapable of persecution. In the 1650s the Quakers had the same freedom of worship among themselves only; their faith compelled them to be missionaries among Christians worshipping falsely.[8]

Belief and action were inseparable to the Quaker. He must damn the antichrist in others and bring about conversions. "Hireling priests," the Quaker name for any ordained or paid minister, were too tolerant of sin and swollen with ceremonies and sacraments. Presbyterians and Independents won the particular contempt of Quakers because many of their ministers, having graduated from Oxford and Cambridge, knew less about the Spirit than common folk did. Herdsmen and fishermen, Quakers said, understood that the Spirit within man governed the interpretation of the Scriptures. Read literally, without the indwelling Light for guidance, the Bible became the "letter that killeth the Spirit." Fox liked to say that a believer needed no man to teach him, but only "an anointing within man to teach him, and that the Lord would teach his people himself." A Puritan preacher interrupted in his service could easily take such a statement as a rejection of the Bible, Christian sacraments, and Christian ministers.[9]

For all their talk about the love of God, Quakers used billingsgate, laced with biblical epithets, against other Christians. After spewing jeremiads, Fox would deny that he was railing; he spoke out of love, he said, while there was still time for repentance. Richard Baxter, the leading Puritan clergyman in western England, and no stranger to bitter religious controversy, wrote in 1657 that hardly a common scold in the past seven years had used against base people so many railing words as the Quakers used "against the faithful servants of Christ. . . . And no servant of Christ who hath learnt of Him to be meek and lowly can believe, if he be well in his wits, that this is the language of the Spirit of Christ." Long after, when Penn was succeeding Fox as the leader of the Quakers, Baxter noted their "extream Austerity," but insisted that their doctrines were

> mostly the same with the Ranters: They make the Light which every Man hath within him to be his sufficient Rule, and consequently the Scripture and Ministry are set light by: They speak much for the dwelling and working of the Spirit in us; but little of Justification, and Pardon of Sin, and our Reconciliation with God through Jesus Christ: They pretend their dependance on the Spirit's Conduct, against Set-times of Prayer, and against Sacraments, and against their due esteem of Scripture and Ministry. They will not have the Scripture called the Word of God: Their principal Zeal lyeth in railing at the Ministers as Hirelings, Deceivers, False Prophets, &c. . . .[10]

Cromwell, who could tolerate almost any Protestant opinion and did in fact tolerate Fox's refusal of hat honor and use of the familiar "thee," condemned the Quaker practice of violating the Christian worship of others. In 1655 he issued a proclamation of religious liberty "for all to hold forth and profess with sobriety, their light and knowledge therein, according as the Lord in His rich grace and wisdom hath dispensed to every man." The government would uphold liberty for "all persons in this Commonwealth fearing God, though of differing judgments," by protecting them against any who "abuse this liberty to the disturbance or disquiet of any of their brethren in the same free exercise of their

faith and worship which himself enjoys of his own." Lately, declared
the proclamation, "Quakers, Ranters, and others" had vilified and interrupted ministers and "daily" reproached congregations of Christians
in public and private meetings. Hereafter, they would be prosecuted as
disturbers of the peace. Until 1655 the law was that one might question
a minister after his sermon, although the Quakers always did far
more.[11]

Driven by religious exaltation and devotion to the Cross, they
reproached other Christians by going naked in public "for a sign." Baxter acknowledged that it was "a Prophetical act," but he did not realize
its significance. As Fox told the vicar of Ulverston in 1652, God made a
Quaker "goe naked amongst you a figure of thy nakednese . . . before
your destruction cometh . . . that you might see that your [you're]
naked from the truth." The Quaker leaders did not reprove the practice, rooted in Isaiah 20:3, for it also showed a central trait of early
Quakerism: the denial of self-will or the evidence of humility before the
Cross. Each Quaker had to find God through Jesus Christ by learning
to "give up self to die by the Cross. . . . Therefore keep in the daily
cross, the power of God, by which ye may witness all that to be
crucified which is contrary to the will of God, and which shall not come
into his kingdom." To become a member of the "Children of Light" as
the Quakers first called themselves, an individual must know his
depravity by confronting the Light within. Conversion required a
psychologically painful and prolonged encounter with self and God.
Before one could be transformed as a person and become reborn as
guiltless as Adam before the fall, he must acknowledge his sins, layer
after layer, and personally experience divine wrath until it turned into
love for the purified one.[12]

The very name "Quaker" reflected the fear and trembling a believer
showed in the presence of the God of Jeremiah. The inward suffering
produced intense physical agitation. "At first," Baxter recalled, "they
did use to fall into Tremblings and sometimes Vomitings in their
Meetings, and pretended to be violently acted by the Spirit; but now
that is ceased; but now they only meet, and he that pretendeth to be
moved by the spirit speaketh; and sometime they say nothing but sit an
hour or more in silence, and then depart." Robert Barclay, writing
about the same time, said in his book *Apology for the Quakers* (1675),
that in the early Quaker meetings the "painful travail found in the soul"
affected the body, so that "oftentimes, through the working thereof, the
body will be greatly shaken, and many groans, and sighs, and tears,
even as the pangs of a woman in travail, will lay hold of it; yea, and this
not only as to one, but . . . sometimes the power of God will break

forth into a whole meeting," everyone quaking, shaking, and groaning as he struggled with the evil in himself, until the Spirit brought serenity and thanksgiving. "And from this the name of *Quakers,* i.e., *Tremblers,* was first reproachfully cast upon us; which, though it be none of our choosing, yet in this respect we are not ashamed of it, but have rather reason to rejoice therefore. . . ." Fox himself attributed the origin of the name to a magistrate who scornfully used it while examining Fox for blasphemy in 1650, although the name in fact existed as early as 1647 to describe the spiritual behavior of others. After the victory at Dunbar in 1650 an officer rode back from his troop to discover the reason for a great commotion among his soldiers.

> When I came thither, I found it was James Nayler preaching to the people, but with such power and reaching energy as I had not till then been witness of. I could not help staying a little, though I was afraid to stay, for I was made a Quaker, being forced to tremble at the sight of myself. I was struck with more terror before the preaching of James Nayler than I was before the Battle of Dunbar, when we had nothing else to expect but to fall a prey to the swords of our enemies. . . . I clearly saw the cross to be submitted to. . . .

The curious aspect of this account is that Nayler, himself a veteran of the battle, had not yet met Fox and was not yet a Quaker.[13]

Primitive Quakerism was very much an embodiment of the youthful experiences of George Fox. In effect he demanded that others reenact his tormented conversion. He was born in 1624 in a tiny village in Leicestershire, the son of a weaver whom neighbors called a "Righteous Christer." The nickname more properly belonged to his son, who at nineteen, after his apprenticeship to a cobbler, left home to wander through the Midlands and learn more about religion. He listened to people of every Protestant persuasion, although he quickly abandoned "the high professors," the university-trained clergy, and consorted mainly with varieties of separatist sects, from whom he probably absorbed many ideas. He saw a turbulent and evil world. Finding no hope in institutions or men, he began receiving "openings" or insights directly from God. Between 1646 and late 1648 he shunned people as much as possible: he was "a stranger to all." So great was his misery he could not express it. But his description of his conversion and his commission to preach is one of the most agonizing and rapturous in English prose. By early 1649 he had "come up in spirit through the flaming sword into the paradise of God," relived the Creation, and by the indwelling Light reached Eden before the Fall. "But I was immediately taken up in spirit, to see another or more steadfast state than Adam's innocency, even into a state in Christ Jesus, that should never fall." His mission was to take others on the same journey. It was a dangerous mission because being taken "into a state in Christ Jesus" could be construed as antinomian blasphemy.[14]

Fox had little schooling and no formal divinity training; education would probably have ruined his ministry. No theologian, he expressed himself carelessly and overbluntly. He was a mystic, a firebrand, and inspired prophet, and, later, an organizer of a sect. But he had nothing new to offer in religious doctrine. Belief in the indwelling Christ who offered universal grace and perfection was certainly commonplace. Henry Lawrence, the president of the Council of State, told the House of Commons during a debate concerning Nayler's declaration that Christ was in him, "I wonder why any man should be so amazed at this. Is not God in every horse, in every stone, in every creature? Your Familists affirm that they are christed in Christ, and godded in God. . . . If you hang every man that says Christ is in you. . . you will hang a good many." Even the Ranters had that "convincement," as Fox conceded, although he said they "fled the Cross." Edwards's *Gangrenae* and Pagitt's *Heresiography* were filled with examples of antinomian heresies. Behmenists, Familists, early Baptists, Diggers, Grindletonians, and many Seekers like William Erbury preached the Light within, the godded man, the reborn innocent. Fox grew up in that religious milieu, which was strongest in the north and west, where he began his mission. Unsophisticated rural folk on the geographic fringes of Puritan centers were most receptive to Fox's preaching. They found in it a way to salvation that was direct and familiar, and they discovered a range of emotional expression that was not otherwise permitted in daily life. Fox was a fundamentalist who suited their wants, and he conducted a great awakening in the style that later revivalist preachers copied.[15]

But Fox's extravagances in statement led him into trouble. In 1650, while traveling through Derby, he stopped with some followers at a "steeplehouse" where many "priests" congregated for "a great lecture." Fox waited for all to finish, then rose to speak about Christ's dwelling within. He and two friends were promptly arrested and brought before "Collonels and Justices and Priests," who examined them for eight hours. Fox told them that all their preaching, sprinklings, and sacraments would never sanctify a man. They asked him whether he was sanctified. "I said, sanctified? yes, for I was in the Paradise of God, and they said had I noe Sinne? Sinne said I Hee hath Taken away my sinne (viz. Christ my saviour) & in him there is noe sinne . . . & soe

They committed mee upon That as a Blaspheamer. . . ." He was sentenced to six months' imprisonment for violating the provision of the act of 1650 against anyone claiming to be God or equal to God, or to have God's attributes, or to have God within him.[16]

The act of 1650 was framed for Ranters, whom Fox despised as filthy beasts. But the early Quakers were frequently mistaken for Ranters. A tract of 1652 condemned "Enthusiasts, Seekers, Shakers, Quakers, Ranters, etc." Ranterism and Quakerism were rival antinomian movements, and after the severe suppression of the Ranters in 1650–1, many converted to Quakerism; but old habits kept cropping out. A magistrate, Durand Hotham, told Fox in 1652 that the Quakers were saving England from being overrun by Ranters, but Hotham was a friend of Fox and privately admitted to him that he had believed in the indwelling Spirit for ten years. Others found blasphemy in such a belief. When Henry More, the Cambridge scholar, wrote that "Ranters and Quakers took their original from Behmenism and Familism," he was connecting the Quakers with blasphemy. Their enemies connected them with much more that was despicable — anarchists of the spirit, "levellers against magistracy and property," and the Anabaptists of Münster. One grand jury denounced "Ranters, Levellers and atheists, under the name of Quakers." Levelling might be inferred from Quaker plain speech and refusal to defer to rank, but the Quakers had no political program. To call them political radicals was absurd. But that Fox should have been condemned under the act against Ranters was not at all strange.[17]

When Fox's term in the Derby jail ended, the magistrate who had sentenced him demanded a steep bond of more than £200 for his release on good behavior. Relatives and friends raised the money, but Fox refused to pledge that he would not return to Derby and proclaim against its "priests." The magistrate, Gervase Bennett, who soon after became a member of the Council of State, furiously struck Fox and ordered him back in jail, this time in the dungeon, and there he stayed for over five months more. Immediately after his release he was preaching again.[18]

In Wakefield, to the north, he converted James Nayler, who became a leader of the early Quaker movement. Nayler, who was eight years Fox's senior, had left home in 1643 to serve in the army. After extensive combat experience he rose to become quartermaster of General Lambert's regiment. He left the army in late 1650 because of illness and took up farming. When Fox met him he was a member of an Independent congregation whose minister had been trained in Boston by John Cotton. Shortly after Nayler's conversion to Quakerism, he was "at the plow," he said, "meditating on the things of God, and suddainly I heard a Voice." It commanded him to leave his family and become a wandering Quaker preacher. Before Nayler left, Fox returned to his community and disputed Nayler's minister; there was a fracas, during which Fox was physically beaten by the congregants, although Nayler supported him. When Nayler left home to preach Quakerism, his minister excommunicated him for blasphemy. Fox and Nayler became intimate friends and remained so until 1656.[19]

That was the year of Nayler's disgrace, after the greatest blasphemy trial of the century. Nayler's death in 1660, shortly after his release from prison, and Fox's survival to 1691, dimmed the memory of Nayler's contribution to Quakerism. Within a few years of his conversion, he rivaled Fox. He was an equally powerful preacher, a superior prose stylist, and a prolific writer of tracts; and unlike Fox, who was abrasive and imperious, Nayler was gentle and considerate. When Baxter later reminisced about the Quakers, he mentioned Penn as their rising leader, did not refer to Fox at all, and said that Nayler had been "their chief Leader." Braithwaite, the leading Quaker historian, called Nayler "the most brilliant of the Quaker preachers," and a non-Quaker authority wrote that he was "a spiritual genius of a high order," whose "depth of thought and beauty of expression deserve a place in the first rank of Quaker literature."[20]

In 1652 Fox and Nayler preached together in northern Lancashire. On one occasion they were both nearly beaten to death by an enraged mob. They recovered at Swarthmore Hall in Ulverston. There Fox converted Margaret Fell, the wife of Judge Thomas Fell, who had been a member of the Long Parliament. Although Fell never converted, he used his influence to protect the Quakers and allowed his home to become their headquarters. Margaret Fell became one of the foremost Quaker missionaries and martyrs after the Restoration; following an imprisonment of four years she married Fox in 1668, although he was ten years younger. She treated him adoringly as the Messiah from the time they met, believing that he was possessed of the living Christ. If her early letters to him had fallen into the wrong hands, Braithwaite wrote, they would have "confirmed the belief that Margaret Fell was bewitched and that Fox was a blasphemer." Others addressed Fox with the same divine submission. He did not reprove them, but years later, when arranging his papers, he crossed out some idolatrous phrases. Even Nayler wrote, "Geo. Fox was denied as dust, but the Spirit that spoke in him is equall with God." Fox himself did not deny that, although on one occasion, when asked whether he was Jesus Christ, he replied, "No, I am George Fox."[21]

For their preaching around Ulverston, Fox and Nayler were charged with blasphemy in October 1652. Judge Fell managed to see that the warrant was not served, but Fox, accompanied by Fell and Nayler, insisted on riding to the Lancaster sessions to answer the warrant. Forty "priests" appeared as witnesses against Fox, but only three testified. The offense was serious, because under the act of 1650 a second conviction for blasphemy required banishment from the country. Shortly before, Fox privately told a friend that he was "the Sonne of God," although someone later changed Fox's manuscript account to read "a sonne of God." There is no doubt that he made unguarded oral statements. Fortunately for Fox, Fell was not the only sympathetic magistrate at his Lancaster trial, and the witnesses offered conflicting testimony about the defendant's exact words. To the first charge, that he had said he "had the divinity essentially in him," Fox denied having said "essentially," although he defended the doctrine of the indwelling Spirit. He also denied the charge of having said "he was equal with God," explaining that "He that sanctified and they that are sanctified are all of one in the Father and Son," and that all who were sanctified were the sons of God. He denied having claimed that he was "the judge of the world," although the testimony against him on that point was clear. To the charge that he had claimed to be as upright as Christ, he argued that "the saints," the true believers, "are made the righteousness of God" and shall be "like him"; Christ brought the saints to "perfection." One of the magistrates declared that Fox had blasphemed while presenting his defense in court. Another asked, directly, "Art thou equall with God?" Fox replied, "My Father and I are one, and as hee is, soo are wee in this present world." Nayler, quickly perceiving the danger in that reply, asked, "Dost thou aske him as a Creature or as Christ dwellinge in him?" When Fox insisted that Christ dwelt in him, Nayler added that nothing was sanctified but the Son, "and the Sonne being one in all, then the thinge sanctified is equal in all."[22]

Judge Fell, relying on the requirement that two witnesses must agree, said they had not; consequently, he quashed the warrant for blasphemy, leaving the issue unresolved. Orthodoxy sought satisfaction from a higher authority. Some Lancashire minisiters, supported by a few local magistrates, petitioned the Council of State in London against the blasphemies of Fox and Nayler. All the old charges were repeated, and the Quaker leaders rushed an answer into print. Even as they denied the accusations, they exposed themselves more by saying, contrary to the act of 1650, "that God will dwell in man and walk in man." Braithwaite concedes that their vivid sense of personal union with Christ led them to identify with the Divine and advocate their own perfection. Tract writers replied and censured Fox and Nayler for blasphemy, but the busy Council of State took no notice.[23]

Nayler and Fox split up after the Lancaster trial, Nayler going into Westmorland where he met with violence and hatred, especially around Kendal. For blasphemous preaching about the resurrection, a warrant was issued against him. He was taken by force and tried by a lynch mob, presided over by a justice of the peace who struck off Nayler's hat with a pitchfork when he refused to uncover. For a while he submitted to theological questions put to him by local ministers. "I witness that Christ [is] in me," he said, but one minister answered that Christ was physically in heaven. He is in heaven spiritually, Nayler answered, not in the flesh. The armed mob was growing ugly, so the justice of the peace decided to remove the trial to a nearby tavern. There Nayler again refused to take off his hat and "thou'd" the magistrate, who immediately jailed him for contempt and vagrancy. Francis Howgill, a Quaker preacher, gathered a group of Friends to protest the treatment of Nayler, and Howgill was locked up with Nayler. The next day the two were transported under guard to the prison in Appleby, further north, to await trial.[24]

In January 1653, two months later, their case came to trial under the act of 1650. But the prisoners were in luck. One magistrate, Gervase Benson, was a local dignitary of great authority who had recently become a Quaker, and another, Anthony Pearson, was sympathetic. Others on the bench were hostile, but Benson and Pearson prevented a verdict of guilty. Pearson instructed the prisoners to remove their hats. They refused, Nayler explaining that they had no contempt for authority but honored God, who did not respect temporal distinctions in people. On a direct command from Pearson to uncover, Nayler pleaded "Conscience sake. . . . Where God commands one thing, and Man another, I am to obey God rather than Man." Benson called for the indictment to be read: the blasphemy consisted in Nayler's having preached "that Christ was in him, and that there was but One Word of God." Pearson asked, "Is Christ in thee?" "I witness him in me." "Spiritual you mean?" "Yea, Spiritual. . . ." "What difference then between the ministers and you?" They, Nayler answered, affirm that Christ rose with a "carnal body, but I with a spiritual." A colloquy ensued on the distinction between the Bible and "the Word of God." Nayler explained his doctrine that "the Word" is spiritual, not seen by the eyes of men but experienced by the Light within. At length, the magistrates fell to disputing with each other. Benson favored a directed acquittal on ground that there was no blasphemy in Nayler's teaching. Others disagreed. In the end, the court decided not to put the case before the jury but to render no verdict, and to keep Nayler and Howgill in prison indefinitely until they answered fresh accusations from local clergymen. The prisoners were not released until five months later. While they were still in the Appleby jail, Anthony Pearson, whose Puritanism had been unsettled by his encounter with Nayler, visited Fox at Swarthmore Hall; he left shaken but unconvinced. When Nayler was released, Pearson invited him to his home, and Nayler brought his judge into the Quaker fold. Pearson traveled with Fox that summer in 1653 and helped save him from another blasphemy charge.[25]

Fox was accused for the third time in Carlisle that summer. He was near the border of Scotland, in a Presbyterian stronghold, and had provoked disturbances on his way north. In Carlisle, despite warnings from the magistrates, he "stood a-top" the cross in the middle of the market at midday and preached his gospel to a curious throng. Soldiers in the audience "were convinced" and protected him. He went to their garrison and convinced more, and on the next day, Sunday, he went to "the steeplehouse," the cathedral church. When the minister finished, Fox rose to speak. People "trembled and shook," he said, "and they thought the very steeplehouse shook and thought it would have fallen down." Friendly soldiers prevented a riot and surrounded Fox. Some were imprisoned for protecting him. But the town hall filled with "officers and justices" and "many rude people" that swore evidence against Fox, "for they were Independents and Presbyterians." Fox was summoned by a warrant.

> And one sware one thing and one sware another thing against me. They asked me if I were the son of God. I said, "Yes." They asked me if I had seen God's face. I said, "Yes." They asked me whether I had the spirit of discerning. I said, "Yes. I discerned him that spoke to me." They asked me whether the Scripture was the word of God. I said, "God was the Word and the Scriptures were writings; and the Word was before writings were, which Word did fulfil them." And so after a long examination they sent me to prison as a blasphemer, a heretic, and a seducer. . . .[26]

Fox was being held until the Assizes, when the county judges held trials with a jury. The news in the county was that Fox was to be hanged. The lord high sheriff, Sir Wilfrid Lawson, according to a letter from Margaret Fell, wanted to execute him at the first opportunity and spread word that he would be tried for his life. Fox reported that "great ladies" and "bitter Scottish priests" came to Carlisle "to see a man they said was going to die." In fact, however, when the Assizes convened, the judges refused to try Fox, leaving him to the local magistrates who had no power to condemn capitally. The judges who had that power probably believed that Fox was guilty of blasphemy; if he was convicted at the Assizes by a jury in a hostile town, the act of 1650 required banishment for the second conviction, and the expectation was that Fox would refuse, allowing no alternative under the act but execution. The judges of the Assizes did not want the responsibility of being the first civil officers to hang a man for his religion since the executions in 1612 of Legate and Wightman. So Fox languished in jail without a trial.[27]

He reported that the judges of the Assizes reviled him, left him to the town magistrates, and encouraged the latter to treat him cruelly, but in fact those whom he blamed probably saved his life. Anthony Pearson and Gervase Benson assisted him too. The two Quaker magistrates from Lancaster traveled to Carlisle, but the jailor refused to let them see Fox. He was transferred from a locked room to a foul dungeon with felons of both sexes, no toilet, and the prisoners "exceedingly lousy . . . almost eaten to death with lice." Pearson formally complained to the Assize judges, defending Fox from the accusations against him and protesting that he should not be left "to the rulers of this town who are not competent judges of blasphemy." Fox himself advertised his situation in letters to Friends and to the town magistrates, as did Pearson and Benson. Weeks passed, enough time for word to reach London. Cromwell and the Nominated Parliament then in session favored broad toleration. Parliament, Fox recorded, "hearing that a young man was to die for religion at Carlisle . . . writ down to the sheriff and magistrates." Carlisle set him free even before the writ arrived from London. After seven weeks of near starvation and brutal clubbings from his jailors, Fox returned to Swarthmore to recuperate, although on the way he turned "thousands" to Christ.[28]

During the next few years Quakerism penetrated southward throughout most of England, as its indomitable preachers worked county by county in pairs. The persecutions that followed them were severe but sporadic and local. By 1654 Fox was in London for the first time, preaching to huge crowds. Nayler, who joined him, was also received as a heroic figure. When Fox departed he left Nayler in charge. For the first time the Quakers were winning converts from better educated, prosperous city people. To eloquence Nayler coupled wit and warmth, and he had the civility of a gentleman with Fox's personal magnetism to boot. Quakerism almost became a London fashion, with Nayler lionized at parties attended by leading politicians and ministers as well as titled ladies. On a trip out of the city Nayler bested more than half a dozen "priests" in a public debate and the crowd shouted, "A Nayler, a Nayler hath confuted them all." But hints of spiritual travail within Nayler began peeping through his triumphs. He could not quash the sin of vanity. Some Quaker women were so smitten with him that they began to reverence him as more than a great preacher, and Nayler did not rebuke them. Nor had Fox when he received adoration. With Nayler, though, the problem became far more serious.[29]

Meanwhile the growing popularity of Quakerism made it the focus of rumors, some vicious, others absurd. William Prynn, the old mutilated Puritan martyr, was one of several who published the libel that the Quakers were really Jesuits and Franciscan friars in disguise sent by Rome to subvert the English people. The government flinched at plots, real and fancied. An officer arrested Fox on suspicion; when Fox would neither swear an oath abjuring Rome nor promise to return home and quit preaching, he was sent under guard to London and imprisoned. Cromwell required from him a pledge that he would not take up the sword against him or his government. Fox complied in a letter unlike anything Cromwell had ever seen. Calling himself "the son of God who is sent to stand a witness against all violence," Fox added, "My weapons are not carnal but spiritual, and 'my kingdom is not of this world.' " The Lord Protector read the letter, interviewed its author, and set him at liberty. As Fox left, Cromwell shook his hand and tearfully said, "Come again to my house; for if thou and I were but an hour in a day together we should be nearer one to the other." That was three weeks after Cromwell's declaration against Ranters and Quakers for disturbing Christian worship.[30]

As 1656 opened, Fox and his companions in Cornwall were thrown into Launceton prison "till the Assizes" in nine weeks. There was talk that the Quakers would be hanged, although their crime was not defined. The lord chief justice of England, John Glynne, presided when the sessions convened, but Glynne aborted the trial when he furiously ordered the Quakers back to prison because they would not uncover before him. At a rehearing, Fox managed to get the charges read — vagrancy, disturbance of the peace, refusal of the oath of abjuration, and perhaps sedition for that refusal. Once again, though, Glynne imprisoned them without trial for their contempt in refusing hat honor. They rotted in Launceton under horrible conditions — excrement was poured on their heads and the jailor beat them — until word reached London. Cromwell promised them liberty if Fox and his companions would go home. They refused; they also refused to pay court and jail costs. Hugh Peters, Cromwell's chaplain, observed that the government could not perform a greater service to the spreading of Quakerism than by making martyrs at Launceton. After eight months, they were freed.[31]

While Fox was at Launceton, Nayler's friends worried about Nayler's head being turned by reverential admirers in London; they persuaded him to travel to Bristol for a religious fair, but his worshippers followed. In Bristol, Nayler decided to visit Fox at Launceton. Fox had already heard about the strange goings-on around Nayler. In a letter of warning, Fox wrote, "Thou became a shelter for the unclean spirits, the beasts of the field, they made thee their refuge." In his *Journal* Fox recorded that Nayler and his companions "ran out into imaginations." A short distance from Launceton, the Nayler group was arrested for vagrancy and jailed at Exeter. On Fox's release he visited Nayler at Exeter and "saw he was out and wrong." At prayers, as Fox admonished the Exeter prisoners, Nayler and his followers left the room — evidence, said Fox, of a "wicked spirit risen up among Friends." He spoke to Nayler the next day. Nayler, remorseful, would have kissed Fox in the Quaker fashion, but "seeing he [Nayler] had turned against the power of God," Fox extended his foot for Nayler to kiss: "the Lord God moved me to slight him and set the power of God over him." So ended the Fox-Nayler relationship. In Exeter prison Nayler was moody, ill, exhausted, and scarcely ate for weeks at a time.[32]

Letters from admirers intending to comfort him aggravated the growing delusion, which he found disturbing, that he James Nayler was a special sign from God. A Quaker, when impelled by the Light within to serve as a sign, experienced spiritual torment and exaltation. To reject the sign implied self-will, a reproach to the divine prompting that betokened the sign. Nayler read the admiring letters, and although they sent a fear through him, he kept them. One follower described him as "King of Israel and Son of Most High." The writer of another letter wished she could present him with gold, frankincense, and myrrh. Still another called him the "son of Zion, whose Mother is a Virgin, and whose birth is immortal." One woman saluted him as the "Prince of Peace" and "fairest of ten thousand, thou only begotten Son of God," and her husband added the postscript, "Thy name is no more to be called James but Jesus."[33]

The "miracle" in Exeter prison involving Dorcas Erbury magnified tenfold the overpowering sense that the God in him had chosen him for a special mission. Dorcas, the daughter of William Erbury the Seeker, had fallen into unconsciousness and seemed dead for two days. Nayler entered her cell, placed his hands on her, and commanded her to rise — and she did. Fox himself had exercised healing powers. Once he cured a deformed boy by laying his hands on him, and on another occasion he claimed that he "raised up" a woman and her child who were dying. Francis Howgill had once called upon the power of God that raised Jesus to make a lame boy walk, and when the miracle failed, Howgill was surprised. No Quaker had raised a person from death, until Nayler seemed to do so in Exeter. His success intensified the hysteria among his worshippers. Fox wrote, "James, thou must bear thy owne Burden, and thy Companyes with Thee, whose Iniquity doth increase, and by thee is not cried against." In late October 1656, Nayler and the Exeter Quakers who had been arrested for vagrancy were freed.[34]

He and eight of his followers traveled from Exeter to Bristol. Their sensational entrance into the city drew crowds even in a downpour. Nayler sat on his horse as if in a trance, while the others, bareheaded, surrounded him and led him through the mud, singing "Holy, holy, holy, Hosannah, Lord God of Israel." They spread their sodden cloaks for his horse to walk upon as he passed through the city streets. The deliberate reenactment of Jesus' entry into Jerusalem on Palm Sunday was intended as a symbol of the imminent coming of Christ—a common enough millenarian belief. The whole group was arrested and sent to the Guildhall for an examination. Ordinarily, local Quakers—Bristol had a thousand—turned out to show sympathy for a Friend in trouble, but Fox had passed through Bristol and sent letters there warning the Quakers not to support Nayler's extravagances. Not one appeared at the Guildhall.[35]

There, before the mayor, the local magistrates and ministers, and the townspeople, Nayler and his followers were searched. The "incriminating" letters of adoration were found on him, used as evidence, and published in lurid accounts. One of the women in his company had in her pocket a description of Jesus that fit Nayler closely; a formal report of Parliament later took notice "how much he resembled . . . the picture usually drawn for our Saviour." During the examination in the Guildhall, the women prisoners sang, cried hosanna, and one kissed Nayler's hand before the horrified magistrates. If any were guilty of blasphemy, they were the Quakers offering worship to Nayler. Whether they believed that he was Christ incarnate is uncertain, but they worshipped the Christ whom they believed to be patently manifest within him. Nayler himself was neither an imposter, as many then believed, nor a fool, nor was he crazy as some historians have thought. He was guilty of bad judgment, excessive zeal, and an incapacity to see himself as others—Fox as well as non-Quaker Christians—saw him. He was the reluctant Jesus in a Passion Play because he had become convinced by the agony of his spirit that God intended him as a sign, both of Immanentism and of Imminence.[36]

The Quakers of the 1650s saw their time as the edge of the Apocalypse. They expected the Lamb's victory over everybody during their lifetime. Much of Quaker preaching was a gloomy prediction that the wrathful day of the Lord was near. "Who waits upon the Lord in his Light," wrote Margaret Fell, ". . . shall see this fulfilled and shall be preserved." Naturally the Second Coming would be preceded by signs of all sorts; Nayler, in a judgment misrepresented by his worshippers, thought he was such a sign, because the strong Light within him made him God's instrument. But he did not believe he was the only sign, the only instrument, the only man through whom the Light worked its mysterious wonders. His interrogators at the Bristol Guildhall, not understanding, quite reasonably saw blasphemy. The misunderstandings between Nayler and them are clear from his examination.[37]

In response to questions he said that he made his extraordinary entrance into Bristol at the command of the indwelling Christ. He did not rebuke those who sang praises, because they were praising the Lord, not him as a man. Promptings from God were not his to rebuke; people about him heeded the Spirit within. No, he was not the "Fairest of Ten-Thousand." He could not help looking as he did, but he denied that his physical appearance was an "attribute" of any sort.

Q.   Art thou the only Son of God?
A.   I am the Son of God, but I have many brethren.
Q.   Have any called thee by the name of Jesus?
A.   Not as unto the visible, but as Jesus, the Christ that is in me.
Q.   Dost thou own the name of the King of Israel?
A.   Not as a creature, but if they give it to Christ within, I own it, and have a kingdom but not of this world; my kingdom is another world, of which thou wotest not.
Q.   Whether or no art thou the Prophet of Most High?
A.   Thou hast said, I am a Prophet.
Q.   Dost thou own that attribute, the Judge of Israel?
A.   The judge is but one, and is witnessed in me, and is the Christ, there must not be any joined with him: if they speak of the spirit in me, I own it only as God is manifest in the flesh, according to God dwelleth in me, and judgeth there himself.[38]

The answers were pure Quakerism. Fox had said the same things to Cromwell. The only christological note that Nayler introduced was his answer "Thou has said it." But pure Quakerism was blasphemy to those who believed that Christ was not within people but physically in heaven. And Nayler's replies lent themselves to misinterpretation. When, for example, they asked him whether he was "the everlasting Son of God," he replied that any in whom Christ dwelt was the everlasting Son, "and I do witness God in the flesh; I am the Son of God, and the Son of God is but one." He meant, as he had said earlier, that he had "many brethren." For Nayler, Christ was the only Son of God and the Son "is but one" dwelling in many. When asked whether he or any of his followers blasphemed, he declared, "What is received of the Lord is true."

    Q. Was Dorcas Erbury dead two days in Exeter, and didst thou raise her?
    A. I can do nothing of myself: the Scripture beareth witness to the power in me which is everlasting; it is the same power we read of in the Scripture. The Lord hath made me a sign of his coming: and that honour that belongeth to Christ Jesus, in whom I am revealed, may be given to him, as when on earth at Jerusalem, according to the measure.

They called that blasphemy, and his answer, "Who made thee judge," also reflected his own refusal to judge his worshippers: "I ought not to slight anything which the spirit of the Lord moves." The entire examination made him seem arrogant beyond belief, if not worse, yet for his part he was reflecting the humility he felt before his God. Any miracle he had performed he attributed to the indwelling Christ; any worship directed at him he had received on the same behalf. Only at the end of the examination did he lose his self-control and violate Quaker precepts. Nayler had offered excessive tenderness to a woman whom Fox had rejected as unclean in spirit; on learning that Nayler favored her, Fox reproved him for treating her like "the mother," that is, the Virgin Mary. The Bristol examiners asked Nayler why he had called her "mother, as George Fox affirms." Nayler exclaimed, "George Fox is a lyar and a firebrand of hell; for neither I, nor any with me, called her so." Long after, Nayler declared that that was the only answer he regretted.[39]

Nayler's worshippers when examined did not make the distinctions that he did, and their testimony did him harm, as if he were guilty of their blasphemies. One woman acknowledged that she should worship him on her knees because "James Nayler will be Jesus, when the new life is born in him." If there was any ambiguity in her statement, she resolved it when she added that Nayler had the spirit of Jesus in him "above all men." Dorcas Erbury's evidence was the most damaging. She insisted that Nayler raised her from the dead and therefore was Jesus. They asked whether Jesus Christ did not sit at the right hand of God, and she replied, "He, whom thou callest Nayler, shall sit at the right-hand of the Father. . . ."[40]

The Bristol magistrates, believing that they were confronted by more than they could cope with, sent a transcript of the proceedings under seal to their deputy in the House of Commons. He reported it to the house, which appointed a committee of fifty-five to investigate and propose action. The committee summoned Nayler, three women including Dorcas, and the man who called Nayler Jesus. Five members of the committee interrogated them in even greater detail than had the Bristol officials. Nayler, of course, was the center of attention. In the end the committee of fifty-five agreed on two charges against him: that he assumed "the gesture, words, honour, worship, and miracles of our blessed Saviour," and that he had assumed His "names and incommunicable attributes."[41]

Nayler replied to the committee as candidly as he had in Bristol, yet the committee took every point as "proved" against him by his own words. They reported that he did not deny being "the only begotten Son of God," although he insisted, "I am the Son of God, but I have many brethren." When the question was asked whether he was the "only begotten Son," he replied, "Thou has said it. . . . Do not ensnare the innocent." The committee resolved that he claimed the title of "the Prophet of the most high God," although he declared, "There be other Prophets besides me." Similarly the committee resolved that he claimed to be king of Israel, when in fact he denied all titles "as a creature," although he acknowledged that the Christ in him was king. When he conceded that others gave the name Jesus "to the Christ that is in me," they resolved that he had assumed the name; yet he denied that he ever used the name for himself. They insistently misconstrued his meaning. At one point he stated, "Nay, do not add to my words; I speak as plain as I can, that all the glory may be given to God, and none to the creature . . . and none to me, as you look upon me as a creature." If his companions attributed anything to James Nayler that belonged to God, "then it is reprovable." He took their remarks as honoring the Lord; otherwise he would have "utterly denied" them. After the committee had examined him for the third and last time, they allowed him a final statement. It was a sockdolager:

I do abhor that any of that honor which is due to God should be given to me, as I am a creature: But it pleased the Lord to set me up as a sign of the coming of the righteous one; and what hath been done in my passing through the towns, I was commanded by the power of the Lord to suffer such things to be done to the outward as a sign. I abhor any honour as a creature.

Thomas Bampfield, a man respected enough to become the next speaker of the house, reported to the House of Commons on behalf of the committee that Nayler was guilty of blasphemy and various misdemeanors.[42]

From the moment that the House of Commons had taken jurisdiction of Nayler's case, his conviction was certain and Cromwell's policy of toleration was in jeopardy. Under the 1653 Instrument of Government, by which Cromwell had become protector, most Christians were free to worship as they pleased. The protectorate was a Puritan Commonwealth tempered by a very broad measure of toleration, even more in fact than in law. Article 35 of the Instrument "recommended" the Christian religion as the religion of the nation and provided for its support, but article 37 protected anyone professing faith in God through Jesus, "though differing in judgment from the doctrine, worship, or discipline publicly held forth." At the time of Nayler's case, no doctrine, worship, or discipline had been defined. The Instrument of Government provided that except for "popery or prelacy" and "licentiousness," no one should be restrained in his religion who did not use his "liberty to the civil injury of others" or "actual disturbance of the peace." The Instrument, which reflected the wishes of Cromwell, his Council of State, and the army, was imposed upon a reluctant Parliament. From the outset Parliament sought to narrow Cromwell's policy of toleration. Members of the house were appalled by his courtesies toward Quakers, his talks with Fifth Monarchists, his dignifying Anglican priests, and his refusal to enforce laws against both Roman Catholic worship and Anglican use of the Book of Common Prayer. Cromwell's policy prevailed because the army backed him. He would have liked the Protestant clergy to agree on a national church comprehensive enough to take in all Protestants, from the sectarians to peaceable Anglicans like Archbishop Ussher. Cromwell drew the line against Socinians, who repudiated the divinity of Christ, and against Ranters, whom he believed opposed to all religion.[43]

Cromwell's hope for a comprehensive national church foundered on sectarian divisions. The Protestant clergy of England bitterly disagreed among themselves; they could not even concur on the fundamentals of the Christian faith. Not even the Presbyterians and Independents could agree, though they were all Puritans; indeed, members of the same sect conflicted among themselves. As time passed the Congregationalists had emerged as the strongest Independent sect, and they grew increasingly conservative. The Independents opposed a national church and uniformity in religion. By the time of the protectorate, the Congregationalists, like their counterparts in New England, favored state support of religion and religious guidance of the state. As time passed the Congregationalists grew closer to the Presbyterians than to the separatistic and voluntary churches of the sects from which Congregationalism had sprung. But even the Presbyterians were divided between latitudinarians like Richard Baxter and those like Samuel Rutherford who looked to Scotland. The principal difference between Congregationalists and Presbyterians was that the former believed that the individual churches should be self-governing, while the latter preferred a centralized ecclesiastical polity of church synods. Both Congregationalists and Presbyterians, who dominated Parliamant in the 1650's, strongly favored an establishment of trinitarian Protestantism along Calvinist lines, and they supported the continuance of tithes. Cromwell too favored tithes till some better substitute might be found.[44]

Cromwell's toleration policy, by seeking to please almost everyone, antagonized the most powerful alliance in Parliament—Congregationalists and Presbyterians. The protector's settlement allowed each parish to choose its minister from lists approved by committees that certified ministerial fitness. Congregationalists, other Independents, Presbyterians, and a few Baptists controlled the committees of certification. In effect England had a plural establishment of various Puritan churches that was wedded, reluctantly, to a constitutional policy of toleration for the numerous gathered churches that supported themselves and existed outside the establishment. It was a strange and divided confederation of Protestant denominations, plus the sects, without doctrines or rites beyond profession of Christ. Anglicanism labored under repressive legal disabilities, but in practice the government in the 1650s—Cromwell and his council—connived at allowing religious liberty for them and any Christians (Socinians always excluded) who did not disturb the state or the worship of others. The persecution of the Fifth Monarchists was centralized but motivated purely by political considerations. The persecution of the Quakers was locally inspired, not centrally, but only because Parliament could not dominate the religious settlement of the Commonwealth, try as it might. Catholics, a despised and untolerated minority, to Parliament's alarm were left unmolested even in London, as were Anglicans, if they worshipped quietly, although the worship of both violated the law. The Venetian ambassador in 1655 reported that the English were "divided into as many faiths as there are heads, and the number of religions equals the number of men." The protector, he observed, favored no sect and it "suits his policy that 246 religions should be professed in London . . . differing greatly from each other and incompatible. This division into so many sects makes them all weak, so that no one [sect] is strong enough to cause his apprehension."[45]

Most Puritans in and outside of Parliament abhorred the sects, abhorred tolerating them officially, and abhorred the de facto toleration of Anglicans and Catholics. And Parliament represented, in the main, the Puritans. They divided on religious matters but not radically on the issue of toleration, and on this issue Parliament probably represented the nation more accurately than did the executive branch and the army. If Cromwell's first protectorate Parliament had had its way, it would have produced what the quarreling divines could not—a confession of faith that subverted the Instrument of Government. If Parliament had had its way, it would have disposed of John Biddle under the Blasphemy Act of 1648. If Parliament had had its way, it would have excluded from the scope of toleration many of the self-supporting gathered churches that used lay ministers. Parliament was particularly rabid in condemning "atheism, blasphemy, damnable heresies, popery, prelacy, licentiousness, and profaneness," all of which it moved to bring exclusively within its jurisdiction and definition. Parliamentary intolerance, representing a Puritan phalanx of conservative Independents, Congregationalists, and Presbyterians, plus a few Particular Baptists (Calvinists), was deadly opposed to the tolerance of the executive and the army. In a blistering attack on their bigotry, Cromwell dissolved his first Parliament in January 1656, after it sat for five months. By dissolving Parliament he saved Biddle and prevented the formation of a national or uniform confession of faith determined by the Commons.[46]

Cromwell's second protectorate Parliament, which met in September 1656, was even more conservative than the first on religious matters. Of 460 who were elected, approximately one hundred were so objectionable that the Council of State, under a power wrested out of the Instrument of Government, excluded them. About fifty more failed to take their seats. The remainder were loyal to Cromwell, but not to the latitudinarian religious provisions of the Instrument. This was the Parliament that passed by a two-to-one majority a severe recusancy act intended to disable the practice of Roman Catholic worship. The same Parliament, which offered the crown to Cromwell, forced a change in the constitution of England by altering the religious provisions of the Instrument. The new constitution of 1657 provided for a "Confession of Faith," to be jointly approved by the protector and Parliament; "no other" profession or worship should "be held forth and asserted" as the public profession, but orthodox trinitarians who believed the Scriptures as the revealed word of God would be tolerated. Socinians, irreligious persons, "Popery," and "Prelacy" would not be tolerated, nor would any who should "revile or reproach the Confession of Faith," or blaspheme, or behave licentiously. By implication Quakerism and dozens of obscure sects, including Familists, Sabellians, Muggletonians, Seventh Day Baptists, Fifth Monarchists, and Ranters, were proscribed.[47]

And this was the Parliament, the "Nayler Parliament," so called by the historian Thomas Carlyle, who floridly satirized it as follows:

> To Posterity they sit there as the James-Nayler Parliament. Four-hundred Gentlemen of England, and I think a sprinkling of Lords among them, assembled from all the counties and Boroughs of the Three Nations, to sit in solemn debate on this terrific Phenomenon; a Mad Quaker fancying or seeming to fancy himself, what is not uncommon since, a new Incarnation of Christ. Shall we hang him, shall we whip him, bore the tongue of him with hot iron, shall we imprison him, set him to oakum [making hemp]; shall we roast, or boil, or stew him; — shall we put the question whether this question shall be put; debate whether this shall be debated; — in Heaven's name, what shall we do with him, the terrific Phenomenon of Nayler? This is the history of Oliver's Second Parliament for three long months and odd.[48]

Carlyle's parody lacked understanding, because the Nayler case raised fundamental constitutional questions that received serious consideration by Parliament. Moreover, the case really tested the limits of tolerance in a Christian commonwealth that enjoyed a greater degree of free exercise of religion than England had ever known, and many members of Parliament, including some rabid ones, sought to rationalize their positions. Not since the Servetus case had there been so important a blasphemy trial, and this one produced the greatest debate on the meaning of blasphemy, and thus on the limits of toleration, in English history. In the end Parliament exercised its *judicial* powers to condemn Nayler for "horrid blasphemy" and sentenced him to grisly corporal punishments followed by an indeterminate period in prison. But the end was not a foregone conclusion. The key votes were close, and the issues so complex that many members could not make up their minds; almost one-third of the house abstained from voting.

From the beginning there was no certainty that Nayler had violated any law or, if he had, what that law was. Was it parliamentary law, common law, natural law, moral law, or biblical law? Was his crime, if he had committed one, divine impersonation, seduction, idolatry, or blasphemy? Was an offense against religion an offense against the state when the head of the state was not the head of a national church? In the absence of ecclesiastical courts, which had been abolished since 1641, was an offense against religion merely a sin, which was cognizable only by God? If Nayler had committed blasphemy, and it was a high crime against God, comparable to treason, could or should the state vindicate the honor of God? What did blasphemy mean? Were there differing degrees and kinds of blasphemy, some capital in nature and others not? If blasphemy was a crime punishable by the state, did jurisdiction over it lie with the regular criminal courts or could Parliament intercede? A trial court had sentenced William Franklin for claiming to be Jesus, in 1650, prior to the enactment of the statute against the Ranters; but no determination had ever been made by the King's Bench, the high court of criminal jurisdiction, that blasphemy was an offense at common law. That did not happen until 1676. The House of Commons had tried and convicted Paul Best for blasphemy in 1646, but they had no law for their action, and even after imprisoning him they never reached a formal decision of a judicial or a legislative nature. The house kept John Biddle in jail without even trying him. During the debate on Nayler's case no one dissented from those who pointed out that Parliament had not judged Biddle in a legal sense. As Lord Chief Justice Glynne told the "Nayler Parliament," "This is a new case before you, and it will be a precedent." He and many others would have let the courts decide the precedent." For Parliament to decide it, some legalists believed, was "dangerous."[49]

Under the Instrument of Government of 1653, which was the Constitution of Great Britain, "the supreme legislative authority" was vested in the lord protector, assisted by a Council of State whose approval he required. Parliaments were to be called every third year, consisting of one house only. Bills enacted by Parliament required the consent of the executive, who might dissolve any Parliament after it had sat for five months. The Instrument vested no judicial authority in Parliament. The House of Lords before its abolition in 1649 could act as the highest court of the land. Did its judicial authority somehow devolve upon the Commons, authorizing them to take jurisdiction of Nayler's case? If so, what law had he broken? A judicial body can apply only the standing law; it cannot otherwise punish. Did Nayler violate the Blasphemy Act of 1648? Significantly, no one during the entire debate on Nayler's case relied on that statute; it was a dead letter. Some members tried to wrest precedents against Nayler from the Bible and even from the act of 1401 for the burning of heretics, *De Haeretico*

Comburendo, but not a member even referred to the act of 1648. They seemed to assume that the Blasphemy Act of 1650 against the Ranters had superseded that of 1648. Francis Rous, a member of Cromwell's council, sought Nayler's death, but declared, "The laws against blasphemy and Ranters are in force, and you may proceed upon them," forgetting that the courts had jurisdiction under that statute and that the penalty for a first offense was only six months. John Thurloe, the secretary of state, declared, "I know no law in force this day against blasphemy; unless it be that of the Old Parliament" — the act of 1650.[50]

Could Parliament proceed against Nayler under its *legislative* authority? If so, Cromwell could veto any bill. Parliament might pass a bill of attainder, that is, a legislative declaration of guilt against the accused and a sentence against him; but all the precedents seemed to show that attainders had been based on some standing law — that, at least, was the legal theory. Alternatively, Parliament might proceed by an ex post facto law, making criminal an act committed earlier and not at the time illegal. Some declared that any attainder in this case must be retroactive, but many warned against the injustice of ex post facto laws. "You are launching into a matter of great consequence," warned Major General Howard. "Whatever you do in this, it may be of ill consequence to posterity." "To take away a man's life by a subsequent law, it is of dangerous consequence," warned Colonel William Sydenham, a councillor. Another councillor, Walter Strickland, urged, "I would have every Englishman be careful in this case. It has been our happiness to be governed by a known law." One theme that ran continuously throughout the debates was that Parliament had no law for what it was doing. Yet some took the view that "Parliament is so sovereign, that it may declare that to be an offence, which never was an offence before." When, however, Major General Thomas Kelsey said, near the end, "This is a new business . . . . You have no law for what you do," he was technically correct.[51]

Because the case was unprecedented, there was no knowledge for sure how to proceed or what to call the crime. Government spokesmen had no fixed position, except perhaps that death was too severe a punishment. Those who insisted that Nayler had committed a "horrid" blasphemy demanded death; avenging the honor of God required an exemplary vindication before the whole nation. That too was a major theme of debate, reiterated monotonously. One of the revengers was Bampfield, who chaired the committee report. He called the moderates the "merciful" party. Although Cromwell was the leader of the merciful party, he kept aloof from the affair until after Parliament rendered its judgment. Only then, when demanding to know by what authority the members had acted, did he reveal that not even he could extenuate Nayler's conduct. He detested giving the least countenance "to persons of such opinions and practices, or who are under guilt of such crimes as are imputed to the said person. . . ." But he did not want Nayler executed. Yet his elder son and successor, Lord Richard Cromwell, announced at a state dinner, well before Parliament voted against capital punishment, that "Nayler deserves to be hanged." The members of the Council of State who held seats in Parliament, although tending to oppose death, reflected a spectrum of opinion ranging from broad toleration to bloodthirsty prejudice.[52]

The lord president of the council, Henry Lawrence, was the one who declared that God was in "every horse, in every stone, in every creature," and added, "If you hang every man that says, 'Christ is in you the hope of glory,' you will hang a good many." Every Quaker said that, he observed. He understood and accepted as tolerably Christian Nayler's distinction between the historical Christ who died in Jerusalem and the Christ that was "in him in the highest measure." Lawrence thought it was a "sad" opinion, no more. He could not call it blasphemy of any sort. "It is hard to define what is blasphemy," he remarked. Doubtless, members thought Arianism was blasphemy, and so too was denying the divinity of Christ, but people's private opinions were not an affair of Parliament. Lawrence acknowledged that he knew Quakers, discoursed with them about religion, and read some of their books. He hoped that most Christians knew "the mystery of Christ manifest in the flesh." Still, he thought that Quakers tended too much toward Arminianism and he would restrain them. But not by punishing for blasphemy.[53]

Major General Philip Skippon was also a member of the council. He called himself "the Christian Centurion," although one scholar called him a bigot and a typical Presbyterian. Skippon recommended that Nayler be "hanged, drawn, and quartered." His views represented nearly half the members who voted. The "growth of these things," he said of Quaker practices, "is more dangerous than the most intestine or foreign enemies. I have often been troubled in my thoughts to think of this toleration. . . . Their [Quaker] great growth and increase is notorious, both in England and Ireland; their principles strike at both ministry and magistracy." Skippon was jealous of God's honor and zealous for it. Nayler's blasphemy was "horrid." The Mosiac law governed the nation, Skippon held, and all who blasphemed should be accountable under it. He raged against "these Quakers, Ranters, Levellers, Socinians, and all sorts" who "bolster themselves under [Articles] thirty-seven and thirty-eight [of the Instrument] of Government, which, at one breath, repeals all the acts and ordinances against them." Nayler was the product of the Instrument's liberty of conscience, and so were the sects. "If this be liberty, God deliver me from such liberty. It is to evil, not to good, that this liberty extends." God's glory had been trampled enough by it.[54]

Major General William Boteler, an Independent, agreed with Skippon, and backed his case with biblical precedents, many far-fetched, to prove that Nayler should be stoned to death. As if they were theologians, soldiers and lawyers vied in construing arcane passages from the Scriptures to support of their arguments that Nayler had committed horrid blasphemy, or ordinary blasphemy, or some other offense. The Bible carried more weight by far than the common law, even more than parliamentary law, because the offense was against religion; Puritans knew their Bible and it yielded more precedents to construe than their secular law. George Smith, one of the judges who hanged Jock of Broad Scotland earlier that year, offered the case of several who were hanged in the sixteenth century for speaking against the Book of Common Prayer; and he reminded Parliament, its laws imposed death on a man who stole a shilling. "Yet we make nothing of robbing God of his glory." If the secular law failed, Judge Smith proposed, the Bible showed the way: death by stoning.[55]

Skippon's rant against Quakers, other sects, and liberty of conscience mirrored a theme of the revengers. They used Nayler's case to discredit the burgeoning sects generally and Quakerism in particular, which they found execrable. As of 1656 Nayler loomed larger and more dangerous than George Fox. Skippon believed that only "Biddle and his sect" were as dangerous as Nayler's. In and outside Parliament Nayler was described as "the chief of the Quakers," "a most eminent Ringleader," and "worst of all the Quakers." One member claimed that Nayler "writes all their books." His prominence, especially in London where he had proselytized so successfully, marked him as a target. After Parliament had sealed Nayler's fate, Colonel Sydenham of the council marvelled at how zealous members were against Nayler, yet were so merciful to his four companions whom Parliament also held in the Gatehouse prison. Bampfield, who had brought in the committee report, recommended that the four be sent "to the House of Correction for three months, and [you] rid your hands of them." And yet, Sydenham declared, they were the greater offenders; they had actually committed idolatry, whereas Nayler "denied all honour to himself." With "no law at all for it," Parliament had "opened a gap to prostitute both life, member, and liberty" by the "arbitrary" power of men who had the votes to do whatever they wanted.[56]

The reason for the distinction in treatment between Nayler and his companions is obvious: he appeared to be the great leader. "Cut off this fellow, and you will destroy the sect," one member urged. Anthony Ashley Cooper of the council sensibly replied that if Parliament killed Nayler, it would make him a martyr and multiply Quakerism. Although Cooper was of the merciful party and spoke abstractly for toleration, his Presbyterianism surfaced when he urged, "I would have you use some endeavour to suppress the growth of them in general." Griffith Bodurda, who found no blasphemy in Nayler, believed that "Millenaries" of "this sort of Quakers" should be "suppressed" as dangerous. Major General William Goffe, a prodigious Bible expert who advocated "amity, love, and charity" while urging death for Nayler as a horrid blasphemer, charged that all the Quakers "go about and revile the ordinances and ministers of Christ, and would tear the flesh off the bones that profess Christ." They were all "beasts" and deserved to die. Judge Smith lamented that England had the reputation among nations as "the great nursery of blasphemies and heresies." Colonel Briscoe too was sure that Quakers "are destructive to human society. . . . Do not they all hold against the essence of Government?" Sir George Downing, alarmed because Ranters and Quakers had increased by the "thousands," recommended that Parliament should "take them all off by a law," if it did not execute Nayler. "It is high time to take a course with them," chimed in Glynne, the chief justice; he knew from his experience that they contemned magistracy, and now "they grow to a great number."[57]

Whether the sects should be tolerated was the broad issue of the Nayler case. A few speakers, including Councillors Walter Strickland, Gilbert Pickering, and William Sydenham, like Henry Lawrence, the head of the council, defended toleration of the sects, Quakers included. "If Nayler be a blasphemer," said Sydenham, "all the generation of them are so, and he and all the rest must undergo the same punishment." Yet, "The opinions they hold," he declared, "do border so near a glorious truth, that I cannot pass my judgment that it is blasphemy." Those who defamed the sects and spoke alarmingly about their growth used the instance of James Nayler to reproach the Instrument of Government's toleration. His blasphemy, they claimed, proved that its lax policy easily degenerated into spiritual anarchy, fanaticism, and gross immorality. The result threatened the safety of the nation and of the Protestant religion. Skippon was correct about Article 38, for it held "null and void" all laws against religious freedom that conflicted with Article 37; but Article 37 only roughly defined that freedom. Captain Adam Baynes, one of the tolerationists who did not believe that Nayler had blasphemed, declared, "the Instrument of Government says, all shall be protected that confess faith in Jesus Christ, which, I suppose, this man does." But Colonel Francis White, in support of the same cause, corrected Baynes by quoting the Instrument to show that Article 37 set a proper limit on religious freedom by restricting it to those who did not injure others or practice licentiousness. Downing, a revenger, hoped that the Instrument would not stand in the way of death for a horrid blasphemer; and Goffe claimed that although he would give his life for the Instrument, "Yet if it hold out anything to protect such persons I would have it burnt in the fire."[58]

Lord Strickland, a tolerationist, called attention to the fact that wherever the Gospel flourished, "most prodigies of heresies and opinions" will be found, "which will happen always, unless you restrain the reading of the Scriptures." The right of each person to think for himself about the Scriptures was at stake, and that was what the Instrument protected. Banish Nayler if you must, Strickland observed, but nothing more. Even banishment would be a "dangerous precedent to posterity. It is against the Instrument to proceed. . . ." Bodurda, on the same side, objected to admitting the power of the civil magistrate in matters of religion. Those who demanded Nayler's death, he declared, kept claiming that the mind of God was clear in this matter, and they repeatedly resorted to biblical texts for various proofs; but, said Bordurda, he was sure that Nayler "would also say, 'The mind of God was clear to him,' and it may be proved just, by as many texts." Colonel Holland summed up the tolerationist view: "Consider the state of this nation, what the price of our blood is. Liberty of conscience, the Instrument gives it us. We remember how many Christians were formerly martyred under the notion of blasphemy; and who can define what it is."[59]

Many definitions were offered and applied to the case, but every member shaped his argument to suit the outcome he sought. By no means were all of the "merciful" party tolerationists. Not that anyone opposed toleration in the abstract. Even Skippon and the other revengers favored their brand of it. The real tolerationists were those who opposed finding blasphemy in the case and construed the Instrument and anything else at hand — the Bible, the examples of Holland and Poland, natural law, moral law, common law, and parliamentary law — to prove their point. All the tolerationists were merciful men, but not all the merciful men were tolerationists. Indeed, most who opposed the revengers opposed death or a brutal sentence, but not a lighter sentence. Few openly claimed that Nayler was guiltless or deserved no punishment whatever. But the revengers took the lead, from the moment Bampfield presented the committee's report, and the others resorted to all sorts of maneuvers to oppose whatever motions the vengeful recommended.

At the very beginning, when the committee reported on December 4, 1656, the revengers wanted to condemn Nayler on the basis of the report, while their opponents demanded witnesses, sworn testimony, and a fair trial. For two days Parliament debated whether Nayler should be given an opportunity to speak against the charges, although they had not agreed on the charges. Those who argued for due process voted with many who confidently expected Nayler to hang himself by confessing his guilt. Most members had never seen him and were curious. Major General John Lambert, a councillor, had known Nayler well. "He was two years my quartermaster," Lambert recalled, "and a very useful person. We parted with him with great regret. He was a man of unblameable life and conversation, a member of a very sweet society of an independent church. How he comes. . . . to be puffed up to this opinion I cannot determine."[60]

On December 6 Nayler was brought before the bar of the house. He refused to kneel or remove his hat; they had expected that and agreed that he might stand, but the sergeant-at-arms took off his hat. The clerk read to him the main sections of the committee's report. Thomas Burton, who recorded the parliamentary debate, was one of the vengeful. He recorded that Nayler, "in effect, confessed," and some historians accepted Burton's judgment. However, Nayler's words show only an admission that the committee had accurately reported what he had said. Nayler hoped that Parliament would not misconstrue his meaning. When questioned for less than half an hour, he told the same story as before, denying any worship paid to him. "I abhor it, as I am a creature." If Christ was in him, they asked, how did he pray to the Christ who died at Jerusalem? To questions on this problem Burton recorded none of Nayler's answers, noting only that he "answered pretty orthodoxly."[61]

After Nayler withdrew and awaited judgment in the Gatehouse prison nearby, the debate rambled and raged for nine long days before the decisive voting. The revengers demanded and won immediate acceptance of the committee's report. "Seeing Nayler must die," one member promptly said, "I desire to know what manner of death it must be." Members roared objections. Questions of procedure and jurisdiction remained to be resolved, let alone the character of the offense; talk of punishment was quite premature. On the evening of December 8, the revengers won another victory when Parliament resolved, without a vote count, that Nayler "upon the whole matter, in fact, is guilty of horrid blasphemy." Not even that was conclusive, because they continued to argue as if every question were still open; often more than one question was before the house at a time, and members, on getting the floor addressed several issues. Everything — procedure, jurisdiction, the offense, its punishment — seemed interwoven. But the overriding issue was clear to all: Would death be the punishment?[62]

When the revengers recommended the use of Parliament's legislative power by passing either an attainder or an ex post facto law, the merciful and the tolerationists demurred at the injustice as well as the danger to posterity. When the revengers recommended Parliament's judicial power as the basis for its sentence, the others claimed that no such power existed, or, if it did, it could not extend to life or limb. When a vengeful Ashe located the source of parliamentary judicial authority in *De Haeretico Comburendo,* the act of 1401 for the burning of heretics, the reply shot back, we will never rake out those ashes; under that law we must all burn as heretics and blasphemers. When the revengers claimed that Nayler had blasphemed and that Parliament should not trifle about the law that authorized the death penalty, the others looked to lesser offenses.[63]

When the revengers insisted that Nayler's blasphemy was "horrid," the others ridiculed the distinction between blasphemy and horrid blasphemy, although they adeptly made distinctions of their own to suit their purposes. Those distinctions between blasphemy and lesser offenses saved Nayler's life. The vengeful claimed that Nayler's offense was the "crime that deposes the majesty of God Himself, *crimen laesae maiestatis,* the ungodding of God," as Major Beake said. The vindictive Downing asserted that blasphemy was the highest offense: "treason against Heaven." No one commented on the blasphemous irony in his reminding the house that Nayler would not remove his hat, "though you be gods in one sense." But the other faction denied that Nayler had blasphemed at all. He had exalted himself, Councillor Strickland admitted, but neither he nor any of his followers claimed that he was Jesus or Christ. He did not allege that "the essence of Christ is in him." He was scandalous, overproud, and sinful, but not a blasphemer, because he honored God; a blasphemer would curse or revile Him. All the mercifuls and tolerationists agreed on that point. Leviticus 24:15–16 proved that capital blasphemy consisted only in reviling God.[64]

Bulstrode Whitelocke, the lord commissioner of the treasury and an eminent jurist, studied the Hebrew text and patiently explained it. He defined the Hebrew words, concluding that this was not a case warranting death. Indeed if those lusting for Nayler's blood had understood the very text that they claimed as the basis for their judgment, they would have known that in Hebrew law the crime of blasphemy could not be committed at all unless the very name of God was cursed. Some divines, Whitelocke conceded, disagreed whether the sacred name must be the express object of the curse, but all agreed that without speaking evil of God and making imprecations against Him, there was no blasphemy. At worst, Nayler's offense came within the fifteenth, not the sixteenth, verse of Leviticus 24, and so merited only a whipping. With a lawyer's fine sense for punctilios, Whitelocke noted that the motion to condemn Nayler for "horrid blasphemy" did not specify that it was blasphemy "against God." In any case, God's mind in the matter was not knowable, and His law did not require death. Nayler's claim that Christ dwelt within him did not constitute blasphemy. That claim, Whitelocke observed, was not uncommon, for even the Lutherans believed in "the ubiquity of Christ." Whitelocke recommended that Parliament turn the case over to the Upper Bench; let the highest judges grapple with the problem. Parliament ought to do nothing more. "One Parliament may count one thing horrid blasphemy, another parliament another thing. The word blasphemy may be as far extended as was heresy." Whitelocke hoped not. Once, opposition to tithes was heresy, and now some said that having compulsory tithes was heresy. Learn from past mistakes, Whitelocke urged. If Nayler died, no man might be safe in the future. Whitelocke's long speech was a marvel of erudite learning in law, religion, and history. If any of his listeners had been undecided, they must have been influenced by his proofs that no law — Mosaic, Gospel, moral, natural, national, or international — supported the death penalty.[65]

But Whitelocke persuaded no one whose mind was already convinced. The vengeful members, challenged time and again to define the particular nature of Nayler's blasphemy, replied that Nayler had assumed the honors and attributes of God or Christ, or they misstated the facts by claiming that he had passed himself off as Christ. Every misstatement provided the others with a chance to correct the record. Those who worshipped Nayler were idolaters, said Pickering, but not Nayler. "Take well what he said for himself as well as against." Pickering recalled that the late John Selden, the greatest parliamentarian, after listening to Paul Best the Socinian, had remarked that Best was a better man than he thought himself to be. "That may be this man's case," Pickering added. Nayler simply gave himself out to be "a prophet, a type, a sign, to warn men of the second coming of Christ. . . ." Samuel Highland stressed that Nayler not only did not revile God; he worshipped Christ. Where was the blasphemy?[66]

To that the revengers replied that because Nayler was a Christian, his

assuming the attributes of Christ magnified the offense. The tolerationists responded that he did not say Christ dwelt wholly or exclusively
in him, and one member reminded the others that Christ himself said
that blasphemy should be forgiven (Matt. 4:19). To the revengers,
however, the doctrine of the indwelling Christ was blasphemous in and
of itself. Blasphemy, they admitted, might in its literal sense mean
speaking evil of God, but its commonsense meaning was that no person
could call himself Christ. Major General Packer replied that if the crime
was against God, no man could decide for Him. Many of us, like Job,
are blasphemers, he said. As for Nayler, he adored, not vilified; he believed in the Father, the Son, and the Holy Spirit. Let him repent, even
if it was only a "show" of repentance. Those wanting his death mis-
interpreted his words in such a way as to require the destruction of all
the sects. The Christian way was moderate and tolerant. "You may as
well condemn a Papist," said Packer, "for worshipping Christ in the
bread and wine, as in this case of Nayler's." Cooper saw in Nayler a
dark carriage and a strong delusion, but not blasphemy, surely not horrid blasphemy. If there was horrid blasphemy, did that mean there was
blasphemy "more horrid, and most horrid? I offer it to you, whether it
were not a greater blasphemy to say he were very Christ." Cooper dared
not say it was blasphemy at all. Nayler, he noted, made a "nice distinction, a vast difference between Christ Jesus dwelling in us, and being
worshipped in a creature." Still others seeking to save Nayler said he
acted without malice, was only a seducer or an imposter, merely disturbed the peace, had high delusions, or set up signs like an idolater.
But he was no blasphemer, let alone a horrid one.[67]

On December 16, the members were finally ready for a conclusive
vote. A motion that Nayler be executed lost by a vote of ninety-six to
eighty-two. The debate suddenly collapsed. Rapid motions were introduced on lesser punishments — that his long hair be cut, that he be
branded with a "B," that his tongue be slit — and were voted up or
down. Finally the motions that passed, all without recorded vote, were
stitched together to produce a sentence:

> Resolved, that James Nayler be set on the pillory, with his head in
> the pillory, in the New Palace Westminster, during the space of
> two hours, on Thursday next, and be whipped by the hangman
> through the streets of Westminster to the Old Exchange, London;
> and there, likewise, to be set upon the pillory, with his head in the
> pillory, for space of two hours, between the hours of eleven and
> one, on Saturday next; in each of the said places, wearing a paper
> containing an inscription of his crimes: and that at the Old Ex-

change, his tongue shall be bored through with a hot iron, and that he be there also stigmatized in the forehead with the letter B.; and that he be, afterwards, sent to Bristol and conveyed into and through the said city, on a horse bare ridged, with his face back, and there also publickly whipped, the next market-day after he comes thither: and that from thence he be committed to prison in Bridewell, London, and there restrained from the society of all people, and kept to hard labour till he be released by the Parliament: and, during that time, be debarred of the use of pen, ink, and paper, and have no relief but what he earns by his daily labour.

The boring of the tongue, implicitly, and the branding with "the letter B," explicitly, signified the crime of blasphemy. The sentence was entered as a judgment of Parliament, that is, a judicial sentence not subject to review by the courts, thus preventing appeals, bailing, or release on habeas corpus.[68]

Debate resumed on the question of whether Nayler should be recalled to the bar to hear the sentence. The vengeful members opposed that, although Chief Justice Glynne had never heard of a case in which a convicted man was not given an opportunity to say why judgment should not be passed against him. A compromise was arranged: they voted to call him back to hear their judgment but not to let him speak against it. Sir Thomas Widdrington, the speaker, told Nayler he had escaped death: "They desire your reformation rather than destruction." Nayler asked what his crime was; he tried several times to say more but was cut off. The speaker pronounced the sentence. As Nayler was led away he said, "God will, I hope, give me a spirit to endure it." Some members were bitter that an Englishman should have been denied his right to speak about the judgment against him.[69]

The first part of the sentence was executed on December 18. "The eyes of the whole nation are upon you in this business," revengers had repeated during the debate. Now the eyes of London were on Nayler. He stood in the pillory near Parliament with a paper pinned to his hat, inscribed "For horrid blasphemy and being a Grand Impostor and Seducer of the People." Although the weather was unusually cold, the bailiff stripped him to the waist after they took him down from the pillory, and bound him to the back of a cart which they drew to the Exchange. The executioner, using a whip of seven cords, each knotted, lashed Nayler at every step. He took 310 lashes. Colonel Holland reported to Parliament that the women who later nursed Nayler's wounds told Holland "there was no skin left between his shoulders and his hips." A Quaker, who watched the punishment and walked alongside the cart, reported that he did not cry out.[70]

In Parliament that day members presented petitions against Quakers from various cities and counties. The revengers wanted a statute against them generally and also a new act against blasphemy. The Quakers were all "levellers," said one, against authority and property. Whitelocke opposed either bill. Sydenham agreed: "It is like the word Lollards or Puritans, under the notion whereof, many godly people are now [buried] under the altar, their blood being poured out. It is of dangerous consequence." Strickland would have no act against blasphemy; punish only disturbers of the peace, he argued. "We may all, in after ages, be called Quakers." Laws against Papists, he reminded, had been turned against "the best Protestants." The proposed bills were consigned to a committee which let them die, although in the following year, 1657, Cromwell accepted from Parliament a new constitution that constricted the liberty of conscience guaranteed by the Instrument of Government.[71]

Londoners, having watched Nayler receive the first part of his punishment, petitioned Parliament to suspend the rest of it. General Lambert, affirming that Nayler was too sick to undergo the remainder, urged that a physician be sent to him. Parliament decided to send "some godly ministers" instead, but postponed the next dose of the punishment for another week. On December 20 crowds were at the doors of Parliament with petitions on behalf of Nayler. After a debate whether to receive some prosperous burghers, the house by one vote allowed thirty to enter. They represented about one hundred; their spokesman was once a chaplain in the New Model Army. They were honest, godly persons who disowned the crime, Lambert said. None was a Quaker. Their petition spoke for "Conscience-Liberty." They claimed that the state should not pass judgment on religious error or blasphemy, and that corporal punishment in such a case was wrong. They had signed the petition, they said, out of "tenderness to the cause of spiritual and civil liberty." Resting their case on Article 37 of the Instrument, they requested that the remainder of the sentence be cancelled. When they withdrew, a debate flared anew on the basic question of whether liberty of conscience meant protection for blasphemers, but "being weary of it," the house adjourned for lunch.[72]

The same petitioners, joined by many others, turned to Cromwell. One petition forwarded to him at this time came from George Fox; it was less a petition than a theological statement of the Quaker position on Immanence written when Parliament first took custody of Nayler. Fox did not mention Nayler by name. The only point of pertinence was a cryptic postscript: "If the seed speake which is Christ . . . it is not blasphemie but truth, but if the seed of the serpent speake and say he is Christ it is the Liar and the blasphemie and the ground of all blasphemie. . . ." Cromwell offered no support to the petitioners for "spiritual and civil liberty." He intervened only with a terse letter to Parliament asking for their grounds of the sentence against Nayler. That provoked a two-day debate on constitutional issues bearing on the adjudicatory powers of Parliament and touching only incidentally on the issue of blasphemy. In the end Parliament proved incapable of formulating a response to the protector. But some of the mercifuls tried to use the issue to obtain a decision on the petition to cancel the rest of the sentence. They lost overwhelmingly, 113 to 59. Members knew that when the deputation of ministers had met with Nayler on Christmas Day, he had still defended his beliefs. Downing shouted, "We are God's executioners. . . . Had you anything from himself, of recantation, it were something. But, as the case is, if ten thousand should come to the door and petition, I would die upon the place before I would remit the sentence you have already passed." Even some of the mercifuls made much of the fact that Cromwell had not asked for a remission of the sentence. And Nathaniel Fiennes, a councillor who had stood with the mercifuls, argued that the petition for remission was "dangerous," because it would "debar the civil magistrate in matters of religion. . . . That is too much liberty."[73]

On December 28th Nayler underwent the second part of the sentence. Burton, one of the revengers, was present among the crowd of "many thousands." They were strangely quiet and sympathetic, and those who were closest and could see the spectacle stood bareheaded. Burton recorded that he went

> to see Nayler's tongue bored through, and him marked in the forehead. He put out his tongue very willingly, but shrinked a little when the iron came upon his forehead. He was pale when he came out of the pillory, but highcoloured after tongue-boring. He was bound with a cord by both arms to the pillory. Rich, the mad merchant [a Quaker] sat bare at Nayler's feet all the time. Some times he sang and cried, and stroked his hair and face, and kissed his hand, and sucked the fire out of his forehead. Nayler embraced his executioner, and behaved himself very handsomely and patiently. A great crowd of people there. . .

A week later Nayler still could not speak.[74]

The final part of the sentence was executed in mid-January in Bristol, as a burlesque of Nayler's entrance there about three months earlier. They transported him to that city sitting on a horse with his face to the rear. In Bristol, they stripped him for the whipping. This time, however, the Quakers of the city turned out en masse to support him; many wept. Bristol had more compassion than Westminster. The authorities allowed one of Nayler's friends to hold the executioner's arm to check his lashes. From Bristol, soldiers conveyed him back to London's Bridewell prison to begin a perpetual imprisonment. He was put to hard labour in solitary confinement and denied a fire to keep him warm in winter.[75]

In February 1658 Nayler, who had been gravely ill, repented by acknowledging that he had been possessed by a dark spirit and had received idolatrous worship. The Spirit of Jesus in him now dictated "lowness, meekness and longsuffering." He wanted Fox's forgiveness, but Fox was unyielding. On September 8, 1659, after nearly three years, the Rump Parliament released Nayler. The army, by then, had deposed Richard Cromwell as the second protector, and it freed many Quakers. Nayler, subdued, returned to preaching. At a London meeting arranged by common Friends, he and Fox appeared on the same platform, but Fox was distant. In 1660, thirteen months after his liberation from Bridewell, Nayler at the age of forty-four, a sick and broken man, died — the victim of a system that could not allow "too much liberty." In that year the Stuart Restoration began. Soon after, the Puritan "priests" who had shrieked for Nayler's life, as well as the Quaker preachers who had reviled those priests, were jailed by the tens of thousands, fellow prisoners.[76]

10

CHRISTIANITY BECOMES THE LAW OF THE LAND

After the Restoration of 1660 England's grand political design nourished persecution of conscience, but the term "blasphemy," like "heresy," passed out of style as the formal designation of most offences against religion. During the preceding period of the Interregnum, the Puritans, who found Old Testament precedents attractive, saw blasphemy in those who repudiated the moral law, rejected the doctrine of the Trinity, impersonated Christ, or worshipped the Christ within. English Protestants of the seventeenth century, confronted with some form of the age-old crime of erroneous religious belief, shied from calling it "heresy." That conjured up the stench of burning flesh at Bloody Mary's Smithfield and the image of mangled bodies under the Spanish Inquisition. Even the Anglican church under Laud and the High Commission had avoided "heresy" as the crime *de jure*. "Nonconformity," the principle usage under the early Stuarts, once again became the generic name of the crime under the later Stuarts. "Nonconformity" differed little in substance from "heresy" or "blasphemy"; yet it somehow implied that although conscience was free, seditious subjects obstinately violated the nation's laws requiring uniformity of religious worship. Calling the crime "nonconformity" avoided the appearance of bigotry, at least in the minds of the persecutors.

The Restoration of the Stuart monarchy revived the English constitution as it had existed prior to the civil wars of the 1640s. Acts of Parliament to which the crown had consented were law once again; all subsequent acts and ordinances were null and void. Thus, the High Commission, the Star Chamber, and the oath *ex officio* were dead, but so too was all law from 1642 to the restoration of Charles II. Thus, the Restoration meant that the Church of England was by law established, that the House of Lords sat as a second chamber, that the Anglican bishops were members of the Lords, and that the House of Commons and the common-law courts might thwart the royal prerogative.[1]

The Restoration also meant that persecution rode booted and

spurred once again. The tragedy of the Stuart Restoration consisted in that fact, but it was a tragedy compounded by paradox. Parliament, which represented the nation, was more Anglican than the Anglican church, and both Parliament and the church vigorously advocated intolerance, while Charles II (1660–85) and James II (1685–88), who had the audacity to violate Parliament's customary legislative powers, championed toleration. Indeed, they went further by advocating the free exercise of religion for all peaceable and loyal subjects, without exception. Thus, the later Stuarts outdid Cromwell and matched even the Baptist theorists, the most consistent friends of religious liberty. The phenomenon was novel: royalist policy was enlightened as to conscience but politically autocratic, while Parliament and the church supported persecution and constitutional government.[2]

Charles II immediately declared himself in favor of "a liberty to tender consciences, . . . [so] that no man shall be disquieted or called in question for differences of opinion in matter of religion, which do not disturb the peace of the kingdom. . . ." Although the king would consent to "such an Act of Parliament," Parliament, dominated by Anglican gentry who had suffered during the Puritan regime, was in a vengeful mood. Anglican gentlemen meant to even the score with the Puritans and did not bother to distinguish Presbyterians from Fifth Monarchists, Quakers, or gathered churches. Anyone not a member of the Church of England was considered a potential subversive. Parliament at first singled out the Quakers for special treatment, although the king had promised a Quaker group that none would suffer for their religion "so long as you live peaceably." The Quaker Act of 1662 inflicted fines and imprisonment on the supposedly dangerous opinions and practices of those who met in great numbers and maintained the illegality of all oaths; for five or more such people to assemble for worship not authorized by law became criminal. The Quakers, of course, conscientiously persisted in their worship and suffered the consequences.[3]

The only official road of Protestantism led to the Church of England. In 1662 the Act of Uniformity reinstated the episcopacy, Anglican rites, the Anglican prayerbook, and Anglican ordination; any minister refusing to give his "unfeigned consent" lost his living. Uniformity and conformity were intended to end the "factions" of "the late unhappy troubles." The Conventicles Act of 1664 extended the principle of the Quaker Act: religious assemblies other than Anglican were outlawed to prevent the growing and dangerous practices of "seditious sectaries and other disloyal persons" who met under pretense of conscience to "contrive insurrections," as the "late experience hath showed. . . ." The Five

Mile Act of 1665 fixed penalties for any noncomformist minister who refused to swear an oath that he would seek no alteration in the ecclesiastical policy. The act took its name from the fact that it excluded a nonjuror from teaching, preaching, or living within five miles of a place where he had served as a minister. The Test Act of 1673 required any person holding government office or receiving money from the government to swear an oath against the Catholic doctrine of transubstantiation and to receive the sacrament of the Lord's Supper according to Anglican usage. Without doubt this body of legislation reflected the intense dislike of Englishmen for Catholics, whom the Anglicans outnumbered 170 to 1, and for Puritans and sectarians of any sort, whom Anglicans outnumbered 20 to 1. Charles II, who was wholly dependent on Parliament for money, consented to all the legislation.[4]

On the whole the Anglicans in church and state simply reinforced conventional anti-Catholic policies and reversed the laws enacted by Puritan governments against Anglicanism. All dissenters suffered, the Quakers disproportionately because their faith compelled them to refuse even to pay fines or give sureties for what the courts called "good behaviour"; in effect, "good behaviour" meant apostasy from Quakerism, if not conversion to Anglicanism. Between 1660 and 1688, one-fourth of the sixty thousand nonconformists who suffered for conscience' sake were Quakers. Estimates of the number of nonconformists who died in prison because of the hideous penal conditions of that era range as high as five to eight thousand. Those figures are doubtlessly exaggerated, but by any reckoning the persecution was widespread and appalling. Richard Baxter, the Presbyterian moderate who himself became a victim of the persecution, conceded that after the Conventicles Act,

> . . . the Fanaticks called Quakers did greatly relieve the sober People for a time; for they were so resolute, and gloried in their Constancy and Sufferings, that they assembled openly . . . and were dragged away daily to the Common Jail; and yet desisted not, but the rest came the next day nevertheless. So that the jail at Newgate was filled with them. Abundance of them died in prison, and yet they continued their Assemblies still. And the poor deluded Souls would sometimes meet only to sit still in Silence. . . . And it was a great question whether this Silence was a religious exercise allowed by the liturgy, etc.[5]

In 1672 Charles II, having concluded that persecution bore only bitter fruit, brazenly exercised his "inherent" royal prerogative as the "supreme power in ecclesiastical matters." He summarily suspended the execution of all penal laws "against whatsoever sort of non-conformists, or recusants," and ordered all his officers to obey. In his "Declaration of Indulgence," the king commanded that to avoid illegal conventicles, all Protestants should be free to worship as they pleased publicly, Roman Catholics privately. Charles went as far as he dared for the "Papists," and he did not mind winning the loyalty of the non-conformists. He was himself religiously indifferent, and he said nothing about the religious value of freedom of conscience. His reasons for the Declaration of Indulgence were realistically based on secular, if not political, grounds. Twelve sad years of experience, he said, showed that coercion settled none of the religious differences among his subjects and did not prevent "seditious conventicles." Exempting dissenters from the penal laws would diminish the political dangers from religious discord, bring peace to the realm, and encourage both commerce and immigration. Parliament, enraged by a renewal of the old Stuart propensity to legislate unilaterally, compelled Charles to revoke his declaration. The church, obsessed by its own ecclesiastical concerns, supported Parliament against the king, although one of the intriguing aspects of the persecution is that secular considerations motivated the church and Parliament, as well as Charles.[6]

The growing prevalence of secular considerations, as contrasted with theological, explains why prosecutions for blasphemy were so infrequent during an era of persecution. The church, although controlled by vengeful Anglicans under Gilbert Shelton, the archbishop of Canterbury, had sound historic reasons for hating sectarians. Yet the church was no monolith. It was hospitable to any Christian who could accept conformity on matters of rites, ordination, and the prayerbook. Many churchmen thought such matters concerned only externals. Ever since Elizabeth's time the church sought to be comprehensive and national; during the Restoration period, it harbored a wide spectrum of religious convictions, ranging from Calvinism to Arminianism to Anglo-Catholicism. Although intensely antipapal and nationalistic, Anglo-Catholicism was a movement within the church that neared as much as possible to the pageantry and ceremonials of Roman Catholicism. The Anglo-Catholic or "High Church" movement composed a distinct minority within Anglicanism, but a politically powerful one. The church also included latitudinarians, who favored the broadest comprehensiveness. The most tolerant of the Anglicans, the latitudinarians were satisfied with subscription to the fundamentals of the Christian faith: acceptance of the Apostles Creed, which included belief in the doctrine of the Trinity and in the Scriptures as divinely inspired. The diversity within the Anglican church produced a decline in a distinctive Anglican theology.[7]

Not even the high-church men claimed theological infallibility or the absolute truth of their beliefs. The episcopacy, with notable exceptions, had practical, not theological, reasons for supporting Parliament's persecution policy. Personal and institutional considerations outweighed theological ones. Bishops no longer persecuted to redeem lost souls or even to save uncontaminated believers from the contagion of heretical opinions. Anglicans rarely disputed with each other on the overweening issue of how to achieve salvation; Anglicanism conceded that religious truth could not be known with certainty. The theological motive for persecution was still triumphant only when antitrinitarians — Socinians, Muggletonians, Deists, freethinkers, or "atheists" — came to official notice or entered as topics of abstract debate. The institutional motive to persevere in the attack on nonconformity was fundamentally secular. At issue was good order and the power to govern the church and to reap the benefits of patronage and perquisites.[8]

The Anglican church had become the true church not because it was right but because it was in power. If it was right, the reason was that it contributed to good order, dignity, the political influence of the episcopacy, and the livings of episcopally ordained priests. If it was right, the reason also was that it was the church established by law: to defy it was wrong because illegal. Anglicanism seemed congruent with the constitution and security of the realm, as well as the well-being of the great majority of Englishmen who were faithful communicants. The theological basis of persecution, the saving of souls, dramatically waned even as the persecution itself reached new peaks. Few Anglicans believed that uniformity was really possible; religious diversity had gone too far for that. The trouble was that external conformity, which was all the church hoped for, had passed the threshold of possibility too; but few Anglicans understood that. Some realized that even external conformity, which barely touched the conscience (as they saw the matter), could be achieved only by extreme measures that England was not willing to undertake: the physical extirpation of dissenters, Protestant and Roman Catholic, by a terrible and systematic exercise of power comparable to the Inquisition and lasting over several generations.[9]

But death for religious differences was no longer an acceptable English way. The Nayler case had proved that, even when the crime was "horrid blasphemy." Despite its panoply of repressive measures, Charles's Cavalier Parliament inflicted moderate penalties for violations. Non-Anglicans could not hold political or religious offices and endured other civil disabilities such as the loss of the right to sue in the courts, or be guardians and trustees, or receive legacies and deeds. The maximum imprisonment under the Act of Uniformity was three months. The Conventicles Act imposed only fines until the third offense, which required "transportation" or banishment for seven years. The Five Mile Act provided for fines and a maximum sentence of six months' imprisonment.

In practice the courts, when confronted with the obdurate recalcitrance of a Quaker or of a principled Baptist like John Bunyan, could keep a man in jail indefinitely for contempt; but he had his own key: he could get out anytime he agreed to sureties for good behavior. The statutes required civil disabilities, fines, and light imprisonment. Conscientious objectors, like Bunyan, who spent twelve years in jail, embarrassed the government and the church. The magistrates who enforced the laws had to choose between ignoring prescribed penal sanctions and increasing them by punishing for contempt. Englishmen could make fine distinctions between punishing for contempt, sedition, or nonconformity, and punishing for conscience. But England did not like making the exercise of conscience a felony. Even the few Cromwellians who fell back on *De Haeretico Comburendo* during the debate on Nayler's case would not have burned anyone. Indeed, it was the Cavalier Parliament of 1677, no less, that repealed the act of 1401 that had established the writ for burning obdurate heretics. Criminal prosecution for "heresy" really died as a result of the reforms of the Long Parliament of 1641. The act of 1677 belatedly recognized that fact. Ecclesiastical courts had returned to business in 1660, and the act of 1677 authorized them to punish for "atheism, blasphemy, heresy, schism, or other damnable doctrine or opinion," but those courts had neither fang nor claw. At most they could only excommunicate.[10]

Parliaments of the Restoration did not argue that conscience should be punished; their position was that conscience pushed to external disobedience of the law raised the specter of seditious conspiracy. To Parliament, nonconformity suggested regicide, treason, revolution, civil war, and the persecution of Anglicanism. Thomas Tomkins, the archbishop of Canterbury's chaplain, wrote that "gathered churches," the backbone of Cromwell's army, "are most excellent materials to raise new troops out of." Samuel Parker, Tomkin's successor and later bishop of Oxford, warned that toleration of different sects meant that if the "grandees" took control, "there is an army." An order for the suppression of nonconformists, in 1683, spoke of the "seditious and rebellious practices of the sectaries" and blamed the nonconformist preachers as the authors of "the late execrable treasons."[11]

The anomaly of the great persecution of 1660 to 1688 is that the theory of toleration grew while the theory of persecution for the sake of religion waned. In state and church, those who argued for persecution relied heavily on political considerations. They imagined that worship outside the church hatched subversive plots. The persecutors demanded law and order — obedience for its own sake as a Christian and a political virtue. The church, for them, was the cement of a safe and sane society. Their persecution policy mirrored their conviction that the state had an obligation to preserve the church so that the church could buttress the state.[12]

Theological reasons for persecution are blind to reason; secular reasons for persecution disintegrate when experience proves them to be unfounded. Religious reasons for toleration meet with prejudiced repudiation; secular reasons for toleration become acceptable when experience validates them. During the Restoration period, excellent tracts were published by Baptists, moderate Independents, Socinians, and Quakers, making the argument for toleration on religious grounds. Even Fox spoke for toleration, although William Penn had no superior among the Quakers. His *Great Case of Liberty of Conscience* (1671) put the religious argument in imperishable terms, but *England's Present Interest Discovered* (1675), his next tract, reached the same conclusions on the basis of political and commercial considerations, and it would eventually prove to be more persuasive. Toleration, however, waited on a second revolution against the Stuarts.[13]

Until then the government prosecuted nonconformists because they subverted church and state. Most prosecutions — and there were thousands — were for violations of parliamentary enactments, but prosecutors abetted by magistrates developed the theory that at bottom the criminality of nonconformity consisted in its seditiousness — subversion of church and state. No court would concede that mere difference of religious opinion was *per se* a crime. That difference had to take on a dangerous political coloration before subjecting victims to penalties.

When John Bunyan was arrested in 1660 for preaching Baptist doctrine, no law existed for prosecuting him until ingenious local magistrates invoked Elizabethan acts against conventicles and for uniformity in religion. The magistrates offered Bunyan his freedom in return for sureties for his good behavior, but he was as intractable as a Quaker. Indomitably he pledged to resume his preaching from the moment prison did not prevent him. The government indicted him for unlawful sermons and conventicles "to the great disturbance of the . . . Kingdom." The magistrate told him that his sort of nonconformity led to "insurrection" and the "ruin of the kingdom." Bunyan's three-month sentence turned into an imprisonment for twelve years; his refusal to abandon his ministry amounted to perpetual contempt, and his mounting fines and jailor's fees made his liberation seem impossible. The law had no way to cope with his spiritual steadfastness, which it had converted into a political crime. Only Charles II's Declaration of Indulgence provided a means of releasing Bunyan. His name and those of others like him were added to a list of pardons, including the remission of fees, intended mainly for the benefit of Quakers. Bunyan had the same experience as the Puritan minister Mathew Mead, who was also arrested in 1660. He wrote: "I have been charged with faction and sedition, nay that I preached rebellion and treason is charged on this sermon, though I mentioned not either the King or his government."[14]

Most of the famous "state trials" of nonconformist ministers were, similarly, prosecutions for seditiousness, which became the common-law synonym for nonconformity. Although seditiousness can be defined in technical terms, the crime, if judged by actual prosecutions, consisted in criticizing or differing from the government — its form, constitution, officers, laws, symbols, conduct, and policies. In effect any comment was seditious that could be construed to have the bad tendency of lowering the public's esteem for the government or of disturbing the peace. When the head of the state was the head of the church, nonconformity or criticism of the church became virtually indistinguishable from sedition.

Field's case of 1662 was a turning point in the law because the King's Bench, the highest criminal court of the realm, resolved the legal issue. Field was indicted for seditious words because he said from the pulpit, "the government of the Church of England is popish, superstitious. . . ." His counsel argued that the matter was "spiritual and ecclesiastical," not against the government, and not within its criminal jurisdiction. The prosecutor argued that Field had, in effect, said that the king was a heretic or a papist "to the disturbance of the Government now established." Field denied that and denied speaking with malice. On conviction, he was disabled from all civil and ecclesiastical offices, fined £500, and jailed until he paid the fine. His motion to arrest the judgment failed, on ground that although he spoke only against the church, "The government of England is all one, and all from one foundation, though in several parts. . . . The ecclesiastick is the prime part of the Government. . . ." Lord Chief Justice Robert Foster pronounced the judgment. A precedent of 1618 had laid down the same rule, that criticism of the church was "*seditious parolls encontre le State de nostre Esglise & encontre le peace del Relme,*" but the precedent had been forgotten until published by a court reporter, using manuscript records, in 1668, six years after Field's case.[15]

After Field's case, nonconformity constituted one form of the crime of seditiousness at common law, even in the absence of any parliamentary enactments. Two years later, in 1664, Chief Justice Robert Hyde, Foster's successor, mercilessly browbeat a Baptist preacher, Benjamin Keach, and bulldozed the jury into convicting him for seditious libel. Keach's crime was publishing a book in which he said such things as "Believers only are the right subjects of Baptism" and "Infants are not to be received into the Church. . . ." Keach was pilloried twice, fined £20, and imprisoned for two weeks. Trials like Keach's continued throughout the Restoration.[16]

One of the cruelest and most sensationally publicized cases was that of Thomas Delaune, a London Baptist who made his living by teaching and translating. In 1683 he published (without imprimatur) a small book entitled *A Plea for the Nonconformists*. His argument was reasoned and temperate, free from the scurrility that characterized partisan writings at that time. The attorney general prosecuted him for seditious libel before the King's Bench presided over by Chief Justice George Jeffreys, whose ferocity earned him the nickname "Bloody Jeffreys." Delaune was convicted, fined, and forced to watch the burning of his book by the hangman. Unable to pay the fine, Delaune was imprisoned in Newgate. Wealthy Baptists could have paid his fine of £67, but he preferred to suffer as a witness for his religion. His wife and child joined him in Newgate and soon died there; after fifteen months, he too died from the foul conditions. The secret presses turned out four editions of his book while he was in Newgate, and they also printed his *Narrative of the Sufferings of Thomas Delaune* (1684). In 1706, Daniel Defoe wrote the introduction to the seventh edition of the book for which Delaune gave his life.[17]

The most celebrated of all the nonconformist ministers who were prosecuted for seditious libel was Richard Baxter. In 1685, at the age of seventy, Baxter was Puritanism's gray eminence. Six lawyers defended him against the prejudiced Jeffreys who had instigated his trial on learning that Baxter's latest book supposedly criticized the bishops of the Anglican church. Baxter had denounced Roman Catholic bishops, but court and prosecution wrested innuendos from his words and called them seditious libel. Jeffreys maligned Baxter throughout the trial, obstructed his lawyers, and harangued the jury on the theme that he was "the main incendiary" in a nonconformist "design to ruin the king and nation." The packed jury whispered a moment and agreed on a verdict of guilty. Jeffreys fined Baxter 500 marks (about £333) and ordered him to prison until he paid it. Baxter's friends who had hired his counsel could have paid the fine, but they realized that Jeffreys would get revenge sooner or later, if Baxter did not suffer some disgrace. Influential friends managed to arrange for his imprisonment in a private home, where he lived comfortably while they pulled strings for him. After seventeen months, James II pardoned him and remitted his fines, leaving Baxter to preach until his death in 1691. The ordinary nonconformist minister was not as fortunate.[18]

Since seditiousness comprehended offenses against religion in cases from Bunyan's to Baxter's, as well as offenses against the temporal government, blasphemy, which was most obviously an offense against religion, became in legal theory a form of seditiousness. In the first Restoration case involving blasphemy, Sedley's case of 1663, the issue of blasphemy was tangential. That crime is basically verbal in character. Sedley's immoral words and conduct provoked a riot, overwhelming the blasphemous aspect of his crime. We have no record of what he said, and his intoxication probably mitigated the verbal offense. Nevertheless, his case is significant because the common-law courts took jurisdiction over what formerly had been a matter exclusively within the authority of the ecclesiastical courts.

Sir Charles Sedley (1639?–1701) became a dramatist and "one of the best gay lyric poets of the century." In his youth he was a notorious rake. He was about twenty-four on the day when he and some friends got roaring drunk at an inn near Covent Garden. According to one account by a contemporary, the revelers in broad daylight went out onto the balcony of the inn "and putting down their Breeches they excrementiz'd in the Street: which being done, Sedley stripped himself naked and with Eloquence preached Blasphemy to the People." Samuel Pepys, the diarist, based his account of the young aristocrat's escapade on the remarks of a friend who observed the trial before the King's Bench. There Sedley stood, Pepys wrote, naked on the balcony, "acting all the postures of lust and buggery that could be imagined, and abusing of the scripture, as it were, from thence preaching a Montebank sermon from that pulpitt, saying that he hath to sell such a pouder as should make all the cunts in town run after him — a thousand people standing underneath to see and hear him." After his speech, Sedley "took a glass of wine and washed his prick in it and then drank it off," and then he took another and toasted the king.[19]

The brief notes of the court reporters speak mystifyingly. One primly recorded that Sedley did "such things, and spoke such words" that were misdemeanors against the public peace "to the great scandal of

Christianity." Thus, the offense, in part at lèast, was verbal and against religion, although the reporters did not mention "blasphemy." In passing sentence against Sedley in 1663, Chief Justice Foster told him that the King's Bench, being custodians of the public morality, meant to punish "profane" actions against Christianity. Foster imposed a fine of 2000 marks, a week's imprisonment, and sureties for good behavior for three years. When asked whether he had anything to say, Sedley is supposed to have remarked that he thought he was the first person "that paid for shitting." He was also the first person (whose case was reported) to be punished by the common law for a crime later called obscenity and, possibly, he was the first to be punished for blasphemy. In later cases the courts would develop the implications of *Rex* v. *Sedley*. During the Restoration the common-law courts began extending secular control over various offenses against Christianity. The law of blasphemy developed in that broad context, connected with crimes such as seditious libel, obscenity, public immorality, profanity, and perjury. But blasphemy always remained a distinct crime.[20]

Very likely the first person to be charged with blasphemy after the Sedley case was Ludowick Muggleton, in 1664. Muggleton had suffered imprisonment for that crime in 1653, under the act against Ranters, after he and Reeve publicly announced their divine commissions as the Two Witnesses. By 1664 Muggleton was the sole prophet of an obscure sect, hardly known outside of London, that bore his name. The Muggletonians discussed the Bible but did not believe in prayer and had no rites. They believed in a deviant but harmless version of Christianity that produced tolerant, morally upright, and industrious people. But they were nonconformists of a type that most Christians then loathed as antichristian, becuase they repudiated the doctrine of the Trinity. Muggleton himself also claimed a power to damn eternally, which might be construed as a divine attribute. That the Muggletonians were few in number, lacking in religious enthusiasm, almost unknown, and not given to worship in any conventional sense probably saved them from blasphemy prosecutions. Their leader, however, was an eloquent man who knew his Bible but had not yet learned to fear man's law.

While traveling in the vicinity of Nottingham, Muggleton got into a religious dispute with some nonconformists, mainly Quakers and Independents. He pronounced the sentence of eternal damnation on several people, who complained to the parish priest. The priest got him arrested and taken before the mayor's court in Chesterfield. During the examination, the priest asked Muggleton whether he believed in the Trinity. 'I answered, No, I did believe there was three Names, or Titles, of Father, Son, and Holy Ghost, but one Person, the Lord Jesus Christ." At the conclusion of the examination, they charged him with blasphemy for denying the Trinity, claiming to be one of the Witnesses referred to in Revelation 11:3, claiming the power to damn and save, and saying that "the Scriptures would do them little good now." On the latter point, Muggleton believed that God would not intervene in the affairs of men until Judgment Day. He was imprisoned in Derby to await trial before the Assize. Muggleton's prosecutors made the mistake of taking his horse. The earl of Newcastle, the local magnate, knew nothing about the religious issue, but he placed a high value of the sanctity of private property. He reproved the major and town recorder for their offense against Muggleton. When the Assize met, the judge allowed Muggleton bail for his appearance at the next session. Muggleton might have sued the town officials, but they arranged to let him disappear, ending the matter. He had spent only nine days in jail. The next time he was charged with blasphemy, he did not get off so easily.[21]

Thomas Hobbes, the political theorist, found himself in a risky situation in 1666, because he had saturated his enduring monument, *The Leviathan* (1651), with his skepticism about Christianity, leaving the faint odor of atheism. Hobbes, in fact, strongly supported a state church, although for political reasons exclusively; he considered only the safety of the state, not the intrinsic values of religion. In October 1666, the House of Commons talked about reviving the writ *De Haeretico Comburendo* to cope with Hobbes. The great fire that had burned London in that year, following the terrible plague of the preceding year, seemed to some of the devout a visitation of divine wrath that ought to be appeased. The House of Commons established a committee to which it submitted for consideration a bill "touching such books as tend to atheism, blasphemy, and profaneness, or against the essence and attributes of God, and in particular . . . the book of Mr. Hobbes called the *Leviathan*. . . ." The bill failed, however, making Hobbes, in the words of Sir James Fitzjames Stephen, "the last person of eminence who went in fear of it [the writ for burning heretics]." Parliament permanently abolished the writ in 1677, as has been noted.[22]

The first person during the Restoration to get into serious trouble for blasphemy was William Penn. In 1668, he had been a Quaker for only a year. His father, Admiral Sir William Penn, who professed whatever the Church of England required, never understood how his son could be so obsessed by religion. Oxford expelled young William after two years for his nonconformity, and he finished his education among the Huguenots in France. After a year of law, he tasted the military life and was a courtier. An accidental encounter with a Quaker preacher in 1667 ended in Penn's conversion, conscripting his prodigious talents into the Quaker and tolerationist causes. A year later, when he was twenty-four, Penn published *Sandy Foundations Shaken*, a tract intended to answer Presbyterian tenets. Pepys called it "Penn's book against the Trinity," indicating why it immediately became notorious. John Evelyn, in his diary, paraphrased a public gazette which reported that Penn had written "a blasphemous book against the deity of our B[lessed] *Lord*." Penn called the Presbyterian version of the Trinity, which was identical to the Anglican, "a fiction." Relying on Scriptures for his argument, he sounded like a Socinian. One passage, intended to reveal the illogic of the doctrine of the Trinity, dangerously verged on ridicule: "And since the Father is God, the Son is God, and the Spirit is God, then unless the Father, Son and Spirit are three distinct nothings, they must be three distinct substances, and consequently three distinct Gods. . . . If each person be God, and that God subsists in three persons, then in each person are three persons or Gods, and from them three, they will increase to nine and so ad infinitum. . . ." Penn's Presbyterian opponent, Thomas Vincent, replied to "the Quaker's hideous blasphemies, Socinian and damnably-heretical opinions."[23]

When the printer of Penn's book was arrested, Penn turned himself in to Lord Arlington, the secretary of state. Arlington consulted the Privy Council. The "Helm of the Church," Penn mistakenly wrote, procured his imprisonment. Arlington and the king himself were responsible. The council ordered Penn to be committed to the Tower of London as a "close" prisoner, meaning that he was to be kept in solitary confinement and denied the usual amenities that political prisoners of his class enjoyed in the Tower. The order of the council explicitly stated the cause of imprisonment: "a blasphemous treatise." The council did not even care that it was unlicensed. While Penn froze in his attic room in the winter and smothered in the summer, the council took its time investigating. It had no power to convict and sentence, but it could hold a person indefinitely while it investigated his offense against the government.[24]

Penn was never formally charged or tried. "That which I am credibly inform'd to be the greatest reason for my Imprisonment," he wrote, "and that noise of Blasphemy, which hath pierced so many Ears of late, is, *my denying the Divinity of Christ, and divesting him of his Eternal Godhead*. . . ." Admiral Penn petitioned the council for clemency to no avail, but managed to send a family retainer to see his son in the Tower. "Thou mayest tell my father . . . these words: That my prison shall be my Grave, before I will budge a Jot; for I owe my Conscience to no

Mortal Man." Those brave words were spoken on Christmas Eve 1668, after less than two weeks in the Tower. Soon after, the king sent his chaplain, Dr. Edward Stillingfleet, the archdeacon of St. Paul's, to convince Penn that he held "blasphemous and heretical opinions."[25]

The choice of Stillingfleet as the king's emissary proved to be fortunate for Penn, for Stillingfleet was then close to the latitudinarians within the church, although he grew more conservative as he rose to a bishopric. Although Stillingfleet could not budge Penn from Quakerism, Penn convinced Stillingfleet that he had never meant to reject the divinity of Christ. He asked Stillingfleet to inform the king that "the Tower is the worst argument in the world to convince me." He also addressed letters to the secretary of state, complaining of his harsh treatment, the fact that he had never had a judicial hearing, and his being held "without legal cause or just procedure, contrary to the privileges of every Englishman." Neither king, bishop, nor council relented. Stillingfleet suggested that Penn put in print a clarification of his views on the Trinity. Penn promptly published *Innocency with Her Open Face Presented by way of apology for the Book Entitled The Sandy Foundation Shaken,* thereby vindicating himself and winning his release. He had suffered in the Tower for eight and a half months. Later, when James II sat on the throne, Penn credited him with using his influence as duke of York in getting Penn his freedom.[26]

While in the Tower, Penn's cause was taken up by the Socinians, doing him no good, nor the Quakers either. Excluding the handful of Socinians and Muggletonians in England, no Christian then conceded that antitrinitarianism was Christian; all, rather, agreed that it was blasphemy. Yet Penn's seeming lapse into Socinianism suggests that more Englishmen were drifting toward it. Thomas Firmin, one of Biddle's converts whom Cromwell once dismissed as a "curl-pate boy," was becoming London's greatest merchant and earned the nation's gratitude for his philanthropy during the great plague of 1665 and the London holocaust of 1666. Firmin never abandoned or hid his antitrinitarianism, although he joined the Anglican church, which required external conformity only. Inquisitions into men's beliefs really had died with the abolition of the High Commission in 1641. Firmin, who was on good terms with nonconformist leaders and Anglican bishops alike, welcomed Penn as a Socinian, but their friendship cooled when Penn wrote the apology that was the price of his freedom.[27]

Penn explicitly declared that although he denied a Trinity of three separate persons in one Godhead, "yet I do not consequentially deny the Deity of Jesus Christ." Penn admitted having read Socinus and, courageously, he praised Socinus's wisdom; "if in anything I acknowledge the verity of his Doctrine, it is for Truth's sake, of which, in many things, he had a clearer prospect than most of his contemporaries." That was a risky acknowledgment, but Penn emerged from the incident as a Sabellian, not a Socinian: for him the three persons of the Trinity expressed different manifestations or aspects of God. That Penn continued to deny the Athanasian creed is unquestionable. Many Anglicans, however, also rejected what Penn called the "Popish School" on the doctrine of the Trinity.[28]

Although Penn repudiated Socinianism, he had unwittingly opened what later became a major theological controversy in England, leading to a new act against antitrinitarian blasphemy in 1698. By 1672 Penn was in the vanguard against the "Biddlean or Socinian Cause," while Henry Hedworth, a follower of Biddle and a friend of Firmin, from the safety of anonymity defended the opinion on Christ of Christians "who for distinction sake call themselves Unitarians, being so called in those places [Holland], where by the Laws of the country they have equal Liberty of Religion with other men. . . ." Hedworth was the first Englishman to call himself a Unitarian. By the end of the century there were many.[29]

A "unitarian" of a different sort, but as thoroughgoing as any in his outright denial of trinitarianism, had been plaguing the Quakers for years with his denunciations of their "bodiless God," the Inner Light. Lodowick Muggleton had published *The Neck of the Quakers Broken* (1663) and *A Looking Glass for George Fox* (1668). Those books attracted more attention than Muggleton bargained for: in 1670 he was a wanted man. His heterodoxy on the Trinity caused his book to be seized and publicly burned as blasphemous, but he went into hiding, evading capture for six years. Penn, having taken on the Socinians, challenged Muggleton too, and his attack, *The New Witnesses proved Old Heretics . . . the Doctrines of John Reeve and Lodowick Muggleton . . . Proved to be Mostly Ancient Whimsies, Blasphemies, and Heresies* (1672), did nothing for the cause of toleration. Muggleton, it is true, had been overgenerous in sentencing Quakers to eternal damnation for their unpardonably "blasphemous" sin of denying his commission. More than half of all his curses were against Quakers, including Fox and Penn. But Muggleton made no exception to his principle of equal practice of conscience for all. To Fox he had written:

I have always loved the persecuted better than I did the persecutor, and I always had compassion upon the afflicted for conscience-sake, though I knew they suffered for a mere lie, as all you Quakers do. Yet I say, whoever doth persecute you for conscience in meeting and worshipping an unknown God (as you Quakers do), I say those men that do persecute you willingly, will be every man of them damned to eternity.

Penn did nothing to reciprocate the sentiment of tolerance toward the Muggletonians or the Socinians. It was Firman, the Socinian, who financed the relief of the French Huguenots (Calvinists), the descendants of those who had burned Servetus, when hundreds of them fled to England for their lives.[30]

In 1675 John Taylor, a yeoman from Guildford in Surrey, uttered words so blasphemous that not even a Socinian tolerationist would defend his liberty of opinion. The magistrates in Guildford kept Taylor in jail while they forwarded a statement of his case to the House of Lords at Westminster. The Lords, perceiving that they might be confronting the most horrendous case of blasphemy since James Nayler's, summoned Taylor under heavy guard and also all the officials and witnesses from Guildford. Three days later Taylor was brought to the bar of the house and his words, as taken down by the mayor of Guildford, were read to him. He admitted that he was the author of the blasphemies. His confession so startled the Lords that they ordered the keeper of the hospital in Bedlam to lock him up "and take Care that the said John Taylor be kept there with Bread and Water, and such Bodily Corrections as may conduce his recovery from Madness wherewith at present he seems possessed." The keeper of Bedlam was under orders to return Taylor in the event that he "shall not be proved to be mad, but persist in the said Blasphemies." Six days later the keeper reported that his treatment proved that Taylor, although persisting in his blasphemies, was not mad. The Lords wisely decided to refer the matter to the highest judges of the land for a recommendation on procedure.[31]

Six months later the judges advised that while the ecclesiastical courts should proceed against Taylor for his "horrid" words, "We are also of the opinion, That inasmuch as many of the said words tend immediately to the Destruction of all Religion and Government," Taylor should be prosecuted in the "King's Temporal Courts, as for a high Misdemeanor." That decision marked a watershed in English law. Never before had the common-law courts taken jurisdiction in a case of blasphemy *per se*.[32]

In early 1676 Taylor went to trial before the King's Bench, presided over by Lord Chief Justice Matthew Hale, England's greatest jurist since Coke. The accusation against Taylor was that he had defamed Christianity by blaspheming God and Christ, having loudly said in public:

Christ is a whore-master, and religion is a cheat, and profession [of Christianity] is a cloak, and they are both cheats, and all the earth is mine, and I am a king's son, my father sent me hither, and made me a fisherman to take vipers, and I neither fear God, devil, nor man, and I am a younger brother to Christ, an angel of God, and no man fears God but an hypocrite, Christ is a bastard, God damn and confound all your gods, Christ is the whore's master.

With embellishment the king's attorney described the words as great blasphemy and scandal to the ruination of Christian "government and society."[33]

Taylor pleaded not guilty, although he acknowledged having said all the words except "bastard." His defense was that he meant the words in a different sense from that placed on them by the prosecution. By whoremaster, for instance, he intended that Christ was the "master of the whore of Babylon," a standard Puritan allusion to the Church of Rome. Taylor, according to the report of the trial, used "such kind of evasions for the rest," but the jury believed the prosecution. Chief Justice Hale sentenced Taylor to stand in the pillory in three different places, wearing a paper saying "for blasphemous words, tending to the subversion of all government." Taylor also had to pay a fine of 1000 marks and find sureties for good behavior for life.[34]

Before passing sentence, Hale delivered the opinion that made Taylor's case the most important from the standpoint of jurisprudence that had ever been or ever would be decided in England on the subject of blasphemy. Two brief versions of Hale's opinion exists, in the notes of the same reporter. In one, Hale acknowledged that although Taylor's words were "of ecclesiastical cognisance," the common law could punish them because they tended "to the dissolution of all government." As in the cases of nonconformist preaching or publishing, the words here were akin to seditious libel, although Hale did not use that term. He defined blasphemy as "contumelious reproaches of God, or the religion establisht," and reasoned that blasphemy, by "taking away religion," left no basis for obligations to government as by oaths. In stating the rule of the case he said that "injuries to God" are punishable by the criminal courts, because the "Christian religion is part of the law itself. . . ." In the other, similar report, Hale said:

And . . . such kind of wicked blasphemous words were not only an offence to God and religion, but a crime against the laws, State and Government, and therefore punishable in this Court. For to say, religion is a cheat, is to dissolve all those obligations whereby

the civil societies are preserved, and that Christianity is parcel of
the laws of England; and therefore to reproach the Christian
religion is to speak in subversion of the law.[35]

The sentence against Taylor was lenient compared with Nayler's and
with the near victory of those who had demanded his death. In that
sense, Taylor's case showed that abhorrence of the crime had diminished. In England at that time people were still being hanged for stealing a shilling or for being witches. Hale himself ordered the execution
of two women convicted for being witches, a capital felony. A fine of
1000 marks against Taylor, a simple farmer, ensured his imprisonment
for life; thus the sentence was not as merciful as it sounds, but it was devoid of the cruelty that characterized Nayler's punishment. The enduring significance of Taylor's case lies in the comprehensive definition of
the crime, "contumelious reproaches" against God or the established
religion, and in the doctrine, which still survives in England, that Christianity is part of the law of the land. No other case on blasphemy had
such far-reaching effects, in America as well as in England. It reverberated down the centuries in many cases in which freedom of religious
opinion or separation of church and state was at issue.[36]

In the year following Taylor's case, the King's Bench convicted
another blasphemer, Lodowick Muggleton. He had been in hiding since
a warrant was issued for his arrest in 1670. As time passed he became
incautious. A lawsuit involving him as the executor of a friend's estate
brought him into an ecclesiastical court in 1676. He was recognized
and arrested on a charge of blasphemy. The indictment referred only to
Muggleton's book of 1663, *The Neck of the Quakers Broken.* An act of
1674 had immunized against prosecution any illegal publications more
than three years old. Accordingly, the only book by Muggleton that
could lawfully be the basis of an indictment was his *Answer to William
Penn,* published in 1673. It contained abundant evidence of his denying
the doctrine of the Trinity and his assumption of the divine attribute of
bestowing eternal blessing and damnation; yet neither the indictment
nor the prosecutor mentioned the book of 1673. Apparently the
government did not know about its existence. The fact that it had been
published anonymously meant nothing; so had the book of 1663. Muggleton's theology and style were unique, and his book of 1673, like the
one of a decade earlier, revealed him as surely as if he had put his name
on the title page.[37]

At the trial in 1677, Muggleton's court-appointed counsel rested his
defense by pointing out that the book of 1663 was written "before the
act of grace." That should have ended the matter. But Hale, a fair man

who had been chief justice for six years, had recently died. His successor, Richard Rainsford, was only a cut above Jeffreys as a tyrant. Jeffreys himself was then the recorder of London. Rainsford took over the prosecution, declaring that anyone capable of writing such blasphemy had the subtlety to antedate its publication. The contention was specious. Fox had replied to Muggleton's 1663 book in 1667; but the defense counsel did not know that, and Rainsford would not let Muggleton speak. A witness stated that Muggleton had acknowledged his authorship of the 1663 book before the lord mayor of London, when he was arrested in 1676. Rainsford took that as proof of guilt. Judge Robert Atkins protested that Muggleton's confession of authorship proved nothing about the date of publication. The witness said that the lord mayor had had a hard time making Muggleton confess his authorship. "We have no law to make a man accuse himself," Atkins replied; "can you make it appear that Mr. Muggleton has writ these books since the Act of Grace?" When the witness said "no," Atkins told the jury that the crown had no case against Muggleton.

Rainsford, however, when charging the jury, harangued them about Muggleton's guilt for many blasphemies, concluding: "And who knows what design this villain had both in church and government: and therefore, Gentlemen, if you do not bring him in guilty, yourselves will be sharers in his curst apostasy." The jury took half an hour to convict. Rainsford than rained abuse on Muggleton, ending with the epithet "murderer of souls." Atkins left the bench, saying audibly, "things are not fairly carried on here." But William Montague, the chief baron of the exchequer, sat on the trial and endorsed everything said by Rainsford, ending by thanking the jury for "so just and pious a verdict" against such a blasphemer. When the judges left the bench, Recorder Jeffreys — "Pilate," Muggleton called him — lashed the prisoner with vile epithets, and then pronounced sentence upon him: to stand in the pillory at three places in London, with a paper pinned to his chest announcing him to be a blasphemer, and at each place to witness the burning of his book, and to pay a fine of £500.

Muggleton, unable to pay the fine, was sent to Newgate. At each place where he stood in the pillory, the crowds "pelted" the sixty-eight-year-old man "with clay, rotten eggs, and dirt in abundance." On the third occasion they stoned him "thick as hail"; his friends who witnessed the event and reported the trial recorded that one stone "broke" the head of the "prophet," making his blood gush. After six months in Newgate, Muggleton's fine was reduced to £100; he paid it and went free. Although he wrote his autobiography in 1677, he kept it from publication until after his death; nor did he publish anything else during the twenty remaining years of his life. The Muggletonians ever after celebrated July 19, the day of his liberation from Newgate in 1677, as a religious festival. His trial and conviction were illegal, but only because his 1673 *Answer to William Penn* was not the basis of the indictment. As a matter of law, denial of the Trinity was blasphemy.

In Old Bailey, the scene of Muggleton's trial, at least three more convictions for blasphemy occurred between 1678 and 1698. In addition to those three there may have been up to sixteen more, plus an unknown number of other convictions outside of London. All were run-of-the-mill cases, showing no movement in the law, nothing unusual in the nature of the crimes, no extraordinary punishments, and no defendants of distinction. To distinguish prosecutions for blasphemous opinions from prosecutions for seditious ones is not possible in many of the cases, but some cases of seditious libel, such as Delaune's and Baxter's, had nothing to do with blasphemy. A legal historian, G. D. Nokes, who attempted to chart all the cases after Taylor's, refused to distinguish blasphemy from seditiousness in any case involving an offense against religion. He reasoned "that when the word blasphemous was first used judicially [in 1676] it was employed to describe an extension of the offense of seditious words. For more than a hundred years after that decision the intimate relationship between seditious and blasphemous offenses seems to have been maintained." Nokes's point on the relationship between seditious and blasphemous opinions is valid, but relatedness is not identicalness. Although all blasphemy in a state that has an established church is a form of seditiousness, not all seditiousness that is an offense against religion is blasphemous.[38]

During the Restoration and after, blasphemy was a distinctive crime. When nonconformity as seditious libel died in consequence of the Toleration Act of 1689, blasphemy remained an offense against religion punishable by the state. The law made distinctions, even when it punished blasphemy as a crime against the state. The law of criminal defamation fanned out into different branches, including obscene libel, seditious libel, and blasphemous libel, or, if the blasphemy was spoken instead of printed, blasphemous utterances. The Toleration Act, followed by the Blasphemy Act of 1698, spurred the demarcation between blasphemousness and seditiousness.

The Toleration Act, a direct consequence of the Revolution of 1688–9, was a reward by Parliament and the Anglican church to the nonconformists for throwing their support against James II. The Toleration Act, to put the same point another way, was a sop to the nonconformists for remaining staunchly anti-Catholic. Few Protestants, except some Baptists and Quakers, advocated religious liberty for Catholics. Few Protestants did not hate Catholics. Memories of Bloody Mary, Torquemada, the St. Bartholomew's Day Massacre, the ravages of the duke of Alva, Guy Fawkes, the revocation of the Edict of Nantes, and other outrages countless in number fixed Catholicism in the Protestant mind as a threat to Protestant and national liberty. Rome, Spain, and France were the leading enemies of England. The very real fear of Catholicism always underlay the fear of granting toleration to Protestant nonconformists. Charles II's Declaration of Indulgence was intended to be an opening wedge for tolerating Catholics and was understood as such by Parliament and the church. James II's policy pushed open the doors to Catholic freedom in England.

James, who succeeded his brother in 1685, openly practiced Catholicism and had a Catholic wife who in 1688 bore him a son and successor. The Stuart dynasty seemed to be leading England back to Rome and to the possible extinction of the English Reformation. James not only gave preference to his coreligionists at the highest levels of government; he formed a standing army that included many Catholics, both officers and men, as a bulwark of his regime. Yet James, although less interested in the Protestant nonconformists than in his Catholic countrymen, really favored religious liberty. His Declaration of Indulgence of 1687 suspended all penal laws related to religion, and pardoned all "nonconformists, recusants [chiefly Catholics], and other our loving subjects for all crimes and things by them committed or done contrary to the penal laws, formerly made relating to religion."[39]

James's policy of religious liberty looked like a means of overthrowing Anglicanism and reviving papistry. Among the Protestant nonconformists, only the Quakers supported James; Penn and the king were good friends. Most others, fearful of relying on the royal prerogative for their freedom and more fearful still of finding themselves allied with Catholics, and thus in a sense allied with the Church of Rome, joined with the Anglicans, their recent persecutors, in condemning royal tyranny. Like Charles before him, James had acted without Parliament by unilaterally abrogating its laws. Unlike Charles, James did not back down. In 1688 he reinforced his Declaration of Indulgence with a command that it be read from the pulpits throughout the realm. When the episcopacy refused, James declared that they had raised the standard of "rebellion." The archbishop of Canterbury and six of the leading bishops pleaded loyalty, but they still refused on good constitutional grounds. James sent them to the Tower of London. While they awaited prosecutions for seditious libel, the Catholic queen of England gave birth to a male heir. At the trial of the Anglican divines, the royal judges divided in their instructions to the jury; the jury's verdict of not guilty was celebrated as a national holiday. The bloodless revolution soon followed, bringing stalwart Protestants, William and Mary of Orange, to the throne of England — and bringing a promised reward to the Protestant nonconformists.[40]

The Toleration Act, which belied its name in form but not in effect, was the product of political necessity, "a nauseous necessity," as a Quaker historian has said. The new king, Parliament, and the church agreed to the act to restore peace to the country. No act more liberal than the very peculiar one passed could possibly have been adopted. A few intellectuals, like Penn and Locke, favored the right of any individual to worship as he pleased, and the historic position of the General Baptists had been that religion, being a private affair between man and God, transcended the state's concern. England overwhelmingly abhorred such principles. The Toleration Act reflected no principle at all, not even that of toleration. Despite the name by which it came to be known, the act was entitled "A Bill of Indulgence." It exempted most nonconformists "from the penalties of certain laws." Parliament did not repeal any of the persecutory laws of the Restoration, thus leaving persecution the rule of the law, but in a state of suspended animation. It was the English way of walking forward into the future — facing backward to the past. In much the same way, prior censorship died in England not because Parliament passed a bill establishing the principle of freedom of the press, and not even because it passed a bill repealing the old licensing laws, but simply because those laws expired and were not renewed.[41]

Under the Toleration Act, laymen who took the requisite oaths to support the new king and to reject transubstantiation were allowed to worship as they pleased in the church of their choice, because they were exempted from the penalties for doing otherwise. Clergymen who subscribed to most of the Anglican Thirty-nine Articles received exemption too from the laws that had suppressed them. Because the articles to which they had to subscribe were not the controversial ones, their consciences went unconstrained. Baptists received a special indulgence: they alone were exempted from the article that required infant baptism. Quakers too received a special indulgence by being allowed to swear that they professed the doctrine of the Trinity and thereby to prove that Unitarianism had not infected them. Not until an act of 1696 were Quakers allowed to affirm rather than swear. The Toleration Act had the effect of making nonconformity lawful if it conformed to the requirements of the act. Nonconformists still had to pay tithes for the established church, and they still endured many civil disabilities. The act was a compound of contradictions and exceptions wrought out of the prevailing system of persecution. Yet secular considerations had triumphed, with the result that where hundreds of thousands had suffered before for conscience' sake, the number fell to a few hundreds of Protestants and a few thousands of Catholics.

Section XVII of the act excluded from its benefits "any papist or popish recusant whatsoever, or any person that shall deny in his preaching or writing the doctrine of the Blessed Trinity, as it is declared in the aforesaid articles of religion." The exclusion of Catholics was to be expected, given the recent revolution against their religion. Yet Protestant monarchs, being above suspicion, found the means, unavailable to their Restoration predecessors, to mitigate the severities against peaceable Catholic subjects. By 1710 the Vatican received from an English agent a report declaring that the English Catholics "enjoy the exercise of their religion totally free"; in fact they felt the sting of double taxation and civil disabilities. Catholics did not actually come within the terms of the Toleration Act until 1778.[42]

The exclusion of antitrinitarians from the act indicates that they were regarded as covert blasphemers. Most clergymen could not accept their opinions as Christian. Some antitrinitarian intellectuals considered themselves freethinking "Deists"; they composed the vanguard of a growing movement, which by 1689 rivaled the Muggletonians in numbers. The Muggletonians, however devout in their Protestantism, still seemed loathsome fanatics. The far more numerous and growing Unitarians fell into a related category. The exclusion of these Protestants from the Toleration Act conclusively shows that most of England still deemed them as execrable as atheists and hardly distinguishable from them.

The Jews constituted a special case. Not more than four hundred of them lived in England at the time of the Toleration Act, none longer than about three decades. They enjoyed freedom of religion, thanks to the Stuarts, although they enjoyed no other civil rights. In 1664, after the Conventicles Act came into force, a movement to bring the Jews within its terms was cut off by Charles II and his Privy Council. Again, in 1673, when leaders of the Jewish community of London were indicted for a "riot," which consisted in their praying in their synagogue, another order of the council quashed the indictment. Later, when thirty-seven Jews were arrested in 1685 for failure to attend the Church of England, James II, the Catholic king, personally ordered his attorney general to allow the Jews "quietly [to] enjoy the free exercise of their religion, whilst they behave themselves dutifully. . . ." Thus, the Jews, never having come within the terms of the Restoration's penal statutes on religion, did not need to be exempted in the Toleration Act from the penalties that had been inflicted on Protestant nonconformists. The Jews continued to suffer long after 1689 from severe disabilities and discrimination, but Protestant England never prosecuted a Jew for blasphemy, nor a Catholic either. The Toleration Act left the Unitarians, however, in a class with blasphemers.[43]

Paradoxically, Unitarianism was surging in strength, mostly within the Anglican church. Not till much later did it become a separate sect. After the suppression of Biddle's little congregation, Unitarianism seemed to survive only among the few whose minds he had touched. They were, however, exceptional minds, and they found secret presses to perpetuate antitrinitarian principles. The movement, or rather the drift, centered around Thomas Firmin, the merchant. His splendid home in Lombard Street was a meeting place for his close friends. Among them were high-placed latitudinarian Anglicans and some dissenters. Most, like Firmin, became or remained communicants of the established church. They had no serious quarrel with its mode of worship or its discipline except on the issue of toleration. In all England, none were more advanced proponents of religious liberty. They also completely rejected the doctrine of the Holy Trinity, but their dispute with the church remained in the church. Although most of them kept their vocal opinions within the group, they published a staggering number of tracts. With rare exceptions, however, they wrote anonymously. To place one's name on the title page of an unlicensed antitrinitarian tract would have been as foolhardy as organizing for independent worship. Secrecy among the Unitarians was the rule. Although they differed from their church on a cardinal doctrine, they believed Anglicanism to comprehend every opinion on the Trinity from the most Catholic to the Deistic. They believed too that the episcopacy included a growing number of "nominal" as opposed to "real" trinitarians. Unitarianism cropped out in unexpected places. When, for example, Milton died in 1674, he left a secret cache of unpublished Unitarian manuscripts.[44]

Firmin's circle included Henry Hedworth, a gentleman scholar and author of many Unitarian tracts; John Locke, the philosopher; Gilbert Clerke, the mathematician and scripturalist, who also wrote Unitarian tracts; Stephen Nye, an Anglican rector, the best and most productive of all the Unitarian writers; and Isaac Newton, the scientist. Remarkably, the three greatest intellectuals of seventeenth-century England—Milton, Locke, and Newton—were covert Unitarians. Hedworth, the literary antagonist of Penn, argued that "the Trinitarians ought to own the Unitarians for Christian Brethren. . . ." Most trinitarians thought otherwise. As early as 1672, Andrew Marvell, the metaphysical poet, complained that "Socinian books are tolerated, and sell as openly as the Bible." A similar complaint issued in 1680 from George Ashwell, an Anglican priest who thought that the Socinians were making headway within the Church of England.[45]

Ashwell was correct, and events seemed to justify his complaint. When William III called a church convocation in 1689 to reform the church, the doctrine of the Trinity divided the Anglican divines so severely that the convocation was paralyzed. While it was in session, Stephen Nye published a withering assault on the Athanasian Creed, triggering a controversy that lasted the remainder of the decade—and after. It had begun, in a way, much earlier, with Penn's *Sandy Foundations* of 1668. By the 1690s the Sabellian views which had put Penn in the Tower were common within the church and at its highest levels. The Trinitarian Controversy began as a purely Anglican affair, first with Nye's anonymous book, then with another by Dr. Arthur Bury, the rector of Exeter College, Oxford. His book of 1690, like Nye's, made many an orthodox minister goggle-eyed. In *The Naked Gospel,* Bury intended to show that during the church's first few centuries of existence it had preached one God and no Trinity. Sympathizing with the doctrine of the primitive church, Bury argued that Christians had perplexed and persecuted each other too long because of bitter differences about the doctrine of the Trinity. When Bury's identity as author of the book was uncovered, a convocation of the entire university consigned *The Naked Gospel* to the flames as heretical and blasphemous, deposed him from office, and fined him. Bury was not, however, without articulate supporters—in print.[46]

Stephen Nye, who was tireless on behalf of the Unitarian cause, rejected the Socinian label because he did not agree on all points with Faustus Socinus or John Biddle. Nye called himself a Christian, thought of himself as a Sabellian, and in print argued for Unitarianism. In 1687, at Firmin's commission, Nye published *A Brief History of Unitarians, commonly called Socinians.* The book was less history than Unitarian propaganda. Firmin distributed free copies of many of Nye's productions, and between 1691 and 1697, Nye, assisted by several others and by Firmin's money, wrote and compiled three substantial volumes, the *Unitarian Tracts.* The first volume reprinted a life of Biddle, several of Biddle's tracts, and Nye's *Brief History.*[47]

The super-orthodox, who heatedly replied to every Unitarian tract, inadvertently aided their opponents' cause by overstating their own position on the doctrine of the Trinity. Some, like William Sherlock and his disciple Joseph Bingham, so exaggerated the distinct persons or substances of the Holy Trinity that they exposed themselves to the charge of polytheism or tritheism. Bingham suffered the same fate as Bury for the opposite reasons. Oxford pronounced a tract by Bingham to be false, impious, and heretical, because of its tritheism. That was in 1695. A year earlier a Unitarian who signed his name to his tract was caught and punished. He was William Freeke, an Oxonian, who foolishly sent copies of his tract to members of both houses of Parliament. The Lords condemned it as an infamous and scandalous libel, without indicating whether it was of the seditious or blasphemous type, and ordered the hangman to burn the tract. Freeke was prosecuted, heavily fined, and forced to make a public recantation. In 1696 someone put into an English translation Aretius's Latin book of 1567, which was published in Bern in justification of the Calvinist execution of "Valentinus Gentilis, the Tritheist"; what made the English edition significant is that its translator wrote in the preface that he thought the book should edify Dr. Sherlock. It was a form of gallows humor. Robert South, a middle-of-the-road Anglican priest, ridiculed Sherlock's tritheism so unmercifully that Nye welcomed South to the rational creed of Unitarianism. [48]

Some Anglican clergymen found the Trinitarian Controversy so unsettling that they embraced the views advocated by Nye. In the course of counterattacking extremists on the right, like Sherwood and Bingham, some moderates and latitudinarians found themselves driven by the force of their logic to the fringes of Sabellianism, if not beyond. William Tillotson, who was the archbishop of Canterbury, and Bishop William Burnet had that experience. Tillotson published some sermons in 1693 in which he praised his friend Firmin, and commented favorably on Socinianism, thereby subjecting himself to criticism that compelled him to deny the accusation that he covertly harbored the dreaded unorthodoxy on the Holy Trinity. Tillotson, who deplored the Athanasian Creed, wrote to Burnet, "I wish we were well rid of it."[49]

Unitarians could never dominate the Anglican church however, or even become a major force within it, because the church used a prayerbook that conditioned worshippers and priests to accept the three persons of the Godhead. Dissenters, who were more familiar with addressing the One Almighty God, found their theological divorce from the doctrine of the Trinity easier to come by. In 1693, Dr. Edmund Calamy, the famous Presbyterian, noting the growth of heterodoxy on the Trinity within his own denomination, saw one side of the disputants "verging toward Arminianism, or even Socinianism. . . ." Thoughtful and unprejudiced people, incited to study the literature of the Trinitarian Controversy, underwent a change of opinion. Their number is indeterminable, but the fallout of the controversy continued well into the eighteenth century and led to the "Arian Movement" within the Church of England and among the dissenters' churches. Indeed, the first dissenter minister who publicly adopted the Unitarian name was Thomas Emlyn, a Presbyterian no less. "Socinians," said one orthodox writer, "under the name of Unitarians," grew bolder and "fill'd the nation" with their writings.[50]

The controversy was infinitely complex because of its metaphysical focus, making any labeling of its contestants controversial. John Locke, for example, explicitly denied being a Socinian, but he told only a half-truth. When his *Reasonableness of Christianity* was published in 1695 the orthodox raked him with obloquy. John Edwards, a worthy son of the author of *Gangrenae*, called Locke a "Socinian," a "Racovian," a "criminal," a "casuist," and a "dissembler" — and Edwards was not all wrong. Locke replied that he had not read Socinus or the Racovian Catechism. In fact, his work showed them plainly and his library included both as well as the works of Dutch and Polish Socinians, those of Biddle and Nye, and the *Unitarian Tracts*. Locke's closest friends were Unitarians. He may not have been a Socinian; Nye, one of Locke's friends, also denied being a Socinian. But Locke, like Nye, spoke only in a very technical sense. By the mid-1690s, the antitrinitarians, who collectively and explicitly called themselves Unitarians, had divided into differing shades of opinion on the Trinity. All, however, shared the opinion that the Bible as construed by human reason led to the conclusion that Jesus, although the Messiah, the Son of God, was human, not God. Scripturalism taught them one God and no Trinity in the Godhead. Arians, Sabellians, Socinians, and Deists — Unitarians all in the 1690s — rejected the Nicene and Athanasian Creeds. They rested on the Apostles Creed as sufficient, fundamental, and scriptural. They were literal scripturalists, to the core. In 1698, when Locke replied to the bishop of Worcester, who tried to draw him out on the subject of the Trinity, Locke declared: "My Lord, my Bible is faulty again, for I do not remember that I ever read in it either of these propositions, in precise words, 'there are three persons of one nature, or, there are two natures and one person.' " God was One.[51]

The Toleration Act, the excesses of the super-orthodox, and the leavening influence of the Enlightenment, then beginning, impelled many Anglicans toward a rejection of the traditional doctrine of the Trinity. Gilbert Clerke once told Baxter that he should not malign Socinians, because they were "the best sort of Christians." Clerke's was a growing opinion, and it frightened the orthodox. They feared that the controversy had gotten out of control, becoming more dangerous with each passing year. Calamy said the "world was wearied out with pamphlets and creed-making." The presses kept disgorging disputatious books and tracts on the Trinitarian Controversy. The interminable theological dispute would have glazed the eyes of medieval scholastics. The orthodox sensed that they were being bested in the analyses of primitive heresies and on such metaphysical points concerning the Trinity as hypostatical union, essences, persons, modes, names, incarnation, attributes, substances, and faculties. Every tract provoked several responses, and the number grew geometrically; the writings multiplied themselves like their long-winded titles, until they would, if piled on the dome of St. Paul's Cathedral, have crushed it by their weight. As the controversy wore on, the orthodox hammered on the theme that the realm was being infected with the pestilence of heterodoxy.[52]

Events in Scotland suggested that a statute against blasphemy might prove necessary or useful in England. In Scotland where the Church of England dispossessed Presbyterianism at the Restoration, blasphemy confronted much harsher laws than in England. The English Puritans had treated Ranter blasphemies mildly, although they came close to killing Nayler; at the time, however, he loomed as a heresiarch. Shortly before, in Scotland the Puritans hanged Jock of Broad Scotland. When the Scottish Anglicans regained control of state and church in 1661, they were fiercer than their English counterparts in their persecutions and their legislation. The Five Mile Act in England was the Twenty Mile Act north of the Tweed. In 1661 the Parliament of Scotland enacted its first statute against blasphemy. The English act of 1648 against Socinianism had fixed capital punishment for the crime, but the statute never came to life. The Scots enforced their law. It had two independent sections. The first applied to any sane person who reviled or cursed God or any of the persons of the Trinity. Cursing or reviling presumably showed deliberate malice. The second part of the act of 1661 applied to those who "obstinately continue" to deny God or any person of the Trinity; since denial might derive from ignorance or momentary passion, the blasphemer might repent. Consequently the act of 1661 made blasphemy against God or the Trinity unrepentant denial or malicious reviling.[53]

Sir George Mackenzie, a Scot who was the king's advocate and formerly a supreme justice of the criminal courts, declared in a book of 1678 that blasphemy was also a crime by the Scottish common law. Mackenzie defined the crime as "divine lease majesty, or Treason," that is, treason against God. The offense consisted in denying to God that which belonged to Him or attributing to Him that which was inconsistent with His divine nature, such as sin. More than a century later, after

Scotland had abolished its blasphemy statutes, another Scottish jurist remarked that to describe blasphemy as treason against God contained "more fancy than propriety."[54]

The first accusation under the act of 1661 occurred twenty years after its enactment, when Francis Bortwick, a Christian who had converted to Judaism, supposedly railed against Christ and his divinity. Bortwick had to be condemned in absentia and declared a doomed outlaw, because he managed to escape to the continent. In 1695, when the Presbyterians were again in control of Scotland, the Scottish Parliament supplemented the earlier statute because it was too tight to cover some opinions that had become current on account of the Trinitarian Controversy. The act of 1695 extended blasphemy to the obstinate denial of, or reasoning against, not only the persons in the Godhead but the literal authority of the Bible and the providence of God in the governance of the world. However, the act of 1695 deferred the death penalty to a third conviction, making it seem an unlikely eventuality. On the first conviction the blasphemer had to make public atonement in sackcloth and on the second to pay heavy fines and remain in prison until his parish was satisfied.[55]

Statutory law and its enforcement by courts sometimes bear slight correspondence when pious shock, bigotry, and the lack of assistance by counsel work against a defendant, as the case of Thomas Aikenhead showed. He was arrested in 1696, imprisoned for several months while awaiting trial, and at the end of the year faced the lord barons who composed the highest criminal court. Aikenhead, still a legal minor, was a medical student at the University of Edinburgh when he caught the "plague of blasphemous Deism"—the phrase of one of the ministers who visited him several times in his prison cell. Later that minister, William Lorimer, faced denunciation as one responsible for Aikenhead's death. At the time of the prosecution Lorimer had preached before the prisoner's judges on the theme of blasphemous Deism. Later, when defending himself against the opinion that he had abetted a judicial murder, Lorimer insisted that Aikenhead remained obstinate for months. Yet Lorimer also declared that on his first visit to the prisoner, "he [Aikenhead] immediately confessed that he . . . was sorry for what he had said, and he desired my prayers."[56]

In fact, before his trial Aikenhead addressed a petition to the court that tried him, in which he made an elaborate orthodox confession of faith. He not only repeatedly professed to "abhorre and detest" the opinions for which he had been indicted; he also embraced the Trinity, the Old and New Testaments, infant baptism, the sacrament of the Lord's Supper, and everything else that Calvin or Knox might have wanted. He repented each specific "atheistical" opinion ascribed to him, saying that he had repeated them only as the views of authors (unnamed) whom he had read, not as opinions he personally held. That he may have lied about that point is irrelevant; he recanted and was not obstinate. Indeed, Lord Anstruther wrote: "We had lately an anomely, and a monster of nature, I may call him, who was execut for cursing and reviling the persons of the Trinity, he was 18 yeers of age, not vicious and extreamely studious. Fountionehall [one of the judges] and I went to him in prison, and I *found a work on his spirit,* and wept that he ever should maintained such tenets. . . ." Anstruther petitioned on the prisoner's behalf for a reprieve but learned that unless the ministers interceded, clemency was impossible. The "ministers," he reported, "out of a pious, though I think ignorant zeal spok and preached for cutting him off."[57]

Lorimer said that George Meldrum, another minister involved in the case, solicited a pardon for Aikenhead, and when that failed, requested a reprieve, "and I joined with him in it." That was the day before the execution. The chancellor took the petition to the Privy Council, the judges attending. After a debate, a plurality of the council sustained the judges' sentence "that there might be a stop put to the spreading of that contagion of blasphemy." That concurs with Lorimer's final judgment. Although he conceded that Aikenhead finally recanted his opinions, Lorimer concluded: "I am far from thinking that the Socinians who deny the Holy Trinity and the eternal Deity of Christ, are such Deists as that poor man was; yet I think the mention of this may serve as a warning to them, to others likewise; for there seems to be but a short passage from Socinianism to Deism." That does not square with Lorimer's statement that Aikenhead died "very penitent, pouring out his soul to Christ . . . and taking shame to himself, and humbly and earnestly begging of God mercy and pardon for Christ's sake."[58]

The Aikenhead case posed two difficult legal questions that seem trivial compared with the decision to execute him as an example to terrorize others. Was Aikenhead guilty under the law? Under what law? The indictment referred, in part, to the crime of blasphemy against "our holy religion," which was not a crime under either of the two statutes of the Parliament of Scotland, both of which the indictment restated. Five witnesses appeared against Aikenhead, all acquaintances of his age. That he denied the persons of the Trinity and the authority of the Bible is unquestionable. But the act of 1695 made death the punishment only for a third offense, and Aikenhead's was a first offense. That act could not have been the basis of his conviction and execution. Nor could the second part of the act of 1661, which required obstinate denial. Abundant proof shows that he recanted often—in prison, before his trial, after his conviction, and at his execution.[59]

The only alternative legal bases for the proceedings were the common law of Scotland or the first part of the act of 1661, which required proof of cursing. Even Mackenzie's definition of blasphemy protected God only, not "our holy religion." Moreover, the king's advocate, Sir James Stewart, never referred to the common law in his prosecution. He stressed Aikenhead's scoffing, ridiculing, railing against and cursing the Bible, the doctrine of the Trinity, and the deity of Christ. The five witnesses agreed that Aikenhead over a period of a year had denied them all, but only one witness swore that the defendant had reviled and cursed. That witness's testimony brought Aikenhead within the terms of the first part of the act of 1661, which imposed death for a first offense even against a defendant who was not obstinate. The key witness was the one who had given Aikenhead the unknown books that led to his blasphemies. The same witness immediately recanted and turned state's evidence to avoid prosecution. His testimony alone convicted Aikenhead under the first part of the act of 1661. Aikenhead confessed to much, but he denied railing, cursing, and ridiculing. In London, John Locke, who gathered the documents of the case, stressed the fact that the prisoner was denied counsel; Locke concluded that the jury that had returned the verdict of guilty had committed perjury.[60]

The only other blasphemy case in Scotland that might have influenced England to enact its own statute against the crime occurred in 1697, later in the year that Aikenhead twisted on the gibbet. Patrick Kinnymount escaped that fate, and Aikenhead became the last man in Great Britain to die for his opinions on religion. The same bench that condemned Aikenhead tried Kinnymount, who had able counsel. His utterances were certainly blasphemous, for among other things he called Christ a bastard. But Kinnymount's ingenious counsel argued that Kinnymount, who repented everything, had uttered the words when drunk. The court rejected the defense of temporary insanity under the influence of whiskey, but committed the prisoner for a first offense only. Long after, Baron David Hume, in his treatise on Scottish criminal law, criticized the judgment in Kinnymount's case. Hume reasoned that intoxication in a case of impetuous and repented blasphemy should be a valid defense against the charge, because the defendant stood to gain no profit from his crime, unlike a drunken thief. Kinnymount's utterances and relatively light sentence showed that Aikenhead's case was all the more a miscarriage of justice, the victim being nothing more than a sacrifice to make a precedent during the Trinitarian Controversy.[61]

The example of Scotland and the unceasing Unitarian barrage during the Trinitarian Controversy finally prodded England into action. Although the censorship laws had expired, in 1697 some dissenting clergymen petitioned William III to stop the Unitarian presses. The year before, in 1696, John Toland, a young friend of John Locke, published his first book, *Christianity not Mysterious.* It triggered a new controversy, "the first act of the warfare between the deists and the orthodox which occupied the next generation," wrote Leslie Stephen. The book infuriated the orthodox, some of whom presented it to the grand jury of Middlesex. Toland prudently left for Ireland, but a grand jury there presented the book, and in 1697 the Irish Parliament, which had not yet learned that heresy was archaic as a legal term except in ecclesiastical courts and convocations, condemned the book to the flames as heresy. The Irish also ordered Toland's arrest. He fled back to England, where he remained under cover until the furor over him died down.[62]

In 1697 John Gailhard published *The Blasphemous Socinian Heresie disproved and confuted,* which he dedicated to the Parliament of England. Gailhard recommended that Parliament take notice of the Scottish Parliament's salutary statutes against blasphemy. Although William III prorogued Parliament before it could enact any sanguinary legislation, the king had wearied of the ceaseless Trinitarian Controversy. He interceded, at last, on the side of religious peace and orthodoxy, commanding the archbishops and bishops, "for the sake of preserving unity in the Church and the purity of the Christian faith concerning the Holy Trinity," to see that theologians muted their publications and preaching. Henceforth, no clergyman could employ invective or scurrility in controversial matters, nor write against the Christian faith by attacking the Holy Trinity. The king promised that his criminal courts and sheriffs would execute all laws against laymen who scandalized or disturbed the peace of the realm by their religious opinions. In Old Bailey in 1698 Susan Fowls was convicted for blasphemy and was pilloried, fined, and jailed; she had passed the bounds of decency by cursing the Lord's Prayer and verbally abusing Christ.[63]

Parliament, which convened again in 1698, was, as usual, more orthodox than the church. The House of Commons beseeched the king to suppress "all pernicious books and pamphlets" that contained "impious" doctrine against the Holy Trinity and "other fundamental articles of our faith, tending to the subversion of the Christian Religion. . . ." The king consented to the passage of a new blasphemy statute, Parliament's real objective. The act of 1698 remains law to this day, although rarely enforced. The courts, using their common law, needed no assistance from Parliament against blasphemy, but a statute carried greater weight than a court decision in forming the public mind. Parliament, with the assent of the king, spoke for the nation and laid down the supreme law. A court merely decided particular cases.[64]

The act of 1698 "for the more effectual suppressing of Blasphemy" provided that any person who had professed the Christian religion should be convicted for blasphemy if he should say anything, in conversation, in the pulpit, or in the press, to deny "any one of the Persons of the Holy Trinity to be God," or deny "the Christian Religion to be true," or deny the divine authority of the Bible. The punishment for a first offense was disablement from any civil, military, or ecclesiastical employment. For a second offense, the punishment was loss of all civil rights, in effect rendering the culprit a nonperson with respect to any suits, legacies, deeds, and trusts; in addition, conviction for a second offense carried the penalty of three years' imprisonment "without bail or mainprize." As usual, England was more lenient than Scotland.[65]

The act of 1698 was intended to thwart the spread of Unitarianism in any of its forms and, more broadly, to protect the Christian religion against harsh criticism. As the century ended, then, blasphemy in England had a variety of meanings, judicial and statutory. John Godolphin, a legal scholar skilled in canon-law matters, had summarized the law of blasphemy in 1678, three years after Taylor's case. Blasphemy consisted in injuring God with contumelious words, "which is when they detract from God the honour due to him, or attribute any evil to him." Mackenzie had provided a similar definition for Scotland in the same year. By coincidence, Godolphin too characterized the crime as "speaking Treason against the Heavenly Majesty" by execrable words that reproached the Deity. Distinguishing heresy from blasphemy, Godolphin wrote that heresy "is an opinion repugnant to the orthodox Doctrine of the Christian Faith, obstinately maintained and persisted in by such as profess the Name of Christ."[66]

In effect, the act of 1698 converted heresy into blasphemy by including as part of the crime of blasphemy denials of the truth of the Christian religion. Similarly, Chief Justice Hale in Taylor's case, when ruling that Christianity was part of the law of the land, found blasphemy in any contumelious reproach against God or against the established religion. Denial of the doctrine of the Trinity, the blasphemous crime in Muggleton's case, also attained statutory endorsement in the act of 1698. Receiving the honors due only to God or claiming divine attributes also fell within the common-law definition of blasphemy. The Toleration Act had in effect excluded from the realm of blasphemy criticism of the established religion, such as denying Anglican doctrines, the episcopacy, the sacraments of the church, and its prayerbook, unless that criticism was accompanied by what the courts might call contumelious reproach or cursing.

Now, by the act of 1698, a simple denial of Christianity or the Bible was blasphemy. In effect the statute was a signal to the courts to cast their nets wider in order to repress criticism that reached the level of an explicit denial of anything Anglican. If prosecutor, judge, and jury concurred, dissident Anglicans like Firmin and all Protestant nonconformists could be exposed to conviction for blasphemy. Unitarians stood in the greatest jeopardy if the law-enforcement agencies fulfilled the letter of the law on blasphemy. That law had been forged by the end of the century as a weapon for subverting the Toleration Act as well as intellectual and religious liberty of opinion. And where blasphemy might not prove the easier crime to prosecute, the law of seditious libel concerning offenses against religion stood as an additional and alternative bulwark of orthodoxy.

EPILOGUE _____

Most of history, being a register of inhumanities, is not fit to repeat itself. It includes prosecutions for blasphemy or, in the more common nomenclature, heresy. Believing that their religion required intolerance to sustain it, Christians praised dead saints and persecuted living ones, making martyrdom sublime, grief ordinary. Example is always more efficacious than precept, terrifying examples the most efficacious of all. Because the rewards of religion were distant, Christians thought that punishment of irreligion or mistaken religion reinforced faith.

Curiously, although blasphemy was a Jewish concept in its origin, its Jewish history is slight. From the time of Moses through the intertestamental period, blasphemy, however feared and decried, was scarcely ever committed, or if committed not prosecuted, or if prosecuted not recorded. That is a striking fact about the Old Testament, which concerns the religion of a people who for centuries kept lapsing into the worship of fertility gods rather than the one living God. Idolatry is an incessant theme of the Old Testament, but blasphemy, its spiritual kin, is nearly unheard of as a crime that the ancient Israelites prosecuted. Except for Naboth's, the case in Leviticus is the only one reported; as time passed the crime of blasphemy became defined so narrowly in Jewish law as to become practically beyond commission.

The Christian history of blasphemy prosecutions is extraordinarily different. The transforming event was Mark's depiction of the trial of Jesus by the Sanhedrin. No longer was reviling God the broadest definition of the crime. It became claiming his kinship, powers, attributes, or honors. When the religion of Jesus became a religion based on belief in his incarnation, resurrection, and offer of eternal salvation, blasphemy expanded still further to encompass not only verbal abuse or denial of Christianity but even the expression of a difference of opinion about it. Regardless of the technical distinctions that can be made between blasphemy and heresy, the two always remained entwined in Christian thought and usage. "Heretics," as Thomas Aquinas so tersely epitomized, "blaspheme against God by following a false faith." In the name

331

of God or His Son or the Holy Spirit, the history of the crime of
blasphemy for the sixteen centuries before 1700 became a sepulcher of
hatreds because of the conviction that the gates of salvation must be
cleared of wrong religious opinions. The Augustinian principle of
persecution to promote the salvation of souls constituted the foremost
justification for prosecuting blasphemy.

Echoing little Peterkin in Southey's poem, "The Battle of Blenheim,"
we may ask, "But what good came of it at last?" All was not lost,
because even death teaches the value of life. Blasphemy as either concept or crime benefited mankind by engendering the claim to freedom
of conscience which pious people, not skeptics, made. That freedom of
conscience came at all to Christendom was probably the result of
perpetual religious fission; the promptings of conscience that seized
men to their innermost depths varied so much that freedom was possible for none unless for all.

Until that fact was realized the atrocities committed on behalf of true
faith victimized an incalculable number of Christians. The Jocks of
Broad Scotland and John Taylors who spoke scurrilously about sacred
things were rare. The blasphemy laws netted, rather, the Servetuses,
Brunos, Ketts, Legates, Biddles, and Naylers who worshipped God and
revered Christ as devoutly as their suppressors. Some of the victims rejected the authority of the pope or sacraments devised by the Roman
Catholic church. Some thought that they had rediscovered the primitive
church. Some followed the example of Jesus by accepting baptism only
as adults. Some professed a Christ who was "so God" he was never truly human and others a Christ so human he was never God. Some
repudiated the fourth-century doctrine of the Trinity as unscriptural.
Some took the Bible too literally, others too symbolically. All these
"blasphemers" were earnest and devout enthusiasts who believed differently from those in authority. Reproaching or reviling God or Christ
was as repugnant to them as to their persecutors, although reproaching
and reviling establishments of religion commonly characterized
religious expression. Inoffensive speech was not the hallmark of Elijah,
Isaiah, or of Jesus himself; Paul, Athanasius, Augustine, Luther,
Calvin, Fox, and other champions of true faith pursued a tradition of
vehement denunciation. Entrance into the kingdom of God was at
stake. That is one reason why some of the greatest figures in Christian
history were not tolerationists. Convinced that they were right about
the only absolute that counted eternally, they believed that all who differed, being wrong, must therefore be offenders against religion. But
persecutors acted out of choice, not necessity, because Christianity
from Jesus to Fox also yielded a tradition of toleration. Protestant
avengers of God's honor chose to denounce offenders against religion as

blasphemers. After the Reformation, "heresy," the once-fashionable name of the crime, deferred to "blasphemy." In England a judicial decision of 1676 held that because Christianity was part of the law, to blaspheme it was a crime against the state. Acts of Parliament before and after that time aimed at punishing particular doctrines as blasphemy.

English precepts naturally made the Atlantic crossing, beginning with the earliest code of laws for the first American colony. Virginia's "Lawes Divine, Morall and Martiall" of 1610 provided death for anyone who spoke impiously against the Trinity or "against God the Father, God the Son, and God the holy Ghost, or against the knowne Articles of the Christian faith." Anyone who blasphemed God's name faced death. For the use of unlawful oaths, taking the name of God in vain, or cursing (the lesser crime of profanity), "severe punishment" awaited the first offense, having a bodkin thrust through the tongue the second, and the ultimate penalty the third. Any word tending to deride the Scriptures was a capital offense. The first body of capital laws of Massachusetts contained similar provisions. Massachusetts regarded Quakers as "a cursed Sect of Hereticks" who "speake and write Blasphemous Opinions," and New Haven followed suit.[1]

Enforcement was softer than statutory threats. Fines, whippings, pillorying, prison, brandings, and banishment were the common punishments. Only Massachusetts actually imposed the death sentence for offenses against religion, but the only "Blasphemous Hereticks" to die were Quakers for the offense, technically, of defying decrees of banishment. Among the seventeenth-century colonies, only Rhode Island had no penalties for blasphemy, and Pennsylvania's sanctions were extremely mild. In Maryland, the celebrated "Act of Toleration" of 1649 applied only to trinitarian Christians; the same statute promised death to Unitarians, Jews, and unbelievers; and to anyone using reproachful language against the Virgin Mary, the apostles, or the evangelists, the statute offered fines, whipping, and banishment. In 1699 Maryland ameliorated its draconianism by emulating a Massachusetts act of 1697 that reserved death for a third offense of blasphemy, defined as cursing, denying, or reproaching the Athanasian Creed, the Scriptures, or Divine Providence and Governance. Six months' imprisonment was the sentence for a first offense, for the second not more than two of the following: Branding with the letter "B," boring through the tongue with a hot iron, severe whipping, and symbolic execution—sitting on the gallows with a rope about the neck. Next to Massachusetts, Connecticut was the most diligent colony of the seventeenth century in enforcing strictures against blasphemy.[2]

During the eighteenth century's Age of Enlightenment the number of blasphemy prosecutions on both sides of the Atlantic diminished. In America, where there were only about half a dozen convictions in all the colonies, the severest sentence was that received by a sea captain in Maryland who blasphemed when scalding pitch burned his foot. He was fined twenty pounds, bored three times through the tongue, and imprisoned for a year. In Great Britain, where the convictions totaled less than a dozen, the cases involved important defendants and serious legal issues. In one, Thomas Emlyn, the first minister to call himself a Unitarian, was convicted for having published a book whose blasphemy consisted in the temperate argument that Christ was a subordinate deity to God. In a case of 1729 that became a leading precedent, Thomas Woolston, a biblical scholar who mocked the literal interpretation of the miracles, lost his appeal to the highest court, which declared, "they would not suffer it to be debated whether to write against Christianity in general was not an offence punishable in the Temporal Courts at common law. . . ." Denying that it meddled with "differences of opinion," the court reaffirmed that because Christianity was part of the law of the land, whatever struck at it "tends manifestly to a dissolution of the civil government," and in this case "struck the very root of Christianity itself. . . ." As the century closed there began a series of trials of publishers and sellers of Tom Paine's *Age of Reason.*[3]

The number of prosecutions and convictions for blasphemy peaked in the first half of the nineteenth century in both England and the United States. Increasingly the defendants were agnostics, deists, and secularists, who, in contrast to the earlier defendants, relied as heavily on freedom of the press as on the liberty of conscience, although with no more success. On this side of the Atlantic the high court of New York, in an 1811 opinion by Chief Justice James Kent, held that a common-law indictment for malicious blasphemy did not violate the state's constitutional guarantees of religious freedom and separation of church and state. Reviling the religion of "Mohamet or of the grand Lama" would not be criminal, for "we are a christian people, and the morality of the country is deeply ingrafted upon christianity. . . ." The Supreme Court of Pennsylvania in 1824 added that to permit the denial of God, contumelious reproaches of Christ, or scoffing of the Scriptures would undermine society. "Without these restraints no free government could long exist. It is liberty run mad, to declaim against the punishment of these offences, or to assert that the punishment is hostile to the spirit and genius of our government."[4]

Two old men, John Adams and Thomas Jefferson, founders of our government, believed otherwise. Speaking of the books of the Bible,

Adams, in an 1825 letter to Jefferson, wrote, "Now, what free inquiry, when a writer must surely encounter the risk of fine or imprisonment for adducing any arguments for investigation into the divine authority of those books? . . . I think such [blasphemy] laws a great embarrassment, great obstructions to the improvement of the human mind. Books that cannot bear examination, certainly ought not to be established as divine inspiration by penal laws. . . . I wish they were repealed." Jefferson wrote voluminously to prove that Christianity was not part of the law of the land and that religion or irreligion was purely a private matter, not cognizable by the state. Nevertheless, in the leading American case on blasphemy, decided in 1838, Chief Justice Lemuel Shaw of Massachusetts repelled arguments based on freedom of the press and of religion when he sustained not only the constitutionality of a state law against blasphemy but also the conviction of a pantheist who declared, in language devoid of scurrility, that Universalists believed in "a god . . . in Christ . . . in miracles, which I do not. . . ."[5]

In all the American decisions the courts maintained the legal fiction that the criminal law punished only malice, never mere difference of opinion. That is, the style rather than the substance of the expression was said to be the target of the law, or, as a Pennsylvania court stated in 1824, the manner rather than the matter determined criminality. In fact, however, what was said, not how, was the decisive factor, because courts almost invariably found "contumelious reproach" in a mere denial of the truths of Christianity, the doctrine of the Trinity, or the existence of God. In England, where there had been seventy-three convictions for blasphemy between 1821 and 1834, a royal commission of 1841 endorsed the same legal fiction as the Pennsylvania court by claiming that "all the recorded instances of prosecution for blasphemy, subsequent to Woolston's case [1729], have been publications of indecent and opprobrious language," so that all sentences were founded "entirely upon the offensive *manner* of writing. . . ." Numerous cases prove otherwise, but the commission appended a footnote that provided the best refutation of its recommendation to preserve the law against blasphemy. The footnote quoted a letter of an Anglican minister who had published an answer to Woolston; he remarked that "if men have an allowance to write against the Christian religion, there must also be considerable indulgence as to the manner likewise. . . . The proper punishment of a low, mean, indecent, scurrilous way of writing, seems to be neglect, contempt, scorn, and general indignation."[6]

Blasphemy is not just a matter of bad taste, but in 1883 Lord Chief

Justice John Coleridge supposedly advanced the law some light-years by ruling that "if the decencies of controversy are observed, even the fundamentals of religion may be attacked without the writer being guilty of blasphemy." He added, however, that the offense consisted in the shock or insult to Christianity or to the opinions of a majority of Christians. That is the theory of the law of blasphemy in the United States too, where no establishment of religion has existed since Massachusetts separated church and state in 1833. The "decencies of controversy" being utterly subjective, most of the authors of the books of the Old and New Testaments as well as leading saints and originators of most Protestant sects would not pass the test of the law.[7]

The most recent blasphemy prosecutions in the United States occurred in 1968. The American cases suggest the probability that the history of blasphemy prosecutions is coming to an end, because of principles implied in opinions of the Supreme Court of the United States. The Court has never had a case on the constitutionality of a law against blasphemy. Acts of Congress empowering the postmaster general to ban from the mails a variety of offensive and subversive literature have never extended to blasphemy. Not until 1940 did the Supreme Court squarely hold that the First Amendment's protection of the free exercise of religion extended to the citizens of the states. Before that time a state might invade religious or irreligious expression without violating the Constitution of the United States. In 1951 the Court held invalid, as a violation of the free-speech clause, a New York statute authorizing a state censorship board to prevent the showing of "sacrilegious" films. Three members of the Court, speaking through Justice Felix Frankfurter, gratuitously but accurately observed that "blasphemy" is a far broader and vaguer term than "sacrilege," which the entire Court believed subjective enough to allow a censor to ban whatever displeased him. Frankfurter also invoked the 1940 precedent to make the point that in the realm of religious faith, differences of opinion are so great and intense that what seems rankling to one group is inoffensive to another. Historically, Frankfurter declared, "Blasphemy was the chameleon phrase which meant criticism of whatever the ruling authority of the moment established as the orthodox religious doctrine." The free-exercise-of-religion clause as well as the free-speech clause was thus a basis of the concurring opinion.[8]

That seems to be the basis too of the ultimate disposition of 1968 prosecutions in Delaware and Maryland. The case that arose in Westminster, Maryland, did not even involve blasphemy, although the prosecution and conviction were based on a 245-year-old blasphemy statute that permitted a sentence of up to six months' imprisonment for blasphemy defined as cursing God or using profane words about Jesus Christ, the Trinity, or any persons constituting the Trinity. Irving West, the defendant in the 1968 case, while being arrested for disorderly conduct told a policeman, "keep your God damn hands off me"—a mere profanity or curse that invoked God's powers but in no way involved "profane words of and concerning our Saviour Jesus Christ." The local magistrate, who was not even a lawyer, had already fined three youths who pleaded guilty under this 1723 statute against blasphemy. The magistrate convicted West and sentenced him to thirty days. The American Civil Liberties Union intervened on his behalf and appealed the conviction. A county circuit judge, Edward O. Weant, Jr., ruled that the state's blasphemy act violated the First Amendment's religion clauses. On appeal, the state argued that blasphemy had become a violation of decency in a secular sense. An appellate court of the state replied, "This effort by the State of Maryland to extend its protective cloak to the Christian religion or to any other religion is forbidden by the Establishment and Free Exercise Clauses of the First Amendment."[9]

Shortly after Judge Weant's ruling, the neighboring state of Delaware decided to abandon the effort of the state police and a local magistrate to enforce Delaware's colonial statute against blasphemy. Two Wilmington teenagers called Jesus a bastard in a high school "underground" newspaper. They were held in jail a few days, then released on bail pending trial. Two years earlier a special panel of lawyers framing a proposed revision of Delaware's criminal code had recommended that the state blasphemy act of 1740 be eliminated; the legislature of the state took no action. But Judge Weant's opinion, holding Maryland's statute unconstitutional in the light of decisions of the Supreme Court of the United States, was noticed in the Delaware press as well as in legal circles. The Delaware statute, which threatened blasphemers with a year in prison, provided no definition of blasphemy whatever, making even easier an effort to strike it down as unconstitutional. After four months, the attorney general's office of Delaware decided not to press charges because "Religious beliefs vary, and we feel everyone has a right to express their own religion and religious belief." The trial judge agreed, adding that the statute was probably unconstitutional. In Butler, Pennsylvania, in 1971, two shopkeepers were charged with blasphemy under a vague state act of 1794. They provoked arrest by displaying posters saying "Jesus Christ—Wanted for sedition, criminal anarchy, vagrancy, and conspiracy to overthrow the established government. Dressed poorly; said to be a carpenter by trade; ill-nourished; associates with common working people, unemployed and bums. Alien; said to be a Jew." The American Civil Liberties Union intervened, and the county prosecutor wisely asked the local magistrate to drop the charges.[10]

Since then no blasphemy prosecutions have occurred in the United States, although local civic groups commonly censure books and movies as blasphemous. In 1977 the Massachusetts legislature, in deference to such groups, voted by two-to-one not to repeal its 1697 statute against blasphemy, although the last prosecutions in that state took place in the 1920s and failed. The 1697 Massachusetts statute ticks away on the books, once like a time-bomb and now more like a dud, ready to fizzle when the right occasion and right prosecutor happen to coincide. Should anyone be convicted in the future under that statute or under any law against blasphemy, anywhere in the United States, the probability is very great that his case would result in a judicial overturning of his conviction and of the law on which it was based.[11]

In Great Britain the situation is quite different, for the Church of England is by law still established and the country has no equivalent of the First Amendment. The blasphemy laws are rarely enforced in Great Britain. Indeed, fifty-six years elapsed between convictions in 1921 and 1977. The most recent case at Old Bailey involved a prosecution of *Gay News,* an obscure homosexual fortnightly, and its editor for having published a poem by James Kirkup, whom distinguished critics and writers have called a respectable man of letters. At the time of the prosecution, Kirkup was a visting professor at Amherst College. The prosecutor at the trial was no bigot; he urged an updated version of Lord Coleridge's 1883 test: "You can say Christ was a fraud or deceiver or Christ may have been a homosexual, provided you say it in a . . . decent way." He thought the poem's manner "so vile that it would be hard for even the most perverted imagination to conjure up anything worse." In Kirkup's poem the Roman centurion at the foot of the cross is a homosexual who fantasizes about having sexual relations with a homosexual Jesus Christ. The poem explicitly describes acts of sodomy and fellatio with the body of Christ immediately after his death. The trial judge, who refused to permit the introduction of professional testimony on the literary merit of the poem or its author, praised the jury's verdict of guilty and imposed fines of £1,000 on the paper and £500 on its editor; the judge also sentenced the editor to nine months in prison but suspended that part of the sentence pending an appeal. In 1978 the Court of Appeals ruled that the crime of blasphemy consisted in indecent, insulting, offensive, vilifying, or immoderate attack on Christianity, Christ, or religion, and the court let the fines stand but quashed the prison sentence.[12]

Whether the conviction and judicial ruling in the *Gay News* case was enlightened or benighted depends on whether one believes that the downfall of society, the subversion of government, or the dissolution of Christianity is at stake because of a disgusting or shocking literary gaucherie. Reasonable men have learned that morality can exist without religion, that Christianity is capable of surviving without penal sanctions, and that blasphemy does not even result in breach of the peace. The use of the criminal law to assuage affronted religious feelings imperils liberty—not greatly, to be sure, because blasphemy prosecutions have become legal relics in the Anglo-American world. But they are reminders that the feculent odor of persecution for the cause of conscience, which is the basic principle upon which they rest, has not yet evaporated.

NOTES

1. The Offense and Its Origins

1. T.S. Eliot, *After Strange Gods* (New York, 1934), 57.
2. *Ibid.*, 55–7.
3. John Godolphin, *Repertorium Canonicum; or An Abridgment of the Ecclesiastical Laws of This Realm* (London, 1678), 559–60.
4. George MacKenzie, *The Laws and Customs of Scotland in Matters Criminal* (Edinburgh, 1678), tit. iii, 1, p.25, and tit. x, 2, p.85.
5. Carl Zollman, *American Civil Church Law* (New York, 1917), 16.
6. Rex v. Gott, 16 Crim. App. Rep. 37 (1922).
7. State v. Mockus, 120 Maine 84 (1921).
8. *New York Times*, Feb. 19, 1926, p.3.
9. *Ibid.*, June 15, 1927, p.6, and *ibid.*, Aug. 28, 1928, p.26.
10. *Ibid.*, Oct. 18, 1928, p.1.
11. Rex v. St.-Martin, 40 *Rev. e Jur.* 411 (1933), and King v. Sterry, *Canadian Bar Rev.*, V (May 1927), 362–5.
12. King v. Sterry, *Canadian Bar Rev.*, V (May 1927), 363.
13. Demosthenes, *In Neareram*, trans. A.T. Murray (Cambridge, Mass., 1956), line 75, p.409, and line 77, p.411, and lines 75, 85–7, 115–17, pp. 409, 417, 419, 441–2; Demosthenes, *Against Meidias*, trans. C.A. Vince (Cambridge, Mass., 1935), lines 43 and 55, pp. 123, 180; Demosthenes, *De Falsa Legatione*, trans. C.A. Vince (Cambridge, Mass., 1935), line 281, p.43; Demosthenes, *Against Aristogeiton*, trans. C.A. Vince (Cambridge, Mass., 1935), lines 79–80, pp. 563–4. See also, J.S. Reid, "Sacrilege," *Encyclopedia of Religion and Ethics*, ed. James Hastings (New York, 1915), II, 40–3. The leading work is Eudore Derenne, *Les procès d'impiété. Intentes aux philosophes à Athines au Vme et au IVme siècles avant J.-C.* (Liège and Paris, 1930).
14. *Plutarch's Lives*, trans. Bernadotte Perrin (Cambridge, Mass., 1951, 11 vols.), *Nicias*, III, 291. For Plato's injunctions against impiety, see Plato, *The Laws*, trans. A.E. Taylor (London, 1960), ix, secs. 853–6, pp. 240–3, and x, secs. 907–10, pp.300–4.
15. Felix M. Cleve, *The Giants of Pre-Socratic Greek Philosophy* (The Hague, 1969, 2 vols.), I, 168. Cleve has the best discussion of Anaxagoras, *ibid.*, 168–328. Scholars do not agree on the dates of Anaxagoras's life and trial. Cleve's dates are much too early. H.T. Wade-Gray, *Essays in Greek History* (Oxford, 1958), 259–60, believes that he was tried in 433 which is too late; we know that Socrates and Anaxagoras never met, but they would have if 433 were correct. I have followed the chronology in A.E. Taylor, "On the Date

of the Trial of Anaxagoras," *Classical Quarterly*, IX (1917), 61–87. See also John Burnet, *Early Greek Philosophy* (London, 1930, 4th ed.), 255–6. For Socrates' reply, see Plato, *On the Trial and Death of Socrates*, trans. Lane Cooper (Ithaca, N.Y., 1941), *Apology*, 60.

16. *Plutarch's Lives, Nicias,* III, 291.

17. Plutarch, *Cimon and Pericles*, trans. B. Perrin (New York, 1910), ch. xxxii, p.149; chs. iv-vi, pp.107–10; ch. viii, pp.112–3; and 226 n. 3.

18. *Ibid.*, ch. xxxii, p.149, and 266 n. 3 See also C.M. Bowra, *Periclean Athens* (New York, 1971), 191–4, and E.F. Benson, *The Life of Alcibiades* (London, 1928), 57–8, 96.

19. Plutarch, *Cimon and Pericles*, ch. xxxi, pp.147–9. See also Bowra, *Periclean Athens*, 190–1; A.R. Burn, *Pericles and Athens* (London, 1948), 152–3; and George Grote, *History of Greece* (N.Y., n.d., 4 vols.), II, 511.

20. Paul Decharme, *Euripides and the Spirit of His Dramas,* trans. James Loeb (New York, 1906), 19–20, 72–3; Nicholas G.L. Hammond, *History of Greece to 322 B.C.* (Oxford, 1959), 404; Gilbert Murray, *Euripides and His Age* (New York, 1913), 57, 188–9; *Orestes*, line 418; *Hippolytus*, line 612; Aristotle, *The Art of Rhetoric*, trans. John Henry Freese (Cambridge, Mass., 1967), III, xv, lines 7–8, pp. 440–1; on Aeschylus, see Murray, *Euripides*, 57, and Leonard Woodbury, "The Date and Atheism of Diagoras of Melos," *Phoenix*, XIX (1965), 199.

21. Thucydides, *History of the Peloponnesian War*, trans. Charles Forster Smith (London, 1921, 4 vols.), III, 231–5, 275–7, 287–93; *Plutarch's Lives, Alcibiades*, IV, 53–61. See also Benson, *Life of Alcibiades*, 152–68, 177–82; Andokides, *On the Mysteries*, ed. with intro. and commentary by Douglas MacDowell (Oxford, 1962), 6–10, 166–76, 182–3, 192–3; R.C. Jebb, *The Attic Orators from Antiphon to Isaeos* (New York, 1962 reprint of 1875 ed., 2 vols.), I, 73–9, 109–19, 281–3.

22. For background on Greek religion, see Jane Harrison, *Prolegomena to the Study of Greek Religion* (New York, 1955, reprint of 3rd ed. of 1922), 150–60, 539; Martin P. Nilsson, *Greek Popular Religion* (New York, 1940), 42–64; W.K.C. Guthrie, *The Greeks and Their Gods* (Boston, 1950), 277–94.

23. Diogenes Laertius, *Lives of Eminent Philosophers*, trans. R.D. Hicks (Cambridge, Mass., 1970, 2 vols.), bk. ix, ch. 8, secs. 49–55, in II, 463–9; Morris Untersteiner, *The Sophists*, trans. Kathleen Freeman (Oxford, 1954), 4–8.

24. Theodor Gomperz, *Greek Thinkers: A History of Ancient Philosophy*, trans. Laurel Magnus (London, 1910, 4 vols.), I, 408; see also *ibid.*, 577–8. See also C.H. Oldfather, trans., *Diodorus of Sicily* (Cambridge, Mass., 1950, 12 vols.), V, 141; Cicero, *De Natura Deorum*, trans. H. Rackham (Cambridge, Mass., 1951), 61, 375; Woodbury, "Date and Atheism of Diagoras," *Phoenix*, XIX (1965), 178–211.

25. Benson, *Life of Alcibiades*, 68–9, 110–11; A.E. Taylor, *Socrates: the Man and His Thought* (New York, 1953 reprint of 1933 ed.), 48–9; Dorothy Stephans, *Critias, Life and Literary Remains* (Cincinnati, 1939), 40–5; Hammond, *History of Greece*, 442–5.

26. The trial of Socrates is reported in Plato's early dialogues, collected in the Lane Cooper edition cited in note 15 above, and in *The Last Days of Socrates*, trans. Hugh Tredennick (Penguin Books, 1954). *The Apology* is the chief source. See also Xenophon, *Memorabilia,* trans. E.C. Marchant (Cambridge,

Mass., 1959). A learned biography is Anton-Hermann Chroust, *Socrates, Man and Myth* (London, 1957). Gregory Vlastos, ed., *The Philosophy of Socrates* (Garden City, N.Y. 1971), is a good collection of critical essays. Karl Popper, *The Open Society and Its Enemies* (London, 1957, 2 vols., 3rd ed.), makes Plato the villain who betrayed and distorted the real Socrates whom Popper saw as the champion of democratic values, equalitarianism, and individualism. The provocative little book by Alan D. Winspear and Tom Silverberg, *Who Was Socrates?* (New York, 1960, 2nd ed.), depicts a youthful democrat who became an old reactionary, guilty as charged. A similar view expressed in moderate terms may be found in A.E. Taylor, *Socrates*, 100–16, and in his earlier work, *Varia Socratica* (Oxford, 1911), 1–39, *e.g.*, Socrates was the "dangerous head of an anti-democratic" conspiracy (*Varia*, 12). Burnet, *Greek Philosophy*, 186–8, also stresses Socrates' politics. For a spirited debate on his religious views and the validity of the indictment against him, see Taylor's *Varia Socratica* and A.S. Ferguson, "The Impiety of Socrates," *Classical Quarterly*, VII (1913), 157–75.

27. Socrates' speech in his defense is in *The Apology;* his life between his conviction and his death is reported in Plato's *Crito and Phaedo*, both reprinted in the Cooper and Tredennick editions.

28. Diogenes Laertius, *Lives*, bk. v, chs. 5–10, in II, 449–53; Alfred W. Benn, *The Greek Philosophers* (London, 1914, 2nd ed.), 245–8; Anton-Hermann Chroust, *Aristotle* (Notre Dame, Ind., 1973, 2 vols.), I, 145–54.

29. For Old Testament chronology I have relied on Theodore H. Robinson, *A History of Israel: From the Exodus to the Fall of Jerusalem, 586 B.C.* (Oxford, 1932), supplemented by H.R. Hull, *Ancient History of the Near East* (London, 1936, 9th ed.). The date of the Exodus from Egypt may have been anywhere between 1600 B.C. and 1250 B.C., although the great scholar William Foxwell Albright, *Yahweh and the Gods of Canaan* (New York, 1968), 159, dated the Exodus as ca. 1297 or 1290. On the composition of the books of the Old Testament, I have followed Harry Gersh, *The Sacred Books of the Jews* (New York, 1968). On the relation between God and ruler, see C.R. North, "The Old Testament Estimate of the Monarchy," *American Journal of Semitic Languages and Literatures*, XLVII (1931), 1–19; Erwin R. Goodenough, "Kingship in Early Israel," *Journal of Biblical Literature*, XLVIII (1929), 169–205; C.J. Gadd, *Ideas of Divine Rule in the Ancient East* (London, 1948), 33–48; Henri Frankfort, *Kingship and the Gods* (Chicago, 1948), 337–44; and Aubrey R. Johnson, "The Role of the King in the Jerusalem Cultus," in S.H. Hooke, ed., *The Labyrinth* (London, 1935), 73–111. Neither the Old Testament nor the Talmud supports the proposition that cursing a ruler was blasphemous. For a contrary view, relying on an inference from Exodus 22:27, see the articles on "Blasphemy" in *Encyclopedia Judaica* (Jerusalem, 1971), IV, 1074, and *The Jewish Encyclopedia* (New York, 1925), III, 237. Herbert Chanan Brichto, *The Problem of "Curse" in the Hebrew Bible* (Philadelphia, 1963), 158, argues that Exodus 22:27 should be translated "Do not act in disrespect of God nor bring under a ban an elected chieftain of your people," leaving no room for the possibility of the crime of blasphemy being committed against a ruler.

30. On stoning, see *The Babylonian Talmud: Sanhedrin* (London: Soncino Press, 1935–48, 34 vols.), eds. I. Epstein *et al.*, I, 275–329.

31. Lev. 4:13–16. On sacrifice, see Johs. Pederson, *Israel: Its Life and Culture* (Oxford, 1940), IV, 299–375.

32. On the Baal cults, see Pederson, *Israel,* IV, 503–23; E. Robertson Smith, *The Religion of the Semites* (N.Y., 1956, reprint ed.), 92–108; Albright, *Yahweh and the Gods of Canaan,* 115–45, 185–91, 226–64; Lewis B. Payton, "Baal," *Encyclopedia of Religion and Ethics,* II, 283–98; "Baal and Baal Worship," *Jewish Encyclopedia,* II, 378–81.

33. 1 Kings 21 describes Naboth's case; Talmud: Sanhedrin, 48b, I, 323–4.

34. Accounts of Rab-Shakeh's blasphemy are in 2 Kings 18–19, 2 Chron. 32, and Isaiah 36–37.

35. Brichto, *The Problem of "Curse" in the Hebrew Bible,* 1–12 and *passim;* Sheldon H. Blank, "The Curse, Blasphemy, the Spell, and the Oath," *Hebrew Union College Annual,* vol. XXIII (Cincinnati, 1950–51), 73–95, 135, 141, 142, 146–9, 151; "Blessing and Cursing," *Encyclopedia Judaica,* IV, 1084–7; Brichto, *The Problem of "Curse" in the Hebrew Bible,* 135, 141, 142, 146–9, 151.

36 Sanhedrin 60a, I, 409.

37. *The New English Bible with the Apocrypha* (New York, 1976), is a convenient collection. R. H. Charles *et al.,* eds., *The Apocrypha and Pseudepigraphd of the Old Testament in English* (Oxford, 1913, 2 vols.), is the fullest collection, with valuable introductions and notes.

38. Brichto, *The Problem of "Curse" in the Hebrew Bible,* ch. 4, esp. pp. 127, 129, 131, 135, 141, 143, 151, 158, 171, 176–7. Emil Schürer, *The Literature of the Jewish People in the Time of Jesus,* ed. Nahum N. Glatzer (New York, 1972), and D. S. Russell, *Between the Testaments* (Philadelphia, 1960), are good introductions to the Septuagint and intertestamental literature. James H. Charlesworth, *The Pseudepigrapha and Modern Research* (Missoula, Mont., 1977), is a useful guide to concordances and indices that allow one to discover the uses of "blaspheme" and its variants. Edwin Hatch and Henry A. Redpath, *A Concordance to the Septuagint and the Other Greek Versions of the Old Testament (including the Apocryphal Books)* (Graz, Austria, 1954, 2 vols.), is invaluable.

39. For other references to blasphemy, see Tobit 1:18; Wisdom of Solomon 1:6, 11; Bel and the Dragon 9; 1 Enoch 94:7, 11; *ibid.,* 94:9, 96:7; Zadokite 7:12, 14:8.

40. Philo, a Greek-Jewish secular author, used "blasphemy" in the Greek sense to mean any sort of slander or evil-speaking (*Flaccus,* 33, and *The Special Laws,* IV, 197). Philo seems also to have meant by "blasphemer" one who "is profane and reviles things sacred"; he did not define blasphemy against God but gave the example of one who ascribed evil to God, *One Flight and Finding,* 83–4. Philo thought the death penalty appropriate for anyone who blasphemed God or "even ventures to utter His Name unseasonably" (*Moses* II, 206). All this is from *Philo,* trans. F. H. Colson and G. H. Whitaker (Cambridge, Mass., Loeb Classical Library, 12 vols.), V, 55; VI, 551; VIII, 131; IX, 321. In the Qumran literature, by contrast, a variety of words were used that could be translated as "blaspheme," *e.g.,* words for curse, reproach, despise, and insult, but without exception they connote blasphemy only when referring to verbal abuse of God. The broadest use of blasphemy that I have found occurs in the "Damascus Rule," where there is a reference to defilers speaking "with a blasphemy of the name of God. (Brownlee, "The Dead Sea Manual of Discipline," *Bulletin of the American Schools of Oriental Researach,* Supplementary Studies, nos. 10–12 [1951], 28).

Qumran. In "The Community Rule," also known as the "Manual of

Discipline," excommunication is the penalty for any person who has uttered the name of God (*ibid.*, 83). In another translation of the same document, Theodor H. Gaster, *The Dead Sea Scriptures* (Anchor Books, 1964, rev. ed.), 60, excommunication, according to Gaster's restoration, applies to one who curses the reader of the Torah or the leader of worship; the phrase supplying the direct object of "curse" is missing in the original document. My colleague, William H. Brownlee, who generously but fruitlessly searched Qumran texts for all usages of "blaspheme" and "blasphemy," has restored a mutilated passage of the "Manual of Discipline" to read "must be put to death" as the punishment for blasphemy of the name of God. (Brownlee, "The Dead Sea Manual of Discipline," *Bulletin of the American Schools of Oriental Research,* Supplementary Studies, nos. 10–12 [1951], 28).

41. Beginners interested in the Talmud should consult Moses Mielziner, *Introduction to the Talmud* (New York, 1968, 4th ed.); Hermann L. Strack, *Introduction to the Talmud and Midrash* (New York, 1959, 5th ed.); Jacob Neusner, *Invitation to the Talmud* (New York, 1973); George Horowitz, *The Spirit of Jewish Law* (New York, 1963); the introduction by Herbert Danby to his translation of *The Mishnah* (London, 1933); Charles Auerbach, *The Talmud: A Gateway to the Common Law* (Cleveland, 1952); Salo W. Baron, *A Social and Religious History of the Jews* (New York, 1952– , 16 vols.), II, 215–321.

42. Sanhedrin 49b, I, 332; see also *ibid.,* 45b, I, 300. On the concept of the unity of God, see Ephraim E. Urbach, *The Sages* (Jerusalem, 1974, 2 vols.), I, 19–36; Louis Jacobs, *A Jewish Theology* (New York, 1973), 21–37.

43. Maimonides, *The Mishnah Torah,* book I, ed. and trans. Moses Hyamson (New York, 1937), Book of Knowledge, Idolatry, 68a, sect. 6. See also, Maimonides, *The Commandments,* ed. and trans. Charles B. Chavel (London, 1967, 2 vols.), II, no. 60, 56–7, on blasphemy and immediately preceding sections of idolatry. An ancient Hebrew phrase, literally translated as "He who puts forth his hand against the Root [God]," denotes both an idolater and a curser of God; see Urbach, *The Sages,* I, 28. Sanhedrin 55b, I, 378; 56a, I, 378, 381.

44. George Foot Moore, *Judaism in the First Centuries of the Christian Era* (Cambridge, Mass., 1927–30, 3 vols.), I, 427. Sanhedrin 90a, I, 602 and 101a, I, 688. Brichto, *The Problem of "Curse" in the Hebrew Bible,* 164, argues that at no point does the Bible enjoin blasphemy as an imprecation against God, for in a system that acknowledges one supreme Deity, cursing or reviling Him cannot be conceived. Brichto concedes that every translation of the Bible and the Talmud speaks of blasphemy in the conventional sense, but alleges that all his predecessors were wrong. See also *Encyclopedia Judaica,* IV, 1073, and Hugo Mantel, *Studies in the History of the Sanhedrin* (Cambridge, Mass., 1965), 274, and linguistic authorities there cited in note 179. On the name of God, its substitutes, attributes, and frequency of use, see "Tetragrammaton," *Jewish Encyclopedia,* XII, 118–20; "Jehovah," *ibid.,* VII, 87–8; Moore, *Judaism,* I, 423–42; Samuel S. Cohon, "The Name of God," *Hebrew Union College Annual,* vol. XXIII (Cincinnati, 1950–51), 579–604; "Name of God," *New Catholic Encyclopedia* (New York, 1967), X, 200–1. From a Greek or Latin equivalent of YHVH based on a mispronunciation of a Hebrew substitute for it, "Adonai," which means "the Lord," Christian theologians of the sixteenth century produced the familiar corruption "Jehovah." Whatever the actual pronunciation of the name, the Old Testament employed the Hebrew Tetragrammaton

instead of the name with great frequency; by actual count, "YHVH" occurs 5989 times. The New Testament invariably translates it as "the Lord."

45. Talmud, Sotah 37b, p. 186, and Yoma 66a, p. 308.

46. On the power of the divine Name, see Urbach, Sages, I, 124–34.

47. Sanhedrin 56a, I, 378; 60a, I, 407–9.

48. Ibid., 56a, I, 378; 60a, I, 407.

49. Ibid., chs. 4–5, I, 199–274. For a later codification of Talmudic criminal procedure, see The Code of Maimonides, The Book of Judges, trans. Abraham M. Hershman (New Haven, 1949), chs. 8–12, pp. 26–36; for a modern work, see Hyman E. Goldin, Hebrew Criminal Procedure (New York, 1952). On the Talmudic background of the right against self-incrimination, see Leonard W. Levy, Origins of the Fifth Amendment (New York, 1968), 433–41. Talmud, Makkoth 4a–5b, pp. 15–25.

50. Sanhedrin 43b, I, 235. On forewarning, see ibid., 8b, I, 36 and 40b–41a, I, 262–5; also Makkoth 6b, pp. 31–34 and Ketubot 33a, p. 181; Maimonides, Book of Judges, ch. 12, sect. 2, p. 34. If forewarning could not be proved in a murder case and the judges were convinced of the defendant's guilt, they could impose a sentence of life imprisonment.

51. Makkoth 7a, p. 35; Sanhedrin 41a, I, 267; 52b, I, 352–3; 89a, I, 589. For the ninth-century statement, see Teshubot Geone Mizrah Uma'arab (Responsa of the Geonim of East and West), ed. Joel Miller (Berlin, 1885), No. 103, quoted in "Blasphemy," Jewish Encyclopedia, III, 237–8, and Horowitz, Spirit of Jewish Law, 185.

2. The Jewish Trial of Jesus

1. On the Sanhedrin, see Sidney B. Hoenig, The Great Sanhedrin (Philadelphia, 1953), and Hugo Mantel, Studies in the History of the Sanhedrin (Cambridge, Mass., 1965).

2. On the Synoptic Gospels, see Frederick C. Grant, The Growth of the Gospels (New York, 1933); Vincent Taylor, The Formation of the Gospel Tradition (London, 1935, 2nd ed.); Martin Dibelius, From Tradition to Gospel, trans. B. L. Woolf (Cambridge, 1971); Rudolf Bultmann, History of the Synoptic Tradition, trans. John Marsh (New York, 1963, rev. ed.); Willi Marxsen, Introduction to the New Testament, trans. G. Buswell (Philadelphia, 1974, 3rd ed.); Werner Georg Kümmel, Introduction to the New Testament, trans. Howard C. Kee (Nashville, 1973, 17th ed.).

3. Mantel, History of the Sanhedrin, 268–73.

4. On John, see Rudolf Bultmann, The Gospel of John: A Commentary, trans. G.R. Beasley-Murray et al.(Philadelphia, 1971); Raymond E. Brown, ed., The Gospel According to John (The Anchor Bible: Garden City, N.Y., 1966–70), vols. 29–29A; C. H. Dodd, Historical Tradition in the Fourth Gospel (Cambridge, 1963). Most scholars agree that John, the last Gospel, was written in the last decade of the first century. Our earliest copy of the text that includes the arrest and trial scenes dates from the fourth century, as in the case of the Synoptic Gospels too. See Kurt Aland, Synopsis of the Four Gospels (n.p., United Bible Societies, 1976 ed.), xvi–xvii. Because the four Gospels were written in the last third of the first century and the earliest extant texts for the trials are so late, we cannot be certain whether there are significant discrepancies. Textual critics working with only the late texts can, nevertheless, discern

changes. For example, Eldon Jay Epp, *The Theological Tendency of Codex Bezae Cantabrigiensis* (Cambridge, 1966), focused on a late fifth-century text, compared it with variants and the fourth-century Codex Vaticanus, and proved that a pronounced anti-Judaic tendency assigned to the Jews and their leaders increasingly greater responsibility for the death of Jesus and also depicted them as more persecutory toward the apostles and the early churches. Epp found the anti-Judaic tendency "striking" and "widespread" (p. 166). On rewriting and revising the Gospels, see *ibid.*, 16. See also Burnett H. Streeter, *The Four Gospels: a Study of Origins* (New York, 1925), 12–45, and Charles Guignebert, *Jesus,* trans. S. H. Hooke (London, 1935), who stated that the texts of the original manuscripts of the Gospels "were regarded, not as personal works which had received from their authors a definite form which might not be tampered with, but as the property of the churches that adopted them. These made use of them in accordance with what they believed to be their own interests and the dictates of the faith, and thought nothing of 'improving' them when they judged it expedient." See generally *ibid.*, 30–50. The statement cannot be proved or disproved.

5. James M. Robinson, *The Problem of History in Mark* (Naperville, Ill., 1957), 54. Bultmann, *Synoptic Tradition,* 374 says: "These works are completely subordinate to Christian faith and worship. . . . the Gospel belongs to the history of dogma and worship." A. E. J. Rawlinson, *St. Mark* (London, 1925), 220, spoke of the Gospel as "Christian propaganda." The quotation on "propaganda material" in my text is from Robert Morgan, "Nothing More Negative," in Ernest Bammel, ed., *The Trial of Jesus* (London, 1970), 137. The use of "propaganda" in relation to the Gospels is not uncommon. See also Walter E. Bundy, *Jesus and the First Three Gospels* (Cambridge, Mass., 1955), 527–8, on Luke's version of the Roman trial; Alfred Firmin Loisy, *The Birth of the Christian Religion* (1935), trans. L. P. Jacks (New Hyde Park, N.Y., 1962), ch. 4; Morton Smith, *Jesus the Magician* (New York, 1978), 38. On the unrecoverability of the historical Jesus, the starting place is Albert Schweitzer, *The Quest of the Historical Jesus,* trans. W. Montgomery (New York, 1961, reprint from the 1906 ed.); see also the works on the Synoptic Gospels cited in note 2 above, especially the book by Bultmann, all of whose works testify to the inevitable failure to recapture the life of the Jesus who actually lived. Bultmann's *Jesus and the Word,* trans. L. P. Smith and E. H. Lantero (New York, 1934), is a demythologizer's existential Christ. Bultmann's mature reflections are in his essay, "The Primitive Christian Kerygma and the Historical Jesus," trans. Carl E. Braaten and Roy A. Harrisville in their collection, *The Historical Jesus and the Kerygmatic Christ: Essays on the New Quest of the Historical Jesus* (New York, 1964), 15–42. James M. Robinson, *A New Quest of the Historical Jesus* (London, 1959), is indispensable.

6. Hans Küng, *On Being a Christian,* trans. Edward Quinn (Garden City, N.Y., 1976), 327. On the obtuseness of the disciples and the mystery of Jesus' identity, see Theodore J. Weeden, *Mark—Traditions in Conflict* (Philadelphia, 1971), 23–44.

7. Oscar Cullmann, *The State in the New Testament* (New York, 1956), 45. According to the *Catholic Encyclopedia* (1908) IV, 520, Jesus was condemned for "sedition and tumult." Sedition was "open resistance, an uprising of a rather large group of persons with the use of—armed or unarmed—force against the magistrates," and the accused were tried under Caesar's law (*Lex Julia*) govern-

ing treason; the name of the crime was *"crimen maiestatis."* See "sedition" and "crimen maiestatis" in Adolph Berger, *Encyclopedia Dictionary of Roman Law,* in *Transactions,* American Philosophical Society, new ser., XLIII, pt. 2 (1953), 418, 695. Any affront to the emperor's authority, dignity, or honor was treason. On Tiberius and the Lex Julia see *Suetonius* (Lives of the Caesars), trans. J. C. Rolfe (London, 1928, 2 vols., Loeb Classics), 1, 373–5. See also C. W. Chilton, "The Roman Law and Treason Under the Early Principate," *Journal of Roman Studies, XLV (1955), 73–81.*

8. Rudolf Bultmann, *Primitive Christianity,* trans. R. H. Fuller (New York, 1956), 71–2. On Jesus as a Jew, works by Jewish authors include Joseph Klausner, *Jesus of Nazareth,* trans. Herbert Danby (New York, 1944); Geza Vermes, *Jesus the Jew* (New York, 1973); Jules Isaac, *Jesus and Israel,* trans. Sally Gran (New York, 1971); Samuel Sandmel, *We Jews and Jesus* (New York, 1973); *idem, A Jewish Understanding of the New Testament* (New York, 1974, rev. ed.). Sandmel's work has had the greatest single influence on my thinking on this subject. See also Sandmel, *The First Christian Century in Judaism and Christianity* (New York, 1969), and *idem, Judaism and Christian Beginnings* (New York, 1978). For more conventional views of Jesus, see Morton Scott Enslin, *The Prophet from Nazareth* (New York, 1961); Günther Bornkamm, *Jesus of Nazareth,* trans. I. and F. McLuskey with J. M. Robinson (New York, 1975).

9. The reply "I am" is not accepted as genuine or is construed as "you say so" by some scholars who accept the Sanhedrin trial as authentic. See D. E. Nineham, *The Gospel of St. Mark* (Penguin Books, rev. ed., 1976), 408; C. E. B. Cranfield, *The Gospel According to Saint Mark* (Cambridge, 1959), 443–4; Vincent Taylor, *The Gospel According to St. Mark* (New York, 1966, 2nd ed.), 568; Bundy, *Jesus and the First Three Gospels,* 518–19. See also Frederick C. Grant, *Translating the Bible* (Edinburgh, 1961), 155–6; Richard Husband, *The Prosecution of Jesus* (Princeton, 1916), 215; Oscar Cullmann, *Jesus and the Revolutionaries* (New York, 1970), 42.

10. Vincent Taylor, *The Names of Jesus* (New York, 1953), 25. See also Ferdinand Hahn, *The Titles of Jesus in Christology* (New York, 1969), 15–42, on the Son of Man; Reginald H. Fuller, *The Foundations of New Testament Christology* (New York, 1965), 34–43, 119–24; Howard Clark Kee, *Community of the New Age* (Philadeiphia, 1977), 129–39; Vermes, *Jesus the Jew,* 160–91; S. Mowinckel, *He That Cometh,* trans. G. W. Anderson (Nashville, 1954), 356–450. The fullest analysis is H. E. Tödt, *The Son of Man in the Synoptic Tradition* (Philadelphia, 1965), which reflects the skeptical account of Rudolf Bultmann, *Theology of the New Testament,* trans. K. Grobel (New York, 1951–5, 2 vols. in one), 26–32.

11. Taylor, *Names of Jesus,* 199; also Taylor, *Gospel According to Mark,* 563, stating that Jesus used the Son of Man saying to make "an explicit claim to be the Messiah." Joseph Klausner, *The Messianic Idea in Israel* (New York, 1955), 223–36, shows the political-religious context of Daniel.

12. On Son of Man, in addition to the works cited in note 10 above, see Norman Perrin, *A Modern Pilgrimage in New Testament Christology* (Philadelphia, 1974); John R. Donahue, *Are You the Christ? The Trial Narrative in the Gospel of Mark* (Missoula, Mont., 1973), 139–87; and esp. "'Son of Man' in Mark," in Samuel Sandmel, *Two Living Traditions* (Detroit, 1972), 166–77.

13. Taylor, *Names of Jesus,* 54, 59, and see his chapters on each of the titles. See also Richard N. Longenecker, *The Christology of Early Jewish Christianity* (London, 1970), 63–119; Hahn, *The Titles,* 136–93 (Messiah), 279–333 (Son of God), 185–93 and 348–50 (Hellenism); Fuller, *Foundations,* discussed each of the titles associated with Jesus three times—under Palestinian Judaism, Hellenistic Judaism, and Christian Hellenism. Vermes, *Jesus the Jew,* Part II on "The Titles of Jesus" includes chapters on Messiah, Son of Man, and Son of God. For an extraordinary interpretation, equating Son of God with a miracle worker or magus, see Smith, *Jesus the Magician,* 39, 100–39, 177. For Hellenistic influences, see also Bultmann, *Theology,* 164–89, and Bultmann, *Primitive Christianity,* 175–9.

14. On Messiah, in addition to the works by Taylor, Longenecker, Hahn, Fuller, and Vermes in the preceding note, see George Foote Moore, *Judaism in the First Centuries of the Christian Era* (New York, 1971 reprint, 2 vols.), II, 323–76. Abba Hillel Silver, *A History of Messianic Speculation in Israel* (Boston, 1959), 16–17, pointed out that messianic hopes were "rife" among Jews in Israel at the time of Jesus, not just because of the Roman occupation but "also because their chronology led them to believe that they were on the threshold of the Millennium." Many claimed to be the messiah.

15. On the Davidic king or Son of David, see Hahn, *The Titles,* 240–78; Vermes, *Jesus the Jew,* 129–59, 153, also 13–14; Klausner, *Messianic Idea,* 519–31. Cf. Enslin, *Prophet from Nazareth,* 54–55, 130–6. Floyd V. Filson, "Capitalization in English Translations of the Gospel of Matthew," in David E. Aune, ed., *Studies in New Testament and Early Christian literature* (Leiden, 1972), 25–30.

16. The Sadducees, although the governing group in Jerusalem at the time of Jesus, were only one of several denominations, sects, and parties (inexact terms), including Pharisees (of whom there were variant groups), Essenes, Baptists, numerous minor sects, and Zealots. Judaism was then, as now, monotheistic but not monolithic. It was a syncretistic religion. Heterodoxy in religious belief and practice prevailed. Heresy, the crime of wrong or erroneous religious belief, was unknown to Judaism during the time of Jesus. The word "heresy" or any equivalent for it does not appear in the Jewish thought of Jesus' time. Orthodoxy and Judaism were incompatible, unless by orthodoxy one merely means worship of God and devotion to the Torah. Orthodoxy did not mean correct doctrine. The two major denominations, the Sadducees and Pharisees, for example, differed on many vital matters yet lived together without reference to heresy. On Jewish sects, see Marcel Simon, *Jewish Sects at the Time of Jesus,* trans. J. H. Farley (Philadelphia, 1967); J. W. Lightley, *Jewish Sects and Parties in the Time of Jesus* (London, 1925); Charles Guignebert, *The Jewish World in the Time of Jesus* (New Hyde Park, N.Y., 1959 reprint), 161–261. Jacob Neusner, *The Rabbinic Traditions About the Pharisees Before 70* (Leiden, 1971, 3 vols.), is definitive, although Louis Finkelstein, *The Pharisees* (Philadelphia, 1962, 3rd ed., rev., 2 vols.), remains very helpful on the Sadducees as well.

17. E. Mary Smallwood, "High Priests and Politics in Roman Palestine," *Journal of Theological Studies,* n.s., XIII (1962), 14–34; Emil Schürer, *The History of the Jewish People in the Age of Jesus Christ,* trans. Sophia Taylor and Peter Christie (Edinburgh, 1885–91, 2nd ed., 5 vols. divided into two "Divisions"), div. II, vol. I, 195–206; Haim Cohn, *The Trial and Death of Jesus* (New York, 1977), 21–37.

18. Rudolf Bultmann, *Form Criticism,* trans. Frederick C. Grant (New York, 1962), 71–2.

19. On John 11:47–53, see Paul Winter, *On the Trial of Jesus,* rev. and ed. by T. A. Burkill and Geza Vermes (Berlin, 1974), 54–5. On Jesus and the Temple, see Donahue, *Are You the Christ?* 103–38; Werner Kelber, *The Kingdom in Mark* (Philadelphia, 1974), 99–116; Donald Juel, *Messiah and Temple* (Missoula, Mont., 1977), 130–6.

20. Cullmann, *Jesus and the Revolutionaries,* 43, found significance in the fact that the entry into Jerusalem was not on a horse in the manner of a warlike Messiah. That misreads Zechariah 9:9. The Messiah there can "command peace" only because of military victory, accomplished with divine aid. Cutting down the enemy and drinking their blood like wine is not the act of a peaceable Messiah.

21. Oscar Cullmann, *The State in the New Testament* (New York, 1956), 14–17. That Josephus, the principal source on Jewish-Roman relations and Jewish uprisings, has nothing on "the insurrection" (Mark 15:7) proves nothing, because the church could have censored his text; what he said about Jesus in *Jewish Antiquities* shows obvious censorship and Christian rewriting, for Josephus could not possibly have described Jesus as the Messiah. *Josephus,* trans. H. St. J. Thackeray *et al.* (Cambridge, Mass., Loeb Classical Library, 1956–65, 9 vols.), IX, 49–51. See also the new translation and completely revised edition of div. I of Schürer, *History of the Jewish People* by Geza Vermes and Fergus Millar (Edinburgh, 1973), 428–41, and S. G. F. Brandon, *The Fall of Jerusalem and the Christian Church* (London, 1954), 110–25. Vermes–Millar, eds., Schürer's *History,* 385, construed Luke 13:1 to mean that Pilate killed a number of Galileans preparing to worship at the Temple. Cullmann, *The State,* 14, thought the passage referred to Pilate's suppression of a Zealot uprising; so too, W. F. Albright and C. S. Mann, *Matthew* (Anchor Bible: Garden City, N.Y., 1971), 344. Robert Eisler, *The Messiah Jesus and John the Baptist,* trans. A. H. Krappe (London, 1931), 457–513, depicts a political Jesus. The only reputable Christian New Testament scholar who takes a similar line is Brandon, *Jesus and the Zealots* (New York, 1967); in his *Trial of Jesus* (New York, 1968), 102, 191, Brandon depicts a military assault on the Temple, led by Jesus, in concert with an attack on the Roman garrison by Zealots, led by Barabbas. Cullmann, *Jesus and the Revolutionaries* and Martin Hengel, *Was Jesus a Revolutionist?* trans. W. Classen (Philadelphia, 1971), present the customary interpretation.

22. On the Zealotic insurrectionists as "robbers" or *lestai* to Josephus, the Romans, and the evangelists, see Hengel, *Was Jesus a Revolutionist?* 13; Cullmann, *Jesus and the Revolutionaries,* 33, 66 n. 3; Gerard S. Sloyan, *Jesus on Trial* (Philadelphia, 1973), 42; William R. Wilson, *The Execution of Jesus* (New York, 1970), 39; Brown, *John* (Anchor Bible), XXIX, 385, 857; Juel, *Messiah and Temple,* 132.

23. The word "council" in the Gospels is the English translation of "synedrion," the Greek for Sanhedrin.

24. Rawlinson, *St. Mark,* 220, used "trumped up," as have many others.

25. *Josephus,* VII, 377 (Loeb Classics ed.).

26. Schürer, *History,* div. II, vol. I, 184–95, assumed that the Talmudic rules were all in force, although he denied the Sanhedrin's power of capital jurisdiction. Husband, *Prosecution,* 151–73, assumed that none were in force but agreed that the Romans reserved exclusive jurisdiction in capital cases. This

became the dominant view after Herbert Danby, who later translated *The Mishnah* (Oxford, 1933), endorsed it in his influential article "The Bearing of the Rabbinical Criminal Code on the Jewish Trial Narratives in the Gospels," *Journal of Theological Studies,* XXI (1919), 51–76. Danby translated Klausner's *Jesus of Nazareth,* the first modern Jewish account. Klausner waffled on the issue of whether any Talmudic rules were operative at the time of the trial of Jesus (pp. 334–5, 340–1). He assumed that the Sadducees completely dominated the Sanhedrin, allowing him to accept a majority condemnation of Jesus by the Sanhedrin for the crime of blasphemy (pp. 343–4). We have no proof that a majority of the Sanhedrin's members were Sadducees. We do not know the proportion of Sadducees to Pharisees as of A.D. 30. Christian scholars followed Danby's view that the Talmudic rules on trial procedure were not in effect in the first century; Wilson, *The Execution,* 122, was a rare exception when he said, vaguely, that "some" of the rules applied, although he did not say which. Jewish scholarship shows no pattern. Winter, *On the Trial,* 32, 98, observed that a Sanhedrin conviction for blasphemy conflicted with the Talmud, but he concluded that the Talmudic tract *Sanhedrin* described only rules of procedure in judicial matters not in force during Jesus' life and therefore irrelevant, because the Sanhedrin that the Gospels described "dealt with an administrative question within the Council's competence, namely, the delivery of a person suspected of sedition to the procurator" (p.39). Mantel, *History of the Sanhedrin,* 268–90, believed that the Sanhedrin never met in Jesus' case and that the trial described in the Gospels was a preliminary hearing. Mantel defended the existence of several of the Talmudic rules as of the time of Jesus, including the ones barring a trial at night, on a festival, or on its eve, but did not mention the rule requiring the agreement of witnesses (pp. 257, 268–90). Cohn, *Trial and Death,* 340, assumed that the Talmudic rules were all in force and measured what the Gospels allege to have happened against those rules; *ibid.,* 71–141 and related notes. Cohn's thesis was unique: the Sanhedrin met informally not to charge Jesus with any offense but to save him from the Romans who had arrested him and were about to try him. The purpose of the meeting, thus conceived, was to persuade Jesus to deny any claims that Pilate might construe as treasonous. Since Cohn trivialized the political character of anything Jesus said or did, the reason for the Roman arrest and condemnation seems obscure.

27. On the Old Testament tradition of criticizing the Temple and its cult, see Walter Schmithals, *Paul and James* (Naperville, Ill., 1965), 21. Schmithals declared that at the time of Jesus, any Jew might with impunity announce the end of the Temple; it was not uncommon for Jews to disregard the Temple cult and its sacrifices. He said that Essenes, Galileans, and Samaritans failed to worship at the Temple "without being molested on that account," and the Hellenistic Jews had only a loose relationship to it. The importance of the Temple to Judaism has been exaggerated: "After all, Judaism survived the destruction of the Temple without a great convulsion." Lloyd Gaston, *No Stone on Another: Studies in the Significance of the Fall of Jerusalem in the Synoptic Gospels* (Leiden, 1970), and Juel, *Messiah and Temple,* contend that Jesus neither said nor did anything to merit the Temple charge. Donahue, *Are You the Christ?* argues that Mark intends his readers to accept the Temple charge against Jesus as having been true; Mark freely composed the trial narrative and included the Temple charge, like the blasphemy charge, as a means of depicting

Jewish rejection of Jesus as well as providing a way for later Christians to understand the Roman destruction of the Temple, which was a catastrophe for Mark's generation, and also to understand that the new Christian community replaced the Temple.

28. On the un-Jewishness of the question, see Klausner, *Jesus of Nazareth,* 342; cf. Rawlinson, *St. Mark,* 222, and Joseph Blinzler, *The Trial of Jesus* (Westminster, Md., 1959), 102–3.

29. Bundy, *Jesus and the First Three Gospels,* 518–9, questioned the "I am" reply on sound grounds and, like Rawlinson, *St. Mark,* 223, and C. G. Montefiore, *The Synoptic Gospels* (London, 1927, 2 vols.), I, 365–6, put the mocking out of the sight of the judges. Klausner, *Jesus of Nazareth,* 343, accepted the high priest's tearing of his robes; Cohn, *Trial and Death,* 129–34, did too, but because Caiaphas anticipated Jesus' Roman crucifixion, not because he heard blasphemy.

30. Nineham, *Gospel of St. Mark,* 408, referred to the "formal judicial act." *Josephus,* II, 445.

31. On the uprising of A.D. 6, see Vermes-Millar, eds., Schürer's *History,* 372–3, and *Josephus,* II, 323–53, and VIII, 489–511. On Theudas, see *Josephus,* IX, 400–1, which includes an editorial note on the discrepancies in the dating of the Theudas event; see also Vermes-Millar, Schürer's *History,* 456–7. Acts of the Apostles made several anachronistic mistakes. Some scholars still insist that because Josephus did not mention the Zealots by name until he reached the year A.D. 66, there was no continuity from Judas the Galilean to the Zealots of 66. Cullmann, in *The State* and *Jesus and the Revolutionaries,* reflects the dominant position today: the Zealots of 66 can be traced directly back to at least the year A.D. 6, but Jesus had no political connections with the Zealots and did not share their views; Josephus concealed the Zealotic line of continuity from Judas of Galilee to 66.

32. Pilate's washing of his hands before the crowd to testify to his innocence in shedding Jesus' blood would be comical but for the fact that it is part of a scene in Matt. 27:24–5 that has fed anti-Semitic fires ever since. Washing the hands was part of Jewish purification rites.

33. "The crucifixion of living persons was not practiced among the Hebrews; capital punishment then consisted of being stoned to death, e.g., the proto-martyr Stephen," in Orazio Marucchi, "The Cross and Crucifix," *Catholic Encyclopedia* (1908), IV, 517. See also Brown, *The Gospel According to John,* 850–1, 877. For a reliable discussion on the un-Jewishness of crucifixion, see Winter, *On the Trial,* 90–102, and Joseph N. Baumgarten, "Does TLH in the Temple Scroll refer to Crucifixion?" *Journal of Biblical Literature,* XCI (1973), 472–81. See also Martin Hengel, *Crucifixion,* trans. J. Bowden (Philadelphia, 1977). A. N. Sherwin-White, in his *Roman Society and Roman Law in the New Testament* (Oxford, 1963), and in his essay, "The Trial of Christ," in D. E. Nineham, ed., *Historicity and Chronology in the New Testament* (London, 1965), argued that the trial before Pilate was technically correct in procedure; in the course of his argument he supported the Gospel truth, making numerous errors. For a discussion of only fifteen of those errors, see T. A. Burkill, "The Condemnation of Jesus: A Critique of Sherwin-White's Thesis," *Novum Testamentum,* XII (1970), 341–2. In Mark 15:15 and Matt. 24:26, Pilate satisfied the Jewish crowd by "delivering" Jesus to be crucified, without passing sentence of death on him, leaving the impression that the Jews did that. In Luke

23:15, Pilate delivered Jesus to the Jewish will. In John 19:16, Pilate "handed him over to them [the Jews] to be crucified." Each Gospel, in whitewashing Pilate, shifted not only the moral but, by implication, the legal responsibility for the crucifixion to the Jews. A. E. Harvey, *Jesus on Trial: A Study in the Fourth Gospel* (Atlanta, 1977), argues, incredibly, that the Gospel of John should be read as an extended trial of Jesus from the standpoint of Jewish law, not figuratively but technically.

34. On the date of A.D. 30 for Jesus' trial, see Blinzler, *Trial,* 72–80; Jack Finegan, *Handbook of Bible Chronology* (Princeton, 1964), 285–325, agreed with A.D. 30 but indicated that the year 33 is a possible alternative. See also George Ogg, *Historicity and Chronology in the New Testament* (London, 1940), 276–7. On the Talmudic tradition, see Cohn, *Trial and Death,* 346–50.

35. Sidney B. Hoenig, *The Great Sanhedrin* (Philadelphia, 1953), 111–13, 211–13, fixed the date at A.D. 66, accepted by Mantel, *History of the Sanhedrin,* 284–5. See also Cohn, *Trial and Death,* 346–9. On post-70 executions, see Winter, *On the Trial,* 102–8. On rabbinic tradition concerning Jesus, see Klausner, *Jesus of Nazareth,* 18–54.

36. That the Romans had exclusive capital jurisdiction is a theme in Schürer, *History,* div. II, vol. I, 187–8; Husband, *Prosecution,* 151–73; Danby, "Bearing of the Rabbinical Criminal Code," esp. pp. 66, 72; Maurice Goguel, *The Life of Jesus,* trans. O. Wyon (New York, 1933), 473–4; Sherwin-White, *Roman Society and Roman Law,* 24–47; F.F. Bruce, *New Testament History* (Garden City, N.Y., 1972), 200; Wilson, *Execution,* 7–14. Brandon, *Trial,* 90–2, wavered between the belief that the Sanhedrin could conduct a capital trial and inflict death and that it required the governor's approval. Blinzler, *Trial,* 157–63, believed that the Sanhedrin held capital powers subject to Roman confirmation of the sentence. Winter, *On the Trial,* 109–28; Cohn, *Trial and Death,* 31–4 and related notes; and T.A. Burkill, *Mysterious Revelation: An Examination of the Philosophy of St. Mark's Gospel* (Ithaca, N.Y., 1963), 280–318, supported the capital competence of the Sanhedrin. So too, Barrett, *St. John,* 445–6, and Robert H. Lightfoot, *St. John's Gospel* (Oxford, 1956), 310. On breach of the peace, see George Horowitz, *The Spirit of Jewish Law* (New York, 1963), 22, and *ibid.,* ch. 14, on capital crimes.

37. Cohn, *Trial and Death,* 105–12 and related notes. For the standard view, followed by most, see Husband, *Prosecution,* 102-36, 149; C.H. Dodd, *More New Testament Studies* (Manchester, 1968), 93; and Danby, "Bearing of the Rabbinical Criminal Code," esp. pp. 57–9, 75–6. Danby described the account by his fellow Englishman, the lawyer A.T. Innes, *The Trial of Jesus Christ, A Legal Monograph* (Edinburgh, 1905, 2nd ed.), as "the best and most restrained" of the many accounts. Innes described blasphemy as "Treason against the Deity" in Jewish law, equated blasphemy with the Roman political offense of constructive treason, and described a Jewish trial that was prearranged by religious zealots to secure the conviction of an innocent man in direct violation of Jewish law. The Jews then switched the charge to treason to procure a conviction by Pilate, whom Innes converted into an English common-law jurist who acted reasonably to safeguard the national interests in peace and security. Wilson, *Execution,* 113–28, followed the theory about a Jewish preliminary hearing, although conducted only by the chief priests, not the Sanhedrin.

38. There are no primary sources that tell us about the respective jurisdic-

tions of the Sanhedrin and the Roman governor. Historians do not agree in the surmises they must make from isolated data, e.g., the remarks of the Roman proconsul in Acts 18:14–15 and the fact that he paid no attention to some Jews beating another (Acts 18:17). The trials of Paul, as reported in Acts, provide the sort of evidence upon which surmises are built. Note how evasive and undocumented is the discussion in Theodor Mommsen, *The Provinces of the Roman Empire,* trans. W.P. Dickson (London, 1909, 2 vols.), II, 187–8.

39. On lynch law, see, *inter alia,* Danby, "Bearing of the Rabbinical Criminal Code," 57, and Wilson, *Execution,* 12. For an unusual account, see Douglas R.A. Hare, *The Theme of Jewish Persecution of Christians* (Cambridge, 1967), 20–30, holding that the Sanhedrin had capital powers, that Stephen was lynched, and that neither he nor Jesus was condemned for blasphemy. George Ogg, *The Chronology of the Life of Paul* (London, 1968), 11–12, uncertainly placed the time of the "lynching" at about the year 36.

40. No Jerusalem court would have considered verbal abuse of Moses as blasphemy. At the time of Jesus, only the Essenes, who eschewed the Temple cult, thought that Moses could be blasphemed. As Hare, *Theme of Jewish Persecution,* 24–5, pointed out, *Josephus,* II, 379, made that Essene belief a distinguishing characteristic of the sect. Blinzler, *Trial,* 162–3, followed by David R. Catchpole, *The Trial of Jesus* (Leiden, 1971), 248–50, interpreted Acts 7:57 as showing an aborted trial followed by lynch law enforcing the injunction against blasphemy. Cohn, *Trial and Death,* 362–3 n. 35, dissenting, observed that if a court assembled, as in Stephen's case, the rule authorizing an on-the-spot lynching of a culprit caught in the act did not apply. Stephen was stoned after a judicial proceeding. Hare's view that Stephen could not have been executed by formal judicial order because he received religious burial rites (p. 23) ignores the fact that the story of Stephen is patterned after that of Jesus. For further discussion, see ch. 3 below, note 15 and related text.

41. Schmithals, *Paul and James,* 13–37, has an insightful but puzzling account of Stephen's case. Schmithals saw Stephen as a Hellenist or gentile Christian who, unlike the Nazerenes or "Jewish Christians," completely rejected the Torah and therefore was executed as an antinomian who threatened the entire Jewish community, the Nazarenes included. They accepted Jesus as the risen Messiah who would return, yet were not molested for blasphemy, and indeed participated in the Temple cult, as Schmithals noted. If Stephen was not a Jew, his crime could not have been apostasy. To call it "false prophecy" is technically incorrect unless Stephen, like other Hellenists, accepted Jesus as divine; even so, false prophecy and its derivatives, such as beguiler, seducer, *mesith,* and deceiver, refer, at least in the Old Testament, to idolaters. To Christians, "false prophecy" was as loose a usage as "heresy" and "blasphemy." Because Stephen's case appears in Acts, the accusation of blasphemy cannot be taken seriously. Stephen's crime remains a puzzle. The Enslin quotation is from his essay "Luke, the Literary Physician," in Aune, ed., *Studies in New Testament,* 138. The Jackson quotation comes from his essay "The Internal Evidence of Acts," in Jackson and Kirsopp Lake, eds., *The Beginnings of Christianity* (London, 1920–33, 5 vols.), II, 149–50.

42. Elias J. Bickerman, "The Warning Inscriptions of Herod's Temple," *Jewish Quarterly Rev.,* XXXVII (1946–7), 387–405; Eisler, *Messiah Jesus,* 517–8, with a photo of the inscription; *Josephus,* III, 413, for Titus.

43. The Roman charge against Paul, which is conjectural, is from George

Edmundson, *The Church in Rome in the First Century* (London, 1913), 93–4; the best accounts are Henry J. Cadbury, "Roman Law and the Trial of Paul," in Jackson and Lake, eds., *Beginnings of Christianity*, V, 297–338, and Winter, *On the Trial*, 112–27. Paul's case also shows the Romans ever looking for Zealots. In Acts 21:38 the tribune mistook Paul as the Zealot leader who had "recently stirred up a revolt and led 4,000 men of the Assassins out into the wilderness."

44. Eusebius, *The Ecclesiastical History*, trans. Kirsopp Lake (Cambridge, Mass., 1953, 2 vols., Loeb Classics), I, 169–79; *Josephus*, IX, 495–6. For James's case, see Hare, *Theme of Jewish Persecution*, 32–4, who argued that Annas proceeded against James from personal hostility, not explained, but that it was not a case of religious persecution; and Brandon, *Jesus and Zealots*, 115–26, 168–9, who argued that James supported the lower priests and Zealots. Danby, "Bearing of the Rabbinical Criminal Code," 57, 66, held that Josephus showed only that the Sanhedrin could not be summoned except with the governor's consent, not that when summoned it could inflict the death penalty. If Danby was right, Annas would have been prosecuted for murder. Eisler, *Messiah Jesus*, 518–9, 540–6, depicted a murder arranged to look like an accident.

45. Montefiore, *Synoptic Gospels*, I, 351. Smith, *Jesus the Magician*, 41, 174, says that "evildoer" was common parlance for magician. In the King James and Revised Standard versions of the Bible, John 18:3 and 18:12 refer to a "band of men" or "band of soldiers." In the New English Bible the translation is "troops." The Greek version of John speaks of a *speira* or cohort and a *chiliarchos* or tribune, thus making the arresting party unmistakably Roman. Blinzler, *Trial*, 66–70, rejected even the possibility that the cohort could be Roman, leaving us to assume that the occupation power allowed the Temple police to organize in para-Roman military units. Dodd, *Historical Tradition*, 73–4, 81, accepted the Roman cohort but noted that the word in Greek could be translated as a "maniple, say 200 men," instead of 600. Dodd's account is amusing because he found no "theological or apologetic" motive for John's introduction of the Romans at the arrest scene; yet John 18:6 has Jesus step forward and identify himself to his captors, whereupon "they drew back and fell to the ground," showing in John's theology the supremacy of Jesus over everyone. John Marsh, *The Gospel of St. John* (Penguin Books, 1968), 585, thought that a Roman cohort of 600 "might not be thought an impossible number" because thousands of Passover pilgrims were available for incitement, and Jesus' triumphal entry suggested that he might "stir up trouble"; but Marsh was puzzled by the fact that the cohort took Jesus to the high priest rather than a Roman official, leaving the interpretation inconclusive. C. K. Barrett, *The Gospel According to St. John* (New York, 1955), 433, accepted the Roman cohort or maniple of 200, and noted that Pilate knew the charge before the Jews made it at the trial (p.443); similarly, Brown, *John* (Anchor Bible), 807–8, 815, 866. Bultmann, *Gospel of John*, 637, 639, questioned whether the Roman soldiers and Jewish police would have worked together; he also thought "unbelievable" that the Romans would have "led the prisoner to the Sanhedrin," but, of course, John does not say that they did. The Sanhedrin does not appear anywhere in John, although Bultmann, *Gospel of John*, 637, 641, 646, amazingly asserted that "it may be allowed as self-evident" that a trial before the Sanhedrin took place; "it has to be imagined that the Sanhedrin is assembled." Bultmann's Ger-

man commentary on John was published in 1957, when his skepticism was spent. Instead of reading legends out of the Gospel, he was reading them into it. In his *History of the Synoptic Tradition,* first published in 1921, he stressed the legendary features in the arrest scene and of the Sanhedrin trial. The question is not whether the Romans arrested Jesus but why they brought him to Annas or Caiaphas, or whether they did. Diverse authorities accept the Roman arrest, including Goguel, *Life of Jesus,* 481, 512; Winter, *On the Trial,* 60–9; Cullman, *The State,* 45; Hengel, *Was Jesus a Revolutionist?* 8; Küng, *On Being a Christian,* 300; Edwin C. Hoskins, *The Fourth Gospel,* ed. F. N. Davey (London, 1947), 509; J. N. Sanders, *A Commentary on the Gospel According to John,* ed. B. A. Mastin (New York, 1947), 382–3. Wilson, *Execution,* 107–9, whose work must be respected, reasonably saw the Romans in John only as reflections of John's theology. One may accept that and yet allow the fact of a Roman arrest. Goguel, *Life of Jesus,* 481, for example, believed that the Romans arrested Jesus for political reasons, at Jewish instigation, but that Pilate, fearing a double-cross by the Jews, required them to condemn Jesus first so that he would be immune to an accusation that he killed an innocent man; yet Goguel believed that "Jesus was not tried by the Sanhedrin" (pp. 511–2).

46. That Bultmann never claimed the Lucan charge to be legendary, inauthentic, or a late accretion suggests that the charge goes back to a primitive church tradition, perhaps the original text of Luke. Luke 23:2 corresponds with Luke 22:6. See Brandon, *Trial,* 119, 146–50.

47. As to the tribute money, the eschatological Jesus whose viewpoint was apocalyptic believed that all things in this life, including the colossal Temple, would soon pass away. Not caring about temporal issues, he therefore could have meant, give Caesar his due in a matter of trifling importance. The Davidic messiah, however, would have thought that because God's earthly kingdom was Israel, paying taxes to Caesar would have violated basic religious and political precepts (Cullmann, *Jesus and the Revolutionaries,* 4). No one can know what Jesus meant. The Gospels allow the impression that he advised payment. But how would a Jewish audience in A.D. 30 have construed Jesus' ambiguous advice? They would have understood him to mean that Caesar had no place in Israel. The Sadducees and the Herodians, who favored restoration of their puppet kingdom under the Romans, would have been alarmed, but probably not the Pharisees and certainly not the Jewish crowd that felt oppressed by Roman taxes. Oscar Cullmann, who thought that Jesus advised payment (money belonged to Caesar and did not matter in the coming kingdom), declared that Jesus regarded the occupation of "Palestine" by the Romans "as a usurpation by violent men, for their totalitarian claim, according to which Caesar demanded what belongs to God" (Cullman, *Jesus and the Revolutionaries,* 43–4).

48. Cohn, *Trial and Death,* 98, assumed that at the time of Jesus the Talmudic rule against self-incrimination was in force; in *Origins of the Fifth Amendment* (New York, 1968), 433–9, I argued that the Talmudic rule against receiving confessions of guilt did not necessarily derive from the requirement of two witnesses and had other rationalizations. Taylor, *Gospel According to St. Mark,* 567; Husband, *Prosecution,* 120–1; Cohn, *Trial and Death,* 114, 126, 134; similarly, Mantel, *History of the Sanhedrin,* 286. "Cunning inquisitor" is the phrase of Blinzler, *Trial,* 129.

49. Finkelstein, *The Pharisees.* One who reads this book, first published in 1938, would not think that the Pharisees had legal or moral responsibility for

Jesus' death. Most Christian scholars who make adverse judgments against the Pharisees know them only from the grossly distorted view of them in the Gospels and show slight familiarity with Jewish scholarship. Among the exceptions is Wilson, who says that the Gospels' picture of the Pharisees "is a distorted and prejudicial caricature" (Wilson, *Execution*, 196).

50. *Josephus*, VII, 375. For "all" condemned, see Nineham, *Gospel of St. Mark*, 408, on Mark 15:43. Bultmann, *Form Criticism*, 72.

51. Danby, "Bearing of the Rabbinical Criminal Code," 54. Cohn, *Trial and Death*, 340; on p.360 Cohn contradictorily declared that "the dictum of a third-century [Talmudic] scholar cannot be relied upon as accurately describing a rule of law which in actual practice must have been obsolete already for more than two hundred years. . . ." The rule requiring witnesses to agree is in Sanhedrin 40a, 41a. Mantel, *History of the Sanhedrin*, 255, claimed on the authority of Josephus that the Talmudic rule was in force requiring a judicial verdict to be given on the same day as the trial, but his citation to *Josephus* is wrong and I cannot find the proof in *Josephus*.

52. Schürer, *History*, div. II, vol. I, 187–8, observed that the Temple gates were locked at night and that the locale for the trial of Jesus was unique in the history of the Sanhedrin; Blinzler, *Trial*, 112–14, accepted the Gospel version of the locale on faith, admitting that he could not explain the uniqueness.

53. Wilson, *Execution*, 121–2.

54. Nineham, *Gospel of St. Mark*, 402. Hahn, *The Titles*, 147.

55. Pal. Talmud, Taanith 65b, quoted in R. Travers Herford, *Christianity in Talmud and Midrash* (London, 1903), 62. On the dating of the Gospels, see John A. T. Robinson, *Redating the New Testament* (Philadelphia, 1976), for the thesis that *all* the Gospels were written *before* A.D. 70 because none mentions the destruction of the Temple in that year. But dozens of details become unintelligible if the composition of the Gospels occurred between A.D. 40 and 65. Robinson did not discuss, let alone solve, any of the problems created by his reading. One may as well argue that the Synoptic Gospels were written after A.D. 70, when the Sadducees had disappeared, because Mark, Matthew, and Luke did not mention them and did not know them. The word "rabbi" used in Matt. 23:7 and several times in John did not come into use until after 70. John 9:22 refers to the Jews having expelled from their synagogues anyone who confessed Jesus to be Christ, but the date of that event, although uncertain, is not earlier than 80 or 85 and perhaps as late as 125. See Hare, *Theme of Jewish Persecution*, 38–9, 48–55; J. Louis Martyn, *History and Theology in the Fourth Gospel* (Abingdon, 1968), 17–41, esp. 40. See Robinson, *Redating*, 7, for the generally accepted dating: Mark was composed between 65 and 75, Luke and Matthew between 80 and 90, and John between 90 and 100. I discuss the Nicene Creed and the dispute about the nature of Christ in the next chapter.

56. Sloyan, *Jesus on Trial*, 48, explained 49–59. Donahue, *Are You the Christ?* 223.

57. Blinzler, *Trial*, 117–21, on the historicity of the trial before the Sanhedrin; "absolute authority," 85; last quotation, 127. Blinzler also insisted that Jesus was convicted "on the basis of his own admission of a capital crime," 105.

58. *Ibid.*, 105–8; Juel, *Messiah and Temple*, 95–106, echoes Blinzler. Klausner, *Jesus of Nazareth*, 343, had previously observed that for a Galilean carpenter to call himself Son of Man in the Danielic sense and say that he would

sit at the right hand of God would have been taken by the Sadducean high priest as blasphemy, but by the Pharisees as nothing but "rash fantasy." But the Sadducees stood for strict enforcement of Old Testament letter whenever possible; Lev. 24:15–16 does not remotely allow for a Sadducean interpretation of blasphemy in anything Jesus said. Catholic priests have recently rejected Blinzler. See Dominic M. Crossan, "Anti-Semitism and the Gospel," *Theological Studies,* XXVI (1965), 189–214; Tibor Horvath, "Why Was Jesus Brought to Pilate?" *Novum Testamentum,* XI (1969), 174–84; Bruce Vawter, "Are the Gospels Anti-Semitic?" *Journal of Ecumenical Studies,* V (1968), 473–87; Jeffrey G. Sobosan, "The Trial of Jesus," *Journal of Ecumenical Studies,* X (1973), 70–90. For books by priests rejecting Blinzler, see Raymond E. Brown *et al., The Jerome Biblical Commentary* (Englewood Cliffs, N.J., 1968); Brown, *John* (Anchor Bible); Sloyan, *Jesus on Trial;* Donahue, *Are You the Christ?*

59. David R. Catchpole, *The Trial of Jesus: A Study in the Gospels and Jewish Historiography from 1770 to the Present Day* (1971), 131–2. In addition to Blinzler, Catchpole relied on G. D. Kilpatrick, *The Trial of Jesus* (London, 1953), a "book" whose text and notes comprise eighteen pages. Kilpatrick's evidence on the point about the Temple consisted of a quotation from a German scholar, Julius Wellhausen, who said, "For proper Jews such a prophecy still counted as blasphemy as in the time of Micah and Jeremiah" *(ibid.,* 11). Presumably the "proper" ones were the accusers, but both prophets were acquitted. Montefiore, *Synoptic Gospels,* I, 355–9, gently destroyed Wellhausen.

60. Listing the important works that repudiated the blasphemy charge as unsupportable is far easier than citing those that support it. Goguel, *Life of Jesus,* is not easy to classify; p. 481 says the appearance of Jesus "before the Sanhedrin cannot be regarded as fictitious. Jesus did actually appear before the Jewish authorities and was judged by the Sanhedrin to be guilty of blasphemy and worthy of death," but pp. 511–12 say, "In reality, Jesus was not tried by the Sanhedrin. . . . There was no trial by the Sanhedrin." Brown, *John* (Anchor Bible), is also difficult to classify. In his translation of John 8:57, he printed Jesus' words, "I am," in full capitals to show the use of the divine name (pp. 354, 367, 818). But Brown insisted that in a "scientific" or "technical" sense, the Sanhedrin could not have found blasphemy, and in his discussion of the question of whether Jesus might have been condemned for usurping divine prerogatives, Brown stressed "the Christian post-resurrectional insight" and refused to find blasphemy as of A.D. 30. Nevertheless, Brown concluded that Jesus' religious views must have been offensive to "Pharisee and Sadducee alike," thus leading to his conjecture that the blasphemy was constructive or "implicitly intruding on God's special privileges." Brown did not reject the historicity of the Sanhedrin trial (pp. 368, 408–13, 801–2). The leading non-Jewish authors, arranged chronologically, who clearly reject the Markan blasphemy account are Loisy, *Birth of the Christian Religion,* 79–87; Robert Henry Lightfoot, *History and Interpretation in the Gospels* (New York, 1934), 146–51; Guignebert, *Jesus,* 461–4, 471; Bundy, *Jesus and the First Three Gospels,* 517–19; Cullmann, *The State,* 44; Burkill, *Mysterious Revelation,* ch. 12; Brandon, *Trial,* 87–92; Wilson, *Execution,* ch. 10, esp. 123–8; Sloyan, *Jesus on Trial,* 61; Donahue, *Are You the Christ?* 96–101. Sanders, *St. John,* found blasphemy only in the Jews, each time they rejected Jesus (pp. 349, 371, 380, 517, 524).

This is the view that Mark intends. Like Brown, Sanders also perpetuated the theory that "I am" is God's name (pp. 148–9, 188–9, 224, 236, 385). See also Severino Pancaro, *The Law in the Fourth Gospel* (Leiden, 1975), 59–64.

61. Catchpole, *Trial of Jesus,* 141, 200, 271.

62. J. Duncan M. Derrett, *Law in the New Testament* (London, 1970), 407, 424, 425, 448, 453–4.

63. Cohn, *Trial and Death,* 98, 359 n. 15, 362 n. 33. Husband, *Prosecution,* 213–14, and Rawlinson, *St. Mark,* 222, spoke of "constructive blasphemy," setting a style still followed, as in Bruce, *New Testament History,* 197. Numbers 15:27–31 mysteriously refers to conscious sinning as being "presumptuously" against the Lord and "reproaching" Him. Whatever that meant, it did not refer to a capital crime, for the penalty was either divine or excommunication: "that soul shall be cut off from his people." "Cut off" cannot be read as if the Inquisition were in progress when the book of Numbers was composed. The next verse shows the contrast. A sabbath-breaker was stoned to death. That his crime was not blasphemy is clear from the fact that Moses treated it as unprecedented, although the case of the blasphemer had occurred earlier. Jesus broke the sabbath on divine authority; the Gospels do not show that the Sanhedrin charged him with blasphemy for that.

64. Husband, *Prosecution,* 225–30, having been unable to find blasphemy in a real or legal sense, held that the Jews convicted Jesus for heresy. Albright and Mann, *Matthew,* 332–3, having rejected the blasphemous nature of a messianic claim and finding no evidence for a decision on a claim to be Son of God, found the blasphemy in the Son of Man saying (without indicating the evidence), and then compounded the crime in Sadducean thought by adding that the implication of resurrection was "certainly heretical," thus convicting all the Pharisaic members of the Sanhedrin. Küng, *On Being a Christian,* 320–1, 328–30, 337–9.

65. Hare, *Theme of Jewish Persecution,* 24, 26.

66. J. C. O'Neill, "The Charge of Blasphemy at Jesus' Trial before the Sanhedrin," in Bammel, ed., *Trial of Jesus,* 72–4.

67. *Ibid.,* 75, 77. For a similar view, see Harvey, *Jesus on Trial,* 51–2, 77–81, and Pancaro, *The Law in the Fourth Gospel,* 53–76.

68. Dodd, *More New Testament Studies,* 98, 99.

69. Conzelmann, *Jesus,* 86; see also Cullmann, *The State,* 42.

70. Cullmann, *The State,* 42–4. Robinson, *Problem of History,* 12.

71. For the spurious custom, see Winter, *On the Trial,* 131–4. As to the name "Jesus," we must keep remembering that the New Testament has familiarized us with Greek versions of Hebrew names. "Jesus" is the Greek for one of the most common Hebrew names, Joshua or the diminutive of it, Jeshu. Origen, a theologian of the third century, considered the name "Jesus Barabbas" offensive or heretical, a reflection of the reason that the name "Jesus" died out. See Adolph Deissmann, "The Name 'Jesus'," in G. K. A. Bell and Deissmann, eds., *Mysterium Christi* (London, 1930), 3–27, esp. 20–2 on Barabbas. See also the following two articles that identify as one man the "Jesus who is called Barabbas" and the "Jesus who is called Christ," as the passage in Matt: 27:17 most likely read originally: Horace A. Rigg, "Barabbas," *Journal of Biblical Literature,* LXIV (1945), 417–56, the fullest study, and H. Z. Maccoby, "Jesus and Barabbas," *New Testament Studies,* XVI (1969), 55–60. Gerald Friedlander, *Jewish Sources on the Sermon on the Mount* (London, 1911), x1,

and George Brandes, *Jesus* (New York, 1926), 108, also identify Barabbas as Jesus of Nazareth. Both Rigg and Maccoby explain that "Barabbas" can mean either "Son of the Father" or "Son of the Teacher" (or "Rabbi"), depending on whether the name is transliterated as Bar Abba or Bar Rabba. See also Brown *et al.*, eds., *Jerome Biblical Commentary*, II, 57, 111, and 161. On the first name of Barabbas, see also Alan Hugh M'Neile, *The Gospel According to St. Matthew* (London, 1961), 411; Streeter, *The Four Gospels*, 87, 95, 101; Rawlinson, *St. Mark*, 227–8; Cranfield, *St. Mark*, 450; Taylor, *St. Mark*, 581; Goguel, *Life of Jesus*, 516; Winter, *On the Trial*, 136–8; Brandon, *Trial*, 113, 190 n. 113, 193 n. 42; Albright and Mann, *Matthew*, 343; Brown, *John* (Anchor Bible), 856, 871. For a different interpretation based on a case of mistaken identity between two men, both named Jesus, see Eisler, *Messiah Jesus*, 472–6.

72. Küng, *On Being a Christian*, 339, said that Pilate was "a tool of the Jewish hierarchy." Charles H. Dodd, *Historical Tradition in the Fourth Gospel*, 96, thought that John's depiction of Pilate was "convincing," and he praised the "psychological subtlety" of the whole Roman trial in John. Such views are common in commentaries on the Gospels. On Pilate as governor, *Josephus*, IX, 43–7; the best secondary account is Brandon, *Jesus and Zealots*, 66–80. See also Cohn, *Trial and Death*, 70–89.

73. Werner Kelber, Anitra Kolenkow, and Robin Scroggs, *Reflections on the Question: Was There a Pre-Markan Passion Narrative?* A Report Prepared for the Markan Task Force of the Society of Biblical Literature, October 1971, 107th Annual Meeting. Seminar Papers (3 vols.), II, 505–85, esp. p. 565.

74. Rawlinson, *St. Mark*, 220. In addition to Brandon's books, cited above, see Wilson, *Execution*, 75–84, and Hans Conzelmann, *The Theology of St. Luke* (New York, 1961), 83–93, and 138–49. See also Robert J. Getty, "Nero's Indictment of the Christians in A.D. 64," in Luitpold Wallach, ed., *The Classical Tradition* (Ithaca, N.Y., 1966), 285–92; P. Winter, "Tacitus and Pliny: The Early Christians," *Journal of Historical Studies*, 1 (1967), 31–40. Samuel Sandmel, *Anti-Semitism in the New Testament?* (Philadelphia, 1978), is restrained and reliable.

75. Vermes-Millar, Schürer's *History*, 484–557. The remark by Winter is from the Epilogue of his *On the Trial of Jesus*.

3. The Age of Christian Heterodoxy

1. For blasphemy as treason, *Shepherd of Hermas*, in Kirsopp Lake, trans., *The Apostolic Fathers* (London, 1932–3, 2 vols., Loeb Classics), II, 271.

2. On the history of the New Testament canon, see Edgar Hennecke, *New Testament Apocrypha*, ed. W. Schneemelcher, trans. R. Wilson (Philadelphia, 1963, 2 vols.), I, 19–42, and F. W. Beare, "Canon of the New Testament," in George A. Buttrick, *The Interpreter's Dictionary of the Bible* (Nashville, 1962, 4 vols.), I, 520–32.

3. On early Christianity, see Philip Schaff, *History of the Christian Church* (New York, 1910, 5th ed., 8 vols.), vols. 1–3; J. F. Bethune-Baker, *An Introduction to the Early History of Christian Doctrine* [to 451] (London, 1942, 7th ed.); Hans Lietzmann, *A History of the Early Church*, trans. B. L. Woolf (London, 1950–1, 4 vols.); Maurice Goguel, *The Birth of Christianity*, trans. H. C. Snape (New York, 1954); Hans Conzelmann, *History of Primitive Chris-*

tianity, trans. J. E. Steely (Nashville, 1973); F. J. Foakes-Jackson, *The History of the Christian Church* [to 451] (New York, 1933). The best and most recent work is Jaroslav Pelikan, *The Emergence of the Catholic Tradition* (100–600), the first of a projected five-volume set on *The Christian Tradition* (Chicago, 1971). I relied on these books for information, not interpretation. The works that I found most suggestive, although not necessarily supportive of my interpretation, included Samuel Sandmel, *The First Christian Century in Judaism and Christianity* (New York, 1969); S. G. F. Brandon, *The Fall of Jerusalem and the Christian Church* (London, 1957, 2nd ed.); Walter Bauer, *Orthodoxy and Heresy in Earliest Christianity,* ed. R. A. Kraft and G. Krodel (Philadelphia, 1971); James A. Robinson and Helmut Koester, *Trajectories Through Early Christianity* (Philadelphia, 1971); and Hans Dieter Betz, "Orthodoxy and Heresy in Primitive Christianity," *Interpretation,* XIX (1965), 299–311.

4. The fullest work is Karl Joseph Hefele, *A History of the Councils of the Church,* trans. H. N. Oxenham (Edinburgh, 1871–95, 5 vols.), considerably expanded and revised in a French translation by Henri Leclercq; I have relied on the English edition, because the French revision did not alter the information I needed. Henry M. Gwatkin, *Studies of Arianism* (London, 1882), does not include the Council of Chalcedon. J. N. D. Kelly, *Early Christian Creeds* (New York, 1972, 3rd ed.), and Kelly, *Early Christian Doctrines* (New York, 1960, 2nd ed.), are also valuable. For brief accounts of the councils, see Foakes-Jackson, *History of the Christian Church* and Bethune-Baker, *Introduction to Early History.*

5. On the councils of 359, Hefele, *History of Councils,* II, 246–70.

6. On diversity in the New Testament, see Günther Bornkamm, *The New Testament: A Guide to Its Writings,* trans. R. H. Fuller (Philadelphia, 1973); Willie Marxsen, *Introduction to the New Testament,* trans. G. Buswell (Philadelphia, 1968). For conflicting views on early Jewish Christianity, see Brandon, *The Fall of Jerusalem and the Christian Church;* George Strecker, "On the Problem of Jewish Christianity," in Bauer, *Orthodoxy and Heresy in Earliest Christianity,* 241–85; Hans-Joachim Schoeps, *Jewish Christianity,* trans. D. R. A. Hare (Philadelphia, 1969); Jean Daniélou, *The Theology of Jewish Christianity,* trans. J. A. Baker (London, 1964). See also note 25 below.

7. Wilfred L. Knox, *St. Paul and the Church of Jerusalem* (Cambridge, 1925), his *St. Paul and the Church of the Gentiles* (Cambridge, 1939), and Günther Bornkamm, *Paul,* trans. D. M. G. Stalker (New York, 1971), are good conventional works. Martin Dibelius and Werner G. Kümmel, *Paul,* trans. F. Clarke (Philadelphia, 1953), is a short introduction. Interesting, unconventional works by Jews are H. J. Schoeps, *Paul,* trans. H. Knight (London, 1961), and Samuel Sandmel, *The Genius of Paul* (New York, 1970). The best Catholic scholarship in English is in Raymond E. Brown *et al., The Jerome Biblical Commentary* (Englewood Cliffs, N.J., 1968, 2 vols.), II, 215–361, on Paul, and Joseph Fitzmyer's "Pauline Theology," in *ibid.,* 800–27.

8. Paul, by contrast, believed in justification "by faith in Christ, and not by the law. . . . If justification were by the law, then Christ died to no purpose" (Gal. 2:16, 21, 3:11). On James, see Marxsen, *Introduction,* 226–32; Bornkamm, *New Testament,* 120–1; Thomas W. Leahy, "The Epistle of James," in Brown, ed., *Jerome Biblical Commentary,* II, 369–77. There is an inexplicable line in James; speaking of the rich, he said "they blaspheme the honorable name

by which you are called" (James 2:7). What was the honorable name? Interpretations vary. Even if we knew whether it was Ebionite, Hebrew, Nazarene, Christian, or something else, we would still not understand what *he* meant by that name.

9. For a variety of interpretations of Mark, see William Wrede, *The Messianic Secret,* trans. J. C. Greig (Cambridge, 1971, first pub. 1901); Willi Marxsen, *Mark the Evangelist,* trans. J. Boyce *et al.* (Nashville, 1969); Werner K. Kelber, ed., *The Passion in Mark* (Philadelphia, 1976); Howard Clark Kee, *Community of the New Age* (Philadelphia, 1977); and Brown, ed., *Jerome Biblical Commentary,* II, 21–61.

10. On Matthew, see Brown, ed., *Jerome Biblical Commentary,* II, 62–114; W. D. Davies, *The Setting of the Sermon on the Mount* (Cambridge, 1966); Werner G. Kümmel, *Introduction to the New Testament,* trans. H. C. Kee (Nashville, 1973, 17th ed.), 101–21; Marxsen, *Introduction,* 146–54.

11. Hans Conzelmann, *The Theology of Saint Luke,* trans. G. Buswell (New York, 1960), is excellent. See also Leander E. Keck and J. Louis Martyn, eds., *Studies in Luke–Acts* (London, 1966).

12. In addition to commentaries on the Gospel of John cited in the notes of the preceding chapter, by R. Bultmann, C. H. Dodd, J. L. Martyn, and R. E. Brown, all of which contain material on John's theology, see R. M. Grant, *Gnosticism and Early Christianity* (New York, 1966, 2nd ed.), 163–74, for Gnosticism in John, and Bruce Vawter, "Johannine Theology," in Brown, ed., *Jerome Biblical Commentary,* II, 828–39.

13. Bornkamm, *New Testament,* 146. See *ibid.,* 73–116; Marxsen, *Introduction,* 17–109; and *Jerome Biblical Commentary,* II, 223–368, for commentaries on each of the Pauline letters. Knox, *St. Paul and the Church,* 146–78, covers Paul's troubles with Gnosticism. On Paul's opponents, especially the Judaizers, see also Helmut Koester, "The Origin and Nature of Diversification in the History of Early Christianity," in Robinson and Koester, *Trajectories,* 143–55. The identity of the author or authors of the Pastoral Epistles and the Epistle to the Hebrews, formerly attributed to Paul, is unknown; Paul probably did not write Ephesians and Colossians either.

14. On the Johannine epistles, see *Jerome Biblical Commentary,* II, 404–13, and Marxsen, *Introduction,* 261–9.

15. Walter Schmithals, *Paul and James* (Naperville, Ill., 1965), 16–37, is most interesting on Stephen's case. Marcel Simon, *St. Stephen and the Hellenists in the Primitive Church* (London, 1958), saw Stephen as a Hellenist Jew of the Diaspora. I think he was a Greek gentile convert to the Nazarenes. Schoeps, *Jewish Christianity,* 43, regarded Stephen's case, even Stephen himself, as fictitious, but construed the text of Acts to depict a person whose antinomianism was anti-cultic enough to warrant the statement by Schmithals, approvingly quoted, that Stephen's execution was "an absolutely necessary act of national and religious self-defense" (p. 26). In my view, the Nazarenes, as a Jewish sect, must have been as opposed to Stephen as were other Jewish sects of the Temple cult. If Stephen was executed for blasphemy, as Simon insists, the reason may stem from the nature of his antinomianism. Simon said that Stephen assaulted the Torah as not being divine Law and as an idolatrous distortion of it (p. 46). That would be equivalent to the unforgivable blasphemy of Matt. 12:31, Mark 3:29, Luke 12:10, rejecting a divine work as demonic.

16. On the date of Paul's conversion, see George Ogg, *The Chronology of*

the Life of Paul (London, 1968), 7, and Jack Finegan, *Handbook of Bible Chronology* (Princeton, 1964), 515. Paul said: "To the Jews I became as a Jew, in order to win Jews; to those under the law I became as one under the law—though not being myself under the law—that I might win those under the law. To those outside the law I became as one outside the law. . ." (1 Cor. 9:20).

17. On *minim,* see R. Travers Herford, *Christianity in Talmud and Midrash* (Clifton, N.J., 1966 reprint), 125–37, 360–90.

18. On the Hymenaeus incident, see Tertullian, *Treatise on Penance,* trans. W.P. LeSaint (Westminster, Md., 1959) 88–9, 247 n. 353.

19. *First Epistle of Clement,* in Lake, ed., *Apostolic Fathers,* I, 89, 91; and *Second Epistle of Clement,* in *ibid.,* 149. Robert M. Grant, *The Apostolic Fathers: An Introduction* (New York, 1964), guesses that Hyginus, a bishop of Rome about 138–42, wrote Clement II.

20. Lake, ed., *Apostolic Fathers,* II, 19, 203, 269, 271.

21. "Mathetes" (Disciple) is a pseudonym; see *Epistle of Mathetes to Diognetus* (ca. 130), in Alexander Roberts and James Donaldson, eds., *The Ante-Nicene Fathers* (New York, 1911–9, 10 vols.), I, 26. "Half a million" is doubtless an exaggeration; see H. H. Ben-Sasson, *A History of the Jewish People* (Cambridge, Mass., 1976), 330–4, 370–2. The best book on Roman persecution of Christians is W. H. C. Frend, *Martyrdom and Persecution in the Early Church* (Oxford, 1965); pp. 104–241 cover the period from the Neronian persecutions to those under Hadrian.

22. *Epistle of Polycarp to the Philippians* (ca. 150), in *Ante-Nicene Fathers,* I, 34, 41.

23. *The First Apology of Justin,* in *ibid.,* I, 160, 164, 173; *Dialogue with Trypho,* in *ibid.,* 212, 239, 264; Athenogoras, *A Plea for Christians* (ca. 177), in *ibid.,* II, 129–48, 173; Tertullian, *Apology* (ca. 204), in *ibid.,* III, 21, 26. See also the letter of Eleutheras to Gaul (ca. 177), in Eusebius, *The Ecclesiastical History,* trans. K. Lake and J. E. Oulton (Cambridge, Mass., 1963, 2 vols., Loeb Classics), I, 413, on "Thysestean feasts and Oedipodean intercourse" (*ibid,* I, 419, 431), for Christian condemnation of the charges as "blasphemy."

24. For a collection of authentic letters by Ignatius, see James A. Kleist, ed., *The Epistles of St. Clement of Rome and St. Ignatius of Antioch* (Westminster, Md., 1961); the quotation on the Docetic blasphemy is in *ibid.,* 92. For the deutero-Ignatius, see *Epistles of Ignatius* in *Ante-Nicene Fathers,* I, 51, 62–4, 68, 88, 89, 113. Hippolytus is in *ibid.,* V, 3–162. See also Einar Molland, "The Heretics Combatted by Ignatius of Antioch," *Journal of Ecclesiastical History,* V (1954), 1–6; Virginia Corwin, *St. Ignatius and Christianity in Antioch* (New Haven, 1960), 52–87; and Cyril Charles Ritchardson, *The Christianity of Ignatius of Antioch* (New York, 1935), 50–4. Ebionism is the subject of Schoeps, *Jewish Christianity.*

25. For "radically anti-Semitic," Grant, *Gnosticism,* 118; *ibid.,* ch. 3 on Jewish Gnostic Christianity. Daniélou, *Theology of Jewish Christianity,* 7–8. Daniélou distinguished three types of Jewish Christians. The first or Ebionites were originally Jews who acknowledged Jesus as a great prophet or Messiah but not as Son of God in the Christian sense. Daniélou did not believe that the members of the Church of Jerusalem, whom he called the Nazarenes, fit the same description. To him, the Nazarenes formed the second type: "This com-

munity was perfectly orthodox in its Christianity but remained attached to Jewish ways of life, without however imposing them on proselytes from paganism." Their "implied divinity of Christ," which Daniélou inferred, enabled him to call them "perfectly orthodox." But if they were orthodox in *that* sense, they could hardly have been accepted as fellow Jews by other Temple sects. The Nazarenes and the Ebionites, who came later, were christianized Jews, although not by Daniélou's classification. His book is about a third type, non-Jewish Jewish Christianity, "Christian thought expressing itself in forms borrowed from Judaism," but "not necessarily connected with it." Thus, Daniélou allowed for Pauline Christianity as a form of Jewish Christianity. But most "Jewish Christians" were not connected at all with Judaism, which they reviled. On Jewish Christianity, see also Adolf Harnack, *History of Dogma,* trans. N. Buchanan (London, 1905, 3rd ed., 7 vols.) I, 286–317; Hans Lietzmann, *Beginnings of the Christian Church* (vol. 1 of his *History of the Early Church*), 177–90. Schoeps, *Jewish Christianity,* is provocative; the best conventional treatment is Goguel, *Birth of Christianity,* which makes the interplay of Judaism, Jewish Christianity, and Christianity one of its major themes. Goguel does not go beyond the first century. Schoeps traces the Ebionites into the second and third centuries and notes their disappearance in eastern Syria in the fifth. Brandon, *Fall of Jerusalem,* traces the Nazarenes to A.D. 70. Sandmel, *First Christian Century,* is excellent.

26. Daniélou, *Jewish Christianity,* 9–10. Justin, *Dialogue with Trypho, a Jew,* in *Ante-Nicene Fathers,* I, 268, 270. The dialogue is unique in the literature of the early church fathers. Trypho listens patiently, even good-naturedly, to torrents of abuse against the Jews, yet at the conclusion wishes Justin a safe voyage and urges him to remember the Jews as friends.

27. On Gnosticism, see Grant, *Gnosticism and Early Christianity;* Hans Jonas, *The Gnostic Religion* (Boston, 1958); and John Dart, *The Laughing Savior* (New York, 1978). Jonas' book is the best. Grant makes a connection between Judaism and Gnosticism. Even a major Jewish scholar makes that connection; see Gershom G. Scholem, *Jewish Gnosticism, Merkabah Mysticism, and Talmudic Tradition* (New York, 1960). In my opinion the use of Old Testament materials by Gnostic writers does not prove that Gnosticism originated in any form of Judaism, and no one has proved that "Jewish Gnosticism" ever existed. Dart's book is a popular account by a responsible journalist, based on *The Nag Hammadi Gnostic Library,* ed. James M. Robinson (New York, 1978). See also Robinson's booklet, *The Nag Hammadi Codices* (Claremont, Calif., 1974), 7–8. Dart (pp. 58–60), following Robinson (and Grant and Scholem), prudently speculated that Christian Gnosticism may have originated in a Jewish Gnostic movement, although Gnosticism was profoundly un-Jewish. As Robinson said in his booklet, Jewish Gnosticism "is a contradiction in terms," because Yahweh became a false and wicked god ignorant of the true God. Yet Robinson thought that a Christian Gnostic movement might have been "the outgrowth of a Jewish Gnostic group." Birger A. Pearson, "Jewish Haggadic Traditions in the Testimony of Truth from Nag Hammadi," in Pearson, ed., *Religious Syncretism in Antiquity* (Santa Barbara, Calif., 1975), 221, imagined that Gnosticism arose from a revolt within Judaism, but he was accurate when he added, "though it is axiomatic that once Gnosticism is present, 'Judaism' has been abandoned." Being religiously Jewish and Gnostic simultaneously was impossible. The contradiction between Chris-

tianity and Gnosticism was similar, but not the same. Christians, whose concept of monotheism and whose interpretation of the Old Testament was not the same as that of Jews, managed to accommodate Gnosticism and Christianity. As I have indicated in the text associated with this note 27, Adolf Harnack sympathetically depicted Christian Gnosticism in his classic *History of Dogma,* I, 227–66, especially because it was a de-Judaized, anti-Semitic, Hellenistic form of Christianity. See also G. Quispel, "Gnosticism and the New Testament," and the "Response" to that essay by Hans Jonas in J. Philip Hyatt, ed., *The Bible in Modern Scholarship* (Nashville, 1965), 252–71 and 279–93.

28. On classifying Gnostics, see Justin, *Dialogue with Trypho,* in *Ante-Nicene Fathers,* I, 212; Harnack, *Dogma,* I, 267–8.

29. *Against Heresies,* in *Ante-Nicene Fathers,* I, 314, 317.

30. On Valentinian, see Grant, *Gnosticism,* 128–47; Jonas, *Gnostic Religion,* 174–205; Schaff, *History,* II, 472–82. For Irenaeus, *Against Heresies,* see *Ante-Nicene Fathers,* I, 415, 429, 462–3.

31. On Marcion, see Jonas, *Gnostic Religion,* 137–46; Grant, *Gnosticism,* 121–8; Schaff, *History,* II, 482–91; Harnack, *Dogma,* I, 267–86; Pelikan, *Emergence,* 71–87.

32. *Against Heresies,* in *Ante-Nicene Fathers,* I, 352, 409, 428, 435; for Irenaeus on specific doctrines, *ibid.,* 408, 419, 458, 462. See also Heggesippus on Marcion, in Eusebius, *Ecclesiastical History,* I, 331.

33. *Ante-Nicene Fathers,* III, 245–6, for Tertullian's *Prescription.*

34. *Ibid.,* 263, 265; see also Tertullian, *Against Marcion,* in *ibid.,* 272, 299, 341, 345. For Tertullian on Judaism and Jewish Christianity, see Jean Daniélou, *The Origins of Latin Christianity,* trans. D. Smith and J. Baker (London, 1977), 139–75, 263–73.

35. S. L. Greenslade, *Schism in the Early Church* (New York, 1952), an excellent book, covers the various schisms and attempts to make distinctions between schism and heresy.

36. On the persecution under Decius and the rise of Novatianism, see Frend, *Martyrdom and Persecution,* ch. 13. Dionysius of Alexandria is in *Ante-Nicene Fathers,* VI, 103.

37. Dionysius of Rome, *Against Sabellians,* in *Ante-Nicene Fathers,* VI, 365, also in a variant translation in Philip Schaff and Henry Wace, eds., *A Select Library of Nicene and Post-Nicene Fathers,* 2nd ser. (New York, 1890–1900), IV, 167–8. Archelaus, *Acts of the Disputation with Manes,* in *Ante-Nicene Fathers,* VI, 188, 189. Stephen Runciman, *The Medieval Manichee* (Cambridge, 1955), and Joseph R. Strayer, *The Albigensian Crusades* (New York, 1971).

38. On Tertullian and toleration, see Foakes-Jackson, *History of the Christian Church,* 206–7.

39. On the heresies of the fathers, see Harnack, *Dogma,* I, ch. 1; Schaff, *History,* II, 548–64; Bethune-Baker, *Introduction to Christian Doctrine,* 119–54; Foakes-Jackson, *History of Christian Church,* 153–79.

40. "Slogans and tags" is from Kelly, *Early Christian Creeds,* 13.

41. Kelly, *Early Christian Doctrines,* 117, 119.

42. I have consistently used books already mentioned by Harnack, Schaff, Bethune-Baker, Foakes-Jackson, Kelly, and Pelikan on the controversies within Christianity, but the interpretation is consistently mine. All the standard works are Trinitarian and orthodox, and except for Pelikan, *Emergence,* 194–200, are

extremely unsympathetic and ununderstanding toward any deviations from the Nicene Creed as construed by Athanasius.

43. Bethune-Baker, *Introduction to Christian Doctrine*, 96–112; Kelly, *Early Christian Doctrines*, 119–23; and Pelikan, *Emergence*, 176–81, are brief introductions to modal monarchianism and Sabellius. For Hippolytus, see *Ante-Nicene Fathers*, V, 125; for Dionysius and Athanasius, see *Nicene and Post-Nicene Fathers*, 2nd ser., IV, 168 and 186.

44. On "rationalistic Unitarians," Schaff, *History*, II, 575. On Paul of Samosata, see also Lietzmann, *From Constantine to Julian* (London, 1953, 2nd ed., vol. III of *History of the Early Church*), 94–102. In A.D. 398 Theodosius II ordered the burning of all unorthodox or heretical writings; see Clyde Pharr, trans., *The Theodosian Code and Novels* (Princeton, 1952), book XVI, title V, ch. 33, p. 456.

45. Kelly, *Early Christian Doctrines*, 118. On the third-century synods against Paul, see Hefele, *History of the Councils*, I, 118–26. This is the principal scholarly work for all church councils; I have relied on it heavily for factual information on all the councils of the fourth century that I mention. See also Eusebius, *Ecclesiastical History*, II, 209–33, and Harnack, *Dogma*, III, 37–48, for Paul. On Athanasius, see *Select Writings and Letters of Athanasius* in *Nicene and Post-Nicene Fathers*, 2nd ser., IV, 113, 156, 355, 407, 446, 474, 485.

46. Frend, *Martyrdom and Persecution*, 477–537, covers the "great Diocletian persecution" of 303–05, concluding at p. 537 that perhaps as many as sixty-five hundred Christians were victims. For Constantine's vision of the cross, see Eusebius, *The Life of Constantine*, in *Nicene and Post-Nicene Fathers*, I, 490, repeated by fifth-century historians, Socrates Scholasticus, *Ecclesiastical History*, and Sozomen, *Ecclesiastical History*, both in *ibid.*, II, 2, 241–2. For Eusebius's rejoicing, see his *Ecclesiastical History*, II, 395, 397. On Constantine, see also Ramsay MacMullen, *Constantine* (New York, 1969), 73, 83–6, 110–12, 115–20.

47. Alexander's account of Arius is in *Ante-Nicene Fathers*, VI, 291–99, esp. 297; Athanasius's account is interspersed throughout his writings; his quotations from Arius are in *Nicene and Post-Nicene Fathers*, 2nd ser., IV, 70, 154, 457–8.

48. On Arianism, see Lietzmann, *Constantine to Julian*, 94–136; Gwatkin, *Studies of Arianism*, a standard orthodox work (vitriolic against Arianism). At p. 18, Gwatkin acquitted Origen of heresy but conceded that he "leaned to Arianism. . . ." On Origen, see also Kelly, *Early Christian Doctrines*, 226. The quotation from Arius is in Athanasius, *Defense of the Nicene Definition*, in *Nicene and Post-Nicene Fathers*, 2nd ser., IV, 154. See Pelikan, *Emergence*, 194–200, for a balanced account of Arius and Arianism.

49. The only extant pre-Nicene statement by Arius was reported by Alexander of Alexandria to Alexander of Constantinople, in *Ante-Nicene Fathers*, VI, 297. Elsewhere in the same letter, Alexander paraphrases Arius, as when writing of "their blasphemous assertion who say that the Son does not perfectly know the Father. . ." 298. See also, Athanasius, *De Synodis*, in *Nicene and Post-Nicene Fathers*, 2nd ser., II, 6, and Sozomen's *History*, in *ibid.*, 252.

50. See Alexander's letter, cited in preceding note, on his synod and its actions; see also Socrates, *Ecclesiastical History*, in *Nicene and Post-Nicene Fathers*, II, 6, and Sozomen's *Ecclesiastical History*, in *ibid.*, 252.

51. Constantine's letter is in Socrates, *Ecclesiastical History*, 6–7. Hefele,

History of Church Councils, I, 231–439, is fullest on the Council of Nicaea. See also Gwatkin, *Studies of Arianism,* 17–51, and Schaff, *History,* III, 618–32.

52. *Epistola Eusebii,* a letter of Eusebius of Caesaria to his diocese, in *Nicene and Post-Nicene Fathers,* 2nd ser., IV, 73–6; Socrates, *Ecclesiastical History,* 6–10; Sozomen, *Ecclesiastical History,* 253–5.

53. The creed is in *Epistola Eusebii,* IV, 75. For discussion, see Kelly, *Early Christian Creeds,* 205–30, and Pelikan, *Emergence,* 200–10.

54. *Epistola Eusebii,* IV, 74–6; also in variant translation in Socrates, *Ecclesiastical History,* 10–12.

55. *Epistola Eusebii,* IV, 76. On the various meanings of the creed to different Christians, see Kelly, *Early Christian Creeds,* 231–62; Kelly, *Early Christian Doctrines,* 231–51; Bethune-Baker, *Introduction to Christian Doctrine,* 155–96; Foakes-Jackson, *History of the Church,* 328–50; Schaff, *History,* III, 632–83. See Socrates, *Ecclesiastical History,* 76, for the action of the council against "impious heresy."

56. Socrates, *Ecclesiastical History,* 12, 14; Sozomen, *Ecclesiastical History,* 255; and editorial preface to *Select Writings of Athanasius,* xix.

57. *Genuine Acts of Peter,* in *Ante-Nicene Fathers,* VI, 265; Eusebius, *Life of Constantine,* in *Nicene and Post-Nicene Fathers,* 2nd ser., I, 539.

58. Harnack, *Dogma,* IV, 1–95, and Hefele, *Church Councils,* II, cover all the councils between Nicaea and Constantinople (381). "Christ-opposing heresy" is from *Nicene and Post-Nicene Fathers,* 2nd ser., IV, xxxviii. On the Arian victory, see Gwatkin, *Studies in Arianism,* 64–92, and the secondary works cited in note 54 above. Pelikan, *Emergence,* 207.

59. Socrates, *History,* 27.

60. Lietzmann, *Constantine to Julian,* 211–35; Hefele, *History of the Councils,* II, 177–270; Gwatkin, *Studies in Arianism,* 156–65. For the "blasphemy of Sirmium," see Athanasius, *Writings,* in *Nicene and Post-Nicene Fathers,* 2nd ser., IV, lxxxviii, 450; Bethune-Baker, *Introduction,* 180; Foakes-Jackson, *History of the Church,* 344–5; Kelly, *Early Christian Doctrines,* 248–9. Sirmium is now Mirovica, Yugoslavia.

61. For Athanasius on the Arian and Semi-Arian councils, see his *De Synodis,* in *Writings, Nicene and Post-Nicene Fathers,* 2nd ser., IV, 451–68. Kelly, *Early Christian Doctrines,* 238, quotes Jerome.

62. Hefele, *History of the Councils,* II, 246–74, covers the councils of Ariminium (Rimini, Italy) and Constantinople, and *ibid.,* 275–339, the councils before the great one in Constantinople in 381. "Every pitch of blasphemy" is in Athanasius, *Writings,* 454 (see note 45 above for fuller reference).

63. Athanasius, *Writings,* 93–5, 106, 436, each from a different "book" in his *Writings.*

64. *Ibid.,* 152, 177–81, 186, 225, 234, 252, 255, 270–2, 296.

65. *Ibid.,* 150–4, 159–60, 457. *Ibid.,* xxxvii, 125–6, 431–2, on Marcellus's heterodoxy; see also Schaff, *History,* III, 651–3, and Gwatkin, *Studies in Arianism,* 81–3. For "heresiarch," see Socrates, *Ecclesiastical History,* 56.

66. Athanasius, *Writings,* 150–4, 168–70, 177, 234, 293–4, 459.

67. *Ibid.,* 294, 458–67. On post-Nicene creeds until 381, see also Kelly, *Early Christian Creeds,* 231–95.

68. Hanson, introduction to Jean Daniélou *et al., Historical Theology,* trans. Hanson *(The Pelican Guide to Modern Theology,* Baltimore, 1969, 3

vols.), II, 17. See *ibid.,* 131–40, for A. H. Coutrain on liturgy. See also Kelly, *Early Christian Doctrines,* 233.

69. On the creeds of 381–451, see Kelly, *Early Christian Creeds,* 296–331. On the councils of Constantinople in 381 and Chalcedon in 451, see also Hefele, *History of the Councils,* II, 340–51, and III, 285–383. Pelikan, *Emergence,* 211 ff., best analyzes the development of orthodox doctrine.

70. The act of 380 is quoted in Schaff, *History,* III, 142. For a variant translation, see book XVI, title I, no. 2, reprinted in Pharr, trans., *The Theodosian Code,* 440. For the sixty-six laws, see book XVI, title V, in *ibid.,* 450–63. William K. Boyd, *The Ecclesiastical Edicts of the Theodosian Code* (New York, 1905), 33–70, is a secondary account of the laws against heresy.

71. Henry Charles Lea, *A History of the Inquisition* (New York, 1955 reprint, 3 vols.), I, 219–24.

72. Julian "the apostate," the pagan emperor, 361–3, boasted of allowing religious freedom to all Christians and pagans, and contrasting himself with Constantius, his predecessor, wrote: "In his reign many of them [Christians of the Nicene-Athanasian persuasion] were banished, persecuted, and imprisoned; and numbers of those who are styled heretics *were put to death,* particularly at Samosata and Cyzicus; and in Paphlagonia, Bithynia, Galatia and many other provinces, whole villages were laid waste and entirely depopulated" (quoted in Greenslade, *Church and State from Constantine to Theodosius,* 57, emphasis added). If the statement by Julian is correct, the execution of the Pricillians in 385 was not the first instance of capital punishment for heresy as most historians state; but nothing in Athanasius's *Writings* supports Julian, and Athanasius would have been the first to catalogue the persecution of Christians under Constantius. Moreover, no law existed fixing the death penalty for an offense against religion, and neither Socrates nor Sozomen records such incidents. The Pricillian episode is discussed in Schaff, *History,* III, 963–7; Foakes-Jackson, *History of the Church,* 408–13, 428; and F. Holmes Dudden, *The Life and Times of St. Ambrose* (Oxford, 1935, 2 vols.), I, 224–40. Dudden, II, 381–92, is best on Ambrose and Theodosius, On Hypatia, see Schaff, *History,* 66–7, and Socrates, *Ecclesiastical History,* 160.

73. St. Augustine, Letter 185, chs. 48–9, in *Letters,* trans. Wilfrid Parsons (New York, 1951–6, 5 vols.), IV, 187–9.

74. Rufinus, *Apology,* in *Nicene and Post-Nicene Fathers,* 2nd ser., III, 465–6.

4. Compelling Heretics to Come In

1. On Augustine's life before conversion, see his *Confessions,* books II–IV, any edition.

2. W. H. C. Frend, *The Donatist Church: A Movement of Protest in Roman North Africa* (Oxford, 1952), is a superb book. Geoffrey Grimshaw Willis, *Saint Augustine and the Donatist Controversy* (London, 1950), is a defense of Augustine. Frederick W. Dillistone, "The Anti-Donatist Writings," in Roy W. Battenhouse, *A Companion to the Study of St. Augustine* (New York, 1955), 175–202, was helpful as were several of the other essays in the anthology.

3. *Saint Augustine, Letters,* trans. Wilfrid Parsons (New York, 1951–6, 6

vols.), I, 187, 203, 368; I have also used the variant translation of Letter 76 in Dillistone, "Anti-Donatist Writings," 186. The other quotations are from Augustine's *Homilies on the Gospel of John,* in Philip Schaff, ed., *A Select Library of the Nicene and Post-Nicene Fathers of the Christian Church* (New York, 1886–90, 14 vols.), VII, 79–80. See also Willis, *St. Augustine,* 130.

4. On the relationship of blasphemy and treason, see Floyd S. Lear, "Blasphemy in the *Lex Romana Curiensis,*" *Speculum,* VI (1931), 445–59. On Augustine's thought on church and state, see John Neveille Figgis, *The Political Aspects of S. Augustine's "City of God"* (London, 1921), 51–80. On Ambrose, see F. Holmes Dudden, *The Life and Times of St. Ambrose* (Oxford, 1935), 499–501. Augustine is quoted from *Letters,* I, 182.

5. *Letters,* I, 186; II, 20; IV, 186. Augustine's letters are usually cited by number and section, so that one may consult any edition. His principal letters on persecution are numbers 87, 93, 173, and above all 185 which in the edition I used is in IV, 141–90. His "letters" are often elaborate essays.

6. *Letters,* V, 146, 149 (Letter 228).

7. *Ibid.,* II, 59, 61, 63–4 (Letter 93).

8. *Ibid.,* II, 64–5; IV, 150–2.

9. *Ibid.,* II, 72–3, 76; IV, 147–8, 162.

10. *Ibid.,* IV, 154–60.

11. *Ibid.,* 161, 165.

12. *Ibid.,* 165, 170.

13. Frend, *Donatist Church,* 258, 263–4, 269, 298–309, 403–11, 435.

14. *Corpus Juris Civilis,* Novel 77, ed. Wilhelm Kroll (Berlin, 1900–5, 3 vols.), III (trans. R. Scholl), 382. Zeger Bernard van Espen, *Jus Ecclesiasticum Universum* (Cologne, 1715, 3 vols.), II, 256–8. John Godolphin, *Reperotorium Canonicium; or An Abridgment of the Ecclesiastical Laws of this Realm* (London, 1678), 559.

15. On capital punishments for heresy before the thirteenth century, see R. I. Moore, "The Origins of Medieval Heresy," *History,* LV (1970), 21–36, and Steven Runciman, *The Medieval Manichee* (Cambridge, 1955), 117–26. Executions were rare. Even into the thirteenth century the decretal of Gregory IX on the subject of blasphemy, as distinguished from heresy, provided only for ecclesiastical punishments ranging from mild penance to excommunication and enjoined the civil power to impose only fines, although heavy (from fifteen to forty gold coins, which only the rich could pay). Aemilius Friedberg, ed., *Corpus Juris Cononici* (Leipzig, 1879–81, 2 vols.), *titulus* XXVI, *De Maledicis,* 826–7; ch. 15 of *ibid.* is on heretics. For the death penalty in the thirteenth century, see Albert Clement Shannon, *Popes and Heresy in the Thirteenth Century* (Villanova, Pa., 1949), 52; this is the best Catholic book on the early Inquisition. The classic and very Protestant account is Henry Charles Lea, *A History of the Inquisition of the Middle Ages* (New York, 1955 reprint, 3 vols.), 1, 220–25, 321–22; the note on p. 322 states that the papal curia framed the legislation requiring the death penalty and sent it to the emperor for signature. On heresy in the Middle Ages, see M. D. Lambert, *Medieval Heresy: Popular Movements from Bogomil to Hus* (London, 1977), the most comprehensive and recent study. See also Jeffrey B. Russel, *Dissent and Reform in the Early Middle Ages* (Los Angeles, 1965); R. I. Moore, *The Origins of European Dissent* (New York, 1977), and Moore's collection of documents, *The Birth of Popular Heresy* (New York, 1975); Gordon Leff, *Heresy in the Later Middle Ages: The*

Relation of Heterodoxy to Dissent, 1250–1450 (Manchester, 1967, 2 vols.); Robert E. Lerner, *The Heresy of the Free Spirit* (Berkeley, 1972); and Walter L. Wakefield and Austin Evans, eds., *Heresies of the High Middle Ages* (New York, 1969), an invaluable and comprehensive collection of primary sources with a helpful editorial apparatus, including a long introduction. Blasphemy was so unimportant a subject in the Middle Ages that historians of heresy, with the exception of Leff, fail to notice it. In a book of 865 pages, for example, Wakefield and Evans do not list "blasphemy" in their index, although I found about forty references to "blasphemy" in the documents. Not one distinguishes blasphemy from heresy. In several of the documents church authorities declare that heretics are blasphemers against God and the faith of the church, or that all blasphemers are heretics; most of the documents that refer to blasphemy identify particular heretical doctrines as blasphemies, *e.g.,* holding Mani to be a person of the Holy Trinity, ridiculing Mass, calling the church abominable names, demeaning the powers of God, assaulting the spiritual powers of the episcopacy, criticizing infant baptism, and alleging that one who has the Spirit within him cannot commit a sin, not even by fornication (Wakefield and Evans, eds., *Heresies,* 90, 120, 140–1, 198, 219, 224, 238, 259, 271, 341, 712). The church did not execute or instigate the execution of anyone for the crime of blasphemy; every person who died for religious opinions was condemned for heresy, although the heresy may have been deemed blasphemous.

16. On the Cathars and on the Albigensian Crusade, which was a series of holy wars that turned into dynastic wars, beginning in 1208 and ending with the fall of Montsegur in 1244, see Lea, *History of the Inquisition,* I, 89–208, and II, 1–112; Austin P. Evans, "The Albigensian Crusades," in *The Later Crusades,* ed. Robert Lee Wolff and Harry W. Hazard (Philadelphia, 1962), 277–324 (vol. 2 of a five-volume set, *A History of the Crusades,* ed. Kenneth M. Setton). For a short, readable book, see Joseph R. Strayer, *The Albigensian Crusades* (New York, 1971), covering the Cathars, the wars, and the early Inquisition, which was organized initially for the express purpose of liquidating the Cathars. Runciman, *Medieval Manichee,* 116–70, is on the Cathars; the preceding pages deal with their precursors, beginning with the Gnostics of the second century. Whether the Cathars descended from Mani is disputable. Walter L. Wakefield, *Heresy, Crusade and Inquisition in Southern France 1100–1250* (London, 1974), is the best up-to-date treatment. See also Lambert, *Medieval Heresy,* 49–164, and Moore, *The Origins of European Dissent,* 168–240.

17. *The "Summa Theologica" of St. Thomas Aquinas,* trans. Fathers of the English Dominican Province (London, 1912–29, 22 vols.), IX, 148–53, available in any edition in Part Two, Second Part, under Question XI, "Of Heresy," articles 1–2.

18. *Ibid.,* 164–9, Quest. XIII, "Of Blasphemy," art. 1–3.

19. *Ibid.,* IX, 153–4, 168–9. The final quotation is from Aquinas's commentaries on the work of Peter Lombard, available only in Latin as *Scriptum Super Sententiis Magistri Petri Lombardi,* ed. Marie Fabien Moos (Paris, 1947–56, 4 vols. in 3), IV, d. 13, qu. 2, art. 3, no. 160, p. 569.

20. *"Summa Theologica,"* IX, 154–55.

21. *Ibid.,* 168–9.

22. Modern Catholic theologians still follow Thomas Aquinas. Arthur Preuss's revision of Anthony Koch, *Handbook of Moral Theology* (St. Louis, 1928), distinguishes between immediate blasphemy (against God) and mediate

(against revealed religion, the church, or the saints); between direct and indirect blasphemy, depending on whether dishonor to God is intended; and between heretical blasphemy ("if it involves heresy") and imprecative blasphemy; in any case blasphemy is *a crimen laesae maiestatis,* the most grievous sin a man can commit" (*ibid.,* 181–2). John A. McHugh and Charles J. Callan, *Moral Theology,* rev. Edward P. Farrell (New York, 1958, 2 vols.), after defining heresy as "an error opposed to faith," distinguishes   between heretical blasphemy and the non-heretical; the former affirms about God something false or denies something true, while the latter "affirms or denies something about God according to truth, but in a mocking or blaming way" (I, 348). The references to "God" mean also the church, the Virgin, saints, the sacraments, the crucifix, the Bible, "etc." Bernard Häring, *The Law of Christ,* trans. E. G. Kaiser (Westminster, Md., 1963, 2 vols.), II, 205–6, is virtually identical in substance.

23. For references to Jews as blasphemers, see the papal letters reprinted in Solomon Grayzel, *The Church and the Jews in the Thirteenth Century* (New York, 1966), 107, 109, 115, 127, 129, 157, 173, 205, 251, 253, 309, 311; see also 337, 341–3.

24. Salo Wittmayer Baron, *A Social and Religious History of the Jews* (New York, 1952 ff., 2nd rev. ed., 16 vols. to date), IX, 6–7 on Alexander; *"Summa Theologica,"* IX, 143. See also Grayzel, *Church and Jews,* 12.

25. For "The Policy of Degradation," see Grayzel, *Church and Jews,* ch. 7. On the legal status of Jews in the Middle Ages, see also Baron, *Social and Religious History,* IX, ch. xl on "Serf of the Chamber," and XI, ch. xlvii, "Citizen or Bondsman." On the massacres, which are all too familiar, one might almost refer to Heinrich Graetz, *History of the Jews* (New York, 1927, 6 vols.) and say *passim.* On 1096 see Baron, IV, 89–106 and 124–47. Baron, XI, 270, concludes his account of the slaughters in Germany in 1348–9 by saying, "Approximately three hundred German communities were annihilated. . . . " For an unusual analytical account, see Norman Cohn, *The Pursuit of the Millennium* (New York, 1971, rev. ed.), 69–139 *passim.*

26. Lea's *Inquisition,* supplemented by his four-volume *History of the Inquisition of Spain* (New York, 1906–7), supplies all the necessary gore on that subject. John L. Motley, *The Rise of the Dutch Republic* (New York, 1856, 3 vols.), II, 155 suggests the murders in the Low Countries. For samples of the savagery during the Crusades, see Stephen Runciman, *History of the Crusades* (Cambridge, 1951–4, 3 vols.), I, 286–7, and III, 123. Runciman's *The Sicilian Vespers* (Cambridge, 1958) is too readable to be bearable. For a one-page pastiche on the massacre of Christians by Christians during the Crusades, see Paul Johnson, *A History of Christianity* (New York, 1977), 246; *ibid., 203* on the papal murders of the emperor's children.

27. Grayzel, *Church and Jews,* 29–32, 251; Baron, *Social and Religious History,* IX, 63–7, 93–6; Graetz, *History of Jews,* III, 573–9; William Popper, *The Censorship of Hebrew Books* (New York, 1969), 7–12. Jean Sire de Joinville, *The History of St. Louis,* trans. J. Evans (Oxford, 1938), 15–16.

28. The quotations are from Baron, *Social and Religious History,* IX, 56–7, 273 n. 18. See also, *ibid.,* 57, 62, 69–70, 87, 272 n. 15; XIV, 30–1, 56–7, 81, 127–8, 158; Graetz, *History of Jews,* III, 585–6, and IV, 213–15; Popper, *Censorship,* 13, 16, 31–7, 46–8.

29. On the Free Spirit movement, see Cohn, *Pursuit,* 148–86, and especially

Gordon Leff, *Heresy in the Middle Ages* (Manchester, 1967, 2 vols.), I, 308–407. See also Robert E. Lerner, *The Heresy of the Free Spirit in the Later Middle Ages* (Berkeley, 1972).
30. Cohn, *Pursuit*, 153–5.
31. See note 29 above for the two historians, Cohn and Leff.
32. Cohn, *Pursuit*, 172–4.
33. *Ibid.*, 180; Leff, *Heresy*, I, 373, 377–8.
34. Leff, *Heresy*, I, 311–4.
35. *Ibid.*, 314, 318, 327, 358, 364–5.
36. For the bull of 1418 and Jerome of Prague, see John Foxe, *The Acts and Monuments of John Foxe* (1565), ed. George Townshend (New York, 1965 reprint, 8 vols.), III, 523, 528. Lea, *Inquisition*, II, organizes the data by country, dispersing the discussion of the Waldensians throughout; for their origins in France, *ibid.*, 145–61. Lea covers the Hussites in his chapter on Bohemia (pp. 427–505), and in the last chapter (pp. 506–67) discusses the Hussites topically and stresses their union with the Waldensians. On the Waldensians, see also Leff, *Heresy*, II, 448–71, and Lambert, *Medieval Heresy*, 67–91, 151–64. Lambert, 272–334, provides a modern account of the Hussites. For briefer accounts of the Inquisition, see A. S. Turberville, *Medieval Heresy and the Inquisition* (London, 1920), and G. G. Coulton, *Inquisition and Liberty* (London, 1938), both of which discuss the Waldensians and Hussites; an apologetic Catholic account purporting to correct Lea is E. Vacandard, *The Inquisition*, trans. B. L. Conway (London, 1908); Father Shannon's *Popes and Heresy* is more critical but limited to the origins of the Inquisition.

5. Protestantism Rediscovers Blasphemy

1. Nathaniel Ward, "The Simple Cobbler of Agawam," in Perry Miller and Thomas Johnson, eds., *The Puritans* (New York, 1938), 232.
2. Earl Morse Wilbur, *A History of Unitarianism: Socinianism and Its Antecedents* (Cambridge, Mass., 1945), 3–112, covers the early Arians of the first half of the sixteenth century and their relationship to the Anabaptists, some of whom were antitrinitarians. The definitive book on the background of this chapter is George Huntston Williams, *The Radical Reformation* (Philadelphia, 1972), which comprehensively covers all the sixteenth-century sectarian movements to the left of the conventionally major Protestant churches throughout Europe, including all varieties of Anabaptists, Spiritualists, and Rationalist antitrinitarians. Williams added a new dimension to "The Reformation" in what is undoubtedly the most original and brilliant book on the subject. Williams does not refer to the problem of blasphemy. His chief concern is the complexity and variety of radical Protestant thought.
3. The best book on the Anabaptists is Williams, *Radical Reformation*. See also E. Belfort Bax, *Rise and Fall of the Anabaptists* (1903; New York, 1970 reprint); Claus-Peter Clasen, *Anabaptism: A Social History, 1525–1618* (Ithaca, N.Y., 1972); William R. Estep, *The Anabaptist Story* (Grand Rapids, Mich., 1975); and Cornelius Krahn, *Dutch Anabaptism* (The Hague, 1968). The quotation from Simons is in Joseph Lecler, *Toleration and the Reformation*, trans. T. L. Westow (New York, 1960, 2 vols.), I, 211.
4. For the Münster episode, see Bax, *Rise and Fall*, 117–256; "The Trial and

Martyrdom of Michael Sattler," in George H. Williams, ed., *Spiritual and Anabaptist Writers* (London, 1957), 138-44. See also Krahn, *Dutch Anabaptism*, 135-64.

5. The judgment against Manz is from Lecler, *Toleration*, I, 200.

6. On Franck, see Rufus M. Jones, *Spiritual Reformers in the 16th & 17th Centuries* (New York, 1914), 64-87. Franck's figure of two thousand is from Lecler, *Toleration*, I, 167. The percentage figures are from Clasen, *Anabaptism*, ch. 11 on "persecution," and Appendix D, "Statistics on the Execution of Anabaptists."

7. Roland Herbert Bainton, "The Development and Consistency of Luther's Attitude to Religious Liberty," *Harvard Theological Review*, XXII (1929), 109, for the first quotation; Lecler, *Toleration*, I, 150, for the second; *ibid.* and Bainton, 115, for the third.

8. Luther's statements of 1523 and 1525 are reprinted in Sebastian Castellio, *Concerning Heretics: Whether They Are To Be Persecuted and How They Are To Be Treated*, trans., with introd., by Roland H. Bainton (New York, 1935), 149, 153; the quotation of 1524 is from Lecler, *Toleration*, I, 153. Luther's reply to the chancellor in 1525 is in *Luther's Works*, eds. Jaroslav Pelican and Helmut T. Lehmann (St. Louis and Philadelphia, 1955-76, 55 vols.), XLIX, 99.

9. Lecler, *Toleration*, I, 152; Bainton, "Development and Consistency," 111, 113. *Luther's Works*, II, 63; XLIX, 110, 262, 410.

10. Bainton, "Development and Consistency," 116, 117.

11. *Ibid.*, 117, 118.

12. *Ibid.*, 118-9; Lecler, *Toleration*, I, 161-3. All quotations are from *Luther's Works*, XIII, 61-7, on Psalm 82:5, part 4 (1530).

13. *Luther's Works*, II; 60; Bainton, "Development and Consistency," 111, 119, 121, 148. Heinrich Graetz, *History of the Jews* (New York, 1927, 6 vols.), IV, 549-52; see also Salo Wittmayer Baron, *Social and Religious History of the Jews* (New York, 1952 ff., 2nd rev. ed., 16 vols. to date), XIII, 216-27.

14. *Luther's Works*, II, 60, 61; IV, 31-2, 204, 334, 399; Bainton, "Development and Consistency," 120.

15. *Luther's Works*, II, 334; XLI, 211, 279, 299, 330. In XLI, see also 11, 13, 80, 81, 172, 234-6, 279, 285, 298, 300, 302, 309, 311, 321, 323, 328, 330, 331, 333, 339, 340, 342, 344, 349, 352, 357, 359, 360, 369, 370.

16. *Ibid.*, I, 179; II, 49, 110; III, 162, 173; XIII, 61; XIV, 95; XLI, 81; XLIX, 141, 233.

17. Lecler, *Toleration*, I, 216 and 248 for Melanchthon and Menius; Castellio, *Concerning Heretics*, 51, 80, and 91 for Brenz, Hedio, and Brunsfels.

18. On Calvin I have relied mainly on the old-fashioned and sympathetic biography by Paul Henry, *The Life and Times of John Calvin*, trans. Henry Stebbing (New York, 1854, 2 vols.). See also Thomas H. Dyer, *The Life of John Calvin* (New York, 1855); Williston Walker, *John Calvin* (New York, 1906); Georgia Harkness, *John Calvin* (New York, 1931); and T. H. L. Parker, *John Calvin* (Philadelphia, 1975). Calvin's *Institutes of the Christian Religion*, ed. John T. McNeill and trans. Ford L. Battles (Philadelphia, 1960, 2 vols.), is based on the final 1559 edition; the first edition was 1536. McNeill's *History and Character of Calvinism* (New York, 1954) is excellent but unfootnoted. The passage from the early edition of the Institutes is quoted in Dyer, *Life of Calvin*, 298. Harkness, *John Calvin*, 109, quotes the passage on predestined infants and also quotes Bainton from an unpublished manuscript by him.

19. Traitor to God ("traistres à Dieu") is from a 1555 sermon on Deuteronomy 15, in John Calvin, *Opera Quae Supersunt Omnia,* ed. Wilhelm Baum *et al.* (New York, 1964 reprint, 59 vols.), XXVII, 245. The French phrase is from Henry, *Life and Times,* I, 353. For Calvin on the pope, Dyer, *Life of Calvin,* 152. Calvin, *Opera,* XXVII, 57, is the source for punishing blasphemies worse than murder. The commentary on Lev. 24:16 is from *ibid.,* XXV, 212, and dishonoring God from *ibid.,* XXIV, 360. Harkness, *John Calvin,* 101–13, discusses Calvin on blasphemy and heresy

20. Calvin, *Opera,* XLIV, 348; X, 56.

21. On Ameaux and his wife, see Henry, *Life and Times,* II, 49, 57–9; *ibid.,* 42–9 on the Libertines.

22. *Ibid.,* 44–8, for the quotations.

23. *Ibid.,* 64–8 on Gruet.

24. Castellio, *Concerning Heretics,* 38–41.

25. Robert Wallace, *Antitrinitarian Biography* (London, 1850, 3 vols.), I, 412–17; I, 139; II, 1–3, 139. Wilbur, *Unitarianism,* 283–4. Richard Copley Christie, *Etienne Dolet, the Martyr of the Renaissance* (London, 1880), 446–7.

26. Christie, *Etienne Dolet,* 450–1; Dyer, *Life of Calvin,* 26–7; Harkness, *John Calvin,* 29–30. Henry, *Life and Times,* I, 363, says that Geneva burned one hundred fifty people for witchcraft in sixty years; see also McNeill, *History of Calvinism,* 172, who states that in one year in the 1540s Geneva burned more than twenty.

27. The best introductions to Servetus are Roland H. Bainton, *Hunted Heretic: The Life and Death of Michael Servetus* (Boston, 1953), and the first third of Wilbur, *Unitarianism.* I relied most on R. Willis, *Servetus and Calvin* (London, 1877), which quotes at length or reprints the important documents in English translation. The primary source is Calvin, *Opera,* VIII, 458–871, containing the Calvin–Servetus correspondence, the trial records, and invaluable supplementary material.

28. *De Trinitatis Errorisbus,* in *The Two Treatises of Servetus on the Trinity,* trans. E. M. Wilbur (Cambridge, Mass., 1932), 50. Bainton, *Hunted Heretic,* 52, quoted Oecolampadius. Willis, *Servetus and Calvin,* 33–4, quotes Zwingli. Wilbur, *Unitarianism,* 58, and Bainton, *Hunted Heretic,* 53, quote Bucer. See also the statement by Calvin in Willis, 433.

29. On Servetus as Dr. Villaneuve, see Willis, *Servetus and Calvin,* 79–156; Wilbur, *Unitarianism,* 114–31; and Bainton, *Hunted Heretic,* 75–127.

30. For summaries of the *Restitutio,* see Willis, *Servetus and Calvin,* 191–230, and Bainton, *Hunted Heretic,* 128–42.

31. Willis, *Servetus and Calvin,* 168; pp. 157–90 cover the Servetus–Calvin correspondence. See also Wilbur, *Unitarianism,* 134, and Stefan Zweig, *The Right to Heresy,* trans. E. Paul (London, 1951), 263, for English translations of Calvin's letter to W. Farel, Feb. 13, 1547, in Calvin, *Opera,* XII, 283. The Cerberus quotation is from Bainton, *Hunted Heretic,* 147, and Willis, *Servetus and Calvin,* 359.

32. The quotations are from Bainton, *Hunted Heretic,* 152–3, 156; also in Willis, *Servetus and Calvin,* 236–7, 246.

33. Quoted in Willis, *Servetus and Calvin,* 346.

34. Willis recounts the trial, *Servetus and Calvin,* 304–479.

35. The charges are reprinted in Willis, *Servetus and Calvin,* 351. Calvin's original thirty-eight articles of impeachment against Servetus are summarized in *ibid.,* 307–11; "an infinity of blasphemies" is on p. 307. A second series of

thirty-eight articles is in *ibid.*, 406–17. The former were based on Servetus's first book, the latter on the *Restitutio*. On Servetus's use of "Trinitarian," see Wilbur, ed., *Two Treatises of Servetus,* 32.

36. Wilbur, *Unitarianism,* 168–9; a different rendering of Calvin's letter is in Willis, *Servetus and Calvin,* 436.

37. For Calvin's letters and the replies of the Swiss cities and churches, see Willis, *Servetus and Calvin,* 428–60. For the reply of Schaffhausen, I have followed Bainton, *Hunted Heretic,* 203.

38. I have followed Bainton, *Hunted Heretic,* 207–9, for a rendering of the verdict and the execution; see also Willis, *Servetus and Calvin,* 480–7, and Henry, *Life and Times,* II, 221–2.

39. Castellio, *Concerning Heretics* (see note 8 above). See also Bainton's "Sebastian Castellio and the Toleration Controversy," in *Persecution and Liberty: Essays in Honor of George Lincoln Burr* (New York, 1931, no. ed.), 183–209. Zweig, *Right to Heresy* (originally entitled *Castellio against Calvin),* is the fullest narrative on Castellio. For an excellent brief account by a liberal Jesuit, see Lecler, *Toleration,* I, 337–64, including the remarks of Melanchthon, p. 331. See Henry M. Baird, *Theodore Beza* (New York, 1889), 61–9, for a summary of Beza's tract replying to Castellio's *Concerning Heretics.*

40. Lecler, *Toleration,* I, 333–4, 338, contains the quoted material.

41. *Defensio Orthodoxae Fidei,* VIII, 476; on Alesius, see Wilbur, *Unitarianism,* 192.

42. Bainton, intro. to Castellio, *Concerning Heretics,* 6. W. K. Jordan, *The Development of Religious Toleration in England* (Cambridge, Mass., 1932–40, 4 vols.), I, 310. On Acontius, see *ibid.,* 303–65; his *Satanae Stratagemata (Satan's Strategems)* is available in modern translation by Charles D. O'Malley (San Francisco, 1940), published by the California State Library for the WPA in bound multilith pages. Baird, *Theodore Beza,* 63–8; Zweig, *Right to Heresy,* 317–23. See also, Walter Rex, "Blasphemy in the Refuge in Holland and in the French Enlightenment," in *Studies on Voltaire and the Eighteenth Century,* ed. Theodore Besterman, *Transactions of the Second International Congress on the Enlightenment,* LVII (1967), 1307–11.

43. Castellio, *Concerning Heretics,* 129.

44. *Ibid.,* 132–3, 137, 139, 248, 280–1.

45. *Ibid.,* 139, 264, 266.

46. *Ibid.,* 284

47. *Ibid.,* 229, 280, 283–4, 286.

48. *Ibid.,* 10, 265; Zweig, *Right to Heresy,* 323–66.

49. On sixteenth-century Italian forerunners of Socinianism, see Wilbur, *Unitarianism,* chs. 6–8, 15, 17. The three books, which bore Castellio's direct influence, were Mino Celso, *Whether Heretics Should Be Subject to Capital Punishment* (1559), Bernardino Ochino, *Dialogues* (1563), and Acontius, *Satan's Strategems* (1565); see Wilbur, *Unitarianism,* 205–8, Jordan, *Development of Religious Toleration,* 309–11, and Lecler, *Toleration,* I, 365–80.

50. Wallace, *Antitrinitarian Biography,* II, 106. The fullest account of Gentile and his trials is Benedictus Aretius, *A Short History of Valentinus Gentilis the Tritheist* (London, 1696), 1–134, originally published in Bern in 1567; Aretius was a supporter of Beza. Gentile's recantation is in *ibid.,* 87. See also Wilbur, *Unitarianism,* 230–7.

51. Aretius, *History of Gentilis,* 36.

52. *Ibid.,* 32.

53. *Ibid.,* 30–1, 40, 42–4, and 55–63 on "the opinion of Arius, wherein Gentilis and he do agree"; also, 114–19 and 127 on Gentiles's "Notorious Blasphemies."

54. *Ibid.,* 132, 134.

55. Joshua Toulmin, *A Dialogue Between a Dutch Protestant and a Franciscan Friar* (London, 1784), 3–7.

56. Earl Morse Wilbur, *A History of Unitarianism: In Transylvania, England and America* (Cambridge, Mass., 1952), 22, 26, 38, hereafter cited as *Unitarianism II.* On the name "Unitarian," first used in Transylvania in 1568 but not the formal designation of the denomination until 1600, see *ibid.,* 47, n. 12. On David, see *ibid.,* 23–80; Wallace, *Antitrinitarian Biography,* I, 245–63; William C. Gannett, *Francis David* (London, 1914).

57. Wilbur, *Unitarianism II,* 36.

58. Wallace, *Antitrinitarian Biography,* II, 248–55, reprints David's sixteen theses and Biandrata's replies.

59. Quoted from Bruno's *Ash Wednesday Supper* (1584), in William Boulting, *Giordano Bruno* (London, 1914), 125. My discussion of Bruno is also based on I. Frith, *Life of Giordano Bruno,* rev. M. Carriere (London, 1887), and John Owen, *Skeptics of the Italian Renaissance* (London, 1893), 245–343.

60. Boulting, *Bruno,* 57; Frith, *Life of Bruno,* 274.

61. Boulting, *Bruno,* 141.

62. *Ibid.,* 142; John Herman Randall, *Making of the Modern Mind* (Boston, 1940), 243.

63. The quotations are from Boulting, *Bruno,* 270, 276, 277. On Bruno before the Inquisition at Venice, see *ibid.,* 254–79, and Frith, *Life of Bruno,* 238–83, invaluable for reprinting English translations of the important documents, including the accusations for blasphemy on pp. 262–5.

64. For the trial in Rome, see Frith, *Life of Bruno,* 284–302, which includes the sentence. Bruno's last words and the statement of the witness are in Owen, *Skeptics,* 328–9.

65. For "images of God," see Ludwig von Bar, *History of Continental Criminal Law* (Boston, 1916), 281. See *ibid.,* 184, 228, 280–1, for various statutes punishing blasphemy.

66. Wilbur, *Unitarianism II,* 444–7; Wallace, *Antitrinitarian Biography,* II, 528–30.

67. Owen, *Skeptics,* 345–419, covers Vanini.

68. Carl E. Jarcke, *Handbuch des Gemeinen Deutchen Strafrechts* (Berlin, 1827–30, 3 vols.), II, 27–46, covers blasphemy in Germany from 1500 to 1800. In eighteenth-century Prussia the penalty was imprisonment for six months. In Austria and Bavaria, Catholic areas, death remained a penalty but the law seemed to be a dead letter. By 1787 Austria sent blasphemers to "the madhouse."

6. The Fires of Smithfield

1. Account by William of Newburgh, trans. in W. O. Hassall, ed., *Medieval England as Viewed by Contemporaries* (New York, 1957), 81–2; Assize of Clarendon, 1166, in George B. Adams and H. Morse Stephens, eds., *Select*

Documents of English Constitutional History (New York, 1929), 17.

2. Henry Charles Lea, *A History of the Inquisition of the Middle Ages* (1887; New York, 1955 reprint, 3 vols.), I, 113-4.

3. W. R. W. Stephens, *The English Church from the Norman Conquest to the Accession of Edward I* (London, 1904), 49; Felix Makower, *The Constitutional History and Constitution of the Church of England* (London, 1895), 384-464; Sir William Holdsworth, *A History of English Law* (London, 1903-66, 16 vols.), I, 614-32; Sir Frederic Pollock and Frederic William Maitland, *The History of English Law before the Time of Edward I* (Cambridge, 1899, 2nd ed., 2 vols.), I, 124-32; Sir James Fitzjames Stephen, *A History of the Criminal Law of England* (London, 1883, 3 vols.), II, 404-13.

4. Pollock and Maitland, *History of English Law*, II, 548; Maitland, "The Deacon and the Jewess," *Roman Canon Law in the Church of England* (London, 1898), 158-79; Lea, *History of the Inquisition*, I, 486; John Foxe, *The Acts and Monuments of John Foxe* [The Book of Martyrs, 1563], ed. George Townsend (New York, 1965 reprint, 8 vols.), I, 486; *The Mirror of Justices*, ed. William Joseph Whittaker with intro. by F. W. Maitland (London, 1895), 59, 135.

5. Thomas Wright, ed., *A Contemporary Narrative of the Proceedings Against Dame Alice Kyteler* (Camden Society, 1843), ix, 1-4, 42-5; *Dictionary of National Biography*, eds. Sir Leslie Stephen and Sir Sidney Lee (London, 1885-1905, 63 vols.), XIV, 1231.

6. Foxe, *Acts and Monuments*, III, 4, 5, 21, 23. Wycliffe's case is also reported in Thomas B. Howell, comp., *A Complete Collection of State Trials and Proceedings for High Treason and Other Crimes* (London, 1816, 21 vols.), I, 67-90 (hereafter cited as *State Trials*).

7. Foxe, *Acts and Monuments*, III, 23.

8. Stephen, *History of Criminal Law*, II, 443-4; H. G. Richardson, "Heresy and the Lay Power under Richard II," *English Historical Review*, LI (1936), 1-28; Foxe, *Acts and Monuments*, III, 38, 100.

9. Foxe, *Acts and Monuments*, III, 110, 116, 118, 125, 127, 286-7.

10. Maitland, *Roman Canon Law*, 174-7; Stephen, *History of Criminal Law*, II, 445-8; Foxe, *Acts and Monuments*, III, 221-9; *State Trials*, I, 163-75; "The Royal Writ for the Burning of Sawtre," in Henry Gee and William John Hardy, eds., *Documents Illustrative of English Church History* (London, 1896), 139.

11. Stephen, *History of Criminal Law*, II, 447-50; Foxe, *Acts and Monuments*, III, 239-40, 353-5; "Act De Haeretico Comburendo, 1401," Gee and Hardy, *Documents*, 133-7.

12. For the number of burnings I have relied on the incidents related in Foxe, *Acts and Monuments*, for the period 1401-1534 in vols. 3-5, not counting those that seem uncertain. John A. F. Thomson, *The Later Lollards* (New York, 1965), was also helpful. Foxe, *Acts and Monuments*, IV, 217-46, covers the inquisition in Lincoln; Philip Hughes, *The Reformation in England* (London, 1950-4; 3 vols.), I, 128-9, gives the figure of 342. On John Huss and Jerome of Prague, see Foxe, *Acts and Monuments*, III, 523, 558. On Joan's case, which I could not confirm, see H. J. W. Coulson, "The Law Relating to Blasphemy,' *Law Magazine and Review*, 4th ser., IX (1883-4), 161.

13. J. V. Bullard and H. Chalmer Bell, eds., *Lyndwood's Provinciale* (London, 1929), 127, 131-2, bk. V, tit. V, chs. 2 and 4.

14. On the rise of Protestantism and the Henrician Reformation in England, see Thomson, *The Later Lollards;* James Gairdner, *Lollardy and the Reformation in England* (London, 1908, 4 vols.); Sir Maurice Powicke, *The Reformation in England* (London, 1961).

15. E. Belfort Bax, *Rise and Fall of the Anabaptists* (1903; New York, 1970 reprint), 332–4; Thomas Fuller, *Church History of Britain,* ed. J. S. Brewer (Oxford, 1845, 6 vols.), III, 175; Edward Bean Underhill, *Struggles and Triumphs of Religious Liberty* (New York, 1858), 98.

16. John Stow, *The Annales of England faithfully collected out of the most authenticall authors, records and other monuments of antiquitie* (1592), 965.

17. *Ibid.,* 973.

18. Foxe, *Acts and Monuments,* IV, 628, 630, 632, 655.

19. *Ibid.,* IV, 697–705; Elizabeth F. Rogers, ed., *The Correspondence of Sir Thomas More* (Princeton, 1947), 558, letter to M. Roper, June 3, 1535.

20. Gairdner, *Lollardy and the Reformation,* I, 453–61; Thomas Wright, ed., *Three Chapters of Letters Relating to the Suppression of Monasteries* (London, 1843), 13–34; James Anthony Froude, *History of England from the Fall of Wolsey to the Death of Elizabeth* (New York, 1865, 10 vols.), I, 294–316, and II, 205–11.

21. W. K. Jordan, *The Development of Religious Toleration in England* (Cambridge, Mass., 1932–40, 4 vols.), II, 43. Hughes, *Reformation in England,* II, 12, for the same period reported only twenty-seven burnings, relying on Foxe as his source, but Foxe rarely reported burnings of Anabaptists.

22. Foxe, *Acts and Monuments,* V, 704.

23. Hughes, *Reformation in England,* II, 105, 114, 128–9, 141, 150–9, 262.

24. John Strype, *Memorials of the Most Reverend Father in God Thomas Cranmer* (1694) (Oxford, 1840, 2 vols.), I, 255–7; Robert Wallace, *Antitrinitarian Biography* (London, 1850, 3 vols.), I, 6, and II, 122–4.

25. John Bruce, ed., *The Works of Roger Hutchinson* (Cambridge, 1842), ii-v; *D.N.B.,* II, 748–9; John Strype, *Ecclesiastical Memorials, Relating Chiefly to Religion . . .* (1721) (Oxford, 1822, 3 vols.), II, 335; Gilbert Burnet, *The History of the Reformation of the Church of England* (1680), rev. Nicholas Pocock (Oxford, 1865, 7 vols.), II, 203–4; for a copy of her sentence, see B. Evans, *The Early English Baptists* (London, 1862–4, 2 vols.), I, 242–3. On Anne Askew, see Foxe, *Acts and Monuments,* V, 536–50.

26. John Proctor, *The Fal of the Late Arrian* (1549), quoted by George T. Buckley, *Atheism in the English Renaissance* (Chicago, 1932), 56–7.

27. Stow, *Annales of the Reformation,* 605; Wallace, *Antitrinitarian Biography,* I, 12–14, and II, 124–7.

28. Hughes, *Reformation in England,* II, 255. Protestant accounts give 288 as the number burned and 419 to 739 when adding those who died in prison; see Evans, *Early English Baptists,* I, 119.

29. Hughes, *Reformation in England,* II, 259–62.

30. Foxe, *Acts and Monuments,* VI, 598, 602.

31. *Ibid.,* VIII, 45, 52, 59, 65, 69–71.

32. *Ibid.,* VII, 636; for Philpot's accusations of blasphemy, *ibid.,* 626, 634, 646, 648, 658, 664, 679, 680.

33. *Ibid.,* IV, 427, 442; VII, 47, 103, 355.

34. *Ibid.,* VII, 631.

35. *An Apology of John Philpot, Written for spitting on an Arian: With an Invective against the Arians,* reprinted in Strype, *Ecclesiastical Memorials,* III, 363–80; Foxe, *Acts and Monuments,* VII, 626.

36. On the Elizabethan Reformation, see A. G. Dickens, *The English Reformation* (New York, 1964); W. H. Frere, *The English Church in the Reigns of Elizabeth and James I* (London, 1904); Hughes, *Reformation in England,* III; J. B. Black, *The Reign of Elizabeth, 1558–1603* (Oxford, 1959, 2nd ed.); M. M. Knappen, *Tudor Puritanism* (Chicago, 1939); Oscar Meyer, *England and the Catholic Church under Elizabeth,* trans. J. R. McKee (London, 1916).

37. David Laing, ed., *The Works of John Knox* (Edinburgh, 1846–64, 6 vols.), V, 207–8, 222–4, *passim.*

38. *Ibid.,* 224–5.

39. *Ibid.,* 228.

40. *Ibid.,* 231.

41. Herbert John McLachlan, *Socinianism in Seventeenth Century England* (London, 1951), 31; *D. N. B.* on Nicholas, XIV, 426–31; Thomas Price, *A History of Protestant Nonconformity in England from the Reformation Under Henry VIII* (London, 1836–8, 2 vols.), I, 293; John Lingard, *History of England from the First Invasion by the Romans to 1688* (London, 1883, 10 vols.), VI, 344. The uncertain sixth case might be that of William Hacket, a wheelwright of Northamptonshire who, about 1601, claimed to be Jesus Christ. Hacket's apostles proclaimed him in the streets of London, causing a "great hurly burly in the City." Hacket was hanged in Cheapside "for his odious blasphemies against God, and high Treason against Queen Elizabeth," and two of his apostles died in jail. John Taylor, *Ranters of Both Sexes* (London, 1651), 6–7. No other source, primary or secondary, mentions the case.

42. Copies of the recantation are printed in Price, *History of Protestant Nonconformity,* I, 294, and Francis Blomefield, *An Essay Towards a Topographical History of the County of Norfolk* (London, 1805–10, 11 vols.), III, 292. The writs *de haeretico comburendo* are printed in Hughes, *Reformation in England,* III, 411–3. The fullest reports of the case are in Underhill, *Struggles and Triumphs,* 179–92, and Evans, *Early English Baptists,* I, 151–64.

43. Foxe's letter, in translation from the Latin, is in Price, *History of Protestant Nonconformity,* I, 294–5; for Elizabeth's opinion, Fuller, *Church History of Britain,* IV, 390.

44. All quotations are from Underhill, *Struggles and Triumphs,* 184, 189, 193.

45. On David Georg, whose Latin pen name was Joris, see Wallace, *Antitrinitarian Biography,* III, 544–51, and Sebastian Castellio, *Concerning Heretics,* trans. with intro. by Roland H. Bainton (New York, 1935), 305–9. On Vittel, see *D.N.B.,* XX, 375–6; on the Familists, see Bax, *Rise and Fall of the Anabaptists,* 338–66; Fuller, *Church History of Britain,* IV, 407–13; John Strype, *Annals of the Reformation and Establishment of Religion* (Oxford, 1824, 4 vols.), II, 282–9.

46. William Burton, *David's Evidence* (1590), 124–5.

47. Stow, *Annales of England* (1592), 1173–4.

48. Blomefield, *Topographical History of Norfolk,* III, 292–3; Wallace *Antitrinitarian Biography,* I, 37–8, and II, 366.

49. *D.N.B.,* IX, 74–5; Burton, *David's Evidence,* 125.

50. Alexander B. Grosart, *The Life and Works of Robert Greene* (New York, 1964 reprint), 259–60.

51. Burton, *David's Evidence*, 125.

52. "The Cases of Bartholomew Legatt and Edward Wightman," in *State Trials*, II, 727–42; Wallace, *Antitrinitarian Biography*, II, 530–4; *D.N.B.*, XI, 846–7.

53. Speech to Parliament, March 1609, in Charles H. McIlwain, ed., *The Political Works of James I* (Cambridge, Mass., 1918), 307.

54. *State Trials*, II, 727.

55. *Ibid.*, 734.

56. Archbishop Abbott to Lord Ellesmere, Jan. 21, 1612, and Jan. 22, 1612, in J. Payne Collier, ed., *The Egerton Papers* (Camden Society, 1840), 447, 448.

57. *State Trials*, II, 730.

58. Wallace, *Antitrinitarian Biography*, II, 534–9; *D.N.B.*, XXI, 195–6. See Mark 3:28–30.

59. For Neile's report, see "The Trendall Papers," Congregational History Society, *Transactions*, I (1902), 199–200.

60. *Ibid.; State Trials*, II, 735, 738.

61. "The Trendall Papers," I, 200.

62. *State Trials*, II, 731.

63. Edward Cardwell, ed., *The Reformation of the Ecclesiastical Laws as Attempted in the Reigns of King Henry VIII, King Edward VI and Queen Elizabeth* (Oxford, 1850), 28–9.

64. Bacon, "Of Atheism," quoted in Buckley, *Atheism in the English Renaissance*, 50.

65. Smith v. Martin (1632), in Samuel Rawson Gardiner, ed., *Reports of Cases in the Courts of Star Chamber and High Commission* (Westminster, 1886), 152.

7. Snatching the Socinian Palm

1. Wilbur K. Jordan, *The Development of Religious Toleration in England* (Cambridge, Mass., 1932–40, 4 vols.), II, 32.

2. For James on Arminius, James O. Halliwell, ed., *The Autobiography and Correspondence of Sir Simonds D'Ewes* (London, 1845, 2 vols.), I, 82. On Vorst, Charles R. Gillett, *Burned Books* (New York, 1932, 2 vols.), I, 98–101; Jordan, *Religious Toleration*, II, 31–2, 335–7.

3. Herbert John McLachlan, *Socinianism in Seventeenth Century England* (London, 1951), 36–7; Earl Morse Wilbur, *A History of Unitarianism* (Cambridge, Mass., 1946–52, 2 vols.), I, 411. The name "Unitarian" was first used in an English tract in 1673 and appeared in a title for the first time in 1687, by which time it was common. See Wilbur, *Unitarianism*, II, 199, 216; McLachlan, *Socinianism*, 294, 302, 310–3, 320.

4. On Socinianism as it emerged in the Racovian Catechism, see Wilbur, *Unitarianism*, I, chs. 29–32. On Baptism, see Thomas Crosby, *The History of the English Baptists* (London, 1738–9, 2 vols.), I, i–lxi, 1–139; Joseph Ivimey, *A History of the English Baptists* (London, 1811, 4 vols.), I, 1–126; W. T. Whitely, *A History of British Baptists* (London, 1932, 2nd ed.) 17–58.

5. Jordan, *Religious Toleration*, II, 32.

6. *Ibid.*, 35–6, 38, 148, 153; Whitely, *British Baptists*, 29.

7. Jordan, *Religious Toleration*, II, 262–6.

8. See *ibid.*, 258–314, for a review of early Baptist works on liberty of conscience. For the quote from Helwys, see *ibid.*, 283. Edward Bean Underhill, ed., *Tracts on Liberty of Conscience and Persecution, 1614–61* (London, 1846), 3–81, reprints Busher's work.

9. Murton's tract of 1615, *Objections Answered by Way of Dialogue,* is in Underhill, ed., *Tracts on Liberty of Conscience,* 85–180, as it was reprinted in 1620 and 1662 under the title, *Persecution for Religion Judg'd and Condemn'd.* For the references to blasphemy, see *ibid.*, 120–4.

10. On Laud, see Hugh R. Trevor-Roper, *Archbishop Laud, 1573–1645* (London, 1962, 2nd ed.), and Jordan, *Religious Toleration,* II, 129–65 *passim.* On Laud's period as primate, see also Samuel Rawson Gardiner, *History of England from the Accession of James I to the Outbreak of the Civil War, 1603–42* (London, 1883–4, 10 vols.), vols. 7–9.

11. "The Trendall Papers," Congregational Historical Society, *Transactions,* I (1902), 194–202.

12. Att.-Gen. v. Fisher (1596), in John Hawarde, *Les Reportes del Cases in Camera Stellata,* ed. William P. Baildon (London, 1894), 41–2; see also *ibid.*, 54, for Wheeler's case. Att.-Gen. v. Miles (1606), in *ibid.*, 301. Vicar's case (1631), in Samuel R. Gardiner, ed., *Reports of Cases in the Courts of Star Chamber and High Commission* (London, 1886), 232–4. No good scholarly book on the Star Chamber exists; the best primary source is William Hudson, *A Treatise of the Court of Star Chamber* (ca. 1635), in Francis Hargrave, ed., *Collectanea Juridica. Consisting of Tracts Relative to the Law and Constitution of England* (London, 1791–2, 2 vols.), I, 1–240.

13. Cawdrey's case (1591), with Coke's additions of 1605, in 5 Coke's Reports 8b, 9a, 40a, 40b. Attwood's case (1618), in Henry Rolle, *Abridgment des Plusieurs Cases et Resolutions del Common Ley* (1668), reprinted in Hargrave, ed., *Collectanea Juridica,* II, 78.

14. See Roland G. Usher, *The Rise and Fall of the High Commission* (Oxford, 1913), and Leonard W. Levy, *Origins of the Fifth Amendment* (New York, 1968), chs. 4–9.

15. Lane's case (1631), in Gardiner, ed., *Reports of Cases,* 188–94.

16. On Bastwick, see Jordan, *Religious Toleration,* II, 159, and III, 279–80; on Burton, *ibid.*, II, 253–4, and III, 358–61; on Prynne, *ibid.*, II, 210. On the trials, see Gardiner, *History of England,* VIII, 226–32; Gardiner, ed., *Documents Relating to the Proceedings against William Prynne, in 1634 and 1637* (London, 1877); William Prynne, *A New Discovery of the Prelates Tyranny* (1641), 33–60; *State Trials,* III, 711–70.

17. On the abortive canons of 1640, see Robert Wallace, *Antitrinitarian Biography* (London, 1850, 3 vols.), I, 65–8; on the mob of Brownists, Usher, *Rise and Fall of High Commission,* 333, and Gardiner, *History of England,* IX, 215.

18. Quotations from Steuart, Pagitt, and Bastwick are in Jordan, *Religious Toleration,* III, 274–81, *passim.*

19. Wallace, *Antitrinitarian Biography,* I, 69–70; *Journals of the House of Commons,* IV, 206, July 14, 1645 (hereafter cited as *Journals H.C.*), and *Journals of the House of Lords,* VI, 494, July 12, 1645.

20. On Best, see McLachlan, *Socinianism,* 149–62; Wilbur, *Unitarianism,* II, 322–7; Wallace, *Antitrinitarian Biography,* III, 161–7.

21. Alex F. Mitchell and John Struthers, eds., *Minutes of the Sessions of the*

Westminster Assembly of Divines (Edinburgh, 1874), 101; D. Laing, ed., *Letters and Journals of Robert Baillie* (Edinburgh, 1841–2, 3 vols.), II, 280.

22. *Minutes of Westminster Assembly,* 101–2, 114, 170, 175, 214; *Journals H.C.,* IV, 284, Sept. 24, 1645.

23. *Journals H.C.,* IV, 420, Jan. 28, 1646.

24. *Ibid.,* 493, March 28, 1646; *Minutes of Westminster Assembly,* 214.

25. *Journals H.C.,* IV, 500, April 4, 1646. On the five members and their views, see Jordan, *Religious Toleration,* III, 56, 329–31, 371–6.

26. Jordan, *Religious Toleration,* 278. *Ibid.,* 280; Wilbur Cortez Abbott, *The Writings and Speeches of Oliver Cromwell* (Cambridge, Mass., 1937–47, 4 vols.), I, 278; Thomas Carlyle, ed., *Oliver Cromwell's Letters and Speeches* (London, 1867, 2 vols.), I, 176; *Letters and Journals of Robert Baillie,* II, 280.

27. Thomas Edwards, *Gangraena or a catalogue and discovery of many of the errours, heresies, blasphemies and pernicious practices of the sectaries of this time, vented and acted in England in these four last years* (1646), part I, 1–39. On Edwards, see Jordan, *Religious Toleration,* III, 281–7. For the recorder of the Westminster Assembly, see *Letters and Journals of Robert Baillie,* II, 361.

28. *Journals H.C.,* IV, 506, 515, 518, 524, 527, 540, 556, 563, 586; V, 296. Paul Best, *A Letter of Advice unto the Ministers assembled at Westminster* (1646), 8. See also Jordan, *Religious Toleration,* III, 92, and McLachlan, *Socinianism,* 153 n. 6.

29. Best, *Mysteries Discovered* (London, 1647), 4 (misnumbered p. 1); "Heads of Proposals," Aug. 1, 1647, in Samuel Rawson Gardiner, ed., *The Constitutional Documents of the Puritan Revolution, 1625–1660* (Oxford, 1906), 321. See also Jordan, *Religious Toleration,* III, 95–104. On Selden, see John Towill Rutt, ed., *Diary of Thomas Burton* (London, 1828, 4 vols.), I, 65; on others quoted, see Edwards, *Gangraena,* part II, 22, 26–7, 123, and part III, 65.

30. Best, *Mysteries Discovered,* 4–5, 10–11, 14–15.

31. *Journals H.C.,* V, 257, July 24, 1647, and *ibid.,* 296, Sept. 8, 1647. McLachlan, *Socinianism,* 160–2; Joshua Toulmin, *A Review of the Life, Character and Writings of the Rev. John Biddle* (London, 1789), iii.

32. Carlyle, *Oliver Cromwell's Letters,* III, 63, for "conspicuous Heresiarch."

33. McLachlan, *Socinianism,* 169. The basic source on Biddle is [John Farrington], *A Short account of the life of John Bidle,* reprinted in English from the Latin edition of 1682, in *Unitarian Tracts* (London, 1691–1701, 5 vols.), I (1691). See also Anthony à Wood, *Athenae Oxonienaes, an Exact History of All the Writers and Bishops who Have Had Their Education in the University of Oxford,* ed. P. Bliss (Oxford, 1813–20), II, 330–2; Wilbur, *Unitarianism,* II, 192–208; McLachlan, *Socinianism,* 164–217; Wallace, *Antitrinitarian Biography,* III, 173–206.

34. Wood, *Athenae,* II, 331, on Usher's reaction. Biddle, *Twelve Arguments drawn out of the Scripture; Wherein the commonly-received Opinion touching the Deity of the Holy Spirit is clearly and fully refuted* (1647), vii–xiv, for the petition to Vane, April 1, 1647.

35. *Journals H.C.,* V, 184, May 26, 1647, and 293, 296, Sept. 6 and 8, 1647.

36. Gillett, *Burned Books,* I, 330; McLachlan, *Socinianism,* 176 n. 5;

Wilbur, *Unitarianism*, II, 196; Wallace, *Antitrinitarian Biography*, I, 111, and III, 158–61.

37. The statute is in C.H. Firth and R.S. Rait, *Acts and Ordinances of the Interregnum, 1642–1660* (London, 1911, 3 vols.), I, 1133–6; see also Jordan, *Religious Toleration*, III, 111–13.

38. On Baptist thought, see Jordan, *Religious Toleration*, III, 452–542. The tracts touching the problem of blasphemy are Samuel Richardson, *The Necessity of Toleration in Matters of Religion* (1647), reprinted in Underhill, ed., *Tracts on Liberty of Conscience*, 235–85; Richardson, *An answer to the London ministers letter* (1649); Henry Danvers, *Certain quaeries concerning liberty of conscience* (1649), and, anon., *A Short Discovery of his Highness the Lord Protector's Intentions* (1651), reprinted in Ivimey, *History of English Baptists*, I, 220–9.

39. *The Petition of Divers Gathered Churches, And others wel affected, in and about the City of London, for declaring the Ordinance of the Lords and Commons, for punishing Blasphemies and Heresies, Null and Void* (1651), 2–4.

40. McLachlan, *Socinianism*, 172, 178, 180. See also David Underdown, *Pride's Purge* (Oxford, 1971).

41. Toulmin, *A Review*, 74; Wood, *Athenae*, II, 301; McLachlan, *Socinianism*, 184.

42. Wood, *Athenae*, II, 360. On Fry, see McLachlan, *Socinianism*, 239–49; Gillett, *Burned Books*, 344-51; *D.N.B.*, VII, 737–8; Wallace, *Antitrinitarian Biography*, III, 206–10.

43. *Journals H.C.*, VI, 123, 125, 131.

44. John Fry, *The Accuser sham'd* (1649), 12, 14–16; McLachlan, *Socinianism*, 241–2.

45. On Cheynell, see *D.N.B.*, IV, 222–4; Wood, *Athenae*, II, 358–61; Gillett, *Burned Books*, I, 351–3; Wallace, *Antitrinitarian Biography*, I, 72–7.

46. Fry, *The Clergy in their Colours* (1650), 14–17, 28, 64.

47. *Journals H.C.*, VI, 536–7, 539–40, Feb. 20 and 22, 1651. Wood, *Athenae*, II, 361; *D.N.B.*, VII, 738.

48. Toulmin, *A Review*, 78–81; McLachlan, *Socinianism*, 185.

49. On Racow and the Racovian Catechism, see Wilbur, *Unitarianism*, II, 408–19, 449–55. *Journals H.C.*, VII, 113–14; Gillett, *Burned Books*, I, 354–5; McLachlan, *Socinianism*, 187–93.

50. Wilbur, *Unitarianism*, II, 204–5, for the Calvinist scholar and Owen; McLachlan, *Socinianism*, 197, for the London Presbyterian; Gillett, *Burned Books*, I, 355–6, for Poole.

51. Biddle, *The Apostolical and True Opinion concerning the Holy Trinity*.

52. Biddle, *A Twofold Catechism: The One simply called A Scripture-Catechism; The Other, a brief Scripture-Catechism for Children. Wherein the chiefest points of the Christian Religion, being Question-wise proposed, resolve themselves by pertinent Answers taken word for word out of the Scripture, without either Consequences or Comments. Composed for their sakes that would fain be meer Christians, and not of this or that Sect. . . .*, Preface, *passim*.

53. *Journals H.C.*, VII, 400, Dec. 12, 1654; *ibid.*, Dec. 13, 1654.

54. *Ibid.*, 416, Jan. 15, 1655.

55. On the licensing laws, see William K. Clyde, *The Struggle for the*

Freedom of the Press from Caxton to Cromwell (London, 1934), 187–8, 299, 314–18.

56. *Ibid.*, 225–9, 232–7, 314, 334–5.

57. Goodwin, *Fresh Discovery of the High Presbyterian Spirit* (1655), reprinted in *ibid.*, 328–37.

58. Toulmin, *A Review*, 117–19; David Masson, *The Life of John Milton* (London, 1859–94, 7 vols.), V, 14, 64. *A True State of the Case of Liberty of Conscience in the Common-wealth of England, Together with a true Narrative of the Cause, and Manner, of Mr. John Biddle's Sufferings* (1655), 2–3.

59. *The Spirit of Persecution Again broken loose, by An Attempt to put in Execution against Mr. John Biddle . . . an abrogated Ordinance . . . for punishing Blasphemies and Heresies. Together with, A full Narrative of the whole Proceedings upon that Ordinance against the said Mr. John Biddle . . .* (1655), 2–6.

60. *Ibid.*, 4–6.

61. *Ibid.*, 19–20; and *A True State*, cited above, note 58.

62. The Instrument of Government, quoted in *Spirit of Persecution*, 9, is reprinted in Gardiner, ed., *Constitutional Documents*, 416.

63. *Spirit of Persecution*, 6, 8–9.

64. *A True State*, 5–12; material quoted on p.10.

65. McLachlan, *Socinianism*, 210; Louise Fargo Brown, *The Political Activities of the Baptists and Fifth Monarchy Men in England during the Interregnum* (Washington, D.C., 1912), 90–1; Clyde, *Struggle for Freedom*, 255, and for Cromwell's order of Aug. 28, 1655, *ibid.*, 323–7. The Anabaptist tract is reprinted in Ivimey, *History of the English Baptists*, I, 220–9.

66. Toulmin, *A Review*, 120; McLachlan, *Socinianism*, 209; James Bradley Thayer, *A Preliminary Treatise on Evidence at the Common Law* (Boston, 1898), 75–80; James Fitzjames Stephen, *A History of the Criminal Law of England* (London, 1883, 3 vols.), I, 209–300.

67. *Publick Intelligencer*, Sept. 29, 1655; Masson, *Life of Milton*, V, 65–6; Wilbur, *Unitarianism*, II, 216–17; McLachlan, *Socinianism*, 209. On Firman, see Wallace, *Antitrinitarian Biography*, III, 372–89; *D.N.B.*, VII, 46–9.

68. Brown, *Baptists and Fifth Monarchy Men*, 91–2; Clyde, *Struggle for Freedom*, 255–6; McLachlan, *Socinianism*, 210.

69. Wilbur, *Unitarianism*, II, 206; Toulmin, *A Review*, 122–3.

70. Rutt, ed., *Diary of Thomas Burton*, III, 118; McLachlan, *Socinianism*, 210–7; Toulmin, *A Review*, 124–30; *A Short Account of the life of John Bidle*, 8–9.

8. Antinomianism Running Amok

1. Clarkson, *The Lost sheep found* (1660), 27. All seventeenth-century tracts cited here were published in London. A. L. Morton, *The World of the Ranters: Religious Radicalism in the English Revolution* (London, 1970), ch. 5, is the only study of Clarkson; ch. 4 is on the Ranters generally. Christopher Hill, *The World Turned Upside Down: Radical Ideas During the English Revolution* (New York, 1973), ch. 9, is the only other treatment of the Ranters. Norman Cohn, *The Pursuit of the Millennium: Revolutionary Millenarians and*

Mystical Anarchists of the Middle Ages (New York, 1970, rev. ed.), has a valuable appendix containing extracts from Ranter and anti-Ranter documents, pp.287-330. Robert Barclay, *The Inner Life of the Religious Societies of the Commonwealth* (London, 1876), appendix to ch. 5, includes abbreviated Ranter documents by Joseph Salmon and Jacob Bauthumley.

2. On the Diggers, see introduction, George H. Sabine, ed., *The Works of Gerrard Winstanley* (Ithaca, N.Y., 1941), and David W. Petegorsky, *Left-Wing Democracy in the English Civil War* (London, 1940), ch. 4. On Clarkson's tract of 1647, see Morton, *World of the Ranters*, 132, and Peter Zagorin, *A History of Political Thought in the English Revolution* (London, 1954), 31-2. For Cromwell, see Wilbur Cortez Abbott, *Writings and Speeches of Oliver Cromwell* (Cambridge, Mass., 1937-47, 4 vols.), III, 435. The Winstanley quotation is from *A New-Yeers Gift for the Parliament and the Armie* (1650), in Sabine, ed., *Works*, 389-90.

3. Gertrude Huehns, *Antinomianism in English History* (London, 1951), unfortunately dismissed the Ranters with a paragraph (p. 109), but is otherwise instructive. The Grindletonians, an obscure sect named after the place of their origin in Yorkshire, believed in universal grace, the indwelling Christ, and the possibility that sin does not exist for Christians; see Hill, *World Upside Down*, 65-8. The Behmenists, a similarly mystical sect, were named for the founder of their movement, Jacob Boehme; see Rufus M. Jones, *Spiritual Reformers in the 16th and 17th Centuries* (1914; Boston, 1959 reprint), which is mainly about Boehme and his English followers, including the Seekers, so named because they looked for the true church, found none, and joined none. On the Familists, see this book, Chapter 6, pp. 179-180. Unlike the Familists and Behmenists, the Seekers did not form a sect. Hill, *World Upside Down*, 148-58, treats the Seekers, as does Rufus M. Jones, *Studies in Mystical Religion* (London, 1909), 449-500, which includes, with little understanding, some references to Ranters.

4. Gilbert Roulston, *The Ranters Bible. Or, Seven Several Religions by them held and maintained* (1650), 1-6.

5. *Copps Return to the Wayes of Truth* (1651), First Errour, describes his upbringing; his account of his conversion is in his first *Fiery Flying Roll* (1649), Preface. For a similar account of a conversion, see George Foster, *The Sounding of the Last Trumpet* (1651), 1-10.

6. Anthony à Wood, *Athenae Oxoniensus* (London, 1721, 2nd ed., 3 vols.), II, 501. *Routing of the Ranters* (1650), 3; *The Ranters Ranting* (1650), 2.

7. *Fiery Flying Roll*, I, 1-5 passim, and, for the long quotation, 6-7.

8. *Ibid.*, 6-8.

9. *Ibid.*, II, 2-4, 13-15, 19. Sabine, *Works of Winstanley*, 262.

10. Cohn, *Pursuit of the Millennium*, and Jones, *Studies in Mystical Religion*, cover the Middle Ages. Jones, 428-48, is good on Familism and on p.445 quotes Ainsworth; on p.455, Murton. See also Barclay, *The Inner Life*, for background on religious mysticism and belief in the indwelling Christ, chs. 5, 9-10. Champlin Burrage, *Early English Dissenters* (Cambridge, 1912, 2 vols.), I, 212-4, reprints Jessop. Roulston, *Ranters Bible*, 2, describes Ranters as Familists. John Tickell wrote *The Bottomles Pit Smoaking in Familisme* (1651).

11. The 1644 quote is from Thomas Clarkson, *A Confutation of the Anabaptists* (1644), 4. Hill, *World Upside Down*, 81, quotes Case; Hill is best on the emergence of radical ideas, but he tends to exaggerate and selects evidence, sometimes out of context, to suit his political interpretation.

12. Edwards, *Gangraena: or a Catalogue and Discovery of many of the Errours, Heresies, Blasphemies and pernicious Practices of the Sectaries of this time* (1646), 116.

13. *Ibid.,* no. 32, p. 22; no. 11, p. 20; no. 77, p. 26; no. 165, p. 35; no. 176, p. 36.

14. *Ibid.,* no 13, p. 20 (quoting *The Bloudy Tenet of Persecution*) and no. 166, p. 35. *A Rout, A Rout* (1649), 1–11 *passim;* pp. 3, 4 and 11 for the quotations.

15. On the Ranter theme, see Coppe, *Fiery Flying Roll,* I, 10; Foster, *Last Trumpet,* 7–10, 14, 17–19; and Salmon, *A Rout,* 2–4. Morton, *World of the Ranters,* 84. The Leveller was Richard Overton, *The Hunting of the Foxes* (1649), reprinted in Don M. Wolfe, ed., *Leveller Manifestoes of the Puritan Revolution* (New York, 1944), 371.

16. Hill, *World Upside Down,* 47, 75, quotes Dell, and 31, Overton. The other Leveller quote is in Abbott, *Writings of Cromwell,* II, 69, and the royalist from G. P. Gooch, *English Democratic Ideas in the Seventeenth Century* (1898; New York, 1959 reprint), 167.

17. The seditious tract was *The Second Part of England's New Chaines* (1649), reprinted in William B. Haller and Godfrey Davies, eds., *The Leveller Tracts, 1647–1653* (New York, 1944), 177 ff. The third *Agreement* is in Wolfe, ed., *Leveller Manifestoes,* 397 ff. See also Pauline Gregg, *Free-born John: A Biography of John Lilburne* (London, 1961), 207–84, and H. N. Brailsford, *The Levellers and the English Revolution* (London, 1961), 481–522. Coppe, *Fiery Flying Roll,* I, 11.

18. Louise Fargo Brown, *The Political Activities of the Baptists and the Fifth Monarchy Men in England during the Interregnum* (Washington, D.C., 1912), 11–18, and B. S. Capp, *The Fifth Monarchy Men* (London, 1972), 14, 20-2, 50-8. The "Fifth Monarchy" was to be the successor of the four "beasts" or empires mentioned in Daniel's vision (Dan. 7:1–14), which millenarians of the seventeenth century construed as Babylon, Assyria, Greece, and Rome. The Fifth Monarchists of England expected the imminent Kingdom of Christ on earth and claimed the religious duty of taking up arms against Cromwell and Parliament in order to usher in the millennium.

19. Holland, *Smoke of the Bottomlesse Pit* (1651), 1–2; Bauthumley, *The Light and Dark Sides of God* (1650), 17; Edward Hide, *A Wonder Yet No Wonder* (1651), 36–7; Lodowick Muggleton, *The Acts of the Witnesses of the Spirit* (1699), reprinted in Joseph Frost and Isaac Frost, eds., *The Works of John Reeve and Lodowicke Muggleton* (London, 1832, 3 vols.), III, 56, where Muggleton said: "So that the Life of a Dog, Cat, Toad, or any venomous Beast, was the Life of God: Nay That God was in a Table, Chair, or Stool. This was the Ranters God, and they thought there was no better God at all." Muggleton, who had known Ranters personally and was briefly attracted to their movement at its outset, wrote *Acts of the Witnesses* in 1677. All books and tracts in *Works of Reeve and Muggleton* contain the pagination of the original editions or, in some instances, of their eighteenth-century reprints. The table of contents is detailed, making it easy to locate any item, despite the fact that the three volumes do not have continuous pagination or an index. See also Coppin, *Divine Teachings* (1649), 8–9; Coppe, *Fiery Flying Roll,* II, 18.

20. Clarkson, *Lost sheep,* 33.

21. Holland, *Smoke,* 3–5; J. M., *The Ranters Last Sermon* (1654), 4, 7;

Clarkson, *Lost sheep,* 28; Bauthumley, *Light and Dark Sides,* 28–31; *The Arraignment and Tryall with a Declaration of the Ranters* (1650), 4; *Routing of the Ranters,* 2.

22. "To the pure all things are pure" is from Titus 1:15, quoted by Coppe, *Fiery Flying Roll,* I, 8, and Clarkson, *A Single Eye* (1650), 10, and Clarkson, *Lost sheep,* 25. See also, Clarkson, *A Single Eye,* 7–9, 11, 15–6, and Clarkson, *Lost sheep,* 26–7; the long quotation is from M. Stubs, *The Ranters Declaration* (1650), 2; *Arraignment and Tryall,* 3; *The Ranters Religion* (1650), 5; *Ranters Bible,* 5; *Strange Newes from Newgate* (1651), 3–4; *Routing of the Ranters,* 4–5.

23. Clarkson, *Lost sheep,* 28; Pagitt, *Heresiography* (1654, 5th ed.), 144; *Strange Newes from Newgate,* 2–3; *Ranters Religion,* 8, also reported the travesty.

24. Clarkson, *Lost sheep,* 25; *Ranters Last Sermon,* 3.

25. Holland, *Smoke,* 4; *Routing of the Ranters,* 6; Winstanley, *A Vindication,* in Sabine, *Works,* 400–1; Bauthumley, *Light and Dark,* 26.

26. John Taylor, *Ranters of Both Sexes* (1651), 4. Sheppard's prologue to his *The Joviall Crew* (1651), opposite title page, is: "Bedlam broke loose? Hell is open'd too. / Mad-men & Fiends, & Harpies to your view / We do present: but who shall cure the Tumor? / All the world now is in the Ranting Humor." Hotham is quoted in *The Journal of George Fox,* ed. John T. Nickalls (Cambridge, 1952), 90. Salmon, *A Rout,* 1; Clarkson, *Lost sheep,* 24–5; Morton, *World of the Ranters,* 87, 112; Stubs, *Ranters Declaration,* 5–6.

27. Holland, *Smoke,* 1, used "atheistical," and Taylor, *Ranters of Both Sexes,* 1, "irreligious." Roulston, *Ranters Bible,* 4, used "Marcions," and "Gnosticks" appears in *Ranters Religion,* 4. *Reliquiae Baxterianae, or . . . Baxter's Narrative,* ed. M. Sylvester (London, 1696), 76–7; *The Journal of George Fox,* ed. Norman Penney (Cambridge, 1911, 2 vols.), I, 47.

28. Winstanley, *A Vindication,* in Sabine, *Works,* 399–403.

29. *Journals of the House of Commons,* VI, 354, Feb. 1, 1650 (hereafter *Journals H.C.*); *Journal of Fox,* ed. Penney, I, 47.

30. *Journal of Fox,* ed. Penney, I, 90; Salmon, *Heights in Depths* (1651), title page for the quotation; *Fiery Flying Roll,* II, 13, 14. Salmon clearly recanted, but *Heights in Depths,* 37–54, is unorthodox on God, heaven, hell, sin, and the Trinity.

31. *Heights in Depths,* p. A4 in Preface ("To the Reader"), and p. 52; Tickell, *Bottomles Pit,* 37–8.

32. *A Single Eye,* 14; *Journals H. C.,* VI, 427, June 21, 1650.

33. *Journals H. C.,* VI, 430 (June 21), 437 (July 5), 440 (July 12), 443–4 (July 19); "A Declaration of the Army," July 19, 1650, in Abbott, *Cromwell,* II, 286; on the Blasphemy Act of 1650, see above, pp. 244–45.

34. C. H. Firth and R. S. Rait, eds., *Acts and Ordinances of the Interregnum, 1642–1660* (London, 1911, 3 vols.), II, 409–12; *Journals H. C.,* VI, 453; Milton, "Of Civil Power," *The Works of John Milton,* ed. Frank Allen Patterson (New York, 1931–8, 18 vols.), VI, 11.

35. "An Act for Relief of Religious and Peaceable People," *"Acts and Ordinances of the Interregnum,* II, 423–5.

36. *Journals H. C.,* VI, 475, Sept. 27, 1650; Clarkson, *Lost sheep,* 30–1.

37. *Weekly Intelligencer,* Oct. 1–8, 1651, quoted in William M. Clyde, *Freedom of the Press from Caxton to Cromwell* (London, 1934), 206, and Morton, *World of the Ranters,* 103; *Routing of Ranters,* 2; *Journals H. C.,* VI,

475, Oct. 1, 1650. Coppe's book was reprinted in January 1650; the house ordered it burned in February; the committee examined him in September, more than six months after the offense.

38. *A remonstrance of the sincere and zealous Protestation of Abiezer Coppe* (1651); *Copps return to the wayes of Truth* (1651), 14, 19–21; Tickell, *Bottomles Pit,* 38.

39. Humphrey Ellis, *Pseudochristus; Or, A true and fanciful Relation of the Grand Impostures, Horrid Blasphemies, Abominable Practices* (1650), 33–8, 42–51.

40. Foster's *Sounding of the Last Trumpet* (1651) sounds like the work of an antinomian Seeker, not a Ranter. Cohn, *Pursuit of the Millennium,* 303, reported that Bauthumley's tongue was bored. I could not verify the fact from a primary source; Morton, *World of the Ranters,* 96, and Hill, *World Upside Down,* 176, retail the same incident. Samuel Rawson Gardiner, *History of the Commonwealth and Protectorate* (London, 1894–1901, 3 vols.), I, 396; Jones, *Studies in Mystical Religion,* 479 n. 2; and Morton, *World of the Ranters,* 104–5, describe the treatment of Ranters in the army. See also *Arraignment and Tryall,* 4; *The Ranters Recantation* (1650), 5; *Routing the Ranters,* 2–3; *Ranters Last Sermon,* 6–7; *Strange Newes from Newgate,* 6.

41. Stubs, *Ranters Declaration,* 4; John Cordy Jeafferson, ed., *Middlesex County Records* (London, 1886–92, 7 vols.), III, 204; *A List of some of the Grand Blasphemers and Blasphemies* (1654), broadsheet; *The Ranters Creed, Being a true copie of the Examination of a blasphemous lot of people called Ranters* (1651), 1–6; Taylor, *Ranters of Both Sexes,* 2–3.

42. *List of Grand Blasphemers,* broadsheet; *A Declaration of John Robins, the false prophet, by G. H., an Ear-witness* (1651), 1–6, which includes statements by Robins in which he exalted himself as the "third Adam" who was divinely inspired, but denied being God or immortal; *Ranters Creed,* 1–6; Taylor, *Ranters of Both Sexes,* 1–6, which alleged, in the subtitle and elsewhere, that Robins "doth Accuse himselfe to be the great God of Heaven." See also Lodowick Muggleton, *Acts of the Witnesses,* in Frost and Frost, *Works of Reeve and Muggleton,* III, 20–3, 45–8; the quotation is on p. 21.

43. Muggleton, *Acts of Witnesses,* in *Works,* III, 20, 42–5; Tany, *The Nations Right in Magna Charta discussed with the Thing called Parliament* (1651), and *Theaurau John his Aurora* (1651); *D.N.B.* on Tany, XIX, 363–4.

44. Norwood wrote the preface to Tany's *Theaurau John his Aurora.* See also *The Case and Trial of Capt. Robert Norwood* (1651), and *A Brief discourse made by Capt. Robert Norwood . . . upon an indictment . . . in Old Bayly* (1652); *List of Grand Blasphemers.* Norwood denied the charges of blasphemy and professed Christianity, yet he was anticlerical and said, "Verily I cannot but abhor the Doctrines and Principles of most Christians," which he condemned as "Doctrines of devils." He embraced antinomianism, and declared we sin "by oppression, by injustice, and by deceit . . ." *Case and Trial,* 7, 13, 15, and 17.

45. Herbert John McLachlan, *Socinianism in Seventeenth Century England* (London, 1951), 226–37, is good on Erbury; see also Hill, *World Upside Down,* 154–9. The primary source is *The Testimony of William Erbury* (1658), which includes his encounter with Cheynell and his denunciation of the Ranters, 3–18, 315–37. On Walker, see *Middlesex County Records,* III, 215, May 25, 1653.

46. *The Works of Reeve and Muggleton* contains books, pamphlets, and let-

ters. Alexander Gordon, who did the *D.N.B.* essay on Muggleton (and on Reeve, Coppe, Tany, and Robins), published two lectures which constitute all the scholarship on Muggletonianism: *The Origin of the Muggletonians: A Paper read before the Liverpool Literary and Historical Society, April 5, 1869* (n.p., n.d.), and *Ancient and Modern Muggletonians,* read before the same society a year later. The only other writings on the subject are James Hyde, "The Muggletonians and the Document of 1729," *New-Church Review,* VII (1900), 215-27, and George Charles Williamson, *Lodowick Muggleton. A Paper Read before Ye Sette of Odd Volumes* (London, 1919), which derives wholly from Gordon.

47. T. B. Macaulay, *The History of England, from the Accession of James II* (London, 1849-65, 5 vols.), I, 164.

48. Muggleton, *Acts of Witnesses,* in *Works,* III, 38-9.

49. *Ibid.,* 47-8. The Reeve quotation is from his *A Transcendent Spiritual Treatise* (1652), in *ibid.,* I, 1-2, reprinting the 2nd ed. of 1756. My description of the Reeve-Muggleton theology is from this work.

50. The trial of 1653 is reported in *Works,* III, 67-78; *A Remonstrance,* in *Works,* I, 15-22.

51. *Journal of Fox,* 182, 195; Morton, *World of the Ranters,* 97, 138; Hill, *World Upside Down,* 176; Forneworth, *Ranter Principles and Deceits Discovered,* 19; Hickcock's *Testimony against the People call'd Ranters,* 2-4. Fox referred to "Ranters" as late as 1668, *Journal,* ed. Nickalls, 622, but he meant rude, disruptive people, a standard by which Fox and all Quakers of the 1650s were Ranters (see next chapter).

52. On Coppin, see *D.N.B.,* IV, 1117-8. For his earlier beliefs on the indwelling God, see *Divine Teachings,* 8-9. His *Truth's Testimony* (1654), 25, reports his rejection of Ranters; that tract describes his later beliefs and five blasphemy prosecutions in which he ably defended himself.

53. Kelsey to Cromwell, 1653, in T. Birch ed., *A Collection of State Papers of John Thurloe* (London, 1742, 7 vols.), IV, 486.

54. Historical Manuscripts Commission, *Report on Manuscripts in Various Collections* (London, 1901), I, 132-3.

55. Kelsey in *Thurloe Papers,* IV, 486. *Mercurius Politicus,* June 26-July 3, 1656, reported the case of Jock of Broad Scotland, reprinted in David Masson, *The Life of John Milton* (London, 1859-94, 7 vols.), V, 92-4.

9. The Quakers Ungod God

1. *The Journal of George Fox,* ed. Norman Penney (Cambridge, 1911, 2 vols.), I, 249-50. This edition is the unexpurgated text, *verbatim* and *literatim.* But this edition and *The Short Journal and Itinerary Journals of George Fox,* ed. Norman Penney (Cambridge, 1925), are extremely difficult to read if only because Fox's style and eccentricities in spelling compound the problems presented by seventeenth-century orthography. *The Journal of George Fox,* ed. John T. Nickalls (Cambridge, 1952), presents in modern English most but not all of the 1911 *Journal* with valuable additions from the 1925 *Short Journal.* As a convenience to the reader I have used, whenever possible, Nickall's 1952 edition and cited it as *Journal* (1952). On occasion the earlier, definitive editions by Penney, which contain invaluable scholarly notes, must be used.

2. Burrough's remarks are from his introduction to Fox, *The Great Mistery*

of the Great Whore Unfolded (1659), reprinted in *The Works of George Fox* (Philadelphia, 1831, 3 vols.), III, 14, and Burrough, *A Word of Reproof* (1659), quoted in Christopher Hill, *The World Turned Upside Down* (New York, 1973), 197. Hill's eagerness to turn the early Quakers into "political radicals" (p. 195), turns the matter upside down; they were nonpolitical and wholly religious. Dewsbury's statement of 1665 is in William C. Braithwaite, *The Beginnings of Early Quakerism* (London, 1912), 280. Braithwaite's is the classic treatment for the period to 1660. Hugh Barbour, *The Quakers in Puritan England* (New Haven, 1964), is the only modern monograph that adds anything of value to Braithwaite.

3. *Journal* (1952), 14, 27, 68. On lamenting the army's failure, see Mabel Richmond Brailsford, *A Quaker from Cromwell's Army: James Nayler* (London, 1927), 24. Nayler's *Lamb's War Against the Man of Sin* (1657) is in his *A Collection of Sundry Books, Epistles and Papers,* ed. George Whitehead (London, 1716), 375–400.

4. *Journal* (1952), 182, 244–5; Braithwaite, *Beginnings,* 195, 446.

5. *Journal* (1952), 36, 92, 242–9; *Journal,* ed. Penney (1911), I, 217–9. Braithwaite, *Beginnings,* 486–99.

6. Barbour, *Quakers,* 257–8, quotes Audland; Braithwaite, *Beginnings,* 136, and on the woman, 199. For the Fox quote, Braithwaite, *Beginnings* 451; *Journal* (1952), 280, gives a variant quotation.

7. *Journal* (1952), 24, 39–40, 51; Braithwaite, *Beginnings,* 444–5.

8. *Journal* (1952), 35. Barbour, *Quakers,* 211, gives the quotations from E. Burrough and George Bishop; his ch. 8 on persecution of Quakers and their theory of toleration is very good.

9. *Journal* (1952), 7, 8, 11, 19–20; Barbour, *Quakers,* 154–7.

10. On Fox's railing as love, see *Journal,* ed. Penney (1911), I, 90–2, 116. For the first Baxter quote, Braithwaite, *Beginnings,* 284; the second, *Reliquae Baxterianae* (London, 1696), 77. On vituperative conduct, see Braithwaite, *Beginnings,* ch. 12.

11. Proclamation of 1655, reprinted in Samuel R. Gardiner, *History of the Commonwealth and Protectorate* (London, 1903, 4 vols.), III, 260–1.

12. *Reliquae Baxterianae, 77; Journal,* ed. Penney (1911), I, 89; *Journal* (1952), 15, 18, 27. On going naked for a sign, see Braithwaite, *Beginnings,* 148–51.

13. On the name "Quaker," *Journal,* ed. Penney (1911), I, 5–9; II, 395; Barclay, *Apology,* proposition xi, sect. 8 of any edition; I used the 8th ed. (Providence, 1940), 359; Braithwaite, *Beginnings,* 57. For the quote of Nayler, see James Gough, *Memoirs* (Dublin, 1781), 56.

14. *Journal* (1952), 8, 10–28.

15. *Diary of Thomas Burton,* ed. John Towill Rutt (London, 1828, 4 vols.), I, 62 (hereafter cited as *Diary of Burton*). On the social backgrounds of the early Quakers and their geographic strengths, see Barbour, *Quakerism,* ch. 3. On religious precursors, see generally Rufus M. Jones, *Spiritual Reformers of the 16th and 17th Centuries* (1914; Boston, 1959 reprint); Rufus M. Jones, *Studies in Mystical Religion* (London, 1909); Robert Barclay, *The Inner Life of the Religious Societies of the Commonwealth* (London, 1876), chs. 5, 9–10. See also my note 3 to ch. 8, above.

16. *Journal,* ed. Penney (1911), I, 2; *Journal* (1952), 51–2.

17. For Fox on the Ranters, *Journal* (1952), 47, 81, 181–3, 195. For the

tract of 1652 and More's statement, see Braithwaite, *Beginnings,* 40, 58. G. H., *The Declaration of John Robins* (London, 1651), I, 6, identified Ranters as Shakers; J. M. (a former Ranter), *The Ranters Last Sermon* (London, 1654), 6, referred to "Ranters, Quakers, Shakers, and the rest of their atheistical crew." See also *The Ranters Creed* (1651), 6. R. Forneworth, *The Ranters Principles* (London, 1654), a Quaker tráct censuring Ranters was written to distinguish Quakers from Ranters. On Hotham, *Journal* (1952), 75, 90, and on the identification of Hotham, *Short Journal,* ed. Penney (1925), 277. Dr. Robert Gell made a similar statement to William Penn about the Quakers' having prevented England from being overrun by the Ranters; see Jones, *Studies in Mystical Religion,* 481. The "leveller" remark, and many like it, is in *Diary of Burton,* I, 169. On the grand jury, Hill, *World Upside Down,* 192; Hill, 195, calls the Quakers "political radicals" to make them fit his ideological straitjacket.

18. *Journal* (1952), 61.

19. Braithwaite, *Beginnings,* 6; *Journal* (1952), 73, 100–1; Brailsford, *Quaker from Cromwell's Army,* 38–9, 41–2, 46–8, 67. Nayler, *A Collection of Sundry Books,* 12, for his "call."

20. *Reliquae Baxterianae,* 76; Braithwaite, *Beginnings,* 241; Alexander Gordon, on Nayler, *D.N.B.,* XIV, 133.

21. *Journal* (1952), 129–30; on Fell, see Braithwaite, *Beginnings,* 105–6. See Barbour, *Quakers,* 148, for Nayler on Fox and Fox's reply to a judge.

22. On Fox's blasphemy case of 1652, see *Journal* (1952), 129–39. On "Sonne of God," see *Short Journal,* ed. Penney (1925), xx, 5, 17, 479 n. 2. On "My Father and I are one," *Journal,* ed. Penney (1911), I, 66, and for Penney's comment, I, 425.

23. *Journal* (1952), 132–9; *Journal,* ed. Penney (1911), I, 62–7; on the petition, *Short Journal,* ed. Penney (1925), 283–4; Braithwaite, *Beginnings,* 108–9, and especially Fox, *Works (The Great Mystery),* III, 585–97.

24. Nayler, *Diverse Particulars of the Persecutions of James Nayler, by the Priests of Westmorland* (1652), reprinted in *A Collection of Sundry Books, Epistles and Papers Written by James Nayler,* 1–10.

25. *The Examination of James Nayler, upon an Indictment for Blasphemy, at the Sessions at Appleby,* in *ibid.,* 11–16. On Pearson, see Brailsford, *Quaker from Cromwell's Army,* 28–9, and Braithwaite, *Beginnings,* 112–13.

26. *Journal* (1952), 158–9; *Short Journal,* ed. Penney (1925), 32–3.

27. *Journal* (1952), 160.

28. *Ibid.,* 160–4. On Cromwell and the Quakers, see W. K. Jordan, *The Development of Religious Toleration in England (1640–1660),* III, 176–9, and Braithwaite, *Beginnings,* ch. 17 on Quaker "Relations with the State." On the Nominated Parliament of 1653, see Gardiner, *Commonwealth and Protectorate,* II, 272–92.

29. *Journal* (1952), 233. Brailsford, *Quaker from Cromwell's Army,* 85–9; Braithwaite, *Beginnings,* 170–200; Emilia Fogelklou, *James Nayler* (London, 1931), 131–7.

30. Brailsford, *Quaker from Cromwell's Army,* 76; Braithwaite, *Beginnings,* 172–3, 178–80, 446; Gardiner, *Commonwealth and Protectorate,* III, 263. For Fox's account, *Journal* (1952), 191–9.

31. *Journal* (1952), 242–66.

32. *Ibid.,* 267–9; Braithwaite, *Beginnings,* 245–8; Brailsford, *Quaker from Cromwell's Army;* 93–100, which on p. 97 includes the Fox letter on "unclean

spirits." For an eyewitness account of the Fox–Nayler schism at Exeter, see Hubberthorne's letter reprinted in Fogelklou, *James Nayler,* 164–7.

33. James Deacon, *The grand Impostor examined, Or, the Life, Trial, and Examination of James Nayler* (1656), reprinted in Howell's *State Trials,* V, 826–42, of which pp. 830–2 includes some of the letters to Nayler. Deacon was an interrogator at the Bristol examination. In addition to his account, other eyewitness reports are Ra[lph] Farmer, *Sathan Inthron'd in his Chair of Pestilence* (1657) and William Grigge, *The Quakers Jesus* (1658). Grigge took the shorthand notes of the Bristol interrogation, *ibid.,* Epistle, answer 2. Farmer's *Sathan Inthron'd,* 4–10, includes a good selection of the letters. Another valuable primary source is Anon., *A True Narrative of the Examination, Tryall, and Sufferings of James Nayler* (1657). Anon, *Memoirs of the Life, Ministry, Tryal and Sufferings of that Very Eminent Person James Nailer, the Quaker's Great Apostle* (1729), is a later collection of the documents of the case, but unique because the long preface is favorable to Nayler and the documents are studded with notes pointing out distortions in the presentation of evidence against him; the author also reprinted some eloquent letters by Nayler on his religious beliefs (*ibid.,* pp. 71–80).

34. On the Dorcas Erbury incident, see Deacon, *Grand Impostor,* in *State Trials,* V, 834, 837. Henry J. Cadbury, *Fox's Book of Miracles* (Cambridge, 1948), is best on "miraculous" cures by Quaker preachers. There are some one hundred fifty entries on cures attributed to Fox; on Howgill and the lame boy, *ibid.,* 12. See also Braithwaite, *Beginnings,* 247, 341. Fox's letter is in Farmer, *Sathan Inthron'd,* 9–10.

35. Most of the primary sources mentioned in note 33 above include accounts of the entry into Bristol. Fogelklou, *James Nayler,* 157–73, contains an excellent account of the Fox–Nayler schism and its effect upon Nayler. See also Brailsford, *Quaker from Cromwell's Army,* 116–18. On Fox's recommendations to the Bristol Quakers, see his *Journal* (1952), 281–2.

36. The primary sources for the Bristol examination are referred to in note 33 above. "Proceedings in the House of Commons against James Nayler for Blasphemy and Misdemeanours," *State Trials,* V, 801–20, of which p. 806 refers to Nayler's resemblance to Jesus. On the same point, see Grigge, *Quakers Jesus,* 68–9, and Farmer, *Sathan Inthron'd,* 25–7. *A True Narrative,* 1–28, reproduces the complete record of the parliamentary committee's interrogations and report. For judgments that Nayler was mad, see the account by David Hume, quoted in *ibid.,* V, 804; David Masson, *The Life of John Milton* (London, 1859–94, 7 vols.), V, 68; Thomas Carlyle, *Oliver Cromwell's Letters and Speeches* (London, 1904, 3 vols.), III, 213; Barclay, *The Inner Life,* 427; Charles H. Firth, *The Last Years of the Protectorate* (London, 1909, 2 vols.), I, 96; Jordan, *Religious Toleration (1640–1660),* III, 221, 223, 226; Theodore A. Wilson and Frank J. Merli, "Nayler's Case and the Dilemma of the Protectorate," University of Birmingham *Historical Journal,* X (1965–6), 46, 47; and, to a lesser extent, Fogelklou, *James Nayler,* 163, 172, 176, 179–80.

37. The Bristol examinations are reprinted in Grigge, *Quakers Jesus,* 4–6. Barbour, *Quakers,* 185, quotes the Fell letter in the context of the prevailing Quaker apocalyptic view.

38. Deacon, *Grand Imposter,* in *State Trials,* V, 832, 834. For a variant report of the same interrogation, see Grigge, *Quakers Jesus,* 7.

39. *State Trials,* V, 834. The woman supposedly called "mother" was Mar-

tha Symonds; for her examination, *ibid.*, 835–6. On her, see Fogelklou, *James Nayler,* 151–5; Farmer, *Sathan Inthron'd,* 9–10, for Fox's letter to Nayler about her.

40. For the Bristol examinations of Nayler's companions, see Deacon, *Grand Imposter,* in *State Trials,* V, 833–8.

41. *Journals of the House of Commons,* VII, 448, Oct. 31, 1656 (hereafter *Journals H.C.*); *State Trials,* V, 805.

42. *State Trials,* V, 805–15; *Journals H. C.,* VII, 448.

43. The Instrument of Government is reprinted in S. R. Gardiner, ed., *Constitutional Documents of the Puritan Revolution* (London, 1906, 3rd ed.), 405–17; the religion clauses, 416. My summary of the religious policy of the Protectorate is from Jordan, *Religious Toleration,* III, 144–202.

44. Jordan, *Religious Toleration,* III, 164–5; *ibid.,* 450–1, on the growth of Congregationalism.

45. *Ibid.,* 156–8; for the quote from the ambassador, 171.

46. *Journals H. C.,* VII, 399; Jordan, *Religious Toleration,* III, 166, 170.

47. Firth, *Last Years,* I, 11–21; Jordan, *Religious Toleration,* III, 188–90. The constitution of 1657 was "The Humble Petition and Advice," reprinted in Gardiner, ed., *Constitutional Documents;* see 454–5, for the religious clause. For the political situation leading to the new constitution, see Firth, *Last Years,* I, 128–200.

48. Carlyle, *Cromwell's Speeches and Letters,* III, 213.

49. Rex v. Taylor, 3 Keble 607 (1676), and 1 Ventris 293 (1676).

50. Instrument of Government, in Gardiner, ed., *Constitutional Documents,* 405–17. *Diary of Burton,* I, 29, 112, 118, 123, 141.

51. *Diary of Burton,* I, 25, 59, 68, 88, 90, 97. On the no-law theme, *ibid.,* 38, 57–8, 87, 120–1, 125, 128, 152, 163, 174; on the omnipotence of Parliament, 58, 108, 125; for Howard, 78; for Sydenham, 86; for Strickland, 88, and see also Wolsey, 89; for Kelsey, 164. Some claimed that the jurisdiction of the defunct ecclesiastical courts devolved upon Parliament, 35, 108, 125, 141–2.

52. On vindicating the honor of God and blasphemy as treason against God, *ibid.,* 25–6, 39, 48, 51, 55, 59–60, 63, 68, 86, 89, 96, 109, 114, 122, 125, 132, 139, 150. On merciful, 90; on Richard Cromwell, 126.

53. *Ibid.,* 62–3.

54. *Ibid.,* 25, 49–50, 63, 107. On Skippon, see Firth, *Last Years,* I, 86, 92.

55. For examples of biblical speeches by major generals, see *Diary of Burton,* I, 99–100 (Packer), 101–4 (Walley), 108–10 (Goffe), 113–14 (Boteler), 122–4 (Kelsey). A note showing all references to the Bible during the course of the debates would have to read *ibid.,* 25–150 *passim.* On Smith, *ibid.,* 87, and Masson, *Life of Milton,* V, 92.

56. *Diary of Burton,* I, 170, 173, 174; Grigge, *Quakers Jesus,* 35.

57. *Diary of Burton,* I, 98, 97, 108–9, 86, 124, 146, 169, in the sequence for the quotations in my text. For other anti-Quaker remarks, see pp. 70, 76, 128, 132, 137 ("they will level the foundations of all government"), and 170. Farmer, *Sathan Inthron'd,* 28, called Quakerism a "medly of Popery, Socinianism, Arianisme, Arminianisme, Anabaptisme, and all that is nought."

58. For statements sympathetic to Quakers, see *Diary of Burton,* 56, 62–3, 65, 69, 86, 88, 99, 120; for Baynes, White, and Goffe, 59, 60, 110.

59. *Ibid.,* 88, 120.

60. *Ibid.,* 33.

61. *Ibid.,* 46–8. Burton's prejudice shows even in the reporting of the debate. In addition to his omission of Nayler's orthodox answers and his stating that Nayler had confessed, Burton omitted a tolerationist speech with the comment that the member, Walter Waller, "said a good deal more to extenuate the crime but I minded it not" (p. 152). At another point Burton gave a few terse lines to several tolerationist speeches, saying it was too dark to take notes, but still later that night he gave ample space to a "very large and handsome speech" by Bampfield against "the merciful men," in which Bampfield advocated death (pp. 90–92). The fullest analysis of the debate by a historian is Jordan, *Religious Toleration,* III, 221–43. Jordan's four volumes are in many respects invaluable and definitive, but he was wholly uninterested in the subject of blasphemy and never treated it as a special problem. To Jordan, blasphemy was merely an aspect of heresy, although he never distinguished the two. He reported the opinions of an extraordinary range of people and sects on toleration, but omitted Quaker opinions. His account of Nayler's case was unreliable and ununderstanding. He simplistically identified the revengers as the Presbyterians, never mentioning Congregationalists and Independents, without whom the revengers would not have been a political force. Jordan gave the impression that the government stood for toleration against the dominant Presbyterian party in Parliament. The government, in fact, was divided, as were Oliver and Richard Cromwell. The protector, having taken no position during the debate, offered no leadership; his councillors who sat in Parliament represented every viewpoint on every question during the Nayler debate. Jordan declared that the Nayler case was of great importance to the development of religious toleration, but without understanding early Quakerism and the differences between heresy and blasphemy, he could not understand the reasons. He regarded Nayler as "obviously mad," "obviously demented," and "plainly unbalanced," and said that he had "messianic delusions." He also said that Nayler had been worshipped "as" the Lamb, rather than that the worship had been directed to the Lamb in Nayler. The distinction is crucial. Jordan declared that Nayler offended "all religious men," yet some who defended him were not offended. More to the point, Nayler himself was a devout Christian, as religious as any member of Parliament, and so were his followers. Jordan saw Nayler as an undoubted blasphemer and claimed that his blasphemy was "universally admitted." Yet many of Nayler's defenders in Parliament denied that he was guilty of blasphemy. Like Burton, Jordan thought that Nayler was "determined to hang himself. He confessed to all the committee's charges against him. . . ." Jordan stated that insanity was not a defense to the charge of blasphemy; but Nayler did not plead insanity; it *was* a defense under the act of 1650, and it was a defense even in Scotland where the Presbyterians were in complete control. The Scottish Act against Blasphemy of 1661 exempted anyone "distracted in his wits" (Baron David Hume, *Commentaries on the Law of Scotland, respecting the Description and Punishment of Crimes* [Edinburgh, 1797, 2 vols.], II, 514). Without considering the cursing of God or atheistic denial and contempt of God, Jordan declared that "no severer test for the principle of religious toleration could have been devised by a satanic mind." Such a statement, from a specialist on toleration, was exaggerated as well as wrong. Firth, *Last Years,* I, 83–106, treats the Nayler case without glaring error; Firth was not interested in the subject of blasphemy. Braithwaite, *Beginnings,* 241–78, has a fascinating account of the Nayler case within the context of early Quaker thought; Braith-

waite too was uninterested in blasphemy as a problem for religious toleration or as a legal or religious concept. He cared about the Quaker mind and the impact of the case on subsequent Quaker behavior and development. The two biographers of Nayler, Brailsford and Fogelklou, stressed colorful details, such as the entrance into Bristol and the execution of the punishment, but they were innocent of any concern for procedure, jurisdiction, or the substantive offense.

62. *Diary of Burton,* I, 53, 79.

63. *Ibid.,* 118–19; see also p.123.

64. *Ibid., 56,* 59–61.

65. *Ibid.,* 128–31, much of which consists of notes by Rutt, the editor of the *Diary of Burton,* from *State Trials.* Whitelocke's speech of Dec. 12 is fully reported there, V, 821–8.

66. *Diary of Burton,* I, 47, 65.

67. *Ibid.,* 66–8, 74, 101–4, 124, 132, 151, 164, for the revengers; for Cooper and Packer, 96–7, 99–101.

68. *Journals H. C.,* VII, 468–9, Dec. 16, 1656; *Diary of Burton,* I, 152–8. Both sources include the vote and the sentence, but Burton provided additional detail on the debate concerning the lesser sentence. *The Diary of Burton,* pp. 161–3, also includes the debate giving the rationale for Parliament's choosing to act judicially rather than legislatively. Boring through the tongue with a hot iron, however cruel, was a humane refinement of the ancient punishment of cutting the tongue off. See John Godolphin, *Reportorium Canonicum; or An Abridgment of the Ecclesiastical Laws of this Realm* (London, 1678), 559. During the Nayler debate a Major Audley said that boring through the tongue "is an ordinary punishment for swearing [profanity], I have known twenty bored through the tongue" (*Diary of Burton,* I, 154).

69. *Diary of Burton,* I, 163, 167, 246.

70. *Ibid.,* 38, 137, 247. For the lashing scene, see *A True Narrative of the . . . Sufferings of James Nayler,* 34–8, written before Nayler underwent the last third of his punishment in Bristol. See also "The Testimony of Rebecca Travers," in *Memoirs of the Life, Ministry, Tryal and Sufferings,* 58–9.

71. *Diary of Burton,* I, 167–73; *Journals H. C.,* VII, 470, Dec. 18, 1656. On the toleration issue and the constitution of 1657, see above, text for note 47 of this chapter.

72. *Diary of Burton,* I, 182–3, 217–21; *State Papers Domestic, Commonwealth and Protectorate,* CXXXI, 1656, Dec. 20, No. 45; *Journals H. C.,* VII, 471; *True Narrative,* 49–56, includes the petitions of the one hundred to Parliament and to Cromwell, prefaced by a plea for religious liberty for Nayler and all Quakers. A copy of the petition to Cromwell, endorsed by him on Dec. 25, 1656, is reprinted in Norman Penney, *Extracts from State Papers Relating to Friends, 1654 to 1672* (London, 1913), 21–3, bearing eighty-eight signatures, including: Joshua Sprigge, a former New Model Army chaplain; Giles Calvert, the printer of Ranter, Leveller, and Quaker tracts; and Edward Bushell, one of the minor heroes in the history of English liberty. In 1670 Bushell was the foreman of the jury that refused, against fierce judicial browbeating, to return a verdict of guilty in the trial of Penn and Mead for inciting a riot—practicing their religion in violation of the act against conventicles. Bushell and his jury were fined, refused to pay, and were sent to jail where they stayed some months before a higher court ruled in favor of the right of the jury to return an honest verdict. See William S. Holdsworth, *A History of English Law* (London, 1938–66, 16 vols., 6th ed., rev.), I, 344–6.

73. *Journal*, ed. Penney (1911), I, 266; *True Narrative*, 55; *Diary of Burton*, I, 217–18, 263; Grigge, *Quakers Jesus*, 16–18.

74. *Diary of Burton*, I, 265–6; *True Narrative*, 42, for the size and behavior of the crowd and for Rich's conduct at the branding.

75. Grigge, *Quakers Jesus*, 19–22.

76. On Nayler's change of attitude, see his "Confessions" written from Bridewell prison, 1658, in Whitehead's introduction to Nayler's *A Collection*, xxv–xxxix; the words quoted are in *ibid.*, xxxv.

10. Christianity Becomes the Law of the Land

1. For general background, see David Ogg, *England in the Reign of Charles II* (Oxford, 1955, 2 vols., rev. ed.), which is superficial on religion and law; Sir George Clark, *The Later Stuarts* (Oxford, 1956, 2nd ed.).

2. A. A. Seaton, *The Theory of Toleration under the Later Stuarts* (1910; New York, 1972 reprint), is excellent; H. F. Russell-Smith, *The Theory of Religious Liberty in the Reigns of Charles II and James II* (Cambridge, 1911), is inferior.

3. Charles's Declaration of Breda, April 4, 1660, reprinted in Henry Gee and W. J. Hardy, eds., *Documents Illustrative of English Church History* (London, 1896), 585–8. For Charles to the Quakers, Clark, *Later Stuarts*, 20. On the Quaker Act, William C. Braithwaite, *The Second Period of Quakerism* (London, 1919), 22–5.

4. On the various statutes, see Gee and Hardy, *Documents*, 594–640, or C. Grant Robertson, ed., *Select Statutes, Cases and Documents to Illustrate English Constitutional History, 1660–1832* (London, 1904), 10–42. The Conventicles Act of 1664 was renewed and made permanent in 1670. For statistics, Clark, *Later Stuarts*, 27.

5. On the state of the Anglican church during the Puritan supremacy, see R. S. Bosher, *The Making of the Restoration Settlement: The Influence of the Laudians, 1649–1662* (New York, 1951), esp. 5–18; William Arthur Shaw, *A History of the English Church During the Civil Wars, 1640–1660* (London, 1900, 2 vols.), an unsympathetic account; William Holden Hutton, *The English Church from the Accession of Charles I to the Death of Queen Anne* (London, 1903), 122–78. On Quakers, see Braithwaite, *Second Period*, 109–15, which includes the estimate that five thousand of the sixty thousand who were imprisoned died in prison. Daniel Defoe, in his introduction to Thomas Delaune, *A Plea for Nonconformists* (London, 1706, 7th ed.), estimated eight thousand. William Penn, *Good Advice* (London, 1687), stated that "more than five thousand persons died under bonds for matters of mere conscience to God" since 1660, in *The Select Works of William Penn* (London, 1825, 3 vols., no ed.), II, 585. The estimates of the number who died in prison seem inflated because a disproportionate number of Quakers were imprisoned, yet only about four hundred fifty Quakers died in prison, when Quakers were about 17 percent of the Protestant dissenter population. Gerald R. Cragg, *Puritanism in the Period of the Great Persecution, 1660–88* (Cambridge, 1957), gives no statistics, but see ch. 2 on "The Pattern of Persecution" and ch. 4 on jail conditions. See also Daniel Neal, *The History of the Puritans, or Protestant Nonconformists* (London, 1822, 5 vols., rev. ed.), V, 19–20. For Baxter, *Reliquae Baxterianae*, ed. M. Sylvester (London, 1696), pt. II, 436.

6. Charles's Declaration of Indulgence is reprinted in Robertson, ed., *Select Statutes*, 42–44. For the evolution of the Indulgence, its impact, and the reasons for its withdrawal, see Frank Bate, *The Declaration of Indulgence, 1672* (London, 1908), chs. 5–6.

7. On the Anglican church during the Restoration, see Hutton, *The English Church*, 179–215; on the High Church party, see Bosher, *Making the Restoration Settlement*, ch. 4; and George Every, *The High Church Party, 1688–1718* (London, 1956), 1–18. On the latitudinarians, see Seaton, *Theory of Toleration*, 45–51, 66–72, 84–92, 205–19; he deals with the high-church men at 107–13, 116–21, 132–41, 154–67, 172, 182, 188–94.

8. Seaton, *Theory of Toleration*, 153.

9. *Ibid.*, 205–18.

10. For the act of 1677, 29 Ch. II ch. 9, *Statutes at Large* (1763), VIII, 417. See Sir James Fitzames Stephen, *A History of the Criminal Law of England* (London, 1883, 3 vols.), II, 468, and Sir William Holdsworth, *A History of English Law* (London, 1938–66, 16 vols., 6th ed., rev.), I, 616–21.

11. Seaton, *Theory of Toleration*, 140–1, 162, 220.

12. *Ibid.*, 146, 183–6.

13. Seaton reviews tolerationist and antitolerationist tracts throughout his *Theory of Toleration*. For tolerationist arguments stressing the secular theme, see especially Seaton, 144–52, and Charles F. Mullett, "Toleration and Persecution in England, 1660–89," *Church History*, XVIII (1949), 30–1. Penn's major tolerationist tracts are reprinted in vol. II of his *Select Works*, as follows: *The Great Case of Liberty of Conscience* (1671), 128–64; *England's Present Interest* (1675), 269–320; *A Persuasive to Moderation* (1686), 504–42. For his secularist position, presented in the works of 1675 and 1686, see also his *Great and Popular Objection against the Repeal of the Penal Laws* (1688), 12–13, and *Three Letters* (1688), 4–5, available only in the originals. As good as Penn but stressing the religious reasons for toleration is Robert Barclay, *An Apology for the True Christian Divinity* (London, 1676, reprinted 1840, 8th ed.), Proposition 14, 486–512. Barclay's *Apology* is the masterpiece of Quaker theology, marking the transition from Fox's feverish evangelism to the cool and placid quietism that would become more characteristic of Quakerism. On Barclay, see Rufus Jones's introduction to Braithwaite, *Second Period*, xxx–xliv.

14. *The Works of John Bunyan*, ed. George Offer (Glasgow, 1856, 3 vols.), I, 47, 56–7, 62, 64. See also John Brown, *John Bunyan* (London, 1928, rev. Frank Mott Harrison), 132–50, 176–8; William W. Whitley, "Bunyan's Imprisonments: A Legal Study," *Transactions*, Baptist Historical Society, VI (1918–19), 1–24; G. Lyon Turner, "Bunyan's License under the Indulgence," *ibid.*, 129–37; Joyce Godber, "The Imprisonment of John Bunyan," *Transactions*, Congregationalist Historical Society, XVI (1949), 23–32. On Mead, see Cragg, *Puritanism in the Great Persecution*, 229, and Bosher, *Making the Restoration Settlement*, 201–02.

15. Attwood or Adwood's case, Michaelmas term, 15 Jac. (1618), is reported in Henry Rolle, *Un Abridgment des plusiers cases et resolutions Del Common Ley* (London, 1668), II, 78. On seditious libel, see Holdsworth, *History of English Law*, VIII, 334–46 and 402–08, for its application to religious offenses; generally, see Leonard W. Levy, *Legacy of Suppression* (Cambridge, Mass., 1960), ch. 1, and Frederick S. Siebert, *Freedom of the Press in England, 1476–1776* (Urbana, Ill., 1952), ch. 13. Field's case is reported in 1 Siderfin 69 and 1 Keble 175, 194, 209, 233.

16. Charles Ripley Gillett, *Burned Books* (New York, 1932, 2 vols.), II, 443–5.

17. *Ibid.,* 449–54, and Benjamin Evans, *The Early English Baptists* (London, 1865, 2 vols.), II, 334–7.

18. The best account of Baxter's trial is in William Orme, *The Life and Times of Richard Baxter* (London, 1830, 2 vols.), I, 443–68; also reported in Howell's *State Trials,* XI, 493–502.

19. On "best gay lyric poet," Albert C. Baugh *et al., A Literary History of England* (New York, 1948), 744. Preaching blasphemy is from Anthony à Wood, *Athenae Oxonienses* (London, 1721, 2nd ed., 3 vols.), II, 1000, whose account Stephen, *History of Criminal Law,* II, 470, accepts. G. D. Nokes, *A History of the Crime of Blasphemy* (London, 1928), 44, is less certain about the blasphemy issue, because the law reports, mentioned in next note, do not refer to it. Pepys is from *The Diary of Samuel Pepys,* ed. Robert Latham and William Matthews (London, 1971 *et seq.,* 9 vols., thus far), IV, 269.

20. 1 Keble 620 (1663); 1 Fortescue, 99, 100; 1 Siderfin 168; for the obscenity, Wood, *Athenae,* II, 1000. Obscenity was not squarely held punishable by the common law until Rex v. Curll, 2 Strange 788 (1727); see also *State Trials,* XVII, 153, and Norman St. John-Stevas, *Obscenity and the Law* (London, 1956), 22–4.

21. Muggleton, *The Acts of the Witnesses* (1696), reprinted in *Works of John Reeve and Lodowicke Muggleton,* ed. John Frost and Isaac Frost (London, 1832, 3 vols.), III, 86–105. A Samuel Sears was charged with blasphemy in 1666 for saying that he was "really Christ and that he should [obscenity deleted] Kings, Princes, and Magistrates" (John Cordy Jeafferson, ed., *Middlesex County Records* [London, 1888, 7 vols.], III, 371); I could not ascertain the disposition of the case.

22. Stephen, *History of Criminal Law,* II, 467.

23. *Diary of Pepys,* V, 446; *The Diary of John Evelyn,* ed. E. S. DeBeer (Oxford, 1955, 6 vols.), III, 521; the *London Newsletter* called *Sandy Foundations* "an infamous and blasphemous pamphlet" (Harry Emerson Wildes, *William Penn* [New York, 1974], 49.) Catherine Owens Peare, *William Penn* (Philadelphia, 1957), 80, quotes Penn on the doctrine of the Trinity. The best account of this episode in Penn's life, reprinting extracts from primary sources, is John Bruce, "Observations upon William Penn's Imprisonment in the Tower of London," *Archaeologia,* XXX (1853), 70–90, where the quote from Vincent appears on p.81. *Sandy Foundations* is reprinted in Penn's *Select Works,* I, 129–56.

24. Bruce, "Penn's Imprisonment," 78–9, reprints Arlington's order of arrest and the confirmatory order of the Privy Council. Penn blamed Henry Henchman, the bishop of London, but Bruce proves that only Arlington, the king himself, and the council were responsible for his imprisonment.

25. Penn, *Innocency with Her Open Face Presented* (London, 1669), 4, for "noise of Blasphemy," reprinted in *Select Works,* I, 157–72; "Thou mayest tell my father . . ." in *A Collection of the Works of William Penn,* ed. Joseph Bessie (London, 1726, 2 vols.), I, 6. On Stillingfleet's mission, *Callendar of State Papers, Domestic, 1668–9,* 146, Jan. 4, 1669. On Stillingfleet, see Seaton, *Theory of Toleration,* 86–92.

26. For Penn to Stillingfleet, see Bruce, "Penn's Imprisonment," 88; for Penn to Arlington, *Works of Penn,* ed. Bessie, I, 154; and for the full text of Penn's letters to Arlington, see Norman Penney, ed., *Extracts from State Papers*

Relating to Friends, 1654 to 1672 (London, 1913), 279–86. Bruce, "Penn's Imprisonment," 90, reprints the order of the council freeing Penn, July 28, 1669. On the intercession of the duke of York, see Robert Wallace, *Antitrinitarian Biography* (London, 1850, 3 vols.), I, 165.

27. On Firmin, see *D.N.B.*, VII, 46–9; Wallace, *Antitrinitarian Biography*, I, 153–78 *passim*, and III, 272–89; Alexander Gordon, *Addresses, Biographical and Historical* (London, 1922), 93–119. See also Herbert John McLachlan, *Socinianism in Seventeenth Century England* (London, 1951), 306–7, for a concise summary of Penn's later account of his rejection of Socinianism and Firmin's response.

28. *Innocency with Her Open Face*, 13; Wallace, *Antitrinitarian Biography*, I, 166–9.

29. McLachlan, *Socinianism*, 312, quotes Hedworth; *ibid.*, 299–315, for the best treatment of Hedworth.

30. On Muggleton's 1670 troubles, see *Acts of the Witnesses*, in *Works of Reeve and Muggleton*, III, 133–6. For Muggleton to Fox, Muggleton's *Looking Glass for George Fox* (London, 1668), 76. *Looking Glass* (1756, 2nd ed.) is reprinted in *Works*, II, with the original pagination of that edition, p. 88 for the quotation. Vol. II includes all of Muggleton's anti-Quaker tracts. Muggleton reproved Fox and the Quakers "for rejoicing in my sufferings, and being sorry magistrates did not punish me" (*Looking Glass*, in *Works*, II, 86). On Muggleton, see Alexander Gordon, *Ancient and Modern Muggletonians: A Paper read before the Liverpool Literary and Historical Society*, April 4, 1870. On Firman, see Wallace, *Antitrinitarian Biography*, I, 176–7.

31. *Journals of the House of Lords*, XII, 688, May 11, 1675; 691, May 14; and 700–1, May 20.

32. *Ibid.*, XIII, 26, Nov. 17, 1675. Rex v. Taylor, 3 Keble 607, 621 (1676).

33. The indictment is reprinted in John Tremaine, *Pleas of the Crown* (Dublin, 1793), 226–7.

34. *Ibid.*, 227; 3 Keble 607, 621.

35. 3 Keble 607, 621.

36. H. L. Stephen, ed., *State Trials, Political and Social* (London, 1899, 2 vols.), I, 211–35, for Hale's witchcraft case. See also J. F. Stephen, *History of Criminal Law*, II, 432–5. For an excellent discussion of the question of whether Hale invented a new crime and whether he was right in holding that Christianity was part of the law of the land, see Nokes, *History of the Crime of Blasphemy*, 49–66, the best part of his little treatise. I shall treat these matters as they arise chronologically.

37. My account of Muggleton's 1677 trial is from Nathaniel Powell, *A True Account of the Trial and Sufferings of Lodowick Muggleton*, reprint of 1808, in Frost and Frost, eds., *Works of Reeve and Muggleton*, III, 1–15. Also, *Acts of the Witnesses* [Muggleton's autobiography, written 1677, first published 1699], in *ibid.*, III, 153–71; all items in *Works of Reeve and Muggleton* contain the pagination of the original tracts of the eighteenth-century reprints. Vol. II contains the tract against Penn.

38. The sources for the three certain blasphemy cases a (1) *News from Newgate: or the female Muggletonian being an account of apprehension and commitment of a certain fanatical woman charged with speaking several horrid blasphemous words* (1678); (2)*The Tryal and Condemnation of Several Notorious Malefactors . . . Also the Tryal of Joseph Hindmarsh, who printed*

and published the *Blasphemous Pamphlet, Entituled, The Presbyterian Pater Noster* (1681); (3) *A Full and True Account . . . of Susan Fowls . . . As also, Of her Tryal and Sentence . . . for Blaspheming Jesus Christ, and Cursing the Lord's Prayer* (1698); *The Second Part of the Boy of Bilson: Or, A True and Particular Relation of the Impostor, Susannah Fowles* (1698). Nokes, *History of the Crime of Blasphemy,* 147–8, 162, lists on his charts sixteen other common-law convictions in Old Bailey for the period 1678–98, all "for offences in relation to religious opinion." All were for seditiousness but perhaps none for blasphemy between 1678 and 1682. There were four cases during that period, none of which I could verify. I would bet that none involved blasphemy. Several pamphlets with the same title, *The Proceedings in* [or *of*] *the Old Bailey* [various spellings] cover the cases of 1683–98. None involved blasphemy, contrary to Nokes. For example, he lists the cases of Delaune and Baxter along with those of Taylor and Muggleton, making no distinctions between seditiousness and blasphemousness. His tables include many cases of the post-1698 period that I know were not prosecutions for blasphemy (Nokes, Appendices B and C). Distinctions, when possible, should be made. Sir William S. Holdsworth, like Nokes, was of the opinion that offenses against religion were seditious because they were simultaneously offenses against the state, but Holdsworth carefully differentiated the separate branches of the law of criminal defamation (*History of English Law,* VIII, 33, 337).

39. Robertson, ed., *Select Statutes,* 249–52, reprints the Declaration of Indulgence of 1687. The leading authority on the reign of James II is still Thomas B. Macauley, *The History of England from the Accession of James II,* ed. Charles H. Firth (London, 1913–15, 6 vols.); on the declaration and its background, see *ibid.,* II, 664–72, 734–58, 862–86, 955–64.

40. Macauley, *History of England,* II, 990–1038. Vol. III covers the flight of James and the accession of William and Mary. For the Anglican church under James II, see Hutton, *The English Church,* 217–33. For a political overview, see Clark, *Later Stuarts,* 116–43. For the trial of the seven bishops, see Howell's *State Trials,* XII, 183–524.

41. Braithwaite, *Second Period,* 190. On the expiration of the licensing laws on the press, see Siebert, *Freedom of the Press,* 260–63. For the Toleration Act, see Robertson, ed., *Select Statutes,* 70–5, or Gee and Hardy, *Documents,* 654–64.

42. On the 1710 report, see George Macauley Trevelyan, *The English Revolution, 1688–89* (London, 1938), 160, concluding with a good discussion of the Toleration Act. The most vivid and provocative treatment is Macauley, *History of England,* III, 1385–92, although his remark that dissenters got as much liberty as under a statute framed by Jefferson was ridiculous.

43. H. S. Q. Henriques, *The Jews and the English Law* (Oxford, 1908), 147–50, 154. The Toleration Act was extended to Catholics in 1778, to Unitarians in 1813, and to Jews in 1846 (*ibid.,* 161).

44. On Firmin, see note 27 above, this chapter. On Unitarianism within the English church, see Wallace, *Antitrinitarian Biography,* I, 252, and Earl Morse Wilbur, *A History of Unitarianism* (Cambridge, Mass., 1946–52, 2 vols.), II, ch. 12. On Milton, see Herbert McLachlan, *The Religious Views of Milton, Locke, and Newton* (Manchester, 1941), 22–66. On real and nominal Trinitarians, Wallace, *Antitrinitarian Biography,* I, 340–2, 362–4.

45. McLachlan, *Socinianism,* 140, 313, 318, for Marvell, Hedworth, and

Ashwell, and 326 for Firmin's circle. See also McLachlan, *Religious Views,*
117–72, on Newton; Wilbur, *Unitarianism,* II, 219–26; Wallace, *Antitrinitarian Biography,* I, 371–5 on Nye, and III, 362–71 on Clerke. On the
subject generally, McLachlan, *Socinianism,* chs. 15–16.

46. Wallace, *Antitrinitarian Biography,* I, 183–4, 196–204; Gillett, *Burned
Books,* II, 533–8; and Every, *High Church Party,* ch. 5, which sympathetically
traces "the High Church hunt for heretical latitude on the doctrine of the Trinity."

47. Wallace, *Antitrinitarian Biography,* I, 218–360, describes each of the
Unitarian tracts and many of the orthodox replies. Herbert McLachlan, *The
Story of a Non-Conformist Library* (Manchester, 1925), 53–87, also reviews
the Unitarian Tracts.

48. Wallace, *Antitrinitarian Biography,* I, 214–5, 236, 258, 327–31, 352,
and III, 389; Wilbur, *Unitarianism,* II, 227–31; Every, *High Church Party,*
79–80.

49. Wallace, *Antitrinitarian Biography,* I, 259–61, 275–9; Every, *High
Church Party,* 77–8; Wilbur, *Unitarianism,* II, 229; McLachlan, *Socinianism,*
335.

50. The quotations are from Wallace, *Antitrinitarian Biography,* I, 233–4,
253. See also McLachlan, *Socinianism,* 334, and on the Arian movement,
Wilbur, *Unitarianism,* II, 236–70.

51. On Locke's religious beliefs, see McLachlan, *Religious Views,* 69–114,
and H. R. Fox Bourne, *The Life of John Locke* (London, 1876, 2 vols.), I,
165–94, 305–11, and II, 31–41, 180–7, 281–93, 404–39, which includes his
controversy with Edwards; on the latter, see also Wallace *Antitrinitarian
Biography,* I, 306–20. For a concise summary, see McLachlan, *Socinianism,*
326–30, which includes Locke's reply to the bishop of Worcester.

52. For Clerke to Baxter, see McLachlan, *Socinianism,* 324.

53. On Scotland during the Restoration, see Clark, *Later Stuarts,* ch. 12.

54. Mackenzie, *The Laws and Customs of Scotland in Matters Criminal*
(Edinburgh, 1678), tit. iii, sec. 1, p. 25; tit. x, sec. 2, p. 85. David Hume, *Com-
mentaries on the Law of Scotland respecting the Description and Punishment of
Crimes* (Edinburgh, 1797, 2 vols.), II, 514.

55. Bortwick's case is reported in Howell's *State Trials,* XIII, 938–40.

56. Anon., "Mr. Macauley's Account of Thomas Aikenhead," *The Christian
Reformer,* XII (1856), 37–8, reprints the statement made by Lorimer in the introduction to an untitled sermon that he published in 1697, defending himself
against accusations of being responsible for Aikenhead's death. Macauley's own
account of Aikenhead's case is in his *History of England,* VI, 2699–2700, in
which he said, "The preachers were the boy's murderers. . . ."

57. Aikenhead's pretrial petition and Anstruther's letter of Jan. 26, 1696,
eighteen days after the execution, are in "Proceedings against Thomas
Aikenhead, for Blasphemy," 1696, in Howell's *State Trials,* XIII, 921–3, 930.
Emphasis added in Anstruther's comment.

58. I have followed Lorimer's account; Macauley's differs. Lorimer claimed
that the chancellor favored a reprieve; Macauley claimed that the chancellor
cast the deciding vote against a reprieve. *Christian Reformer,* XII, 37–8, and
Macauley, *History of England,* VI, 2700.

59. The account in *State Trials,* XIII, 917–40, includes all pertinent
documents except Lorimer's statement. John Gordon, *Thomas Aikenhead*

(London, 1856), and the same author's *Supplement to "Thomas Aikenhead"* are virulently anticlerical tracts in defense of Macauley's account.

60. *State Trials,* XIII, 926–7, for the evidence of Mungo Craig, and 917–8, 925–9 for Locke.

61. "The Trial of Patrick Kinnymount, for Blasphemy," 1697, *State Trials,* XIII, 1273–82. See Hume, *Commentaries on the Law of Scotland,* II, 40–1.

62. Wallace, *Antitrinitarian Biography,* I, 384–5, on stopping the presses. On Toland, see *D.N.B.,* XIX, 918, and Sir Leslie Stephen, *History of English Thought in the Eighteenth Century* (3rd ed. of 1902; New York, 1949 reprint, 2 vols.) I, 101–19; see also, John Orr, *Deism: Its Roots and Fruits* (London, 1934), 116–24. For Toland's reception in Ireland, see *Journal of the House of Commons of the Kingdom of Ireland* (Dublin, 1763, 2nd ed.), II, 903–4, Sept. 9, 1697.

63. Wallace, *Antitrinitarian Biography,* I, 376–77; Every, *High Church Party,* 81. For the case of Susan Fowls, see note 38, above, this chapter.

64. Wallace, *Antitrinitarian Biography,* I, 385.

65. For the act of 1698, see *Statutes of the Realm* (London, 1812–28, 11 vols.), VII, 409: 9 Gul. III ch. 35.

66. Godolphin, *Reportorium Canonicum; or An Abridgment of the Ecclesiastical Laws of this Realm consistent with the Temporal* (London, 1678), 559–61.

Epilogue

1. "Articles, Lawes, and Orders, Divine, Politique, and Martiall for the Colony in Virginea," sects. 2–3, 5, in Peter Force, ed., *Tracts and Other Papers, Relating Principally to the Origin, Settlement, and Progress of the Colonies in North American* (New York, 1947 reprint ed., 4 vols.), III, no. 2, p. 10. William H. Whitemore, ed., *The Colonial Laws of Massachusetts . . . together with the Body of Liberties of 1641* (Boston, 1890), 14, 60; Charles J. Hoadley, ed., *Records of the Colony or Jurisdiction of New Haven, 1653–1665* (Hartford, 1858), 238.

2. Rufus M. Jones, *The Quakers in the American Colonies* (New York, 1966 reprint), 70–88, covers the execution of the Quakers. For the "Act of Toleration," really entitled "An Act concerning Religion," see William H. Browne *et al., Archives of Maryland* (Baltimore, 1883–), I, 244–6; for the act of 1699, *ibid.,* XXII, 523. For the Massachusetts act of 1697, see Abner C. Goodell *et al.,* eds., *The Acts and Resolves, Public and Private, of the Province of Massachusetts Bay, 1692–1786* (Boston, 1869–1922, 21 vols.), I, 297.

3. For the captain, Petition of Ann Pauley, Nov. 14, 1710, Colonial Office Series 5, Vol. 717, no. 19, P.R.O., London. George Mathews, *An Account of the Trial, on 14th June, 1703, Before the Court of Queen's Bench, Dublin, of the Reverend Thomas Emlyn* (Dublin, 1839), 10–37. Rex v. Woolston, 1 Barn. K. B. 162–3 and Fitz-G. 64–66 (1729). The first of the *Age of Reason* trials was Rex v. Thomas Williams (1797), in Thomas B. Howell, *Complete Collection of State Trials* (London, 1816–28, 34 vols.), XXVI, 654–713. The last batch of *Age of Reason* trials is the subject of William H. Wickwar, *The Struggle for the Freedom of the Press, 1819–1832* (London, 1928), chs. 3 and 7.

4. People v. Ruggles, 8 Johns Rep. (N.Y.) 290, 294 (1811); Updegraph v. Comm., 11 Serge & R. (Pa.) 394, 406 (1824).

5. Adams to Jefferson, Jan. 23, 1825, in Lester J. Cappon, ed., *The Adams–Jefferson Letters* (New York, 1971 reprint, 2 vols. in one), 606–7. For Jefferson, see his letter to Adams, Jan. 24, 1814, in *ibid.,* 422–3; to Thomas Cooper, Feb. 10, 1814, in *The Writings of Thomas Jefferson,* ed. Andrew A. Lipscomb and A. A. Bergh (Washington, D.C., 1904–5, 20 vols.), XIV, 85–97; to John Cartwright, June 5, 1824, in *ibid.,* XVI, 48–51; Jefferson, *Reports of Cases Determined in the General Court of Virgina,* preface and appendix, reprinted in William Addison Blakely, ed., *American State Papers Bearing on Sunday Legislation* (New York, 1970 reprint), 208–19. Shaw's opinion is in Comm. v. Kneeland, 37 Mass. 206 (1838), reprinted in Leonard W. Levy, ed., *Blasphemy in Massachusetts: Freedom of Conscience and the Abner Kneeland Case. A Documentary Record* (New York, 1973), 425–39.

6. On the number of English convictions, see Reg. v. Lemon (C.A.), 3 *Weekly Law* R. 404, 412 (Aug. 11, 1978). The Pennsylvania case is Updegraph v. Comm., 11 Serg. & R. 394, 405–6 (1824). *Reports from the Royal Commission on the Criminal Law. Sixth Report. May 3, 1841* (London, 1841), 84.

7. Regina v. Ramsey and Foote, 15 Cox's Cr. Cas. 231, 238–9 (1883).

8. Cantwell v. Conn., 310 U.S. 296 (1940); Burstyn, Inc. v. Wilson, 343 U.S. 495, 529 (1952).

9. *Baltimore Sun,* July 22 and 23, Aug. 9, 1968; May 2, 1969; April 7, 1970; *Time,* May 16, 1969, p. 72; Maryland v. West, 9 Md. App. 270 (1970).

10. Wilmington (Del.) *Evening Journal,* May 26–29, Sept. 30, 1969; *New York Times,* May 29, 1969, p. 41. For the Pennsylvania case, see *Civil Liberties,* the ACLU newsletter, Sept. 1971, and *New York Times,* April 25, 1971, p. 18.

11. *Boston Globe,* Nov. 30, 1977, p.3.

12. The 1921 conviction was in Rex v. Gott, 16 Cohen's Cr. App. Rep. 86, 87. The *Gay News* trial was reported in the *Times* of London, daily from July 4 to July 12, 1977. See also comment in 127 *New Law Journal* (London) 701–2 (July 21, 1977), and for the appeal, Reg. v. Lemon, 3 *Weekly Law* R. 404–23 (Aug. 11, 1978).

INDEX

Abbot, Archbishop William, 191, 193, 196-97

Acontius, Jacobus, 144, 192

Act of Toleration, 333

Act of Uniformity, 223, 298, 302

Acts of the Apostles, 46, 70, 71, 72

Acts of Parliament, 297-98, 333

Adams, John, 334-35

Adams, Mary, 249

Adoptionists, 84

Aeschylus, 10

Against Calvin's Book, 147

Against Heresies, 79

Against the Horrible Blasphemies of Servetus, 144

Against Marcion, 80-81

Agnew, Alexander (Jock of Broad Scotland), 256-57, 286, 324, 332

Agnosticism, 9, 12, 14. *See also* Atheism

Ahab, King, 18-19

Aikenhead, Thomas, 325-27

Ainsworth, Henry, 230

Albigensian Crusade, 82, 111, 115, 161

Alcibiades, 10-12, 13, 14, 63

Alesius, Alexander, 144

Alexander of Alexandria, 73, 87, 88, 89, 90, 98

Alexander of Hales, 114

Alva, Duke of, 149, 317

Amaury of Bene, 117

Ambrose, Bishop of Milan, 99, 105

Ameaux, Pierre, 132

American Association for the Advancement of Atheism, 5

American Civil Liberties Union, 337, 338

American Colonies, 333-34

Anabaptism, 122, 123-25, 126, 128, 130, 135, 143; in England, 168, 169, 173, 174, 175, 176, 177, 178, 179, 180, 188, 189, 230

Anaxagoras, 7-9, 10, 14

Andocides, 11

Anglicanism, 122, 173, 175, 184, 188-89, 191, 194, 196, 197, 214, 231-32, 279-81, 297-300, 302, 308, 317, 320-24, 330, 338

Anglo-Catholicism, 300-1

Annas (the Elder), 36

Annas (son of Annas the Elder), 48

Anstruther, Lord, 326

Answer to William Penn, 314, 316

Antichrist, 70, 88, 89, 138, 165, 170, 210, 259, 260

Antinomianism, xiv, 118, 224-57, 266

Antioch, Synod of, 85

Anti-Semitism, 23, 62, 74, 75, 77, 79, 129. *See also* Jews and Judaism

Antitrinitarianism, xv, 86, 134, 135, 150, 163, 171, 172, 212, 225

Apology for the Quakers, 264

Appollinarists, 165

Aquinas, St. Thomas, xi, xiv, 63, 104, 110, 111-14, 115, 119, 121, 126, 190, 331

Archelaus, Bishop of Mesopotamia, 82

Archer, John, 199

Aretius, Benedictus, 148-49, 322

Arianism, xi, 76, 85, 86, 88, 89-97, 99, 109, 117, 323; versus Athanasianism, 88, 89-97; in England, 165, 168, 172, 173, 174, 175, 176, 180, 182, 183, 202, 203; Protestantism and, 122-23, 128, 130, 134, 147

"Arian Movement," 323

Aristotelianism, 153, 154

Aristotle, ix, 15

Arius of Alexandria, 87, 88, 90, 91-92, 93, 95, 96-97, 122, 135, 204

Arlington, Lord, 309
Arminianism, 188-89, 191, 193, 208, 285, 300
Arminius, Jacobus, 188
Arundel, Archbishop Thomas, 166
Ashtaroth (deity), 17, 18
Ashwell, George, 321
Askew, Anne, 172
Aspasia, 9, 10
Assheton, John, 171, 172
Athanasianism, 76, 88, 89-97, 226
Athanasius, 85, 86, 87, 89, 90, 92, 94, 95, 96-97, 98, 202, 204, 332
Atheism, x, 3, 75, 89, 156, 178, 187, 193, 203, 212, 267, 301
Athenagoras, 75
Atkins, Robert, 315
Audland, John, 261
Augustine, St., xi, xiv, 84, 95, 104-7, 108, 109, 121, 126, 332

Baal cults, 17-18, 19, 25
Babylonian captivity, 33
Bacon, Sir Francis, 187
Bainham, John, 170
Bainton, Roland, 131
Bampfield, Thomas, 279
Baptists, ix, xiv, 77, 123, 189-93, 194, 197, 198, 208-10, 216, 221-22, 280, 298, 303, 305, 316, 318
Barabbas, 61
Barclay, Robert, 264
Bar Kochba, 76
Barrowists, 191
Barton, Elizabeth (the nun of Kent), 170
Basilidism, 76, 78
Bastwick, Dr. John, 197, 199
Bauthumley, Jacob, 236, 237, 248
Baxter, Richard, 241-42, 263, 264, 268, 280, 299, 305-6, 316
Baynes, Captain Adam, 287-88
Becker, Johannes, 120
Becket, Archbishop Thomas a, 161
Beghards and Beguines, 117-19

Behmenism, 226, 230, 235, 266, 267
Bellarmine, Cardinal Robert, 110, 155
Bennett, Gervase, 267
Benson, Gervase, 270, 272
Best, Paul, 199-205, 207, 208, 211, 217, 225, 283, 291
Beza, Theodore, 143-44, 147, 148, 173
Biandrata, Dr. Giorgo, 150, 151, 152
Bible, 3, 16-17, 122, 135, 145, 163, 189, 199, 217, 237, 250, 252, 263, 271, 286, 288, 323, 329, 330, 334-35
Biddle, John, 205-7, 208, 210, 211, 213-23, 225, 231, 246-47, 250, 256, 281, 311, 320, 321, 323, 332
Bilney, Thomas, 169-70
Bingham, Joseph, 321-22
Black magic, 7
Black mass, 10
Blasphemer Slain, The, 214
Blasphemoktomia, 207
Blasphemy Act of *1648*, 210, 243, 244, 281, 283, 284, 324
Blasphemy Act of *1650*, 246, 284
Blathory, Stephen, 151, 152
Blinzler, Josef, 55-56
Bocher, Joan. See Joan of Kent
Bond, William, 256
Boniface VIII, Pope, 163
Book of Common Prayer, 194, 196, 223, 279, 286
Bornkamm, Günther, 69
Bortwick, Francis, 325
Boteler, Major General William, 286
Braithwaite, William C., 262, 268
Brandon, S. G. F., 62
Brenz, John, 131
Brethren of the Free Spirit. See Free Spirit movement
Brownists, 191, 194, 198
Bruno, Giordano, ix, 152-55, 156, 157, 332
Brunsfels, Otto, 131
Bucer, Martin, 136
Bullinger, Heinrich, 173

Bultmann, Rudolf, 52
Bunyan, John, 302, 303-4, 306
Burnet, Bishop William, 322
Burrough, Edward, 259
Burton, Reverend Henry, 197
Burton, Thomas, 289, 295
Burton, William, 180, 182
Bury, Dr. Arthur, 321
Busher, Leonard, 192, 193
Byzantium, 86, 109-10

Caesar, Julius, x
Caiaphas (high priest), 36-37, 39, 40-42, 46, 49, 50, 51, 53, 54-55, 96
Calamy, Dr. Edmund, 322, 323-24
Calvin, John, xi, xiii, 122, 131-33, 135, 137-44, 147, 148, 172, 173, 174, 190, 325-26, 332
Calvinism, 122, 125, 147, 150-52; in England and Scotland, 172, 175-77, 186-88, 190-91, 197-209, 214, 232, 252, 262, 322; of Knox, 176-77
Cambridge University, 200, 262
Canaan (Palestine), 17-20
Case, Thomas, 231
Castellio, Sebastian, 143, 144-47, 176, 192-93
Catchpole, David R., 56-57
Catharism, 111, 114, 115, 118, 121, 161, 162
Cavalier Parliament, 301-2
Charicles, 13
Charlemagne, 110
Charles I, King, 193, 227, 233, 234
Charles II, King, 297-300, 301, 304, 317, 319
Cheynell, Francis, 198, 212, 213
Christianismi Restitutio, 135, 137, 138, 139, 140, 141, 142
Christianity: Arianism versus Athanasianism, 88, 89-97; impiety and, 63-64, 80, 88, 89, 95; Jesus and, 64, 65, 66, 70, 71, 76-77, 79, 82, 83; Jews and, 64, 65, 66, 67, 68, 71, 72, 74-75, 76, 77, 81, 86, 88, 96, 99; martyrology, 48; pre-Nicene period, 63-100; Trinitarian controversy, 81-100, 103. See also *names of religions*
Christianity not Mysterious, 328
Church of England. *See* Anglicanism
Church of Strangers (London), 172
Cicero, 12
Clarkson, Laurence, 224, 225, 226, 227, 233, 237-38, 239, 241, 244, 246, 248
Clement, 98
Clement VIII, Pope, 117
Cleon, 9
Clergy in their Colours, The, 212
Clerke, Gilbert, 320, 323
Cohn, Haim, 50-51, 52, 58
Cohn, Norman, xiv
Coke, Sir Edward, 195, 312
Cole, Peter, 180, 181, 182
Coleridge, John, 335-36, 338
Comfort for Believers, 199
Concerning Heretics, 144-45, 147, 192
Confession of Faith touching the Holy Trinity, 210
Congregationalism, 194-95, 279-80, 281
Conscientious objection, x
Constantine, Emperor, 86-87, 90, 91, 92, 93, 94, 95
Constantius, Emperor, 94
Conventicles Act, 298, 299, 302
Conzelmann, Hans, 60
Cooper, Anthony Ashley, 287, 292
Copernicus, Nicolaus, 153, 154
Coppe, Abiezer, 225, 226-30, 233, 234, 236, 237, 239, 243, 244, 246-47, 248, 255
Coppin, Richard, 236, 255-56
Coptic Christians, 116
Corpus Juris Civilis, 110
Corpus Christi College, 181
Cotton, John, 267
Council of Antioch (*341*), 97
Council of Antioch (*361*), 97

Council of Ariminium, 94-95
Council of Arles, 94
Council of Assembly, 11
Council of Chalcedon, 65, 97
Council of Constantinople, 65, 94, 97
Council of Milan, 94
Council of Nicaea, 64-65, 81, 95, 96, 137
Council of Sirmium, 94
Concil of Trent, 136
Courtney, Archbishop William, 163-63
Court of High Commission for Ecclesiastical Causes, 181, 193, 195-96, 198, 250
Court of Star Chamber, 193, 195-96, 198
Coverdale, Miles, 173
Cranmer, Archbishop Thomas, 170, 171, 172, 173, 174, 186
Critias, 13
Cromwell, Oliver, 203, 205, 210-11, 219-23, 224-25, 234, 247, 248, 249, 256, 263-64, 272, 273, 276, 279, 280-81, 298, 302, 310
Cromwell, Lord Richard, 285, 296
Cromwell, Thomas, 170
Cullman, Oscar, 31, 37, 61
Cyrillus, Patriarch, 99

Damasus, Pope, 98
Danby, Herbert, 52
Daniel, 33, 35, 40
David, Francis (David Ferencz), 150-52, 183
David, King, 15, 35
Decius, Emperor, 81
"Declaration of Indulgence" (Charles II), 300, 304, 317
Defense of the Orthodox Faith Against the Prodigious Errors of Michael Servetus, 144, 147
De Haeretico Comburendo, 166, 170, 179, 184, 283-84, 290, 302, 308
Deism, 180, 301, 319, 320, 323, 325, 326
Delaware, 336, 337

Dell, William, 233
Demosthenes, 7
Derrett, J. Duncan, 57-58
Detection and Refutation of False Knowledge, The, 79
De Trinitatis Erroribus, 136,
Dewsbury, William, 258
Diagoras of Melos, 9, 12-13, 14-15
Diaspora, 22, 67, 74
Diggers, 224, 231, 234, 235, 239, 240, 266
Dionysius, Bishop of Alexandria, 82
Dionysius, Bishop of Rome, 82, 85, 98
Diopeithes, 8
Divine Teachings, 255-56
Docetism, 68, 70, 75, 76, 81, 111, 133, 150
Dodd, C. H., 60
Dolet, Étienne, 134, 135
Donahue, Father John R., 55
Donatism, 76, 81, 104-5, 106-8, 109, 165
Dualism, gnostic, 81, 111

Early Baptists, 266
Ebionism, 66, 76, 88
Edict of Nantes, 317
Edward VI, King, 170-71, 172, 173, 174
Edwards, John, 323
Edwards, Thomas, 203, 204, 232-33, 250, 266
Egypt (ancient), 6, 15
Eleusinian mysteries, 10, 11, 12, 13
Elijah, 107, 332
Eliot, T. S., 3, 4, 5, 6
Elizabeth I, Queen, 153, 196, 300
Emlyn, Thomas, 323, 334
England (to 1700), 161-330; Christianity, as law of the land, 297-330; ecclesiastical courts, 161-62; Edwardian reformation, 170-74; Elizabethan policy, 175-83, 187; fires of Smithfield, 161-87; Henrician Reformation, 167-70; impiety, 172; Inquisition, 166-67, 168;

James I policy, 183-86, 187, 188-93, 213; Jews and Judaism, 161, 162, 199, 250, 319-20; Marian period, 172-75, 187; Middle Ages, 161-67. See also *names of religions*

England's Present Interest Discovered, 303

Enlightenment, xv, 333-34

Enslin, Morton S., 47

Epistle to the Ephesians, 73

Erasmus, Desiderus, 133-34, 135

Erbury, Dorcas, 274, 277-78

Erbury, William, 250-51, 266, 274

Essenes, 59, 71

Eugenius IV, Pope, 117

Euripides, 9-10, 12

Eusebius of Caesaria, 48, 76, 86, 88, 90, 91, 93, 95, 96

Eusebius of Nicomedia, 88, 90, 92, 93

Evans, Austin, xiv

Evelyn, John, 309

Excommunication, 28, 73, 85, 163, 193, 268

Ezekiel, 21

Fairfax, Lord, 200

Family of Love (the Familists), 178, 180, 181-82, 195, 196, 198, 226, 227, 230, 231, 235, 266, 267, 282

Farel, William, 138

Faulkner, Richard, 250

Fawkes, Guy, 317

Fell, Margaret, 268, 271

Fell, Thomas, 268, 269

Fiennes, Nathaniel, 295

Fiery Flying Roll, A, 228, 229, 243, 246

Firmin, Thomas, 222, 310, 312, 320, 322, 330

First Amendment, ix, xi, xv, xvi, 4, 336, 337

First Crusade, 115

Five Mile Act of 1665, 298-99, 302, 324

Flekwyk, Hermann Van, 149-50

Forneworth, R., 255

Foster, George, 226, 248

Fourth Lateran Council, 115

Foster, Robert, 304-5, 307

Fowls, Susan, 328

Fox, George, ix, 234, 240, 242, 243, 255, 258-60, 261, 263-75, 276, 277, 286, 294-95, 296, 303, 314, 315, 332

Foxe, John, 165, 170, 171, 179

Franck, Sebastian, 125

Frankfurter, Felix, 336

Franklin, William, 226, 247-48, 283

Freake, Bishop Edmund, 181

Frederick II, Emperor, 116, 161

Free Exercise Clauses (First Amendment), 337

Freeke, William, 322

Free Spirit movement, 117-20, 121, 133, 225, 230

Free Will Ranters, 248

Freud, Sigmund, 239

Fry, John, 211-13, 225

Gadbury, Mary, 247, 248

Gailhard, John, 328

Galen (physician), 136

Galilaeans, 77

Galileo, 153

Gamaliel, 41, 42, 46, 51

Gangraena, 203, 204, 266, 323

Gay News case, 338-39

Gentile, Giovanni Valentio, 147-49

Georg, David, 179-80

Gideon, 18

Glynne, John, 273, 283, 293

Gnosis, 70

Gnosticism, 65, 70, 74, 76, 77-81, 118, 119, 241. See also *names of sects*

"God damn," 21, 24

Godolphin, John, 329

Goffe, Major General William, 287, 288

Goodwin, John, 204, 216, 217-18

Gratian, xiv, 110

Great Case of Liberty of Conscience, 303

Greece (ancient), 7-15; impiety in, 9-15
Greek Orthodox Church, 109-10
Gregory IX, Pope, 116
Gregory XI, Pope, 163
Gregory, Bishop of Alexandria, 95
Grindletonians, 226, 266
Gruet, Jacquet, 132, 133, 135
Gui, Bernard, xiv, 110

Hahn, Ferdinand, 53
Hale, Matthew, 312, 313-14, 329
Hammond (or Hammante), Matthew, 180, 181, 182
Hanson, R. P. C., 97
Hare, Douglas R. A., 58
Harnack, Adolph, 78, 79
Hatzer, Ludwig, 134
Hebrew language, 21-22, 25, 32, 34, 37, 57
Hedio, Caspar, 131
Hedworth, Henry, 311, 320
Helwys, Thomas, 191-92, 193
Henrician Reformation, 167-70
Henry II, King, 161
Henry IV, King, 166
Henry VI, King, 167
Henry VIII, King, 167, 168-69,170
Heresiography, 199, 266
Hezekiah, King of Judah, 20
Hibbord, Thomas, 256
Hickcock, Richard, 255
Highland, Samuel, 291
Hilary of Poitiers, 92, 94
Hippocrates, 9
Hippolytus, 10
Hippolytus of Rome, 76, 77, 85
Hobbes, Thomas, 308
Hohenstaufen, House of, 116
Holland, John, 236, 240, 293
Holmes, Oliver Wendell, ix-x
Homosexuals, x, xiii, 338
Hotham, Durand, 240, 243, 267
House of Commons, 164, 198-207, 211, 221-22, 231, 234, 243-46, 250, 259, 266, 278, 279, 281, 283, 297, 308, 328
Howgill, Francis, 258, 270, 275

Hughes, Philip, 172-73
Huguenots, 308, 312
Hume, Baron David, 327
Husband, Richard W., 50-51
Huss, John, 121, 167
Hyde, Robert, 305
Hymenaeus, 73
Hypatia, 99

Idolatry, 46, 89
Ignatius of Antioch, 76, 77, 98
Impiety, 7, 107; in ancient Greece, 9-15; early Christianity and, 63-64, 80, 88, 89, 95; in England, 172
Index of prohibited books, 136-37
Infant baptism, 123
Innocency with Her Open Face Presented by way of apology for the Book Entitled The Sandy Foundation Shaken, 310
Innocent III, Pope, xi, xiv, 114, 115, 118, 161, 165
Innocent IV, Pope, 116
Inquisition, xiv, 82, 104, 111, 115, 116, 121, 259; in England, 161, 166-67, 168; Protestantism and, 127, 133, 134, 136, 138, 140, 141, 149, 153, 154-55, 156
Institutes of the Christian Religion, 131, 138
Iraenaeus, Bishop of Lyons, 77, 78-79, 80, 83, 98
Isaiah (prophet), 20, 332
Islam, 109, 115, 116, 130
Israelites (ancient), 15, 17-28, 331; trial of Jesus, 29-62. *See also* Jews and Judaism

Jackson, Robert, x
James (brother of Jesus), 51, 66-67
James the Just, 48
James I, King, 183, 188-93, 213
James II, King, 298, 306, 310, 316-18, 319
Jefferson, Thomas, xii, xv, 83, 145, 334-35
Jeffreys, George, 305, 306, 315

Jegon, Bishop John, 191
"Jehovah" case (Canada), 5-6
Jeremiah, 40
Jerome, 100
Jerome of Prague, 121, 167
Jerusalem, Assyrian siege of (*701* B.C.), 20
Jessop, Edmond, 230
Jesus, ix, x, xi-xii, xiii, 5, 13, 114, 133, 141, 150, 189, 260, 264, 268, 275, 323, 331, 332, 337, 338; divinity of, xi-xii, 3; early Christianity and, 64, 65, 66, 70, 71, 76-77, 79, 82, 83; Jewish trial of, 29-62; preaching of, 32; Son of Man claim, 32-33, 35, 40, 43, 46, 48, 54, 57, 58, 59, 69; unreliability of Gospels as history, 52-53
Jesus College (Cambridge University), 200
Jewish Christians, 70, 76-77
Jews and Judaism, xiv, 65, 331, 333; early Christianity and, 64, 65, 66, 67, 68, 71, 72, 74-75, 76, 77, 81, 86, 88, 96, 99; in England, 161, 162, 193, 199, 250, 319-20; as God's chosen people, 35; Luther and, 128, 129; Matthew's Gospel and, 68; Middle Ages, 103, 106, 111, 112, 114-17; Protestantism and, 128, 129, 130, 133; Roman persecution of, 74-75. *See also* Israelites (ancient); Mosaic law; Torah
Jezebel, 19, 107
Joan of Kent (Joan Bocher), 171-72, 174, 176, 177, 178
Jock of Broad Scotland. *See* Agnew, Alexander
Johannines, 76
John (Apostle), 46, 51
John the Baptist, 51
John Sigismund II, Prince of Transylvania, 150-51
Jordan, W. K., 144
Joseph of Arimathea, 42, 51
Josephus, 41, 48, 51
Joshua, 41

Journal, 274
Joyce, James, ix
Judas of Galilee, 41
Justinian I, Emperor, 110
Justin Martyr, 75, 76, 77, 78, 80, 83

Kali (goddess), x
Kallen, Horace, 5
Kelsey, Major General Thomas, 256, 284
Kent, James, 334
Kepler, Johannes, 153
Kett, Francis, 181-82, 332
King, Richard, 249
Kinnymount, Patrick, 327
Kirkup, James, x, xiii, 338
Kneeland, Abner, xv
Knox, John, 173, 176-77, 325-26
Küng, Hans, 31, 58, 61

Lake, Mary, 239
Lambert, M. D., xiv
Lambert, Major General John, 289, 294
Lambs War, The, 259-60
Lane, Richard, 196, 197
Langton, Archbishop Stephen, 162
Latimer, Hugh, 173, 176
Latitudinarians, 300, 310
Laud, Archbishop William, 185, 186, 193-98, 199, 202, 231-32, 297
Lawrence, Henry, 266, 285, 287
Lawson, Sir Wilfrid, 271
Lederede, Bishop Richard, 163
Leff, Gordon, xiv
Legate, Bartholomew, 183, 184, 186, 188, 190, 272, 332
Lerner, Robert E., xiv
Levellers, 204, 224-25, 227, 229, 233, 234, 235, 239, 246, 247, 267, 285
Leviathan, The, 308
Lewes, John, 180, 181, 182
Libertines, 132-33
Light and Dark Sides of God, 248
Lilburne, John, 225, 233, 234
Lincoln, Abraham, 83
Locke, John, xv, 146, 318, 320,

323, 327, 328
Logos (of the Fourth Gospel), 82, 83, 85, 87, 91
Lollard Bible, 165
Lollards, 163, 164, 165-66, 168, 294
Long Parliament, 268, 302
Looking Glass for George Fox, A, 311
Lorimer, William, 325
Louis IX, King, 116
"Love That Dares to Speak Its Name, The", x
Luther, Martin, xi, 72, 122, 125-30, 134, 135, 136, 173, 332
Lutheranism, 122, 123, 125, 127, 130-31, 135, 143, 150, 172
Lyndewood, Bishop William, 167

Macaulay, Thomas Babington, 251
Maccabees, 22
Mackenzie, Sir George, 324-25, 327, 329
Madison, James, xii
Magnus, Albertus, 119
Maimonides, 24
Maitland, Frederic William, xiii
Mani, 82
Manichaeism, 82, 98, 99, 104, 111, 118, 165
Manz, Felix, 124-25
Marcellus, Bishop of Ancyra, 96
Marcion, 79-80
Marcionites, 76, 78, 79-81, 92, 226, 241
Marvell, Andrew, 320-21
Mary I, Queen, 171, 172-75, 297, 317
Mary II, Queen, 318
Maryland, 333, 336-37
Massachusetts, 5, 333, 335, 336, 338
Mead, Mathew, 304
Melanchthon, Philipp, 130, 143, 173
Meldrum, George, 326
Meletians, 76, 81
Menanderism, 76
Menius, Justus, 130-31

Mennonites, 123, 149
Midianites, 18
Milton, John, xv, 146, 320
Monotheism, 64
Montague, William, 315
Montanism, 76, 81
Montefiore, C. G., 48-49
Moore, R. I., xiv
More, Henry, 267
More, Sir Thomas, 170
Morton, A.L., 233, 241
Mosaic law, xiii, 23-28, 39, 51, 54, 66, 71, 73, 129, 172, 176, 194. *See also* Talmud
Moses, xiii, 15-18, 21, 24, 25, 33, 58, 59, 71, 237, 331
Moslems. *See* Islam
Muggleton, Lodowick, 249, 250, 251-55, 307-8, 311-12, 314-16, 326
Muggletonianism, 251-52, 255, 282, 301, 307, 310, 312, 316, 319
Münster episode of *1533*, 123, 125, 189
Murton, John, 192-93, 230

Naboth (elder of Jezreel), 19-20, 331
Naked Gospel, The, 321
Naylor, James, xiii, 258, 265-79, 282-94, 295-96, 301, 312, 314, 324, 332
Nazarenes, 46, 47, 59, 65, 66, 70, 72
Nebuchadnezzar, 21, 105, 108
Neck of the Quakers Broken, The, 311, 314
Neile, Bishop Richard, 185-86, 194
New Haven Colony, 333
Newton, Sir Isaac, xv, 320
New Witnesses proved Old Heretics...the Doctrines of John Reeve and Lodowick Muggleton...Proved to be Mostly Ancient Whimsies, Blasphemies, and Heresies, The, 311
Nicanor, 22
Nicene Creed, 65, 76, 90-97, 103, 122-23, 149, 185, 204,

210, 321, 322, 323
Nicholartanes, 226
Nicklaes (or Nicholas), Henrick,
 178, 179, 180, 182, 230, 245
Nicodemus, 42, 51
Nicolaitanism, 76
Nineham, D. E., 51, 53
Nokes, G. D., 316
Novatianism, 81-82, 83-84, 92,
 99
Nye, Stephen, 320, 321, 322, 323

Oates, Titus, 11
Objections Answered, 192
Oecolampadius, Johannes,
 135-36
O'Neill, J. C., 59-60
"On the Scope of the Magistrate's
 Authority", 126
Oral Law, 39, 64
Orestes, 9-10
Origen, 83, 87, 98
Ory, Matthieu, 139
Ossius of Cordoba, 87, 90
O'Toole, Adam Duff, 163
Overton, Richard, 225, 234
Owen, John, 214
Oxford ecclesiastical court of
 1166, 161
Oxford University, 161, 164-65,
 206, 207, 212, 214, 226, 262,
 321, 322

Paganism, 65, 112; theories of
 gnosis, 70
Pagitt, Ephraim, 199, 238, 266
Paine, Tom, ix, xv, 334
Parker, Samuel, 302
Parris, George van, 172
Particular Baptists, 281
Passion narrative, 31, 52, 61
Patripassianism, 85
Paul, St., 47-48, 66, 67, 69, 70,
 106, 108, 118, 121, 203, 226;
 early Christian beliefs and, 68,
 71-74, 89; Luther and,125-26
Paulinists, 76
Paul of Samosata, 85-86, 88
Pearson, Anthony, 270, 271,
 272
Peasants' War of *1525,* 124,

125, 127
Peeters, Jan, 178, 179
Pelikan, Jaroslav, 93
Penn, Admiral Sir William, 308,
 309-10
Penn, William, ix, 193, 262,
 263, 268, 303, 308-12, 318,
 321
Pennsylvania, 333, 334, 335,
 337-8
Pentateuch, 22, 24
Pepys, Samuel, 306, 309
Pericles, 8, 9, 10
Peter (Apostle), 31, 32, 34, 46,
 51, 67, 68, 74, 98
Peters, Hugh, 273-74
Pharisees, 29, 30, 41, 50, 51,
 57-59, 61, 66, 71, 77
Phidias, 9, 10, 14, 63
Philetus, 73
Philpot, John, 174-75, 176
Photinus, Bishop of Sirmium, 96
Pickering, Gilbert, 287, 291
Pilate, 35, 36, 42-43, 44, 49, 50,
 51, 54, 61, 62
Plato, 7, 13
Plutarch, 7, 8, 13
Polycarp, Bishop of Smyrna, 75
Poole, Reverend Matthew, 214
Predestination, 147, 190, 232
Presbyterianism, in England,
 183-84, 195-200, 202-4, 208,
 210, 211, 218, 223, 226, 232,
 233, 242, 244, 250, 256, 262,
 271, 279, 280, 285, 287, 298,
 309, 322, 324, 325. *See also*
 Calvinism
Prescription Aginst Heretics, 80
Pricillian heresy, 99
Pricillius, Bishop of Spain, 99
Primitive Christianity Revived, 262
Protagoras of Thrace, 9, 10, 12,
 14
Protestantism: blasphemy and,
 122-57; Jews and, 128, 129,
 130, 133; trinity doctrine and,
 123, 135, 137-38, 142,
 144-45, 147-49, 153. See also
 names of sects
Prynne, William, 197, 273
Pseudepigrapha, 22, 23

Ptolemy, 136
Puritanism, in England, 168, 175, 189, 190-191, 194, 198-99, 202, 236, 239-40, 252, 263, 266, 271, 279, 280-81, 296, 298-99, 305, 313, 324
Purvey, John, 165

Quaker Act of 1662, 298
Quakerism, ix, xiv, 223, 226, 234, 235, 240, 242, 245, 250, 251-52, 255, 298, 299, 302-4, 307-10, 316-18, 333; in England, 258-96

Rab-Shakeh, 20-21, 23, 24
Racovian Catechism, 189, 190, 213-14, 215, 217, 323
Rainborough, William, 246
Rainsford, Richard, 315
Ranterism, 117, 205, 224, 225, 230, 231, 232-55, 258, 259, 263, 264, 266, 267, 273, 279, 282-84, 285, 287, 324
Rawlinson, A. E. J., 62
Real Presence in the Mass, 121
Reasonableness of Christianity, 323
Reeve, John, 251-55
Reformation, xiv, 121, 163, 167-70, 173, 194, 317. See also names of reformers
Refutation of All Heresies, The, 76
"Refutation of Servetus's Errors," 141-42
Religion's Peace; or, A Plea for Liberty of Conscience, 192
Religious foundations, blasphemy and, 3-100; early Christianity, 63-100; offense and origins, 3-28; Jewish trial of Jesus, 29-62
Remonstrance from the Eternal God, A, 254-55
Return to the wayes of Truth, 247
Revolution of 1688-89 (England), 316-17
Rex v. Sedley, 307
Rex v. Taylor, xiii

Ridley, Nicholas, 173, 176
Robbins, John, 26, 249, 251, 253
Robins, Joan, 249
Robinson, James M., 30
Rogers, John, 173-74
Roman Catholic Church, ix, xiv, 5, 65, 72, 332; in England, 164, 166, 172-75, 177, 182-83, 187, 198, 203, 204, 262, 279, 281, 299-301, 305, 316-18; Luther and, 126-27, 128, 129-30; Middle Ages, 103-21; Protestant Reformation and, 122, 124, 125, 134, 150, 152, 156; triumph of, 103
Roman Empire, xiii, 63, 110; Christian heterodoxy, 63-100. See also Israelites (ancient)
Roman law, 45, 155
Roulston, Gilbert, 230
Rous, Francis, 284
Rout, A, A Rout, 233, 240-41, 243
Routing of the Ranters, The, 240
Rufinus (presbyter), 100
Rump Parliament, 211, 296
Russell, Jeffrey B., xiv

Sabellianism, 76, 82, 87, 95-96, 122, 282, 311, 321, 322, 323
Sabellius, 82, 85, 86, 95-96
Sacco, Nicola, 5
Sacramentaries, 168
Sadducees, 35-36, 39, 41, 48, 53-54, 56, 57, 77
St. Bartholomew's Day Massacre, 317
St. John's College, 212
Salmon, Joseph, 226, 233, 240-41, 243-44, 248
Samosatans, 76
Sandy Foundations Shaken, 309, 321
Sandys, Bishop Edward, 179
Sanhedrin, 20, 26-27, 72-73, 100, 331; loss of capital jurisdiction, 44, 45; trial of Jesus, 29-62
Sanhedrin (tractate), 44
Santayana, George, xii

Satan's Stratagems, 144, 192

Sattler, Michael, 124

Saturnilians, 78

Saul of Tarsus. *See* Paul, St.

Sawtre, William, 165-66

Sayer, William, 191

Scambler, Bishop Edmund, 182

Sedley, Sir Charles, 306-7

Seekers, 226, 230, 235, 251, 266, 267

Selden, John, 204, 291

Seleutian Donatism, 226

Semi-Arianism, 76, 89, 91, 93, 94, 95, 97

Sennacherib, King, 20

Servetus, Michael, ix, xi, xiii, 135-43, 144, 146, 147, 172, 177, 180, 186, 282, 312

Seventh Day Baptists, 282

Shakers, 267

Shaw, Lemuel, 335

Shelomethes, 226

Shelton, Archbishop Gilbert, 300

Shepherd of Hermes, The, 63, 74

Shepherd's Crusade, 115

Sheppard, Samuel, 240

Sherlock, William, 321-22

Short Declaration of the Mistery of Iniquity, A, 192

Short Parliament, 197

Sicilian Vespers, 116

Simonianism, 76, 78

Simons, Menno, 123

Single Eye All Light, no Darkness; or Light and Darkness One, A, 244, 246

Sirach, 23

Sirmium Creed, 94

Skepticism, 14, 308

Skippon, Major General Philip, 285-86, 287, 288

Slovan, Father Gerard S., 55

Socinianism, xiv, 122, 147, 150, 156, 231, 244, 246, 279, 285, 291, 301, 303, 309-11, 312, 321, 323, 324, 326; in England, 171, 188-223. *See also* Unitarianism

Socinus, Faustus, 135, 147, 150, 151, 189, 310-11, 321, 323

Socrates, ix, 8, 13-14, 63

Socrates Scholasticus of Constantinople, 93-94

Son of Man claim, 32-33, 35, 40, 43, 46, 48, 54, 57, 58, 59, 69

Sorcery, 7, 163

Sorrell, Elizabeth, 249

South, Robert, 322

Spiritual Libertines, 133

Stephen, 46, 47, 54, 71, 73

Steuart, Adam, 198

Stewart, Sir James, 327

Stillingfleet, Dr. Edward, 310

Strickland, Walter, 284, 287, 288, 290, 294

Stuart Restoration, 223, 296, 297-98, 302

Swinderby, William, 165

Sydenham, Colonel William, 284, 286, 287, 294

Talmud, 19, 21, 23-28, 39, 40, 44, 50, 52, 57, 116, 117

Tany, Thomas (Theaurau John), 249-50, 251, 253, 259

Taylor, John, 240, 312-14, 316, 329, 332

Taylor, Vincent, 32, 34, 50

Temple, destruction of (A.D. 70), 27, 38-39, 44

Ten Commandments, 15, 39, 225, 237, 243, 244

Tertullian, xiv, 75-76, 77, 80-81, 83, 98, 99, 111

Test Act of 1673, 299

Testimonies concerning the One God and the Persons of the Holy Trinity, 210

Tetragrammaton, 25-26, 57

Theodosian Code, 99, 103, 109

Theodosius, Emperor, 94-95, 97-98, 99, 105

Theognis of Nicaea, 92, 93

Thirty-nine Articles, 175, 194, 196, 318

Thirty Tyrants, 13, 14

Thucydides, 10

Tidford, Thomas, 249

Tillotson, Archbishop William, 322

Titus, 71, 73

Toland, John, 328
Toleration Act of *1689*, 316, 317-20, 323, 329-30
Torah, 42, 45, 50, 52, 54, 66, 67, 69, 71, 72
Tournon, Cardinal de, 135
Transubstantiation, 165, 170, 173, 260, 299
Trendall, John, 194
Trinity, doctrine of the, ix, xi, xii, 4, 63, 68, 118, 163, 180, 184, 185, 187, 189, 191, 200, 201, 206, 211-12, 213, 253, 254, 297, 300, 307-11, 318, 321, 322-27, 328, 332, 337; early Christian era controversy, 81-100, 103; Protestantism and, 123, 135, 137-38, 142, 144-45, 147-49, 150, 153
True Levellers, 224-25
True Levellers Standard, The, 224
Turwert, Henry, 178, 179
Twofold Catechism, The, 214-15, 216, 218-19
Tyszkiewicz, Iwan, 156, 157

Unitarianism, ix, xi, xv, 85, 96, 122, 135, 147, 150-52, 333, 334; in England, 171, 182, 183, 185, 310, 319-23, 327-29; *See also* Antitrinitarianism; Socinianism
Unitarian Tracts, 321, 323
U. S. Constitution, x, xv
U. S. Supreme Court, ix, 4, 336
University of Paris, 117, 136, 153
Uriah, 40
Usher, Archbishop James, 206, 279

Valentinianism, 78, 79, 92
Valentinus, 79
Vanini, Julius Caesar, 156, 157
Vanzetti, Bartolomeo, 5
Venerable Bede, 110
Vermes, Geza, 35

Villeneuve, Michel de, 136, 137
Vincent, Thomas, 309
Virginia, colony of, 333
Virgin Mary, 114, 116, 119, 124, 178, 333
Vittel, Christopher, 180, 230
Vorst, Konrad van den, 188, 189

Wakefield, Walter L., xiv
Waldensians, 121, 135, 161
Waldo, Peter, 121
Walker, Henry, 251
Walwyn, William, 204
Webberley, John, 207, 208, 212
Weigel, Katherine, 134
Westminster Assembly of Divines, 200, 201, 203, 207, 212
Whitehead, Alfred North, xii
Whitelocke, Bulstrode, 290-91
Whitgift, Archbishop John, 179
Widdrington, Sir Thomas, 293
Wightman, Edward, 184-85, 186, 188, 190, 272
Wildman, John, 225
Wilkinson, Robert, 255
William III (of Orange), King, 318, 321, 328
Williams, Roger, 193, 232
Wilson, William R., 53
Winstanley, Gerrard, 224, 225, 240, 241, 242
Winter, Paul, 62
Witchcraft, 4, 131, 163, 237

Yahweh, 16, 18, 19, 20, 21, 24, 35
YHVH, 25, 26, 40, 57

Zealots, 34, 37, 38, 41, 48, 49
Zechariah, 37
Zeffirelli, Franco, xi
Zoroastrianism, 77
Zurkinden, Nicholas, 143
Zwingli, Ulrich, 124, 125, 135, 136, 173
Zwinglianism, 123, 130